THE

WEST AND CENTRAL FLORIDA EXPEDITIONS

of Clarence Bloomfield Moore

Classics in Southeastern Archaeology

Stephen Williams, Series Editor

Publication of this work has been supported in part by grants and donations from the following agencies and institutions.

Southeastern Archaeological Conference
The Seminole Tribe of Florida/Genealogy
The Florida Archaeological Council
The Florida Anthropological Society
Mrs. Joan Miller
Panamerican Consultants, Inc.
Dan Josselyn Memorial Fund

THE WEST AND CENTRAL FLORIDA EXPEDITIONS *of Clarence Bloomfield Moore*

Edited and with an Introduction by
JEFFREY M. MITCHEM

The University of Alabama Press
Tuscaloosa and London

The works by Clarence B. Moore reproduced in this volume were published originally in 1895, 1900, 1902, 1903, 1905, 1907, 1918, 1919, and 1921.

∞

The paper on which this book is printed meets the minimum requirements of American National Standard for Information Science-Permanence of Paper for Printed Library Materials, ANSI Z39.48-1984.

Library of Congress Cataloging-in-Publication Data

Moore, Clarence Bloomfield.
The west and central Florida expeditions of Clarence Bloomfield Moore / edited and with an introduction by Jeffrey M. Mitchem.
p. cm.—(Classics in southeastern archaeology)
Includes bibliographical references and index.
ISBN 0-8173-0951-9 (pbk. : alk. paper)
1. Indians of North America—Florida—Gulf Coast—Antiquities. 2. Moore, Clarence Bloomfield—Journeys—Florida—Gulf Coast. 3. Archaeological expeditions—Florida—Gulf Coast. 4. Archaeological expeditions—Florida—Oklawaha River Region 5. Excavations (Archaeology)—Florida—Gulf Coast. 6. Excavations (Archaeology)—Florida—Oklawaha River Region. 7. Gulf Coast (Fla.)—Antiquities. 8. Oklawaha River Region (Fla.)—Antiquities. I. Mitchem, Jeffrey M. II. Series.
E78.F6 W46 1999
975.9'01—dc21 99-6085

British Library Cataloguing-in-Publication Data available

Contents

Preface

Thirteen of Clarence B. Moore's papers are reproduced in this volume. Most of these deal with Moore's work in west peninsular Florida, but the first three describe work in central and northeast Florida. His many research expeditions in east peninsular Florida and in northwest Florida are included in two other volumes in the *Classics in Southeastern Archaeology* series.

In the essay that follows, I provide an overview and update of research on sites reported by Moore in west Florida. Although I do not claim that the overview is complete, my hope is that it will be a useful tool for archaeologists who need background information on sites investigated by Clarence B. Moore.

I could not have accomplished writing the introduction or compiling Table 1 without the help of the staff at the Florida Master Site File in Tallahassee, Florida. Site File Supervisor Dr. Marion F. Smith Jr. and several of his employees (Heather Pearcy, Steve Amiss, Charles Branham, Gerald Ferguson, and Kim Heinz) were helpful in answering questions, searching databases, and allowing me work space on a number of occasions. I would also like to express my appreciation to Joan P. Morris, Archives Supervisor at the Florida Photographic Collection of the Florida State Archives, for the photograph reproduced as Figure 2 in the introduction.

Cynthia Cerrato was of great help in providing details about Clarence B. Moore, the boats he used, and the dates he was in Florida. Robert J. Austin, George M. Luer, and B. William Burger answered questions I had about sites and shared knowledge about Moore's work in the Tampa Bay and Charlotte Harbor areas. Margo Schwadron kindly provided copies of unpublished letters referring to Moore and his boat, the *Gopher*. Karen Jo Walker helped clarify some questions I had about some of the sites in southwest Florida. Keith Ashley provided information on northeast Florida archaeology and Moore's work there. Dr. Lewis N. Wynne, Executive Director of the Florida Historical Society and Debra T. Wynne, archivist at the Florida Historical Society's Tebeau-Field Library of Florida History, generously provided copies of two letters that Clarence Moore had sent to the first president of the Florida Historical Society. Thank you all for sharing your expertise.

This volume would not have happened without the special help of Dr. James J. Miller, the State Archaeologist of Florida. When he found out that we were searching for clean copies of original Moore publications, Jim cheerfully stepped forward, loaning copies of virtually all of Moore's publications on Florida. The true significance of this gesture is realized when one considers that each volume had to be taken apart, each page photographed, and then rebound. The process entails loss of the original bound edge of each page.

Four colleagues read and commented on drafts of the introduction: Rochelle A. Marrinan, William H. Marquardt, James J. Miller, and Stephen Williams. Although I did not follow all of their suggestions, they made many constructive criticisms that enhanced the manuscript. I appreciate their insights and advice.

Special thanks go to Judith Knight at the University of Alabama Press. Always cheerful and helpful, she was a joy to work with. Kathy Swain's copyediting improved the clarity of this introduction. And finally, my thanks to Bonnie and Katie for putting up with my clutter on and around the kitchen table.

Editorial Note

This volume contains the works of Clarence Bloomfield Moore on west and central Florida. Most sections have been presented by facsimile reproduction. In these facsimile sections, a few blank pages appear. These pages are blank in the originals and are the reverse sides of pages bearing plates or other illustrations. No text has been omitted.

The last four sections, which appeared originally in a variety of published formats, have been typeset for this volume in the format of the *Journal of the Academy of Natural Sciences of Philadelphia*, but they have been transcribed almost exactly as originally published. Editorial interventions consist only of the addition of bracketed page numbers showing original pagination, the regularization of chapter titles and subheadings, and the silent correction of a few typographical errors.

To find the original publication data for the works included in this volume, see the listing for Moore in the References Cited on pp. 44–45.

THE WEST AND CENTRAL FLORIDA EXPEDITIONS *of Clarence Bloomfield Moore*

Introduction
Clarence B. Moore's
Work in Western and Central Florida, 1895–1921

Jeffrey M. Mitchem

The name Clarence Bloomfield Moore (1852–1936) is familiar to every archaeologist interested in the southeastern United States. His seemingly indefatigable travels and investigations resulted in dozens of illustrated publications that are important records of information about archaeological sites all over the Southeast. The scientific value of his publications increases as more of the sites he investigated are destroyed by development or other factors. Although no definitive biography of Clarence B. Moore has been written, a brief synopsis is provided in the introduction to Moore's Moundville volumes by Vernon James Knight Jr. (1996) in the first reprint in the *Classics in Southeastern Archaeology* series. Additional biographical information is provided in works by Brigham (1936), Davis (1987), and Wardle (1956).

Although some modern archaeologists may decry Moore's field methods, all are impressed by his prodigious, prompt reporting of his discoveries. It is also clear from his works that Moore had read the available literature pertaining to previous work in Florida, and he was in frequent contact with other archaeologists and specialists, both professional and amateur. The quality, timeliness, and thoroughness of his publications far exceeded the efforts of his contemporaries.

Clarence B. Moore's initial interest in the archaeology of Florida was stimulated by reading published works of Andrew E. Douglass, Jeffries Wyman, and other pioneers of Florida archaeology. While a student at Harvard, he probably met Jeffries Wyman, the first curator of the Peabody Museum of Archaeology and Ethnology, and it is likely that Moore got his first taste of excavation under the tutelage of Wyman in January 1873 at a shell midden on the St. Johns River (Murowchick 1990:64; Stephen Williams, personal communication 1997). Moore then proceeded to devote considerable time and effort to east and central Florida.

His reason for switching his focus to the western part of the peninsula is clear when one reads the first page of his initial west coast paper (Moore 1900:351). Moore had been shown the spectacular wooden and painted artifacts excavated at Key Marco by Frank Hamilton Cushing (1896) and was clearly hoping to duplicate Cushing's success. Moore was not to find another site like Key Marco, however, and his disappointment is obvious in a sentence on the second page of the report: "Never before had we set out so thoroughly prepared for work and never did our efforts meet with so little success" (Moore 1900:352). Nevertheless, fortunately for us, Moore did devote more time to the western part of the state, and his publications, collections, and field notes are in many cases the only records we have from archaeological sites that were subsequently destroyed by development.

Study of Moore's collections in various museums, along with his written records, was instrumental in the initial formulations of cultural chronologies for Florida (Goggin 1949c, 1952; Willey 1948a, 1949; Willey and Woodbury 1942). For the western part of the peninsula, Gordon R. Willey (1949) established the cultural chronology that is still largely valid today, and he included much of Moore's information in his synthesis of the spatial distribution of sites and the time sequence of various artifact types (Fairbanks 1982:1–2).

The works reprinted here include all of Moore's papers describing his researches on the west coast of peninsular Florida, along with a few that deal with the eastern and central parts of the state. C. B. Moore invested considerable effort in Florida and devoted more pages of published reports and articles to Florida than to any other state. Because of the great number of pages, it was necessary to devote three volumes of reprinted works to the state: one on northwest Florida, one on east Florida, and the present volume on west and central Florida.

When it came time to divide the works into three parts, some problems became apparent. First, Moore's expeditions were often wide-ranging, covering great expanses of territory that did not necessarily fit our tripartite division. Several of the expeditions overlapped different parts of the state. Second, if the works were divided strictly by geographical location, the number of pages in each volume would vary a great deal. There was a significant variance in the number of pages on east and west Florida, with the former outnumbering the latter. To bring the east and west volumes closer to equal numbers of pages, we moved three papers from 1895 (on work in northeast and central Florida) from the east volume to the present one. In addition, sections on Levy and Citrus Counties from two of Moore's (1902, 1918) works on northwest Florida were added to the present volume because research on these counties was included in some of his other west peninsular Florida publications.

Another problem arose while lists of Moore's papers on Florida were being compiled. Citations of his works in books and articles often gave different dates of publication. This is at least partly because he subsidized most of his publications (Wardle 1929:119) and often had quantities of copies printed separately for distribution to colleagues, sometimes in a different year than the official publication. To resolve this dilemma, I decided to use dates cited by Moore himself in the "Writings on Archaeology" list he included in several of the later volumes of his works.

A Chronological Outline of Moore's Florida Expeditions

From Moore's field notebooks and the guide to them prepared by Davis (1987), along with his published accounts, we can reconstruct the chronology of his Florida work. From the dates of his field notebooks, one would assume that his first research in Florida was in 1891 along the St. Johns River and its tributaries in the eastern part of the state. Nonetheless, from a passing remark in one of his publications, it seems that his first Florida work was in January 1873 in a shell mound (probably 8PU4) north of Palatka (Moore 1892a:137; Murowchick 1990:64). A brief remark in another paper indicates that he also excavated at the Bluffton Mound (8VO23) in March of 1879 (Moore 1894a:45).

Moore's concentrated research in the St. Johns drainage began in 1891, and he continued working in the region until 1895. A brief note in one of his publications (Moore 1892b:292) indicates that he had also conducted excavations on the west coast of Florida prior to 1892. After a few years' work in Georgia, South Carolina, and Alabama, he returned to Florida in 1900, this time concentrating on the central Gulf Coast of Florida. In 1901, he began focusing on northwest Florida, along with forays into Mississippi and Alabama. Northwest Florida continued to attract his attention until 1903, when he also worked on sites farther south along the Gulf Coast, as far south as Tampa Bay.

From 1904 until 1906, Moore combined investigations in diverse parts of Florida with significant work in Alabama, Mississippi, and Georgia. His Florida research during this period extended from the southwest coast to the area around Lake Tohopekaliga in the central part of the state. He also continued work in northwest Florida and carried out major excavations at Crystal River in Citrus County. In the winters of 1906 and 1907, he undertook research in the Ten Thousand Islands region of the southwest coast.

Beginning in 1907, Moore switched his focus to states and river valleys to the west and north of Florida. According to his field notebooks (Davis 1987) his last Florida fieldwork was in 1918, but a passing mention in one of his later publications (Moore 1921a:12) makes it clear that he was still conducting fieldwork on the southwest Florida coast as late as 1920. An article by H. Newell Wardle (1929:119–120) reveals that Moore traveled to Florida from January until April of 1929, although no mention is made of his conducting excavations on this trip.

Moore's papers are reprinted here in chronological order. This should help the reader because he often made mention of similar or contrasting artifacts or situations at other sites where he had worked. He also returned to several sites to carry out additional investigations.

Florida Sites Investigated by C. B. Moore

I am one of many archaeologists who has used Moore's works in my research. One of the first tasks when investigating a site or region where Moore excavated is to determine what state site file number(s) represent his sites. Another bothersome aspect of such research is that many sites have more than one common name or the names have changed since Moore's time. To make this volume a more valuable and "user-friendly" research tool, I have compiled Table 1. This table lists the sites sequentially as they are described in the reports reprinted herein and gives the most common names, the site numbers, and the period(s)/cultural affiliation(s) of occupation as they are recorded in the Florida Master Site File. This site file is the State of Florida's official repository for information and records on Florida archaeological and historic sites. Maintained by the Florida Department of State's Division of Historical Resources in Tallahassee, the site file is an essential resource for researchers.

One caveat should be mentioned in connection with Table 1. For some of the sites where Moore worked, it is difficult or impossible to determine the exact location from his maps and descriptions, and possibly in a few cases the same site may have received two site numbers, especially if he visited a single site on several occasions. I carefully checked both the written locational information and maps at the Florida Master Site File to avoid this problem, but some of the files are incomplete.

Table 1. Site Names and Numbers from Moore's Work in West, Central, and Northeast Florida

Moore's Site Name	Site Number	Other Site Name(s), [Components]
Johnson Mound	8DU10	[St. Johns I, Ib]
Shields Mound	8DU12	Mound near Mill Cove [Deptford, St. Johns IIb]
Gilbert Mound	8DU11	[St. Johns Ia, Ib]
Monroe Mound	8DU13	[St. Johns I, Ia, Ib]
Grant Mound	8DU14	[Late Swift Creek, St. Johns Ia, Ib, IIa]
Low Mounds South of Grant Mound:		
Mound A	8DU15	Low Mound A [St. Johns Ia]
Mound B	8DU16	Low Mound B [St. Johns II]
Mound C	8DU17	Low Mound C
Mound D	8DU18	Low Mound D
Mound E	8DU19	Low Mound E [Late Archaic]
Low Mounds near Horse-Shoe Landing:		
Mound A	8DU21	Horseshoe Landing Mound A [St. Johns I]
Unnamed (smaller)	8DU22	Horseshoe Landing Other Mounds
Unnamed	8DU23	Brutus Mound
Broward Mound	8DU20	[St. Johns I]
Low Mounds near Reddie Point:		
Unnamed (larger)	8DU25	Reddie Point Mound A [St. Johns Ia, Ib]
Unnamed	8DU26	Reddie Point Mound B [Preceramic]
Mound at Daniel's Landing	8DU27	Daniel's Landing Mound [St. Johns]
Low Mounds at Alicia:		
Mound A	8DU30	Low Mound A Alicia; Alicia Mound A [St. Johns I]
Mound B	8DU31	Low Mound B Alicia; Alicia Mound B [St. Johns Ia]
Denton Mound	8DU24	[St. Johns I, Ia, Ib]
Two Low Mounds at Chaseville:		
Unnamed	8DU28	Chaseville Mound A [Preceramic]
Unnamed	8DU29	Chaseville Mound B [Preceramic]
Low Mounds at Floral Bluff	8DU32	Floral Bluff Mound [St. Johns I]
Sand Mounds on Murphy Island:		
Unnamed (northernmost)	8PU20	North Mound, Murphy Island [St. Johns Ia, IIc, European]
Southernmost Mound	8PU21	South Mound, Murphy Island [St. Johns IIa]
Mounds near Ditch Creek:		
Unnamed	8PU53	Mound A, Ditch Creek [St. Johns]
Unnamed	8PU54	Mound B, Ditch Creek [Preceramic]
Mounds near Palmetto Landing:		
Unnamed (northernmost)	8MR19	Palmetto Landing Mound 1; Shiner Pond Mound 2 [St. Johns I]
Unnamed (southernmost)	8MR20	Palmetto Landing Mound 2; Shiner Pond Mound 3
Unnamed	8MR21	Palmetto Landing Mound 3; Shiner Pond Mound 1
Unnamed	8MR22	Palmetto Landing Mound 4; Shiner Pond Mound 4
Unnamed	8MR23	Palmetto Landing Mound 5

Moore's Site Name	Site Number	Other Site Name(s), [Components]
Unnamed (MacDonald)	8MR24	Palmetto Landing Mound 6 [Orange, St. Johns I]
Unnamed	8MR25	Palmetto Landing Mound 7
Mound near Silver Springs	8MR33	[St. Johns Ia, Ib]
Gamble Mound	8MR39	[St. Johns Ia]
Hopson Mound	8LA47	[Swift Creek, Weeden Island, St. Johns Ia, Ib]
Mound near Higley	8LA48	Higley Mound
Mound near Umatilla	8LA49	
Mound near Fort Mason	8LA43	Fort Mason Mound
Mound on Lake Eustis (large)	8LA50	Mound A Lake Eustis
Mound on Lake Eustis (small)	8LA51	Mound B Lake Eustis
Mound near Tavares	8LA52	Tavares Mound [St. Johns Ia, Ib]
Unnamed (smaller)	8LA53	Small Mound near Tavares [St. Johns IIc]
Mound at Barclay's	8LA44	Barclay's [St. Johns IIa, IIb, IIc]
Richmond Mound	8LA55	[St. Johns II]
Low Mound near Helena	8LA56	[Weeden Island, St. Johns Ia, Ib]
Mound near Old Okahumpka	8LA57	Old Okahumpka [St. Johns IIb]
Four Mile Bayou	8PI41	Bayshore Homes [Late Weeden Island]
Disston City	8PI28	
New Cadiz	8PI29	
Point Maximo	8PI19	Maximo Mounds; Maximo Point; Sheraton Midden [Archaic, Manasota, Weeden Island, Safety Harbor, 19th century, 20th century]
Point Maximo	8PI31	Maximo Park; Maximo Beach [Archaic, Manasota, Weeden Island, Safety Harbor, Spanish, 19th century, 20th century]
Mound on Pine Key	8PI1692	Tierra Verde, Cabbage Key Mound [Safety Harbor]
Mound on Pine Key	8PI51	Tierra Verde, Cabbage Key Middens [Weeden Island, Englewood, Safety Harbor]
Mounds near Point Pinelos	8PI108	Hirrihigua Mound; Mound at Bethel's Camp [Safety Harbor]
Unnamed (Armistead)	———	
Unnamed (near Safety Harbor)	8PI2	Safety Harbor; Philippe Park [Safety Harbor, Historic, Spanish 1]
Mounds on Alafia River:		
Unnamed (Riverview)	8HI21	Riverview
Shell Bluff	8HI22	[Late Weeden Island, Safety Harbor]
Mill Point (shell ridges A)	8HI16	Mill Point 1 [Late Weeden Island, Safety Harbor]
Mill Point (sand ridge B)	8HI17	Mill Point 2 [Late Weeden Island, Safety Harbor]
Mill Point (mound D)	8HI18	Mill Point 3 [Late Weeden Island, Safety Harbor]
Mill Point (sand mound E)	8HI19	Mill Point 4 [Late Weeden Island, Safety Harbor]
Mill Point (mound F)	8HI20	Mill Point 5 [Late Weeden Island, Safety Harbor]

Moore's Site Name	Site Number	Other Site Name(s), [Components]
Bullfrog Creek	8HI12	Bullfrog Mound
Mound near Little Manatee River	8HI1	Thomas Mound; Hoey Mound [Manasota, Safety Harbor]
Indian Hill	8HI2	Cockroach Key; Indian Key [Manasota, Late Weeden Island]
Terraceia (irregular mound)	8MA83	Terra Ceia, Johnson Burial Mound
Terraceia (shell deposit)	8MA83D	Terra Ceia, Boots Point Shell Midden [Safety Harbor, 19th century]
Terraceia (oblong mound)	8MA83B	Bickel Mound; Madira Bickel Mound [Weeden Island, Manasota, Safety Harbor]
Three small mounds near Erie P.O.:		
Unnamed, one (Foy property)	8MA50	Honey Mound [post-Archaic]
Unnamed, two (Brubacher)	———	
Unnamed (Cow Point Island)	8MA12	Cow Point Midden [Manasota]
Unnamed (near Sarasota Bay)	———	
Unnamed (near Snell's Bayou)	8SO20	Weber Mound [Weeden Island, Safety Harbor]
Unnamed (1/2 mile S. Sarasota)	8SO44	Sarasota Bay Mound [Weeden Island, Safety Harbor]
Indian Old Field	8LL39	Indian Field [Caloosahatchee IV, V, Spanish 1, 19th century]
Mound on Pine Island	8LL40	Pine Island 8 [Caloosahatchee V, European]
Mondongo Island	8LL52	[Precolumbian]
Joseffa Island	8LL51	Useppa Island; Collier Inn [Middle Archaic–Caloosahatchee IIB, V]
Josselyn Key	8LL32	Josslyn Island [Caloosahatchee I–III, Spanish 1]
Demorey Key	8LL31	Demere Key [Glades II-III, Spanish 1–2, European, British, American]
Mound Island	8LL2	Mound Key; Johnson's Key [Caloosahatchee I–V, Spanish 1]
Mound Island (burial mound)	8LL3	Mound Key Burial Mound [Caloosahatchee I–V, Spanish]
Little Marco Island	8CR50	
Marco	8CR48	Key Marco [Archaic, Glades I–III, Seminole]
Goodland Point	8CR45	Goodland Point Midden [Glades I–IIIc]
Goodland Point (burials)	8CR46	Goodland Point Burial Site [Glades]
Blue Hill, Horr's Island	8CR41	Horr's Island 5 [Weeden Island, Glades II–III, European]
Caximbas Hill	8CR107	Caxambas [Archaic, Glades I]
Gomez' Old Place	8CR28	Shell Key
Dismal Key	8CR27	[Glades I–IIIb]
Fikahatchee Key	8CR22	Fakahatchee Key
Russell's Key	8CR17	Russell Key [Glades]
Wiggins' Key	8CR11	Sandfly [Glades, American, 19th century]
Chokoloskee Key	8CR1	[Preceramic, Seminole]
Turner's River	8CR2	Turner River I [Glades I–IIb, American]
Watson's	8MO63	Watson's Place [Glades, American]
Mound on Hog Island	8LV26	Hog Island 1

Moore's Site Name	Site Number	Other Site Name(s), [Components]
Unnamed shell-heap on the mainland	8LV42	Shell Mound [Preceramic]
Mound on Pine Key	8LV40/2/7	Pine Key Mound; Graveyard Island; Palmetto Island; Rattlesnake Island; Hog Island [Swift Creek, Weeden Island]
Mound near the Shell-Heap	8LV41	Mound near Shell Heap, Levy Co.
Mound near Fowler's Landing	8LV1	Fowler's Landing, larger mound [Weeden Island]
Smaller Mound near Fowler's Landing	8LV14	Fowler's Landing, small mound
Clark Place	———	
Jennings Landing	8DI19	
Fannin	8GI5	Fannin Mound 1
Mound ENE of Fannin	8LV130	Fannin Mound 2
Fayetteville	8DI18	Fayetteville Mound [Weeden Island?]
Rocky Landing	8DI20	
Mound near Cedar Keys	8LV38	Lutterloh Mound
Mound near Gigger Point	8LV3	Gigger Point [Weeden Island]
Mound near Dry Creek (1st)	8LV16	Mound A near Dry Creek
Mound near Dry Creek (2nd)	8LV17	Stonewall Pond [Weeden Island or Safety Harbor?]
Mound near Burns' Landing	8LV11	Burns' Landing
Mound near Bear Landing	8LV18	Bear Landing [Weeden Island]
Mound near Rock Landing	8CI17	
Mound near the Shell-Heap, Crystal River	8CI1	Crystal River; Spanish Mound [Deptford, Swift Creek, Weeden Island]
Mound near Crystal River Settlement	8CI10	
Mound near the Chassahowitzka River	8CI3	Chassahowitzka River [Late Weeden Island, Safety Harbor?]
Mound near Indian Bend	8HE2	[Late Weeden Island]
Mound near Bayport	8HE1	Bayport [Weeden Island, Safety Harbor]
Mound near Indian Creek	8HE3	Indian Creek Mound
Mound near the Wekiwachee River	8PA1	Wekiwachee River [Weeden Island]
Mound near the Pithlochascootie River	8PA2	Oelsner Mounds [Late Weeden Island, Safety Harbor]
Mound near Tarpon Springs	8PI3	Safford Mound [Deptford, Swift Creek, Weeden Island, Safety Harbor]
Mound on Hog Island	8PI9	Hog Island Mound
Mound near Clearwater	8PI10	Clearwater Mound
Mound near John's Pass	8PI4	Johns Pass Mound [Safety Harbor]
Mound on Long Key	8PI11	Long Key Mound
Mound near Kissimmee	8OS24	Bass Mound [St. Johns II]
Lanier Mound	8OS26	Lanier Point
Mounds near Brown's Landing:		
Unnamed (2 miles SW)	8OS21	Brown's Landing Mound A; Southport Mound [St. Johns II, Spanish, Historic]

Moore's Site Name	Site Number	Other Site Name(s), [Components]
Unnamed (3/4 mile SW)	8OS22	Brown's Landing Mound B
Unnamed (3/4 mile east)	8OS23	Brown's Landing Mound C
Mound near Frier Cove	8OS20	Frier Cove
Mound near Lee's Landing	———	
Mound near McCool's Landing	8OS19	McCool's Landing
Mound near St. Elmo's Landing	———	
Mound near Hickory Bluff	8CH5	Hickory Bluff Mound [Safety Harbor]
Mound in Gasparilla Sound	8CH2	Gasparilla Sound Mound [Safety Harbor]
Cayo Pelau	8CH1	Cayo Palu, Carapileu [Weeden Island, Safety Harbor, Caloosahatchee IIA–V]
Canal on Pine Island	8LL34	Pine Island Canal
Mound near Punta Rassa	8LL8	Shell Creek [Caloosahatchee III–V]
Nameless Key near Marco	8CR35	Addison's Key
Lossman's Key	8MO54	Lostmans Key [Transitional, Glades]
Cutler	8DA8	Cutler Mound [Glades II–III]
Battey Place	8LL33	Pineland; Battey's Landing [Caloosahatchee I–V, Spanish 1]
McIlvaine's Key	8CR53	McIlvane Key [Glades I–III, Historic]
Crawford Place	8CR55	Crawford's Key; Shell Island [Glades I–IIIa]
Pumpkin Key	8CR25	[Glades II]
Mounds on Hog Island:		
Unnamed (on shell ridge)	8LV27	Hog Island 2
Unnamed (larger)	8LV39	Hog Island 3
Mound in Cedar Keys	8LV43	Cedar Keys Mound
Aboriginal Cemetery in Cedar Keys	8LV4	Aboriginal Cemetery in Cedar Key [Weeden Island]
Unnamed (1 mi. north of Spanish mound)	8CI448	Williams A D Mound; A. D. Williams Mound
Mound on the Greenleaf Place	8CI11	Greenleaf Place

It is unfortunate that Moore was not able to illustrate more artifacts, especially from the smaller, less exciting sites. In many cases, he excavated sites completely, and it is not possible to determine temporal or cultural affiliations from his published descriptions of the sometimes small numbers of artifacts recovered. Because of this, many of the affiliations listed in Table 1 may be incomplete or incorrect. I included additional affiliations when they could be gleaned from Moore's writings or other sources. Those needing more information can study Moore's collections in museums (for the locations of many of these, see Goggin 1952:Appendix A, Mitchem 1989, Rouse 1951, and Willey 1949) or in his original field notes (Davis 1987).

For those readers not familiar with the geography or county names of Florida, I have included two aids that should help in understanding the discussions that follow. The first is Figure 1, a map of peninsular Florida (the panhandle of northwest Florida is omitted), with the present boundaries and names of Florida counties indicated. The shaded counties are those with sites discussed by Moore in the present volume. Readers should note, however, that a number of the county boundaries have changed since Moore's time, especially in southwest Florida. The second aid is Table 2, a list of the county abbreviations used in the following discussion and in Table 1. The site-numbering system of the Florida Master Site File uses these two-letter designations to denote counties.

Many of the sites that Moore investigated have been the subject of additional research in subsequent years. Because of space limitations, it is impossible to list here every citation and to discuss every research project that has been conducted on these sites. My aim is to summarize some of the more notable studies and findings that were stimulated by Moore's pioneering work. Those desiring more complete information about individual sites are referred to the Florida Master Site File.

Moore's collections ended up in many different institutions, with material from a single site sometimes divided between several museums. Extensive studies of collections by John M. Goggin (1949a, 1952) and Willey (1949) provide descriptions of artifacts and cultural affiliations for many of the sites, but advances in dating techniques have shown that many of the specific dates they proposed for the various culture periods were incorrect. In Table 3, I present a chronological chart based on publications by Jerald T. Milanich (1994), William H. Marquardt (1992b:Table 2), Michael Russo (1992:Figure 2), and John W. Griffin (1988:Figure 6.3) with currently accepted dates for the various archaeological cultures. Because the present volume includes Moore's research in both west and east Florida, Table 3 includes chronologies for both regions.

The first three reprinted papers in the present volume report the results of Moore's work in northeast and central Florida during the first six months of 1895 (Moore 1895a, 1895b, 1895c). The first major site on which he reported excavations was the Shields Mound (8DU12), at which he had conducted limited excavations the previous year (Moore 1894b:204–205). This flat-topped Mississippian period mound and ridge complex is one of several contemporaneous sites in the area that yielded stone and copper artifacts. Although Goggin (1952:84) dated the site to St. Johns IIa times, recent researchers place it in St. Johns IIb (ca. A.D. 1050–1513) (Milanich 1994:269–270; Thunen and Ashley 1995:6–7). Some of the sherds and projectile points illustrated by Moore (1895a:Figures 4 and 11) indicate that earlier components were present as well.

The Grant Mound (8DU14) was another mound that Moore had first investigated the previous year (Moore 1894b:200–204). His 1894 excavations yielded copper and galena artifacts, and he had seen many artifacts of exotic origin in local private collections (1894b:203). These initial results led to a major effort in 1895, with Moore spending five weeks at the site with a large field crew (1895a:473). The artifacts from the mound indicate a St. Johns IIa date, with Thunen and Ashley (1995:6) suggesting a range of A.D. 800–1300. Artifacts from elsewhere on the site suggest that there is also an earlier St. Johns Ia (A.D. 100–500) component (Williams and Goggin 1956:47).

Much has been written about the Grant Mound since Moore's time. The two copper objects known as "Long Nose God Masks" (Moore 1895a:Figures 39–42) have been the focus of particular attention (Williams and Goggin 1956:23–24, Figures 10 and 11). The remarkable similarity of these and other artifacts to specimens from Mississippian sites elsewhere in the greater Southeast and Mississippi Valley re-

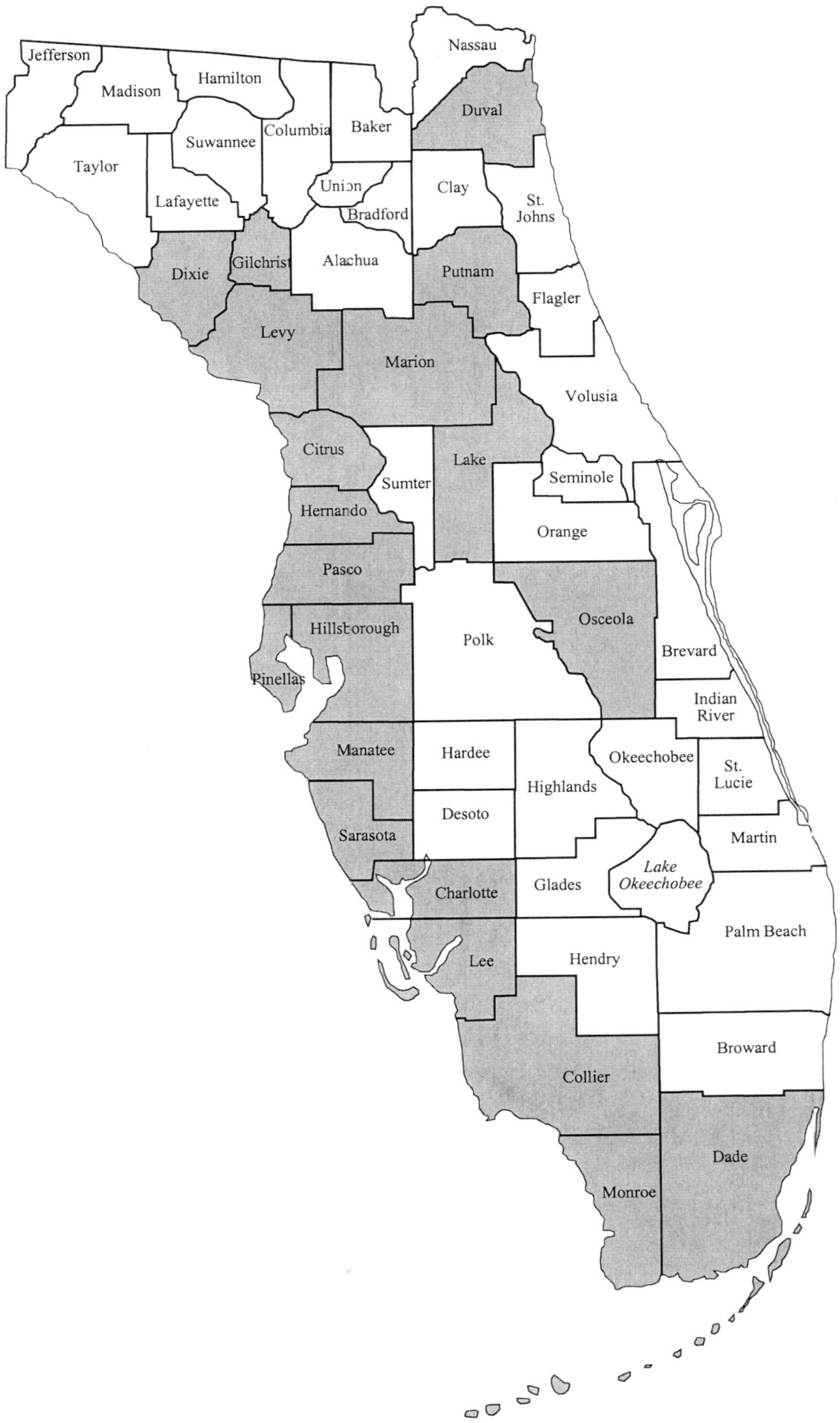

Figure 1. Map of peninsular Florida with county names and boundaries marked. Shaded counties are those containing sites discussed in this volume. Drawn by Charles B. Poe.

Table 2. Florida Master Site File County Abbreviations

Abbreviation	County
CH	Charlotte
CI	Citrus
CR	Collier
DA	Dade
DI	Dixie
DU	Duval
GI	Gilchrist
HE	Hernando
HI	Hillsborough
LA	Lake
LL	Lee
LV	Levy
MA	Manatee
MR	Marion
MO	Monroe
OS	Osceola
PA	Pasco
PI	Pinellas
PU	Putnam
SO	Sarasota

veals that the people of the northern St. Johns region were involved in exchange networks that extended as far as Oklahoma (Goggin 1952:54; Griffin 1946:77, 88; Mitchem 1996:234; Williams and Goggin 1956:49–50). On the basis of ceramic types, Michael Russo (1992:118) has suggested that both the Shields and Grant Mounds may be part of a local St. Marys culture rather than the broader northern St. Johns cultural system.

Pre-Mississippian period sites were also investigated by Moore in northeast Florida. He illustrated Swift Creek Complicated Stamped vessels and sherds from Alicia Mound B (8DU31) (Moore 1895a:Plates LXXX and LXXXI), some of which exhibit identical paddle designs from nearby Early Swift Creek sites (Ashley 1995:32; Sears 1957:27, Plate IIB). In addition, Weeden Island influence in the region is clearly revealed by pottery vessels from the Gilbert (8DU11), Monroe (8DU13), and Denton Mounds (8DU24) (Moore 1895a:Plates LXXI, LXXIII, LXXXIII, and LXXXIV).

The second reprinted paper by Moore (1895c) deals solely with excavations at two mounds (8PU20 and 8PU21) on Murphy Island in the St. Johns River. One of these had been described by botanist John Bartram in 1765–1766 (Goggin 1952:31). Moore (1894a:15) first visited these sites in late 1892 or 1893, but the owner refused permission for excavations at that time. One of the sites had been partially excavated some years earlier by a local doctor, Frederick D. Lente (1877).

Most of Moore's 1895 work was concentrated on the northernmost Murphy Island mound (8PU20). The most remarkable items he illustrated were several copper artifacts. Two of these (1895c:Figures 59 and 61) appear to be the metal remains of copper-covered panpipes (or conjoined tubes). Although the mound had an obvi-

Table 3. Regional Chronologies of Florida (Archaeological Cultures)

Dates	Peninsular Gulf Coast	Caloosahatchee (S.W.)	Glades (South)	St. Johns (East)	St. Marys (N.E.)
A.D.	Seminole A.D. 1725–1850	Seminole A.D. 1750–1850	Seminole A.D. 1725–1850	Seminole A.D. 1763–1850	Protohistoric A.D. 1600/ 1700–1850?
1800					
1750				St. Augustine A.D. 1565–1763	
1700	Safety Harbor A.D. 900–1725 (includes Englewood)	Caloosahatchee V A.D. 1500–1750	Glades IIIc A.D. 1513–1725		
1650					
1600					St. Johns II/ Savannah A.D. 800– 1600/1700
1550				St. Johns IIc A.D. 1513–1565	
1500					
1450		Caloosahatchee IV A.D. 1350–1500	Glades IIIb A.D. 1400–1513	St. Johns IIb A.D. 1050–1513	
1400					
1350			Glades IIIa A.D. 1200–1400		
1300		Caloosahatchee III A.D. 1200–1350			
1250					
1200					
1150		Caloosahatchee IIB A.D. 800(?)–1200	Glades IIc A.D. 1100–1200		
1100					
1050			Glades IIb A.D. 900–1100		
1000				St. Johns IIa A.D. 750–1050	
950					
900					
850	Weeden Island/ Manasota A.D. 200–900		Glades IIa A.D. 750–900		
800					
750		Caloosahatchee IIA A.D. 650–800(?)			Colorinda/ Swift Creek A.D. 100–800
700			Glades I late A.D. 500–750	St. Johns Ib A.D. 500–750	
650					
600		Caloosahatchee I 500 B.C.–A.D. 650			
550					
500					
450			Glades I early 500 B.C.–A.D. 500	St. Johns Ia A.D. 100–500	
400					
350					
300					
250	Swift Creek A.D. 150–300				
200					
150					
100	Deptford/ Early Manasota 500 B.C.– A.D. 150				
A.D. 50				St. Johns I 500 B.C.– A.D. 100	Deptford/ St. Johns I? 500 B.C.– A.D. 800
0					
50 B.C.					
100					
150					
200					
250					
300					

Table 3. *Continued*

Dates	Peninsular Gulf Coast	Caloosahatchee (S.W.)	Glades (South)	St. Johns (East)	St. Marys (N.E.)
B.C.					
350					
400					
450					
500					
550	Late Archaic 3000–500 B.C.	Terminal Archaic ("Transitional") 1200–500 B.C.	Late Archaic 3000–500 B.C.	Orange 5 1000–500 B.C.	Transi- tional? 1000– 500 B.C.
600					
650					
700					
750					
800					
850					
900					
950					
1000					
1050				Orange 4 1250– 1000 B.C.	Orange? 1500– 1000 B.C
1100					
1150					
1200					
1250		Late Archaic 2000–1200 B.C.			
1300				Orange 3 1450–1250 B.C.	
1350					
1400					
1450					
1500				Orange 2 1650–1450 B.C.	
1550					Orange 2300– 1500 B.C.
1600					
1650					
1700				Orange 1 2000–1650 B.C. (may begin earlier)	
1750					
1800					
1850					
1900					
1950					
2000					
2500		Middle Archaic 5000–2000 B.C.		Mount Taylor (Middle Archaic) 5000–2000 B.C.	
3000					Preceramic Late Archaic 2300–4000 B.C.
3500	Middle Archaic 5000–3000 B.C.		Middle Archaic 5000–3000 B.C.		
4000					
4500					Not defined
5000					
5500	Early Archaic 7500–5000 B.C.	Early Archaic 6500–5000 B.C.	Early Archaic 7500–5000 B.C.	Early Archaic 7500–5000 B.C.	
6000					
6500					

Table 3. *Continued*

Dates	Peninsular Gulf Coast	Caloosahatchee (S.W.)	Glades (South)	St. Johns (East)	St. Marys (N.E.)
B.C.					
7000		Late Paleoindian 8500–6500 B.C.			
7500					
8000	Paleoindian 12,000?–7500 B.C.		Paleoindian 12,000?–7500 B.C.	Paleoindian 12,000?–7500 B.C.	
8500					
9000		Early Paleoindian 11,500?–8500 B.C.			
9500					
10,000					
10,500					
11,000					
11,500					
12,000					

Sources: Griffin 1988; Marquardt 1992b; Milanich 1994; Russo 1992.

ous superficial postcontact component, Moore recovered a meteoric iron object from a deep undisturbed context (1895c:514). The probable Hopewellian affinities of these objects have been noted by several authors (Brose 1979:145–146; Goggin 1949c:27, 1952:49–50; Greenman 1938; Griffin 1946:63).

Goggin (1952:87) assigned the northern mound to the St. Johns Ia period (ca. A.D. 100–500), along with an intrusive St. Johns IIc (A.D. 1513–1565) component. Moore (1895c:515–516) provided little description of artifacts from the southernmost mound (8PU21), but Goggin (1952:87) postulated that it dated from the St. Johns IIa period (A.D. 750–1050). On the basis of the island's geographical position and European artifacts recovered from 8PU20, Milanich (1994:270) has suggested that this island may have been the location of Edelano, an aboriginal village mentioned by French explorers in the 1560s (but for an alternative view, see Beasley 1997).

The third reprinted paper reports Moore's (1895b) investigations along the Ocklawaha River, which flows into the St. Johns River from the western side. Moore (1895b:518) noted that the river was narrow and winding and very shallow in places. It is well known that he used a stern-wheel steamboat, the *Gopher of Philadelphia,* in his travels and excavations (Knight 1996:3–4; see also a later section of this essay), but the winding nature and shallow depth of the Ocklawaha precluded use of the *Gopher* on this river. Research by Cynthia Cerrato (1996) reveals that Moore used another steamboat, the *Alligator,* for travel and work along the Ocklawaha.

The *Alligator* (Figure 2) was built in 1888 and was probably customized for Moore's use, with space for artifact analysis and storage and a photography laboratory on the lower deck. When loaded, the boat had a draft of only one and a half feet, and had a paddlewheel that was located farther forward on the craft than on the *Gopher* (Cerrato 1996). Moore apparently chartered the boat at Palatka for one of his exploratory trips along the St. Johns River and some of its tributaries north of Sanford, but decided to buy the boat at some point (Cynthia L. Cerrato, personal communication 1996; Moore 1891). It is not known how long Moore owned the *Alligator*. Earlier in 1891, he had chartered another boat out of Palatka, the *Osceola* (Mitchem 1999:Figures 2 and 3; Moore 1891).

An interesting anecdote about Moore's research on the Ocklawaha in early 1895 was recorded by Frederick R. Swift (1903:47–49). Swift was a wealthy salesman from New York City whose hobbies were yachting and hunting. He spent several winters in Florida beginning in the 1890s (Swift 1903). The anecdote is worth quoting in its entirety because it contains some details about Moore's activities and his boat, although Swift regarded Moore as an eccentric.

> We were about to tie up at noon when a series of unearthly whistles shook me into the shivers. I was watching what I thought was a deer ahead fording the river, but I dropped my gun in amazement.
>
> Again it sounded, and I counted five, the signal of a steamer in distress. I had heard and read of all kinds of apparitions but never of a steamer's ghost. There never had been a steamer through this narrow, shallow stream. That was an impossibility. Then what could it be?
>
> I climbed to the top of the cabin house and could distinctly see, a mile away through a break in the trees, a boat I recognized in a sheep's tail-shake. It was the *Alligator*, owned by Dr. Moore, of Philadelphia. That explained everything. Dr. Moore has a fad. And he can't seem to get over it. His fad is hunting for Indian relics, and he's chased them from coast to coast. Every winter for years I have met him in some out-of-the-way place on his digging expeditions in Florida. And as long as he's alive I suppose he'll keep right on at the same old game. He's rich enough, so I shan't stop him.
>
> As for myself, I hunted with him one day, but it was too monotonous. It struck me as being a very dead kind of sport. I felt at the end of the day as if I wanted to stick up one of the Indian skulls and shoot at an eye-hole to see if it wouldn't wink once more. The Doctor has published several large-sized works nobly illustrated with pictures of an only good Indian's bones. The books are not intensely exciting and the largeness is in their size and not in circulation.
>
> The *Alligator* is a small-sized edition of an Ocklawaha steamer, about sixty feet long and twelve wide. She was built expressly for the Doctor and only draws a foot and a half of water, loaded. The Doctor appears in Florida about September, bringing with him his cook, his steward, his engineer, and captain. Then he hires his waiters and other help in Palatka, including about twenty colored gentlemen to do the excavating.
>
> I suppose the Doctor is the best Indian mound hunter in the world. I never could tell how he ever trailed them as he was shy on dogs and the two he did have seemed to be poor mongrel brutes, and no use for sport. He seemed to sniff them from afar, but that don't look probable, as the relics had been *passe* too long. What he ever did with his game was a mystery to me. There was a photograph factory on board, but no tallow dip or phosphate store. And I know he told me once that he got seven thousand pieces out of one mound.
>
> So we kept on for another mile and came upon the relic hunter and his boat in

Figure 2. Clarence B. Moore's *Alligator* on the Ocklawaha River, probably in 1900. Photograph courtesy of the Florida State Archives. Used by permission.

> distress. The water had deepened and the current was running strong. The bow of the boat had lodged up against one bank, the current had struck the stern, which married the other bank, and there she was, stuck fast.
>
> The *Lela Bell* went into business as a tug boat, and after an hour's pulling we got the *Alligator* off. Then, as we were both booked for the same way, we joined hands. For two weeks we were together, and as the Doctor had some friends with him who played the usual Philadelphia game of poker, I passed many an enjoyable evening. We parted company about ten miles from Lake Griffin, as the Doctor sniffed a mound [Swift 1903:47–49].

At most of the Ocklawaha sites, Moore found few artifacts, and his descriptions were often cursory, but the illustrations allow tentative temporal placement in many cases. For the Mound near Silver Springs (8MR33), Goggin (1952:96) assigned an age of St. Johns Ia to Ib (ca. A.D. 100–750), no doubt a result of Moore's (1895b:Plate LXXXV) illustration of a Deptford Linear Check Stamped vessel from the site. At the Hopson Mound (8LA47), the predominance of Dunns Creek Red pottery suggests a St. Johns Ia or early Ib (ca. A.D. 100–600) date (Milanich 1994:247).

The Tavares Mound (8LA52), which had already been disturbed prior to Moore's excavations, yielded mainly plain, red-colored pottery (Moore 1895b:536). If this was Dunns Creek Red, the mound would most likely date to St. Johns Ia or early Ib, as in the case of 8LA47. Moore's (1895b:Plate LXXXVI) illustration of a Weeden Island Incised sherd corroborates this general dating of the site.

Moore (1895b:539) made brief mention of a nearby smaller mound (8LA53), which had yielded European metal artifacts and glass beads. Decades later, this site was investigated by Frederick W. Sleight (1949), who recovered three pottery vessels and numerous glass beads and a glass pendant from the disturbed soil. One of the vessels (Sleight 1949:Figure 9a) was of the type Sarasota Incised. This type is typical of the Englewood phase (ca. A.D. 900–1100) of the Safety Harbor culture (Milanich 1994:389; Mitchem 1989:557–561), and the Tavares vessel may indicate exchange with the Gulf Coast. The glass beads were primarily undiagnostic seed beads, but the glass pendant description indicates it is probably a Punta Rassa Teardrop Pendant, a type typically found on late-seventeenth-century contact sites in Florida (Goggin n.d.; Mitchem 1993:403–404). Considered together, these artifacts imply a late prehistoric date for the mound, with a later intrusive component.

The presence of St. Johns Check Stamped at the Barclay's site (8LA44) indicates that it probably dates to St. Johns IIa (beginning A.D. 750) or later (Milanich 1994:247). The mention of two glass beads on the surface (Moore 1895b:539) points to a postcontact date or component.

The cursory description of the Low Mound near Helena (8LA56) includes mention of sherds decorated with red pigment and curves of punctations (Moore 1895b:541). These may refer to Dunns Creek Red and Weeden Island types, which would probably date within a range of A.D. 100–750 (St. Johns Ia or Ib).

The Mound near Old Okahumpka (8LA57) yielded late prehistoric pottery and part of a copper plate decorated with a repoussé dancing human figure (Moore 1895b:542–543). The only sherd illustrated by Moore (1895b:Figure 91) is almost identical to a sherd from a Safety Harbor site in Pasco County (Mitchem 1996:Figures 6 and 7), and the Old Okahumpka site, like 8LA53, appears to show contact with the Mississippian period Safety Harbor Culture on the Gulf Coast. Willey (1949:557), in his work on Florida Gulf Coast archaeology, noted that the Lake County region showed affinities to both the St. Johns area and the Gulf Coast. The probable date range for the site is A.D. 1100–1300 (Mitchem 1996:229).

The copper plate from Old Okahumpka (Goggin 1949d:Figure 11; Mitchem 1996:Figure 3) depicts the lower half of a dancing figure and is nearly identical to plates from the Spiro site in Oklahoma and a site in Jackson County, Alabama (Hamilton et al. 1974:157–159; Phillips and Brown 1978:Figure 217). It has been proposed (Mitchem 1996:234; Phillips and Brown 1978:206–208) that the Mississippian period populations in the northern half of Florida were involved in the *Busycon* shell trade with Mississippian groups to the north and west, which provides a plausible explanation for the presence of exotic copper artifacts at such sites as Old Okahumpka and those in the northern St. Johns region.

The remaining papers reprinted in this volume deal primarily with Moore's investigations along the Gulf Coast of Florida. Moore (1900:351) was attracted to this part of Florida by the interesting discoveries made by Frank Hamilton Cushing at Key Marco a few years earlier (Cushing 1896; Gilliland 1975, 1989).

The first site he reported was what is now known as the Bayshore Homes site

(8PI41). Moore (1900:352–353) referred to it as "Four Mile Bayou," named for an inlet to the west (the waterway that leads to Cross and Long Bayous). This is probably the site mentioned by S. T. Walker (1880a:403), where he was refused permission to excavate. It included three mounds and a shell midden. Other than his references to check-stamped pottery, Moore (1900:352) did not mention any artifacts from the site. William H. Sears (1960) conducted excavations in one of the mounds and in the midden and recorded information on the remaining two mounds while they were being destroyed by development. From what he termed Mound B (Moore's mound "300 yards in a northerly direction from Mr. Girard's Place" [Moore 1900:352]), Sears (1960:24) recovered 118 burials, but estimated that as many as 500 people had originally been buried there. The skeletal remains were later analyzed by Charles E. Snow (1962). Ceramics recovered in Sears's (1960:29–31) excavations demonstrated that the site dated from late Weeden Island times (ca. A.D. 700–900 [Milanich 1994:224–227]).

The site complex on Maximo Point (8PI19 and 8PI31) has been the subject of a great deal of archaeological investigation. The site was first recorded by S. T. Walker (1880a:404–405, 1880b:419), who excavated a few test pits, but he was unable to map the site due to the heavy vegetation. Moore (1900:353–354, Figure 1) succeeded in producing a map of the complicated shell middens and earthworks and dug a few small excavations where the landowners gave permission. Neither Walker nor Moore described any artifacts from the site.

Modern excavations at various parts of the site complex were conducted by Sears (1958), Bushnell (1962), students of Florida Presbyterian College (Lazarus 1963), Williams (1979), and Boyle et al. (1986). These investigations revealed evidence of occupation dating from as early as the Archaic (ca. 7500–500 B.C. [Milanich 1994]) through Safety Harbor (A.D. 900–1725), with Weeden Island and Safety Harbor assemblages predominating (Mitchem 1989:75–79). A Florida Cut Crystal bead and some small Cornaline d'Aleppo beads collected by Walker (now in the collections of the National Museum of Natural History, Smithsonian Institution) indicate some occupation in the late sixteenth or seventeenth centuries (Deagan 1987:168, 180), and more recent Spanish artifacts undoubtedly date from the 1843–1848 fishing *rancho* of Antonio Maximo, the first nonaboriginal settler at the site (Austin and Hardin 1987:271; Bethell 1914:7; Mitchem 1989:79).

Moore's (1900:355) "Mound on Pine Key" is part of the Tierra Verde site complex (8PI1692 and 8PI51), located on what is today known as Cabbage Key. The mound was first visited by Walker (1880a:404), who excavated four human crania and a bone ornament inlaid with copper. Moore (1900:355) did not illustrate artifacts from the site, but mentioned incised and punctated sherds.

Prior to the mound's destruction by development in the 1960s, avocational archaeologists (Warren et al. 1965) dug at the site, followed by major excavations by Sears (1967). These investigations demonstrated beyond doubt that the mound was a Safety Harbor (ca. A.D. 900–1725) burial mound, probably dating to the earlier part of the time range (Mitchem 1989:80–85). The site produced the best-known collection of Safety Harbor decorated ceramics (most from a cache at the east edge), and Sears (1967) was able to demonstrate continuity with earlier Weeden Island pottery styles and possible influence from other areas of the Southeast. Dale L. Hutchinson's (1993) analysis of the skeletal material from Sears's excavations revealed that at least forty-eight individuals were buried there, some of whom suffered from treponematosis.

The Hirrihigua Mound (8PI108) is probably the mound on the Henderson property near Point Pinelos (now called Pinellas Point) in which Moore excavated (1900:355–356). Part of this mound is still preserved as a small park in a residential neighborhood. It was first described and drawn by Walker (1880a:405–407, Plate VI[3 and 4]), who referred to it as "Mound at Bethel's Camp." His minor excavations turned up only a few sherds, which he did not describe. Moore (1900:356) likewise found few artifacts, none of which he illustrated. More than two decades later, the site was visited and photographed by David I. Bushnell (1926:126–127, Figure 121), who collected only shells from it. The site is generally assumed to be a Safety Harbor mound (Mitchem 1989:91), but it could also date from late Weeden Island times.

The burial mound at Shell Bluff (8HI22), south of the Alafia River (Moore 1900:356), probably dates from late Weeden Island times (ca. A.D. 700–900 [Milanich 1994:224]). This proposed dating is based on analysis of a small collection from the site in the Florida Museum of Natural History and results of 1980 salvage excavations on remains of this mound or one in the immediate vicinity (Mitchem 1987).

On the north side of the Alafia River, the complex of features at Mill Point (Moore 1900:356–357, Figure 2) have been assigned five site numbers (8HI16, 8HI17, 8HI18, 8HI19, and 8HI20). Moore did not describe any artifacts from the site. A small collection from 8HI16 in the Florida Museum of Natural History (Mitchem 1989:Table 12) indicates either a late Weeden Island or Safety Harbor date. The configuration of the site argues for its having been a Safety Harbor town (Mitchem 1989:117). Unfortunately, most of the site has been destroyed by industrial development.

The Bullfrog Mound (8HI12) had already been largely removed for road fill when Moore (1900:357–358) visited the area. This shell midden was described, mapped, and drawn by Walker (1880b:417, 422, Plate IV[1]), who noted its tremendous size. James Shepard (1886:905–906) also commented on the great size of the site, but indicated that large quantities of shells were being used to produce lime. Unfortunately, the time period of the site's construction is not known. The site had been completely destroyed by 1904 (Moore 1905:304).

Moore's "Mound Near Little Manatee River" (1900:358–359) is most commonly known as the Thomas Mound and was the subject of two WPA excavations during the period from 1935 to 1937 (Lyon 1996:116). Results of the first project were reported in detail by Willey (1949:113–125), along with analysis of some additional collections. The results of the second were briefly summarized by J. Clarence Simpson (1937:111–113), then included in a more comprehensive report on eleven sites by Ripley P. Bullen (1952:7–20). These projects revealed that the mound was a burial mound first used by people of the Manasota culture (A.D. 300–700), who "practiced early Weeden Island burial ceremonialism" (Milanich 1994:221). The mound continued to be used by the succeeding Safety Harbor culture people, beginning about A.D. 900. The presence of glass beads and looking-glass fragments (Moore 1900:359), plus additional European artifacts found during the WPA work, indicates that the mound was probably still being used during the Tatham and Bayview phases of the Safety Harbor culture (Milanich 1994:389).

The Indian Hill site reported and illustrated by Moore (1900:359–360, Figure

4), now known as Cockroach Key (8HI2), was likewise the subject of WPA excavations in 1936 (Lyon 1996:116). The first record of the site was probably by Walker (1880b:418–419, 422, Plate IV[2]), though he failed to mention that the complex of shell middens was located on an island. Although Moore did not describe any artifacts from the site, the analyses of the WPA excavations (Bullen 1952:20–25; Willey 1949:158–172) reveal that Cockroach Key was probably occupied from early Manasota (ca. 500 B.C.–A.D. 400) through late Weeden Island (A.D. 700–900) times (Luer and Almy 1982; Milanich 1994:224).

After discussing Indian Hill/Cockroach Key, Moore (1900:360–362) provided cursory descriptions of several sites south of Tampa Bay. He mentioned three features of the Terra Ceia site (8MA83), located on Terra Ceia Island. Although Moore reported no artifacts from Terra Ceia, Bullen (1951) conducted major excavations and analysis of collections from the various sites on the island, which are all considered part of a single complex. Bullen's work demonstrated that the main occupation of the sites dates from Manasota (500 B.C.–A.D. 700) and prehistoric Safety Harbor (A.D. 900–1500) (Milanich 1994:221–222, 389). More recent excavations at the part of the site known as Boots Point Shell Midden (8MA83D) by B. William Burger (1988) recovered late-sixteenth-century Spanish and aboriginal remains.

Heading up the Manatee River, Moore (1900:360) dug in three small mounds near what was at that time the Erie Post Office. One of these, belonging to a Mr. L. P. Foy, was probably 8MA50, known as the Honey Mound (Burger 1982:193). Burger (personal communication 1997) noted that records for this site indicate that sherds were present, but the types were not identified. Moore (1900:360) found only scattered bones in this site and the two nearby mounds. These two mounds (on land owned by Mr. Louis Brubacher) were apparently never recorded in the Florida Master Site File (B. William Burger, personal communication 1997).

Although we cannot identify some of the other sites Moore (1900:362) dug in Manatee County, two of them are sites that have been recorded in the Florida Master Site File. The mound near Snell's Bayou (now known as Whitaker Bayou) was probably the Weber Mound (8SO20), which was investigated by Bullen (1950:22–27) during its destruction in 1950. Artifacts from the burial mound (Bullen 1950:Figure 5; Luer 1992b:228; Mitchem 1989:223; Monroe et al. 1982:15, 83–84) suggest that it dated from late Weeden Island and Safety Harbor times (ca. A.D. 800–1500).

The mound one-half mile south of Sarasota (Moore 1900:362) was the Sarasota Bay Mound (8SO44). Although Moore did not find burials or artifacts worthy of description, burials and pottery were discovered by workmen building a house on the site in the 1920s (Grismer 1946:12). Salvage excavations in 1968 by Ripley P. Bullen recovered poorly preserved skeletons and sherds prior to the mound's destruction (Monroe et al. 1982:89–90). The Florida Master Site File lists Weeden Island and Safety Harbor components (ca. A.D. 200–1500) for the site (Mitchem 1989:226).

Moore continued working his way south and arrived at Pine Island. He first visited an extensive shell midden, Indian Old Field (8LL39), where he apparently did not excavate (Moore 1900:362). Excavations and surface collections at the site by personnel from the University of Florida in 1952 indicate a late prehistoric and/ or early contact component and glass beads from a nineteenth-century Seminole occupation (Mitchem 1989:275–277, Table 41). More recent work by George M. Luer (1989a:99–105, 1989b) resulted in additional evidence from these time periods.

Less than a mile from Indian Old Field, Moore (1900:362–363) trenched a burial mound, now known as Pine Island 8 (8LL40). The European artifacts he recovered indicate the presence of a Caloosahatchee V (A.D. 1500–1750) component in the mound (Marquardt 1992b:Table 2). Moore (1905:305–308) returned to the site in 1904 and completely excavated the remainder (Luer 1989a:97–99). He noted quantities of European goods accompanying burials throughout the mound in the latter investigations and concluded that the entire mound was of postcontact construction (Moore 1905:308). Goggin (1949a:298) identified a sherd illustrated by Moore (1905:Figure 6) as Safety Harbor Incised, but Mitchem (1989:281–283) identified this as Fort Walton Incised, *var. Sneads* (Scarry 1985:219, Figure 5b). If this latter identification is correct, it suggests contact with northwest Florida, although the nature of that contact is open to question.

The Pine Island 8 Mound was associated with a pond and a canal, both of which were constructed by the aboriginal inhabitants (Luer and Wheeler 1997:Figures 9 and 10). The mound no longer exists, and the site was recently described as "a crater in a mangrove swamp" (George M. Luer, personal communication 1997).

Brief visits were made at two nearby islands, Mondongo (8LL52) and Joseffa (now known as Useppa [8LL51]). Moore (1900:363) decided not to dig at either place, though he noted both were covered with shell middens. Useppa Island has been the subject of several investigations since Moore's visit. Work by John W. Griffin (1949), Milanich et al. (1984), and Marquardt (1992b:Table 2, 25–29, 1999) demonstrated that human occupation of the island lasted from Middle Archaic times (ca. 5000 B.C.) through the Caloosahatchee IIB period (ca. A.D. 1200), with additional settlements beginning in the nineteenth century.

Moore (1900:363) was unsuccessful in finding anything on Josslyn Island (8LL32). Recent work under the direction of William H. Marquardt (1984, 1992a) has revealed occupation on the island spanning the period of ca. 500 B.C. to A.D. 1350, including parts of the Caloosahatchee I through III periods (Marquardt 1992b:Table 2).

At Demorey (or Demere) Key (8LL31), Moore's (1900:363–366) work revealed that a curious conch-shell faced platform that had been described and drawn by Cushing (1896:338–341, Plate XXVIII) was actually of modern construction. The Florida Master Site File also lists earlier components for this site.

Moore's (1900:366–369) endeavors on Mound Island (now known as Mound Key) were disappointing, in both the main site (8LL2) and the burial mound (8LL3). He corrected Cushing's (1896:347–348) earlier measurements and provided a drawing of the mound and an associated canal (Moore 1900:Figure 7). Both before and since Moore's visit, a tremendous number of collections have come from these two sites, and they are in many different repositories (see summary in Mitchem 1989:258–267). These collections include artifacts dating from Caloosahatchee I through V (ca. 500 B.C.–A.D. 1750), with an especially large number of late-sixteenth- and seventeenth-century Spanish artifacts (Mitchem 1989:265). The location of the island and these Spanish artifacts have prompted archaeologists to propose that this island was the site of Calos, the principal town of the Calusa Indians and the residence of their paramount chief, Carlos (Goggin and Sturtevant 1964:182–183; Widmer 1988:5).

Moore (1900:369) then began exploring parts of the Ten Thousand Islands, noting that the name underestimates their true number. After mentioning shell ridges and mounds on Little Marco Island (8CR50), he arrived at Key Marco, with obvious anticipation. Both Charles Durnford (1895) and Frank Cushing (1896) had excavated marvelous wooden and other organic artifacts from the muck in an area (8CR49) between some shell ridges (Gilliland 1975, 1988, 1989; Snapp 1996). Much to his dismay, Moore (1900:369–371) found nothing in his excavation of an adjacent muck deposit (8CR48), but he did obtain a collection of shell and stone plummets and shell gorgets/discs from a local resident. Moore (1900:380) correctly inferred that Cushing's preserved wooden artifacts had resulted from continuous immersion in wet muck soil and that wooden implements were probably common in aboriginal Florida, but most had not been preserved.

Several projects have focused on Marco Island since Moore's visit. Vernon Lamme (1978:55) indicated that Matthew Stirling of the Smithsonian Institution worked there in the early 1930s. In 1963, local avocational archaeologists excavated in a midden deposit near Cushing's 8CR49 (Van Beck and Van Beck 1965; Wing 1965), revealing artifacts dating to Glades II and early Glades III (ca. A.D. 750–1300). Wilburn A. Cockrell (1970) investigated pre–A.D. 500 occupation in 1967 and 1969. Randolph J. Widmer (1996) has recently conducted additional work at Moore's 8CR48 and was able to confirm an occupation date of A.D. 500–900 for the site.

From Goodland Point (8CR45 and 8CR46), Moore (1900:371–376) excavated and purchased a number of temporally undiagnostic shell and stone artifacts. He illustrated two bird head adornos (Luer 1992a:52, Figures 1b and 1c; Moore 1900:Figures 20 and 21). The sites were visited by Aleš Hrdlička (1922:24) and other researchers, but Goggin (1949b) was the first to analyze collections from 8CR45. His analysis revealed occupation spanning Glades I through Glades IIIc (ca. 500 B.C. to post–A.D. 1513).

After leaving Goodland Point, Moore (1900:376–377) made brief mentions of several keys and islands with shell features and sites on them, but he did little digging. One site Moore visited, the Blue Hill burial mound on Horr's Island (8CR41), was the subject of excavations in 1930 by Matthew W. Stirling (1931:167, 171, Figure 143). Stirling then returned in 1931 to conduct more extensive excavations (Lamme 1978:55; Stirling 1933). Unfortunately, no report on the excavations was ever completed. Recent research on Horr's Island (although not at the Blue Hill site) has revealed a substantial Archaic occupation (Russo 1991, 1994, 1996). Moore described a mound on Chokoloskee Key (8CR1) and purchased stone, bone, and coral artifacts from the site, some of which he illustrated (Moore 1900:Figures 22–28).

The Turner River site (8CR2) has been the subject of considerable research since Moore's visit. Hrdlička (1922:36–39) was greatly impressed by the site. Excavations by William Sears in 1955 (Sears 1956) and subsequent research by the National Park Service (Griffin 1988:239–244; Taylor 1985:71) produced a date range of late Glades I through IIb (ca. A.D. 500–1100).

In his conclusion to this paper, Moore (1900:380) noted that, on the basis of Cushing's (1896) discoveries at Key Marco, wooden artifacts were probably once abundant in the Florida sites. Subsequent research has demonstrated that this was indeed the case (Purdy 1988), though evidence is normally found only in continuously wet sites. Moore (1900:380–394) concluded the paper by illustrating and discussing a number of shell tools from southwest Florida sites.

The fifth reprinted paper is an excerpt from a long work on research in northwest Florida (Moore 1902). This section describes excavations at some sites in Levy County. Because Moore's other work in that county is also reprinted here (Moore 1903), the decision was made to include the excerpt in this volume. The complete 1902 work (including this excerpt) is reprinted in the volume on northwest Florida (Brose and White 1999).

The Mound on Hog Island (8LV26) had been dug into prior to Moore's (1902:348) visit. He did not mention finding any artifacts and devoted little time to this sand-covered shell midden (Moore 1902:348). Willey (1949:315) mentioned the site, but the time period of occupation is unknown.

In describing the location of the next two mounds, Moore (1902:348–349) made reference to a very large shell heap (8LV42) on the nearby mainland, which he considered to be the northernmost of the exceptionally large shell middens on the west coast (Dorian 1980:46–47). There is no indication that he excavated in this site, however, probably because the landowner's house was on top of it (Moore 1902:349).

There is some confusion about the Mound on Pine Key, the next site Moore (1902:348–349) investigated. Moore's description of the location indicates that it is on an island about a quarter mile from 8LV42. Notes in the Florida Master Site File indicate that the Mound on Pine Key was first assigned the site number 8LV40, but it is probably the same site recorded as Graveyard Island (8LV2) and Palmetto Island (8LV7). The confusion is due to the fact that the many small islands in the Cedar Key region have been known by multiple names. The likelihood that the three site numbers represent the same site is supported by the fact that sherds from the Graveyard Island (8LV2) and Palmetto Island (8LV7) collections in the Florida Museum of Natural History were pieces of the same vessels that fit together (Borremans and Moseley 1990:32).

Moore's (1902:349) work at the Pine Key Mound demonstrated that it was actually a cemetery covering about a quarter acre. Despite a great deal of former digging, his workers encountered mass deposits of bone as well as single burials, both flexed and secondary (bundle) interments (Moore 1902:349). Moore (1902:349) mentioned check stamped and complicated stamped pottery, but noted that most of the ceramics were apparently undecorated.

Notes in the Florida Master Site File and in Willey (1949:308, 311–312) indicate that this site was probably dug into by Decatur Pittman in the 1880s, whose massive collection from the site is now curated at the Florida Museum of Natural History (Willey 1949:311–312). Two other collections from the same site (listed as 8LV7) in the same museum were amassed by T. Van Hyning in 1924 and St. Clair Whitman in the early twentieth century. Bradenton collector Montague Tallant probably also dug there in the early twentieth century (Willey 1949:308). John M. Goggin and University of Florida students excavated a ten x ten foot square on the east edge of the site in 1952, but no report was written. Visits to the site in 1989 revealed that the site had experienced additional looting in more recent decades (Borremans and Moseley 1990:32).

The collections from 8LV40/2/7 in the Florida Museum of Natural History, along with Moore's (1902:349) description of artifacts, reveal that the site dates from Weeden Island times (A.D. 200–900), including an early Weeden Island Swift Creek component (A.D. 150–300) (Milanich 1994:211–214).

Moore (1902:349) next presented a brief report on the Mound near the Shell-Heap (8LV41), located about three hundred yards from the great shell mound (8LV42). Major trenching of this mound revealed that it was constructed of alternating layers of oyster shells and sand, but only a few fragments of human bone and "rude earthenware" were noted by Moore (1902:349). On the basis of the limited description, it can be inferred that it was a prehistoric burial mound dating from sometime after the introduction of pottery (ca. 2500–2000 B.C.).

The remainder of this excerpt from the 1902 paper is primarily a summary of Moore's (1902:349–355) observations on pottery and burial customs from his work in Florida, both in the peninsula and in the northwest part of the state. Moore (1902:352) believed that the pottery from the northwest Florida coast was much better made and more beautiful than that found in the peninsula, and he hypothesized that the finest wares found in the peninsula were imported vessels. Nonetheless, technological studies from peninsular Florida indicate that most pottery was being produced locally, including ornate Weeden Island mortuary vessels (Cordell 1984, 1992). Moore (1902:352–355) also discussed intentional perforation of mortuary vessels, massive deposits of vessels on the eastern edge of mounds (especially prevalent on the northwest Florida coast), urn burials, and the rarity of cremation in Florida mounds. In these discussions and the accompanying footnotes, Moore demonstrated his breadth of knowledge and familiarity with the pertinent scientific literature of the day.

The longest paper reprinted here is Moore's report on his work during 1903, when he explored sites along the Gulf Coast from the Suwannee River to Tampa Bay (Moore 1903). The first site he visited was Fowler's Landing (8LV1), from which he recovered and illustrated a number of decorated vessels and sherds (Moore 1903:364–371). The site was a Weeden Island (ca. A.D. 200–900) burial mound, probably dating to the earlier part of the range (Willey 1949:307). After a brief account of a nearby small mound (8LV14), where he found only one sherd, he illustrated a unique copper "fish-spear" found near Fannin on the Suwannee River (Moore 1903:371–373, Figure 9). It is impossible to determine the date of manufacture of this implement, and the site where it was found has not been located.

Moore (1903:373) then provided a summary discussion of five sites (8DI19, 8GI5, 8LV130, 8DI18, and 8DI20) that he investigated along the Suwannee River. It is impossible to tell the temporal or cultural affiliations from his descriptions, with the possible exception of 8DI18 (Fayetteville Mound), where descriptions of the decorated sherds probably refer to Weeden Island types.

After trenching the Lutterloh Mound (8LV38) with negative results, Moore (1903:374–377) proceeded to Gigger Point (8LV3), a major Weeden Island period burial mound. After digging here with some success, he continued exploring mounds in Levy County (8LV16, 8LV17, and 8LV11), none of which can be dated based on his descriptions (Moore 1903:377). Nevertheless, collections by John M. Goggin from the second of Moore's (1903:377) Mounds on Dry Creek (8LV17, also known as the Stonewall Pond site) included sherds of Pasco Plain, St. Johns Plain, St. Johns Check

Stamped, and a punctated gritty ware (Jones and Borremans 1991:29). These types suggest either a Weeden Island or Safety Harbor date for the mound.

His work at Bear Landing (8LV18) revealed that it was a badly disturbed burial mound, and he illustrated a crude incised bowl (Moore 1903:377–378, Figure 15). Descriptions of some of the vessels suggest that the site might date from Weeden Island times.

After fruitless exploration of a mound near Rock Landing (8CI17), Moore (1903:379–413) arrived at Crystal River (8CI1). This was his first and most extensive episode of work at this famous site. He was so impressed that he returned two additional times (Moore 1907a:406–425, 1918:571–573). The site yielded a diverse variety of artifacts of pottery, shell, copper, stone, and other materials. Moore's three episodes of work at the site were concentrated on the burial complex, consisting of a tiered sand mound surrounded by a sand embankment.

Only a few excavations have been carried out at the multicomponent Crystal River site since Moore's time, but it has been the subject of an enormous amount of interpretation and speculation (Weisman 1995; Willey 1949:316–323). The obvious similarity of some of the artifacts to Hopewell artifacts from Ohio and elsewhere was noted in Moore's (1903:409–410) initial report, as a result of his correspondence with Charles C. Willoughby of the Peabody Museum at Harvard University. Later authors also recognized the similarities (Brose 1979; Greenman 1938; McMichael 1964; Sears 1962; Willey 1948b; Willey and Phillips 1958:160). Some scholars have posited connections with Veracruz, Mexico (Bullen 1966; Ford 1966, 1969; McMichael 1960, 1964), and other authors claim there is astronomical significance to the layout of the site (Hardman 1971; Williamson 1984).

Crystal River has Deptford and Weeden Island components, demonstrating that it was occupied between about 500 B.C. and A.D. 900. Whether it was occupied after A.D. 900 is open to debate. Brent R. Weisman (1995) wrote an excellent overview that summarizes published and unpublished research on the site, as well as an analysis of the many artifacts recovered by Moore and others.

When he left Crystal River, Moore (1903:413–414) investigated a nearby mound (8CI10) with negative results, then excavated several burials at a mound on the Chassahowitzka River (8CI3). Willey (1949:324) suggested that this mound probably dates to late Weeden Island times, though the bird head rim adorno (Luer 1992a:54, Figure 1d; Moore 1903:Figure 63) might indicate a Safety Harbor component. Moore (1903:414–415) continued south, digging several trenches in the Mound near Indian Bend (8HE2). This was probably a late Weeden Island burial mound (Willey 1949:326).

Near Bayport, Moore (1903:415–424) excavated a burial mound (8HE1). From his illustrations of sherds, it is clear that this was a Weeden Island burial mound that was also used in early Safety Harbor times, the latter evidenced by a sherd of Englewood Incised (1903:Figure 66) and part of a Safety Harbor Incised bottle (1903:Figure 71). From this site, Moore (1903:424) investigated another mound (8HE3), in which he encountered no artifacts.

Near the Wekiwachee (now spelled "Weekiwachee") River, Moore (1903:425–426) excavated many burials from a sand mound (8PA1). From illustrated sherds and other collections, Willey (1949:328–329) dates this mound to Weeden Island times (ca. A.D. 200–900), probably late Weeden Island.

At the Pithlochascootie River, Moore (1903:426–433) investigated a burial mound (8PA2) that had been previously reported by S. T. Walker (1880a:392–394). It was associated with a platform mound, and both are now known as the Oelsner Mounds. A master's thesis by Michael S. Garner (1993) summarized the early work at the site, along with a report of the results of more recent testing. The site dates from late Weeden Island, with a Safety Harbor component (Garner 1993; Mitchem 1989:44–45).

Although he did not dig there, Moore (1903:433) made mention of a mound near Tarpon Springs (the Safford Mound, 8PI3), where both Walker (1880a:396–399) and Cushing (1896:352–354) had excavated. William H. Holmes (1903:126–127, Plates CI–CIV, CVI–CIX) illustrated a number of the vessels excavated by Cushing, most of which were clearly Weeden Island types. Bullen et al. (1970) and Smith (1971:131–133) later analyzed the collections from the site, revealing occupation from Deptford through Safety Harbor times (ca. 500 B.C.–A.D. 1500). Phyllis Kolianos (1998) recently relocated the site, parts of which may be intact.

It is impossible to determine the date of occupation for the Mound on Hog Island (8PI9) or the Mound near Clearwater (8PI10) because Moore (1903:433–434) did not report any artifacts from either site. At John's Pass (8PI4), Moore (1903:434–436) again dug at a site previously investigated by Walker (1880a:401–403). After Moore's visit, this mound was also excavated by Bethell (1914:54–55) and surface collected by Ostrander (1960). Sherds illustrated by Moore and Ostrander indicate that the site is a Safety Harbor (post–A.D. 900) burial mound. A glass bead and a silver bead reported by Walker (1880a:401) indicate that at least part of the occupation was postcontact (A.D. 1500–1725).

The last site described by Moore (1903:436–438) in this paper is another mound investigated earlier by Walker (1880a:403–404, Plate V), the Long Key Mound (8PI11). Because Walker had described it as being in the shape of a turtle, Moore (1903:Figure 89) drew a careful plan view map of the site. Although he noted hematite-stained sand and one human burial, Moore found no artifacts.

The next paper by Moore (1905) reports the results of his 1904 fieldwork. Moore (1905:299) noted that this field season was a disappointing one. It was devoted to work in the interior region of central Florida and along the southwest coast. The work in the Kissimmee region was hampered by difficulty of travel in the weed-clogged canals and Kissimmee River, for which Moore (1905:299) chartered a small steamer and a flatboat because the *Gopher* was unable to travel to the region from the Gulf Coast. The Kissimmee work was abandoned when the boiler on the chartered steamboat was damaged in an accident.

Around Lake Tohopekaliga, Moore (1905:300–302) visited nine mounds. The Mound near Kissimmee (also known as the Bass Mound, 8OS24) yielded check stamped and incised sherds. The Florida Master Site File gives a St. Johns II affiliation for the site, which would date ca. A.D. 750–1565 (Milanich 1994:247). The long sand ridge known as the Lanier Mound (8OS26) cannot be dated on the basis of Moore's (1905:300) description.

The Mounds near Brown's Landing (8OS21, 8OS22, and 8OS23) were cursorily excavated by Moore (1905:300–301). These three sites were further investigated in a survey by Hardin et al. (1984). One of them, 8OS21 (Moore's "2 miles in a southwesterly direction," also known as the Southport Mound), was the subject of major excavations in 1996 because it is located where a landfill is planned (Robert J. Austin, personal communication 1996). Glass beads recovered in the 1996 project reveal a postcontact component dating to the late sixteenth or seventeenth century (Mitchem et al. 1998).

Of the remaining four mounds in the region, only two have site numbers (Frier Cove [8OS20] and McCool's Landing [8OS19]). The brief description of Moore's (1905:301–302) excavations at these mounds precludes determining temporal or cultural affiliation.

The rest of the 1905 paper pertains to the region from Charlotte Harbor south through the Ten Thousand Islands, into the Florida Keys, and up the east coast as far as Lake Worth. The sherds illustrated from both the Hickory Bluff Mound (8CH5) and the "Mound in Gasparilla Sound" indicate that they were Safety Harbor sites (Mitchem 1989:238–239; Moore 1905:Figures 1–5). Both had been badly disturbed prior to Moore's visit.

There is disagreement among archaeologists about the identification of Moore's (1905:302) "Mound in Gasparilla Sound." Willey (1949:345) identified it as the Gasparilla Sound Mound (8CH2), a Safety Harbor burial mound on Gasparilla Island (or Boca Grande Key). He noted that its exact location was not known (Willey 1949:345). Mitchem (1989:238) concurred with Willey's designation. Nevertheless, George M. Luer (personal communication 1997) believes that the site was actually a mound on Cayo Pelau (8CH1) rather than the Gasparilla Sound (8CH2) site. Moore (1905:302) described the site's location as "on a key believed to be nameless, the first key north of Boca Grande Pass, in Gasparilla sound." Luer (personal communication 1997) has pointed out that Gasparilla Island is an outer barrier island that defines the western edge of Gasparilla Sound and the north end of Boca Grande Pass, and he does not believe that Moore would have described the island as the first large island north of Boca Grande Pass and *in* the sound. Cayo Pelau has been the subject of uncontrolled digging for many decades (Mitchem 1989:232–238) and has yielded Safety Harbor pottery such as the sherds illustrated by Moore (1905:Figures 4 and 5). We will probably never know with certainty which island Moore was describing.

After discussing some conclusions based on his work so far, Moore (1905:305–308) visited Pine Island, where he had previously worked in 1900. He described some of the sites in the area, including the first mention of the aboriginal canal (8LL34) that crosses the island (Luer 1989a; Luer and Wheeler 1997; Moore 1905:305). He devoted the remainder of this visit to completing excavation of the Pine Island 8 Mound (8LL40), which he had partially excavated in 1900 (Moore 1900:362–363). The results of both excavation episodes at this site were discussed earlier in this essay.

The next site Moore (1905:308–309) investigated was the Shell Creek Mound (8LL8) near Punta Rassa. This burial mound yielded Safety Harbor pottery (1905:Figures 11–14) and one glass bead. Allerton et al. (1984:40) described four sheet silver incised tablets from the site that were recovered in 1972 and also mentioned a number of glass, crystal, and silver beads in private collections. Other private collections include Safety Harbor pottery types, with a few specimens of Weeden Island types

(Mitchem 1989:269). The European items suggest a late-sixteenth- and/or seventeenth-century date of contact. The location of the site indicates it is probably a Calusa burial mound used from Caloosahatchee III–V times (ca. A.D. 1200–1700), with a possible earlier component.

The next several sites visited by Moore (1905:309–314) were ones that he had investigated in 1900. At Mound Island (8LL2) and Marco (8CR48), he collected a number of pendants and other temporally undiagnostic artifacts. Among the pendants he obtained were some from the "nameless shell key, near Marco" (Moore 1905:311), which is now known as Addison's Key (8CR35). Moore (1905:311–314) continued south, surface collecting and purchasing collections from local residents at Goodland Point (8CR45), Wiggins Key (8CR11), and Chokoloskee Key (8CR1), all of which he had investigated in 1900. At Chokoloskee Key, he obtained three wooden artifacts that had been recovered from muck deposits (Moore 1905:Figures 28–31). The last site he described was Lossman's Key (8MO54, also called Lostmans Key), where he did no digging.

The remainder of his journey was summarized in two sentences (Moore 1905:315), after which he devoted the rest of the paper to illustration and discussion of *Busycon* shell tools. Some of these came from five sites he did not describe at any length: Cutler (8DA8), Battey Place (8LL33, now known as Pineland), McIlvaine's Key (8CR53), Crawford's Key (8CR55), and Pumpkin Key (8CR25). Two of these sites have been the subject of recent research. Major excavations have been completed at the Pineland site (Marquardt 1992b:48–54), revealing occupation lasting from Caloosahatchee I through early Spanish contact (ca. A.D. 300–1550). In a study of the Rookery Bay area, Weisman and Newman (1995:137–138) determined that 8CR55, which is also known as Shell Island, has artifacts dating from late Glades I through Glades IIIa (ca. A.D. 500–1400). Recent excavations by Widmer (1997) support this dating. Shell mining has destroyed approximately three-fourths of the site (Widmer 1997). Weisman and Newman (1995:137) also reported that the shell mound on McIlvaine's Key has been destroyed.

The next reprinted paper is Moore's (1907a) account of his second visit (in 1906) to the Crystal River site. The account of his third visit (Moore 1918:571–573) is included in a later paper reprinted in this volume. Moore's work at Crystal River was discussed earlier in this essay.

Moore's (1907d) paper on his 1906–1907 work in the Ten Thousand Islands is reprinted next. All of the sites he visited were ones about which he had previously written. Virtually the entire paper is given over to illustrating and discussing plummets, shell tools, and other objects of shell and stone either collected from the surface of sites or obtained from local residents.

The tenth paper reprinted here is an excerpt from one of Moore's (1918) reports on his work on the northwest Florida coast. The excerpt is included in this volume because it concerns work in Levy and Citrus Counties. He first described two mounds on Hog Island, both of which had been dug into by others (Moore 1918:568). One (8LV27), on a shell ridge, was composed of sand and shell and included human burials. The second mound (8LV39) was larger, but Moore (1918:568) did not report burials from this one. He made no mention of artifacts from either mound.

Moore (1918:568–569) then traveled to the town of Cedar Keys (now called Cedar Key), where his crew excavated three holes in a sand-and-shell mound known as Cedar Keys Mound (8LV43). He reported stone celts and shell beads from the previously disturbed site, as well as human burials and an ornament of sheet copper (Moore 1918:568–569). It is not possible to determine a date of occupation from the artifacts as described.

At the Aboriginal Cemetery in Cedar Keys (8LV4), Moore (1918:569–571) did some digging in a prehistoric cemetery that had been extensively dug by others prior to his work. He encountered primary burials in flexed and extended positions, most of which were in shell-filled graves (Moore 1918:570). Although he did not recover any artifacts other than two or three sherds, Moore contacted one of the previous excavators of the site (W. L. Bryant, Director of the Buffalo Society of Natural Sciences, Buffalo, New York), who sent him photographs of pottery and other artifacts (Moore 1918:Figures 39 and 40). From the reproduced illustrations and one of the sherds recovered by Moore (1918:Figure 41), it is clear that the pottery is Weeden Island Incised, dating the cemetery to the Weeden Island period (A.D. 200–900 [Milanich 1994:208–221]).

Willey (1949:309) expressed the opinion that the site may have originally been a mound, most of which had been dug away by previous excavators. In 1989, B. Calvin Jones (1992) investigated Weeden Island period burials from the Lions Club site (8LV284) in the general vicinity of 8LV4. The two burial areas are probably part of a single site (Jones 1992:4; Borremans and Moseley 1990:26).

The next few pages of Moore's (1918:571–573) paper report the results of his final visit to Crystal River (8CI1). His work at this site was discussed earlier in this essay. At the end of his discussion of Crystal River, Moore (1918:573) made passing mention of a sand mound about one mile to the north, in which his digging proved fruitless. This mound may have been the A. D. Williams Mound (8CI448), the only site in the vicinity listed in the Florida Master Site File.

The final site described by Moore (1918:573–574) in this paper was the Mound on the Greenleaf Place (8CI11). This previously disturbed sand mound contained secondary burials, stone tools, and mica. From the description provided, it is impossible to determine the time period of its construction.

Moore's interest in shell tools is evident in the final three papers reprinted here. The first *American Anthropologist* article (Moore 1919) began with an indignant Moore responding to statements made by Aleš Hrdlička (1919:62) in a Smithsonian Institution publication implying that the southwestern coast of Florida had never been explored and that no sites had been investigated there. After setting the record straight, Moore (1919:401–402) briefly discussed and illustrated some shell tools that he had collected from sites in the area. Two years later, Moore (1921a) published a short article about shell tools from southwest Florida in the same journal, the next paper reprinted here.

Although Moore donated most of his artifacts to the collections of the Academy of Natural Sciences of Philadelphia, he also (Moore 1907d:463, 1918:573, 1919:402) sent some to the Museum of the American Indian (Heye Foundation) in New York and to various museums in South America. The final paper reprinted here (Moore 1921b) was originally published by the National Academy of History in Quito, Ecuador, and illustrated some of the shell tools from southwestern Florida that Moore donated to that institution. Moore's text accompanying the photographs was largely paraphrased from his 1921 *American Anthropologist* article.

Some Anecdotes about C. B. Moore and the *Gopher of Philadelphia*

Earlier in this essay, I mentioned that Clarence B. Moore had used several steamboats in his Florida work, including the *Alligator,* the *Osceola,* and the *Gopher.* The *Gopher of Philadelphia* was Moore's primary boat, the one he used in most of his Florida research and in virtually all of his work in other states (Knight 1996:3–4).

The *Gopher* was first piloted by George W. Rossignol, who handled these duties until 1899 or 1900 (Moore 1900:352). As of 1900, Captain J. S. Raybon of Tampa took over, also acting as advance scout for Moore prior to each field season, locating sites accessible by steamboat and getting landowner permission to excavate (Knight 1996:3).

The *Gopher* was apparently kept docked at or near Tampa during the summer and fall when Moore was in Philadelphia doing his analysis and writing. There are several bits of information about the steamboat and Clarence B. Moore in a series of letters written in 1920 and 1921 by Mr. Charles T. Earle of Bradenton (known as Bradentown at that time), Florida. Mr. Earle was concerned about the probable impending destruction of the Shaw's Point archaeological site (8MA7) at the mouth of the Manatee River and collected artifacts from the site over a seven-year period, which he sent to the Smithsonian Institution (Schwadron 1997:63). The planned real estate development of the site never took place, and it is today part of De Soto National Memorial (Schwadron 1997:65). Along with the artifacts, Earle also wrote many letters to Jesse W. Fewkes, who was Chief of the Bureau of American Ethnology from 1918 until the beginning of 1928 (Judd 1967:26–29).

In his desperate attempts to help save the site, Earle contacted Moore, as noted in one of his early letters to Fewkes: "I wrote and asked Mr. Clarence Moore if he had ever visited the Snead's Island group or the large sand burial mound on my place (near Shaw's Point) and he answered that he had not" (Earle 1920a). Earle was disappointed that Moore had not indicated any desire to excavate at Shaw's Point. He elaborated on his interaction with Moore in a later letter to Fewkes, including a note about the *Gopher.*

> I have read Mr. Clarence Moore's "Certain Antiquities of the Florida West Coast," (1900) and found it sadly lacking in that essential attribute, "espirit de corps." I realize that it is valuable to a student, and it has helped me much, but it is very discouraging to a beginner.
>
> Last year when Mr. Moore returned from his cruise among the Ten Thousand Islands, I, standing on the beach at Shaw's Point, saw his boat, the "Gopher," steam serenely by this prehistoric settlement on a bright spring morning, going on up the Bay. I had just written a few weeks before describing these places to him. He replied that little had been found on Tampa Bay and he had never visited the places I located in my letter [Earle 1920b].

Earle's disappointment seems to have evolved into something resembling paranoia a few months later, resulting in letters not only to Fewkes (Earle 1920c) but also to Dr. Charles D. Walcott, Secretary of the Smithsonian Institution (Earle 1920d).

Dear Sir [J. W. Fewkes]:

Early this morning, while the tide was low, I went up to Shaw's Point in hopes of finding a jewel or so, but as I stepped out upon the beach and looked seaward what did my wondering eyes behold but a sternwheel steamboat steaming up the Bay!! There she was, big as life and twice as natural, with her smokestack pouring out volumes of pitchpine smoke and her wheel kicking up a foamy wake that stretched out behind her like a string of white shell beads! Is it necessary to add that her name was *Gopher*? Needless to say, I found no relics that trip, for I just could not make my eyes behave—lest she turn and come into this river. Where she is from I cannot say, but where she is going I can easily guess—to Tampa to be fitted out for another seasons work on the Gulf coast. After all she may come here—and explore the section she has passed by so many times. For you see, while in Tampa undergoing repairs some of her crew may meet some of the Tampa Sand and Shell Company's employees who might tell about finding a skeleton in a deposit of oyster shell thirty feet deep in Manatee River—and then—?? [Earle 1920c].

Sir [C. D. Walcott]:

In the temporary absence of Dr. Fewkes will you please read the enclosed letters, and let me explain that I have been uneasy ever since I saw the steamboat "Gopher" go up Tampa Bay a few days ago, fearing that Mr. Clarence B. Moore may now turn his attention to this locality and get these Indian relics.

Two years ago I wrote Mr. Moore describing the mounds in this vicinity, and he replied that he had never visited this shore of Tampa Bay.

I hope all of these antiquities will go to your Museum [Earle 1920d].

It was necessary for Fewkes (1920) to defend Moore, which provides insight into how Moore was viewed by some of his professional contemporaries.

Dear Sir:

Your letter of November 3, addressed to the Secretary of the Smithsonian Institution, has been referred to me. I do not know as anything could be done should the Gopher land in the vicinity in which you have been working. It is very good of you to be so interested in the National Museum, but Mr. Moore's contributions to the science of archaeology have been of the highest order and anything that falls into his hands would be eventually well housed or described in his publications. I do not think you need to worry [Fewkes 1920].

Fewkes's letter seems to have calmed Earle's fears of Moore working at Shaw's Point. There was only one mention of the *Gopher* in Earle's later letters to Fewkes: "Last Saturday (the 9th) the steamer "Gopher" passed up the Bay, going to Tampa to be laid up for the summer, I suppose" (Earle 1921).

Clarence B. Moore and the *Gopher* were certainly familiar, if not understood, to many residents of the west coast of Florida. An excerpt from another of Earle's letters to Fewkes gives an example.

I have again talked with Mr. George Breeze of Bradentown, who is the foremost local authority on shell mounds in their relation to shell roads, having superintended the destruction of several, including Shaw's Point. . . . Mr. Breeze told me this interesting bit of scientific history: "Years ago there used to be an old, dilapidated steamboat, her name was the 'Gopher'; she just drifted up and down this coast looking for mounds. In the summer time she was laid up in Tampa, and every winter she would cruise down the coast looking for all kinds of curiosities." He expressed surprise to know she is still afloat and able to be of service. He was also surprised to know she was connected with a big museum, having thought at the time that she belonged to only an idle curio hunter, and lamented that she didn't ever come in and study that wonderful Shaws Point mound. Now it's gone, and here's the man who destroyed it [Earle 1920e].

These anecdotal accounts are important because they support the notion that the *Gopher* was docked at Tampa between field seasons, and they also reinforce the fact that Moore was still conducting fieldwork in Florida (Moore 1921a:12) at least as late as 1920, contrary to what is suggested by his curated field notes (Davis 1987).

A final bit of anecdotal evidence about the *Gopher* comes from an unpublished paper by John W. Griffin (1981). In this paper, Griffin noted that he had heard that the *Gopher* sank at a dock in Tampa in 1926, but he could not verify it (Griffin 1981). Perhaps studies of newspaper accounts or other historical records will be able to verify this claim someday.

Few Floridians are aware that Clarence B. Moore was an ardent supporter of the Florida Historical Society in its early days. The archives of the Florida Historical Society's Tebeau-Field Library of Florida History contain two letters from Moore to the president of the society. Not only did Moore donate copies of his own writings to the society, but also he was instrumental in obtaining other works that he thought were essential for the study of Florida archaeology and early history. With the kind permission of Lewis N. Wynne, Executive Director of the Florida Historical Society, both letters are quoted here in their entirety.

House-boat Gopher, Ft. Myers, Fla.
Jany. 21, 1907.
Hon. Francis P. Fleming, President.

Dear Sir,

I will remember our pleasant acquaintance in the past and am greatly pleased to hear from you and to learn of the organization of which you are the head, namely the Florida Historical Society.

I have often wondered why such a society was not started in Florida and it is gratifying to know that so good a beginning has been made as is shown by the pamphlet you so kindly sent me.

It will give me great pleasure to give to your Society such of my writings on Florida as you do not already possess, and I am writing by this mail to an agent in Phila. to send to you, as soon as he can procure it, the Travels of William Bartram which I notice is not on your list.

As to the collection of antiquities, I fear I cannot promise much at present as I have absolutely no personal collection, and the collection of the Academy of Natural

Sciences is so condensed that nothing farther can be taken from it. On my return to Phila. (In April, when I hope to send you the books) I will see what can be done, and I shall keep my eyes open this winter among the Keys of southwestern Florida, where some interesting objects may be obtained.

With my kindest regards I am

Most sincerely yours

Clarence B. Moore

P.S. My address for some days will be St. James City, Lee County, Florida [Moore 1907b].

St. James City, Lee Co. Fla.
Feby. 4, 1907.
Hon. Francis P. Fleming, President,

My dear Sir,

The book expert in Phila. who attends to matters for me, has written me that he has succeeded in buying a fine copy of William Bartram's "Travels" which he has sent by express to your society.

I have no doubt you are familiar with these "Travels." If you have not read that part which relates to Florida, a great treat is in store for you, to know how the old St. Johns appeared in the latter part of the eighteenth century. Bartram's adventure with the rattlesnake and the Seminole Indians is delightful.

The copy of this book sent your society is a gift from me with my best wishes.

Incidentally, I may say what no doubt you know already, that the father of William Bartram published a small work on Florida, which is now very rare. You may not recall, however, that in this work Bartram speaks of the existence of the bison in Florida, and when he speaks of Florida he means the Florida of the present day, saying it is bounded on the north by the St. Mary's River. In various books about the bison an effort is made to trace its southern most habitat in former times but the farthest definite statement made locates the bison on St. Simons Island.

Jeffries Wyman, in his "Shell Mounds of the St. Johns River, Florida," speaks of the bison in Florida but does not give a correct reference to the elder Bartram though I think he intended to refer to him as I think the number of the page is correctly given. Wyman died before his book was printed and no doubt the reference was partly omitted by others in correcting the proof.

Incidentally, I may say your Society ought to have Wyman's book and perhaps the Peabody Museum, Cambridge, Mass., where it is on sale will present you with a copy should you write just how your society is situated.

The volume on Florida which I sent recently (your kind letter of acknowledgement for it and for Bartram's "Travels" is just handed to me) is one I happened to have on the boat. On my return to Phila. I hope to send you a number of other of my volumes one of which relates to mounds in the immediate vicinity of Jacksonville.

With Kindest regards I am
Most sincerely yours
Clarence B. Moore [Moore 1907c]

These letters not only demonstrate Moore's thorough familiarity with the literature pertaining to the area but also reveal his well-known generosity (Wardle 1956).

Clarence B. Moore's Contributions to West Florida Archaeology

It should be obvious to anyone who peruses the papers reprinted here that knowledge of Clarence B. Moore's investigations in Florida and the resultant publications are indispensable to any researcher involved in Florida archaeology. His publications are the only record we have for many of the sites, and even though he destroyed a number of the sites through excavation (which is, after all, the nature of archaeological excavation), many more are now gone because of development, the use of shell for road material, and vandalism.

Moore was careful about taking accurate measurements of mounds and other features (at times using a theodolite) and recording these in his field notes and publications. In some cases, these corrected erroneous measurements recorded by other researchers (e.g., Moore 1900:367). He also constructed plan view maps of some sites (e.g., Moore 1900:Figure 1, 1903:Figure 89), often with the help of his assistant Dr. Milo G. Miller, and these are of inestimable value to modern archaeologists in studying site layouts and extents before more recent alterations.

Moore was also an accomplished photographer (Davis 1987:8), with a darkroom or photographic laboratory on board at least one of his boats (Swift 1903:49). It is unfortunate that so few field photographs of sites are included in the publications. There are stories that after Moore's death in 1936, the people who cleaned out his house destroyed many glass photographic negatives (Stephen Williams, personal communication 1996). We can only guess at what archaeological information was included among those negatives and mourn their loss.

The results of Moore's excavations were used by John Goggin, Gordon Willey, and other pioneers of modern Florida archaeology in defining the initial culture historical frameworks of prehistory in the state. His collections in various museums were valuable in the formulation of the artifact typologies we use today, and the availability of his field notes (Davis 1987) provides opportunities for additional research on his work (e.g., Cerrato 1996).

The enduring value of Clarence B. Moore's work in west Florida is demonstrated by looking at the References Cited section of any major synthesis of Florida archaeology or study of particular sites or time periods in the western part of the peninsula. Because he was primarily interested in mounds and earthworks, his reports tend to lack information about Archaic and Paleoindian sites, as well as postcontact sites (other than aboriginal sites containing European material). His publications mainly featured the "fancy" artifacts, with less regard for stratigraphic interpretation or context, but these details were often recorded in his field notes.

The results of Moore's investigations helped to put Florida on the archaeological map, so to speak, in terms of pointing out relationships to other parts of eastern North America. One example in the accompanying papers (Moore 1895a:452–468, 473–488) is his work at the Shields (8DU12) and Grant Mounds (8DU14), where he recovered native copper artifacts and other objects that show clear affinities with the Mississippian phenomenon often referred to as the Southeastern Ceremonial

Complex. Nearly identical artifacts are found in contemporaneous sites all over the Southeast and Mississippi Valley, and Moore's work revealed that north Florida populations were actively participating in Mississippian exchange networks (Goggin 1952:54; Griffin 1946:77, 88; Mitchem 1996:234; Williams and Goggin 1956:49–50).

In both east and west Florida, Moore (1895c, 1903:379–413, 1907a:406–425, 1918:571–573) discovered strong evidence of Hopewellian influence in Florida at the Murphy Island (8PU20) and Crystal River (8CI1) sites. Moore and several of his colleagues (1895c:509, 1903:410, 1907a:421–422) recognized the similarity of many of the objects to artifacts recovered from the classic Hopewell sites in Ohio and surrounding areas. Over the intervening decades, archaeologists have continued to debate the nature of the connections between the Florida Hopewellian manifestations and those elsewhere (Brose 1979; Greenman 1938; Griffin 1946:63–65; Willey and Phillips 1958:160–162).

As would be expected, on the basis of additional research, some of Moore's conclusions have been shown to be incorrect (e.g., Moore 1905:304). Nevertheless, his body of work has formed the basis for much of the subsequent work in Florida and the greater Southeast. One can only speculate how the course of archaeological research in the Southeast would have been different if Moore had been able to duplicate Cushing's (1896) discoveries at Key Marco.

Archaeologists owe a debt of gratitude to Clarence B. Moore for publishing his findings. I hope that this reprint will not only stimulate newfound gratitude for his efforts but also encourage fresh research in some of the regions where he worked.

References Cited

Allerton, David, George M. Luer, and Robert S. Carr
1984 Ceremonial Tablets and Related Objects from Florida. *The Florida Anthropologist* 37:5–54.

Ashley, Keith H.
1995 The Dent Mound: A Coastal Woodland Period Burial Mound Near the Mouth of the St. Johns River, Florida. *The Florida Anthropologist* 48:13–34.

Austin, Robert J., and Kenneth W. Hardin
1987 Conserving a City's Prehistory: St. Petersburg's Archaeological Survey and Planning Project. *The Florida Anthropologist* 40:266–274.

Beasley, Virgil
1997 The Location of Edelano, a Timucua Village Encountered by the French Huguenots: 1564–1565. Paper presented at the 54th Annual Meeting of the Southeastern Archaeological Conference, Baton Rouge.

Bethell, John A.
1914 *Pinellas: A Brief History of the Lower Point.* Independent Job Department Press, St. Petersburg.

Borremans, Nina Thanz, and Michael E. Moseley
1990 *A Prehistoric Site Survey of the Cedar Keys Region of Coastal Levy County, Florida.* Department of Anthropology, University of Florida, Gainesville. Submitted to the Division of Historical Resources, Florida Department of State, Tallahassee.

Boyle, Diane, Todd Gray, and Gunnar Helgason
1986 *A Preliminary Report of 8-Pi-19, The Sheraton Maximo Site, 1986.* Department of Comparative Cultures, Eckerd College, St. Petersburg. Submitted to the City of St. Petersburg Planning Department.

Brigham, Clarence S.
1936 Clarence Bloomfield Moore [Obituary]. *Proceedings of the American Antiquarian Society* (New Series) 46:13–14.

Brose, David S.
1979 An Interpretation of the Hopewellian Traits in Florida. In *Hopewell Archaeology: The Chillicothe Conference,* edited by David S. Brose and

N'omi Greber, pp. 141–149. Midcontinental Journal of Archaeology Special Paper No. 3. Kent State University Press, Kent, Ohio.

Brose, David S., and Nancy M. White (editors)
1999 *The Northwest Florida Expeditions of Clarence Bloomfield Moore.* University of Alabama Press, Tuscaloosa.

Bullen, Ripley P.
1950 Tests at the Whittaker Site, Sarasota, Florida. *The Florida Anthropologist* 3:21–30.
1951 *The Terra Ceia Site, Manatee County, Florida.* Florida Anthropological Society Publications No. 3. Gainesville.
1952 *Eleven Archaeological Sites in Hillsborough County, Florida.* Report of Investigations No. 8. Florida Geological Survey, Tallahassee.
1966 Stelae at the Crystal River Site, Florida. *American Antiquity* 31:861–865.

Bullen, Ripley P., William L. Partridge, and Donald A. Harris
1970 The Safford Burial Mound, Tarpon Springs, Florida. *The Florida Anthropologist* 23:81–118.

Burger, B. William
1982 *Cultural Resource Management in Manatee County, Florida: The Prehistoric Resources Base.* Unpublished Master's thesis, Department of Anthropology, University of South Florida, Tampa.
1988 The DeSoto Trail Project: Preliminary Report on Investigations in the Southeastern Tampa Bay Area. Ms. on file, Department of Anthropology, Florida Museum of Natural History, Gainesville.

Bushnell, David I., Jr.
1926 Investigation of Shell and Sand Mounds on Pinellas Peninsula, Florida. In *Explorations and Field-Work of the Smithsonian Institution in 1925,* pp. 125–132. Smithsonian Miscellaneous Collections 96(4). Washington, D.C.

Bushnell, Frank
1962 The Maximo Point Site—1962. *The Florida Anthropologist* 15:89–101.

Cerrato, Cynthia L.
1996 C. B. Moore on the Ocklawaha River: No Place for a *Gopher. The Florida Anthropologist* 49:261–266.

Cockrell, Wilburn A.
1970 *Glades I and Pre-Glades Settlement and Subsistence on Marco Island (Collier County, Florida).* Unpublished Master's thesis, Department of Anthropology, Florida State University, Tallahassee.

Cordell, Ann S.
1984 *Ceramic Technology at a Weeden Island Period Archaeological Site in North Florida.* Ceramic Notes No. 2. Occasional Publications of the Ceramic Technology Laboratory, Florida State Museum, Gainesville.
1992 Technological Investigation of Pottery Variability in Southwest Florida. In *Culture and Environment in the Domain of the Calusa,* edited by William H. Marquardt, pp. 105–190. Institute of Archaeology and Paleoenvironmental Studies Monograph No. 1. University of Florida, Gainesville.

Cushing, Frank Hamilton
1896 Exploration of Ancient Key Dwellers' Remains on the Gulf Coast of Florida. *Proceedings of the American Philosophical Society* 35(153):329–448. Philadelphia.

Davis, Mary B. (compiler)
1987 *Field Notes of Clarence B. Moore's Southeastern Archaeological Expeditions, 1891–1918: A Guide to the Microfilm Edition.* Huntington Free Library, Museum of the American Indian, Bronx, New York.

Deagan, Kathleen A.
1987 *Artifacts of the Spanish Colonies of Florida and the Caribbean, 1500–1800. Volume I: Ceramics, Glassware, and Beads.* Smithsonian Institution Press, Washington, D.C.

Dorian, Alan W.
1980 *Literature Search and Partial Cultural Resource Inventory of Chassahowitzka, Cedar Keys, and Lower Suwannee National Wildlife Refuges.* Archeological Research Reports No. 10. Southeast Conservation Archeology Center, Tallahassee.

Durnford, Charles Day
1895 The Discovery of Aboriginal Netting, Rope, and Wood Implements in a Mud Deposit in Western Florida. *The American Naturalist* 29:1032–1039.

Earle, Charles T.
1920a Letter to J. Walter Fewkes, dated February 20, 1920. On file, National Anthropological Archives, National Museum of Natural History, Smithsonian Institution, Washington, D.C.
1920b Letter to J. Walter Fewkes, dated May 6, 1920. On file, National Anthropological Archives, National Museum of Natural History, Smithsonian Institution, Washington, D.C.
1920c Letter to J. Walter Fewkes, dated October 26, 1920. On file, National Anthropological Archives, National Museum of Natural History, Smithsonian Institution, Washington, D.C.
1920d Letter to Charles D. Walcott, dated November 3, 1920. On file, National Anthropological Archives, National Museum of Natural History, Smithsonian Institution, Washington, D.C.
1920e Letter to J. Walter Fewkes, dated October 21, 1920. On file, National Anthropological Archives, National Museum of Natural History, Smithsonian Institution, Washington, D.C.
1921 Letter to J. Walter Fewkes, dated April 13, 1921. On file, National Anthropological Archives, National Museum of Natural History, Smithsonian Institution, Washington, D.C.

Fairbanks, Charles H.
1982 Introduction. In *Archeology of the Florida Gulf Coast.* Reprinted. Florida Book Store, Gainesville. Originally published 1949, Smithsonian Miscellaneous Collections Vol. 113. Washington, D.C.

Fewkes, J. Walter
1920 Letter to Charles T. Earle, dated November 24, 1920. On file, National Anthropological Archives, National Museum of Natural History,

Smithsonian Institution, Washington, D.C.

Ford, James A.

1966 Early Formative Cultures in Georgia and Florida. *American Antiquity* 31:781–799.

1969 *A Comparison of Formative Cultures in the Americas.* Smithsonian Contributions to Anthropology Vol. 11. Smithsonian Institution Press, Washington, D.C.

Garner, Michael S.

1993 *An Archaeological Survey of the Oelsner Mounds Site.* Unpublished Master's thesis, Department of Anthropology, University of South Florida, Tampa.

Gilliland, Marion S.

1975 *The Material Culture of Key Marco, Florida.* University of Florida Press, Gainesville.

1988 Marco's Buried Treasure: Wetlands Archaeology and Adventure in Nineteenth Century Florida. In *Wet Site Archaeology,* edited by Barbara A. Purdy, pp. 255–261. Telford Press, Caldwell, New Jersey.

1989 *Key Marco's Buried Treasure: Archaeology and Adventure in the Nineteenth Century.* University of Florida Press, Gainesville.

Goggin, John M.

1949a The Archeology of the Glades Area, Southern Florida. Ms. on file, P. K. Yonge Library of Florida History, University of Florida, Gainesville.

1949b Cultural Occupation at Goodland Point, Florida. *The Florida Anthropologist* 2:65–91.

1949c Cultural Traditions in Florida Prehistory. In *The Florida Indian and His Neighbors,* edited by John W. Griffin, pp. 13–44. Inter-American Center, Rollins College, Winter Park, Florida.

1949d A Southern Cult Specimen from Florida. *The Florida Anthropologist* 2:36–38.

1952 *Space and Time Perspective in Northern St. Johns Archeology, Florida.* Yale University Publications in Anthropology No. 47. Yale University Press, New Haven.

n.d. An Introduction to Spanish Trade Beads and Pendants, Sixteenth and Seventeenth Centuries. Ms. on file, Bureau of Archaeological Research, Division of Historical Resources, Florida Department of State, Tallahassee.

Goggin, John M., and William C. Sturtevant

1964 The Calusa: A Stratified, Nonagricultural Society (With Notes on Sibling Marriage). In *Explorations in Cultural Anthropology: Essays in Honor of George Peter Murdock,* edited by Ward H. Goodenough, pp. 179–219. McGraw-Hill, New York.

Greenman, Emerson F.

1938 Hopewellian Traits in Florida. *American Antiquity* 4:327–333.

Griffin, James B.

1946 Cultural Change and Continuity in Eastern United States Archaeology. In *Man in Northeastern North America,* edited by Frederick Johnson, pp. 37–95. Papers of the Robert S. Peabody Foundation for Archaeology, No. 3. Phillips Academy, Andover, Massachusetts.

Griffin, John W.

1949 Notes on the Archaeology of Useppa Island. *The Florida Anthropologist* 2:92–93.

1981 The Role of the Archaeologist in the CRM Process. Paper presented at the Annual Meeting of the Florida Historical Society, St. Petersburg. Ms. on file, John Wallace Griffin Papers, National Anthropological Archives, National Museum of Natural History, Smithsonian Institution, Washington, D.C.

1988 *The Archeology of Everglades National Park: A Synthesis.* Southeastern Frontiers, Inc., St. Augustine, Florida. Submitted to Southeast Archeological Center, National Park Service, Tallahassee.

Grismer, Karl

1946 *The Story of Sarasota: The History of the City and County of Sarasota, Florida.* M. E. Russell, Sarasota.

Hamilton, Henry W., Jean Tyree Hamilton, and Eleanor F. Chapman

1974 *Spiro Mound Copper.* Memoir No. 11. Missouri Archaeological Society, Columbia.

Hardin, Kenneth W., Janice R. Ballo, and Mark J. Brooks

1984 *Cultural Resource Assessment Survey of the Proposed Southport Sanitary Landfill Site, Osceola County, Florida.* Piper Archaeological Research, Inc., St. Petersburg. Submitted to Environmental Science and Engineering, Inc., Tampa.

Hardman, Clark, Jr.

1971 The Primitive Solar Observatory at Crystal River and Its Implications. *The Florida Anthropologist* 24:135–168.

Holmes, William H.

1903 Aboriginal Pottery of the Eastern United States. *Twentieth Annual Report of the Bureau of American Ethnology, 1898–1899,* pp. 1–201. Smithsonian Institution, Washington, D.C.

Hrdlička, Aleš

1919 Anthropological Survey of the Southwestern Coast of Florida. In *Explorations and Field-work of the Smithsonian Institution in 1918.* Smithsonian Miscellaneous Collections 70(2):62–65. Washington, D.C.

1922 *The Anthropology of Florida.* Florida State Historical Society Publications No. 1. DeLand.

Hutchinson, Dale L.

1993 Analysis of Skeletal Remains from the Tierra Verde Site, Pinellas County, West-Central Florida. *The Florida Anthropologist* 46:263–276.

Jones, B. Calvin

1992 *Archaeological Evaluation of Lions Club Lot in Cedar Key, Florida: Salvage of Historic Burials and Preservation of Weeden Island (Pasco) Burial Area.* Florida Archaeological Reports No. 9. Bureau of Archaeological Research, Division of Historical Resources, Florida Department of State, Tallahassee.

Jones, Paul L., and Nina T. Borremans
1991 *An Archaeological Survey of the Gulf Hammock, Florida.* The Seahorse Key Maritime Adaptations Program, Institute of Archaeology and Paleoenvironmental Studies, University of Florida, Gainesville. Submitted to Bureau of Historic Preservation, Division of Historical Resources, Florida Department of State, Tallahassee.

Judd, Neil M.
1967 *The Bureau of American Ethnology: A Partial History.* University of Oklahoma Press, Norman.

Knight, Vernon James, Jr.
1996 Introduction: The Expeditions of Clarence B. Moore to Moundville in 1905 and 1906. In *The Moundville Expeditions of Clarence Bloomfield Moore,* edited by Vernon James Knight, Jr., pp. 1–20. University of Alabama Press, Tuscaloosa.

Kolianos, Phyllis
1998 "Vanished" Mound Found: Relocating 8PI3, Safford Mound. Paper presented at the 1998 Annual Meeting of the Florida Anthropological Society, Gainesville.

Lamme, Vernon
1978 *More Florida Lore Not Found in History Books.* Star Publishing Company, Boynton Beach, Florida.

Lazarus, William C.
1963 A Potter's Tool of the Safety Harbor Period. *The Florida Anthropologist* 16:3–4.

Lente, Frederick D.
1877 The Mounds of Florida. *Semi-Tropical* 3:129–137, 193–203. Jacksonville.

Luer, George M.
1989a Calusa Canals in Southwestern Florida: Routes of Tribute and Exchange. *The Florida Anthropologist* 42:89–130.
1989b A Seminole Burial on Indian Field (8LL39), Lee County, Southwestern Florida. *The Florida Anthropologist* 42:131–133.
1992a Mississippian-Period Popeyed Bird-Head Effigies in West-Central and Southwest Florida. *The Florida Anthropologist* 45:52–62.
1992b Urban Archaeology in the City of Sarasota, Florida: The Whitaker Archaeological Site Complex. *The Florida Anthropologist* 45:226–241.

Luer, George M., and Marion M. Almy
1982 A Definition of the Manasota Culture. *The Florida Anthropologist* 35:34–58.

Luer, George M., and Ryan J. Wheeler
1997 How the Pine Island Canal Worked: Topography, Hydraulics, and Engineering. *The Florida Anthropologist* 50:115–131.

Lyon, Edwin A.
1996 *A New Deal for Southeastern Archaeology.* University of Alabama Press, Tuscaloosa.

Marquardt, William H. (editor)
1992a *Culture and Environment in the Domain of the Calusa.* Institute of

Archaeology and Paleoenvironmental Studies Monograph No. 1. University of Florida, Gainesville.

1999 *The Archaeology of Useppa Island.* Institute of Archaeology and Paleoenvironmental Studies Monograph No. 3. University of Florida, Gainesville, in preparation.

Marquardt, William H.

1984 *The Josslyn Island Mound and Its Role in the Investigation of Southwest Florida's Past.* Miscellaneous Project Report Series No. 22. Department of Anthropology, Florida Museum of Natural History, Gainesville.

1992b Recent Archaeological and Paleoenvironmental Investigations in Southwest Florida. In *Culture and Environment in the Domain of the Calusa,* edited by William H. Marquardt, pp. 9–57. Institute of Archaeology and Paleoenvironmental Studies Monograph No. 1. University of Florida, Gainesville.

McMichael, Edward V.

1960 *The Anatomy of a Tradition: A Study of Southeastern Stamped Pottery.* Ph.D. dissertation, Indiana University, Indianapolis. University Microfilms, Ann Arbor.

1964 Veracruz, the Crystal River Complex, and the Hopewellian Climax. In *Hopewellian Studies,* edited by Joseph R. Caldwell and Robert L. Hall, pp. 123–132. Scientific Papers Vol. 12. Illinois State Museum, Springfield.

Milanich, Jerald T.

1994 *Archaeology of Precolumbian Florida.* University Press of Florida, Gainesville.

Milanich, Jerald T., Jefferson Chapman, Ann S. Cordell, H. Stephen Hale, and Rochelle A. Marrinan

1984 Prehistoric Development of Calusa Society in Southwest Florida: Excavations on Useppa Island. In *Perspectives on Gulf Coast Prehistory,* edited by Dave D. Davis, pp. 258–314. University Presses of Florida, Gainesville.

Mitchem, Jeffrey M.

1987 Salvage Excavations at the Gibsonton Site, Hillsborough County, Florida. *The Florida Anthropologist* 40:224–228.

1989 *Redefining Safety Harbor: Late Prehistoric / Protohistoric Archaeology in West Peninsular Florida.* Ph.D. dissertation, University of Florida, Gainesville. University Microfilms, Ann Arbor.

1993 Beads and Pendants from San Luis de Talimali: Inferences from Varying Contexts. In *The Spanish Missions of La Florida,* edited by Bonnie G. McEwan, pp. 399–417. University Press of Florida, Gainesville.

1996 The Old Okahumpka Site (8LA57): Late Prehistoric Iconography and Mississippian Influence in Peninsular Florida. *The Florida Anthropologist* 49:225–237.

1999 Clarence B. Moore's Research in East Florida, 1873–1896. In *The East Florida Expeditions of Clarence Bloomfield Moore,* edited by Jeffrey M. Mitchem. University of Alabama Press, Tuscaloosa.

Mitchem, Jeffrey M., Robert J. Austin, and Scott E. Mitchell

1998 Investigations at the Southport Mound: A Protohistoric and Historic Period Burial Mound in East-Central Florida. Paper presented at the Annual Meeting of the Society for Historical Archaeology, Atlanta.

Monroe, Elizabeth B., Sharon Wells, and Marion Almy

1982 *Historical, Architectural, and Archaeological Survey of Sarasota, Florida.* Miscellaneous Project Report Series No. 51. Florida Division of Archives, History and Records Management, Bureau of Historic Sites and Properties, Tallahassee.

Moore, Clarence B.

1891 Field Notes, unnumbered notebook. "Cruise of the Osceola" and "Cruise of the Alligator." Ms. on file, Huntington Free Library, Bronx, New York.

1892a A Burial Mound of Florida. *The American Naturalist* 26:129–143.

1892b Mounds in Florida. *The American Antiquarian and Oriental Journal* 14:292–295.

1894a Certain Sand Mounds of the St. John's River, Florida. Part I. *Journal of the Academy of Natural Sciences of Philadelphia* 10:4–128.

1894b Certain Sand Mounds of the St. John's River, Florida. Part II. *Journal of the Academy of Natural Sciences of Philadelphia* 10:129–246.

1895a Certain River Mounds of Duval County, Florida. *Journal of the Academy of Natural Sciences of Philadelphia* 10:448–502.

1895b Certain Sand Mounds of the Ocklawaha River, Florida. *Journal of the Academy of Natural Sciences of Philadelphia* 10:518–543.

1895c Two Sand Mounds on Murphy Island, Florida. *Journal of the Academy of Natural Sciences of Philadelphia* 10:503–517.

1900 Certain Antiquities of the Florida West-Coast. *Journal of the Academy of Natural Sciences of Philadelphia* 11:350–394.

1902 Certain Aboriginal Remains of the Northwest Florida Coast. Part II. *Journal of the Academy of Natural Sciences of Philadelphia* 12:128–358.

1903 Certain Aboriginal Mounds of the Central Florida West-Coast. *Journal of the Academy of Natural Sciences of Philadelphia* 12:361–438.

1905 Miscellaneous Investigation in Florida. *Journal of the Academy of Natural Sciences of Philadelphia* 13:298–325.

1907a Crystal River Revisited. *Journal of the Academy of Natural Sciences of Philadelphia* 13:406–425.

1907b Letter to Francis P. Fleming, dated January 21, 1907. On file, Tebeau-Field Library of Florida History, Cocoa, Florida.

1907c Letter to Francis P. Fleming, dated February 4, 1907. On file, Tebeau-Field Library of Florida History, Cocoa, Florida.

1907d Notes on the Ten Thousand Islands, Florida. *Journal of the Academy of Natural Sciences of Philadelphia* 13:457–470.

1918 The Northwestern Florida Coast Revisited. *Journal of the Academy of Natural Sciences of Philadelphia* 16:514–580.

1919 Notes on the Archaeology of Florida. *American Anthropologist* 21:400–402.

1921a Notes on Shell Implements from Florida. *American Anthropologist* 23:12–18.

1921b *Shell Implements from Florida.* Boletín de la Academia Nacional de

Historia No. 1. Quito, Ecuador.

Murowchick, Robert E.
1990 A Curious Sort of Yankee: Personal and Professional Notes on Jeffries Wyman (1814–1874). *Southeastern Archaeology* 9:55–66.

Ostrander, Ozzie
1960 The Johns Pass Mound. *The Florida Anthropologist* 13:77–79.

Phillips, Philip, and James A. Brown
1978 *Pre-Columbian Shell Engravings from the Craig Mound at Spiro, Oklahoma,* part 1. Paperback edition. Peabody Museum Press, Cambridge.

Purdy, Barbara A. (editor)
1988 *Wet Site Archaeology.* Telford Press, Caldwell, New Jersey.

Rouse, Irving
1951 *A Survey of Indian River Archeology, Florida.* Yale University Publications in Anthropology No. 44. Yale University Press, New Haven.

Russo, Michael
1991 *Archaic Sedentism on the Florida Coast: A Case Study from Horr's Island.* Unpublished Ph.D. dissertation, Department of Anthropology, University of Florida, Gainesville.
1992 Chronologies and Cultures of the St. Marys Region of Northeast Florida and Southeast Georgia. *The Florida Anthropologist* 45:107–126.
1994 Why We Don't Believe in Archaic Ceremonial Mounds and Why We Should: The Case from Florida. *Southeastern Archaeology* 13:93–109.
1996 Southeastern Archaic Mounds. In *Archaeology of the Mid-Holocene Southeast,* edited by Kenneth E. Sassaman and David G. Anderson, pp. 259–287. University Press of Florida, Gainesville.

Scarry, John F.
1985 A Proposed Revision of the Fort Walton Ceramic Typology: A Type-Variety System. *The Florida Anthropologist* 38:199–233.

Schwadron, Margo
1997 *An Archeological Investigation of Shell Ridges at Shaw's Point (8MA7), De Soto National Memorial, Bradenton, Florida.* Unpublished Master's thesis, Department of Anthropology, Florida State University, Tallahassee.

Sears, William H.
1956 The Turner River Site, Collier County, Florida. *The Florida Anthropologist* 9:47–60.
1957 *Excavations on Lower St. Johns River, Florida.* Contributions of the Florida State Museum, Social Sciences No. 2. University of Florida, Gainesville.
1958 The Maximo Point Site. *The Florida Anthropologist* 11:1–10.
1960 *The Bayshore Homes Site, St. Petersburg, Florida.* Contributions of the Florida State Museum, Social Sciences No. 6. University of Florida, Gainesville.
1962 Hopewell Affiliations of Certain Sites on the Gulf Coast of Florida. *American Antiquity* 28:5–18.
1967 The Tierra Verde Burial Mound. *The Florida Anthropologist* 20:25–73.

Shepard, James
1886 Shell Heaps and Mounds in Florida. *Annual Report of the Smithsonian Institution for 1885,* pp. 902–906. Washington, D.C.

Simpson, J. Clarence
1937 Part IV. Florida State Archaeological Survey. *Second Biennial Report to State Board of Conservation, Biennium Ending June 30, 1936,* pp. 107–152. Florida State Board of Conservation, Tallahassee.

Sleight, Frederick W.
1949 Notes Concerning an Historic Site of Central Florida. *The Florida Anthropologist* 2:26–30.

Smith, Samuel D.
1971 Excavations at the Hope Mound with an Addendum to the Safford Mound Report. *The Florida Anthropologist* 24:107–134.

Snapp, Annette L.
1996 The Durnford Collection. *The Florida Anthropologist* 49:267–273.

Snow, Charles E.
1962 *Indian Burials from St. Petersburg, Florida.* Contributions of the Florida State Museum, Social Sciences No. 8. University of Florida, Gainesville.

Stirling, Matthew W.
1931 Mounds of the Vanished Calusa Indians of Florida. *Explorations and Field-Work of the Smithsonian Institution in 1930,* pp. 167–172. Washington, D.C.
1933 Report of the Chief. *Forty-eighth Annual Report of the Bureau of American Ethnology to the Secretary of the Smithsonian Institution, 1930–1931,* pp. 1–21. Washington, D.C.

Swift, F. R.
1903 *Florida Fancies.* G. P. Putnam's Sons, Knickerbocker Press, New York.

Taylor, Robert C.
1985 *Everglades National Park Archeological Survey: Season 3.* Southeast Archeological Center, National Park Service, Tallahassee.

Thunen, Robert L., and Keith H. Ashley
1995 Mortuary Behavior Along the Lower St. Johns: An Overview. *The Florida Anthropologist* 48:3–12.

Van Beck, John C., and Linda M. Van Beck
1965 The Marco Midden, Marco Island, Florida. *The Florida Anthropologist* 18:1–20.

Walker, S. T.
1880a Preliminary Explorations Among the Indian Mounds in Southern Florida. *Annual Report of the Smithsonian Institution for 1879,* pp. 392–413. Washington, D.C.
1880b Report on the Shell Heaps of Tampa Bay, Florida. *Annual Report of the Smithsonian Institution for 1879,* pp. 413–422. Washington, D.C.

Wardle, H. Newell
1929 Wreck of the Archeological Department of the Academy of Natural

Sciences of Philadelphia. *Science* 70(1805):119–121.
1956 Clarence Bloomfield Moore (1852–1936). *Bulletin of the Philadelphia Anthropological Society* 9(2):9–11.

Warren, Lyman, Francis Bushnell, and Gerard Spence
1965 Six Contributions to the Hand Motif from the Safety Harbor Burial Mound on Cabbage Key, Pinellas County, Florida. *The Florida Anthropologist* 18:235–238.

Weisman, Brent R.
1995 *Crystal River: A Ceremonial Mound Center on the Florida Gulf Coast.* Florida Archaeology No. 8. Bureau of Archaeological Research, Florida Department of State, Tallahassee.

Weisman, Brent R., and Christine L. Newman
1995 An Introduction to the Archaeology of Rookery Bay, Gateway to Florida's Ten Thousand Islands. *The Florida Anthropologist* 48:133–145.

Widmer, Randolph J.
1988 *The Evolution of the Calusa: A Nonagricultural Chiefdom on the Southwest Florida Coast.* University of Alabama Press, Tuscaloosa.
1996 A Glimpse of Life at the Key Marco Site, 8Cr48, A.D. 500–900. Paper presented at the 53rd Annual Meeting of the Southeastern Archaeological Conference, Birmingham.
1997 Recent Investigations at the Shell Island Site, 8Cr55, Collier County, Florida. Paper presented at the 54th Annual Meeting of the Southeastern Archaeological Conference, Baton Rouge.

Willey, Gordon R.
1948a Culture Sequence in the Manatee Region of West Florida. *American Antiquity* 13:209–218.
1948b The Cultural Context of the Crystal River Negative Painted Style. *American Antiquity* 13:325–328.
1949 *Archeology of the Florida Gulf Coast.* Smithsonian Miscellaneous Collections Vol. 113. Washington, D.C.

Willey, Gordon R., and Philip Phillips
1958 *Method and Theory in American Archaeology.* University of Chicago Press, Chicago.

Willey, Gordon R., and Richard B. Woodbury
1942 A Chronological Outline for the Northwest Florida Coast. *American Antiquity* 7:232–254.

Williams, J. Raymond
1979 *Excavations at the Maximo Point Site, Pinellas County, Florida.* Department of Anthropology, University of South Florida, Tampa. Submitted to Division of Archives, History and Records Management, Florida Department of State, Tallahassee.

Williams, Stephen, and John M. Goggin
1956 The Long Nosed God Mask in Eastern United States. *The Missouri Archaeologist* 18(3):3–72.

Williamson, Ray A.
1984 *Living the Sky.* Houghton Mifflin, Boston.
Wing, Elizabeth
1965 Animal Bones Associated with Two Indian Sites on Marco Island, Florida. *The Florida Anthropologist* 18:21–28.

Certain River Mounds of Duval County, Florida

BY

CLARENCE B. MOORE

CERTAIN RIVER MOUNDS OF DUVAL COUNTY, FLORIDA.

By Clarence B. Moore.

The three succeeding papers give the results of our work in Florida, from January 16th to June 16th, 1895. These results, though mainly cumulative, having been arrived at with great care, are, we think, worthy of publication.

We wish to return thanks for valuable assistance to Professor Cope, to Professor Putnam, to Dr. E. Goldsmith, and to Prof. H. A. Pilsbry for identification of numerous shells.

Again we express our indebtedness to Dr. M. G. Miller for continuous assistance in the field and in the preparation of these papers.

C. B. M.

August, 1895.

Such mounds of Duval County as are considered in this paper, border that portion of the river between Jacksonville[1] and the sea, a distance of about twenty miles by water. The large mounds of this territory have been noticed in Part II of our previous report,[2] the smaller, often slight elevations, frequently covered with underbrush and unknown to the inhabitants of the neighborhood, escaped our notice during our previous work in this section, which was not so thorough as that on the upper portion of the river where the territory has been gone over literally dozens of times.

It is evident that this part of the river sustained a considerable population in former times, rendered possible, perhaps, by the great abundance of oysters in the waters near the river's mouth, where the low marshes are still studded with shell-heaps and a few years back contained deposits of great size.[3]

It will be noticed that the great mounds of this portion of the river resemble Mt. Royal, near Lake George, as to contents, while on the other hand, the low, irregular ridges which seem characteristic of the extreme lower portion of the river, differ considerably in the nature of the objects inhumed, from the mounds of the St. Johns farther south. Mica, so abundant in these low mounds and ridges, was rarely met with and in but small quantities on the river south of Jacksonville.[4] Again, deposits of numerous pebbles and pebble hammers together, almost

[1] The reader will bear in mind that the St. Johns, whose general course above is south to north, turns abruptly to the east at Jacksonville.

[2] "Certain Sand Mounds of the St. Johns River, Florida," Jour. Acad. Nat. Sci., Vol. X.

[3] Stowe Island, in the Sisters Creek, when first visited by us, had a deposit of oyster shells thirty feet in height. Since that time the mass has been reduced by shipments to the jetties.

[4] Abundance of mica was present in one mound of the Ocklawaha.

unknown on the upper river, were found in great abundance in the low mounds near the sea. The same may be said of numbers of mussel shells buried in association.

One point characterizing this whole region, the low mounds in common with the great, was the comparative abundance of tobacco pipes. From all the sand mounds south of Jacksonville but seven tobacco pipes rewarded our labors, while over double this number were taken from a circumscribed district between Jacksonville and the sea.

The grooved axe, present in Georgia and farther north, was absent from the mounds of this section in common with those of other portions of Florida investigated by us.

Mounds Described in this Paper.

Johnson Mound.	Broward Mound.
Shields Mound.	Reddie Point (2).
Gilbert Mound.	Daniel's Landing.
Monroe Mound.	Denton Mound.
Grant Mound.	Chaseville (2).
Low Mounds South of Grant Mound (5).	Alicia (2).
Horseshoe Landing (3).	Floral Bluff.

Johnson Mound.

This symmetrical and previously uninvestigated mound lay in the pine woods about one-half mile in a northerly direction from the first landing on St. Charles Creek, a stream emptying into the St. Johns just east of the town of New Berlin.

The mound, which had a height of 7 feet 4 inches and a diameter at the base of 65 feet, was totally destroyed with the courteous consent of the owner, William A. Johnson, Esq., of Wilmington, N. C.

The mound was composed of a peculiarly dry sand of a light yellow shade, with occasional bits of charcoal scattered throughout and a limited number of fire-places. Pockets of sand tinged cherry color by the artificial use of the red oxide of iron, increasing in number and in size toward the center, were encountered throughout the mound.

In all, human remains were met with at eleven points. In one case the burial was in anatomical order. In the remainder but limited portions of the skeleton were represented. The bones were past all possibility of preservation—a somewhat peculiar fact in view of the dry condition of the sand.

Sherds were very limited in number, the majority being undecorated, though three or four bore a complicated stamped pattern. No vessels or considerable portions of vessels were encountered.

Singly, loose in the sand, were: three arrowheads; one bit of mica; a small "celt" and several pebbles.

With human remains was a portion of a conch (*Fulgur*).

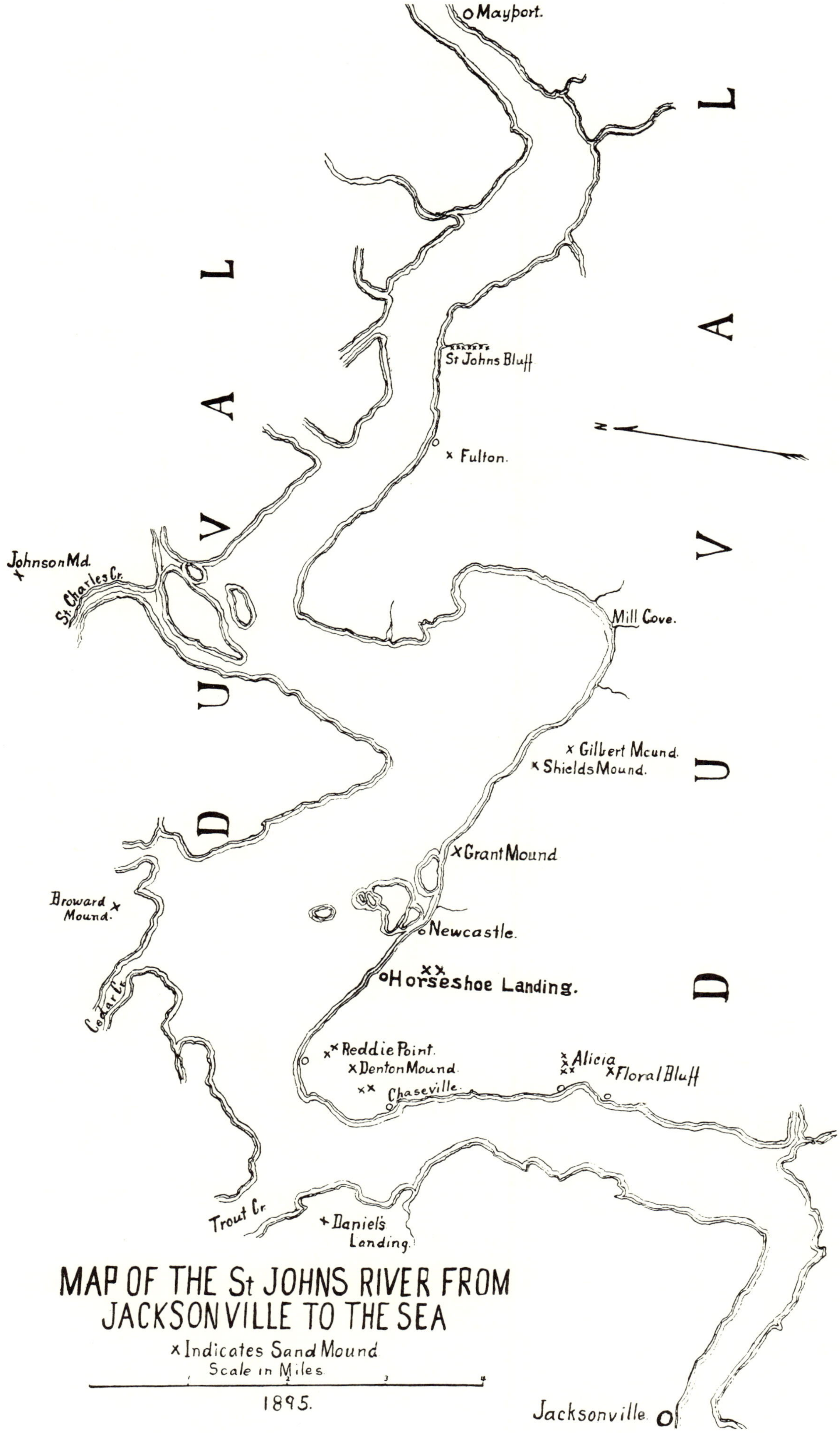

MAP OF THE St JOHNS RIVER FROM JACKSONVILLE TO THE SEA

× Indicates Sand Mound

Scale in Miles

1895.

Three feet from the surface, with a few decaying fragments of human bones, were two flat pieces of fine-grained sandstone,[1] one roughly given the shape of a hatchet, the other resembling a keystone—a form sometimes met with in Florida mounds. With these were: a pebble about two inches in diameter; a coarse sandstone hone; seventeen chips of chert; two columellæ of marine univalves with part of another; a portion of the body whorl of a conch; one incisor of a large rodent, and several masses of certain fresh-water mussels—three to four dozen in all—laid one within the other. These mussels, *Unio Shepardianus*, Lea,[2] are not reported farther south than Georgia nor are any fresh-water mussels present in the tide water of this portion of the St. Johns or of its tributary creeks. Moreover, the mussels of the St. Johns are distinctive. These shells were doubtless an importa-

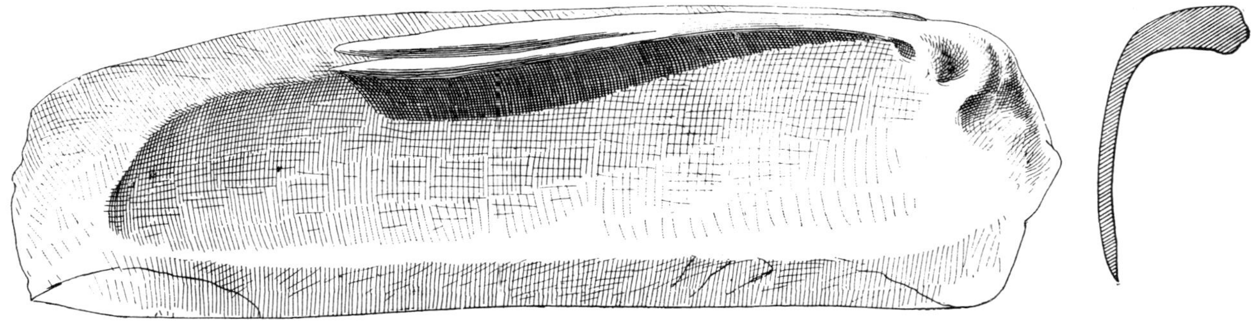

Fig. 1.—Mussel shell used as knife. Johnson Mound. (Full size.)

tion, and, as Fig. 1 shows, were peculiarly adapted for use as knives, for which we know mussel shells to have been employed by the later Indians.[3]

Almost in the immediate center of the mound, separately, were: a tubular bead of sheet copper; a fragment of sheet copper about 1 inch by 1.5 inches; a minute bit of the same material, and a portion of a sheet copper ornament about 5 inches long with an average width of 2.5 inches. This fragment lay with human remains about 4.5 feet from the surface and was too badly decayed for determination as to its original shape.

Nothing in the Johnson mound gave any evidence of intercourse with the Whites.

SHIELDS MOUND.

The Shields mound, near Newcastle, in section 35, township 1, has been briefly noticed by us in our Report on the mounds of the St. Johns,[4] where it is described

[1] The rocks from which were made the various objects of stone, described in this paper and the two succeeding ones, have been determined with care by Dr. E. Goldsmith of the Academy of Natural Sciences of Philadelphia. Exact determination has not been possible as, fearing to mutilate specimens, we have not furnished material for microscopic slides and for chemical analysis, which the careful petrologist requires.

[2] "Observations on Unio," I, Plate XIII, Fig. 38.

[3] "A pair of mussel shells sharpened on a gritty stone." Heckewelder's "Indian Nations," page 205. Cited by Holmes.

[4] "Certain Sand Mounds of the St. Johns River, Florida," Part II, Jour. Acad. Nat. Sci., Vol. X.

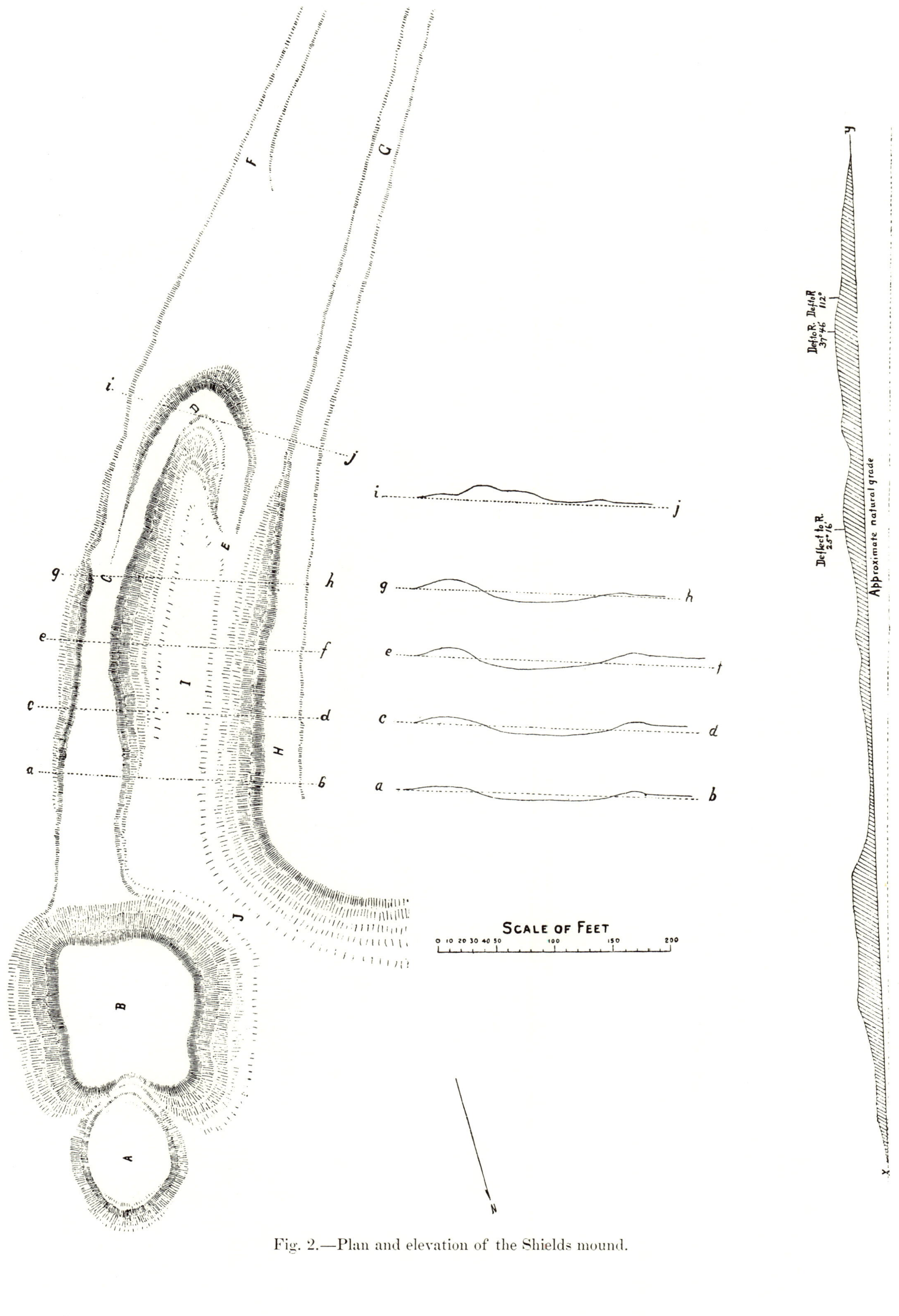

Fig. 2.—Plan and elevation of the Shields mound.

as a mound near Mill Cove. As all our readers may not have access to the work in question, at the risk of repetition, we give certain details as to size and shape of the mound.

About 150 yards from the river's bank, which at this point forms a bluff commanding the stream for miles, is a great platform mound entirely unlike in form any aboriginal earthwork on the river. Its shape is not circular, as we have stated in our Report, but slightly oblong with rounded corners; its base diameter, about 214 feet; the diameter of its summit plateau, 115 feet by 133 feet. Situate upon rolling ground, its height depends upon the point from which the measurement is taken, a fair average being 18 feet. A graded way leads up to the summit plateau on the side toward the river, while certain curious ridges, one running directly from the mound, extend in a southerly direction for a considerable distance in the rear until lost in the surrounding level. Investigation indicated these ridges to have been made for some purpose other than sepulture. We are largely indebted to F. W. Bruce, Esq., engineer in the employ of the United States Government at the jetty at the mouth of the St. Johns, for the accompanying plan and elevation of the Shields mound and its adjuncts (Fig. 2). We have requested Dr. M. G. Miller, who assisted at the survey, to notice these curious ridges in detail.

"From the southern margin of the mound B a long ridge (see plan) runs in a southerly direction for a distance of about 500 feet. With a height of about one foot where it joins the mound, the ridge gradually rises until at C it attains an altitude of 8 feet 10 inches above the level to the east. Beyond C is a marked depression from which the ridge again rises, reaching its greatest altitude, 13 feet 8 inches, at D, from which, making an abrupt turn northward, it descends gradually to the point E. The southern slope at D is so abrupt as to be difficult of ascent.

"From C a narrow terrace leads down the eastern side of the main ridge and continues, with gradually decreasing altitude to F from where a low ridge, varying in height from ten inches to six inches, extends a distance of about 350 feet, to be lost in the surrounding territory.

"About eighty-five feet to the west of this is a similar low ridge, G, leading northward along the margin of a well-marked terrace, H.

"Limited by this terrace and the main ridge is a basin, I, which has two outlets, one at E leading to the space between the two low ridges, and the other at J, between the mound and the terrace H as it turns to the west.

"About 600 yards southwest of the mound lies a small lake, to which the space between the low ridges F and G may have served as a covered way. Unfortunately, the territory in which these ridges lie has been under cultivation and it is impossible to decide as to their original extent and character.

"At ab, cd, ef, gh, ij, are given the contours between corresponding points on the plan, while at XY is given the sectional elevation of the mound and main ridge."

EXCAVATIONS.

Seventeen days of seven hours each, during parts of April and May, 1895, with an average force of thirty-one men, exclusive of those engaged in directing the work, were devoted to the investigation of the Shields mound.

The entire mound was encircled somewhat above the margin of the base and work prosecuted for about two days, the discovery of a few interments, none over three feet from the surface, being the only result.

Next, the entire eastern slope, commencing a little in from the margin, was removed for a distance of twenty-seven feet, where the trench, at this point 175 feet in breadth, had approached to within eleven feet in a horizontal line of the edge of the summit plateau. From this point the trench, reduced to a breadth of 115 feet, was carried along the base, as before, a farther distance of twenty-one feet, or ten feet beyond the margin of the plateau, as shown by accompanying diagram (Fig. 3).

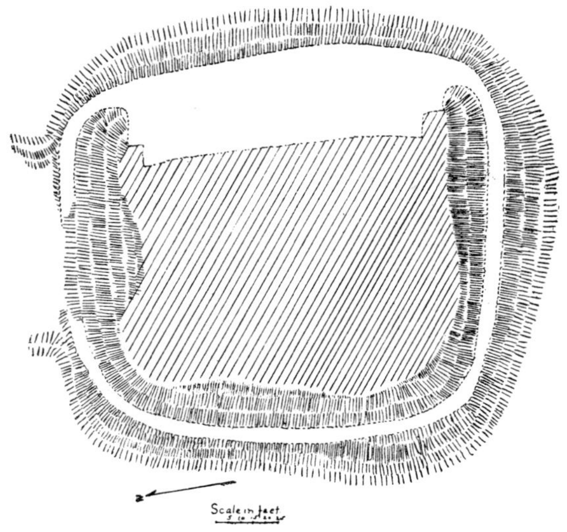

Fig. 3.—Diagram of excavations in Shields mound. Clear space represents portion excavated to base; section lines, portion excavated to depth of seven feet.

In this considerable portion of the mound comparatively few interments were found—possibly two dozen—none at a greater depth than three feet, nor were there any accompanying relics, with the exception of a few shell beads.

Next, the entire plateau, with about five feet of adjacent slope was dug through to a depth of from six to eight feet from the surface.

COMPOSITION OF MOUND.

No uniform stratification is apparent in the Shields mound. The base is not absolutely determinable, though a streak of sand from two to six inches in thickness, discolored by charcoal, was taken as indicating it, the light yellow sand beneath it being free from admixture of any foreign substance. Above this was a stratum of dark yellow sand from three to five feet in thickness, containing considerable charcoal in scattered particles, and this stratum continued to the point where the investigation ceased. Above it the composition of the mound varied at every stage of the digging. Yellow sand, yellowish brown sand streaked with small layers of white sand, pockets of gray sand calcined by fire with abundant charcoal, small pockets of brick red sand and layers and pockets of oyster shells and midden refuse containing sherds and fragmentary bones of lower animals, made up an almost indescribable whole. In the central portion of the broad summit plateau, extending to the eastern margin, was a very irregular layer, at places five feet in thickness, though this was exceptional. This layer, varying in shade from light chocolate to brick red, was due to intentional admixture of the red oxide of iron with the sand—a practice whose occurrence is frequently noted in our Report on the mounds of the St. Johns.

We append a description of a fairly representative section of the mound taken at the junction of the eastern slope with the summit plateau, going down:

2 feet, 8 inches—Sand of brick red and of chocolate color.
11 feet, 8 inches—Irregular and local strata; pocket of gray sand showing effects of fire, with much charcoal; occasional pockets of shell; pockets of yellow sand darkened by plentiful admixture of charcoal.
2 feet, 8 inches—To base. Pure yellow sand with occasional particles of charcoal.

HUMAN REMAINS.

In that portion of the mound beneath the plateau, interments were, as a rule, in the last stage of decay, frequently marked by a few crumbling fragments, isolated teeth, or even a line of small disintegrating particles of bone—hardly more than a yellowish stain. It was, therefore, impossible to give the exact number of interments met with, or, in many cases, to determine the form of burial. At not less than 150 points human remains were encountered, presenting both methods of sepulture—the bunched variety and the burial in anatomical order. In most cases, careful examination showed an unnatural juxtaposition indicating the interment of the remains when denuded of flesh.

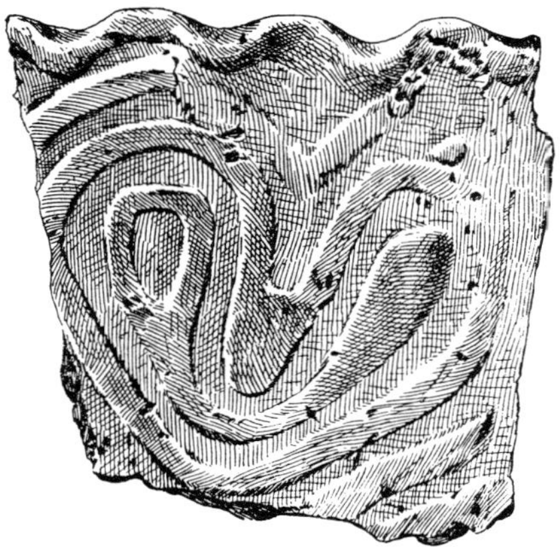

Fig. 4.—Sherd with stamped decoration. Shields mound. (Full size.)

With four exceptions, when the burials were encountered at a depth of six feet, all human remains lay within four feet of the surface.

In the western portion of the plateau, six feet from the surface, virtually in contact, were six crania associated with but one vertebra and two clavicles. This burial, however, was entirely exceptional.

In the central portion of the summit plateau, 3.5 feet from the surface, was a quantity of small fragments of human bones and of bones of lower animals, charred and calcined. With them were a number of human bones entirely unaffected by fire.

Two pathological specimens and a number of platycnemic tibiæ were sent to the United States Army Medical Museum at Washington. One of these tibiæ had an index of fifty; that is to say, its lateral diameter was but one-half of the diameter taken antero-posteriorly at the point of entrance of the nutrient artery. This is the lowest index ever met with by us in Florida or recorded by anyone as from that State. Most of our readers will recall, however, platycnemia is no longer regarded as a racial characteristic.

No crania were recovered save in fragments.

EARTHENWARE.

Occasional sherds were met with in all parts of the mound, especially with the midden refuse. In the material beneath the summit plateau, so far as explored by us, they were, however, infrequently encountered, though at times oblong pieces and triangular bits doubtless intentionally given the outline of the arrow point, were encountered in close association with human remains. Undecorated earthenware predominated. The square and the diamond-shaped stamps were represented

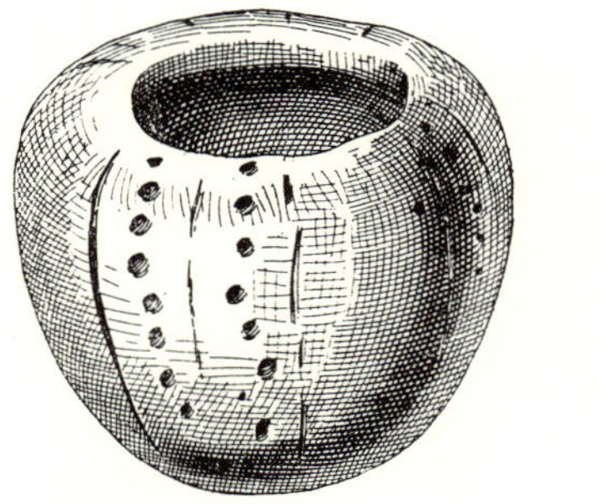

Fig. 5.—Toy vessel of earthenware. Shields mound. (Full size.)

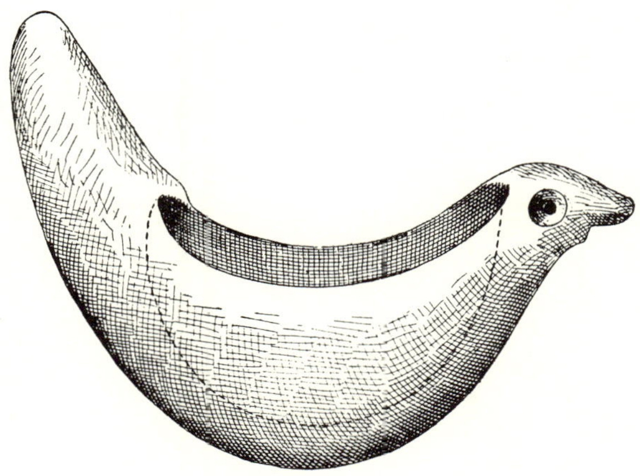

Fig. 6.—Bird-shaped vessel of earthenware. Shields Mound. (Full size.)

with the occasional occurrence of the complicated stamped decoration, though not of the patterns found so abundantly in several neighboring low mounds, but wanting in the great Grant mound less than one mile distant. Fig. 4 shows a complicated stamped decoration from the Shields mound.

Portions of two vessels in fragments, with cord-marked decoration, were colored inside and out with crimson pigment. Margins corresponding to missing parts gave evidence of ancient fracture, and it was clear that here, as in many other mounds demolished by us, broken, and consequently otherwise useless, vessels had been utilized for mortuary purposes.

During the investigation, nine entire vessels, none of so much as one quart capacity, were met with, including three unfortunately badly broken at the time of discovery. None were of special interest as to shape or decoration, and all were imperforate as to the base, if we except a toy vessel shown in Fig. 5.

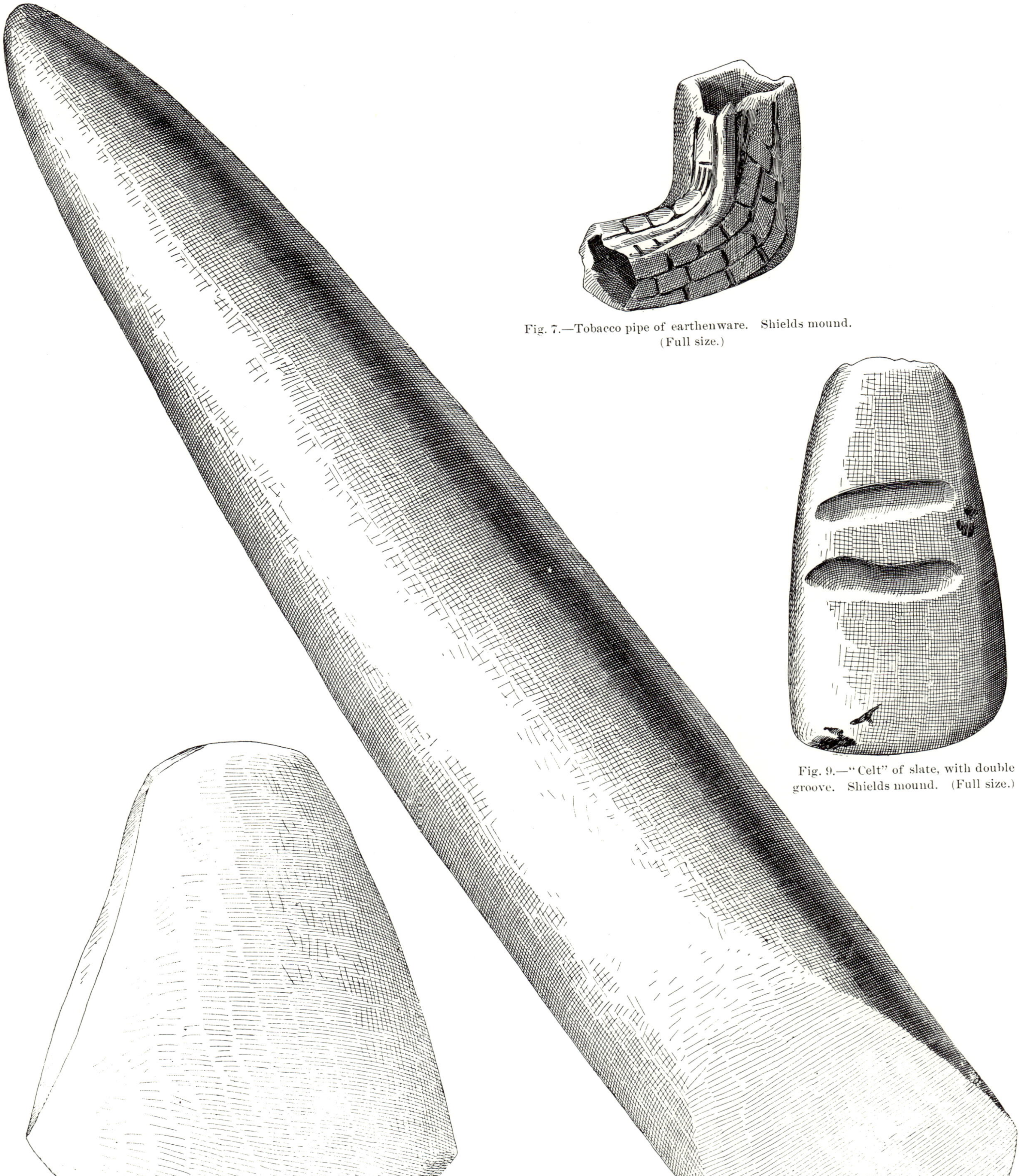

Fig. 7.—Tobacco pipe of earthenware. Shields mound. (Full size.)

Fig. 9.—"Celt" of slate, with double groove. Shields mound. (Full size.)

Fig. 10.—Implement of sedimentary rock. Shields mound. (Full size.)

Fig. 8.—Polished hatchet of igneous rock. Shields mound. (Full size.)

A diminutive vessel, representing a sitting bird and to a certain extent recalling Tennessee forms of earthenware, was the only variation from common types (Fig. 6). Height, 2 inches; length, 3 inches; depth of bowl, .8 of one inch.

Two tobacco pipes of earthenware were found during the investigation. One, of ordinary type, somewhat broken, had an encircling line of indentations just beneath the outer margin of the bowl.

The other, an interesting specimen, was decorated as shown in Fig. 7. Maximum length, 1.7 inches; height, 1.5 inches.

STONE.

Polished Hatchets.—Twelve polished hatchets, or "celts," were taken from the Shields mound. Their material has not been exactly determined. One, of fine-grained, compact rock of igneous origin, was within a small fraction of 13 inches in length, which is considerably more than that of any hatchet heretofore met with by us in Florida, and close to the limit of length attained by any other so far reported from any section (Fig. 8).

We are indebted to Mr. E. P. Upham of the National Museum, for the information that a polished "celt" from Alabama, 13.5 inches in length, is probably the longest in that institution.

One small "celt" of slate, 3 inches in length, has two deep transverse parallel grooves on one side and a single one on the other (Fig. 9). These grooves may have been made by the sharpening of implements. If not, and the grooves were made for the purpose of attachment to a handle, this is the nearest approach to the grooved axe ever, we believe, reported from Florida.

A chisel of sedimentary clay rock, 8.6 inches in length, was the only implement of the type discovered in the mound.

A handsome cutting implement of fine-grained sedimentary rock differed somewhat in form from any Florida implement we have seen (Fig. 10).

Arrow and Lance Points.—In the Grant mound, less than one mile away, arrow and lance points were of comparative rarity, as we shall presently see. In the Shields mound, on the contrary, they formed an important feature among the mortuary inhumations. In all, one hundred and fourteen were taken from the mound, the great majority of chert, a few of hornstone and of chalcedony. Numerous types and sizes are represented, none offering any unusual feature. On the tangs of some, considerable bitumen adheres showing the method of attachment to the shaft.

It is possible that some of the points classed by us as arrow heads may have served as knives, fastened into short handles for the purpose. Fig. 11 shows a number of selected lance and arrow points from the Shields mound.

Tubes of natural formation.—These objects, probably natural formations around some perishable material, such as wood, are occasionally found in the Florida mounds and were no doubt utilized as ornaments, though the larger may

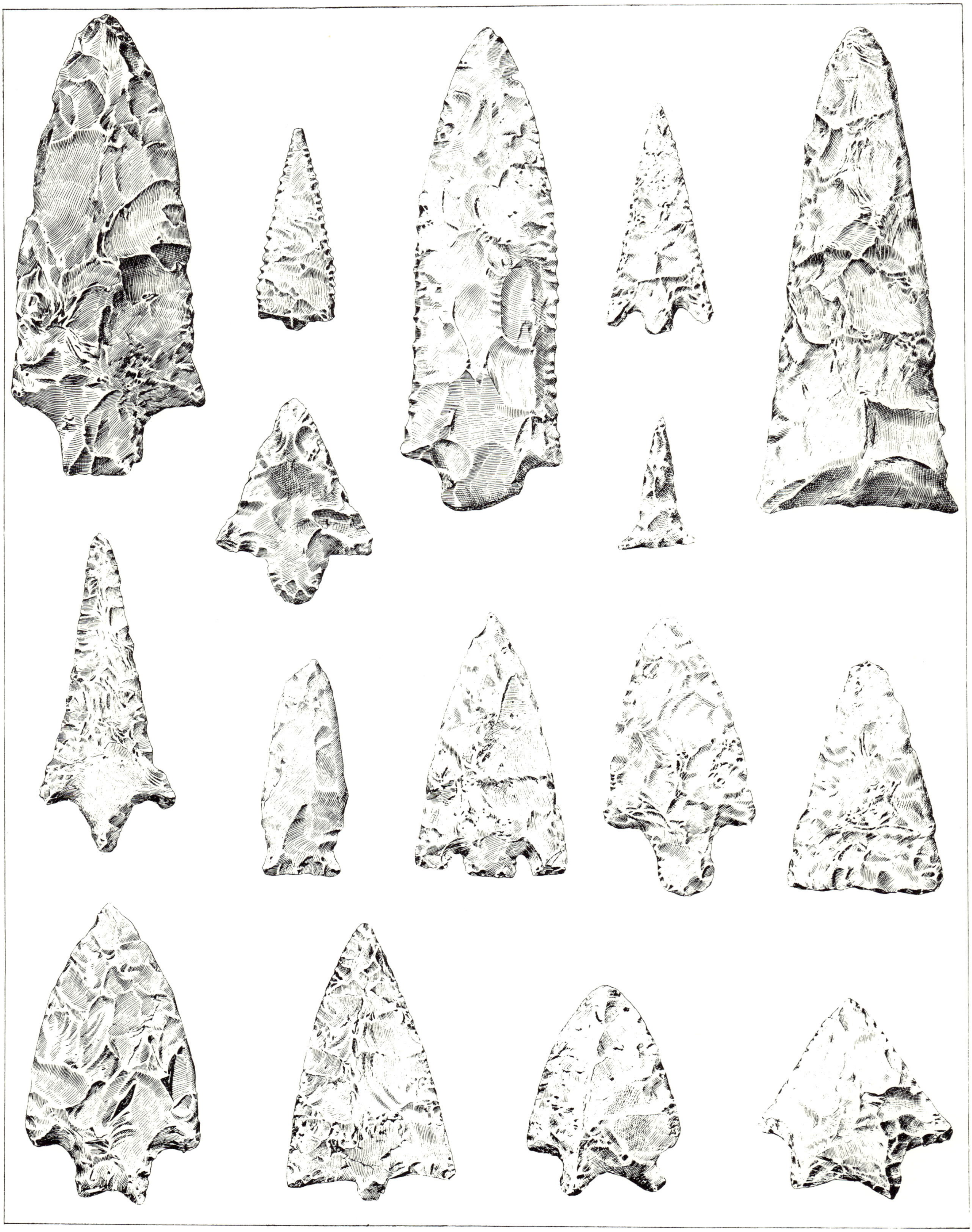

Fig. 11.—Arrow and lance points. Shields mound. (Full size.)

have served in lieu of tobacco pipes. Twenty-six of these objects, from 1 inch to 4.5 inches in length, were taken from the mound, and in every case, where determination was possible, they were found with human remains. One of these curious objects is figured in Part I of our Report as coming from Mt. Royal.[1]

Spade-shaped implements.—This curious type, discussed at some length in Part I, has been reported from Florida, we believe, by us alone, three specimens having been taken by us from Mt. Royal. Two of these implements, about fourteen inches and eight inches in length respectively, were taken from the Shields mound, associated with human remains. They are probably of *Saussurite*, though for obvious reasons we have not permitted mutilation for microscopic examination. In type they differ somewhat from the Mt. Royal specimens. The end of the shaft is neither tapered nor squared but left rough and unfinished. The wings are much broader, those of the larger specimens being about 3.75 inches across. Each has four nicks, or tally marks, on either wing. The larger is shown in Fig. 12.

Ornaments.—With a small earthenware vessel and human remains was a pebble of sedimentary origin, pierced through the center. A little to one side of the perforation another had been attempted and abandoned.

A fragment of clear quartz crystal, 1.4 inches in length, found loose in the sand, forms part of what must have been a beautiful pendant, flat on one side, convex on the other. It is grooved for suspension.

A "banner stone" in the form of a double-bladed axe, of the type figured by us[2] in Part II

[1] *Op. cit.*
[2] *Op. cit.*

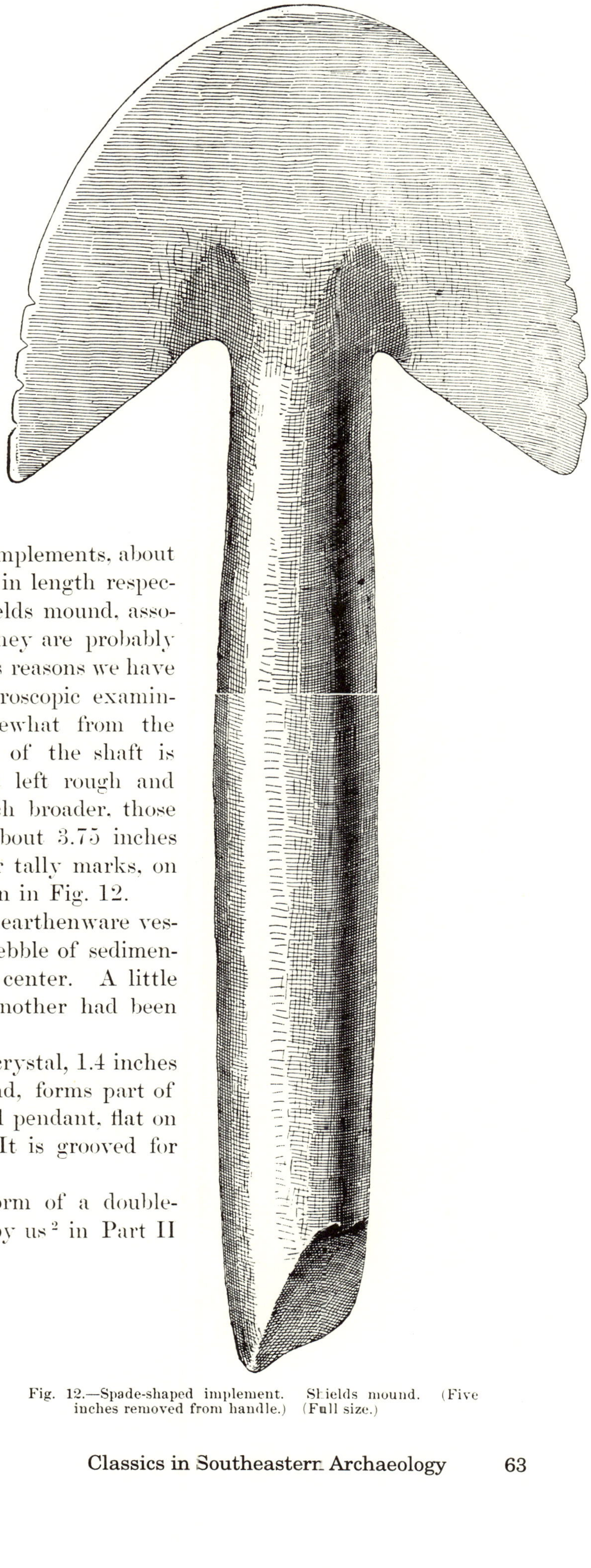

Fig. 12.—Spade-shaped implement. Shields mound. (Five inches removed from handle.) (Full size.)

as coming from the smaller mound at Thornhill Lake, Volusia County, was found at a depth of one foot, where it lay with two arrowheads. The material is of dark

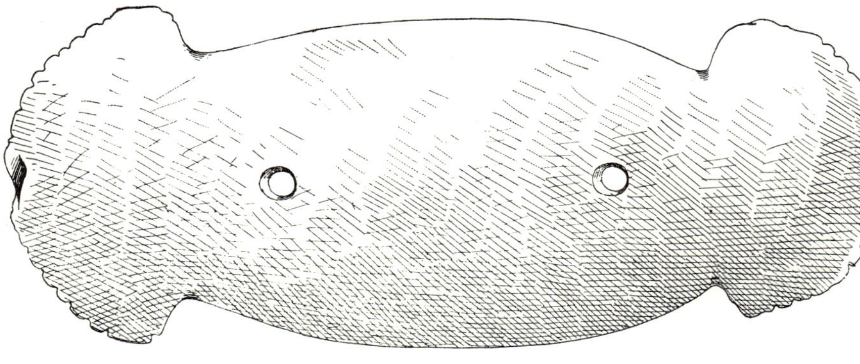

Fig. 13.—Gorget of schistose rock. Shields mound. (Full size.)

chocolate claystone beautifully banded. Height, two inches; breadth, about 2.5 inches; maximum thickness, about .7 of one inch.

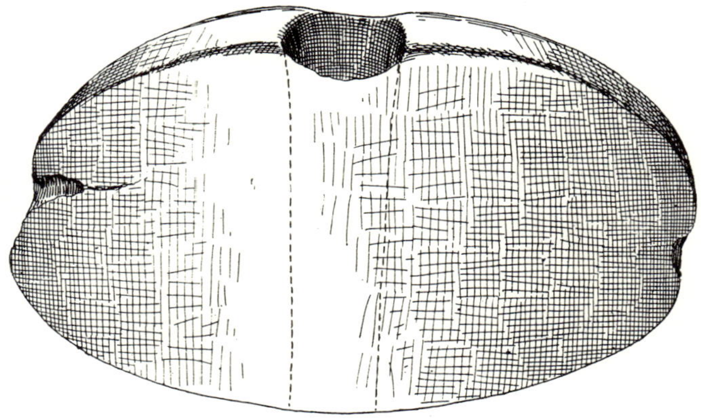

Fig. 14.—"Banner stone" of soft claystone. Shields mound. (Full size.)

Another graceful ornament of a schistose rock of slaty texture, lay at a depth of three feet, with human remains. It is doubly perforated and has many notches at either end. Length, 4.5 inches; breadth, 1.7 inches; thickness, .4 of one inch (Fig. 13).

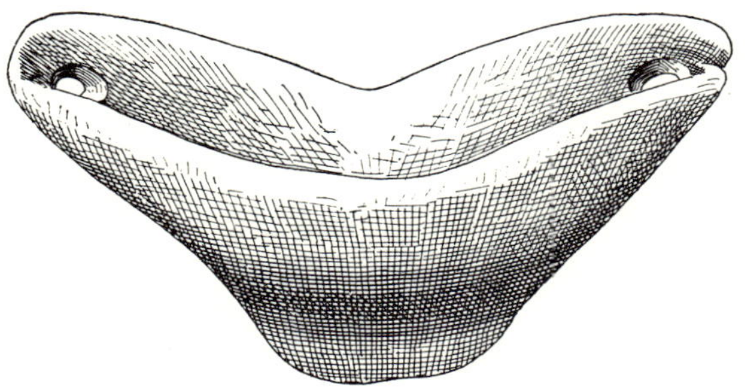

Fig. 15.—Boat-shaped pendant. Shields mound. (Full size.)

Four feet from the surface, with the small earthenware pipe already figured and two arrowheads, was a "banner stone," probably of soft claystone, shown in Fig. 14. Breadth, about 3.4 inches; height, 1.7 inches; maximum thickness, .9 of one inch.

A curious little boat-shaped pendant, presumably of soft claystone, of a form new to us, was found with human remains and numerous shell beads, three feet from the surface. A perforation at either end serves for suspension. A deep groove not possible to show in the cut is on the base. Height, 1.3 inches; width, 2.7 inches; maximum thickness, 1.1 inches (Fig. 15).

A small sedimentary pebble evidently split during perforation, lay beneath a cranium, three feet below the surface. With the two parts were an arrowhead and a chip of chert.

Tobacco pipe.—But one tobacco pipe of stone came from the Shields mound. The material was *Steatite* and the type that of other stone pipes of the neighborhood. It was associated with human remains at a depth of three feet, and with it were an arrowhead and a few shell beads. Height, 3.7 inches; maximum length, 3.8 inches; orifice of bowl, 1.4 inches by 1.5 inches; orifice of stem, 1.2 inches by 1.3 inches (Fig. 16).

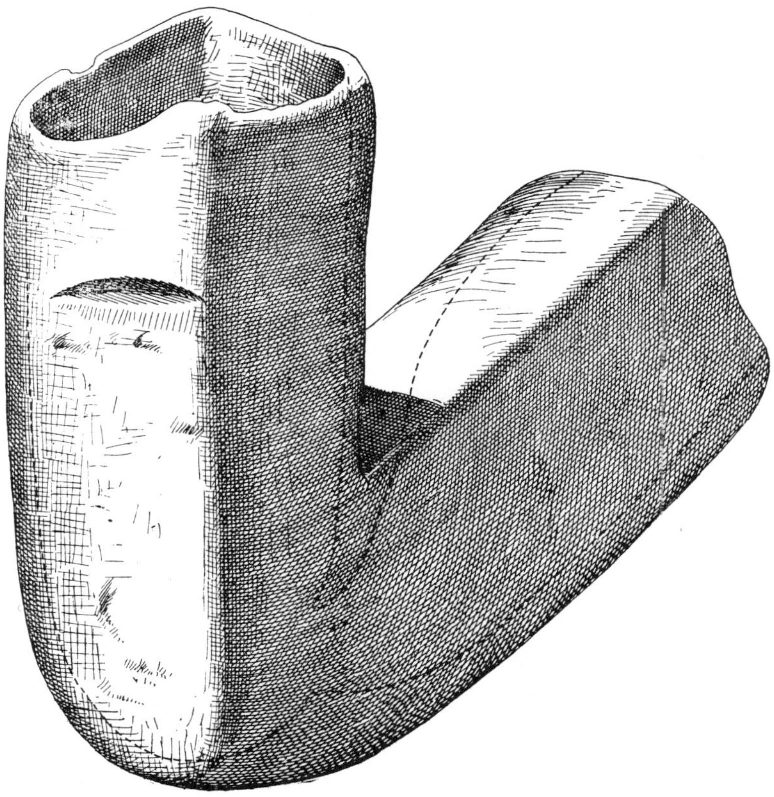

Fig. 16.—Tobacco pipe of soapstone. Shields mound.
(Full size.)

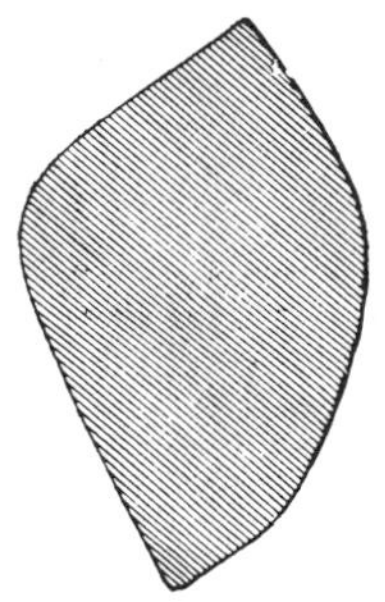

Section of Fig. 17.
(Full size.)

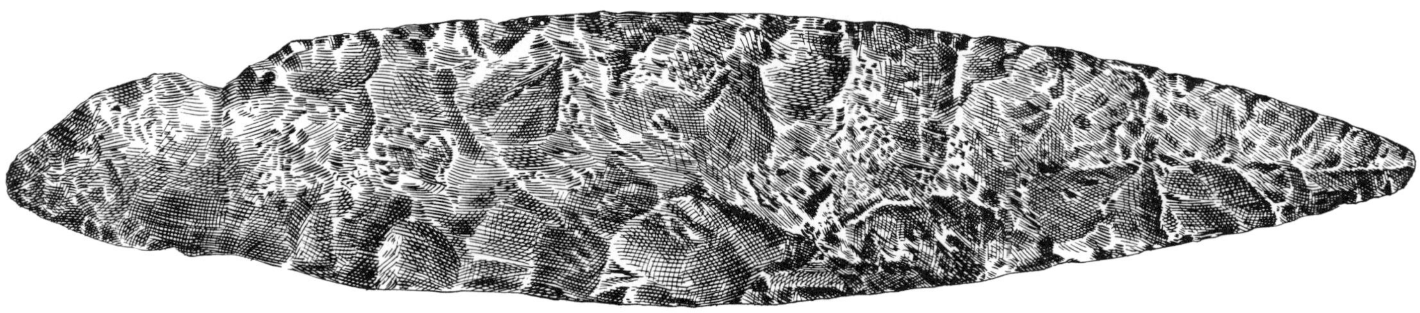

Fig. 17.—Weapon of chipped chert. Shields mound.
(Full size.)

Miscellaneous.—Two and one-half feet from the surface, in a mass of crimson pigment, with human remains, was a double pointed implement—possibly a weapon—of chipped chert, about seven inches in length with a maximum thickness of .8 of one inch. The section is triangular. The cut fails clearly to represent the two sides of the triangle. This type, so far as our experience extends, has not heretofore been discovered in Florida mounds (Fig. 17).

Together, with human remains, 1.5 feet from the surface, were: a leaf-shaped implement of chipped chert, one end unfortunately missing, with a length of 5.5 inches, and a maximum thickness of about .4 of one inch; a portion of a dagger or lance head about 4.5 inches in length, probably of crystaline sandstone; a sandstone hone, and a part of the lower jaw of a bear.

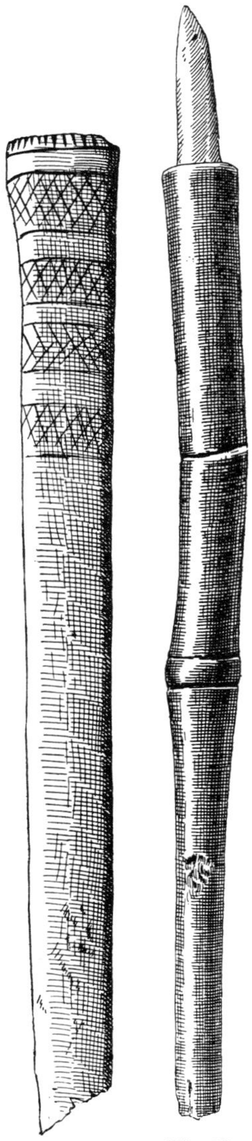
Fig. 18. Fig. 19. Portions of bone pins. Shields mound. (Full size.)

One implement of chert was rudely chipped to serve as a hammer.

One bit of sandstone, about the size of half of a closed hand, had a considerable cavity worked for some unknown purpose.

Two cylindrical beads of undetermined rock were found together, while from another portion of the mound came a part of what had been a beautiful bead or small pendant of red jasper, oblong with rounded corners.

Three small cubes of galena came from various depths.

Throughout that portion of the mound beneath the summit plateau were broken arrowheads, chips and spalls of chert, bits of sandstone and quartz pebbles, found singly.

But one or two small sheets of mica were encountered.

BONE.

Bone pins in considerable number were present in the Shields mound, often six or more with one interment. Their condition, as a rule, was fragmentary, none being so well preserved or so artistically carved as those we have figured in another report as coming from the Tick Island mound, Volusia County, Florida. Some show certain attempts at decoration (Figs. 18 and 19), while others have rudely carved heads. In other cases a shank projecting from the upper end shows traces of bitumen, indicating the former presence of a head of some perishable material, probably wood.

In close proximity to human remains was a section[1] of a leg of a turkey—doubtless a wild turkey, though determination is impossible—with the core of a spur. It is not

[1] Tarso-Metatarsal.

unlikely that this portion of a turkey leg and spur may have been used as a decoration for the lobe of the ear. At the time of the occupation of the mouth of the St. Johns by the French Protestants, in the third quarter of the sixteenth century, it was customary for the aborigines to wear ornaments of considerable size buttoned into or thrust through, the lobe of the ear. In Fig. 20 we reproduce a portrait of an Indian warrior decorated with the leg and claws of some large bird, from Plate XIV of the "*Brevis Narratio*."[1] The artist, Jaques Le Moyne, was one of the few survivors of the ill-fated garrison of Fort Caroline, massacred in time of peace by the Spaniards, "not as Frenchmen, but as Lutherans." Fort Caroline cannot have been much over one league distant from the Shields mound.

Fig. 20.—Indian Warrior of Sixteenth Century.

COPPER.

Considering the interesting types in stone taken from the Shields mound, one would look for more varied forms in copper. In addition to a number of fragments of sheet copper five small sheets of familiar type were taken separately from various depths.

A portion of a large undecorated ornament of sheet copper, centrally perforated, 6.5 inches by 7 inches, lay near the surface. With it were fragments of vegetable fabric.

A curiously shaped object of wood with circular section, bent somewhat at one end, has a pin fitted into it evidently to connect with a missing portion containing a socket. The wood has been overlaid with copper which remains at places. This fragment is too imperfect for identification.

[1] "*Brevis Narratio*," published by DeBry, Frankfort-on-the-Main, 1591.

A handsome double-pointed pin or piercing implement, a fraction over 12 inches in length, completes the meager list of copper from the Shields mound.

SHELL.

Large beads of shell were represented by few specimens, and the usual small discoidal beads were of by no means such frequent occurrence as in some other mounds. As usual, when found, they lay with human remains.

A few small shells (*Olivella*), longitudinally perforated, also were present with one burial.

One interesting feature of the Shields mound has not been noticed by us elsewhere. It was an aboriginal custom from Canada to Florida to inter with the dead, canine teeth of large carnivores, usually pierced for suspension. In the Shields mound were many such canines, the majority probably belonging to the bear, though a smaller one, submitted to Professor Cope, proved to be of the gray wolf. Sometimes with these teeth and sometimes alone, invariably with human remains, we believe, were a considerable number of pendants of shell, shaped and perforated in what seems to be a close imitation of the animal teeth also used as pendants. In Fig. 21 we show a canine of some large carnivore, the prototype of the form in shell given in Fig. 22.

One columella of a marine univalve and a portion of a body whorl, probably of *Fulgur*, worked to a certain extent, were found together.

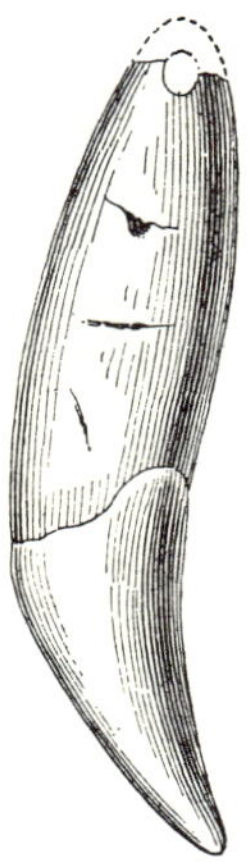

Fig. 21.—Tooth of large carnivore, used as pendant. Shields mound. (Full size.)

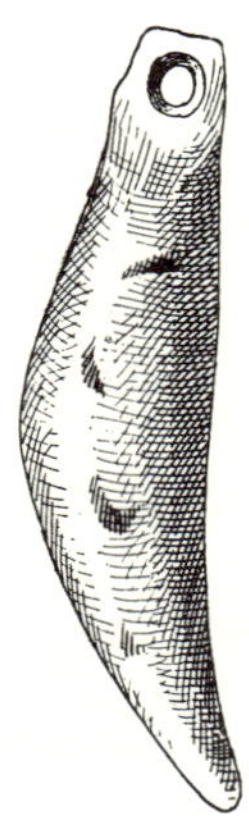

Fig. 22.—Pendant of shell. Shields mound. (Full size.)

A conch (*Fulgur carica*) from which a considerable portion of the body whorl had been cut, probably to furnish material for beads or for gouges, lay loose in the sand.

Near human remains, several feet from the surface, were three conchs (*Fulgur perversum*). Two have no unusual marks. The third, however, in addition to the regular hole so often found in the body whorl opposite the aperture, had three small perforations evenly made by some tool, at various points on the body whorl.

With one burial were twenty conch shells (*Fulgur*).

MISCELLANEOUS.

Associated with skeletal remains was a tooth, probably of a drum fish.

The enamel coverings of four teeth of the man-eating shark, were found during the investigation. Two of these lay together, three feet from the surface, associated with human remains.

Upon the surface of the mound were bits of concrete indicating its occupation as a place of abode at a period previous to that of the existence of the frame house of the present owner, Mr. Shields, destroyed by fire some years since. Nails, bits of glass and the like, were found at a certain depth in the mound in excavations made and filled by ourselves the year previous. In addition, in excavations of limited area, possibly post-holes, and in one case, perhaps the foundation of a chimney, filled with disturbed material and debris, were bits of rusty iron, buttons, a glass bottle, bits of china, a brass bolt, a half-penny of William IV of England, and other articles of White origin. These relics of a late occupation of the mound were sometimes not far removed from purely aboriginal objects and brought forcibly to our mind how readily a careless or inexperienced investigator, or one drawing conclusions from incomplete reports, might formulate erroneous deductions as to the period of the origin of the mound.

REMARKS.

Before proceeding to base conclusions upon the results of the somewhat incomplete investigation of the Shields mound, several facts must be borne in mind, which, though previously noted, for emphasis are referred to here.

The few burials discovered toward the margin of the mound were at no great depth, the maximum being about three feet. The great bulk of sand beneath the eastern slope, lying between the point at which some of these burials were discovered and the margin of the summit plateau, contained no interments whatever. In this mass of material, as we have stated, were strata of midden refuse with oyster shells, bones of lower animals, fire places and all the marks of prolonged occupation. It is probable that these strata extend through the mound. In fact, a large bed of oyster shells was discovered in a central position about seven feet from the surface of the summit plateau. In this bed was a circular hole 8 to 10 inches in diameter, and about 4.5 feet in depth, which may have contained a pole or post during a period when that level was used for domiciliary purposes.

No burials were found in that part of the mound dug down by us at a greater depth than six feet, and those at that depth were very exceptional. While we freely admit the slight dependence to be placed upon conclusions in respect to a mound which has not been totally demolished, we are inclined to believe that the great Shields platform mound was gradually built, and during this period used as a place of domicile; subsequently being utilized on the summit plateau for mortuary purposes.

That the burials in the summit plateau were not intrusive was clearly shown by the unbroken layer of colored sand above.

With undisturbed interments were no objects save those of purely aboriginal origin, though, as we have stated, and as might be expected in ground beneath a site used for residence in recent times and most probably during the English and Spanish occupation, at various points superficially were a number of objects found in use among the Whites. Under these circumstances there would seem to be no reason to assign to the burials beneath the summit plateau of the Shields mound a period other than one antedating the coming of Europeans.

Gilbert Mound.

The Gilbert mound stood in the pine woods, in full view of the road, about one-quarter of a mile southeast of the Shields mound. Its outline was that of an egg, its greatest height 4 feet 9 inches, being at the broadest portion from where it sloped gradually to the level of the surrounding territory. It was 86 feet in length, its maximum lateral diameter being 53 feet.

It was completely demolished, with the cordial consent of the owner, Mr. W. A. Gilbert, of Jacksonville, Florida.

The mound, unstratified, was composed of yellowish sand with occasional pockets of red sand in connection with some of the deposits of relics.

Human remains were encountered at various depths, superficially, in the body of the mound and below the level of the surrounding territory. In all, human remains were noted at twenty-seven points in the mound, though it is possible that a trench dug by a former investigator may have removed a certain number in addition. In no case did interments noted by us, which were of the bunched variety, include the entire skeleton. In a number of cases isolated crania were found and once, two skulls associated with no other bones. Again, the cranium was accompanied by the shaft of a long bone, while in one instance nothing was found but a portion of a tibia, curiously enough accompanied by art relics.

Virtually no sherds lay scattered loose throughout the sand, though numbers of fragments of vessels were found, usually with human remains. When put together, these fragments did not represent complete vessels. They belonged to vessels of ordinary type, of small or medium size and undecorated. In no case was stamped pottery met with, neither the stamped decoration of squares and diamonds so frequently found on the sherds of the two great neighboring mounds nor the complicated stamp of various intricate patterns so plentiful in the low mounds in the immediate vicinity.

Five and one-half feet below the surface, with an isolated cranium, was a globular bowl with inverted rim surrounded by an interesting raised decoration. The base is without perforation. Its height is 4.5 inches; its maximum diameter 6.4 inches; diameter of orifice, 2.8 inches (Plate LXXI, Fig. 1).

About two feet from the surface, associated with human remains, were two graceful vessels entirely intact. The larger (Plate LXXI, Fig. 2) of less than one pint capacity, is of fairly good material carefully smoothed. Its height is 3.6 inches; its maximum diameter, 3.9 inches, while the aperture, from which the rim turns out slightly, has a diameter of 2.9 inches. There are two perforations for suspension.

The smaller vessel, with a height of 3.3 inches, a maximum diameter of 3.3 inches, and a diameter at opening of 2.6 inches, has a perforation at either side for suspension. The rim is slightly scalloped and to a small extent everted. The body of the bowl is decorated as shown in Plate LXXI, Fig. 3. The material is of good quality.

In the southern margin of the mound, three feet below the surface, considerably below the level of the surrounding territory, near human remains, was a vessel of about one pint capacity, from which portions of the rim, old breaks, were missing. Height, 3.9 inches; maximum diameter, 4.4 inches. The base is imperforate. Its incised decoration lacks uniformity. The most interesting portion is shown in Plate LXXII, Fig. 1.

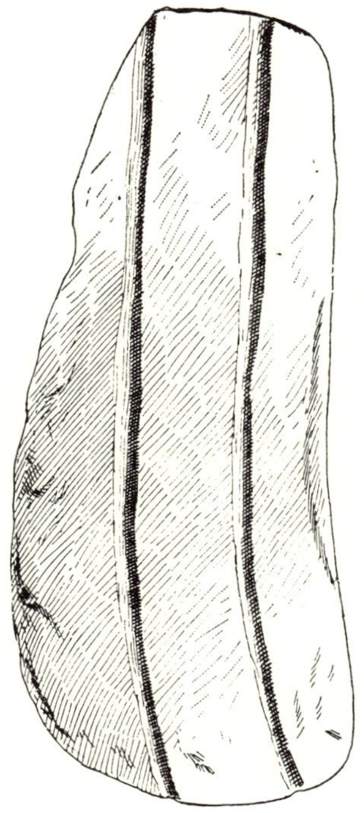

Fig. 23.—Chisel of shell. Gilbert Mound. (Full size.)

In caved sand was a toy vessel about two inches in height with imperforate base and flaring rim which was unfortunately damaged by contact with a spade.

A number of additional vessels of ordinary type and size, without decoration, were recovered during the investigation. Some were intact, while others had been intentionally mutilated as to the base.

Loose in the sand, near the base, was a mass of cherty material about 5 inches by 3.5 inches by 2.75 inches. Its shape was ovoid. It was doubtless fashioned to do duty as a hammer. A somewhat smaller mass of coralline limestone, not so regularly shaped, lay unassociated, about 3 feet from the surface.

Sheets of mica, of somewhat irregular shape, some so large as 7 inches square, came from various depths. Some had perforations for suspension or for fastening to garments. These sheets of mica, as a rule, were associated with pebble hammers, chips of chert, bits of shell and of sandstone.

Two and one-half feet from the surface, probably on the base, as the mound sloped considerably at that point, with part of the shaft of one human long bone, were one rounded piece of sandstone, one bit of chert, two pebbles, one small fragment of earthenware, and many marine mussel shells (*Modiola plicatula*). These shells lay in bunches, one within the other, showing them to have been inhumed without the animal, and therefore not as food. About 18 inches below this curious medley was an undecorated bowl, imperforate as to base, of about one quart capacity.

A chisel or gouge, of shell, found alone, had two incised parallel grooves extending the length of one side (Fig. 23).

In the central portion of the mound, about 6 feet from the surface, with human remains, including a tibia of considerable pathological interest,[1] were: five arrow heads of chert; two chisels neatly wrought from the lip of *Strombus*; one *Fulgur*; bits of sandstone; various fragmentary portions from columellae of marine univalves, showing grooves, probably the initial step in the manufacture of some ornament.

Near the base, with human remains, were a piercing implement of bone, the articular portion remaining; a bit of coquina; part of a cannon bone of a deer, a fragment of buck-horn, and a considerable number of marine mussel shells.

In various other parts of the mound, curious collections, somewhat similar to those described, were met with. With one lot was a small chisel of stone, polished at one end and roughened at the other.

Nothing in any way indicating intercourse with the Whites was discovered in the Gilbert mound.

Monroe Mound.

The Monroe mound lay about one quarter of a mile southeast of the Grant mound (see map), in a peach orchard, the property of Mr. George J. Monroe, of Joliet, Illinois. Its height had been reduced by cultivation. Its shape was somewhat irregular. Its length was about 63 feet; its breadth about 5 feet less. At the center of the broader portion, the maximum height of the mound was 3 feet 2 inches. A deep depression on the west showed whence the material of the mound had been derived.

There had been no previous investigation.

The mound was completely destroyed, being dug through at a depth of about 3 feet below the level of the surrounding territory.

It was evident that the mound had been constructed in the following manner. First, a fire was built on the surface, possibly to destroy the underbrush. Next, a pit of the area of the intended mound was dug to a depth of about 3 feet. In a central portion of this pit was made a deposit of human remains with certain artifacts to be described later. Then the pit was filled with the sand previously thrown out, through which was plentifully mingled charcoal from the surface fire. During the process of filling, various relics, but no human remains, were deposited, and covered by the sand. When the pit was filled to the general level, a great fire was made over its entire area as was evidenced by a well marked stratum of sand discolored by fire and containing particles of charcoal, extending entirely through the mound at the level of the surrounding territory. Upon this the mound proper was constructed and various bunched burials and art relics introduced.

In all, human remains were encountered eleven times, once at the base of the pit, the remainder in the body of the mound. The burials were of the bunched variety, but small portions remaining.

[1] Sent to the United States Army Medical Museum, Washington, D. C.

Sherds were fairly numerous, some of superior quality with lined decoration artistically executed. Others of less excellent material were undecorated or bore complicated stamped decoration of the type seen in neighboring low mounds (Plate LXXII, Fig. 2). The common square stamp and diamond shaped stamp were present but twice in the mound and then superficially.

At a depth of 1.5 feet, apparently unassociated, was an undecorated bowl of about three quarts capacity, with a perforation of base made subsequent to manufacture, which afterwards fell into pieces too small for restoration.

At the same depth, in a different portion of the mound, was a vessel of heavy ware of much better quality than usual. Its outline is elliptical. Small handles, one of which is partly missing, extend horizontally from either end. On the rim, which is .7 of one inch in breadth, and on the handles, is incised decoration. Height, 2 inches; present length, 5.7 inches; width, 4.5 inches. The base shows perforation after manufacture (Plate LXXIII, Fig. 1).

With a burial about 1 foot from the surface, though no doubt at a greater depth before long continued cultivation of the mound, were one polished hatchet and a fragment of a marine shell. With these were great numbers of fragments of various vessels, though in no case was the entire vessel represented.

About 1 foot down was a vessel with intricate stamped decoration, of about one quart capacity. Its base was intact. No human remains were noticed in its vicinity.

Four feet from the surface, unassociated, was a mass of graphite about 2 inches by 1.5 inches by 1 inch. One side was slightly pitted, the other deeply so.

Apparently unassociated with human remains, 4 feet from the surface, together, were: five arrow points of chert; one flake of the same material, used as a cutting instrument; one sheet of mica, and four worked masses of sandstone and of chert. One foot farther in, on the same plane, together, were: one pebble; one small mass of chert; one bit of coquina; two drinking cups wrought from *Fulgur perversum*, with perforated bases, one within the other, containing a number of marine mussel shells. With these lay an interesting little vessel, undecorated, with three compartments intact save a small portion missing from the base of one. The nature of this fracture would indicate the result of accident rather than an intentional perforation of the base. Length, 5.8 inches; maximum width, 3 inches; depth, 1 inch (Plate LXXIII, Fig. 2).

Almost in the center of the bottom of the pit of which we have already made mention, about 4 feet from the surface, were several decaying fragments of a cranium and a portion of the shaft of a long bone. With these was a boss of sheet copper with deep central indentation through the middle of which is a perforation for attachment. On the outside a knot of the original cord still remains. With this ornament was a lance head of copper, 7.6 inches in length, with a maximum breadth of 1.8 inches. This interesting piece, unlike anything else in copper we have seen in Florida, has almost a cutting edge at the sides with slightly increasing thickness to a maximum of .1 of one inch in the middle. A notch is at either side of the base by which it was doubtless fastened to the shaft. One would hardly expect a weapon of copper of this thickness to be of much effect against any but unprotected bodies. Highly polished, it would have an attractive appearance and may have been used for ceremonial purposes (Fig. 24).

With one burial were two shell beads each about .75 of one inch in length.

Several vessels of medium size and uninteresting as to type, were taken from various depths, as were a number of pebbles, always several together.

REMARKS.

It may be well to note here that pebbles which seem of so little value to us, and whose presence in these low mounds must strike many of our readers as curious, were to be had in this section of Florida by importation alone, and were distinctly of value either for use as small hammers or as raw material for the manufacture of pendants and the like.

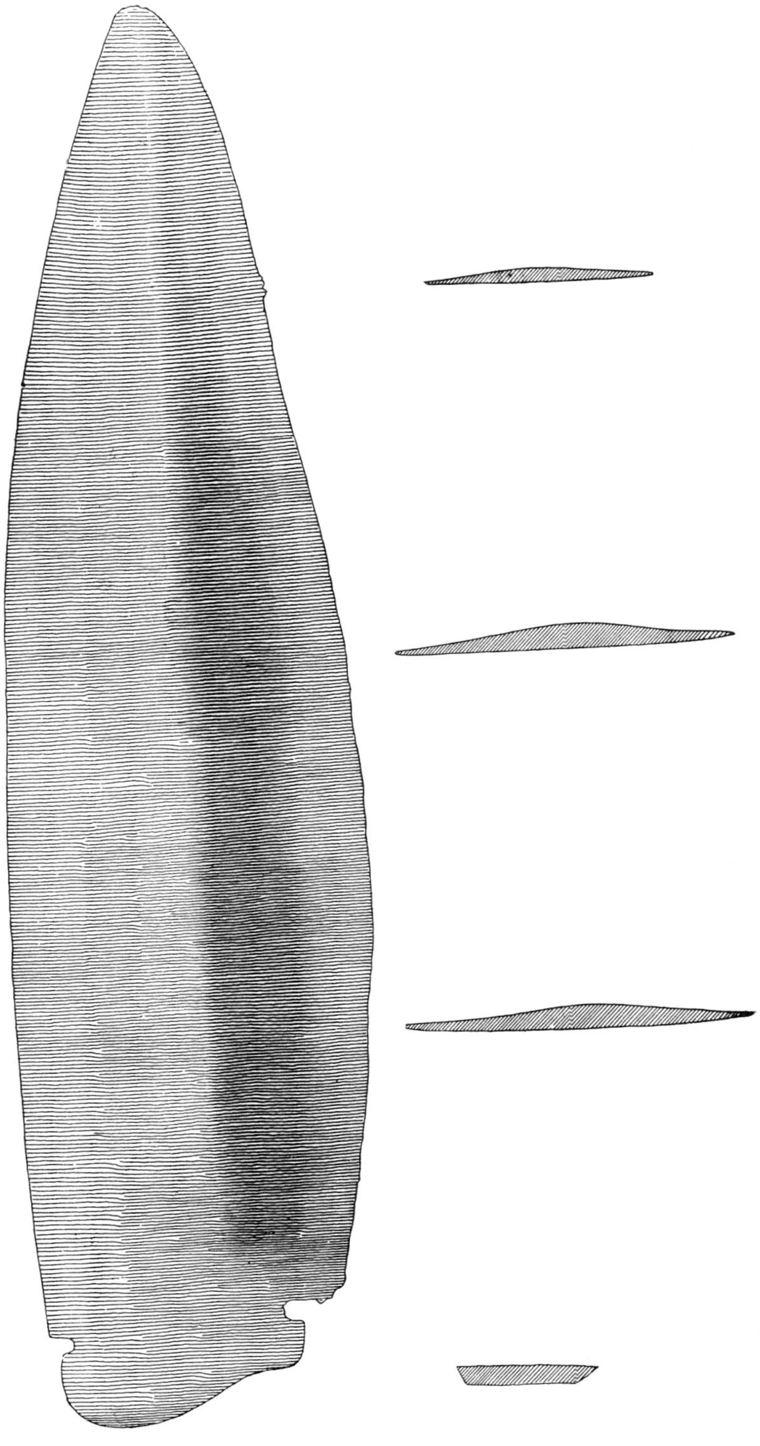

Fig. 24.—Lance-head of copper. Monroe mound. (Full size.)

Nothing discovered in the Monroe mound points to an origin other than aboriginal.

Grant Mound.[1]

The Grant Mound,[2] near New Castle, Duval County, Florida, in Section 35, Township 1, stood on the southern bank of the St. Johns River, on a bluff 25 feet in height. Its situation is noted on the Government chart relating to this portion of the river. It lay about one mile in a westerly direction from the Shields mound.

The height of the mound, taken from the present level of the bluff on the west, was 26 feet 8 inches. On the eastern side is an abrupt dip of the land and a measurement from this quarter would have given an exaggerated idea of its altitude. The base of the mound, as we shall see later, was marked by a layer of oyster shells. From this base line, taken on the western side where no natural depression exists, the height of the mound was 30 feet 9 inches and even this considerable altitude must be increased by at least one foot to allow for material removed by us at a previous investigation, as was shown by trees growing on the summit. It is evident, then, that the territory around the margin of the mound, which was composed, to a depth of several feet, of dark loamy sand and scattered oyster shells, either was a deposit belonging to a period subsequent to the erection of the mound and had consequently lessened its height by about four feet, or previously existing, had been dug into to a depth of four feet.

Fully one-third of the mound on the north, undermined by the river previous to our investigation, had fallen into the stream, and it is probable that had not the hand of man anticipated its destruction, a limited term of years would have seen the mound entirely absorbed by the river—to a certain extent a consolation for the loss of so notable a landmark.

In shape the mound was the usual truncated cone. Its base diameter was 216 feet and that of the summit plateau but 24 feet. The western slope was at an angle of 28°, the others somewhat less steep, though, taken as a whole, the mound was one of the most symmetrical we have met with.

Two low ridges, one somewhat better marked than the other, almost parallel, start a short distance from the southernmost portion of the mound, and, after a time, merge in the surrounding level. Investigation failed to reveal either interments or art relics in them, and it is presumable that these causeways were used as approaches, like others found in connection with Florida mounds.

The mound was totally demolished by an average force of forty-three men, exclusive of those supervising the work, digging seven hours per day during a period of five weeks of March and April, 1895.

[1] A short account of a former investigation of this mound was given in our "Certain Sand Mounds of the St. Johns River, Florida," Part II, Jour. Acad. Nat. Sci., Vol. X.

[2] See frontispiece.

COMPOSITION OF MOUND.

No uniformity of stratification was observed in the construction of the Grant mound. The bluff on which it was built had previously served as a place of abode for the aborigines whose kitchen refuse, in the shape of oyster shells, fragments of bone, and of earthenware, mingled with black loamy sand and charcoal, formed an irregular layer sometimes five feet in thickness.

This layer constituted the base of the mound.

Upon this base, through the outer portions of the mound, ran a layer of sand intentionally given a cherry color by the use of *Hematite*, from twelve to eighteen inches in thickness, which, gradually ascending, was lost, its place being taken, at certain points, by an irregular stratum of pure white sand with a maximum thickness of about two feet.

While the great bulk of the mound was composed of yellowish sand, there were very numerous pockets and local layers of considerable size of white sand, fine and again coarse and angular; of brown sand; of gray sand; of sand dyed a beautiful cherry, and of oyster shells mingled with black loam and midden refuse. A superficial layer of rich brown loam had a varying thickness of from two to three feet. The usual particles of charcoal were encountered throughout the mound.

At one point on the western side of the central portion of the mound was a striking combination of shades. Above the shell base was a layer of sand black in color through admixture of loam, six inches in thickness. This was surmounted by a band of white sand about ten inches through, above which was a stratum of sand of a chocolate tint, about three-quarters of a foot in breadth. Next came a layer one foot in thickness of sand of stone color, which was surmounted by seven inches of sand tinged a bright cherry. Above these layers were masses of yellowish sand with occasional strata of brown sand and of blackish sand containing oyster shells. This conformation, it must be borne in mind, was not representative of other portions of the mound.

Water-worn sherds, some from central portions of the mound, gave evidence that a portion of the material had been brought from the river front below.

Scattered oyster shells were frequently met with throughout the entire mound and to such an extent was their distribution that, by constant contact with the spade and thus exciting vain hopes of the discovery of more valuable articles, they considerably interfered with the interest of the search.

HUMAN REMAINS.

Skeletal remains in the Grant mound were singularly disproportionate in number to the vast bulk of material present, and emphasized more clearly than ever before in our experience how much needless labor was sometimes undertaken by the aborigines for their dead. Many men in our employ dug for days without encountering a vestige of human remains and in the entire eastern and southeastern portion of the mound virtually none was present while in no part (excluding the side bordering the river, as to which we are not in a position to speak) had any interments been made within nineteen feet from the margin of the base.

During our first investigation, which included a superficial portion of the mound containing but few skeletal remains, no burials in anatomical order were met with, such as were encountered being of the bunched variety exclusively.

In point of fact, however, as was demonstrated by the demolition of the mound, the burial in anatomical order largely predominated, though both forms were met with. On the base, especially, few, if any, bunched burials were brought to our notice.

More forcibly than ever before was brought to our attention the opposite state of preservation of bones presumably of approximately the same age. At times, in various portions of the mound, the skeleton was represented by remains with hardly a greater consistence than putty, while again, often at no great distance from the base, the bones were fairly well preserved. Such remains lay near oyster shells from which, doubtless, the infiltration of lime was a potent factor in preservation.

In the Grant mound, as in all other mounds we have investigated, the great majority of skeletal remains was unaccompanied by relics of any sort.

No crania were preserved, the facial bones being in all cases crushed or wanting through decay and the vaults usually to a certain extent broken in.

Marked examples of platycnemia[1] and of the pilastered femur were noted, and these, with specimens bearing evidence of inflammation and others showing fracture, were sent to the United States Army Medical Museum at Washington.

After a careful examination of the bones from the Grant mound we were impressed, as has been the case during all our mound work in Florida, with the exceedingly limited number of fractures present among them, probably much less than would be encountered among modern skeletal remains. Presumably the level country, the sandy soil, the absence of ice and of horses and of vehicles, of scaffolding and of machinery, and of many other things incidental to civilization, militated against accidents to the human structure.

LOCATION AND ASSOCIATION OF RELICS, ETC.[2]

The proceeds of the demolition of the Grant mound were disappointing in so much as, contrary to our expectation, few new types or specimens of remarkable interest, were encountered. In fact, the eastern and southeastern portions of the mound were virtually barren, as was that part 25 feet in all directions from the

[1] The reader will recall that this flattening of the tibia is no longer regarded as a racial characteristic but rather the result of muscular traction upon the bone, in running and climbing. *Mémoire sur la Platycnémie chez l' Homme et chez les Anthropoïdes. Dr. Manouvrier. Mémoires de la Société d' Anthropologie de Paris. Tome troisième, deuxième Série Paris*, 1883–1888, *page* 469, *et seq.*

[2] The reader of our "Certain Sand Mounds of the St. Johns River," Part II, will recall that at the previous investigation of the Grant mound we found one sheet-copper ornament, a number of beads of the same material, two small vessels of earthenware and a number of "celts" of polished stone.

margin of the base, save on the north where the encroachment of the river, to which we have referred, prevented determination. The objects discovered, comparatively few, when we consider the enormous mass of sand removed, were mainly confined to the north and northwest portions of the mound surrounding the summit plateau. Beneath the plateau itself the discovery of relics was comparatively infrequent. All the tobacco pipes found by us and five previously taken out by persons well known to us, were from the northern, or river, side of the mound.

So great was the height of the mound that frequent slides of masses of sand were unavoidable, and thus exact depths of objects found were often unobtainable, though at times close estimates were to be made since sections of the mound, sliding down a few feet as a whole, retained their integrity, holding undisturbed human remains and associated objects.

In describing various articles from the Grant mound we shall not give in all cases exact details as to objects found in association, but shall content ourselves with a few representative examples of "finds" of various relics encountered together and in the immediate neighborhood of skeletal remains, stating at the same time that, as we have said, most burials were without accompanying relics when found;[1] that shell beads, usually unassociated with other objects, were the most frequent tribute to the departed; that beads and sometimes ornaments, of sheet copper, were occasionally found with the beads of shell and that stone hatchets, singly, in pairs or very rarely three at one time, occasionally lay with the bones, sometimes associated with other objects.

About four feet from the surface, in the northern slope, a short distance apart, were two drinking cups wrought from *Fulgur perversum.* Into each a skull had been crushed to fragments by weight of sand. With one were a number of large shell beads and several ellipsoidal objects of shell. About one foot above was a large fossil shark's tooth.

Beneath the cranium of a skeleton in anatomical order, 20.5 feet from the surface, in a mass of crimson pigment, were a tobacco pipe of sandstone and several shell beads.

Together, with human remains, in contact with, and partially enclosed in, a mass of red pigment, were many shell beads; several small sheets of mica, one cut square with central perforation, doubtless for attachment; small beads of sheet copper; numerous fragments of sheet copper; a large tobacco pipe of *Steatite,* and one human molar with incised line around the crown and a central perforation for suspension.

In the eastern side of the mound, with human remains, were: a shell drinking cup; many shell beads; small beads and very fragmentary ornaments of sheet copper; a mass of red pigment about the size of a cocoanut; a tobacco pipe of undecorated earthenware of the usual type found in the mound, and a disc of lime-

[1] It is possible that objects of wood, fur, vegetable fabric and other perishable materials, when not in contact with copper, may have, in some cases, disappeared without leaving a trace.

stone 1.5 inches in diameter and .2 of one inch in thickness, centrally perforated and overlaid with sheet copper on one side. These objects were about six feet from the surface.

PEARLS.

With shell beads, near human remains, were two symmetrical pearls perforated as is the case in the mounds. The larger pearl is .35 of one inch by .25 of one inch.

SHELL.[1]

Beads.—Shell beads in great abundance, always with human remains, were present in the Grant mound. Though great numbers of the smaller forms were not recovered, nevertheless a box 14 inches by 10.25 inches by 5.75 inches, was entirely filled. The beads were of every shape, discoidal, spherical, barrel-shaped, tubular, of various sizes. One discoidal bead of shell, of about one inch diameter, had been overlaid with copper.

Two beads found 10 feet down in the northern slope, with other beads and associated with human remains, were of graceful and unusual pattern; the larger, with a length of 1.2 inches and a maximum diameter of .5 of one inch; the other somewhat smaller (Fig. 25).

Fig. 25.—Beads of shell. Grant mound. (Full size.)

In a few instances, numbers of small elongated marine shells (*Olivella* and *Marginella*) longitudinally perforated, lay in lieu of beads with human remains. These little shells were in use for a like purpose in post-Columbian times.

Drinking cups.—The reader will recall that the conch (*Fulgur perversum*) was utilized by the aborigines as a drinking cup by the removal of the columella and a portion of the body whorl.

Nine such drinking cups were met with during our last investigation, usually associated with other objects. Some of these were perforate as to the base; others were intact.

Pendants.—A number of pendent ornaments of shell, mostly resembling in type others described and figured by us elsewhere, were found throughout the mound. One, cylindrical in shape (Fig. 26) is of somewhat unusual design for Florida. Its length is 3.2 inches. The perforation begins at one side, meeting one from the top.

Another pendant, found with a long tubular bead of shell, is of a somewhat elongated pear shape with one side flattened.

A graceful ellipsoidal ornament of shell from the mound is shown in Fig. 27.

Miscellaneous.—Four columellæ of marine univalves were found during the excavation.

[1] The reader is referred to Holmes' exhaustive memoir "Art in Shell." Second Annual Report, Bureau of Ethnology. 1880-1881.

FIG. 27.—Ellipsoidal object of shell. Grant mound. (Full size.)

FIG. 26.—Pendant of shell. Grant mound. (Full size.)

A cockle shell (*Cardium*) contained a certain amount of crimson pigment, but whether it had been used as a receptacle for paint, an aboriginal use for certain shells in California, or whether the pigment was accidentally obtained through proximity to one of these masses present throughout the mound, we are unable to say.

EARTHENWARE.

Thirty-five vessels of earthenware were taken from the Grant mound, none of so much as one quart capacity. Some had the base intact; others a hole knocked through after baking, though the great majority were of the "freak" style of mortuary pottery with perforation in the base made prior to baking. None bore any traces of soot or evidence of use over fire. These vessels, as a rule, did not seem to be associated with human remains, though, in the case of many which came from sand caved from above, absolute determination was impossible. The material of all was of the usual flimsy sort used for vessels made for mortuary purposes.

In Plate LXXIII, Fig. 3, is shown a bowl 1.8 inches in depth with a maximum diameter of 5.3 inches. In common with all other vessels in the Grant mound, it shows no sign of use over fire and is probably of the mortuary variety.

In Plate LXXIV, Fig. 1, we have a vessel doubtless of a similar type, though in both cases the base has been perforated after completion. Height, 2 inches; length, 6.9 inches; maximum breadth, 4.8 inches.

A specimen of the pure "freak" variety is shown in Plate LXXIV, Fig. 2. The perforation at its base was made previous to baking. The form is entirely new to us. Height, 4.2 inches; maximum diameter, at rim, 3 inches.

Plate LXXIV, Fig. 3, represents a portion of a vessel with perforations of side and base. The motive for constructing a vessel of this sort is not apparent. Very recently vessels each with numerous perforations at the base have been found

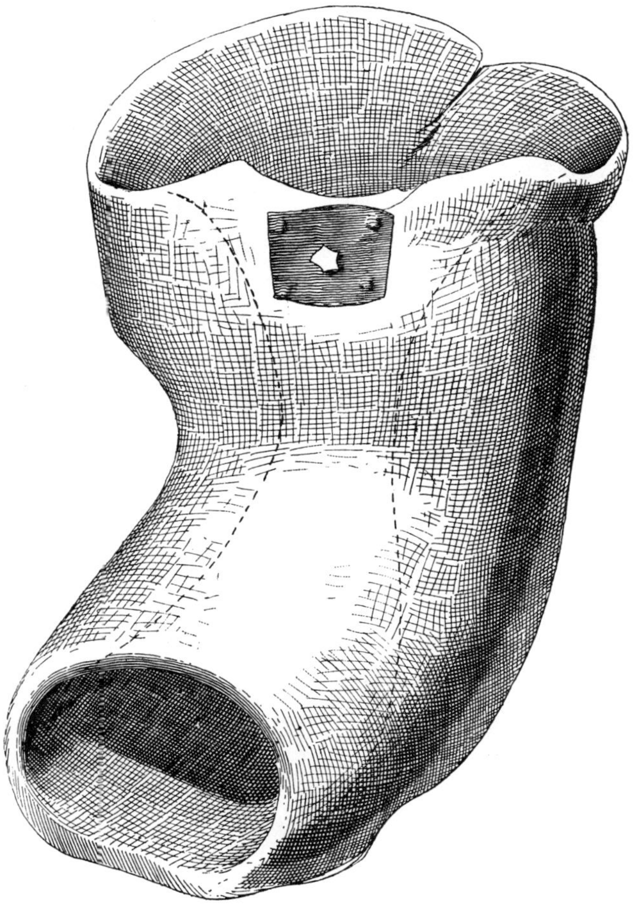

Fig. 28.—Tobacco pipe of earthenware. Grant mound. (Full size.)

in certain Kentucky mounds. These are supposed to have served as colanders or sieves, like those in use in southern Mexico for straining the cactus fruit. In the case of our vessel, however, such cannot have been the case, as a perforation at the base, made previous to baking, has a maximum diameter of almost 1 inch. It is perhaps an emphasized form of "freak" mortuary ware.

A vessel of a type entirely new to us was recovered in a somewhat fragmentary condition. The form calls to mind certain tobacco pipes, but in this specimen the perforation is wanting. Two small holes, one on either side of the rim, served for suspension (Plate LXXV, Fig. 1). Length of base, 5.3 inches; width of base, 2.2 inches; full height, 3.1 inches; maximum diameter of bowl, 2.7 inches; diameter of orifice, 1.7 inches.

Plate LXXV, Figs. 2 and 3, are doubtless types of mortuary ware. The larger has a perforation at base made prior to baking; the smaller, imperforate as to the base, has two small holes for suspension.

A bowl of about one quart capacity, with incised and stamped decoration beneath the margin, has but one of the two holes, one on either side, usually made for suspension. As the base has a large perforation made previous to baking, it is probable the potter was not over-careful as to the bestowal of details not likely to be called into requisition.

One small vessel with perforation of base made prior to completion, has a small hole on either side of this perforation and none

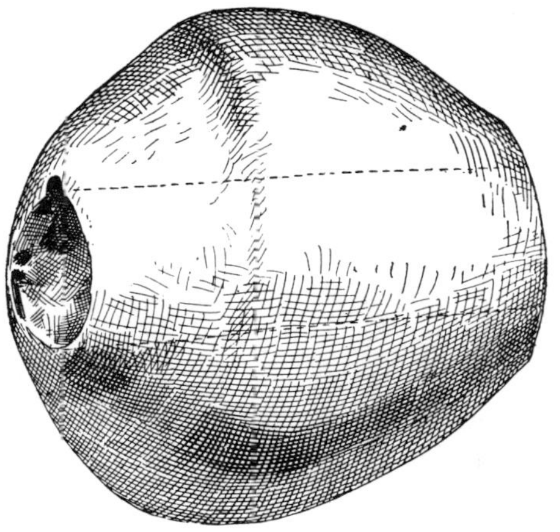

Fig. 29.—Bead or pendant of, earthenware. Grant mound. (Full size.)

beneath the rim. We have never before seen this proceeding and are at a loss to account for its motive.

Another bowl, with the usual small perforations beneath the margin on either side, has, about one inch below the rim in the other two sides, holes about three-quarters of an inch in diameter, carefully cut.

A number of other vessels from the Grant mound, though of considerable interest, will not be particularly described here, since, to a certain extent, they resemble vessels from other mounds referred to, and figured in, our previous reports.

Sherds were of infrequent occurrence in the Grant mound. Some bore the usual stamped squares and diamonds, but in one instance only was there brought to our notice the complicated stamp of such frequent occurrence in many low neighboring mounds.

But two tobacco pipes of earthenware were recovered. The larger, with length of stem 2.8 inches, height of bowl 3 inches, orifice of bowl 1.7 inches by 2.8 inches, had, when found, a small ornament of sheet copper fastened beneath the margin of the orifice, facing the smoker, by an encircling cord which crumbled into dust (Fig. 28).

A somewhat smaller tobacco pipe of ordinary type came from a depth of 6 feet, with human remains and many associated objects.

A large bead or pendant, of earthenware, was of equal proportions in height and in length, 2.3 inches (Fig. 29).

STONE.

Hatchets or "celts."—In all, 117 hatchets, or "celts," were taken by us from the Grant mound during the second investigation. Their material has not been separately determined, the majority, however, being from rocks of igneous origin, while an occasional sedimentary or metamorphic rock is represented. None of these rocks are found in Florida.

Twelve feet from the surface, just beneath a skeleton with which were beads of shell, was the most perfectly symmetrical and beautiful "celt" it has been our good fortune to find. The material, light green in color, is believed to be an altered *Felsite*. The semi-circular outline of the cutting edge has been conferred with wonderful precision. This implement is of the pure Santo Domingo type. The cuts by no means convey a fair idea of the appearance of the original. Length, about 5.5 inches; maximum breadth, about 2.6 inches; maximum thickness, about 1.5 inches (Figs. 30 and 31).

Arrow and lance heads.—The interment of arrow and lance points with the dead was largely a matter of fashion. In the Shields mound, less than one mile distant, they were very abundant, as was the case in Mt. Royal, which closely resembled the Grant mound in many particulars. In the Grant mound but fifteen were taken out by us. None was of unusual size or of especial interest.

Tobacco pipes.—Three pipes of soapstone, variously associated, came from the Grant mound. One of these was about the size and form of the one figured from the Shields mound. The others were somewhat smaller though of the same type. One had two lines rudely incised on one side and one on the other.

A tobacco pipe of sandstone came from a depth of 20.5 feet, beneath a cranium with a mass of red pigment and shell beads. Length of bowl and stem, 3.4 inches; diameter of bowl, about 1.7 inches (Fig. 32).

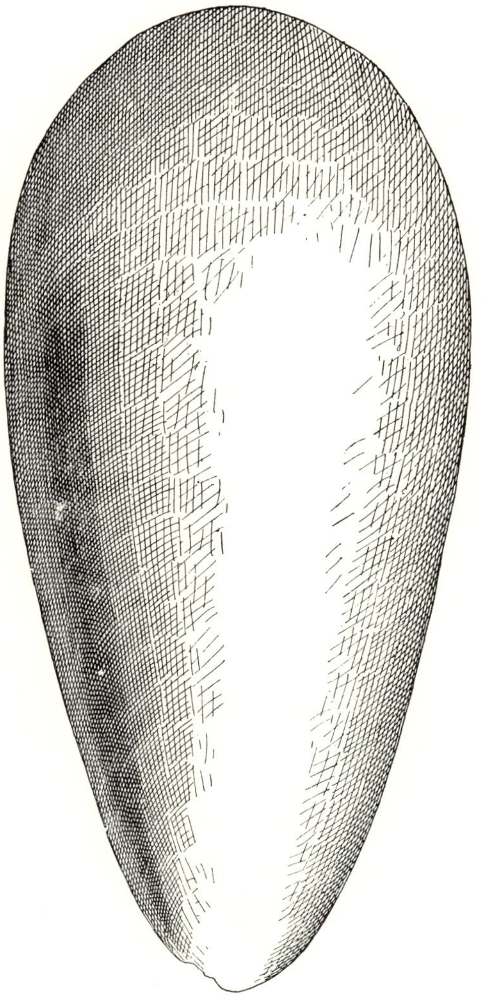

Fig. 30.—"Celt" of altered *Felsite*. Grant mound. (Full size.)

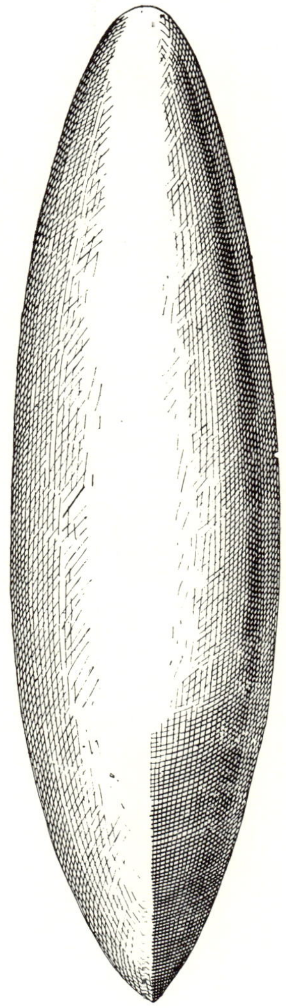

Fig. 31.—Same, side view. (Full size.)

Another tobacco pipe of sandstone, with bowl nearly at right angles to the stem, lay in caved sand. Height of bowl, 2.5 inches; length of stem, including báse of bowl, 2 inches; diameter of bowl, about 1.7 inches (Fig. 33).

Pendants.—A pendant, probably of fine-grained *Diorite*, 2.5 inches long with maximum diameter of 1.2 inches, lay in caved sand (Fig. 34).

A pear-shaped pendant of quartz, grooved at the neck for suspension, about 2 inches in length, has a maximum diameter of about 1.6 inches.

Tubes.—During the excavation several tubes of sandstone and of coquina, were met with. In addition, six curious natural formations, such as we have referred to in our account of the Shields mound, were recovered separately.

Miscellaneous.—Several sandstone hones and a few loose pebbles and chips of

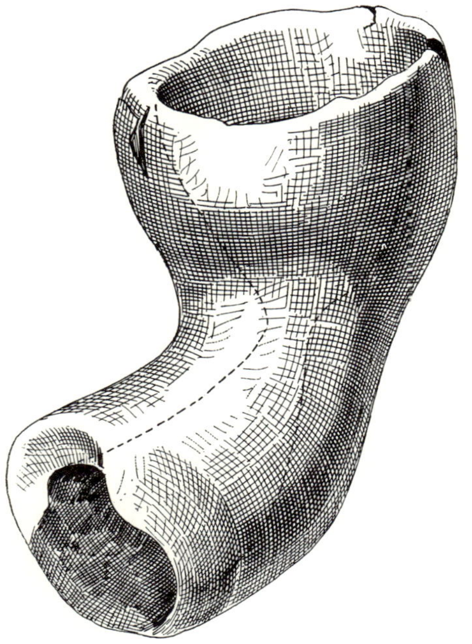

Fig. 32.—Tobacco pipe of sandstone. Grant mound. (Full size.)

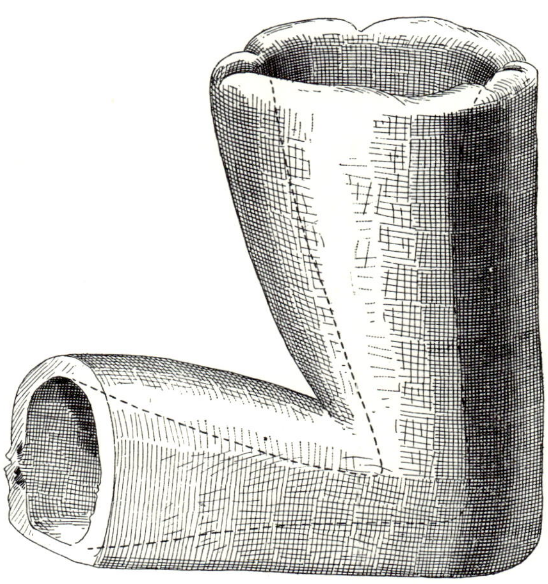

Fig. 33.—Tobacco pipe of sandstone. Grant mound. (Full size.)

chert were encountered separately. Mica was noted but twice, in each case thin sheets perforated for attachment. Fifteen masses of galena, some about one-half the size of the closed hand, came from various depths.

BONE.

A feature of the Grant mound was the great quantity of bone piercing implements and pins interred with human remains, sometimes a considerable number at one spot. Most, in a very fragmentary condition, were not preserved. None showed unusual or artistic forms. Fig. 35 represents a fragment with incised decoration. A considerable number, entire or but slightly fragmentary, are preserved in our collection with all the contents of the St. Johns and Ocklawaha River mounds at the Academy of Natural Sciences of Philadelphia.

COPPER.

The yield of copper from the Grant mound was somewhat disappointing, being, as a rule, a repetition on no very large scale of the usual types of ornaments of sheet copper and of other materials overlaid with sheet copper.

In many places in the mound mere traces of the copper remained and at times a discoloration of bones or of beads was the only evidence of the former presence of the metal.

Upon a number of occasions a single bead of sheet copper, not over one-third of an inch in length, lay with many beads of shell, showing the scarcity of the material.

As in other mounds no two ornaments of sheet copper were alike, and the sheets were slightly irregular in length, in breadth, and in thickness.

What we have before noted, namely, the almost entire absence of copper implements of any sort in Florida,[1] was emphasized in the Grant mound, where no object of that character was present save pins or piercing implements and even these may have done duty in the hair.

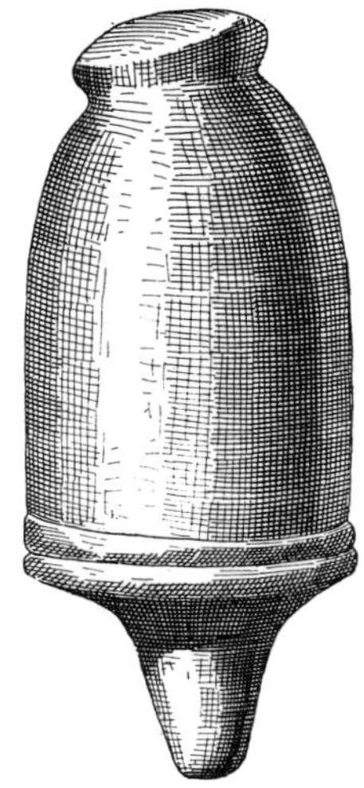

Fig. 34.—Pendant ornament. Grant mound. (Full size.)

Fig. 35.—Fragment of bone pin. Grant mound. (Full size.)

As in other mounds, the copper of the Grant mound was at times wrapped in bark or in vegetable fabric, a custom, as we have before stated, prevailing in other parts of the United States and in Canada, and, curiously enough, the occurrence of the same custom is noted in England, where, upon one occasion at least, prehistoric bronze was wrapped in linen.[2]

In addition to a considerable number of sheet copper ornaments, in a fragmentary condition, nine of the usual type consisting of repoussé bosses and beaded lines were recovered entire, or nearly so, from the Grant mound, two of which we show, full size, in Figs. 36 and 37.

One ellipsoidal bead of sheet copper, of the same shape though somewhat smaller than the one recovered during the previous investigation of the mound and figured[3] in Part II, came, with human remains, from the western slope of the mound. In addition, four beads of the same material, though more elongated in shape, were met with, the largest being 2.75 inches in length with a maximum

[1] From the interesting "Notes on Primitive Man in Ontario," by David Boyle, we learn that the reverse of this is true in Ontario where such specimens of copper as are found are almost invariably tools or weapons.

[2] Cited by Clodd. "The Story of Primitive Man," page 165.

[3] *Op. cit.*

Fig. 36.

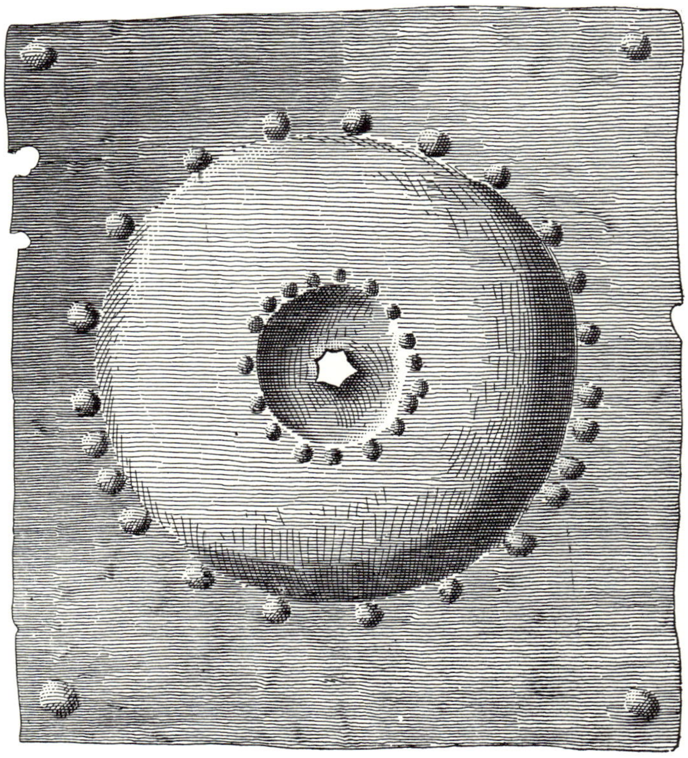

Fig. 37.
Ornaments of sheet copper. Grant mound. (Full size.)

diameter of .75 of one inch. Smaller beads of copper were found in considerable numbers.

A large bead of wood, 1.6 inches by 1.3 inches, spheroidal in shape, had been overlaid with sheet copper, portions of which still adhere.

Seven pins or piercing implements of copper, the longest 13 inches in length, were found variously associated at different depths. All seem to have been made by hammering sheet copper into the required shape.

A disc of limestone, 2 inches in diameter, with a central perforation, overlaid with sheet copper on one side, and a somewhat smaller disc of shell or of limestone of the same type, came from different portions of the mound. With the smaller was an earthenware pipe.

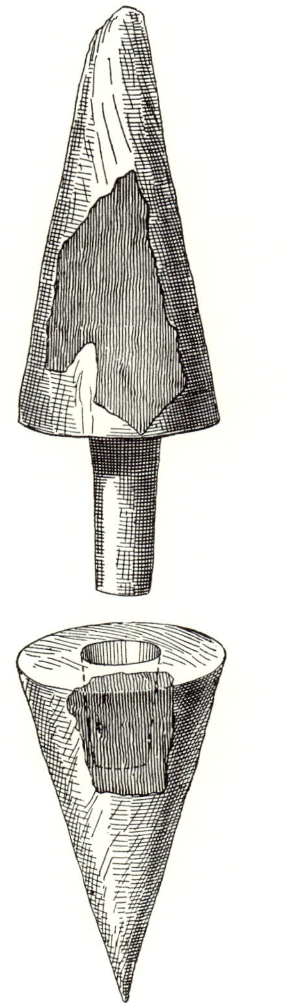

Fig. 38.—Ornament of wood overlaid with sheet copper. Grant mound. (Full size.)

Two discs, probably of limestone, overlaid with sheet copper, with shanks extending from the lower central portions, were found together near human remains and were doubtless used as ear plugs. A somewhat similar ornament is figured by us[1] in Part I as coming from Mt. Royal.

About 13.5 feet from the surface, near together, associated with human remains and a mass of red pigment, were two cones of wood, 3.2 inches and 1.7 inches in height, respectively, each with base diameter of 1 inch. These cones had been overlaid with thin sheet copper which had preserved the wood. Portions of the coating were still adherent. From the base of the larger cone projected a pin .9 of one inch in length, exactly fitting into a socket having a depth of .6 of one inch in the base of the smaller cone. This pin was not an integral portion of the cone from which it projected, but had been let into a small socket and secured with bitumen.

These interesting specimens, unique so far as we know, were carefully allowed to dry and then treated with shellac.

It is not unlikely that these objects form two parts of an ear ornament, one worn on either side of the lobe, the pin passing through the perforated portion (Fig. 38). The difference between the length of the pin and the depth of the socket would be about made up by the thickness of the lobe of the ear.

During the investigation an ornament, or, more probably, two somewhat similar ornaments, of sheet copper, were laid bare at a depth from the surface of about

[1] *Op. cit.*

20 feet. Before this copper could be removed a section of the mound fell from above burying the objects beneath tons of sand and breaking them, to a certain extent, as we learned hours later when they were recovered. It was apparent at the same time, however, by the carbonated edges of certain fractures that the ornaments had undergone some breakage previous to the caving of the sand.

The larger ornament consists of a shield, or escutcheon, shaped concavo-convex sheet of copper, with a maximum length of 2.6 inches and a maximum width of 2.2 inches. This shield has repoussé decoration, probably intended to represent the human face, the raised portion of the decoration being on the concave side of the shield. Near the margin, about .7 of one inch from the upper edge, is a small perforation on either side as shown in Fig. 39. From the convex side of the shield, where the design is depressed, the remaining portion of a band of copper, about 1.3 inches broad, projects (see section, Fig. 40). It is slightly bent, but has the appearance of having at one time been at right angles to the shield and having been bent by weight of sand. Near the shield lay a band of copper, 3.5 inches in length, and of the same breadth as the portion fastened to the shield. The ragged edge at either end, however, is carbonated, showing an early fracture. One portion of this band, which

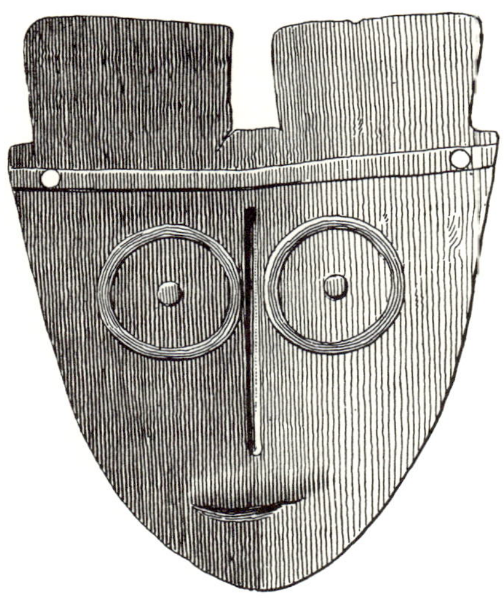

Fig. 39.—Ornament of sheet copper. Grant mound. (Full size.)

Fig. 40.—Transverse section of same. (Full size.)

is heavily carbonated, being cleared by acid, shows a straight line of rivets, running transversely, where it had probably been joined to the tongue projecting from the shield.

The shield-like portion of the second ornament is somewhat smaller, having a maximum length of 2.3 inches, and a maximum width of 1.9 inches. It is thinner than the larger shield, from which it differs in that it has repoussé decoration on the convex side alone, the concave side being undecorated and the excised portion from the upper part in the concave side does not end squarely, but has its base in the form of an upright wedge. Vegetable fabric, not shown in the cut (Fig. 41), adheres to the convex side which shows considerably less convexity than the larger shield. From the convex side, as in the case of the other specimen, a band of sheet copper, irregularly bent over, probably by weight of sand, projects as represented in section (Fig. 42a). Near the shield lay a band of copper about 2.5 inches in length, of the same breadth as that portion projecting from the shield. The line of fracture shows a recent break as does that of the band on the ornament. As the two portions do not join, it is probable an intervening portion is missing. This band of copper differs from that probably belonging to the larger shield, which is made of but one thickness of copper, in that it is constructed of one sheet bent upon itself to give double thickness, the edges meeting at the margin.

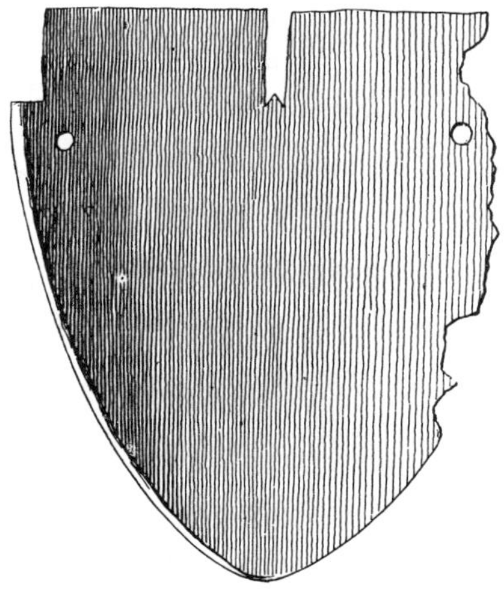

Fig. 41.—Ornament of sheet copper. Grant mound. (Full size.)

Dr. M. G. Miller, who has made a careful examination of the method of construction of these ornaments, writes as follows:

"The surfaces of both shields were obscured by a thick coating of carbonate, the removal of which required the use of acid

"The smaller ornament consists of two plates. That on the concave side, smooth, undecorated and showing no fissure in the median line, was made from a solid sheet. The plate of the convex surface is composed of two sheets each cut according to the pattern shown in Fig. 42c and united in the following manner: First, the tongue, D, was bent to a right angle with the remaining portion. Then the sheet of the other side being prepared in a corresponding fashion, the two were brought together in such a way that the tongues were in apposition and the margins overlapped at E and F, Fig. 42b. Rivets along these margins, as indicated at E, F, in Fig. 42b united the sheets, while the edges of one tongue were bent around those of the other as shown by the dotted lines. The plate thus formed was decorated as represented in the cut, and attached to its companion by applying it against the convex surface and turning its edges around the margin of that plate and pressing them tightly against the other side (Fig. 42a and dotted lines on 42b). More rivets than those represented in the cut may have been used in the formation and union of the plates, but fear of serious injury to the

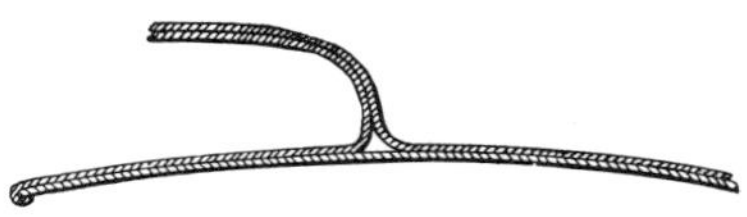

Fig. 42a.—Transverse section. (Full size.)

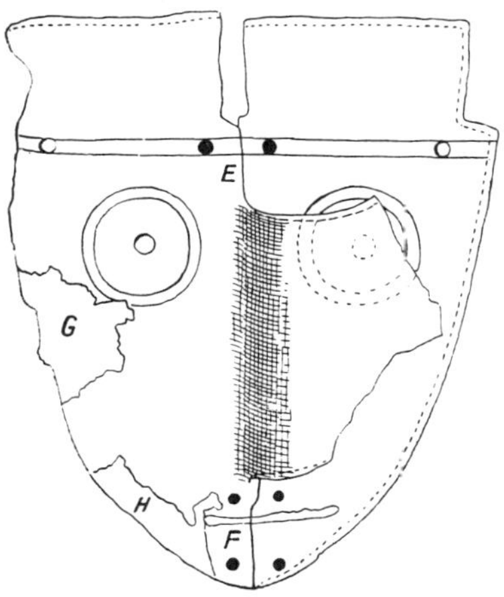

Fig. 42b.—Convex surface. (Full size.)

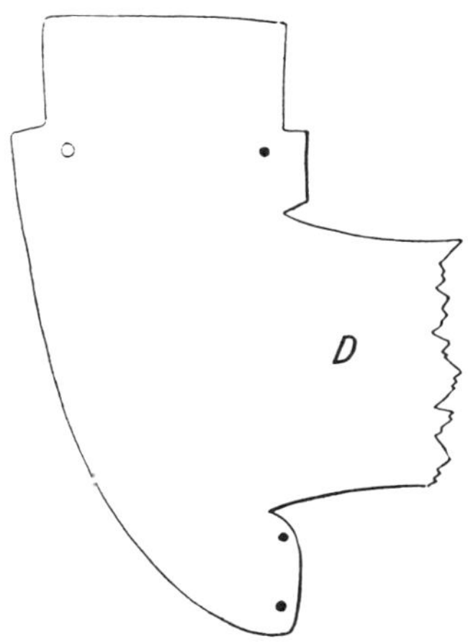

Fig. 42c.—Pattern of one-half of convex sheet. (Full size.)

specimen restricted the search. At G and H are indicated places where the convex plate has fallen away exposing the plate beyond.

"The larger ornament was examined on both surfaces as carefully as its condition would allow, but no rivets were discovered. It was, however, apparently constructed after the fashion of the convex sheet of the smaller ornament, as shown by the overlapping at the point, by the fissure along the median line of the concave surface and by the apposed tongues projecting from the convex surface."

REMARKS.

It is probable that the demolition of the Grant mound was a work as extensive and as carefully conducted as anything of the kind ever undertaken in this country. During the entire investigation not one object in any way connecting the mound with a period subsequent to White contact, was discovered. Under the circumstances, we think the mound and its contents may safely be assigned to a period prior to the arrival of Europeans.

Low Mounds South of Grant Mound.

About 500 yards in a southerly direction from the Grant mound, in dense underbrush, was a series of low elevations of irregular shape, which had been considered of natural formation, by persons who knew of their existence.

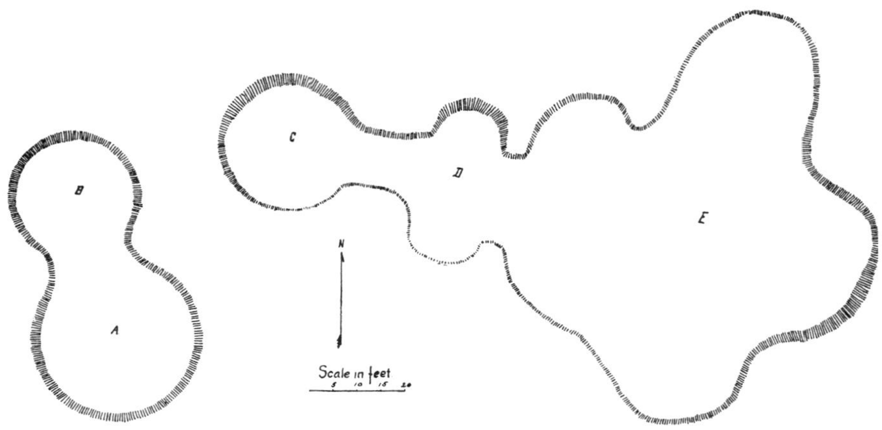

Fig. 43.—Plan of low mounds south of Grant mound.

It was difficult to determine whether these earthworks consisted of one curved ridge with occasional depressions, or a number of low intersecting mounds. For purposes of description we shall treat them as a series of mounds as figured in accompanying plan (Fig. 43). The mounds were totally demolished by permission of James B. Grant, Esq., the owner.

Mound A. Height, 4 feet; diameter of base, 36 feet. But two burials were discovered in this mound, both of the bunched variety, one representing portions of two skeletons. In addition, two bones were found separately. All skeletal remains, and, with trifling exceptions, all artifacts were deposited near the margin.

In the southern margin, about 1 foot below the surface, was a small vase, imperforate as to the base, with interesting decoration as shown in Plate LXXV, Fig. 4. A portion of the rim is wanting. This vase was apparently unassociated with human remains.

Two feet down in the S. S. W. margin, unassociated with human remains, were two bowls, each of about three quarts capacity. The material is inferior. Traces of red pigment are visible exteriorly.

With a bunched burial in the southern margin, 3.5 feet from the surface, were: one pebble-hammer; one rounded mass of stone about 2.75 inches in diameter, flattened on one side and slightly pitted at places; one columella of a large marine univalve, considerably affected by decay.

A polished stone "celt" lay 3.5 feet from the surface, about 1 foot above a bunched burial.

With no human remains in association, or, at least, with none remaining, 4 feet from the surface, were: one small "celt"; one slab of bituminous slate, 5 inches by 6.25 inches by .75 of one inch, rudely cut in the form of a keystone; three sheets of mica.

One and one-half feet down was a bowl with inverted brim, of about one quart capacity, bearing traces of red pigment. Immediately beneath were: three incomplete arrow-heads; a portion of another; ten fragments of chert and of sandstone, showing workmanship to a certain extent. No human remains were encountered near these relics.

Several other vessels of ordinary type, crushed by weight of sand, were met with in the mound and numerous sherds of good material, with the complicated stamp of Georgia and of Carolina, lay loose in the sand. This intricate stamped decoration is not met with on the St. Johns River farther south than Dunn's Creek, ten miles above Palatka.

Mound B. Height, 2 feet; diameter of base, 28 feet. With the exception of one fire place, no evidence of human origin was encountered.

Mound C. Height, 3 feet; diameter of base, 30 feet. One small sherd alone was recovered from this mound.

Mound D. Height, 3 feet 4 inches; major and minor axes respectively 36 feet and 17 feet.

Together, toward the center, with a few fragments of human remains, in sand dyed with red *Hematite*, 4 feet from the surface, were: eleven conchs (*Fulgur carica*); numerous shells of salt-water mussels; many sections of columellæ of marine univalves; several small bits of stone.

In the margin, about 3 feet down, was a pocket of cherry colored sand leading to a mass of crimson pigment, followed, on the same plane, by a seam of cherry sand, about 1 foot in length, connecting with another mass of pigment.

No human remains were discovered in association, nor were there apparently any farther traces of skeletal remains in any other portion of the mound.

Mound E. Five feet eight inches in height; major and minor axes 91 feet and 78 feet respectively.

This mound was dug through with great care at a level considerably below that of the surrounding territory.

At but four points in the mound were skeletal remains encountered. All interments were of the bunched variety, in no case representing the full complement of bones.

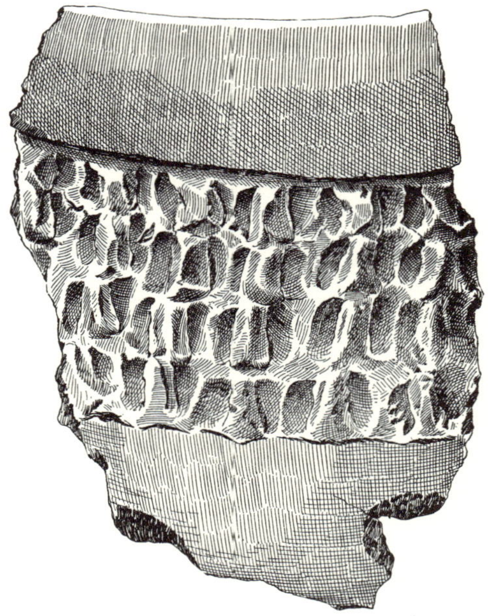

Fig. 45.—Sherd showing pinched decoration. Low mounds south of Grant mound. Mound E. (Full size.)

Fig. 44.—Sherd with complicated stamped decoration. Low mounds south of Grant mound. Mound E. (Full size.)

The mound was literally filled with earthenware—whole vessels, fragmentary ones, and sherds. Many sherds bore complicated stamps, one of which we show in Fig. 44. Another had a pinched decoration (Fig. 45).

With an isolated cranium, 2 feet 8 inches from the surface, lay a piercing implement of bone, badly decayed, with a number of large fresh-water mussel shells

(*Unio Jayanus*, Lea), pierced through the impression of the anterior adductor muscle, to enable them to be worn strung as a necklace. These large shells with the nacreous portion in evidence, must have made an effective showing. In addition, were portions of columellæ of marine univalves and a vessel of earthenware. This vessel, 12.2 inches in height, has a maximum diameter of 8 inches. It is centrally constricted and decorated and has decoration below the margin. It is imperforate as to the base and absolutely intact, and is by far the finest specimen of earthenware recovered by us from any Florida mound. Considerable soot remaining upon it shows it to have been in actual use (Plate LXXVI).

With a small earthenware pot was a graceful ovoid vessel of good material, handsomely decorated beneath the rim (Plate LXXVII). Its height is 7.2 inches; its maximum diameter, 5 inches. Considerable soot still remains upon it, showing culinary use for so ornamental a vessel. A portion of the rim and body is wanting through a fracture previous to inhumation as the missing portions were not present with the remainder of the vessel. Below the line of the fracture is a perforation with a semi-perforation a short distance away. It is evident that the intention was, by boring holes in the broken portion, to attach it to the remainder, a purpose for some reason abandoned.

A small bowl with two compartments, somewhat crushed, of a type already noticed by us, lay about 1 foot down with many fragments of various vessels. It has been entirely restored. Length, 5.1 inches; width, 3 inches; height, 1.3 inches.

In the northern slope, 5 feet down, were two vessels together, unaccompanied by skeletal remains. One, a bowl of ordinary type but of good material, holding about three quarts, has traces of red pigment inside and out. The rim projects. It is imperforate as to base and otherwise intact with the exception of several cracks produced by pressure.

The other, gourd-shape, of yellow ware, absolutely intact save a slight chipping at the mouth, lay on its side. It is unornamented save for traces of red pigment. Height, 9.6 inches; maximum diameter, 7.7 inches; diameter of aperture, 2 inches (Plate LXXVIII). About 1 foot above these vessels was a layer of charcoal nearly 4 feet in length.

About 1 foot below the surface, with fragments of various vessels, was a vessel with two compartments, and a handle somewhat resembling a third, though much shallower. Small holes had been broken through the bottom of each compartment. In Plate LXXIX, Fig. 1, the vessel is shown, the handle to the front. Length across compartments, 6 inches; across handle and partition, 5.1 inches; height, 1.5 inches.

About 2.5 feet below the surface, with a mass of crimson pigment about the size of a cocoanut, and apparently not in proximity to human remains, were: sheets of mica; two pebble hammers; two chips of chert; a bit of clayey substance about the size of a chestnut; the head of a shell pin with shank missing through decay; a mass of bituminous clay about 2.5 inches by 3 inches, evenly pitted on one side to the size of about the first joint of a human thumb.

In a central portion of the mound, 3 feet down, together, each resting on its base which showed intentional perforation after manufacture, with no traces of human remains apparent, were five vessels of ordinary type, each of about two quarts capacity. The material was very inferior, several dropping to pieces after discovery. The only decoration was traces of red pigment exteriorly.

Surmounted by crimson sand, 3 feet 9 inches down, together, were: one large tobacco pipe of earthenware of ordinary pattern; one thick sheet of mica 3 inches by 4 inches; and a bit of a marine shell. Here again no skeletal remains were encountered.

In the E. N. E margin of the mound, 2 feet down, were two vessels together, one in somewhat fragmentary condition, in addition to the loss of a portion of its base. This vessel, of medium size, offered no novelty as to type. Its decoration is parallel lines running diagonally. The second vessel, of ware fully equal to any found by us in the Florida mounds, has a capacity of about five quarts. Bowl-shaped in form, its rim, 1.5 inches in breadth, is inverted horizontally. It is interiorly decorated with crimson pigment. Portions of the vessel broken, but not detached, by pressure of sand, were readily fastened into place. Within it were seven pebbles and two chips of chert. Near by, on the outside, were two pebble hammers and one small bit of chert. No human remains were evident in association.

In the margin of the mound, unassociated with human remains, together, were two small undecorated vessels, rude and of ordinary type. Their bases are intact.

About 4 feet down was an isolated cranium, badly decayed, lying in cherry sand. One foot distant, in the same plane, lay a pebble hammer of considerable size, showing use, and pitted on one side.

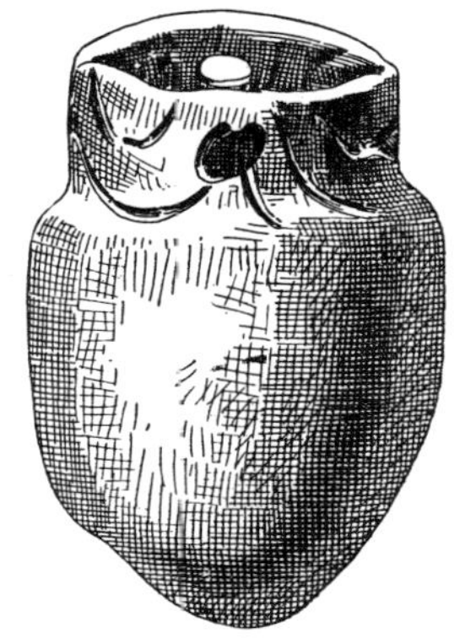

FIG. 46.—Toy vessel of earthenware. Low mounds south of Grant mound. Mound E. (Full size.)

Together, in the southern margin, were many fragments of a small bowl and a globular bowl of about one quart capacity, the bottom of which had been knocked out, and, with the exception of a small portion, placed within the vessel.

Two and one-half feet from the surface, in the southern margin, apparently apart from human remains, together, were: three small undecorated vessels of ordinary type and poor material, imperforate as to bases; two curious toy vessels, unbroken, with side perforations for suspension, one showing decoration (Fig. 46). In addition was a cylindrical vessel with slightly round imperforate base, the rim somewhat flaring. The decoration is of the complicated stamp variety. This vessel was slightly broken by contact with the spade. With all these were a number of pebbles, chips of chert, and pieces

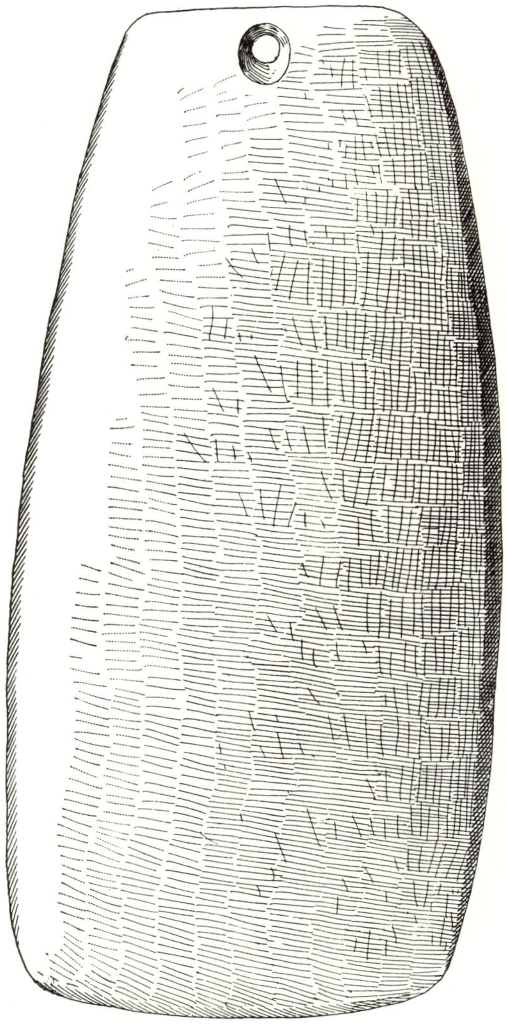

FIG. 47. Pendant of banded slate. Low mounds south of Grant mound. Mound E. (Full size.)

of marine shell which probably at one time had some definite shape. Again, human remains were wanting.

In the northwest slope, together, unassociated with human remains, were two rough undecorated bowls, one imperforate as to base, the other showing perforation intentionally conferred. With these were: one "celt" of polished stone; one small boss of sheet copper; bits of sandstone and a number of pieces of chert resembling small rude arrowheads.

Four feet from the surface, without association, in red sand, was a pendant of polished banded slate, 5.5 inches by 2.5 inches, with maximum thickness of about 1 inch (Fig. 47).

Two feet down, apart from human remains, were a polished hatchet of stone and a fragmentary ornament of sheet copper with central double perforation.

A small vessel of ordinary type lay 3.5 feet from the surface. With it was an undecorated cylindrical vessel with rounded imperforate base and slightly flaring rim. Height, 7.25 inches; maximum diameter, 4 inches; aperture, 3.75 inches. With these, placed one within the other, were several cockle shells (*Cardium*).

Occupying a central position in the mound, 5 feet from the surface, in pale cherry sand, was a curious medley of objects with fragmentary remains of an adolescent at one extremity and probably the entire skeleton of a young child at the other. Included in the deposit were: bits of charcoal; a large clay tobacco pipe of the usual type; a curious object of polished sedimentary rock (Fig. 48); a slab of syenitic rock, entirely smooth and slightly concave on one side, probably a sharpening stone; several phalanges of the deer; part of the core of a buck horn; two "celts"; hammer stones; pebble hammers; pebbles; a small fragment of bitumen; many worked portions of columellæ of marine univalves; numerous chips of chert, some very diminutive; one arrowhead; bits of coquina; sheets of mica; a small bit of clayey substance; one small undecorated earthenware bowl; one cutting implement of chipped chert; many large and small beads of shell; a circular ornament of sheet copper.

Throughout the mound were various other bowls of ordinary type, some imperforate; pebbles; bits of marine shells and the like, variously associated and often in pockets of cherry or reddish sand.

At various points were considerable deposits of bits of earthenware representing parts of different bowls, but in no case sufficient for restoration.

REMARKS.

These low mounds offer, so far as the earthenware is concerned, a striking contrast to their near neighbor, the great Grant mound. In that mound the earthenware, almost entirely of the "freak" mortuary variety, showed no marks of domestic use, while the vessels in the low mounds were in many cases evidently originally intended for culinary purposes and bore on their bases and sides the soot received during domestic use. Earthenware of complicated stamped decoration, virtually absent from the Grant mound, abounded in these low neighboring mounds.

As we have stated, human remains were encountered at but four points in the largest mound. That so great a heap of sand should have been thrown up for so few interments seems unlikely, in view of the number of art relics found in every portion. In mounds where relics are inhumed in a general way, they are found in a central position and somewhat superficially. We deem it not unlikely that all traces of other interments in this mound have entirely disappeared.

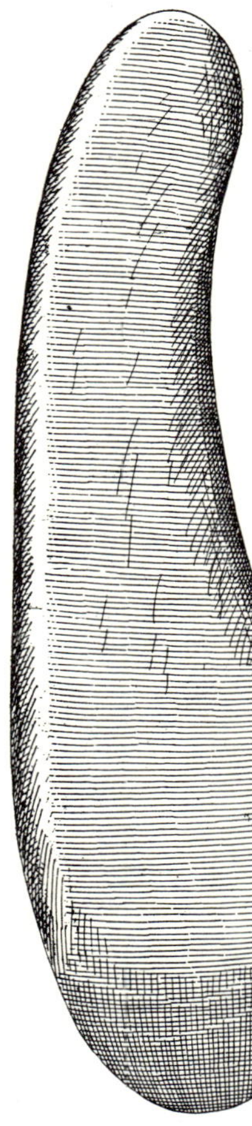

Fig. 48.—Unidentified object of sedimentary rock. Low mounds south of Grant mound. Mound E. (Full size.)

Nothing was discovered in these low mounds in any way connecting them with a period other than pre-Columbian.

Low Mounds near Horse-shoe Landing.

These low mounds and ridges lie about 500 yards in a southerly direction from the landing. They were thickly covered with "scrub" and had sustained no previous examination. Our investigation was conducted with the kind permission of J. B. Parsons, Esq., the owner.

Mound A, the easternmost, was somewhat irregular in shape, and had an average diameter of base of 50 feet. Its maximum height was 3 feet 7 inches. It was completely demolished.

Human remains were encountered but four times, in each case but a small portion of the skeleton being represented.

Sherds were infrequently met with. Several bore the complicated stamp of the type encountered in neighboring low mounds. Three undecorated vessels of medium size and of poor material came from various depths. One of these, on four sides, about equidistant, showed careful chipping away of material without perforation. The base had been treated in a similar manner over an extent about 2.5 inches in diameter. We have before met with chipping of this nature at one or possibly two points on the surface of certain vessels, but never before have we noticed it executed with such evident intent.

Three feet down was a small hatchet of stone and two arrow heads in a pocket of sand blackened by fire. No skeletal remains were in association.

Together, unassociated with human remains, 3 feet down, were eleven fragments of stone including four partially completed arrowheads, the end of a polished chisel, and six bits of chert. In addition, variously associated, were small "celts," mussel shells, smoothing stones, pebbles and arrowheads. Several of these arrowheads were coated as to the tangs, with bitumen which bore the impress of some long-fibred wood, probably reed or cane.

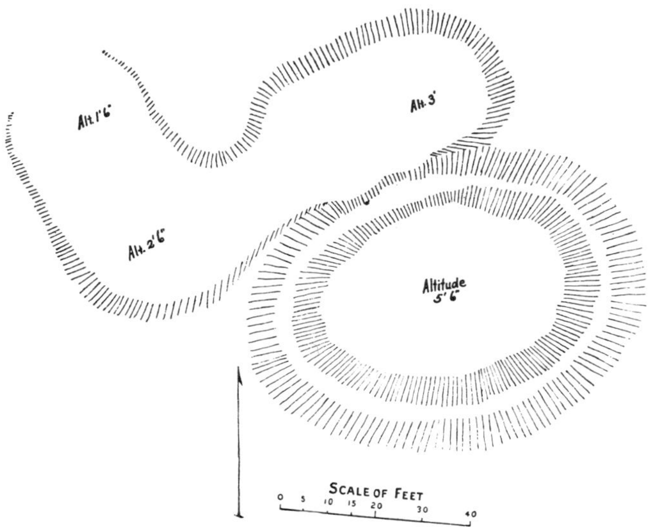

Fig. 49.—Plan of Brutus mound.

Certain other smaller mounds in the immediate neighborhood were partially investigated with negative results.

About one-quarter of a mile in a southerly direction from the low mounds, was a mound on the property of an old colored man named Brutus. Its shape was somewhat unusual (Fig. 49).

A careful investigation, not, however, carried to complete demolition, indicated its erection for other than sepulchral purposes.

Broward Mound.

This symmetrical mound, in the pine woods, about one-quarter of a mile northwest from Cedar Creek Landing, had a height of 8 feet, a breadth of 60 feet across the base.

It was totally demolished with the courteous permission of its owner, Napoleon Broward, Esq., of Jacksonville.

Above the level of the surrounding territory was an irregular layer, from 6 inches to 14 inches in thickness, of pure white sand often containing beds and pieces of charcoal. The remainder of the mound was of yellowish sand with local streaks and pockets of white sand throughout and several small seams of cherry-colored sand in the northeastern portion.

Human remains were not present in the marginal portion of the mound, but were encountered toward the center at twelve different places. The usual bunched burial of fragmentary portions of the skeleton prevailed. Four times, isolated crania were encountered. Again, shafts of a femur and tibia lay with a pelvis and a single vertebra. In one case two long bones represented an entire burial, and again a single humerus was found unassociated. The bones, in the last stage of decay, were encountered at different depths, from the base to within a short distance of the surface.

Sherds were infrequently met with.

Two and one-half feet from the surface, near no human remains, was an interesting cylindrical cup 4.4 inches in height, with a diameter of 2.8 inches. It is absolutely intact. The base is flat, permitting the maintenance of an upright position. There are two holes for suspension at opposite sides of the rim. It has interesting incised and punctate decoration (Plate LXXIX, Fig. 2).

Chippings, flakes, and cores of chert, so abundant in some mounds, were wanting in this one.

In all, five polished stone hatchets were met with, four separately in caved sand, one about 2 feet from the surface. None seemed to be in the neighborhood of human remains.

A serrated arrowhead of chert lay, unassociated, 1 foot from the surface.

A pebble about 2 inches long, showing use at either end, completed the list of art relics taken from the mound.

REMARKS.

The Broward mound is typical of a certain class of sand mounds met with on the St. Johns in that the considerable amount of material was wholly disproportionate to the small number of interments.

In another respect also it was typical of certain mounds of the river. All relics were comparatively centrally located, and, so nearly as could be determined, at no great distance from the surface and unassociated with skeletal remains, showing the inhumation of art relics to have been made in common toward the completion of the mound. There were, however, it must be remembered, many mounds on the St. Johns, not embraced in this class, where artifacts were discovered from the margin throughout and associated with human remains. Of this class of mounds were that at Tick Island, Thursby mound, the mound at Blue Creek and others.

Nothing in the Broward mound gave evidence of White contact.

Low Mounds near Reddie Point.

About one-quarter of a mile in from the landing at Reddie Point were two low mounds on the property of Dr. Anita Tyng.

Fig. 50.—Sheet of mica given the outline of a lance point. Larger mound near Reddie Point. (Full size.)

The larger mound had a base diameter of 80 feet. The territory is reported to have been in use for years as a cotton field, and the mound had been virtually leveled. At three points near the margin were deep depressions from which the material had been taken. The mound was dug through at a depth varying from 4 feet to 6 feet below the surface. It was composed of yellowish sand, unstratified, with the usual charcoal and fire places.

Human remains, infrequently met with and fragmentary, were found so far down as 4 feet.

Earthenware was represented by several vessels of ordinary type and size, undecorated and of poor quality. All showed portions missing from the base through intentional fracture. Other pots had important portions missing, and evidently had been utilized for mortuary purposes.

Sherds were mainly undecorated, some, however, bearing an intricate stamped design (Plate LXXIX, Fig. 3).

Two "celts" and two arrowheads were found separately, and numbers of pebbles and pebble hammers variously associated. Mica was in comparative abundance. One sheet had been rudely given the outline of a lance point (Fig. 50).

Four feet from the surface, with human remains and shell beads, some over one inch in length, was a neatly made ornament elliptical in shape, with central perforation. The material is of sedimentary origin, composed mainly of iron pyrites. Length, 1.3 inches; breadth, 1.2 inches (Fig. 51).

Apparently unassociated was a mass of somewhat deteriorated *Hematite*, about the size of a clenched hand.

A small fragment of sheet copper lay with human remains.

Near an isolated lower jaw were three small ornaments of sheet copper, of

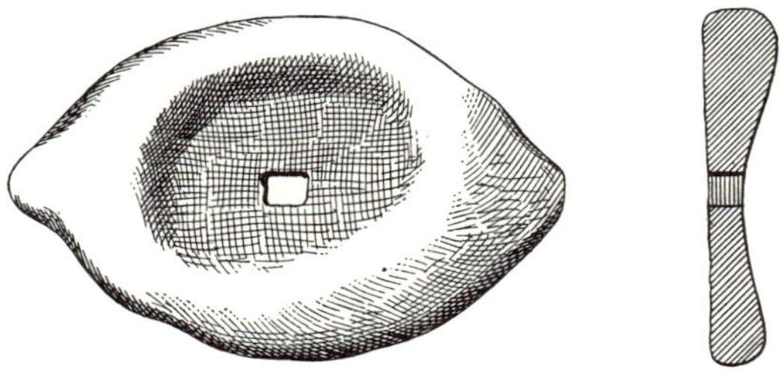

Fig. 51.—Gorget. Larger mound near Reddie Point. (Full size.)

Fig. 52.—Ornament of sheet copper. Larger mound near Reddie Point. (Full size.)

about the same size, oblong with rounded corners (Fig. 52) and a portion of another. At the end on one side of each of the three unbroken ones was a flat circular deposit of bitumen, used for purposes of attachment.

About 25 yards east of this mound was another with a height of about 1.5 feet and a diameter of base of 60 feet.

It was completely dug through.

No copper was present in this mound. In other respects it resembled many mounds of the neighborhood as to deposits of mica, pebble hammers, arrowheads and the like.

Mound at Daniel's Landing.

This mound, about one-quarter of a mile in a northerly direction from the landing, had long been under cultivation, and had previously been dug into to a considerable extent.

Its height was 2.5 feet; its diameter of base, 60 feet. It was virtually demolished.

The usual fragments of shell, mica, etc., were present with fragmentary human remains.

Low Mounds at Alicia.

On the property of John G. Driggs, Esq., of Jacksonville, to whom our thanks are tendered for permission to investigate, at Alicia, about 400 yards in from the landing, were four low mounds.

Mound A. Height, 3.5 feet; diameter of base, 45 feet. This mound was about two-thirds demolished by us, human remains in small fragments being encountered at three points. Near the center was a mass of sandstone pitted on either side, weighing about ten pounds. Nothing else of interest was encountered.

Joining mounds A and B was a causeway about 28 feet long, 1 foot 4 inches in height, with an average width of 12 feet at the base.

Mound B. A considerable portion of this mound had been carted away for use in the neighboring orange grove. The discovery of many art relics is said to have been made at the time. The height of the remainder of the mound was about 18 inches. Judging from trees still remaining, the original maximum altitude was from 3 feet to 4 feet. The diameter of the base was 86 feet.

The mound was carefully dug through by twenty men during two and one-half days.

The sand was of a brownish color, apparently from the effect of fire and a considerable intermingling of particles of charcoal. This combination extended about 2 feet below the level of the surrounding territory. Relics were found from the margin in, both above and below a dark line showing a large percentage of charcoal, which ran through the mound at the level of the surrounding territory and seemingly marked where a fire had been built after the filling of an excavation.

Human remains were represented by small fragments in the last stage of decay.

As much of the contents of this mound suggest those of many low neighboring mounds, we shall not give in detail the various associations of pebbles, pebble-hammers, mica, chips of chert, hones of sandstone, marine shells and fragments of shell contained therein.

Three "celts" were met with, several arrowheads, small pendants of shell, and at one point a large mass of crimson pigment.

Near the base, that is to say about 2 feet below the general level, or 3.5 feet down, together, were: two pebbles; a toy pot; a shark's tooth, and 142 minute chippings of chert.

Earthenware constituted the feature of the mound, and was encountered in great abundance, though, with two or three exceptions, so poor was the material that vessels were recovered in a very fragmentary condition. Certain large vessels and numerous smaller ones, inhumed with portions missing and badly crushed by weight of sand, were abandoned.

Sherds were abundant and, in common with fragmentary vessels, presented various intricate stamped designs shown in Plate LXXX, and Plate LXXXI, Figs. 1 and 2.

Lined and punctate decoration also was represented on fragmentary vessels and sherds, while in one case the use of a small tubular stamp was apparent, showing a circular prominence surrounded by a depression.

Of the larger vessels, some of so much as about four gallons capacity, none was capable of restoration. Four vessels were recovered intact, and nine in a more or less imperfect condition. Four vessels were imperforate as to the base; the remainder, and apparently all others interred in the mound, had suffered intentional mutilation of the base after completion.

Two small bowls lay together, one containing the other. A vessel of good material, thick and heavy, somewhat globular, with sloping rim, is decorated with red pigment inside and out. A portion of the base is missing. Maximum diameter, 5.8 inches; depth, 3.4 inches; diameter of orifice, 3.6 inches (Plate LXXXI, Fig. 3).

An interesting vase was recovered virtually intact. Its height is 9 inches; maximum diameter of body, 4 inches; diameter of aperture, 4.2 inches. The imperforate base is flat with a diameter of about 1.75 inches. Interesting incised and punctate decoration surrounds the rim to a depth of about 2.5 inches. On one side are two perforations about 1.5 inches apart, nearly three inches below the rim. Their use is not apparent (Plate LXXXII).

One tobacco pipe of earthenware came from the mound. The type is the same as that found in the neighboring mounds with the exception that, on the part facing the smoker, two raised parallel lines, one at either side, run the entire length of the pipe.

The two remaining mounds at Alicia, each about the size of mound A, were not investigated.[1] One had been utilized as a place of burial within recent years.

Denton Mound.

About one-half mile east of Chaseville, in thick undergrowth, was a ridge or possibly three intersecting mounds of irregular shape, the largest to the east, two smaller side by side to the west. The length of the ridge was 77 feet. The eastern end was 40 feet across; the western, 30 feet. The maximum height, which was near the eastern extremity, was 2.5 feet. These low mounds were not before supposed to be aboriginal remains, and had undergone no previous investigation.

They were completely dug through with the consent of the owner, James L. Denton, Esq., of Jamaica, N. Y.

The usual yellow sand and charcoal were present.

Human remains were few and very fragmentary.

Sherds were infrequently met with. One small bowl, undecorated, was broken by contact with a spade. An undecorated globular vessel, perforated through the base after completion, has a height of about 2.5 inches, and a diameter of 3.75 inches approximately.

Three feet from the surface was a vessel of great interest, in numerous fragments, crushed contemporary with or previous to inhumation and with certain missing portions chipped off by use of a pointed tool. This vessel, of excellent material and graceful design, with incised decoration of straight diagonal and of curved lines, has on one side, the repoussé head of a duck, neatly made. The upper portion of a similar head is on the opposite side. As we have said, this form of ornamentation, so novel for Florida, is, in this case, repoussé, and was not modelled previously and fastened on by pressure, as is the case of the human head from the mound near Old Okahumpka, described in this volume. These two examples of such use of effigies of heads are the only ones to come under our notice in Florida. The height of this interesting vessel is 7.75 inches; its maximum

[1] Since writing the above these mounds were investigated with negative results.

diameter, 10.5 inches; diameter of aperture, 4.5 inches. It is shown, pieced together, in Plate LXXXIII, while in Plate LXXXIV, Fig. 1, we give a front view of the head.

We have above alluded to the chipping off of portions of vessels with pointed implements. In Part II of our report on the St. Johns mounds we spoke of many sherds not broken but detached by piercing implements, and stated that this curious custom seemed to be confined to a limited area bordering the lower portion of the St. Johns River. Since the publication of that report we have noted the occurrence of these peculiar sherds and of vessels intentionally deprived of certain parts by the aid of pointed implements, at points throughout a wide area, including a mound on the Econlockhatchee Creek, Orange County, about thirty-five miles by water south of Sanford, and certain mounds of Crescent Lake, Putnam County.

A sheet of mica and a handsome arrow point of jasper were the only other art relics discovered in the mound.

About 10 feet south of the western extremity of the Denton mound was a mound about 1 foot in height and 20 feet across the base. In the center, about 2.5 feet down, was a small layer of charred human bones. Two or three sherds completed the contents of the mound.

Two Low Mounds at Chaseville.

On the property of Mr. I. Harrington, who readily granted permisson to explore, was the site of a mound which had been entirely leveled and carted to an adjacent field. The diameter was about 30 feet. It probably once had a height of about 2 feet.

Fig. 53.—Lance-head of chert. Mound at Chaseville. (Full size.)

It was completely dug through at a depth of 2.5 feet below the surface. The usual mica, chips of chert, fragments of marine shells, variously associated, were present, and in addition, a noble barbed lance-head of reddish chert, 5 inches in length, lying with a shell chisel at a depth of 2 feet (Fig. 53). No human remains were met with.

A few yards from the mound just described, on the property of Mrs. Mary Bennevis, was a mound 1 foot in height, with a diameter of base of about 20 feet.

About 1.5 feet from the surface was a central deposit of human bones representing parts of various skeletons. No others were met with.

Loose in the sand and singly were: one undecorated bowl in fragments; one cube of lead sulphide; one arrowhead; one bit of pottery intentionally given the outline of the arrow point and various sherds.

Low Mounds at Floral Bluff.

By the roadside, about 300 yards inland from the landing at Floral Bluff, on the property of Mr. G. H. Shepard, to whom we wish to express our thanks, was an asymmetrical mound, or, more properly, a V-shaped ridge, having its maximum height of 4.5 feet in the western arm, about 50 feet from the apex which points almost due south. The western arm has a length of 170 feet; the eastern, about 30 feet less. The maximum width of the western arm was 46 feet; that of the eastern, 37 feet.

The most prominent portions of the ridge were dug through at considerable depth.

Human remains—mere fractional portions of the skeleton—were encountered seven times, all within an area of a few square yards, beneath the highest portion of the ridge.

With human remains, about 3 feet down, was a large tobacco pipe of earthenware, one portion filled with bitumen and with a considerable quantity near by. This pipe, somewhat broken, had all portions present. About 1 foot above was a smaller tobacco pipe of earthenware in many fragments and incapable of restoration.

About 3.5 feet from the surface, near human remains, was a vessel of bean-shaped outline of about one quart capacity. Its base is intact. Traces of red pigment are inside and out (Plate LXXXIV, Fig. 2). With it were many pebbles and chips of chert.

At various depths were nests of fragments of parts of different vessels, and one deposit of many minute chippings of chert.

1

2

3

MOORE: SAND MOUNDS OF DUVAL COUNTY, FLORIDA.

1, 2, 3. VESSELS OF EARTHENWARE, GILBERT MOUND. (FULL SIZE.)

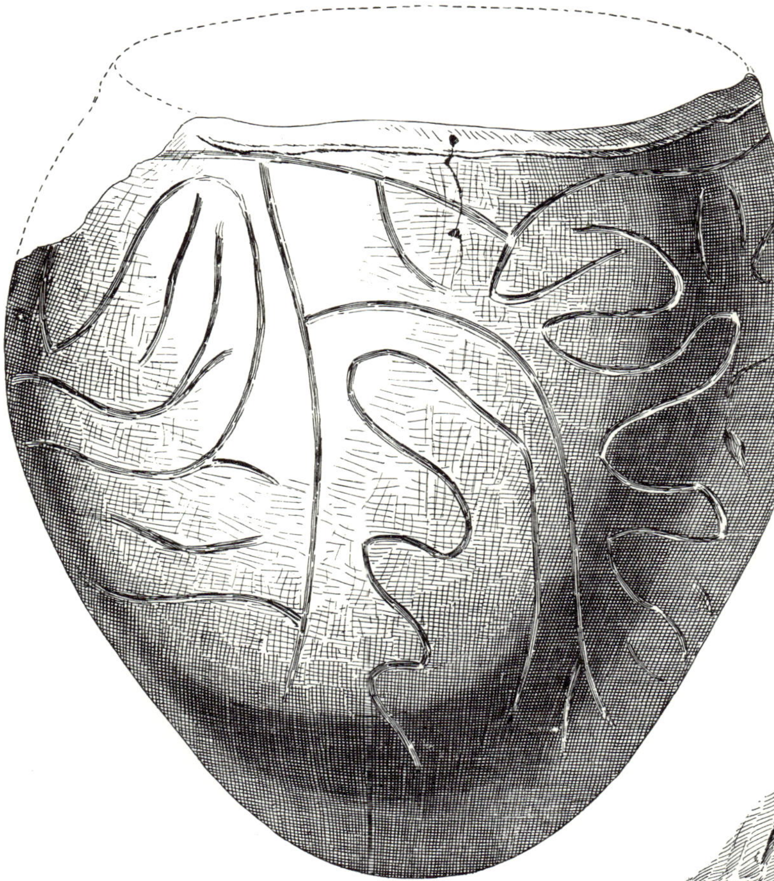

1

2

MOORE: SAND MOUNDS OF DUVAL COUNTY, FLORIDA.

1. EARTHENWARE VESSEL WITH CURIOUS INCISED DECORATION, GILBERT MOUND. (FULL SIZE.)
2. SHERD WITH COMPLICATED STAMPED DECORATION, MONROE MOUND. (FULL SIZE.)

1

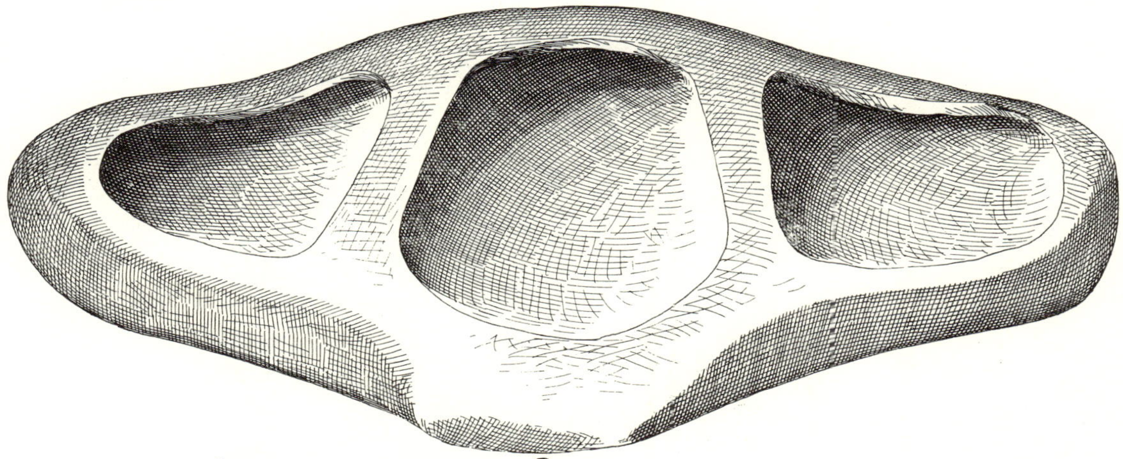

2

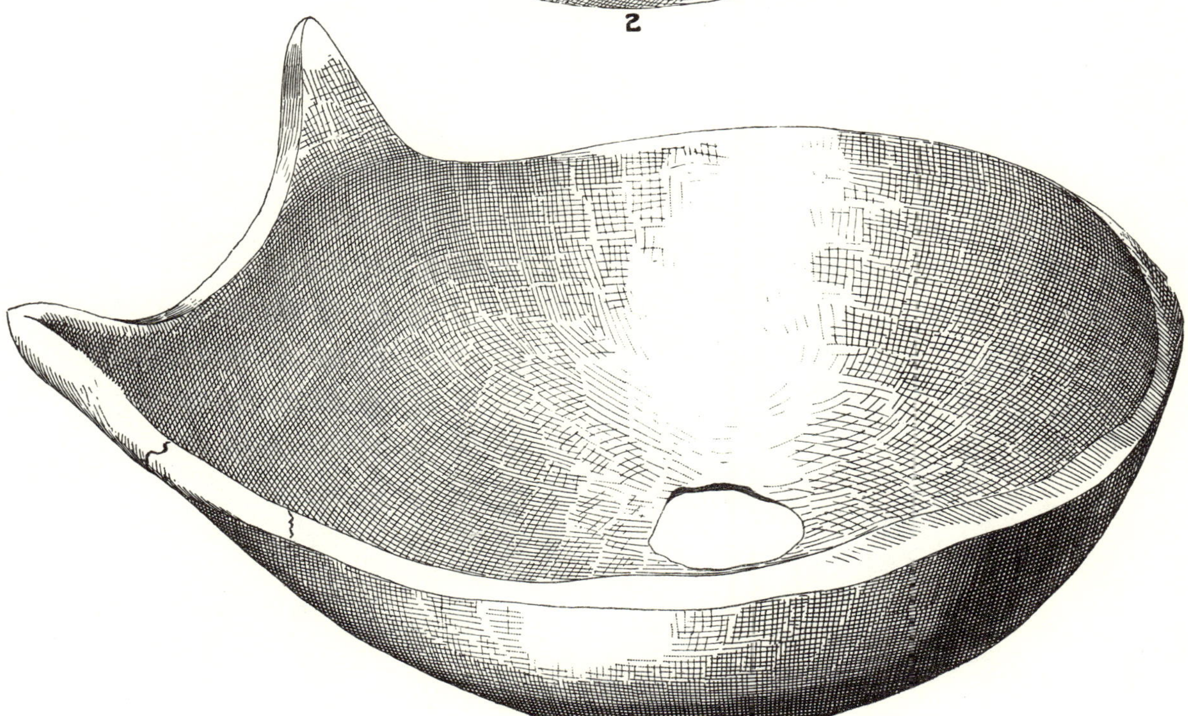

3

MOORE: SAND MOUNDS OF DUVAL COUNTY, FLORIDA.

1. BOWL OF HEAVY EARTHENWARE, MONROE MOUND. (FULL SIZE.)
2. CURIOUS EARTHENWARE VESSEL WITH THREE COMPARTMENTS, MONROE MOUND. (FULL SIZE.)
3. MORTUARY VESSEL OF EARTHENWARE, GRANT MOUND. (FULL SIZE.)

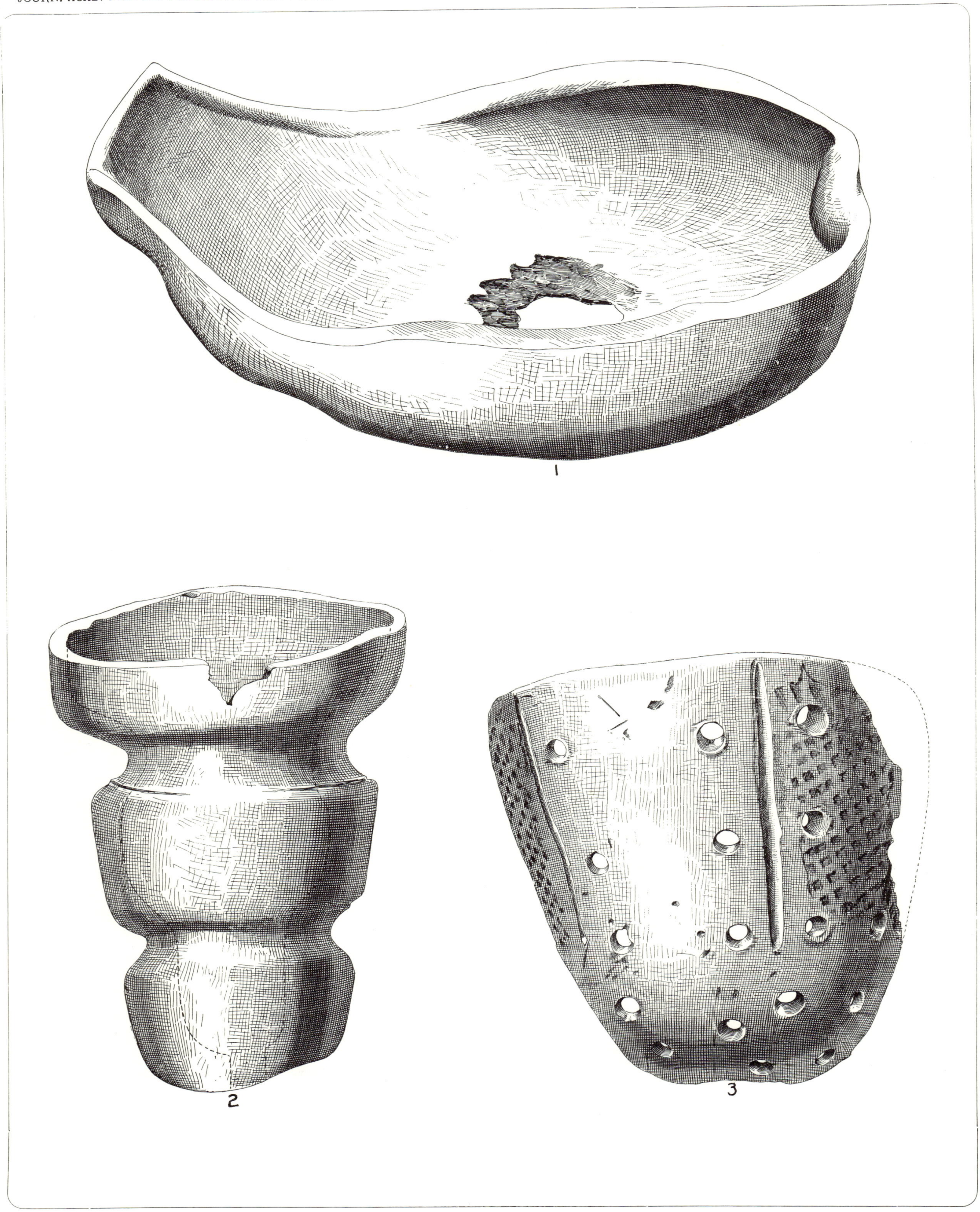

MOORE: SAND MOUNDS OF DUVAL COUNTY, FLORIDA.

1 AND 2. MORTUARY VESEELS OF EARTHENWARE, GRANT MOUND. (FULL SIZE.)

3. FRAGMENT OF FERFORATED VESSEL, GRANT MOUND. (FULL SIZE.)

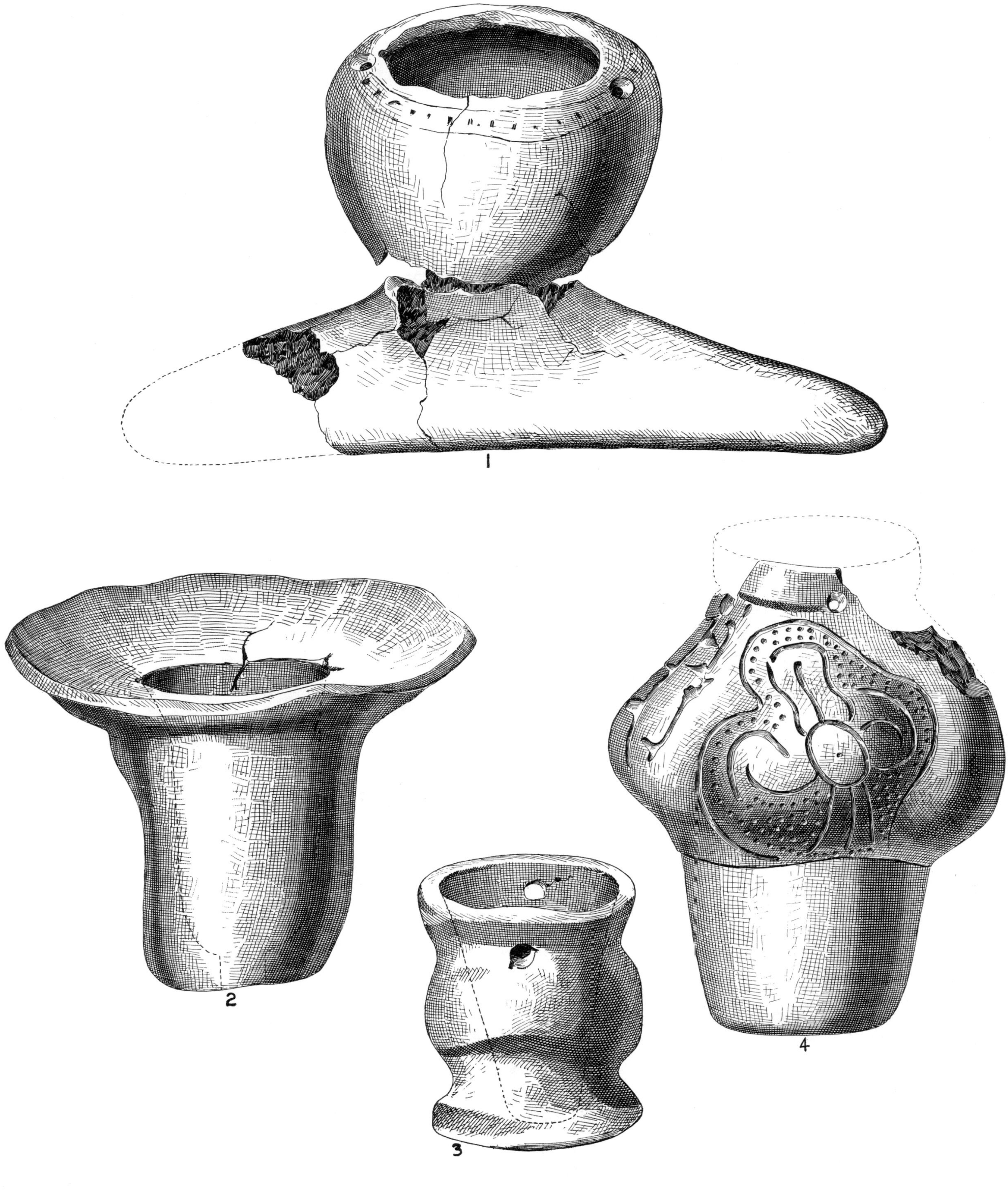

MOORE: SAND MOUNDS OF DUVAL COUNTY, FLORIDA

1. CURIOUS VESSEL OF EARTHENWARE, GRANT MOUND. (FULL SIZE.)

2 AND 3. MORTUARY VESSELS OF EARTHENWARE, GRANT MOUND. (FULL SIZE.)

4. VASE OF EARTHENWARE, MOUND A, LOW MOUNDS SOUTH OF GRANT MOUND. (FULL SIZE.)

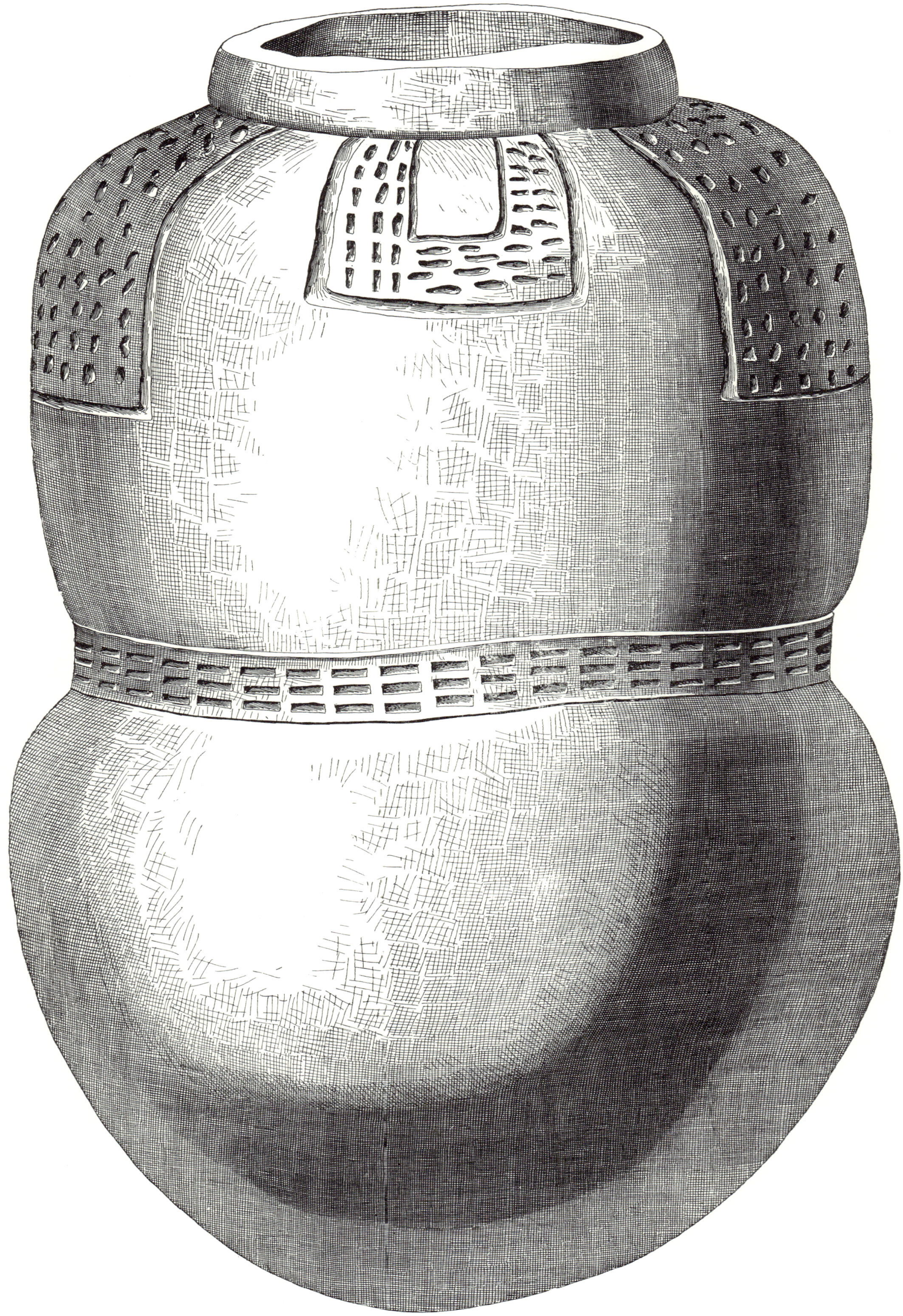

MOORE: SAND MOUNDS OF DUVAL COUNTY, FLORIDA.

VESSEL OF EARTHENWARE, LOW MOUNDS SOUTH OF GRANT MOUND. MOUND E (SEVEN-EIGHTHS SIZE).

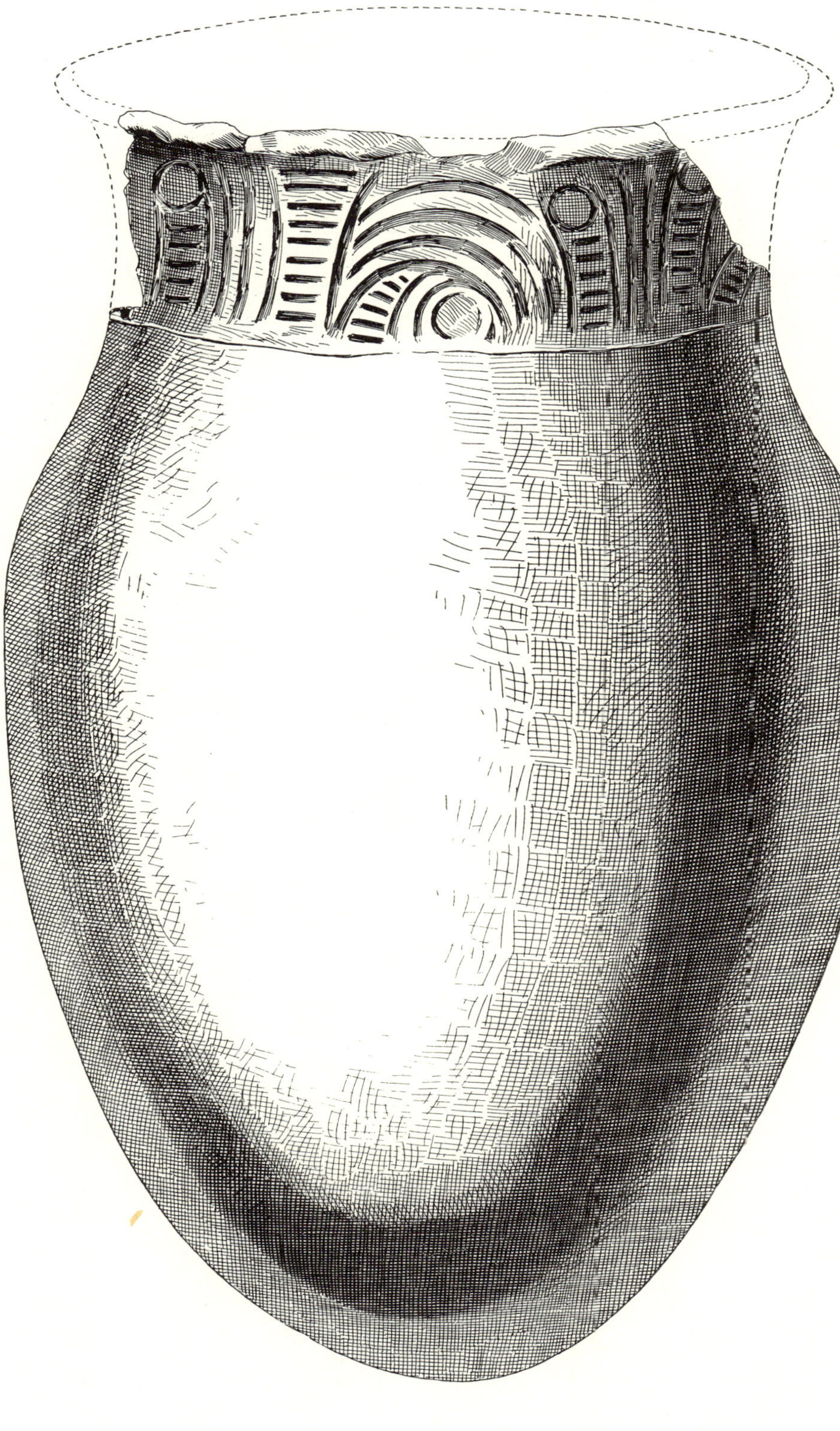

MOORE: SAND MOUNDS OF DUVAL COUNTY, FLORIDA.

OVOID URN OF EARTHENWARE. LOW MOUNDS SOUTH OF GRANT MOUND. MOUND E (FULL SIZE).

MOORE: SAND MOUNDS OF DUVAL COUNTY, FLORIDA.

GOURD-SHAPED VESSEL OF YELLOW WARE, LOW MOUNDS SOUTH OF GRANT MOUND, MOUND E. (FULL SIZE).

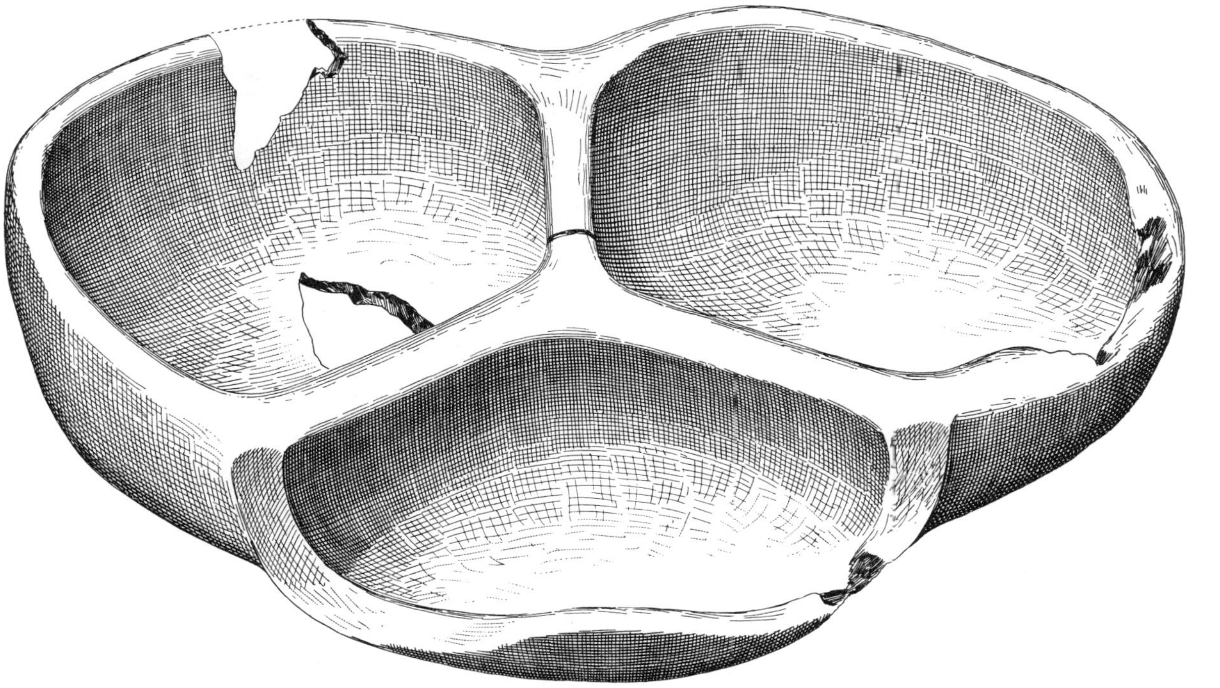

1

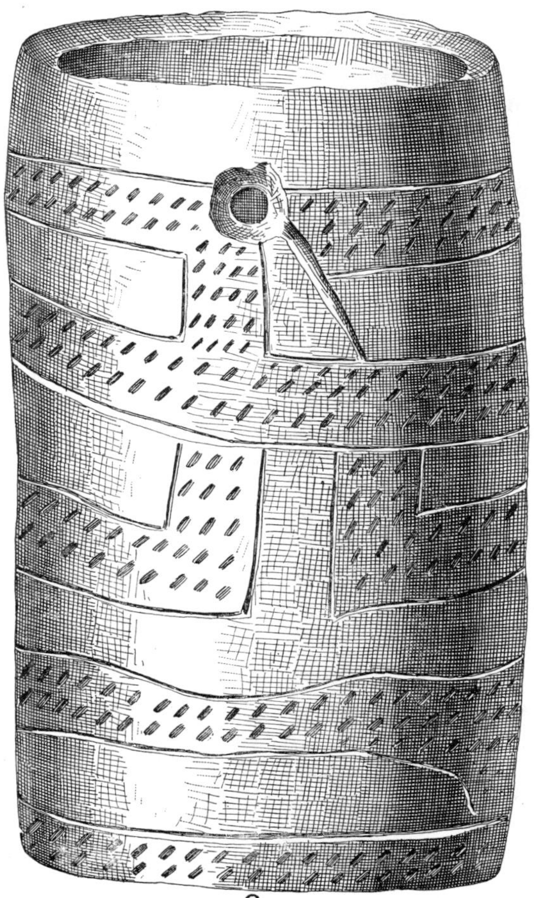

2

3

MOORE: SAND MOUNDS OF DUVAL COUNTY, FLORIDA

1. EARTHENWARE VESSEL WITH TWO COMPARTMENTS AND HANDLE, LOW MOUNDS SOUTH OF GRANT MOUND, MOUND E. (FULL SIZE).
2. CUP OF EARTHENWARE, INCISED AND PUNCTATE DECORATION, BROWARD MOUND. (FULL SIZE.)
3. SHERD WITH COMPLICATED STAMPED DECORATION, LARGER MOUND, REDDIE POINT. (FULL SIZE.)

MOORE: SAND MOUNDS OF DUVAL COUNTY, FLORIDA

FRAGMENTS OF EARTHENWARE VESSELS WITH COMPLICATED STAMPED DECORATION, LOW MOUNDS AT ALICIA, MOUND B. (FULL SIZE.)

1

2

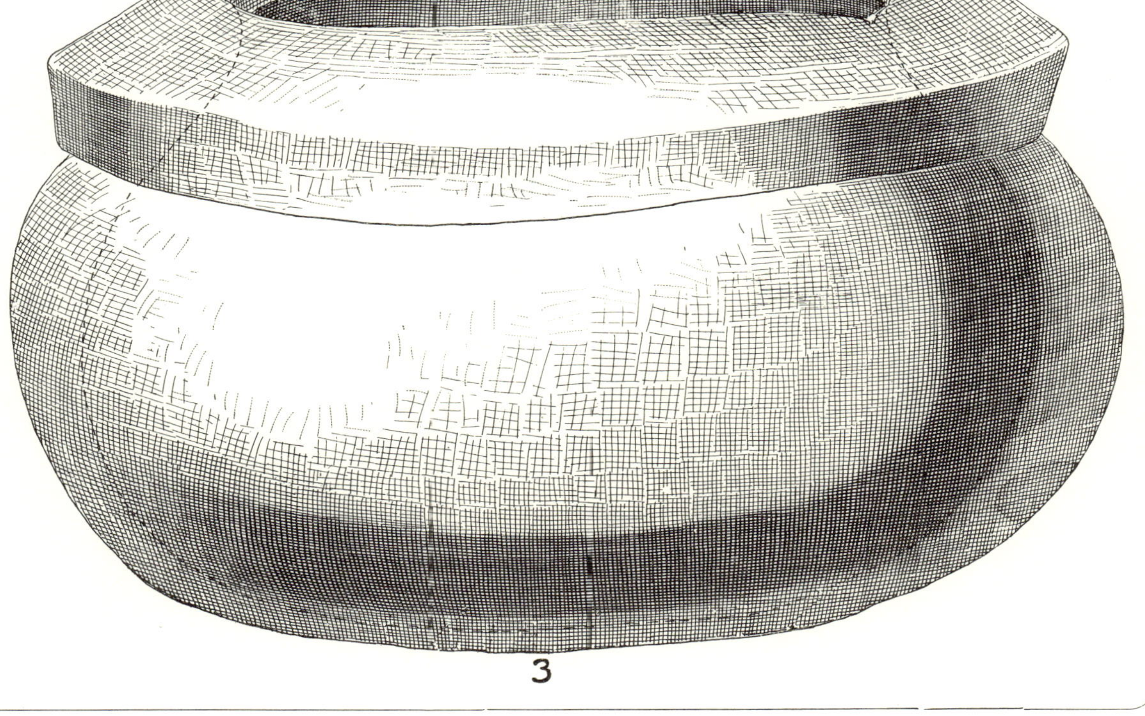

3

MOORE: SAND MOUNDS OF DUVAL COUNTY, FLORIDA.

1 AND 2. SHERDS WITH COMPLICATED STAMPED DECORATION, LOW MOUNDS AT ALICIA, MOUND B (FULL SIZE.)

3. VESSEL OF HEAVY WARE, LOW MOUNDS AT ALICIA, MOUND B. (FULL SIZE.)

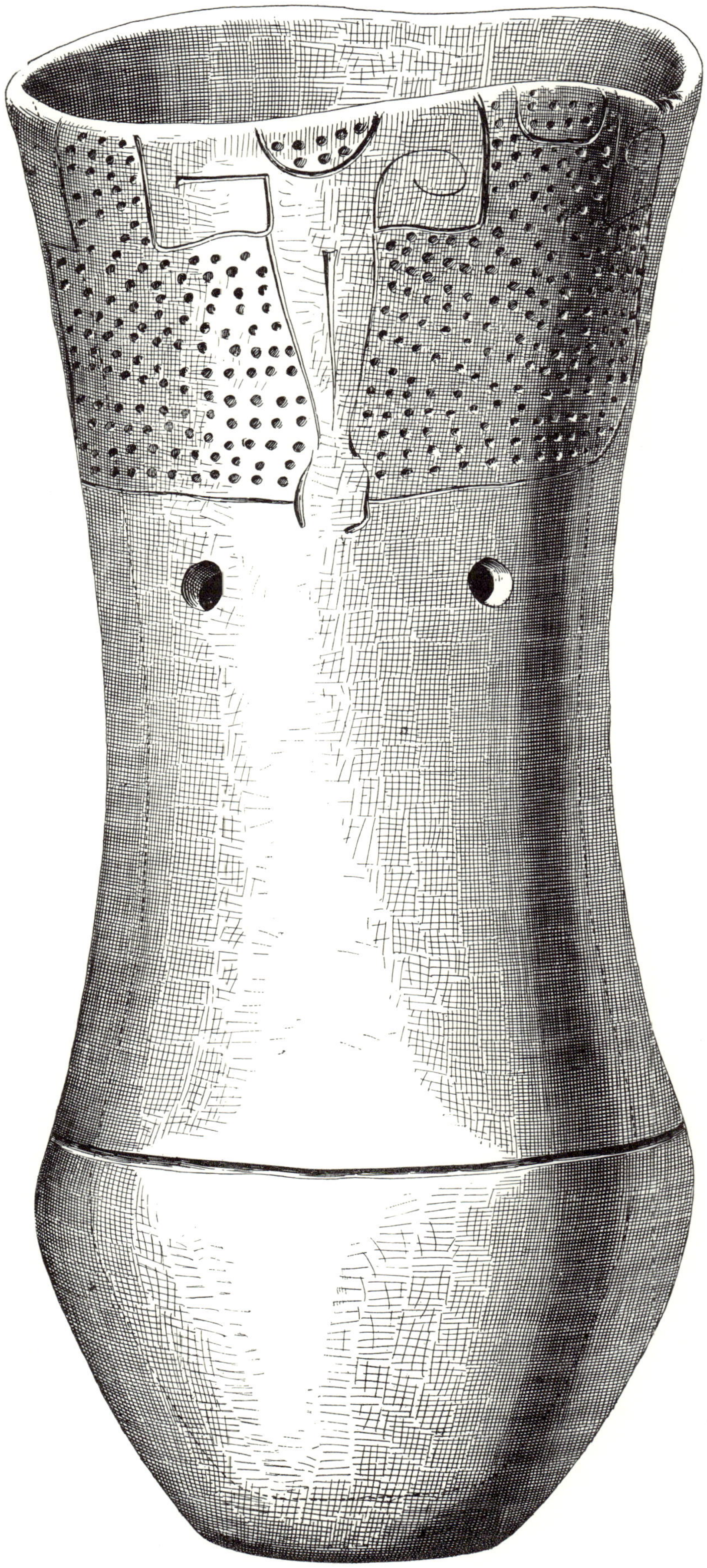

MOORE: SAND MOUNDS OF DUVAL COUNTY, FLORIDA.

VASE OF EARTHENWARE, INCISED AND PUNCTATE DECORATION, LOW MOUNDS AT ALICIA, MOUND B. (FULL SIZE.)

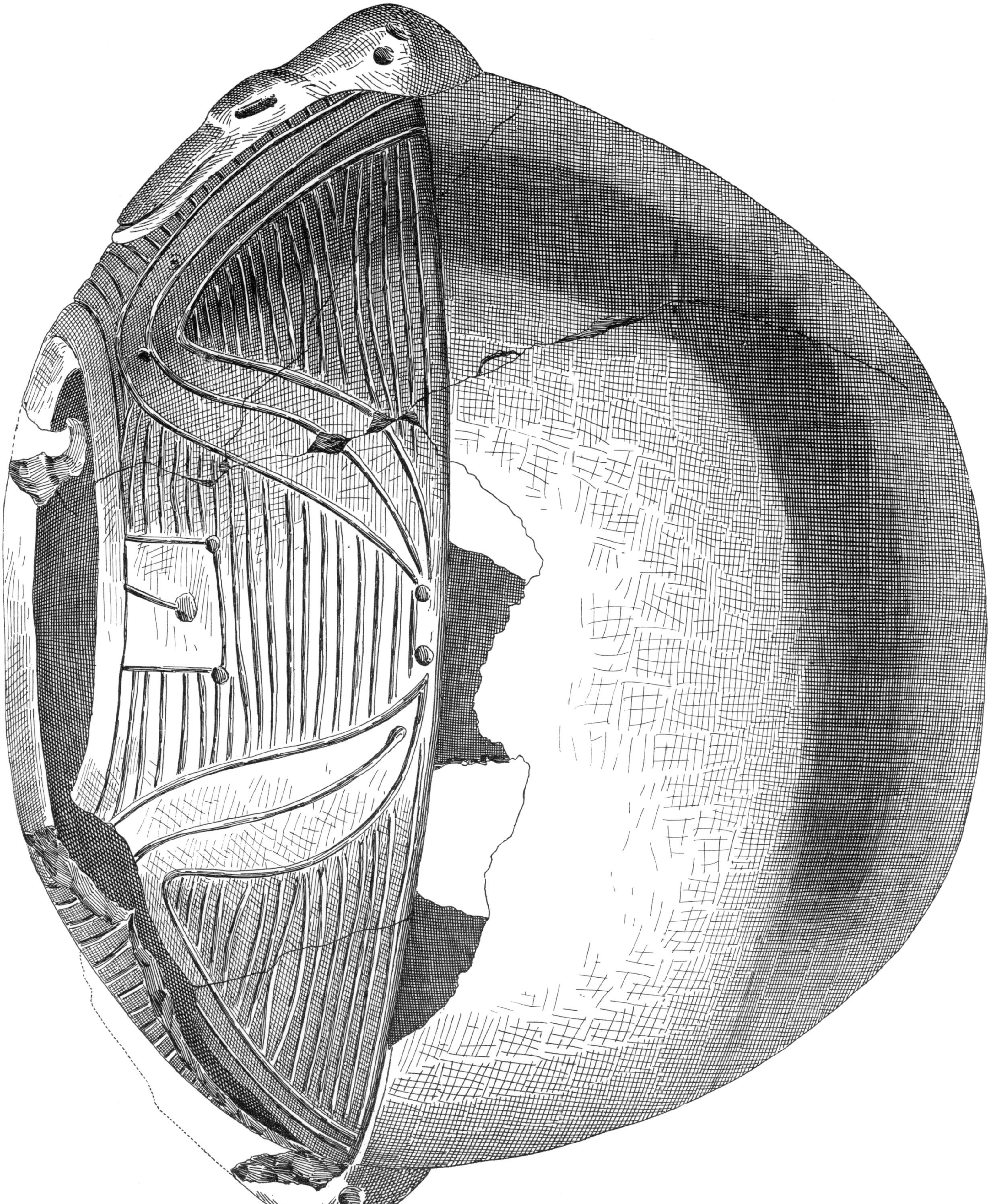

MOORE: SAND MOUNDS OF DUVAL COUNTY, FLORIDA

VESSEL WITH INCISED DECORATION AND REPOUSSE DUCK HEADS, DENTON MOUND. (FULL SIZE.)

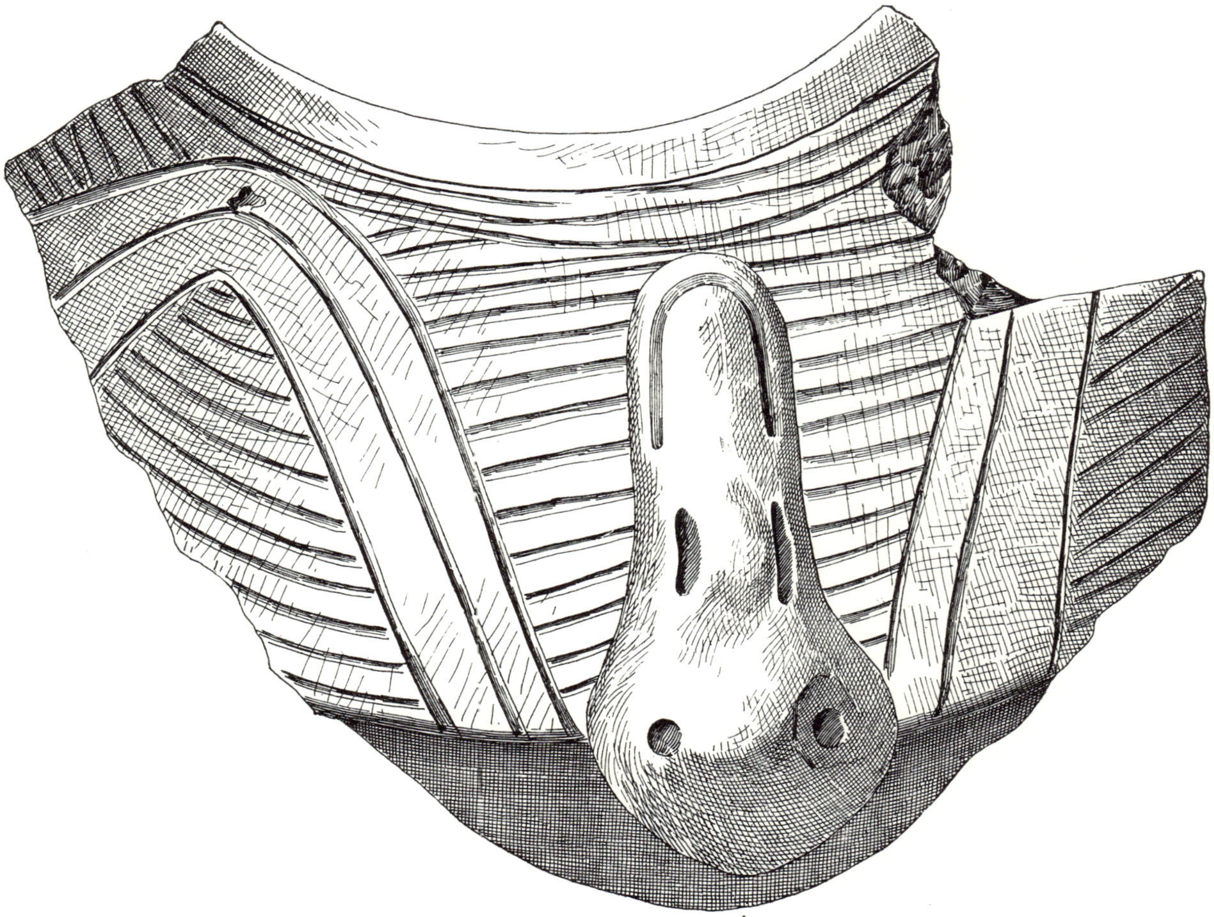

1

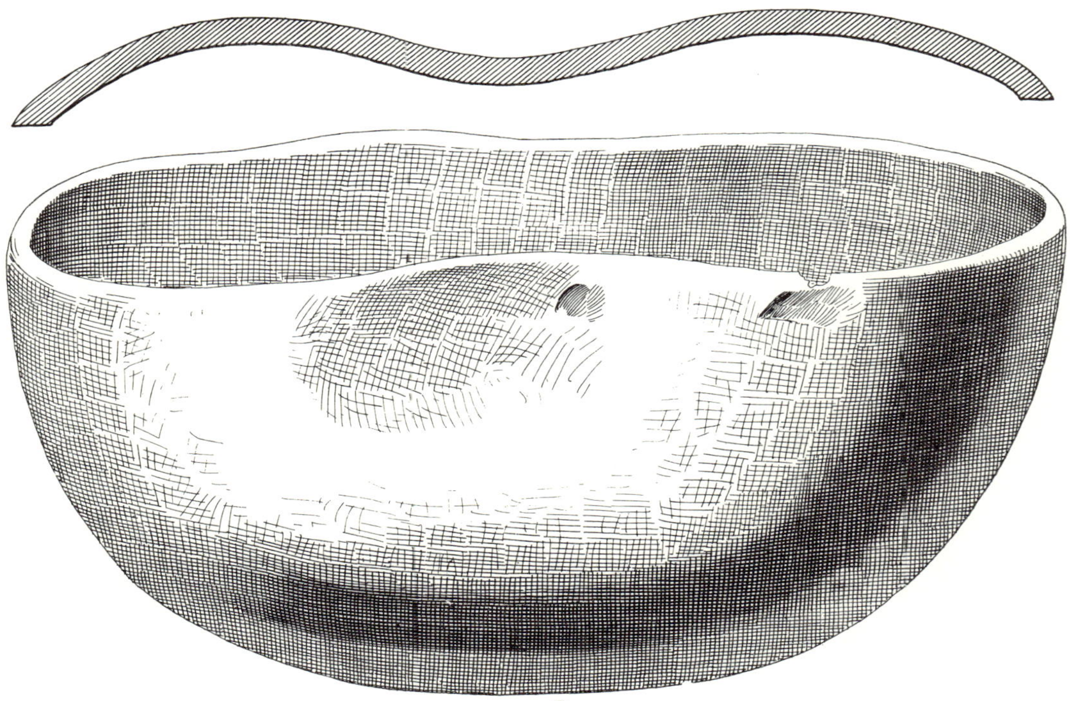

2

MOORE: SAND MOUNDS OF DUVAL COUNTY, FLORIDA.

1. FRAGMENT OF EARTHENWARE VESSEL, DENTON MOUND. (FULL SIZE.)

2. BEAN-SHAPED VESSEL OF EARTHENWARE, WITH HORIZONTAL SECTION OF PORTION OF MARGIN. LARGEST MOUND, FLORAL BLUFF. (FULL SIZE.)

Two Sand Mounds on Murphy Island, Florida

BY

CLARENCE B. MOORE

TWO SAND MOUNDS ON MURPHY ISLAND, FLORIDA.

By Clarence B. Moore.

Murphy Island, on the eastern bank of the St. Johns River, by water ten miles south of Palatka, Putnam County, is separated from the mainland by a small stream known as Murphy Creek.

Two sand mounds and a considerable shell deposit on Murphy Island were briefly noticed by us in Part I, "Certain Sand Mounds of the St. Johns River, Florida."[1]

Unfortunately, during our investigation of the mounds of the St. Johns, we were unable to come to terms with the owner of the property, but have, however, availed ourselves of an arrangement subsequently made.

Neither of the sand mounds on Murphy Island is believed to have sustained any previous investigation, with the exception of a small hole in one, made by a party of excursionists from Palatka during part of one day in the early "seventies."

The northernmost mound, visible from the steamboat landing, was one of the most symmetrical earthworks we have encountered in Florida. Its shape was almost a perfect truncated cone; the slope of the sides being at an angle of thirty degrees. The diameter of base was 80 feet; that of the summit plateau, 21 feet; the height, 11 feet 9 inches.

Large sweet-orange trees and towering palmettoes grew on the top and sides.

The mound was totally demolished by us during four and one-half days of June, 1895.

The body of the mound was composed of the whitish sand of the surrounding territory, with the marginal portions, 4 feet or 5 feet in, dyed a light pink through intentional admixture of the red oxide of iron. Pockets of pink sand and of light chocolate colored sand, some of considerable size, were encountered throughout the mound. The material of the mound was notably cohesive as through a certain admixture of clay. Although a considerable deposit of *Paludinæ* and *Ampullariæ* with fire places, fragmentary bones of lower animals and all the usual midden refuse, exists within a short distance of the site of the mound, no shells were encountered at any depth beneath the immediate surface where cultivation would not explain their presence. We were informed that superficial shells had been hauled from the adjacent shell heap to serve as a fertilizer.

[1] Journ. Acad. Nat. Sci., Vol. X.

HUMAN REMAINS.

Burials were of the bunched variety, which, our readers will recall, consists of piles of bones previously denuded of flesh by exposure to the elements. In this case separate interments were often represented by isolated crania or by various long bones of one skeleton or of several individuals.

Certain burials found near the surface with iron implements and glass beads had also the appearance of belonging to the bunched variety of interment, though of these we may not speak positively as they had possibly been subjected to disturbance by subsequent cultivation of the mound and the setting out and removal of orange trees.

In that portion of the mound included in the slope and not covered by the summit plateau, human remains were noted at forty-eight different points, many of these deposits, however, including the remains of a number of individuals.

In that portion of the mound beneath the summit plateau, that is to say, a mass of material about 12 feet high and 21 feet in diameter, interments were so numerous at places and so frequently in contact—single crania, bunches of long bones, and great layers of human remains, in places over one foot in thickness—that all efforts to record the number of individuals represented, were abandoned. Moreover, in many places—and this applies also to other portions of the mound—mere discoloration of the sand or at most yellowish powder, marked the former presence of bones.

No human remains were encountered at a depth greater than 12 feet, though certain objects of aboriginal design were fully one foot lower.

No skeletal remains were preserved.

EARTHENWARE.

The earthenware of this mound was of markedly inferior quality and design.

In the northern portion of the mound, including about one-third of the circumference, beginning near the margin and extending in for about 15 feet, between 2 and 3 feet from the base, was a curious layer of bits of earthenware and considerable fragments of vessels. These sherds were not laid in close proximity but at irregular distances, here and there, as though strewn upon that portion of the mound during its erection. No human remains were encountered with these sherds.

None but comparatively small vessels were recovered intact, though, from a considerable depth, near the center of the mound, four vessels of several quarts capacity each, but fragmentary and incomplete, were found in association. Several large fragments and one complete vessel had basal supports which we have noted as present in but three or four other mounds of the St. Johns. The use of feet on early aboriginal earthenware is unusual in any section of the United States, and we are informed that the clay pots found in Ontario are round bottomed and without supports.[1]

It has been suggested that feet on aboriginal vessels of earthenware might possibly be attributed to an imitation of metallic forms obtained from the Whites. So far as our experience goes we are strongly inclined to doubt this, since we have always obtained earthenware with basal supports from depths to guarantee original deposits in mounds where evidence of European influence, if present at all, was superficial. Moreover, the European kettle with feet, if we mistake not, had three supports, while the pottery of the Florida mounds, when supplied with feet, has four.

While the bases of a majority of the vessels of the mound showed perforation after manufacture, some were entire, and a few samples of the "freak" variety of ready made mortuary pottery, with perforation of base previous to baking, also were present. This perforation of the base of earthenware by the aborigines of the Peninsula was done, it is believed, to free the soul of the vessel to accompany the spirit of the dead to the land beyond.

As a rule, though with occasional exceptions, vessels seemed to be unassociated with human remains, though taking into consideration the advanced state of decay of some of the bones, exact determination was impossible. It is not unlikely, however, that most of the earthenware was put into the mound in a general way, and not to accompany individual interments.

In all, twenty-five vessels of earthenware were found in the Murphy Island mound in a condition to justify removal. These, in common with vessels in fragments and isolated sherds, were almost invariably at considerable depth—some so low as 13 feet from the surface. None bore stamped, punctate, or incised superficial ornamentation. One small vessel of the "freak" mortuary variety, 2.5 inches in height with a diameter of 2.7 inches across its laterally extending rim, and 1.65 inches through the body, was covered with crimson pigment inside and out. The base showed perforation prior to baking.

One vessel, 4.4 inches in height with a diameter of 3.5 inches, had a rude fluting around the body surmounted by the remains of an encircling projecting band 1.5 inches below the aperture. The entire bottom had been knocked out. This vessel lay 12 feet down with another broken vessel.

About 7 feet down were three bowls, the largest with a diameter of 14 inches, containing the other two, one within the other. Near by lay a fourth. These vessels, incomplete at the discovery, later fell into pieces, rendering restoration impossible—no great loss, so poor was their quality and so ordinary their type. We have already made reference to them.

Ten feet from the surface was an imperforate pot resembling a crucible in shape. Height, 3 inches; diameter at mouth, 2.2 inches; diameter at base, 1 inch.

[1] "Notes on Primitive Man in Ontario," by David Boyle, Toronto, 1895, page 31.

With it was a toy vessel also intact as to the base, having a height of 1.5 inches; a diameter at aperture of 1.4 inches, and .9 of one inch across the base (Fig. 54).

A spool-shaped object of earthenware, with edges slightly broken, has a height of 3 inches; a diameter at each expanded end of 2 inches; a diameter through the body of 1.5 inches. These spool-shaped objects of earthenware probably belong to the "freak" variety. We have figured one[1] from the mound at Davenport on the Ocklawaha, and found a somewhat similar specimen in the mound in the pine woods near Duval's, Lake County.

Fig. 54.—Toy vessel of earthenware. Northernmost mound, Murphy Island. (Full size.)

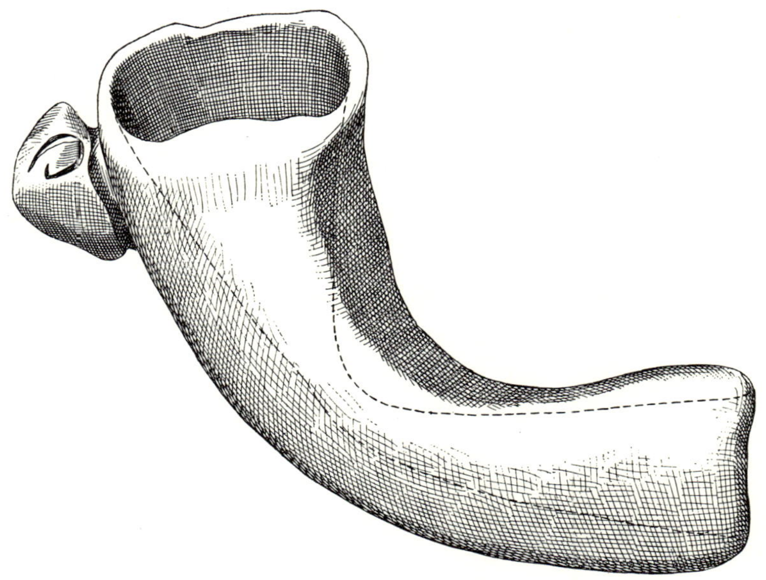

Fig. 55.—Tobacco pipe of earthenware. Northernmost mound, Murphy Island. (Full size.)

The remaining vessels from the mound at Murphy Island offered no feature worthy of remark.

But two tobacco pipes of earthenware were recovered from the mound. One of the usual type found on the lower river, was in fragments, with several considerable portions missing; the other (length, 3.5 inches; orifice of bowl, 1.6 inches by 1.2 inches; orifice of stem, .7 of an inch by 1 inch) is of especial interest, having a rude projecting animal head below the distal margin of the bowl as shown in Fig. 55.

A curious pendant of earthenware, rude and of poor material, came from 11 feet from the surface. Length, 1.8 inches; maximum diameter, .7 of one inch (Fig. 56).

An earthenware pendant or bead, with transverse perforation, found loose in the sand, is shown in Fig. 57. Length, 1.5 inches; diameter, .6 of one inch.

[1] *Op. cit.*, Part II, Plate XXVIII, Fig. 1.

Near human remains, was a ring of earthenware, 1.6 inches in diameter, .7 of one inch across

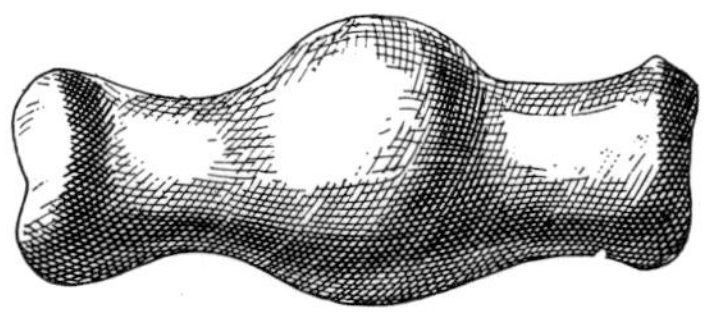

Fig. 56.—Pendant of earthenware. Northernmost mound, Murphy Island. (Full size.)

the opening, and .3 of one inch in thickness. It was found 7 feet from the surface (Fig. 58).

COPPER.

The reader of our report on the mounds of the St. Johns may recall that between Jacksonville and Lake Washington—the end of navigation—aboriginal copper was met with in but four mounds. It was, therefore, especially gratifying to find a variety of objects of this metal in the principal mound on Murphy Island.

Well in toward the center, in the northern

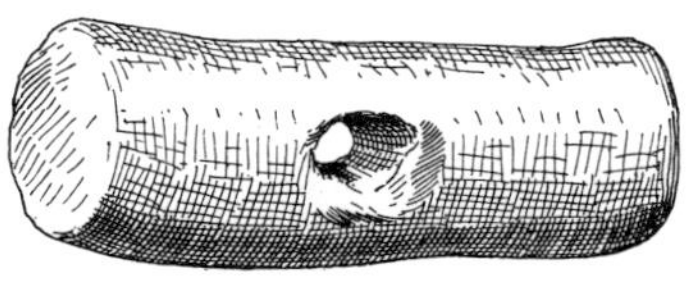

Fig. 57.—Pendant of earthenware. Northernmost mound, Murphy Island. (Full size.)

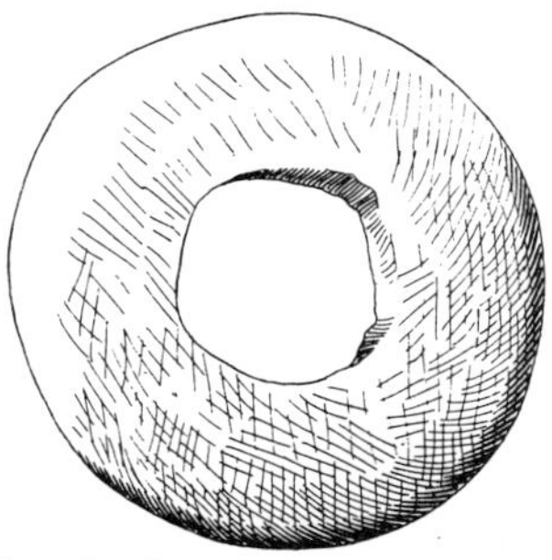

Fig. 58.—Ring of earthenware. Northernmost mound, Murphy Island. (Full size.)

portion of the mound, at no great distance apart, but each with a separate interment, 12 feet from the surface, were: (1) fragmentary remains of an ornament of wood overlaid with very thin sheet copper. One side is flat, the other repoussé. The breadth is about 2.2 inches; its original length is undeterminable. With it was a large sheet of mica. (2) An ornament of sheet copper, bent over and repoussé as shown in Fig. 59. A part of one side is missing

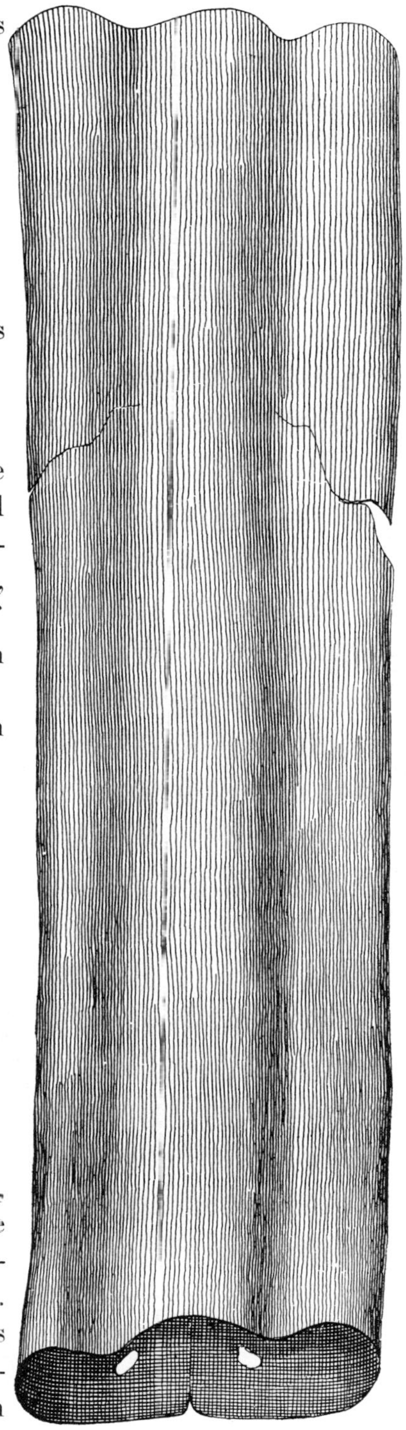

Fig. 59.—Ornament of sheet copper. Northernmost mound, Murphy Island. (Full size.)

Fig. 60.—Crescent of copper. Northernmost mound, Murphy Island. (Full size.)

through corrosion. At one end of the broken side are two perforations. Length, about 7 inches; width, about 2 inches. (3) An ornament of thin sheet copper apparently at one time coating a tube of some long-fibered substance like cane. It was recovered in several fragments, but probably when entire had a length of about 8 inches, with a slightly irregular diameter averaging 1.5 inches. (4) A fine specimen of sheet copper, entirely unbroken, and not materially affected by corrosion, representing the crescent moon. Distance between horns, 10.3 inches; maximum width, 1.7 inches; thickness, .04 of one inch. About one-half inch from the central part of the convex margin of the body, 1.7 inches apart, are two perforations by the aid of which this ornament, in early times doubtless highly polished, could be fastened to the chest or suspended from the neck, the horns pointing down (Fig. 60).

Toward the center, in the eastern portion of the mound, 12 feet from the surface, with human remains, together, associated with a pendant of shell, were: (1) apparently a number of separate discs, each about 1.8 inches in diameter, of sheet copper firmly cemented together through corrosion and too greatly carbonated to permit any successful attempt at separation. (2) A disc of sheet copper, centrally concavo-convex, about 2 inches in diameter. (3) A much corroded object of sheet copper, apparently of the sort known as spool-shaped, supposed by some to have served as an ear-plug, by others, as a button or stud for garments. Similar objects have frequently been figured as coming from Ohio mounds and elsewhere. Diameter of upper and lower portions, about 1.8 inches. (4) An ornament of sheet copper consisting of a disc centrally perforated and symmetrically bent and repoussé, as shown in Fig. 61, with section. Maximum diameter, about 2.1 inches.

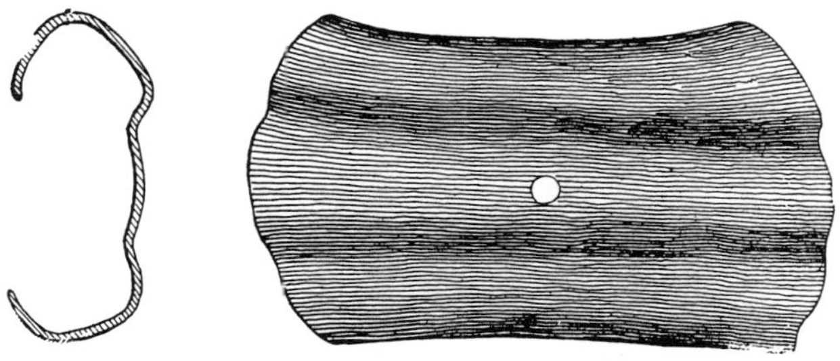

Fig. 61.—Ornament of sheet copper. Northernmost mound, Murphy Island. (Full size.)

Loose in caved sand was a small disc 1 inch in diameter. Within its slight concavity lay remains of wood.

SHELL.

Twenty-two specimens of shell drinking cups wrought from *Fulgur perversum* by the removal of the columella and a part of the body whorl, were taken from the mound. Some were intact; others showed an intentional perforation of the bottom. So far as we could determine, these drinking cups, though coming from different points, were all from within a few feet of the surface.

The quantities of small beads so often found with interments were not met with in this mound. At two points, beads from .5 of one inch to one inch in diameter—thirty in all—were encountered with human remains, while perhaps one dozen others were gathered from various portions of the mound.

Two feet from the surface, with human remains, were two shell discs with diameter of about 3 inches and 2.5 inches respectively, probably cut from the body whorl of *Fulgur*. The smaller had near the margin a double perforation for suspension. In neither was any decoration apparent.

A somewhat smaller disc was found loose in the sand.

Two shell pins, the larger 5 inches in length, lay together, near human remains, 2.5 feet from the surface. Two others, somewhat smaller, also with skeletal remains, were about 2 feet down. A fifth pin was recovered loose in the sand. These pins were all of types previously figured by Mr. Holmes in his exhaustive "Art in Shell," by others, and by ourselves in our account of the mound at East Palatka, Putnam County.

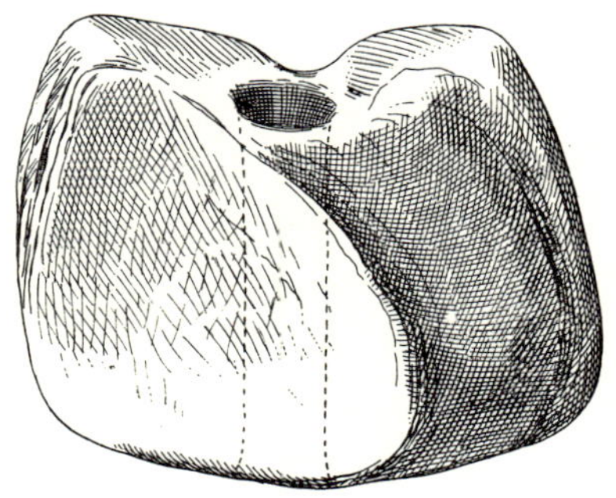

Fig. 62.—Ornament of shell. Northernmost mound, Murphy Island. (Full size.)

An interesting ornament, as shown in Fig. 62, was probably cut from the lip of the great marine *Strombus*. Its length is a little less than 2 inches; its breadth, about 1.3 inches. It had evidently formed a central ornament in a string of little shells (*Olivella*) longitudinally perforated, as one of these still lay in its perforation.

With a layer of human bones, 8 feet down, were four chisels of shell, probably cut from the lip of *Strombus*, approximately from 2 inches to 4 inches in length. With them were two stone "celts" and a columella of some large marine univalve. These columellæ, as we have pointed out elsewhere, were probably removed from the shell for shipment, to be manufactured into beads and ornaments.

Several other chisels of shell were found variously associated.

STONE.

During the demolition of the mound, sixty-six hatchets, or "celts," of smooth or polished stone, from about 2 inches to 12 inches in length, were taken from the mound. These hatchets—mainly of igneous rock—presenting no points of difference from other mound specimens, were not separately determined as to material.

A cutting implement of chipped chert, about 3 inches by 6 inches, flat on one side, lay 3 feet from the surface with human remains and several pebbles.

A pitted hammerstone, about 2.6 inches by 4 inches, was apparently unassociated.

Mica was found in but three places.

Twenty-six arrow and lance points of chert and of chert breccia were found separately, at various depths and a number of others associated with various objects. None presented anything unusual as to type.

Ten feet down, in a pocket of red *Hematite*, near human remains, together, were: twelve arrow and lance points; a sharpening stone of claystone, almost rectangular, about 6.3 inches by 3 inches, with an average thickness of about .3 of one inch; one "celt"; a heart-shaped bit of rock, apparently claystone, 3.8 inches by about 2.5 inches, used for sharpening pointed tools, grinding beads, or both, as shown by grooves on either side across its widest part; a small bit of sandstone; one flake of chert, and twenty-two chips of the same material. We have frequently remarked the inhumation of great numbers of fragments, chips, and flakes of chert, especially in the smaller river mounds between Jacksonville and the sea, while from Mt. Royal, near Lake George, Putnam County, we took 951 associated masses of chert, averaging about the size of a hen's egg. Lieutenant-General Pitt Rivers, in his monumental work,[1] speaks of great numbers of flakes, chips, and cores of flint (which is almost the same as our chert) found by him in the barrows.

Four quartz pebbles; one core of chert; three fragments of fossil bone, shaped to a certain extent, the largest rectangular, about 1.6 inches by 2.5 inches, with an average thickness of .5 of one inch, were found in association. Fossil bones are not infrequently met with in Florida in the clay and in the bottom of streams.

Two and one-half feet from the surface, in immediate association, were: a pebble hammer of quartz, 5 inches long; fifteen smaller pebbles and pebble hammers; three small bits of sandstone; one fragment of an apparently clayey substance; four arrow heads of chert; a small natural formation, tubular in shape; ten bits of fossil bone, some worked to a certain extent; one unidentified object of the same material, about 3 inches long, 1.5 inches high, with an average thickness of 1.6 inches; a portion of a tooth of a fossil shark; an astragalus of a fossil llama,[2] and a small fragment of striated rock.

Three feet from the surface was another curious medley consisting of: one bit of fossil bone; two rude arrow heads of chert; one pebble hammer; four small pebbles; one chip of chert; four bits of sandstone; two pieces of coquina, and one small fragment of *Steatite*.

All together, 4 feet down, were: sixteen bits of fossil bone from .5 of one inch to 3 inches in length, some by their even edges showing a certain amount of work; ten pebble hammers; thirty small pebbles, one pebble partially ground for suspension, an incipient pendant; seven fragments, of sandstone and of other rocks; two chert arrow heads; one tubular bead of soapstone, about .75 of one inch in length.

In addition to these curious deposits there lay separately throughout the mound, pebble hammers, sharpening stones, and certain natural formations in the form of tubes, largely used by the aborigines, similar to one figured by us in Part I of our Report on the St. Johns mounds as coming from Mt. Royal, and found in such numbers in the Shields mound, Duval County.

[1] "Excavations in Cranborne Chase, near Rushmore." Printed privately. Three volumes, 1887—1892. England.

[2] Identified by Professor Cope. Three species of fossil llama from Florida have been described by Leidy.

Loose in the sand was a cuboidal mass of carbonate of lime, with rounded corners, about the size of an English walnut, while apparently unassociated was a mass of undetermined rock about the same size, spheroidal, depressed at the poles. A flat pebble of clayey material, about 2 inches by 4 inches, with a maximum thickness of .8 of one inch, has four perforations apparently of natural formation around twigs. These perforations, doubtless, the aborigines had been quick to utilize.

Two small pendants, one of crystalline granular rock, possibly of igneous origin, the smaller of *Agalmatolite*, lay with human remains, 8 feet from the surface, with a small shell chisel. Their shape is triangular and each has a countersunk perforation for suspension. In addition, the larger, 1.1 inches in length with a maximum width of .6 of one inch and a thickness of .2 of one inch, has a curved groove extending across one side (Figs. 63 and 64).

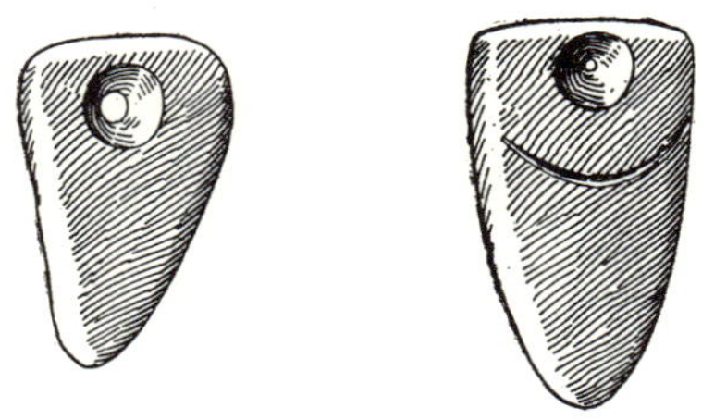

Figs. 63 and 64.—Pendent ornaments. Northernmost mound, Murphy Island. (Full size.)

Nine feet down, with human remains, was a handsome banner stone of a crystalline rock in which the silica projects while the felspathic material is much decomposed—possibly a *Granulyte*. It is laterally and longitudinally perforated. Two shoulders with median grooves encircle it. A small portion is broken from one side. Length, 3.4 inches; minimum diameter of shaft, .6 of one inch; maximum diameter of shaft, .8 of one inch; diameter of smaller shoulder, 1 inch; of larger, 1.1 inches (Fig. 65).

A graceful pendant of a crystalline granular rock, probably syenitic, came from a depth of 5 feet with a "celt." Human remains were in association. At either

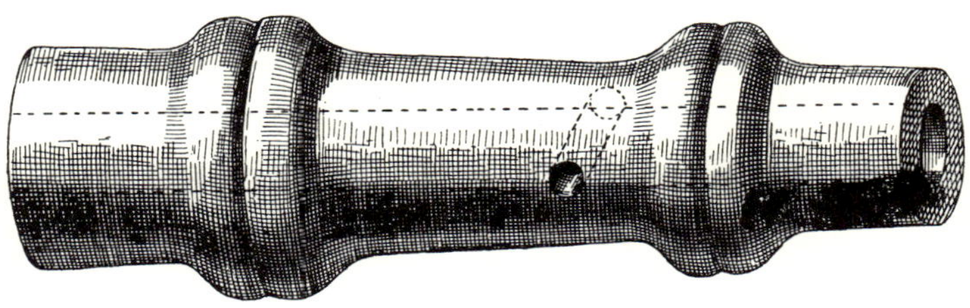

Fig. 65.—Ceremonial of stone. Northernmost mound, Murphy Island. (Full size.)

end is a rim, while from one end is a small projection as shown in Fig. 66. Length 2.6 inches; diameter of body, 1.3 inches; diameter of larger rim, 1 inch; of smaller rim, .7 of one inch.

A fusiform pendant, probably of steatitic material, grooved at one end for suspension, strongly resembles in shape pendants of shell found by us in the mound on Tick Island and figured in Part II of our Report. Length, 3.7 inches; maximum diameter, 1 inch (Fig. 67).

A curiously shaped pendant of steatitic rock, having a length of .9 of one inch and a maximum diameter of 1.2 inches, lay with a burial 6 feet from the surface (Fig. 68).

Two pendants of quartz were found separately in the mound. One, a rough fragment about 1 inch in length, is rudely grooved at one end. The other, a crystal, 1.9 inches in length with a maximum diameter of .5 of one inch, is neatly grooved and shows considerable wear (Fig. 69).

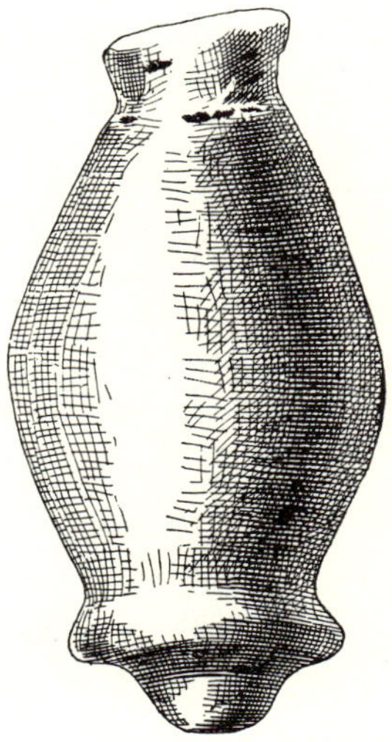

Fig. 66.—Pendant of syenitic rock. Northernmost mound, Murphy Island. (Full size.)

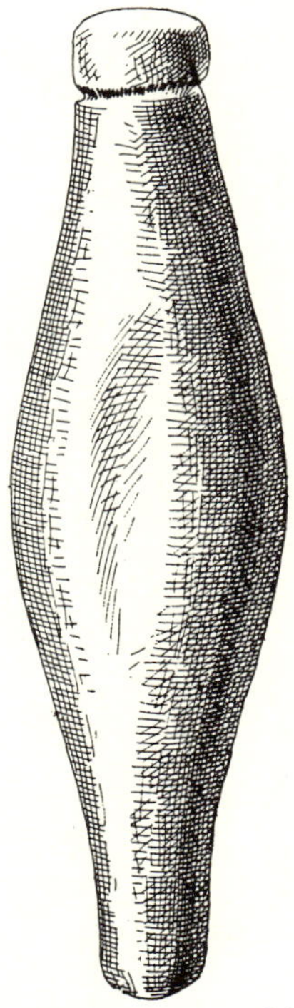

Fig. 67.—Pendant of steatitic material. Northernmost mound, Murphy Island. (Full size.)

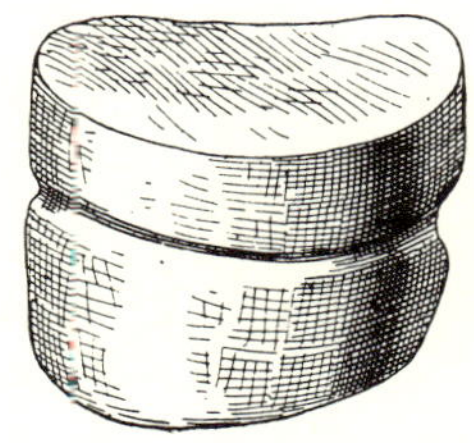

Fig. 68.—Pendant of steatitic rock. Northernmost mound, Murphy Island. (Full size.)

Fig. 69.—Pendant of quartz crystal. Northernmost mound, Murphy Island. (Full size.)

We have, in a former Report, quoted Laudonnière's statement as to presents of fine crystal made by southern Indians.

At various depths, though at no great distance from the surface, singly, were seven beads of soapstone, some cylindrical, others oblong, varying in length between 1.1 inches and 2.2 inches.

INTRUSIVE DEPOSITS.

Two and one-half feet from the surface, with a burial and a chisel of stone, was a comb apparently made of leather, with scroll decoration on either side.

With a burial three feet down were an iron or steel axe with long narrow blade, and an unidentified tool of the same material. With these implements, of necessity obtained from the Whites, were a number of long blue cylindrical beads of glass and spherical polychrome beads of the same material.

Together, accompanying a burial, 1.5 feet from the surface, were a long knife, two chisels, a triangular chisel or tomahawk, and an unidentified tool, all of iron or of steel.

An implement resembling a modern grubbing hoe, and a narrow bladed axe, both of steel or of iron, lay together with fragmentary human remains about 2 feet from the surface. Near by was a hatchet of polished stone. It is not unlikely that these implements of metal were placed in the neighborhood of a pre-existing deposit of stone, nor is it unlikely that all belonged to the same period, since implements derived from White contact did not at once supplant all products of aboriginal art.

AN OBJECT OF UNDETERMINED DERIVATION.

Twelve feet from the surface, toward the central portion of the mound, in association with human remains was taken out, in our immediate presence, an object resembling the lower portion of a small nail (Fig. 70). Its length is .8 of one inch. It is affected by the magnet, and is therefore iron or steel or iron ore.

Fig. 70.–Unidentified object. Northernmost mound. Murphy Island. (Full size.)

It may be well to explain to the general reader that the aborigines were unable to reduce iron from its ores, and that this metal in a native state, if it exists at all on this earth, is of extreme rarity, and that the only iron in aboriginal use in pre-Columbian times was that obtained from meteorites, as is shown by the high percentage of nickel present when analytically tested. There is no reason why the aborigines of Florida should not have been possessed of some small piercing implements of meteoric iron. Unfortunately, the original material of this specimen cannot be determined by analysis, as it weighs but 215 milligrams and is corroded through and through.

It seems unlikely that aborigines in a way to obtain iron and other products of White contact such as lead, pewter, brass, bronze, glass, china, glazed earthenware, etc., should have scrupulously kept them from the body of the mound wherein lay the great majority of the burials, after placing upon the base a portion of a single nail.

It may be well, moreover, to state in this connection that not one spadeful of sand was thrown back from this mound save in our presence, and that, in addition, three persons trained to careful mound work for years, were present at all times to aid us. Furthermore, after the discovery of superficial iron, if possible, greater vigilance than ordinary was exercised by all, no part of the mound being left without constant inspection. In addition, the work at this mound was done at the close of the season by picked men mostly for many months in our employ. It is, therefore, unlikely that any deposit in the mound escaped us.

REMARKS.

The contents of the northernmost mound on Murphy Island are of considerably above the average interest. The numerous fragments of fossil bone are new to us, while the collections of pebble hammers, chips of stone, and the like, buried together, have not been met with before above Jacksonville, though in low mounds between that point and the sea, they are common enough. The period when the mound was built depends upon the nature of the small piece of iron discovered at the base, and of this we have already spoken.

SOUTHERNMOST MOUND, MURPHY ISLAND.

About two hundred yards in a southerly direction from the mound we have just described is another in full view of the river, did not a thick growth of sour orange trees intervene. The height of the mound is 10 feet; its diameter of base, 70 feet. A number of large forest trees grew upon it. Irregular ridges, evidently artificial, not directly connected with the mound, ran in an easterly direction from it.

Owing to the presence of many orange trees around a portion of the margin, the entire mound was not demolished.

A trench 103 feet wide at the beginning, including the south, southeast and southwest parts of the circumference, was carried in until over one-half the mound had been removed.

The mound proved structurally of great interest. From the start, with its base at about the level of the surrounding territory, was a black layer of midden refuse surmounted by a stratum of sand artificially colored by the use of the red oxide of iron, sometimes pink, and again a bright cherry. Above this was mottled sand containing various local streaks and layers. As the work progressed a second layer of midden refuse was observed.

At the center of the mound, the strata, though somewhat irregular in thickness, were about as follows:

Superficial 4 feet.—Mottled sand, pink, white, and gray at places.
1.5 feet.—Black loam, solidly packed, containing midden refuse, sherds, bones of lower animals, charcoal, and very occasional shells.
6 inches.—Cherry colored sand with pockets, extending into the layer below.
2 feet 10 inches.—Mottled sand.
1.5 feet.—Black loam—midden refuse.
7 inches.—Sand brownish in color, resembling a stain.

Beneath this was pure white sand showing occasional signs of mottling and containing scattered particles of charcoal and at least one worked fragment of chert. There was no definite base line, and how much of this white sand may have been filled into a previous excavation there was no method to determine.

During the entire investigation but seven burials were encountered, all of the bunched variety and none deeper than 5 feet from the surface. In association were several small bits of pottery, a chipping of chert, and, together, two pins of bone.

Occasional sherds were in the midden refuse, and two small imperforate bowls were found separately in the same material. A few arrow heads lay loose in the sand and in the loam.

This curious mound, evidently a place of abode during two extended periods, had been subsequently used, to a small extent in the upper portion, for sepulchral purposes.

In default of total demolition we do not feel justified in drawing conclusions as to this mound.

Certain Sand Mounds of the Ocklawaha River, Florida

BY

CLARENCE B. MOORE

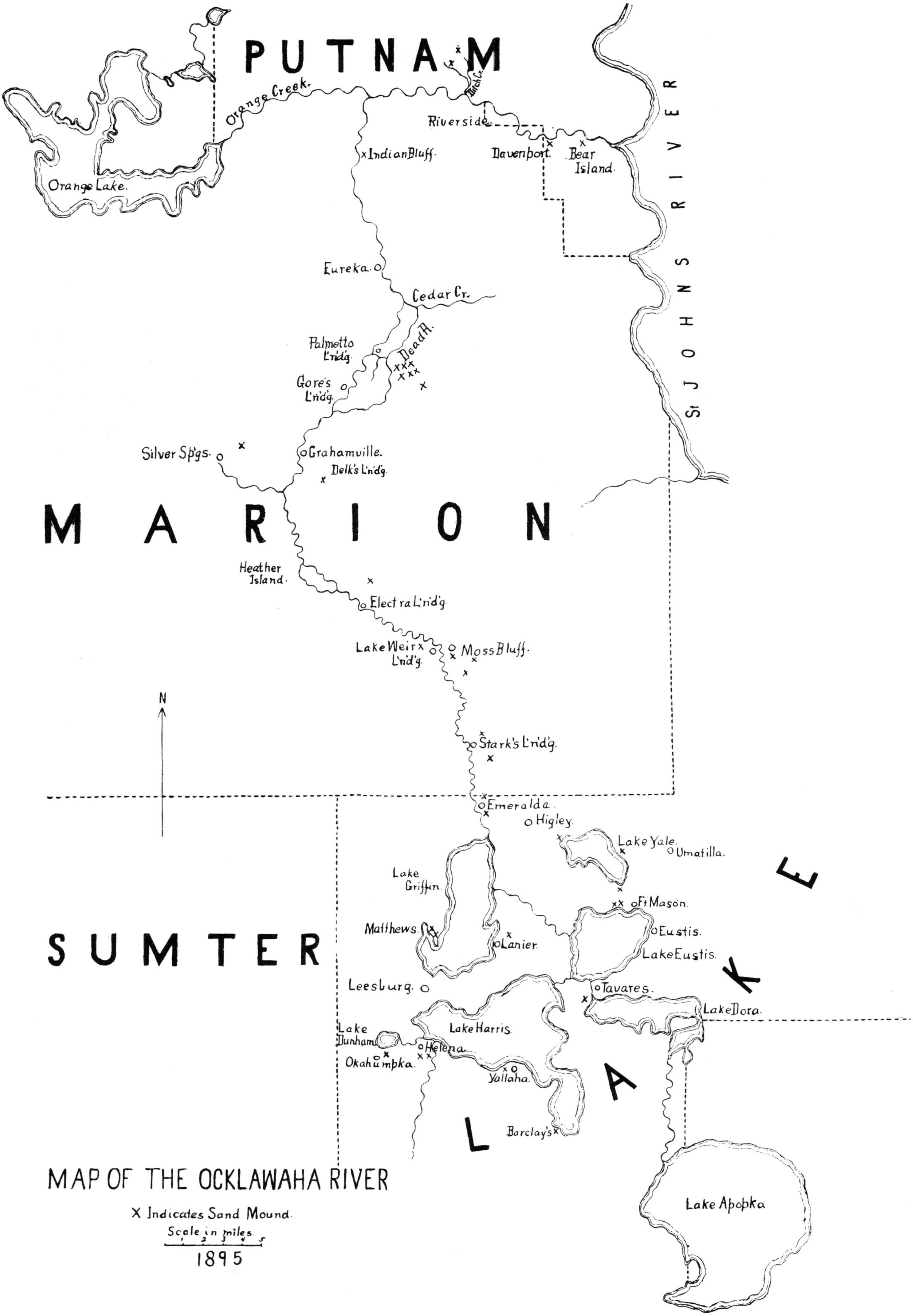

MAP OF THE OCKLAWAHA RIVER

X Indicates Sand Mound.

Scale in miles

1895

CERTAIN SAND MOUNDS OF THE OCKLAWAHA RIVER, FLORIDA.[1]

By Clarence B. Moore.

The Ocklawaha River, whose narrow, winding and rapid current enters the St. Johns from the western side of that river, about twenty-five miles above Palatka, has its source in Lake Apopka (see map) though the head of navigation is at the channel between Lakes Eustis and Dora.[2] From Lake Apopka, running in a northerly direction, it traverses Lake Dora, Lake Eustis and Lake Griffin and continuing first through marsh and then through swamp land and joining Orange Creek, an unnavigable stream, it turns abruptly to the east, pursuing this course until its union with the St. Johns.

Passing through a portion of Lake County, traversing the county of Marion and skirting on the south about one-half of Putnam County, the Ocklawaha, irrespective of curves, has a length of about seventy-five miles. So tortuous, however, is the stream that these figures convey not the faintest idea of the distance to be travelled by water in a journey from the outlet of the river to its source.[3]

In comparison with the St. Johns, the Ocklawaha had little to offer the aborigines as a place of abode. From the mouth to the union with the stream from Silver Springs (where the acquaintance of the tourist with the river usually comes to an end) the Ocklawaha runs between cypress swamps with very occasional bits of solid land; while above, the course of the stream is through saw-grass marshes offering an equal paucity of landing places.

It is therefore evident that the archæologist exploring this stream, fully cognizant of the fact that the aborigines were no mean judges of living sites, must set out with a less sanguine spirit than would be justified on the St. Johns, especially as it is doubtful whether the lower Ocklawaha, obstructed, at every turn as it must have been, by huge trunks of fallen cypresses, offered in early times a channel of communication. In point of fact, the paucity of shell-heaps and their restricted

[1] The mound on Bear Island and that at Davenport, within a few miles of the mouth of the Ocklawaha River, have been described in Part II of our "Certain Sand Mounds of the St. Johns River, Florida." Jour. Acad. Nat. Sci., Phila., Vol. X.

[2] The channel between Lakes Eustis and Dora has, at places, scarcely two feet of water. In addition, two immovable bridges bar the way.

[3] A table of distances used on the line of steamers plying on the river, gives as 101 miles the distance by water between the point of union with the St. Johns and the entrance into Silver Springs Run, somewhat less than one-half the length of the Ocklawaha, and this, be it remembered, is a less tortuous portion of the stream than that farther south. Between Alligator Landing and Moss Bluff on the upper river, the distance by land is given as three miles by those in a position to know, and as five times that number when the journey is made by water.

size, insignificant if compared with the great shell deposits of the St. Johns, testify to a scanty population.

From the mouth to the end of navigation the territory bordering the Ocklawaha was found to contain no mound over eight feet in height[1] and very few approaching even that altitude. It has been, therefore, in the power of the ignorant treasure seeker, or of the "relic hunter," even with his limited time and means, seriously to impair the archæological value of many of these mounds by the removal of central portions—an impossibility in the case of the greater earthworks of the St. Johns.

As the reader will see, the mounds of the river proper were virtually barren, while no rich harvest was yielded by those of the "lake" country beyond.

This investigation was conducted with steam motive power and an abundant force of men during portions of January and March and all of February, 1895.

We append a list of mounds investigated on the Ocklawaha River, to be followed by a detailed account of those offering any interest either structurally or as to human remains or relics of aboriginal art.

Ditch Creek (2).
Indian Bluff.
Palmetto Landing (7).
Delk's Landing.
Silver Springs.
Electra Landing.
Lake Weir Landing.
Moss Bluff (3).
Stark's Landing (2).
Hopson Mound.
Near Higley.
Near Umatilla.
Near Fort Mason.
Lake Griffin (3).
Lake Eustis.
Near Tavares.
Barclay's.
Near Yallaha.
Richmond Mound.
Near Helena.
Okahumpka.

Mounds near Ditch Creek, Putnam County.

Ditch Creek enters the Ocklawaha from the left, going down, about eighteen miles by water from the river's mouth. About one mile up the creek is a landing, and from this landing, about four hundred yards W. N. W., was a mound 1.5 feet in height and 45 feet in diameter of base. It had apparently lost somewhat in height by the trampling of cattle.

It was totally demolished.

It consisted of gray, loamy sand with the usual admixture of charcoal. At one point were two bits of human femur; at another, charred fragments of human bones. Numerous chips, flakes, and two cores of chert were found and one bit of plain undecorated earthenware.

[1] The mounds of Lake Harris, though not properly belonging to the Ocklawaha River, are included in this paper. The territory bordering this lake had one mound of an altitude greater than the limit given above.

About one mile north of the landing at Ditch Creek was a mound 4 feet 9 inches in height and 60 feet through the base. It was much spread out, probably by trampling of cattle and bore marks of previous superficial investigation.

It was completely dug through with the kind permission of J. J. Cummings, Esq., of Beaufort, S. C.

Bunched burials were comparatively numerous, and all or nearly all within 1 or 2 feet of the surface, though, of course, at greater depth when the height of the mound was unimpaired. With one burial were charred turtle bones, while with several were associated calcined fragments of human remains.

About 2 feet down, not far from the center of the mound, was a considerable mass of calcined fragments of human bones mixed with those of lower animals in similar condition. These apparently were not in proximity to any interment.

Throughout the mound were sherds of fairly good quality for Florida, some decorated with red pigment, others with incised lines, etc.

With the exception of the sherds and of a rude and somewhat fragmentary cutting implement chipped from chert, no relics were met with.

Mounds near Palmetto Landing, Marion County.

Palmetto Landing on the Ocklawaha River is said to be about seventy-seven miles by water from the river's mouth. About one mile in an easterly direction from the landing were five mounds at no great distance apart, while about one-half mile and one mile respectively farther in the same direction were two others.

Nearest the landing were two symmetrical mounds with base margins almost in contact at one point. The northernmost had a height of about 5 feet with a base diameter of about 52 feet; the southernmost, a height of 6 feet 3 inches and a diameter of base of 57 feet.

These mounds were completely demolished.

They consisted of coarse yellow sand, unstratified and almost, if not entirely, devoid of the usual intermingled charcoal.

No human remains nor indications of burial nor, with one exception, sherds of any description were encountered.

A number of cores and chippings, of chert with two rude chipped cutting implements of the same material, lay loose in the sand. No other relics of any sort were found.

Fifty-five paces in an easterly direction from the northernmost of the twin mounds was another, with a height of 4 feet 4 inches and 48 feet across the base. The entire central portion of this mound was dug out with no return.

Eighty-five paces northeast of the preceding mound was another, 4 feet 3 inches high with a diameter of base of 55 feet. Absolutely nothing was obtained from this mound.

About 20 paces farther was a fifth mound 3.5 feet high. The base had a diameter of 53 feet. Again careful investigation was absolutely unrewarded.

On the property of Mr. R. D. MacDonald, about one-half mile farther to the east, was an unsymmetrical mound of yellow sand, 7.5 feet high and 71 feet through the base. This mound was not demolished. A certain amount of investigation yielded nothing.

Still farther on, about one-half mile in the same direction, was a beautiful little mound 4 feet in height with a diameter of base of 68 feet. It was built on the edge of a small lake which bordered a portion of its margin, while the remainder was surrounded by a trench about 24 feet wide and 1 foot in depth, which, in the wet season, made an island of the mound.

It was totally demolished, the task being a very difficult one owing to the presence of great quantities of scrub palmetto roots.

The mound was unstratified. Its material was coarse white sand. The usual charcoal was not noticed. A few sherds, undecorated save one which showed marks of red pigment, were scattered through the sand as were a few flakes of chert and a fragmentary lance head.

Almost centrally situated in the mound, at three separate points, each about 18 inches from the surface, were fragmentary human remains, while a small excavation made by a previous visitor showed fragments of human bones in the sand.

This mound illustrates the amount of work at times undertaken by the aborigines to make a limited number of interments.

We can form no conclusion as to the five mounds nearest the landing. They may have been erected for domiciliary purposes, but it is worthy of remark that no village site refuse was found upon them. But, for that matter, we have never in Florida found any marks of habitation upon any mound which, through absence of human remains and products of aboriginal industry, we have been inclined to assign to the domiciliary class.

Mound near Silver Springs, Marion County.

This mound, about one mile in an easterly direction from Silver Springs, had a height of 4 feet 2 inches, with a base diameter of 50 feet. A trench surrounding it, from which its material had been taken, gave an appearance of considerably greater altitude to the mound.

The mound had undergone much previous exploration. A trench had been dug on one side from the margin to the center, and the upper central portion had been excavated to a depth of about 2 feet.

The mound was totally demolished, being dug through, as is our habit, at a level considerably below that of the surrounding territory. Its material was yellow sand without stratification, but with the usual intermingling of particles of charcoal. In various parts of the mound, especially on the base, were small pockets of sand showing marks of fire.

Burials were of the bunched variety, but human remains, when found, were in the last stage of decay. At one point on the base was a layer of intermingled bones representing a number of individuals. No human remains were saved.

EARTHENWARE.

Great numbers of sherds, usually undecorated, some, however, bearing traces of red pigment, and, in two instances at least, ornamented with graceful curves and lines, were met with. A number of fragmentary vessels were found which had evidently been interred in an incomplete condition, as careful search failed to reveal the missing portions. This utilizing of otherwise useless earthenware was very prevalent among the makers of the mounds in Florida. Fragments of various vessels showed perforation of the base subsequent to manufacture.

One small vessel, somewhat broken (Plate LXXXV, Fig. 1), with everted brim and stamped decoration on the body, had four feet for support, a somewhat uncommon occurrence in Florida, though we have met with it on the St. Johns in

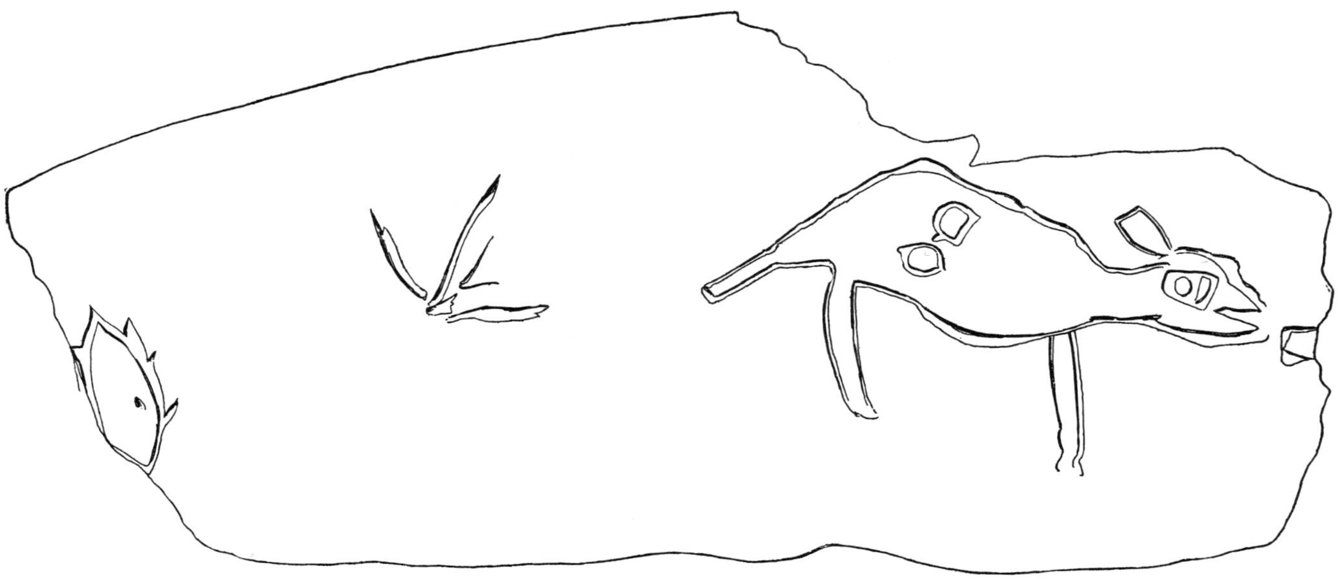

Fig. 71.—Diagram of incised delineation. Mound near Silver Springs. (Full size.)

the mound at Racey Point, and have seen basal supports on fragments from the mound at Tick Island and on vessels from Murphy Island.

In a portion of the mound at some distance from previous excavations, so far as the most careful investigation could determine, at 3 feet from the surface, in sand where the closest scrutiny could discover no previous disturbance, was found, in our immediate presence, a portion of a small bowl of earthenware. The remainder was not discovered, and was probably not present in the mound. The hollow portion of this fragment contained a solid mass of roots probably belonging to scrub palmettoes on the surface of the mound. Upon examination by us it became apparent that incised figures were on the fragment, one probably representing a deer, and that others had been on the missing portion, since incomplete figures were at the broken margins at either side. A close inspection showed that a certain amount of soot, gained doubtless during the entirety of the vessel while in use for culinary purposes, still remained upon the fragment, and that the incised figures were cut through this soot, or after the abandonment of the vessel for domestic use. It is, therefore, evident either that the decoration is aboriginal, but made subsequent to the vessel's final contact with the flames, or that our judgment as to undisturbed sand, in the absence of stratification, is at fault, and that the fragment was a recent addition to the mound, left by some previous investigator. It is shown diagrammatically in Fig. 71.

We have submitted this fragment to Professor Putnam and append the opinion of this high authority.

"Thanks for allowing me to see the fragment of pottery from the Florida mound. It is a very interesting piece of incised work, and again shows the rude character of the art of the people who buried their dead in the sand mounds of Florida.

"That the cutting is not recent I think is shown by the edges of the lines, and also by the fact that in the lines forming the front leg and foot there are little

Fig. 72.—Incised delineation of human figure. Shell-heap of Mulberry mound. (Full size.)

particles of mica that seem to be cemented to the bottom of the incised lines. Now this, it seems to me, could not have happened if the cutting were of recent date and the bowl put into the mound only a short time ago.

"There is every indication, to my mind, that the carving was made by the people who buried their dead in that mound, and no indication of fraudulent work. The whole thing is in keeping with what you have found before.

"We took a piece of similar pottery from Florida and cut lines upon it of the same character, and we found that in making a very slight line we cut into the black interior of the pottery, and the edges were sharp. Whereas, the edges of your specimen are smoothed over, as if considerable handling had taken place since they were cut. If you will try this on a piece of the same kind of pottery you will at once see the difference between the lines on the bowl and the lines that you cut."

The incised delineation of an animate object on earthenware has never before been encountered by us in a sand mound, and but once previously in a shell-heap.

In the island shell-heap constituting Mulberry mound, Orange County, Florida, from a depth of 10 feet, were thrown out, in our presence, two fragments of the same earthenware vessel, which, upon being fitted together, showed incised delineation representing a human head and portion of the body, the remainder of the body having been on parts of the vessel not left in that portion of the shell-heap.

Incised delineation of the human form on early earthenware, it may be interesting to know, is believed to be represented by this specimen alone within the limits of the United States and probably beyond. We have given in "The American Naturalist"[1] a full account of our work at Mulberry mound, and have borrowed from it, for comparison, a representation of the incised figure (Fig. 72). Certain parts of the delineation, represented in the cut as less distinct than others, are not of unequal depth, but still contain a certain amount of soot, a relic of pre-historic fires. This point, of considerable interest, shows the decoration to have been made during the entirety of the pot, and not to have been scratched on a detached sherd subsequent to breakage.

STONE.

Flakes and chippings of chert were present in the mound in unusual numbers. Four arrowheads and one drill, also of chert, were met with separately.

A small polished cutting implement of compact igneous rock was in caved sand.

On the base, near the margin of the mound, was a small object of sandstone, probably an ornament, a little short of 2 inches in length. Its shape is ellipsoidal, flattened on one side. A median groove is confined to the curved portion.

In immediate association, 4.5 feet from the surface, lay eleven masses of chert showing cleavage, varying in length from 3 to 9 inches, evidently material for implements. Some were several pounds in weight.

SHELL.

At depths showing them to be of original deposit were two chisels probably from the lip of *Strombus* and a gouge from the body whorl of *Fulgur*. One chisel lay with human remains. The other was with a copper bead.

COPPER.

Three cylindrical beads of copper were found during the excavation, all apparently of original deposit. These differed from beads of the same material found by

[1] August, 1893.

us on the St. Johns, on which river all beads are of thin sheet copper or of wood, limestone, or shell, overlaid with a thin coating of metal. The copper beads from this mound are more massive, and, while the method of manufacture by hammering to overlap the edges was the same, the thickness of copper employed was greater.

MISCELLANEOUS.

The tooth of a fossil shark lay 3 feet from the surface. A notch on either side had served as a medium of attachment by cord or sinew.

REMARKS.

In no portion of the mound was anything found in any way indicating contact with the Whites.

Gamble Mound, Marion County.

This mound, about one-quarter mile from Stark's Landing, on property of Mr. R. Gamble, of Tallahassee, to whom we wish to express our indebtedness, was demolished by us during three days in February, 1895. We take occasion here to return thanks also to Mr. T. J. McKinnon, superintendent of the grove.

The mound, long under cultivation, had been reduced to a height of 5 feet 8 inches. The diameter of the base, increased by material from summit and sides, was 76 feet.

The mound was composed of yellow sand, unstratified, with the usual particles of charcoal intermingled. In the sand were present throughout the mound, pockets of fire-whitened sand and deposits of charcoal. One at least of these deposits of charcoal had been made subsequent to the extinction of the fire, as sand unaffected by the flames was mingled with the charcoal.

Throughout the mound, at about the level of the surrounding territory, was a layer of an approximate thickness of 3 inches, composed of fire-whitened sand, mingled with small particles of charcoal. At places in this layer, pockets of sand, nearly one foot in thickness, showing marks of fire, and containing considerable charcoal were met with.

No occurrence of human remains was noted until well on toward the central portion of the mound, when fragmentary bones, indicating the bunched burial, were found, though by no means in numbers proportionate to the size of the mound.

Sherds, plain and stamped in squares, were met with at every depth; also several portions of vessels with base supports. In the eastern margin of the mound, on the base, 2 feet from the surface, was an undecorated bowl 4.5 inches in diameter at aperture and about three inches high. The base has two perforations made subsequent to manufacture, one through the agency of a pointed tool.

Six and one-half feet from the surface was an ellipsoidal object of shell without perforation. These objects are not uncommon in the mounds.

STONE.

Five and one-half feet from the surface was a pendent ornament wrought from a nodule of chert, globular in shape, with grooved projection for suspension. Traces of bitumen surround the groove. The ornament lay in a pocket of fire-whitened sand, though no traces of heat are upon it, and the presence of bitumen

Fig. 73.—Pendant made from chert nodule. Gamble mound. (Full size.)

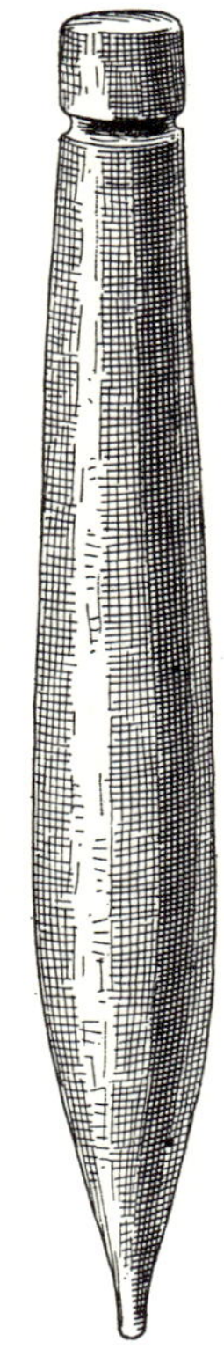

Fig. 74.—Pendent ornament. Gamble mound. (About full size.)

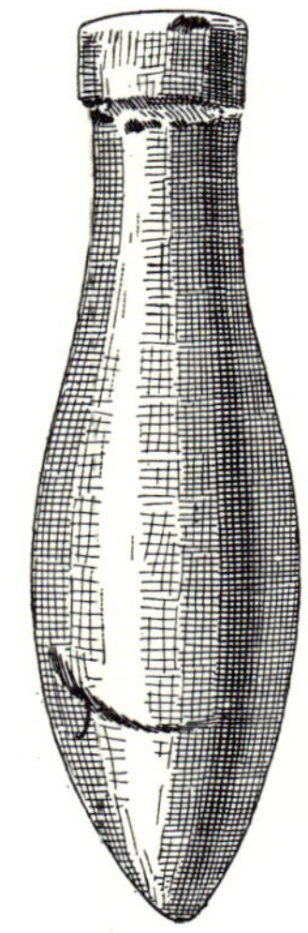

Fig. 75.—Pendant of silicified fossil bone. Gamble mound. (Full size)

shows the deposit to have been made after the extinction of the fire. Length, about 2.5 inches; maximum diameter, 1.7 inches (Fig. 73).

A graceful pendant of slate, of a type not met with by us elsewhere, was recovered from previously disturbed sand. Former explorers state that from the small excavation made by them, an exactly similar ornament was recovered. The shape of the pendant is cylindrical, swelling out somewhat at and below the center and then tapering to a point. A groove surrounds the upper portion. Length, 3.7 inches; maximum diameter, .5 of one inch (Fig. 74).

A pendant, probably of silicified fossil bone, in shape somewhat suggesting our "Indian clubs" used for exercise, though thicker at the handle, has a length of 2.6 inches, a maximum diameter of .75 of one inch. Considerable bitumen surrounds the groove and upper portion of the ornament (Fig. 75).

From a depth of 5 feet came a pendant of a sedimentary rock approaching *Agalmatolite*, somewhat similar in shape to the preceding. The lower portion is missing. Its length is 3.5 inches; its maximum diameter, .8 of one inch (Fig. 76).

A pendent ornament of sedimentary rock, elliptical in outline, flattened on

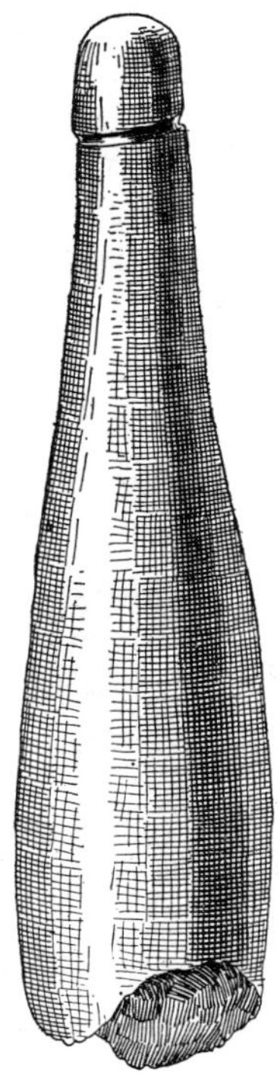

Fig. 76.—Pendent ornament. Gamble mound. (Full size.)

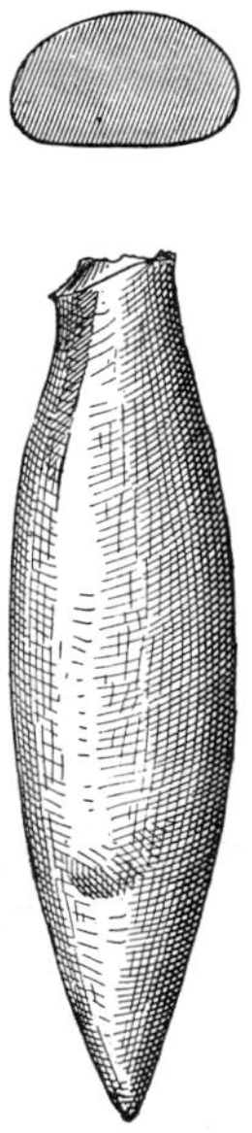

Fig. 77.—Pendent ornament. Gamble mound. (Full size.)

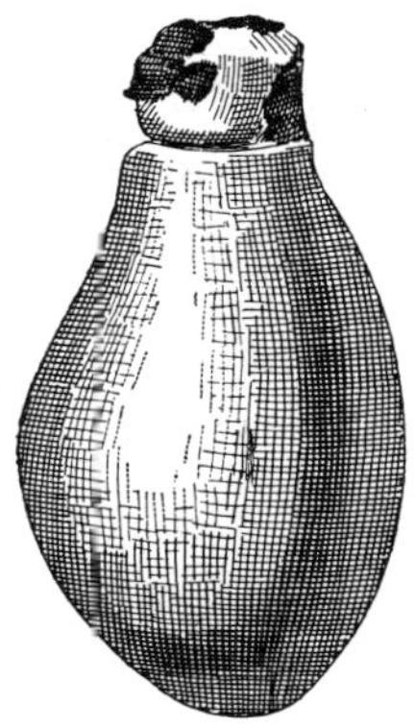

Fig. 78.—Pendant of igneous rock. Gamble mound. (Full size.)

one side, with a small portion missing above the groove, has a length of 2.3 inches with a maximum diameter of .6 of one inch (Fig. 77).

A pear-shaped pendant of some igneous rock, with a length of 1.9 inches and a maximum thickness of 1 inch, came from a depth of 3.5 feet. This specimen also has bitumen adhering to the upper portion. A part of one side is missing (Fig. 78).

On the base, in a pocket of fire-whitened sand, was an ovoid pendant of limestone, unfortunately somewhat injured by contact with a spade. Length, 2 inches; maximum width, 1.4 inches.

So far as careful search would indicate, none of these pendants were associated with human remains, though it is of course possible that all traces of the former presence of bones may have disappeared. It is worthy of note that the inhumation of pendants seemed to prevail in this mound, and that these pendants were uniformly grooved for suspension, bitumen, upon certain occasions at least, having been used to aid in attaching the cord or sinew. We shall see later how, in the mound at Tavares, the pendants, as a rule, had perforation, in which case the use of bitumen would be needless, and it was apparently not employed.

A sheet of mica, 2 inches by 3 inches, came from a depth showing original deposit. Sheets of mica, so abundant in the low mounds between Jacksonville and the sea but seldom found in the larger ones, are of very rare occurrence and found only in small quantities in the mounds of the St. Johns River above Jacksonville.

Two and one-half feet from the surface was a portion of a superb lance head or dagger, of chalcedony, 6 inches in length. Judging from the point of fracture, the weapon may have been of considerably greater size. Weapons of this character are virtually absent from the mounds of the Ocklawaha and of the St. Johns though the type is not unknown in Florida. Some years ago a hoard of similar ones was unearthed by the workmen of a construction train, not far from Palatka. The find, seven in all, if our memory serves, was unfortunately scattered, though one, which we have seen, is in the possession of Andrew E. Douglass, Esq., of the Museum of Natural History, New York, and one of the smaller specimens, which also we have examined, of milk white chert, 11 inches in length, is owned by Mr. Fry, of Palatka.

An arrow head of chalcedony lay at a depth of 6.5 feet. Throughout the mound were various chippings of chert.

COPPER.

In caved sand was a bead .25 of one inch in length, of copper somewhat thicker than the usual sheet copper of the mounds of the St. Johns.

Fig. 79.—Pendant of copper. Gamble mound. (Full size.)

A massive bead, or rather a pendant of copper, has a maximum diameter of .86 of one inch; maximum thickness of band, .34 of one inch; maximum width of band, .58 of one inch. A groove showing continued wear was apparent on the inner surface (Fig. 79). During all our work on the St. Johns River we have found no ornaments of copper other than those wrought from thin sheets, and why beads of the Ocklawaha, which are made in the same manner, as their overlapping margins testify, are more generously supplied with metal, we are unable to decide.

CONCLUSIONS.

Nothing from the Gamble mound suggested an origin other than pre-Columbian.

HOPSON MOUND, LAKE COUNTY.

At Emeralda, in the orange grove of Robert L. Hopson, Esq., of that place, to whom we are indebted for cordial permission to investigate, was an interesting little mound. It had long been under cultivation, and had suffered considerable diminution in height through the agency of the plow. It had sustained but little previous examination. Its height was 4 feet 2 inches; its base diameter, 42 feet. It was carefully dug through at a level considerably below that of the surrounding territory, since, in nearly all the Florida mounds examined by us, some sort of excavation seems to have been made previous to the erection of the mound proper.

The upper 3 feet was composed of yellow sand, beneath which was sand of a dark color to a depth of 2 to 3 feet. Charcoal was abundant, and numerous fire-places were encountered throughout the mound. Several pockets of sand colored red with *Hematite* were at various depths.

HUMAN REMAINS.

Human remains were numerous. The usual bunched burial prevailed, with, in addition, isolated bones scattered throughout the mound. None was in condition to justify preservation.

One foot from the surface, though of course originally at a considerably greater depth, lay a skull in fragments, the shaft of a femur, a large part of a humerus, and an os innominatum, entirely unaffected by fire, in immediate association with fragments of charcoal and small portions of calcined bones, some unmistakably human and others too small for identification.

At various other points in the mound were fragments of human bones affected by fire.

STONE.

Six polished "celts," as a rule unassociated, were found separately at from 3 to 6 feet from the surface. None exceeded 4 inches in length.

At various depths in the mound, separately, were twelve arrow points, while together, about 6 feet down, almost in contact with a fire place, were four arrow heads. These sixteen projectile points, all of chert or of chert breccia, were in each case in a more or less imperfect condition. We have noticed in many mounds a strong aboriginal tendency to be rid of imperfect objects through mortuary deposit and to discharge a duty with as little cost as possible.

Separately, were three pendants of quartz, grooved for suspension, none over two inches in length, one tapered to a point, somewhat resembling an arrow head.

At at least half a dozen points in the mound, sometimes associated with human remains and with other objects, were sheets of mica, some so large as 3.5 inches by 5 inches. One had the form of a circle with a diameter of 3.25 inches.

A few chippings of chert were scattered throughout the mound.

SHELL.

At various points, always with human remains, were beads of shell, at times in considerable numbers. Some were very minute, others nearly 1 inch in length.

As a rule, separately and at all depths, were a number of ellipsoidal objects of shell, imperforate, none over 1 inch in length.

A considerable number of mussel shells were at one point in the mound.

COPPER.

A small tubular bead of copper lay 3.5 feet from the surface, while, with a large number of shell beads 1 foot down, were minute fragments of thin sheet copper.

With human remains, 5 feet 2 inches from the surface, lay an ornament of sheet copper, 1.3 inches by 1.5 inches. Four flutings ran parallel to the lesser diameter. Unfortunately, this object was badly injured by a blow of a spade.

Five feet from the surface, with human remains and associated with many shell beads, a thick sheet of mica, a small shark's tooth, three canines of some large carnivore (one perforated for suspension, the others broken at a point preventing determination), a pendant of quartz, and a small ellipsoidal object of shell, was a disc of thin sheet copper, about .66 of one inch in diameter, resembling certain ones taken by us from Mt. Royal, and figured in one instance in our account of that mound.

EARTHENWARE.

The chief feature of this interesting little mound was the earthenware with which it was filled. Sherds were abundant at all points, while vessels in fragments were numerous, and unbroken ware not uncommon. In the case of one sherd, interesting raised decoration was noticed around the aperture; another bore incised ornamentation; but with these two exceptions, the sherds, when ornamented, showed the use of crimson pigment exclusively, usually consisting of a uniform coat.

No gritty ware was present in the mound, and, as a rule, the pottery was of very inferior quality.

Three feet from the surface, unassociated, was a small globular pendant of earthenware, with projecting neck grooved for suspension.

Three neatly made beads of earthenware of about the same size, the dimensions of one being 1.1 inches by 1 inch by .8 of one inch, lay together with a portion of an arrow head, 3.5 feet from the surface.

Many vessels, some evidently of considerable size, were represented by portions only, and these, being in comparatively small fragments, were not preserved.

An interesting vessel, scaphoid in shape, imperforate as to the base, with inverted rim, had a uniform coat of crimson pigment inside and out. It was found unassociated, 3 feet from the surface. Length, 2.8 inches; width, 2.3 inches; average height, 1.4 inches: diameter of aperture, 2 inches by 1.3 inches (Plate LXXXVI, Fig. 1).

An undecorated circular bowl, with perforation of bottom made after baking, lay apparently unassociated, 3 feet 8 inches from the surface. Height, 2.2 inches; diameter of opening, 4.2 inches.

Near a fire-place, with charred human remains, 5 feet 2 inches from the surface, was a vessel of inferior ware but of interesting design, consisting of two nearly circular bowls joined, originally with projecting handles 1 inch in length, one from the outside of each. One handle was missing through breakage. Each bowl had a portion of the base knocked out after completion. Dimensions of one bowl, applying to both in the main: height, 1.4 inches; length, 2.8 inches; width, 2.4 inches (Plate LXXXV, Fig. 2). This unusual form of a double bowl, may be a highly conventionalized form representing the open bivalve. We have seen the type before, on one occasion from Mt. Royal, and several times from the low mounds bordering the St. Johns between Jacksonville and the sea. General Thruston figures[1] an artistic double vessel much more directly pointing to the shell, as from Tennessee.

Two and one-half feet from the surface was a globular bowl with perforation of base after baking. A small hole on either side of the mouth had served for the purpose of suspension. This vessel, with a height of 3.7 inches, a maximum diameter of 4.5 inches and a diameter at aperture of 3 inches, was completely filled with mussel shells. We do not recall the discovery by us before of any object in vessels from Florida mounds with the exception of certain pebbles in one instance, and an occasional vessel of inferior size placed within a larger one.

A globular vessel and a bowl, both undecorated and both wanting a portion of the bottom through breakage done after manufacture, lay together, 4 feet 8 inches from the surface.

Six feet down, beneath human remains, was an imperforate bowl with oval section, decorated with red pigment inside and out. Depth, 2 inches; length, 4.2 inches; breadth, 3.6 inches.

An unassociated vessel, 3 feet 6 inches down, with oval aperture and with portion of bottom knocked out, had a coating of red pigment on the outside and on the inside a band of the same color 3 to 4 inches in width, beginning at the margin. Height, 8 inches; average diameter of aperture, 10.5 inches. This vessel was somewhat broken by pressure of sand.

With fragments of a large bowl 1.5 feet from the surface, was an urn with flaring rim and red pigment decoration on outside and part way down the interior. Height, 7.7 inches; maximum diameter, 8.8 inches; width of top with rim, 6.8 inches; diameter of aperture, 5.5 inches. A portion of the bottom is missing through breakage after manufacture. Near this urn lay an undecorated globular vessel of ordinary type.

One foot three inches from the surface, with human remains immediately above, were two flaring basins of the same pattern and of approximately the same size, recalling in shape a basin from Thursby mound shown in Plate XXVI, Fig. 1, in Part II of our Report on the St. Johns mounds. Traces of red pigment are apparent on both sides of one and interiorly on the other. Height, 4.5 inches; maximum diameter, including the flaring rim, 18 inches. One bowl lay face down, while the other, also inverted, lay upon it, covering about one-half its base.

[1] "Antiquities of Tennessee."

Associated with human remains, about 5 feet from the surface, were two trough-shaped vessels of earthenware. With them was another of similar pattern with one of the ends omitted in manufacture, while a fourth showed marked concavity of one end (Plate LXXXV, Fig. 5). These specimens of mortuary "freaks" in earthenware had each a perforation in the base made previous to baking. Traces of red pigment were apparent on some. But one of the four was in perfect condition. Largest, 6 inches by 3.5 inches by 1.5 inches high. Smallest, 4.1 inches by 2.8 inches by 1.2 inches high.

Five feet from the surface, though not at the same point as the vessels just described, the smaller inverted within the other, were two trough-shaped vessels nearly similar to the others but imperforate as to the base. The larger, 5.6 inches by 3.1 inches by 1.4 inches high, has traces of red pigment inside and out (Plate LXXXV, Figs. 3 and 4). The smaller is undecorated. Its dimensions are approximately 5 inches by 2.5 inches by 1.3 inches high. We have never before met with this curious type of earthenware.

At various depths were four other vessels of ordinary type, somewhat crushed by weight of sand but capable of restoration.

REMARKS.

Nothing in any way indicating contact with the Whites was discovered in the Hopson mound.

Mound near Higley, Lake County.

About one mile south of Higley, on property belonging to Mr. Hart, in whose absence we are indebted to Mr. W. J. Young, of Higley, for permission to investigate, was a mound in pine woods, within sight of the western bank of Lake Yale, 5 feet 4 inches in height, with a diameter of base of 65 feet. This mound had previously been dug into to a considerable extent, the immediately central portion having been removed. The mound had doubtless in former times been of considerably greater altitude.

It was totally destroyed.

It was composed of yellow sand with occasional pockets of white sand and sand scarlet from admixture of *Hematite*.

Human remains, fragmentary and much decayed, were infrequently met with.

Sherds were mostly plain, though one of good material showed very neat square stamped decoration, separated at intervals by parallel, perpendicular, incised lines (Plate LXXXVI, Fig. 2).

With human remains, 2 feet from the surface, about 1 foot apart, were two polished hatchets. One arrow head came from a depth of 3 feet. From a like depth was taken an oblong, flat, perforated pendant of shell, with rounded corners, 1.7 inches long, 1.2 inches wide, .7 of one inch thick.

Beyond these, no objects of interest were encountered.

REMARKS.

The amount of previous investigation sustained by this mound renders accurate conclusions impossible.

Mound near Umatilla, Lake County.

This mound, about two and one-half miles west of Umatilla, lay in the grove of Mr. R. McS. Byrnes. Mr. J. F. Holton, superintendent of the grove, kindly consented to the investigation. The mound had long been under cultivation, and was evidently much reduced in height. It had, moreover, sustained much pre-

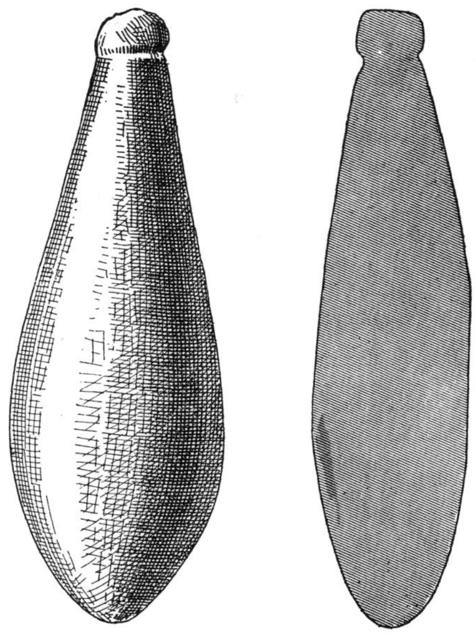

Fig. 80.—Pendant of shell with antero-posterior section. Mound near Umatilla. (Full size.)

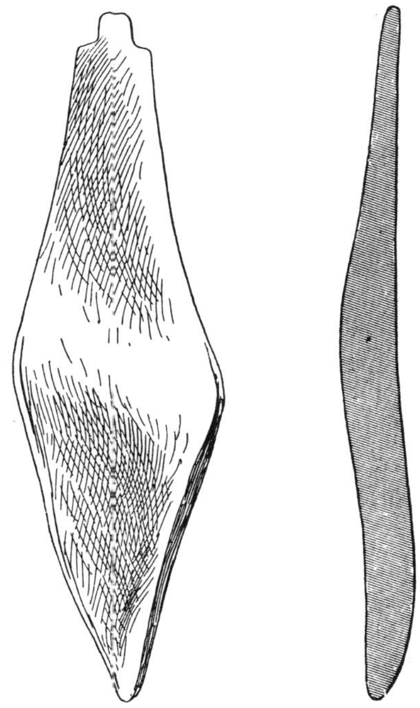

Fig. 81.—Pendant of shell. Mound near Umatilla. (Full size.)

vious examination with a reported yield of numerous objects of interest. Its height was 4 feet; its basal diameter, 46 feet. It was completely dug through.

No stratification was apparent, yellow sand with the usual admixture of charcoal composing the mound. Occasional fire-places were scattered throughout. Scattering pockets of white sand and numerous streaks and pockets of sand, pink from the use of the red oxide of iron, were present.

Human remains in the usual bunched form of burial were abundant.

From depths indicating original deposit came: one small bowl of earthenware, imperforate as to base, with single perforation for suspension on either side below the margin and with punctate and incised linear decoration, as shown in Plate LXXXVI, Fig. 3 (height, 2.3 inches; maximum diameter, 2.4 inches); a small, rude, undecorated, oblong vessel with rounded corners and perforation of base subsequent to completion; separately three arrow heads, thin and carefully made; two shell pendants, one wrought from the lip of the great marine univalve, *Strombus gigas* (Fig. 80), the other, diamond shaped, from the body whorl of the conch (*Fulgur*) (Fig. 81); a number of shell beads with human remains.

REMARKS.

Nothing from this mound gave evidence of other than aboriginal art.

MOUND NEAR FORT MASON, LAKE COUNTY.

About one mile northwest of Fort Mason, just south of Lake Yale, on the property of Mr. G. D. Jackson, was a mound 50 feet in diameter of base and 2 feet in height, though considerable depressions from which material had been taken gave the mound the appearance of greater altitude.

The mound was completely demolished, the excavation being carried to a level considerably lower than that of the surrounding territory. Mr. W. J. Gladwell, manager of the property, to whom, in the absence of the owner, we are indebted for permission to dig, informed us that the land containing the mound had been cleared by him two years previously, and that subsequent cultivation had lessened the height of the mound by about one foot.

Unlike other mounds demolished by us on the Ocklawaha, the method of burial in this mound was in anatomical order in various forms of flexion. In all, fifteen skeletons were encountered, in such condition, however, that no crania were preserved. In the majority of cases, skeletons lay from 1 foot to 18 inches beneath the surface.

Sherds were fairly numerous, but not in association with human remains. They lay loose in the sand, and were probably gathered with it from the surface during the formation of the mound. The majority were undecorated; the square stamp appeared upon one or two occasions, and once a punctate decoration.

With one burial was an iron spike; with another, an iron or steel hunting knife 9 inches in length, including the projection for the handle, no other trace of which remained. Both knife and spike were badly affected by rust.

Three skeletons had each one polished stone "celt" in association. Another "celt" lay loose in the sand.

With a skeleton, in contact with the lower jaw and cervical vertebræ, were: beads of shell and numerous minute shells (*Olivella*) longitudinally perforated for use as beads; a carbonized ball about 1 inch in diameter, of bark or some kindred material many times rolled upon itself; a tubular bead of sheet silver with overlapping edges, 1.3 inches in length and .3 of one inch in diameter, and a tubular bead of sheet copper 2 inches in length and .25 of one inch in diameter. Whether this copper bead was wrought from metal obtained from the Whites or was a purely aboriginal ornament made from native[1] copper, we have not determined by analysis, which, however, could readily be done.

It may not be out of place here to explain to the reader who may not have seen our monograph on aboriginal copper, contained in Part II of our Report on the St. Johns River mounds, that chemical analysis can readily distinguish *native* copper from the product of *smelting* of any ores obtainable in Europe during any possible mound-building period. In the first place, native copper, in use among our aborigines, was purer than the copper resulting from early smelting processes. And again, lead, almost universally present in the products of European smelting, is never found in native copper. Moreover, any copper that has been in a state of fusion contains a small percentage of *combined* oxygen which is entirely absent from native copper. Still further, most native copper is free from arsenic, while in Europe the copper supply was obtained from highly arsenical *sulphide ores*. Even now, arsenic cannot be totally eliminated from copper and was much less readily excluded in early times.

To return to the mound. A large shell bead wrought from the lip of *Strombus* lay with a skeleton, while elsewhere in the mound were a *Fulgur perversum* and a curved cylindrical ornament of shell, with tapering ends, possibly for use in the lobe of the ear.

On the surface of the mound was a copper or brass-coated convex bit of wood, almost circular, with double perforation.

Throughout the mound were four arrow heads and a number of chippings and flakes, of chert; also a small chipped "celt" somewhat broken.

With human remains was a small bowl with stamped decoration, the bottom of which had been knocked out subsequent to manufacture.

REMARKS.

In this interesting little mound we have a good example of the tumuli raised in undoubtedly post-Columbian times[2] for mortuary purposes. Here we have the polished "celt" at the same depth in the mound as iron, and other objects probably of European origin are found side by side with articles purely aboriginal. It is interesting to note the survival of the perforation of the base in pottery—the killing of the vessel—to a comparatively late period.

MOUND ON LAKE EUSTIS, LAKE COUNTY.

On the northern shore of Lake Eustis, about one mile west of Fort Mason, in a field belonging to Mr. J. T. Wofford, were two low mounds about fifty yards

[1] The reader will recall that native copper is copper found in nature, with no elements in chemical combination.

[2] In all the mounds examined by us in Florida, including virtually every known tumulus on the St. Johns River, in addition to those described in this paper, we have encountered but two mounds—this, and one near Bayard Point, Clay County, about 4 feet in height—where articles of European make were other than superficial. July, 1895.

apart. The larger one, the nearer to the lake, was completely dug through by permission of the owner. Its height was 2 feet 5 inches; its base diameter, 48 feet.

The most careful search failed to reveal any trace of human remains.

Loose throughout the sand were: numbers of chips and flakes, of chert; two bits of quartz; a hone of sandstone with double groove, and several rude cutting and piercing implements of chipped chert, whole and fragmentary.

MOUND NEAR TAVARES, LAKE COUNTY.

In the "scrub," about one mile southwest from the town of Tavares, the county seat of Lake, was a mound about 5 feet in height and about 50 feet across the base. It had sustained considerable previous investigation. It was completely dug down by us.

Its composition was peculiar. The northern portion, unstratified, was of pure white sand, while the section to the south was made up of sand of a brownish yellow color. The usual charcoal and fire-places were present.

Bunched burials were in considerable numbers. The very fragmentary condition of the bones rendered useless any attempt at preservation.

No whole vessels were discovered nor any represented by a full complement of fragments. Sherds were fairly numerous and at times indicative of large vessels. Undecorated fragments and those adorned with red pigment predominated. One, with somewhat striking ornamentation, is shown in Plate LXXXVI, Fig. 4.

A portion of a small oblong dish with rounded corners had the somewhat unusual addition of feet.

No copper was met with in the mound but a portion of a human clavicle dyed a bright green indicated the former presence of the metal.

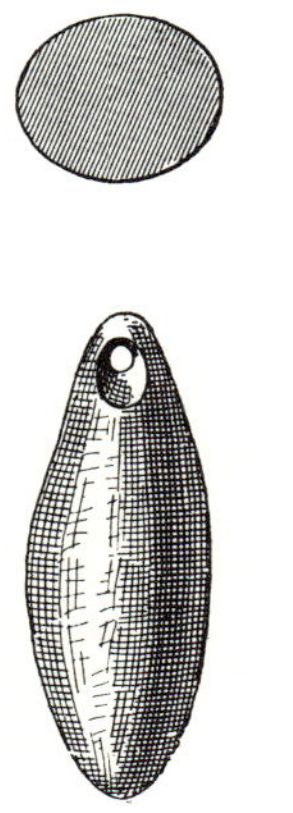

Fig. 82.—Pendant of igneous rock. Mound near Tavares. (Full size.)

Two and one-half feet from the surface, with human remains, together, were a number of shell beads and four ellipsoidal objects shaped from columellæ of marine univalves, 3 inches to 5 inches in length. Singly, in various portions of the mound, were five similar objects of shell, two pear-shaped pendants of like material, and two shell beads of considerable size.

A cube of galena, 1.4 inches by 1 inch by .7 of one inch, apparently shows wear on one side.

As in the case of the Gamble mound, the feature of the mound near Tavares was pendent ornaments.

A graceful ellipsoidal pendant of fine-grained, compact rock of igneous origin, 1.3 inches in length, is perforated at one end for suspension (Fig. 82). Another, of a compact crystalline igneous rock, *Dolerite* or *Diorite*, pear-shaped, has a rim for suspension.

A small pendant of banded red jasper lay loose in the sand.

Found separately, but from the same portion of the mound, were four pendent ornaments, two of syenitic and two of sedimentary rock, ranging in length between 3.4 inches and 2.9 inches, each perforated at one end, three transversely, one from front to back, and more or less rounded at the other end (Figs. 83, 84, 85, 86). In one instance, one side has an incised longitudinal line. In the case of three others the line is represented by a deep groove. One is highly polished. This type is new to us, though we have figured[1] something similar in Part I as coming from the low mound in the pine woods back of Duval's, Lake County, a duplicate of which, as to type but larger, is shown in "The Archæological Collection of the United States National Museum," Charles Rau, figure 322, page 90.

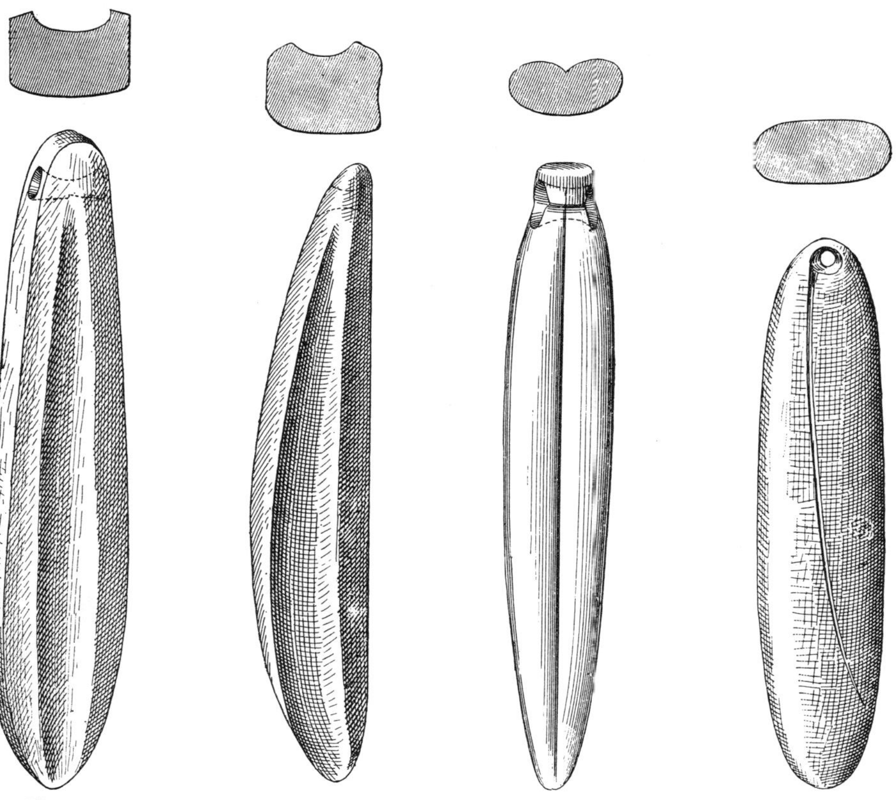

Fig. 83. Fig. 84. Fig. 85 Fig. 86.
Pendent ornaments. Mound near Tavares. (Full size.)

An interesting discovery, since the type, we believe, is hitherto unreported from Florida, was an effigy of igneous rock, probably *Diorite*, representing a bird at rest. The length is 2.1 inches; maximum width, 1.2 inches. The wings are clearly defined, while the tail spreads out to afford a means for suspension. The head, unfortunately, is missing. This type, the bird amulet, is well known to

[1] *Op. cit.*

archæologists as found in many sections,[1] though this particular specimen offers many points of variation from the forms usually encountered (Fig. 87).

Separately, in two cases with human remains and once in caved sand, were three polished "celts," one having a length of 10 inches.

At various depths were: several fragmentary arrow heads of chert; two small and gracefully shaped points of like material; a lance head of chipped chert, 4.7

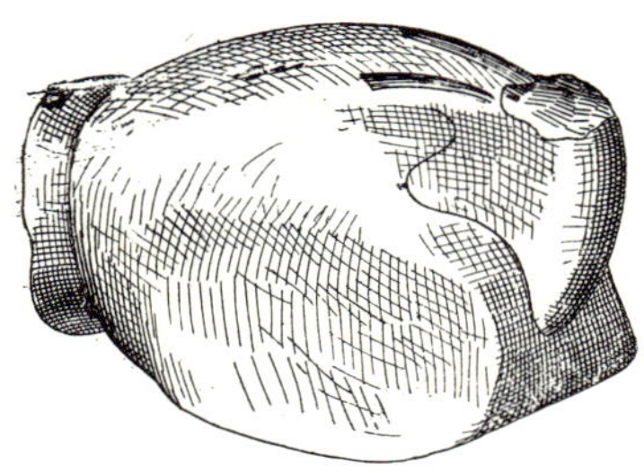

Fig. 87.—Bird amulet of igneous rock. Mound near Tavares. (Full size.)

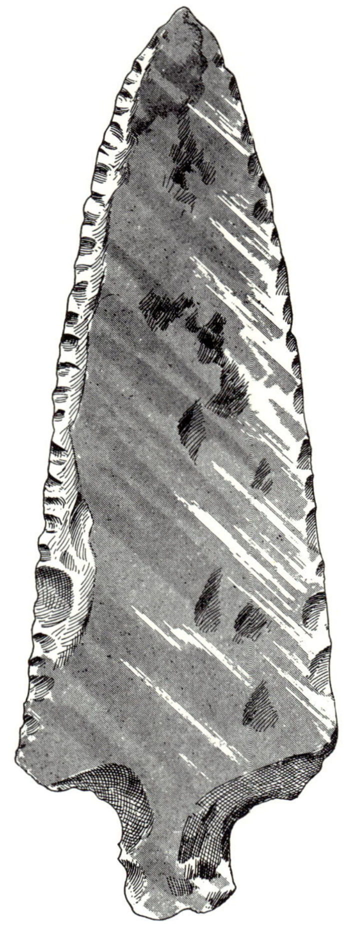

Fig. 88.—Polished spear head of red jasper. Mound near Tavares. (Full size.)

inches in length; another slightly larger, of red jasper, with a high polish on either side, a very unusual feature (Fig. 88).

A number of chippings of chert lay scattered throughout the mound.

We see no reason to ascribe to this mound an origin other than pre-Columbian,

[1] "Notes on Primitive Man in Ontario," David Boyle, page 67, *et seq.*
"Antiquities of the Southern Indians," C. C. Jones, page 374, *et seq.*
"Ancient Monuments, Miss. Valley," Squier and Davis, page 239.
"Smithsonian Arch. Coll.," Charles Rau, page 53.
"Primitive Industry," Abbott, chap. XXVI.

though a much smaller mound in the neighborhood, completely dug through by relic hunters, is generally reported to have contained articles of brass or of bronze, while at the time of our visit glass beads were present on its surface.

Mound at Barclay's, Lake County.

On the southernmost extremity of Lake Harris is the property of Mr. C. M. Barclay, upon which was a mound 2.5 feet in height with a diameter at base of 55 feet. It had long been under cultivation. A trench nearly traversing the mound and other excavations had been made by members of the family of Mr. Barclay, to whom our thanks are due for permission to demolish the mound.

The mound was composed of yellowish and brownish sand intermingled; the "dumps," or individual loads, being unusually well marked. In the northernmost portion streaks and pockets of brick-red sand were present, as was the usual charcoal throughout, often in pieces of considerable size.

But few interments were encountered by us, though the bunched form, scattered bones, and in one case, an original burial plainly in anatomical order, were present.

At various depths, always with human remains, were five polished hatchets of stone, three separately, two with the same burial.

Loose in the sand, were various flakes, chippings and broken arrow heads of chert, and four small, delicate ones of the same material.

Sherds were undecorated, or stamped in squares or diamonds. One small vessel, considerably broken, with bottom knocked out, had beneath the rim two encircling lines of punctate markings.

We obtained from Mr. Barclay, whose son, he assured us, found it in the mound, a bead of copper, 1.8 inches in length, with a maximum diameter of .6 of one inch. The shape is nearly ellipsoidal, though the ends do not agree as to diameter. It is made of copper hammered over in the usual fashion, and is more massive than any ornament of copper met with by us on the St. Johns, recalling in weight though not in shape, a heavy copper ornament from the Gamble mound.

A number of small shells (*Olivella*) used for beads, lay with one skeleton.

Two beads of blue glass were picked up on the immediate surface, but most careful search failed to reveal any in the body of the mound. One point noticeable in the majority of the Florida mounds was clearly emphasized in this one. While the height of the mound was but 2.5 feet above the surrounding level, it was necessary to go down 6 feet 4 inches from the surface before evidence of artificial construction came to an end, showing that, before the building of the mound, an excavation of some sort had been made. This custom obtained upon the St. Johns also, where, it will be remembered, when mounds were built upon pre-existing shell-heaps, one layer of burials was placed in the shell.

Richmond Mound, Lake County.

The Richmond mound, at Helena, near the southwestern shore of Lake Harris, was 12 feet high and 90 feet across the base. Pines of large size grew upon its surface. Though considerable previous investigation had been attempted in a desultory way, yet, so great was the bulk of the mound, that comparatively little material had been removed and the mound presented a symmetrical appearance.

Former explorers and residents of the neighborhood concurred in reporting negative results from previous investigation. Testimony of this character in relation to mound work may usually be accepted with safety.

We are indebted to the Reverend John F. Richmond, whose residence is near Helena, for cordial permission to investigate, and to his family for many courtesies.

The mound was totally demolished during six and one-half days of seven hours each with an average force of sixteen men surrounding the mound and throwing back.

There was no uniformity of stratification. The level of the surrounding territory was marked by a layer of brownish sand with a certain intermixture of charcoal and an occasional fire-place. Above, the body of the mound was composed of yellow sand of irregular thickness surmounted by a number of feet of brown sand. From the base almost to the summit were pockets and local layers of sand artificially colored a brick-red. One of these layers, from 1 to 6 inches in thickness, began on the southernmost side and continued at least half-way through the mound.

During the entire investigation, evidence of not exceeding ten interments, apparently of the bunched variety, was met with. During the second day, two crania were found separately at about 3 feet from the surface. On the fourth, a burial was found 9 feet down, while during the last day's work an interment was encountered at no great distance from the base. The burials were all in the last stage of decay, and were associated with no relics of any sort.

During the fifth day's work, one polished stone hatchet was met with near the surface. On the sixth day, five were discovered, of which four were comparatively superficial, while one was in caved sand. Six arrow heads lay separately, loose in the sand, one at a depth of 7 feet.

Sherds were of extreme rarity. On the base with charcoal, were two fragments of earthenware with a square stamped decoration.

REMARKS.

The Richmond mound is another example of the mass of sand sometimes thrown up for comparatively few interments. The hatchets found 2 or 3 feet from the top, were doubtless put in in a general way at the completion of the mound.

One would look for more interments and for a greater supply of art relics in a mound of this size where such care was shown as to construction.

Low Mound near Helena, Lake County.

In the grove of Messrs. Steiner Brothers, near Helena, was a mound which years of cultivation had reduced to a height of less than 2 feet and whose diameter, excluding later additions from above, was about 45 feet. We are indebted to Mr. William Henry Bennett, superintendent of the grove, for permission to investigate.

The mound, which was entirely dug through at a level considerably below that of the surrounding territory, was of yellowish sand, brownish at places, probably through admixture of organic matter.

The usual fire-places and fragments of charcoal in the sand, were observed.

Interments and art relics were virtually confined to the northwest portion of the mound, continuing well in toward the center; first, single burials, then almost a continuous layer. In all, fully thirty bodies were at least partially represented.

Sherds were abundant, both plain and decorated, with red pigment and a few ornamented with punctate curves. No whole vessels were discovered.

Numbers of flakes, chips and cores and imperfect and broken arrow heads lay at all points throughout the mound. With one burial were minute remnants of an ornament of thin sheet copper, while with another were small fragments of the metal with two flat oblong bits of earthenware, about 1 inch by 1.3 inches each, with rounded edges and central perforation, evidently cut from a broken vessel. These had not been overlaid with the copper, but simply interred in association (Fig. 89.)

With a single burial, not far from the northwestern margin was a highly polished and beautifully made pendent ornament of a rock which we have not identified through hesitation to mutilate so beautiful a specimen. In type it resembles one from the mound at Tavares, though in addition to the median groove on one side, it has incised line decoration at the upper end while the lateral perforation unites with one from the top to allow perfect perpendicularity of suspension. Length, 3 inches; maximum diameter, about .4 of one inch (Fig. 90).

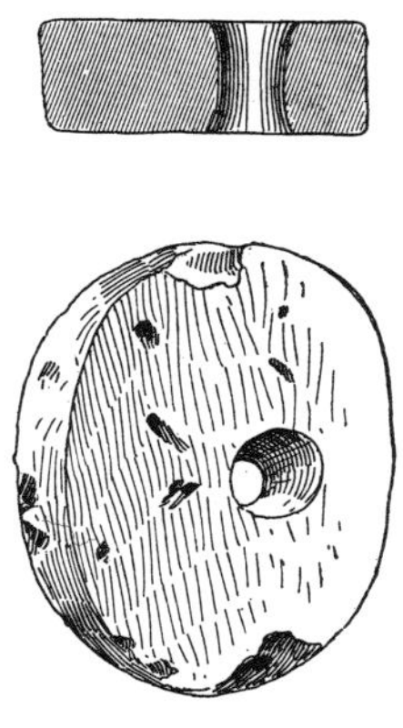

Fig. 89.—Ornament of earthenware. Low mound near Helena. (Full size.)

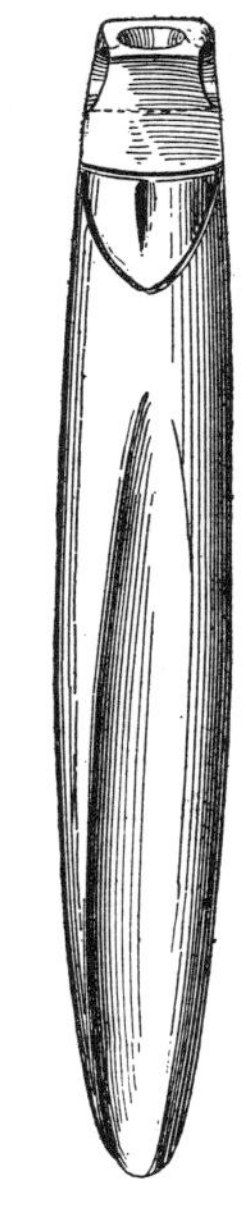

Fig. 90.—Pendent ornament. Low mound near Helena. (Full size.)

Mound near Old Okahumpka, Lake County.

About one-half mile, in a northwesterly direction from Old Okahumpka, in the orange grove of Robert A. Green, Esq., of Ocala, was a low mound, for years under cultivation and doubtless much reduced in height. Its altitude at the time of its total demolition by us was less than 2 feet above the surrounding level though most of the human remains and accompanying art relics came from a depth of from

Fig. 91.—Fragment of vessel of earthenware. Low mound near Old Okahumpka. (Full size.)

3 feet to 4.5 feet from the summit of the mound. The diameter of the base was about 40 feet.

The mound was composed of brownish sand apparently changed from the yellow of the surrounding territory by admixture of organic matter. It was unstratified. The usual scattered bits of charcoal and fire-places were present.

Human remains were numerous, the bunched form of burial being indicated.

In this mound, all art relics were in immediate contact with human remains. Pockets and streaks of sand colored by *Hematite* were not present.

STONE.

Numerous chips of chert were present in the mound, also one arrow head of the same material.

Seven "celts" of the usual rocks were found separately with human remains, and upon one occasion two lay in contact with long bones, one on either side of the mass.

With a bunched burial was a rude "celt" of sandstone, associated with a copper ornament.

EARTHENWARE.

Sherds, plain or decorated with red pigment, were very numerous. No vessels, whole or approximately so, were encountered.

We have obtained from Mr. Russell W. Bennett, of Helena, a sherd which he informs us was ploughed up from this mound. This fragment of earthenware, shown in Fig. 91, is of considerable interest, as possessing the only plastic effigy of the human face ever seen by us in Florida. This face, apparently modeled by hand, appears to have been constructed separately, and pressed onto the clay of the vessel previous to baking.

The reader will recall that this joining of heads to earthenware was prevalent in other sections. Upon but one other occasion in Florida have we seen a head of any sort serving as a decoration on the side of a vessel of earthenware and in that case a portion of a vessel from a low mound near the mouth of the St. Johns had the head of a duck, not added to it by pressure, but repoussé.

COPPER.

With bones tinged green from contact and in association with a few small shell beads were the remains of a long tubular bead of copper overlaid on a cylinder of fibrous wood.

Eighteen inches from the surface was a heavy bead of copper .7 of one inch by .6 of one inch, in contact with a human lower jaw which formed part of a bunched burial.

With a burial about 4.5 feet from the top of the mound was a sheet of copper, 2.8 inches by 6 inches, bent under and crumpled at one end. The two shorter and one larger side show a clean-cut edge, but the uneven appearance of one larger side proves but a portion of the plate to have been inhumed. The state of this copper sheet precludes inspection of the entire ornamentation which is repoussé and seems to be of an interesting character, entirely dissimilar from the usual lines of semi-perforations. With it were bark and some fibrous material, a rude "celt" of sandstone and a small core of chert.

SHELL.

With a burial were fifty-six beads of shell, many of unusual size, the largest 1.9 inches in length. Many were not symmetrical but were apparently perforated portions of great marine univalves such as are figured as massive beads in Holmes' "Art in Shell." With the beads was a polished stone hatchet.

REMARKS.

There seems to be no reason to connect this mound with a period subsequent to the coming of the Whites.

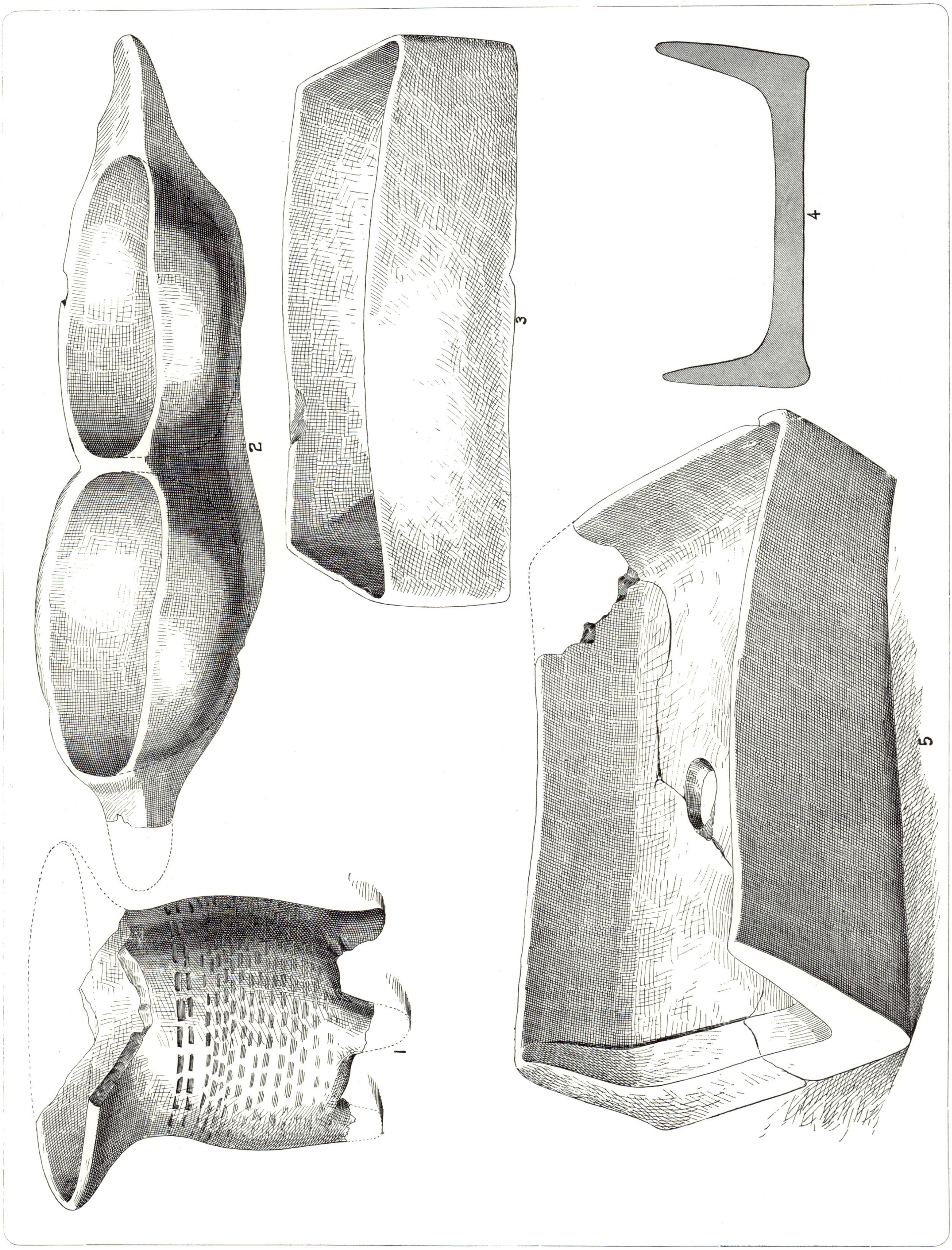

MOORE: SAND MOUNDS OF OCKLAWAHA RIVER, FLORIDA.

1. VESSEL OF EARTHENWARE WITH BASAL SUPPORTS, MOUND NEAR SILVER SPRINGS. (FULL SIZE.)
2. VESSEL OF EARTHENWARE WITH DOUBLE COMPARTMENT, HOPSON MOUND. (FULL SIZE.)
3. OBLONG DISH OF EARTHENWARE, HOPSON MOUND. (FULL SIZE.)
4. TRANSVERSE SECTION OF NUMBER 3. (FULL SIZE.)
5. OBLONG DISH OF EARTHENWARE, HOPSON MOUND. (FULL SIZE.)

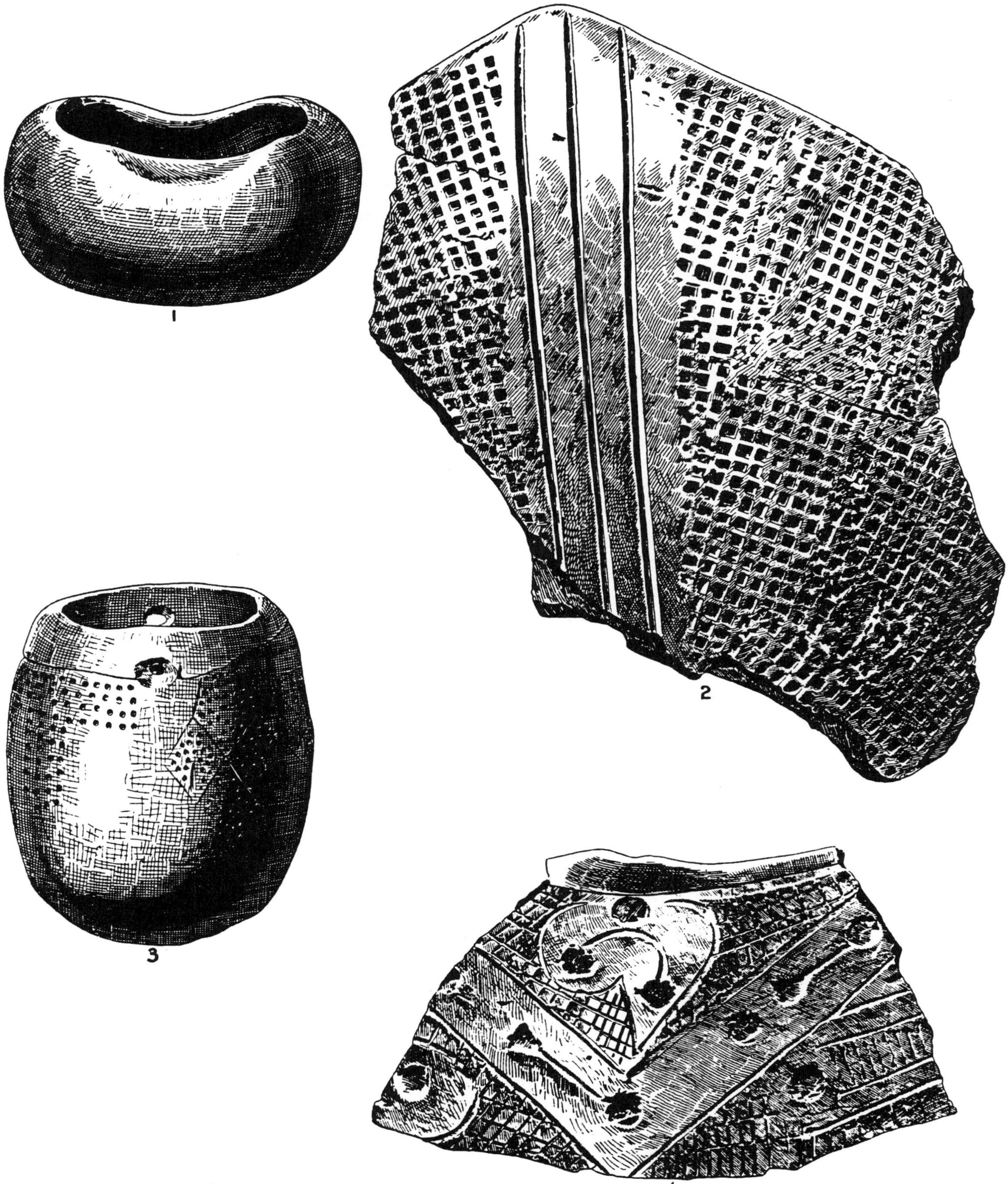

MOORE: SAND MOUNDS OF OCKLAWAHA RIVER, FLORIDA.

1. BOAT-SHAPED VESSEL OF EARTHENWARE, HOPSON MOUND. (FULL SIZE.)
2. SHERD WITH STAMPED AND INCISED DECORATION, MOUND NEAR HIGLEY. (FULL SIZE.)
3. VESSEL OF EARTHENWARE, INCISED AND PUNCTATE DECORATION, MOUND NEAR UMATILLA. (FULL SIZE.)
4. SHERD, MOUND NEAR TAVARES (FULL SIZE).

Certain Antiquities of the Florida West-Coast

BY

CLARENCE B. MOORE

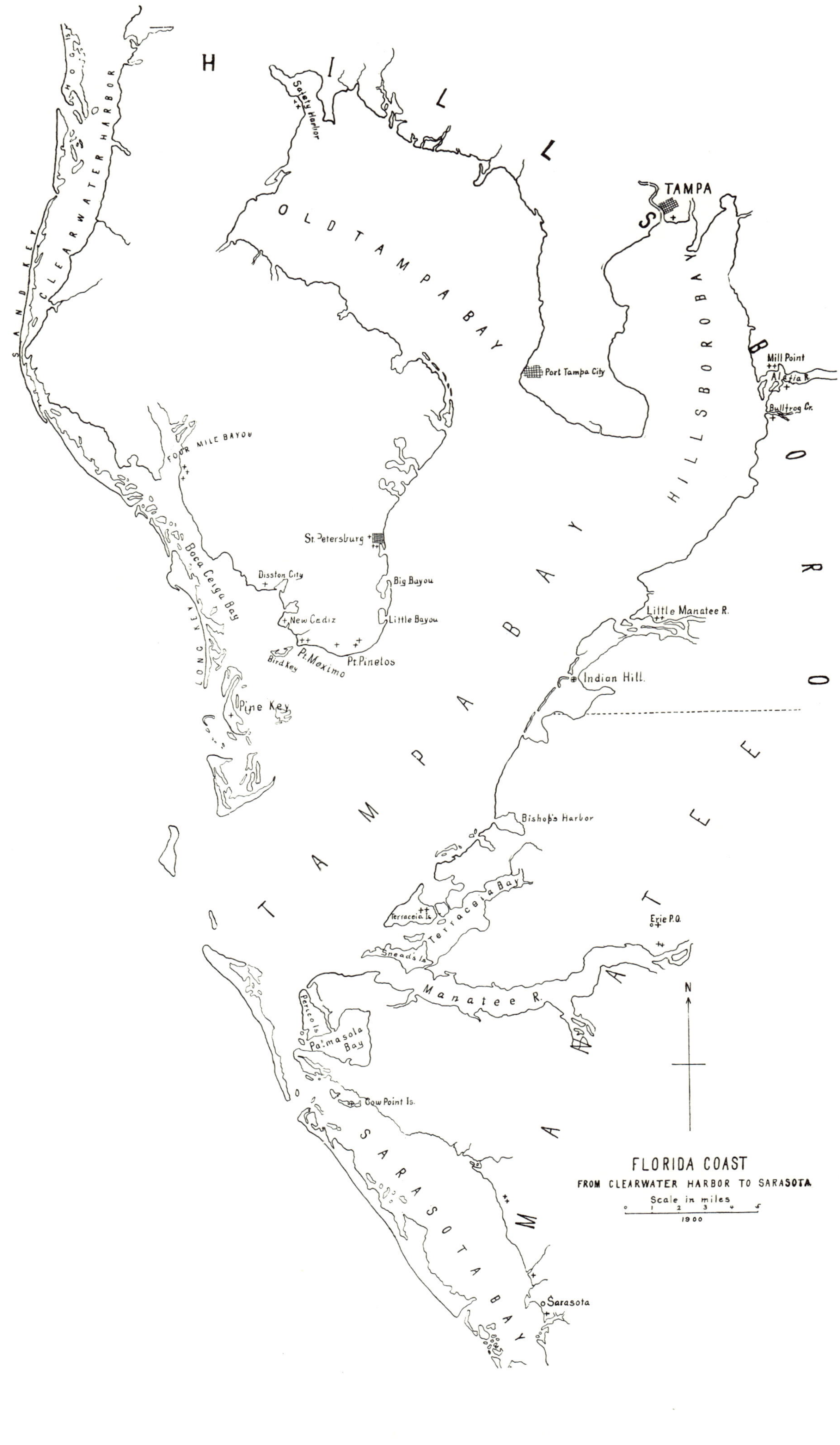

FLORIDA COAST

FROM CLEARWATER HARBOR TO SARASOTA

CERTAIN ANTIQUITIES OF THE FLORIDA WEST-COAST.

By Clarence B. Moore.

During the past eight years we have made certain investigations of aboriginal remains in the southern United States with the aid of a large flat-bottomed steamer containing a corps of assistants and numbers of trained men to dig. The results of these investigations have been embodied in reports appearing in the Journal[1] of the Academy of Natural Sciences of Philadelphia, where the collections made by us during our work are deposited.

Several years ago we explored the mounds bordering the Florida east-coast, following the footsteps of Mr. Andrew E. Douglass, of the Museum of Natural History, New York, finding, as he did, but little of comparative interest in the mounds of that section.[2]

A certain amount of investigation of the aboriginal remains of the west coast of Florida has been made by Mr. S. T. Walker, the results appearing in the reports of the Smithsonian Institution, Washington, D. C., for the years 1879 and 1883.

The data obtained by Mr. Walker, while of interest, were not of a nature to encourage farther archæological work on the west coast, and had it not been for the remarkable discoveries made in the muck on the upper end of the island of Marco, almost the northernmost key[3] of the Ten Thousand Islands, which border the Florida west-coast along the counties of Lee and Monroe, it is not likely a visit would have been made by us to the Florida west-coast. But when the magnificent collection, mainly of objects of wood, was shown us by Mr. Frank Hamilton Cushing, and we had studied his brilliant preliminary report,[4] we resolved to visit the west coast of Florida, and did so during about three and one-half months of the winter of 1900, to make a reconnoissance, as it were, to determine whether or not a series of seasons could profitably be spent by us in making a thorough examination of what might prove to be so rich a field.

1 "Certain Sand Mounds of the St. Johns River, Florida." Parts I and II, Journ. A. N. S. P., Vol. X, 1894.

"Certain Sand Mounds of Duval County, Florida. Two Mounds on Murphy Island, Florida. Certain Sand Mounds of the Ocklawaha River, Florida." Journ. A. N. S. P., Vol. X, 1895.

"Certain Aboriginal Mounds of the Georgia Coast." Journ. A. N. S. P., Vol. XI, 1897.

"Certain Aboriginal Mounds of the Coast of South Carolina. Certain Aboriginal Mounds of the Savannah River. Certain Aboriginal Mounds of the Altamaha River." Journ. A. N. S. P., Vol. XI, 1898.

"Certain Aboriginal Remains of the Alabama River." Journ. A. N. S. P., Vol. XI, 1899.

2 "Additional Mounds of Duval and Clay Counties, Florida. Mound Investigation on the East coast of Florida. Certain Florida Coast Mounds North of the St. Johns River." [Privately printed.]

3 An island, from the Spanish *cayo*.

4 "Exploration of Ancient Key-dweller Remains on the Gulf Coast of Florida." Proceedings of the American Philosophical Society, Vol. XXV, No. 153.

During the summer of 1899, G. W. Rossignol, formerly captain of our steamer, and thoroughly familiar with aboriginal remains, accompanied by a companion knowing the territory, made a journey along the coast from Anclote Key on the north to the Caloosahatchee river on the south, including the shores of Tampa Bay. Great numbers of mounds and shell heaps were located by him and the addresses of the owners[1] secured, from nearly all of whom we obtained in advance permission to investigate, so that our labors were greatly expedited. Never before had we set out so thoroughly prepared for work and never did our efforts meet with so little success.

Our journey extended from near Clearwater Harbor on the north to Tampa Bay, and to such mounds on the Bay as seemed of most interest, including parts of the Alafia, the Little Manatee and the Manatee, rivers; through Sarasota Bay; down Pine Island Sound, including some of the keys described by Mr. Cushing; part of the Caloosahatchee river; Estero Bay with Mound Island; Key Marco; and the Ten Thousand Islands to the Chatham river, not far from the North-west Cape.

Four Mile Bayou, Hillsboro County.

Four Mile Bayou was the northernmost point on the coast visited by us.

On the east side of Four Mile Bayou, beginning at a small bayou that connects with the greater one, is a ridge of shell, 640 paces in length, running parallel with the water and only a few yards back from high water mark. The ridge, which runs N. by W. and S. by E., has been cut into to a certain extent by the removal of shell for use on streets of the town of Clearwater Harbor. The section exposed showed no artifacts other than a few bits of pottery with the check stamp. One hundred yards from the northern end the ridge is 64 feet across and 5 feet high. Two hundred yards farther along its altitude is 3 feet 7 inches; its breadth, 76 feet. Five hundred yards from the northern extremity it is 79 feet across and 4 feet 10 inches high. The southern end, for the last 150 feet, has a breadth of 50 feet and is 8 feet 6 inches high.

On the east side of Four Mile Bayou, on the property of Mr. J. F. Girard, living near by, is a mound 4 feet high and 58 feet across the base. This mound had a top layer of shell and black loam 1.5 feet thick. Next came about 1 foot of yellow sand and finally a layer of shell and loam about 1 foot 4 inches in thickness. A central excavation and lateral trenching indicated this mound to be of a domiciliary character.

About 300 yards in a northerly direction from Mr. Girard's place, in woods, on property belonging to Mr. George T. Chamberlain, of Tampa, is a mound thickly covered with scrub growth, having an irregular basal outline. Excavations, whence came material for the mound, are near its base, and a person standing at the bottom of one of these would form an incorrect idea as to the height of the mound, which, measured from the western side, apparently from the

[1] To owners of mounds who so readily and so cordially granted us permission to dig, we wish to tender our warm thanks.

general level, is 18 feet. The diameter of the mound north and south is 150 feet; east and west, 116 feet. The summit plateau is 60 feet by 28 feet.

Considerable digging led us to believe the mound to be of irregular local layers of shell and sand, covered with sand which, at the summit plateau, is about 3 feet in thickness. A few burials closely flexed were met with, none at a greater depth than 3 feet. While there was not sufficient digging to enable us to determine positively, it is our belief that this mound is of a domiciliary character with superficial burials.

About 150 yards N. N. W. from the mound just described, also on the property of Mr. Chamberlain, is another mound, the N. E. slope of which has been eaten away by a small stream.

Excavations made previous to our visit, and the great section laid bare by the stream, showed no presence of shell or indication of interments.

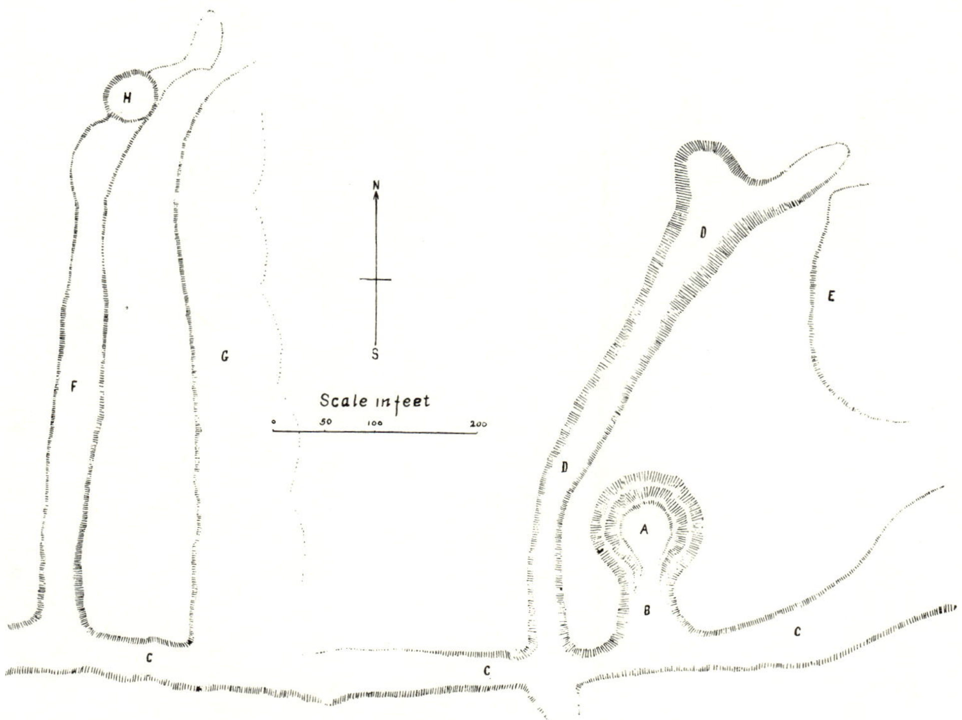

FIG. 1.—Plan of mounds and causeways, Point Maximo.

Disston City and New Cadiz are on the mainland a few miles south of Big Bayou. Small sand mounds on properties belonging to Mr. Martin Campos and Mrs. R. Barnett, yielded neither human remains nor artifacts.

POINT MAXIMO, HILLSBORO COUNTY.

Following the coast line down we come to Point Maximo. About half a mile in an easterly direction inland are several very interesting aboriginal works on the property of Mr. R. Strada, of St. Petersburg, Fla., who refused permission to dig. Thickly covered by palmettoes, is a mound marked A on the plan (Fig. 1), apparently of sand and shell, now having a small frame cabin on the summit. This mound, which is referred to by Mr. S. T. Walker,[1] nearly circular as to outline of base, has a diameter at base of a little over 100 feet. The height is 10 feet above the general level.

From the southern side of the mound a broad ridge of shell (B) connects the mound with another ridge (C) running parallel to the water. The remainder of the base is surrounded by an excavation from 1 to 2 feet in depth below the general level, though seemingly much deeper when looked down upon from ridges adjacent to the mound. In a westerly direction from the mound is a curious ridge (D), 700 feet long, running in a northeast by easterly and southwest by westerly direction, with a maximum height of 6 feet 9 inches and a maximum breadth of 70 feet. This causeway does not seem to be a deposit of shell, formed during aboriginal occupation, but rather built for a purpose, as parts of it are of shell and sand mingled; parts, shell and sand side by side; parts, all sand. Beginning near the northeastern terminus of the ridge another causeway (E), mainly of sand, extends about 250 feet in a southerly direction where it turns to the east, having approached at this point within 50 feet of the ridge (C), which leaves the southern side of the mound. The area enclosed between these ridges is about 1 foot 3 inches below the general level, and doubtless furnished material for the causeways.

Beginning with, and nearly at right angles to, the shell ridges (C) fronting the water, about 500 feet in a westerly direction from the principal mound, two embankments (F, G) extend in a northerly direction about 500 feet, terminating at a mound of sand (H) about 3 feet 6 inches above the general level and 55 feet across the base, approximately. The embankments converge from 131 feet between them where they leave the shell ridge to 17 feet where they join the mound.

The westernmost causeway is well defined; is of sand, where excavations were made; is from 35 feet to 53 feet in breadth and 1 foot 6 inches in height. The eastern embankment is less well marked and merges, on the other side, with the surrounding country. Two excavations of moderate size were made in the sand mound; one without result; the other yielding human remains, badly decayed, just below the surface.

The space included between the ridges varies from 2 feet 8 inches to 1 foot in depth, and has somewhat the appearance of a canal. Presumably the removal of material for the ridges is responsible for the depression.

In the territory back of Point Maximo are other embankments of considerable size which were not investigated by us through refusal of permission by the owner. Numerous small shell ridges not included in the plan lie to the east of mound A back of shell ridge C.

[1] Smithsonian Report, 1879, p. 404.

Mound on Pine Key, Hillsboro County.

Pine Key is one of the islands at the entrance to Tampa Bay. The mound described by Mr. Walker, is on the southernmost portion of Pine Key, which is divided into two parts by a small bayou. The mound, which is most difficult to find, being surrounded by trees and scrub growth, is about 300 yards in an E. S. E. direction from the southern end of a sheet of water called the Duck Pond, or about 50 yards in an easterly direction from a tongue, or continuation extending beyond the end of the lake. The tongue, itself apparently of artificial origin, is connected with the mound by a canal of irregular breadth, nowhere exceeding 58 feet, which, leaving the tongue at right angles, goes directly to the mound. The canal, at the present time, is not over 2 feet 3 inches in depth, though banks on either side make it appear considerably more.

The mound, which is very irregular, varies from 60 feet to 85 feet in diameter of base and is about 6 feet in height, taken from the general level. Deep depressions near parts of the base show whence the material for the mound was derived.

A number of small and shallow excavations were apparent.

Seven of our men dug 3.5 hours on parts of the mound previously undisturbed. The mound is made of unstratified white sand. Burials were met with at six points from 1 foot below the surface to 6 feet in depth. These burials were closely flexed in a manner to be described more particularly in our account of a mound on the Little Manatee river. With one burial were a number of massive beads of shell. With others were bits of earthenware vessels having incised and punctate decoration.

Mounds near Point Pinelos, Hillsboro County.

Point Pinelos is the southernmost extremity of the peninsula which bounds Tampa Bay on the west. On the property of Mr. Wm. B. Henderson, of Tampa, about three-quarters of a mile in from Point Pinelos, following a course N. W. by W., is an oblong mound with rounded corners, extending longitudinally almost due east and west. Its major diameter of base is 155 feet; its minor diameter, 47 feet. The summit plateau is 105 feet in length and 30 feet across at the center. Each extremity of the plateau is 19 feet across. Mr. S. T. Walker (Smithsonian Report, 1879, p. 407) gives this mound as No. 10 on his list, and gives the height as 25 feet. The exact altitude above the surrounding level is 16 feet 6 inches, and above the mass of sand which surrounds the base, 12 feet 6 inches. From the summit plateau to undisturbed sand at the base of the mound is a depth of 17 feet. The sides of the mound are precipitous, ascending at an angle of 30 degrees.

A graded way extends from the exact center of the southern side of the summit plateau almost due south, a distance of 112 feet. This causeway, made of sand with a sprinkling of shell, is 34 feet broad at its union with the mound and 23 feet across, 12 feet from its terminus.

The labor of seven men working five hours on a trench beginning 46 feet from the western end of the north side of the mound indicated the mound to be of irregular layers of sand and of shell, the exterior being of sand. Several bits of rude, undecorated ware, one fragmentary bone piercing implement, a bit of chert lance-head were the only relics met with.

One hundred and thirty feet N. from the eastern end of the mound is an excavation of circular outline, 91 feet in diameter and 6 feet 7 inches deep, from which sand for the mound was taken. Another excavation 94 feet by 78 feet, similar in character and of the same depth, lies 125 feet E. S. E. from the eastern end of the mound.

A number of low sand mounds in the neighborhood of the one described gave no feature of interest.

There are several low mounds near St. Petersburg, which have been dug into. In addition, in the town, on the property of Mr. J. A. Armistead, of St. Petersburg, who granted permission to investigate, are two mounds in a field. One is conical, of shell and very steep; the other, of sand, has a rather unpromising appearance.

At the northern extremity of old Tampa Bay, near Safety Harbor, permission to dig was refused.

Near Tampa are two mounds which have been dug through by treasure seekers, it is said.

Mounds on Alafia River, Hillsboro County.

The Alafia river runs into Hillsboro Bay, a part of Tampa Bay.

Riverview is a small settlement about 5 miles up the Alafia river. About 1 mile farther up on the opposite side of the river, somewhat back from the landing, is an unstratified sand mound where considerable digging was without result.

About one-half mile above the mouth of the river is Shell Bluff, the property of Mr. R. E. Gibson, in whose orange grove is a low, irregularly shaped sand mound about 2 feet in height, with a diameter of 55 feet at present time. Owing to presence of orange trees, trenching only was attempted. A considerable number of burials were met with, flexed and lying on the left side as a rule. No artifacts were with the remains.

Mill Point is less than one-half mile above the mouth of the Alafia river, on the right-hand side going down. At this point are a number of aboriginal works which are shown on the accompanying plan (Fig. 2). Investigation was made by us with the consent of Mr. W. B. Henderson, of Tampa, to whom we are indebted, in addition, for kindness shown us in other ways.

Along the banks of the river are shell ridges (A) with a maximum height of 8 feet. In rear of these ridges are shell fields and other ridges running back, not shown on the plan. Parallel with the water of a sort of bay to the east of the point, is a steep ridge of sand (B) terminating abruptly at either end, containing local layers of shell. A certain amount of investigation in this ridge, which is 148 feet long, about 62 feet wide at the base and somewhat over 11 feet high, gave no indication of interments. A roadway about 30 feet wide at its central part slopes upwards and joins the ridge about at right angles, near the center of the western side. The length of this roadway from its beginning to the mid-line of the ridge is 82 feet. Off the northern end of the ridge is a depression (C) with sloping sides, having a maximum depth of 4.5 feet, a maximum breadth of 56 feet and 96 feet in length. From this depression doubtless came material for the ridge. A short distance west of the ridge is a mound (D) very much spread out, which, apparently, has been under cultivation in earlier times. Its basal dimensions are 80 feet by 68 feet; its height, 4.5 feet. Various excavations showed it to be of white sand with a certain intermixture of loam, and local layers of shell. A few fragments of human bones lay near the surface.

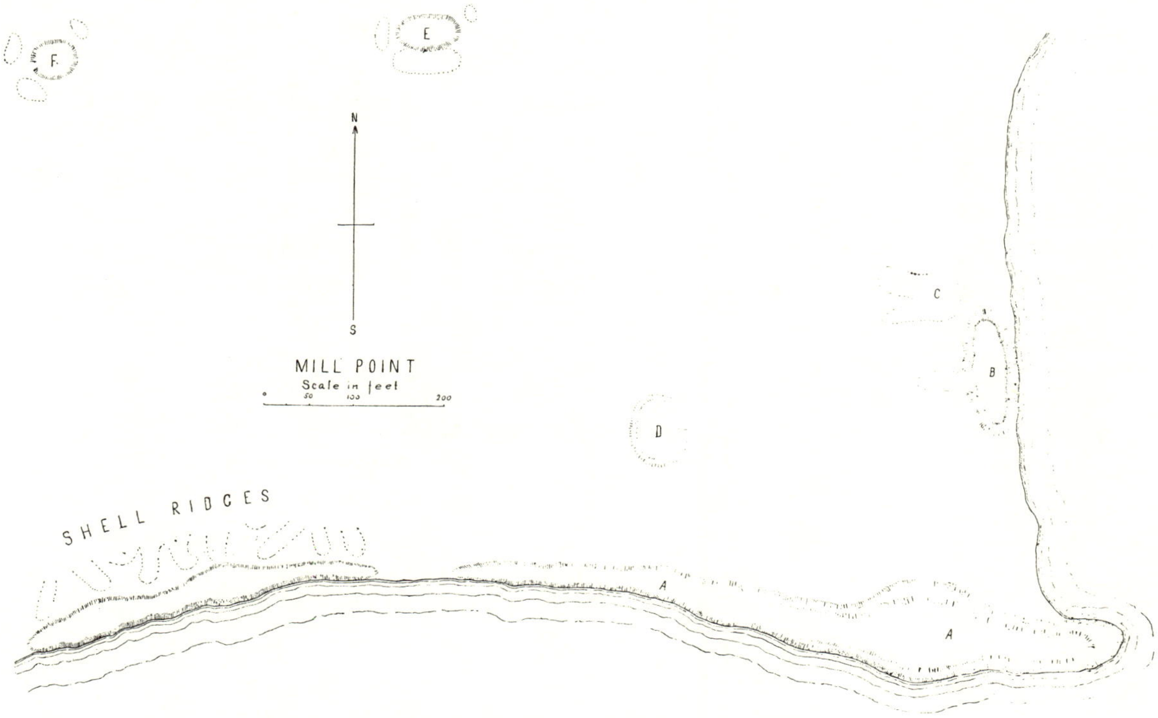

FIG. 2.—Plan of mounds and causeways near Mill Point.

Several hundred yards from this mound, in a northerly direction, in pine woods, on property of Mr. L. G. Newman, of Tampa, is a sand mound (E) about 3 feet in height. Considerable digging showed it to be domiciliary. A similar mound (F) but a short distance from the other yielded no result. Depressions around these mounds are shown in broken lines.

Bullfrog creek is a tributary of the Alafia river. On this creek was formerly a shell heap of considerable size. It is referred to by Mr. Walker in his list of shell heaps of Tampa Bay and its location given on a plan. This mound has since been largely demolished to furnish shells for the streets of Tampa, and its destruction was watched with interest by many. We are informed on all sides that no object of interest was met with during the work, and as this so closely agrees with our experience of the shell heaps of the west coast, we are inclined to accept it.

MOUND NEAR LITTLE MANATEE RIVER, HILLSBORO COUNTY.

On the north side of the Little Manatee river, about 1.5 miles up, is the residence of Mrs. Cordelia Hoey, on the summit of a great aboriginal shell heap, possibly one of those seen by DeSoto and his men. A short distance in a northerly direction from the house is a mound thickly covered with scrub, into which a small trench had been dug prior to our visit. The mound, irregularly circular and rather rugged as to its surface, has a base diameter of about 58 feet, a height of 6 feet. From the southwest side of the mound an aboriginal canal, almost straight, runs a distance of 238 feet to the water. Leaving the mound the canal is 64 feet across, converging to a width of 36 feet at its union with the water. The canal, in common with the field through which it runs, has been under cultivation, and consequently is irregular as to sides and bottom. The maximum depth is now 3 feet 3 inches, though, according to Mr. Hoey, twenty years ago, when first he came to the place, the sides were steeper and the canal about 2 feet deeper, so that high tides entered the field until a dam was placed across the mouth of the canal.

Beginning in the marginal part of the northeast side of the mound, a trench 35 feet across at the beginning was run 29 feet in to the center of the mound, where the trench had converged to a width of 9 feet. The mound was of pure white sand, unstratified. At the very outset burials were encountered. In all, 112 burials were met with, classing as such human remains with which the cranium was present and omitting a limited number of bones found loose in the mound. These burials were in a much greater state of flexion than we have usually seen in our mound work. The prevailing form of interment was a squatting position, the feet on a level with the pelvis, the legs against the thighs and these drawn up against the body. The upper arms were against the sides with the forearms sometimes raised parallel to the upper arms and sometimes on the chest, reaching to the neck. The head was bent over and forced down between the thighs, sometimes to the pelvis. Certain skeletons lay on the side with the same general arrangement of the extremities and the skull pressed over against the knees. So compact were these bundles of bones, which were not the bunched burial so often met with, where separate bones, not in order, are loosely piled in a heap, that we believe the skeletons in this mound, perhaps denuded of flesh, but held together by ligaments, were enveloped in wrapping of some sort and tightly bound with cord or sinew. One of these bundles of the average size was 23 inches long and about 26 inches in circumference.

The crania were so decayed and so injured by roots of palmetto scrub which covered the mound, that none was preserved.

In connection with human bones lying loose in the mound, and with probable denudation of flesh from the skeletons prior to interment, the reader will recall that it was near Tampa that DeSoto rescued Juan Ortiz, a member of a former Spanish expedition, who was found guarding from wild beasts, dead bodies of aborigines, exposed for a period prior to interment.

Under two crania was sand made pink by admixture of hematite. With, or in the immediate vicinity of, burials were: a shell drinking cup; a well-made bead of shell; a number of blue glass beads and two bits of lookingglass; a spear-head of chert; a large flake of the same material, doubtless used as a knife; a pebble hammer; a smoothing stone, apparently of lime rock; a fossil shark's tooth over 4 inches in length, considerably worked at the base, probably for hafting;[1] a polished pendant of stone, minus a portion of the base; a stone pendant, badly broken; a pendant, probably of fine-grained sandstone,[2] representing the head of a bird, of which, unfortunately, most of the bill is wanting (Fig. 3). Pendants in the form of birds have infrequently rewarded our search in southern mounds. In a mound near Tavares, Lake County, Florida, we found a bird amulet of igneous rock, the head of which was wanting.[3] We have seen, described and figured,[4] a beautiful pendant representing the head of a duck, which came from the Turkey creek mound, among a cache of other pendants, and is now in possession of Andrew E. Douglass, Esq., of the American Museum of Natural History, New York.

FIG. 3.—Pendant. Mound near Little Manatee river. (Full size.)

Throughout the mound were sherds mostly plain, though some bore incised, and some punctate, markings. One had stamped decoration.

About 400 yards E. by N. from the mound just described, in pine woods, is a mound 3 feet high and 72 feet in diameter, the property of Mr. J. A. Darcey, living nearby. A central excavation yielded neither burials nor artifacts.

INDIAN HILL, HILLSBORO COUNTY.

About 3 miles down Tampa Bay from the mouth of the Little Manatee river is an island known as Indian Hill, probably eight acres in extent, almost covered by an aboriginal deposit of shells, including oyster, clam, conch (*Fulgur*), cockle (*Cardium*), *Pecten*, *Strombus gigas*, *Strombus pugilis*, *Fasciolaria gigantea*, *Fasciolaria tulipa*. Part of the shell deposit is made of irregular mounds and ridges. At one extremity, however, the deposit rises steeply, forming a great heap seemingly composed of three mounds with depressions between. The circumference of base is 423 paces. The largest of these heaps has a height of 30 feet above the surrounding shell deposit and 36 feet 7 inches above water level. We believe, after personal inspection of the majority of Florida shell heaps and careful inquiry as to the rest,

[1] A shark's tooth similarly treated, was found by us in a mound on Ossabaw Island, Georgia, and is described in our "Certain Aboriginal Mounds of the Georgia Coast."

[2] Theodore D. Rand, Esq., of the Academy of Natural Sciences, has kindly identified all rocks referred to in this Report. As we have not furnished Mr. Rand with sections of the specimens, the determinations are not considered final by him.

[3] "Certain Sand Mounds of the Ocklawaha River, Fla.," Journ. Acad. Nat. Sci. Phila., Vol. X.

[4] "A Cache of Pendent Ornaments," p. 190, Journ. Acad. Nat. Sci. Phila., Vol. XI.

that the shell deposit at Indian Hill exceeds in height any in the State, though considerably greater altitudes for other sites have been given by writers who base their assertions upon estimate. In Fig. 4 we give a photograph showing the great deposit at Indian Hill, extending completely across the background of the picture, with the house of the owner of the island, Mr. F. B. Walker, occupying the westernmost extremity of the heap. Unfortunately, it is beyond the power of the camera to show the slope or comparative height of mounds owing to undue prominence given to the foreground.

Close to the great shell heap is another, also of shell, very symmetrical, with upward slope of 28 degrees, in places. This mound, shown in the photograph in front of the greater heap, oblong with rounded corners, extends 76 feet in a N. E. and S. W. direction. Its minor diameter is 55 feet; its height above the general level of the surrounding shell is 12 feet 4 inches. At the S. W. end of the mound a trench was run in from the margin 21 feet, converging from 41 feet at the beginning to 20 feet at the end. The mound was built of layers of small oyster shells and strata of crushed shell and blackened debris. During the excavation, human remains were met with at seventeen points and in other places while caving the sides of the excavation at the end. No remains lay at a depth greater than 4 feet, while the majority were just beneath the surface. With three exceptions the burials consisted of parts of disarranged skeletons. Two skeletons lay much flexed, on the side; the other, face down and partly flexed. No artifacts were with the remains.

At one end of this mound lay numbers of small shells (*Strombus pugilis*) with two perforations for a handle, in the body whorl below the periphery and much chipped and worn at the beak. These and similar shells, lying here and there over the entire deposit, had doubtless served as hammers, probably to open shell-fish for food.

In a southerly direction, along the east shore of Tampa Bay, is Terraceia Island, Manatee Co. On this island (see map), on the property of Mr. L. W. Johnson, is a low irregular mound, in which were found a few flexed burials without artifacts.

About 150 yards N. N. W from this mound is a shell deposit, with the usual ridge leading to it.

On property of Dr. L. R. Warren, of Braidentown, Florida, not far from the other remains on Terraceia Island, is a large oblong mound running north and south, with the usual graded way leading to it.

Up the Manatee river, Manatee Co., near Erie P. O., are three small mounds, on properties belonging to Messrs. L. P. Foy and Louis Brubacher, in which were found only a few scattered bones.

On the southern extremity of Cow Point Island, Sarasota Bay, Manatee Co., on property of Mr. C. W. Thigpen, are an aboriginal shell deposit and two low burial mounds, in which were present closely flexed burials without artifacts.

FIG. 4.—Principal shell heaps, Indian Hill, Tampa Bay.

Near the shore of Sarasota Bay, on property of Mr. J. H. Gillespie, of Sarasota, are three low sand mounds, much dug into previous to our visit, in which we found practically nothing.

Near Snell's Bayou, Manatee Co., in sight of the water, is a mound on property of Mrs. F. E. Brooks, of Birmingham, Michigan, whose winter home is near the mound. The mound, of brown sand, is 109 feet across the base and 10 feet in height. A central trench was without result.

About one-half mile in a southerly direction from Sarasota, Manatee Co., a few yards from the water, in oak and palmetto scrub, is a mound on the property of Mr. Adolph Zakezewski, of Philadelphia, Pa. The mound is 20 feet high with somewhat irregular basal outline, and about 130 feet across. Considerable digging done previous to our visit showed no trace of human remains along the sections, nor were our excavations more successful. The mound, which is probably of a domiciliary character, seems to be of gray sand without shell.

Mound on Pine Island, Lee County.

Southward from Charlotte Harbor is Pine Island Sound in which is Pine Island. About three miles down, on the eastern side of the island, is a small key supposed to be about three acres in extent. This island rises in places to a considerable height owing to an aboriginal deposit of shells, whence its name,—Indian Old Field.

About three-quarters of a mile in a W. N. W. direction from Indian Old Field, on Pine Island, is a mound a trifle over 5 feet in height and 60 feet across the base. It is situate away from the mainland proper, on what is known as a sandspit,—territory not usually covered by tides but subject to overflow during unusually high ones. It seems curious for aborigines to have chosen such a spot for a place of interment when solid ground in abundance was so near at hand.

The mound, on property of the late J. H. Kreamer, Esq., of Philadelphia, Pa., was but partly investigated by us. A trench, 28 feet across at the beginning, was started at the northeast side of the mound where wash of tides had carried away a portion, leaving an abrupt section. The trench, converging to 24 feet at the end, was carried in a distance of 20 feet. The mound, unstratified, was of gray sand. At the base and below, where were a number of burials, the sand was black from admixture of loam. At the beginning of the excavation were numbers of fragments of pottery, belonging to different vessels, placed thickly together. Nearby were several shell drinking cups and a number of conch-shells.

Interments met with at thirty-eight points, consisted of burials loosely flexed and others closely drawn together like those we have described from the mound on Little Manatee river. There were also several masses of disconnected bones and skeletons disturbed by burials made afterward, though probably by the same tribe.

With the burials were three "celts" of iron or steel; glass beads, on three occasions; two tubular sheet silver beads with overlapping edges; one kite-shaped pendant of thin sheet silver, decorated with a repoussé cross (Fig. 5); a handsome lance-head of hornstone, 4 inches long; a lance-head of chert; two arrowheads of chalcedony; a tooth of a fossil shark, perforated for use as a pendant. With the basal burials and with the sub-basal ones, some of which were 6.5 feet beneath the surface, were no artifacts. The burials on and below the base, in every case but three, were closely flexed, while the flexion in the body of the mound was loose in character. The burials with European objects, however, were not intrusive, but belonged to the period when the part of the mound in which they were was made.

FIG. 5.—Pendant of silver. Mound on Pine Island. (Full size.)

At the northern end of Pine Island Sound are several islands, among which Mondongo and Joseffa were visited by us. These islands, though thickly covered with aboriginal deposits of shell, are not of the pile-dweller type, since the islands are of sand, a number of feet in height, on which the debris of aboriginal meals has been thrown. Though Mr. F. P. Roach,. owner of Joseffa Island, placed it at our disposition, we had by this time done so much fruitless digging into the shell of the west coast that we did not feel justified in taking time from what we believed to be a richer district farther south.

JOSSELYN KEY, LEE COUNTY.

Josselyn Key, in Pine Island Sound, off the northwestern end of Pine Island, has been described by Mr. Cushing. There is a large shell deposit on the island with courts, canals, mounds and platforms. We made a number of excavations in the muck of various courts and canals, finding absolutely nothing.

DEMOREY KEY, LEE COUNTY.

This island lies about two and one-third miles S. S. E. from Josselyn Key. Here our men made numerous excavations in the muck, finding it from 1 to 3 feet in depth. Nothing was obtained beyond several bits of coarse earthenware.

Mr. Cushing has described Demorey Key with considerable detail, and it was there he found the "truncated pyramid" with the wall of conch-shells described by him,[1] and shown in Plate XXIX and, in elevation with the rest of the key, in Plate XXVIII. Mr. Cushing says: "The most remarkable feature of this key was a flat, elongated bench, or truncated pyramid, that crowned the middle elevation. I discovered this merely by accident. In order to gain a general idea of the key, which was almost as much overgrown with luxuriant and forbidding vegetation as had been the wilder key first explored, I climbed high up among the skinny and crooked limbs of a gigantic gumbo limbo that grew directly from the inner edge of

[1] *Op. cit.*, pp. 10 and 11.

this elevation. Luckily, great festoons of tough vines clung to the lower limbs of this tree, for in shifting my position, I slipped and fell, and was caught by these vines, to the salvation of my bones, probably, since by the force of the fall some of the vines were torn away, revealing the inner side of this platform and the fact that it was almost vertically faced up with conch-shells; their larger, truncated and spiral ends, laid outward and in courses so regular, that the effect was of a mural mosaic of volutes. I hastily tore away more of the vines, and found that this faced-up edge of the platform extended many feet in either direction from the old gumbo limbo. I may say here, that on occasion of two later visits I cleared the façade of this primitive example of shell architecture still more; was enabled, indeed, when I last visited the place—since I was then accompanied by a considerable force of workmen—to entirely expose its inner side and its southern end. Thus was revealed—even more completely than is shown in Plate XXIX—a parallelogramic and level platform, some three and a half feet high and twelve yards in width, by nearly thrice as many in length. It was approached from the inner side by a graded way that led obliquely along the curved ascent up from the mangrove swamp, to a little step-like, subsidiary platform half as high and some twelve feet square, which joined it at right-angles, just beyond the point shown at the extreme right of the picture here given. The top of this lesser step, and the approaches to either side of it, were paved with very large, uniform-sized clam-shells, laid convex sides upward, and as closely and regularly as tiles. The lower or southern end of the main platform was rounded at the corners, and rounded also on either side of the sunken ascent midway, in which the longer of the graded ways I have described terminated. Contemplating the regularity of this work, its central position and its evident importance, as indicated by the several graded ways leading to it from distant points, I could not doubt that it had formed the foundation of an imposing temple-structure, and this idea was further carried out by the presence at its northern end of two small, but quite prominent altar-like mounds."

Although Mr. Cushing seems carefully to have looked into this matter, we believe him to be mistaken in attributing an aboriginal origin to this wall of conch-shells.

We four times visited Demorey Key with a force of men to dig.

The elongated bench described by Mr. Cushing is a portion of an ordinary aboriginal shell ridge, which seemed to us to have been somewhat flattened to serve as a site for a modern house and garden. In fact, we are informed by "Johnny" Smith, Mr. Cushing's guide, that at the time of his visit to Demorey Key, a house, partly in ruins, occupied a portion of this level space just by the little platform. When we first visited the key (March, 1900), we saw a frame house which must have occupied the site of the older one. This house also had been removed when last we stopped at the key.

The wall of conch-shells, shown in our plan (Fig. 6) by the solid line A to B, does not surround a parallelogram, but extends about 100 feet only on the inner, or eastern side, where it distinctly leaves the straight line to go around a gumbo limbo tree, as shown at C. This alone we think sufficient to prove the comparatively modern origin of the wall. At the southeastern corner it circles about a lemon tree at D and comes to an end. There is no sign of a wall in the southwestern corner, there being there only a loose heap of large shells, mostly conchs. Such

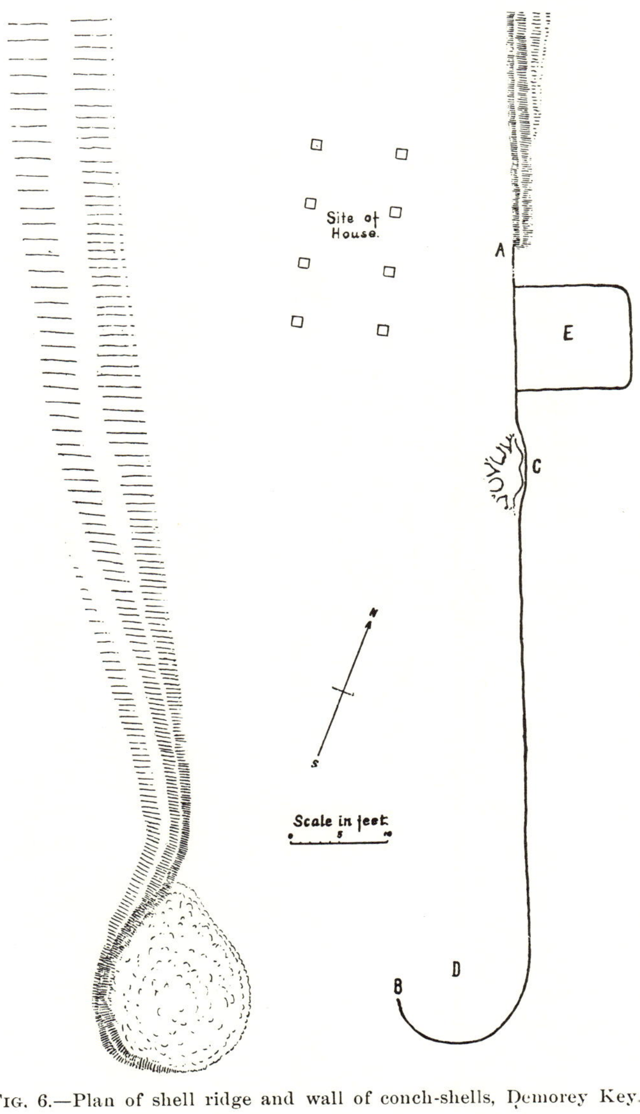

FIG. 6.—Plan of shell ridge and wall of conch-shells, Demorey Key.

heaps are very frequently met with on the shell islands which have been cultivated, since the large shells interfere with the hoe and the plow. At Chokoloskee, in the Ten Thousand Islands, great piles and ridges of these shells, collected within the last few years, are to be seen. At Josselyn Key are similar heaps of shells thrown loosely together, which Robert Allen, the captain of our steamer, informed us he had seen in process of collection by Josselyn, the former owner of the key. Several such piles are in close proximity to the leveled space at Demorey Key.

There is no defined outline of a parallelogram save along the wall, the other portions being the simple, gradual slope of an ordinary shell ridge.

The wall itself seemed to us to have been built by some settler in the present century, primarily to serve as a sort of retaining wall to keep in place great numbers of conchs which lie loosely behind the wall, and thus when loam was superimposed, to broaden his vegetable garden. The slope of the shell heap on the inner side is much steeper than on the outer side where it was not necessary to build a wall.

We removed portions of the shell wall at various places and dug into the mass of material beyond at the level of the base, finding glass, iron and earthenware, one bit with a glaze.

We examined also the subsidiary platform referred to by Mr. Cushing and shown on our plan at E. The pavement of large clam shells, the convex side upward, described by him, no longer remained, though here and there were clam shells mostly with the convex side upturned. Young Smith, a brother of Mr. Cushing's guide, informed us that he had lived upon Demorey Key after Mr. Cushing's visit, and had displaced many of these shells. Digging into the platform we discovered it to be made of loose conchs with a certain amount of undisturbed, black loam on top, in all a little over one foot in thickness. Just below this loam, and over the conch-shells, was a large fireplace leading us to suppose that the platform had been built for use as a kitchen. Beneath was the black surface loam of the shell heap. One foot down, among the conch-shells of the platform, and just above the black loam of the original surface, under the fireplace, we found a number of large pieces of glass showing marks of fire.

Mound Island, Lee County.

Mound Island, or Johnson's Key, as it is also called, is in Estero Bay, about seven miles in a straight line in a southeasterly direction from Punta Rassa, and may be reached by a sheltered way behind islands, or from the Gulf through Carlos Pass.[1] Mound Island, where we were courteously received by Mrs. F. M. Johnson in the absence of her husband, the owner, is, in our opinion, the most typical of all the Key-dwellers islands. We were informed by Mrs. Johnson that its area is about 140 acres. A survey we have seen makes it about 128 acres in extent. In addition to a general shell deposit over most of the island, and numerous graded ways, courts, small canals and at least one hooked-shaped breakwater at the mouth of a canal, a great canal, still admitting water in the highest tides, running nearly N. E. and S. W., bisects the island. Beginning in the northeastern portion of the island, this highway for canoes, a little farther on, passes the burial mound of the island, and at about two-thirds of its length goes between embankments of shell,

[1] Government Chart, No. 174, shows Little and Big Carlos Pass. They are now united. Mound Island lies nearly two miles in an easterly direction from the Pass.

at places over 20 feet in height, having on its left the great precipitous shell-heap which gives the island its name. In Fig. 7 we show a representation of this mound with part of the main, or dividing, canal, sketched from an elevation to the north.

Mr. Cushing, in his brilliant preliminary report (page 19 *et seq.*), speaks of Mound Island at some length. At the foot of page 19 he says, "It consisted of a long series of enormous elevations crowned by imposing mounds that reached an average altitude of over 60 feet." Mr. Cushing here has given an estimate as the actual height, and we feel impelled to call attention to this since we have repeatedly gone on record that no shell deposit of Florida reaches a height of 40 feet. In point of fact the principal mound of Mound Island is 31 feet above sea level at half tide, and 30 feet, 2.5 inches in height if measured from the general level at the base. These measurements were made and repeated with a theodolite, and we believe them to be accurate. Different stages of tide might modify the first measurement by a foot or two either way.

FIG. 7.—Principal mound with portion of main canal. Mound Island.

Persistent excavations were made by us in the muck of the canals and courts at Mound Island, which was sometimes 3 or 4 feet in depth, resulting in the discovery of a few bits of earthenware only and a handsome implement wrought from a conch-shell, unfortunately without a handle. The result of our work was a bitter disappointment to us, as we had gone to Mound Island fully prepared with a band of diggers and with a portable pump to keep down the water while engaged in the muck.

The burial mound in the northeastern part of the island, to which we have referred, lies in a mangrove swamp. It is 65 feet across the base and about 11 feet in height. It is composed of sand and loamy material with a certain admixture of shell. We dug into this mound to a certain extent, finding nothing of particular interest. Many relics, however, mostly of European origin, have come from it.

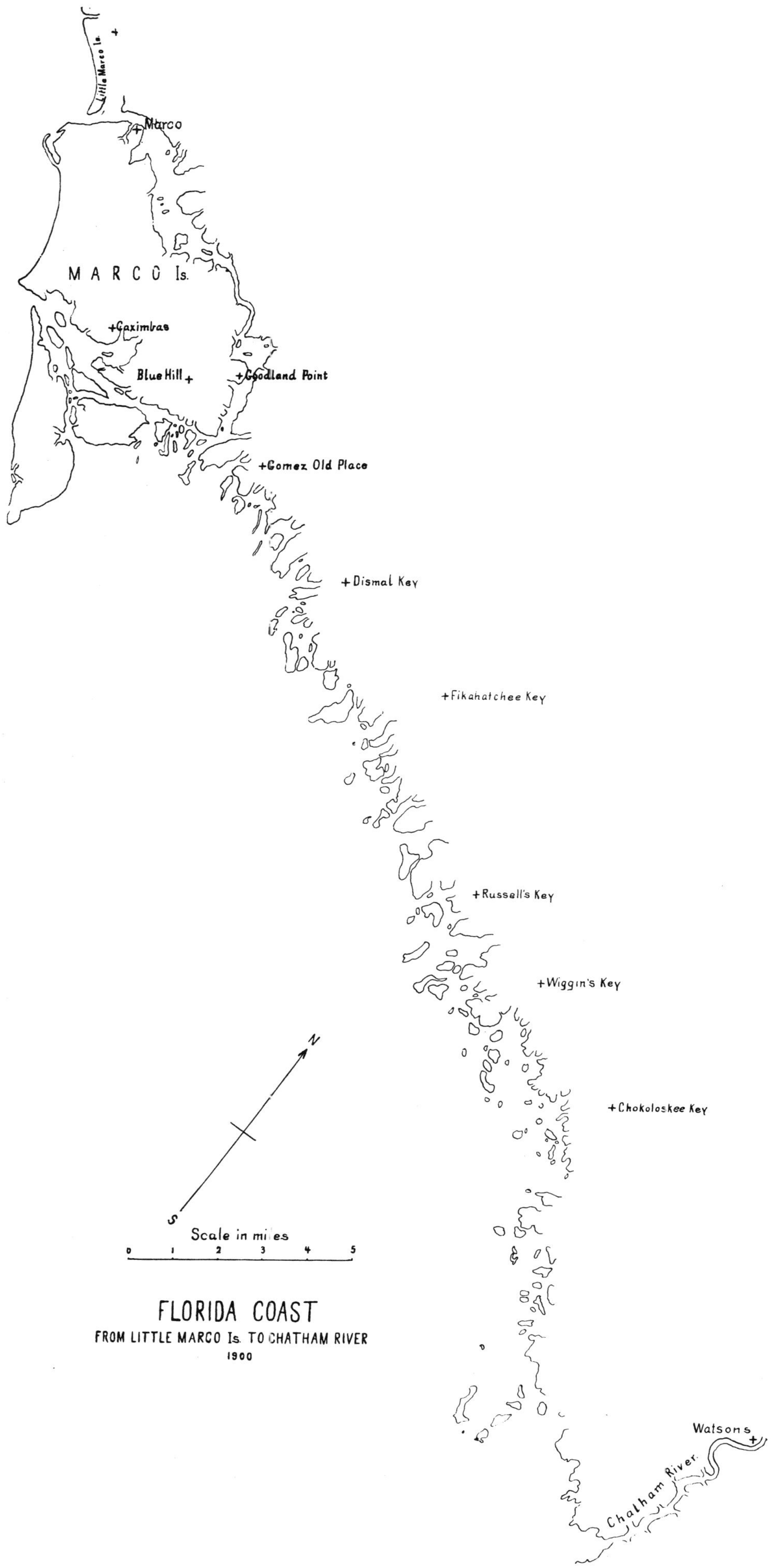

FLORIDA COAST
FROM LITTLE MARCO Is. TO CHATHAM RIVER
1900

Some of these, we believe, have been presented to the Museum of Science and Art of the University of Pennsylvania by Mr. Joseph Willcox.

Little Marco Island, Lee County.

The Ten Thousand Islands, whose name is not conferred in a poetical way, but probably falls short in describing the number, beginning with Little Marco Island in the north, thickly fringe the coast line of part of the counties of Lee and Monroe to the Northwest Cape, a distance of about seventy miles, in a straight line.

These keys, formed by oyster bars, sand and the roots of the mangrove tree, are from a few feet to a number of miles in area, and are, as a rule, just above the level of the sea. But an insignificant proportion of these islands have been utilized by the Key-dwellers.

All published maps of this part of Florida are grossly inaccurate in respect to the Ten Thousand Islands, locating key settlements on the mainland, reversing their positions and the like, while Government charts skip most of the islands, the task being too difficult to cope with.

The map given by us, mainly taken from the Government chart, shows, as it does, below Key Marco, only the outlines of the outer tier of islands, and, in addition, indicates the location of the shell islands visited by us. These islands do not lie in open water, but are enclosed in a labyrinth of other keys.

On the eastern side of Little Marco Island is a shell settlement with the usual ridges and mounds of moderate size.

Marco, Lee County.

Marco, on the northernmost end of Key Marco, by far the most important of the Ten Thousand Islands (see map), is where Mr. Cushing made his marvelous collection of objects of wood and of shell in the muck at the bottom of a small triangular court, enclosed between ridges of shell.

All the territory in and around Marco, including its canals, its courts and its mounds of shell, was cordially placed at our disposition by W. D. Collier, Esq., of Marco, the owner, and investigation was made by us in the muck of courts in the immediate vicinity of the one so advantageously explored by Mr. Cushing. Absolutely nothing rewarded our efforts.

From Mr. G. E. Cuthbert, of Marco, we obtained a collection of objects ploughed up during cultivation, among which were many rather rude "sinkers" of shell and others somewhat resembling them, but too carefully made to have served for other than ornamental purposes. In Fig. 8 are shown selected specimens of this kind from the Ten Thousand Islands, including Marco; Goodland Point, Key Marco; and Chokoloskee Key.

In the Marco collection are four shell discs. One, with two perforations, is evidently a gorget; one is imperforate; one has a small central perforation, while the remaining one has a much larger hole in the middle. All these are shown in Fig. 9.

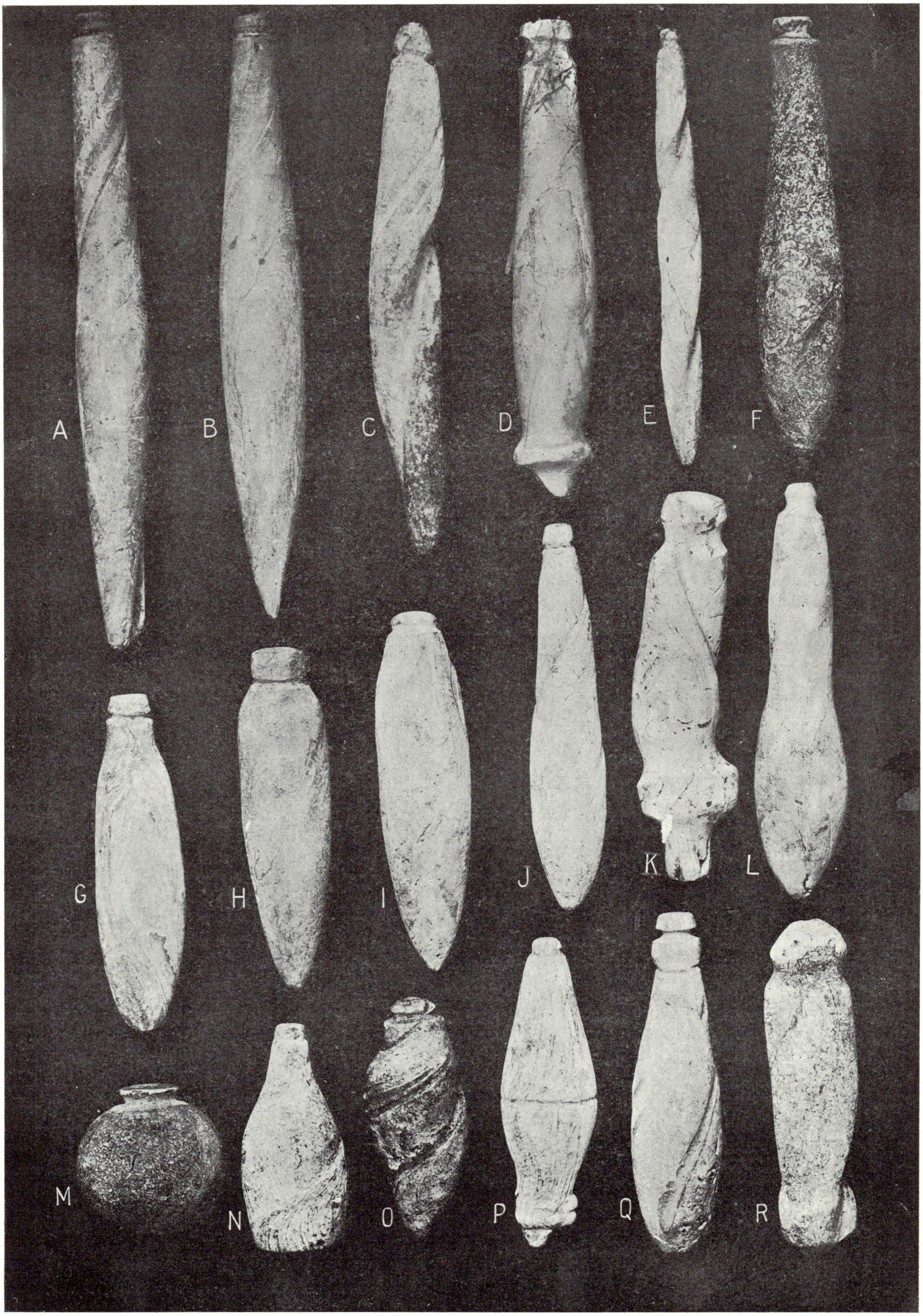

FIG. 8.—Ornaments of shell. Ten Thousand Islands. (Full size.)

There were also a number of rude sinkers of coralline limestone and one, globular in shape, of coral.

A curious type found among the Florida keys, consisting of oblong strips of shell, is represented by four specimens in the Marco collection. These objects

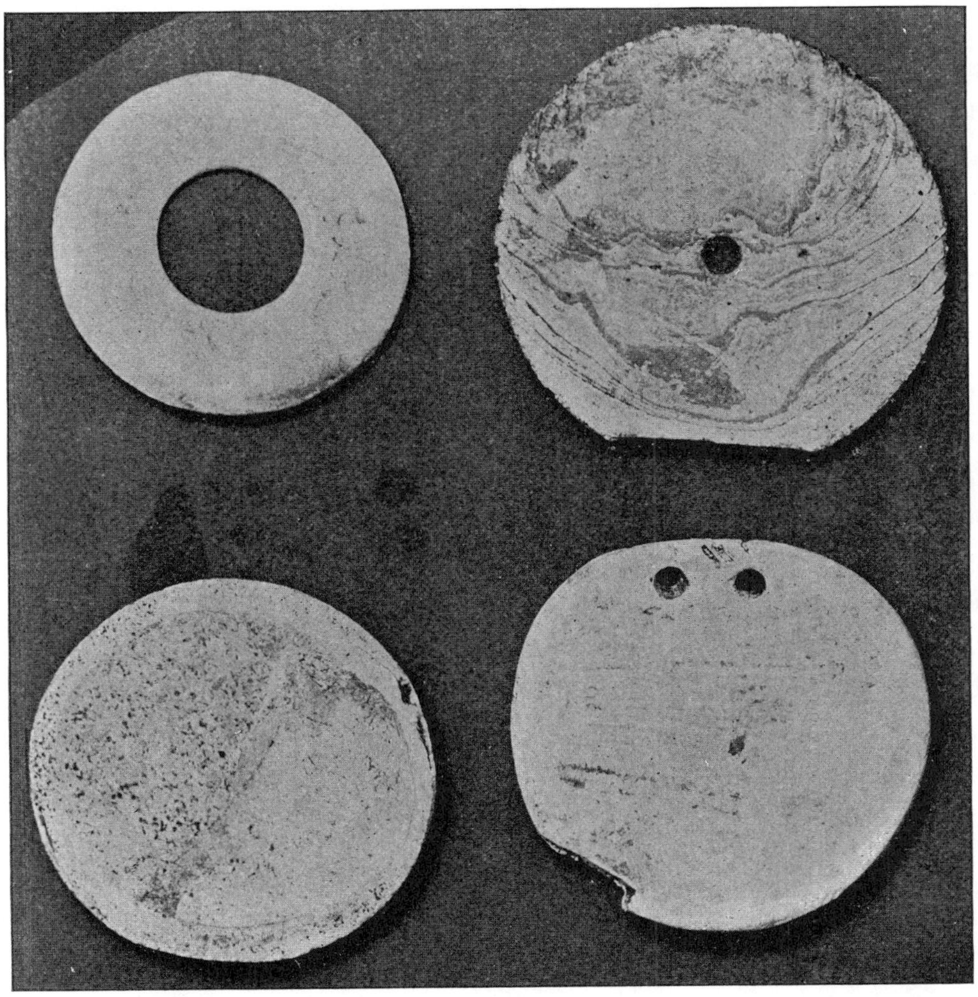

FIG. 9.—Discs of shell, Key Marco. (Full size.)

might seem to be unfinished were it not that the margins are carefully worked, and some show a high polish as from use.

A neatly-made chisel, probably of argillyte, 3.4 inches in length, is polished and has a circular section. On one end is a bevelled cutting edge; on the other, a blunt point.

GOODLAND POINT, MARCO ISLAND, LEE COUNTY.

Goodland Point, about six miles farther down the east side of Marco Island, on its southeastern extremity, has a great expanse of shell deposit which was put at our service by Mr. Samuel Pettit, the owner. In the mangroves, about one-half mile from the landing, are a number of low, irregular undulations, which seem to have served as places of burial for the aboriginal settlement. Considerable previous digging had been attempted. An imperfect examination indicated that parts of disjointed skeletons had been buried just below a shell deposit, and subsequently about one foot of loam had been piled above.

FIG. 10.—Disc and "sinkers" of limestone. Goodland Point. (Full size.)

With a femur, a tibia, fragments of a fibula, parts of a radius, were four arrowheads, or knives, of chert.

One small mound had twelve shell drinking cups just beneath the surface. Though the mound was less than half demolished by us, over twenty of these cups were met with.

From the sons of Mr. Pettit we got a considerable collection of objects found during cultivation of the place, including several beautiful shell pendants; many

FIG. 11.—"Celt" of shell. Goodland Point. (Full size.)

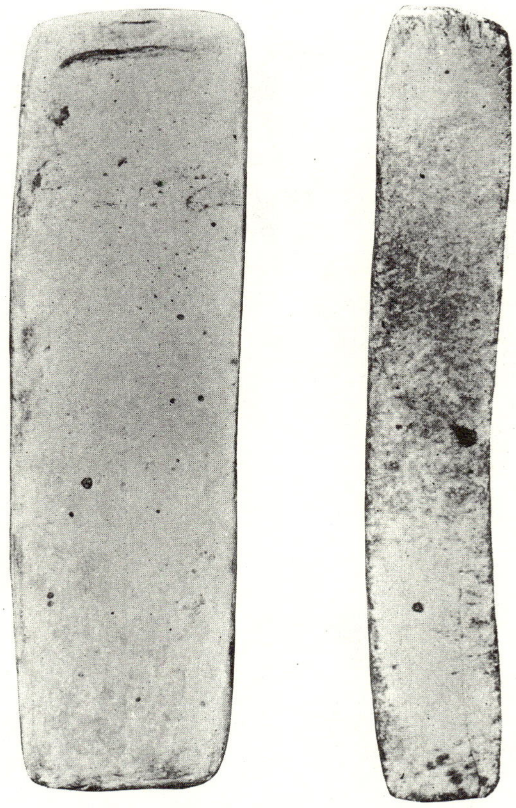

FIGS. 12, 13.—Objects of shell. Goodland Point. (Full size.)

FIG. 14.—Object of shell. Goodland Point. (Full size.)

rude "sinkers" of shell and of coralline limestone; a perforated disc of soft limestone which, with some typical stone "sinkers," is shown in Fig. 10; a beautiful and perfect "celt" of shell, wrought from the lip of *Strombus gigas*, about 7.5 inches long, of a type not found out of Florida in the United States, but present in certain West India islands (Fig. 11); two smaller "celts" of shell; three narrow, oblong strips carefully cut from the body whorl of a large marine univalve, of the type we have referred to as found at Marco, two of which are shown in Figs. 12, 13; a shorter and wider oblong section of shell, much polished (Fig. 14); two centrally perforated discs of shell shown in Figs. 15, 16; a scoop-shaped object of shell with rough incised decoration (Fig. 17); another, spoon-shaped, also of shell (Fig. 18); a chisel of igneous rock, with bevelled cutting edge, similar in type to the one from Marco, though somewhat larger.

FIGS. 15, 16.—Discs of shell. Goodland Point. (Full size.)

One of the most interesting features of this collection is a beautifully wrought implement, probably of claystone, of a type not found in the National Museum, we are informed by Professor Holmes. At one end is a carefully made bevelled cutting edge; the other end originally tapered to a fine point. This specimen, Mr. Pettit's son informed us, was found intact by him, but having been allowed to fall, it broke into a number of pieces. These pieces, with the exception of a small fragment from the pointed end, which he had lost, have been put together by us. The present length is 13.12 inches, though the reproduction makes it a little greater; the maximum diameter is .56 of an inch (Fig. 19).

With the objects of shell and of stone obtained by us at Goodland Point were two earthenware heads of birds, one probably representing a turkey head (Fig. 20); the other, the head of a predatory bird, perhaps an eagle (Fig. 21).

These heads, which doubtless served as handles of vessels, are interesting, owing to the section whence they came, since no such heads were met with by us else-

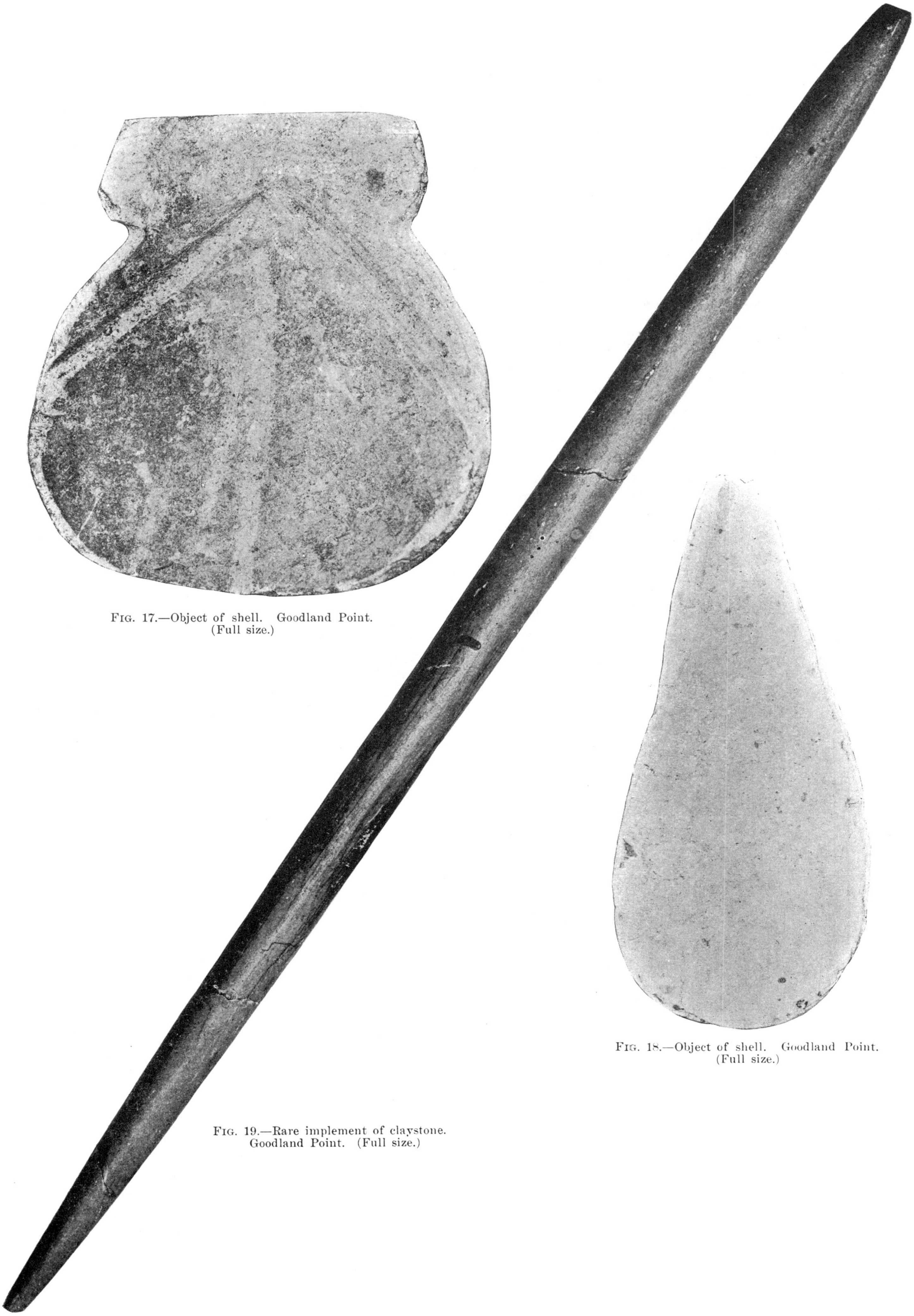

Fig. 17.—Object of shell. Goodland Point. (Full size.)

Fig. 18.—Object of shell. Goodland Point. (Full size.)

Fig. 19.—Rare implement of claystone. Goodland Point. (Full size.)

where on the southwestern coast of Florida, or, we think, have been described by others as coming from there.

The heads show considerable excellence of design and workmanship, and far exceed, in these respects, any bird-head handles met with by us in other parts of Florida, with one exception.

Mr. S. T. Walker, in the Smithsonian Report for the year 1883, describes and figures certain earthenware bird-heads from Florida, but these came from the extreme northwestern coast of that State, not far from the Alabama line, and, moreover, are of little artistic excellence.

In the mound at Ginn's Grove, St. Johns river, Orange County, we found a beautifully painted and incised head of a predatory bird,[1] which Professor Holmes describes in his "Earthenware of Florida."[2]

FIG. 20.—Earthenware head of turkey. Goodland Point. (Full size.)

FIG. 21.—Earthenware head of predatory bird. Goodland Point. (Full size.)

Elsewhere on the St. Johns we have found bird-head handles of vessels, but these others were rude in character.

It is interesting to note a groove cut around the base of the neck of the predatory bird, showing that, after the separation from the vessel, the head was used as a pendant.

Blue Hill, on Horr's Island, about one mile S. W. from Goodland Point, has a

[1] "Certain Sand Mounds of the St. Johns river, Florida." Part I, p. 87. Plate XV, Fig. 4.
[2] Page 124, Journ. Acad. Nat. Sci. Phila., Vol. X.

considerable aboriginal shell deposit and a sand mound about 6 feet in height, which has been thoroughly dug through.

Caximbas Hill is a wind formation on the southwestern part of Marco Island. Nearby is a considerable shell deposit.

Proceeding in a southerly direction among the Ten Thousand Islands, we visited Gomez' Old Place on a small nameless key reached from the Gulf through a pass about two miles east of Coon Key, and continuing in about one mile in a northerly direction. The key, at present writing (1900), is uninhabited. It covers probably about 30 acres of interesting shell deposit, partly surrounding a basin that fills with the rising tide.

Dismal Key, Lee County, lies about 2 miles north of Horse Key, an outside island about 5 miles E. S. E. from Coon Key Pass, which is the southern entrance to Marco. This unsurveyed key has a great shell deposit with the usual mounds and the like.

Fikahatchee Key, Lee County, unsurveyed, perhaps 150 acres in extent, can be reached by an inland passage at high tide, or from the Gulf through a nameless pass and continuing in among the islands for from three to four miles. In any event, a pilot is requisite. On this island is an extensive shell deposit. A family living on the key occupies a house partly built upon piles.

Russell's Key may be reached from the Gulf by entering the islands about three miles above Sandfly Pass and continuing in among the keys another three miles. This key, which has large aboriginal shell deposits, perhaps 60 acres in extent, is occupied by Mr. J. W. Russell and Mr. M. M. Gaston with their families.

Wiggins' Key on Sandfly Pass,[1] about one mile from the Gulf, on the right-hand side going out, has extensive shell deposits and two small burial mounds of sand and shell which have been much dug into. Our excavations, made with permission of Mr. J. Wiggins, the owner, were unrewarded.

This place is shown on maps as in the northern limits of the county of Monroe, but at the present time this territory, extending south below Chokoloskee Key, is claimed by Lee County, and, it is said, probably will be obtained by it.

Chokoloskee Key, Monroe County.

This island lies in the lower part of Chokoloskee Bay, a sheet of water back of the maze of islands bordering the Gulf.

The island is unsurveyed. It is roughly circular and is said to be somewhat

[1] See Government Chart, No. 173.

Fig. 22.—Unidentified object of limestone. Chokoloskee Key. (Full size.)

Figs. 23, 24.—"Sinkers" of coral. Chokoloskee Key. (Full size.)

Fig. 27.—"Sinker" of limestone. Chokoloskee Key. (Full size.)

Fig. 25.—Canine of bear, used as pendant. Chokoloskee Key. (Full size.)

Fig. 26.—Implement of argillyte. Chokoloskee Key. (Full size.)

Fig. 28.—Net "sinker" of shell. Chokoloskee Key. (Full size.)

over one-half mile in diameter. It is almost entirely covered with great shell deposits, including lofty peaks, graded ways, canals and the like. Rising from the mangrove swamp at the edge of the northern part of the island, is a mound of shell of abrupt ascent, a fraction over 27 feet in height, if measured from the level of low water. Running in from the southern section of the island are two graded ways enclosing a canal. These ways terminate in mounds facing each other. The easternmost mound, slightly the higher, on its western side, where it rises from the canal, has a slope of thirty-three degrees. Its height above the level of the bottom of the canal is 18 feet 4 inches, and 22 feet 4 inches above low water level. From Mr. McKinney, postmaster at Chokoloskee, and from others, we obtained an interesting collection of artifacts, including shell pendants; shell "sinkers;" two shell "celts;" a shell disc; a small "celt" of decomposed rock; a handsomely made heart-shaped object of limestone, with perforation, which seems too carefully wrought for use as a "sinker" and too large for a pendant (Fig. 22); two "sinkers" of coral (Figs. 23, 24); a pendant made from a canine tooth of a large bear, probably

FIG. 29.—Net "sinker" of clam shell. Turner's river. (Full size.)

Ursus floridanus, grooved for suspension (Fig. 25); a very rare type of implement, probably of argillyte, perhaps used as a piercer (Fig. 26); a net "sinker" of coralline limestone (Fig. 27); a net "sinker" of the shells of the reef-building mollusc, *Vermicularia nigricans*, Dall[1] (Fig. 28).

We have found on the keys a number of perforated "sinkers" of this material, but all others were of irregular outline, unworked as to the margin.

Near the mouth of Turner's river, which enters Chokoloskee Bay in an easterly direction from the key and not far from it, is a considerable shell deposit

[1] Identified by Professor Pilsbry of the Academy of Natural Sciences.

where we found, among other objects, a sinker made from a clam-shell (Fig. 29). It is interesting to recall that Mr. Cushing found in the muck at Marco "chipped and notched fragments of heavy clam shells" in place on fishing nets.

Watson's, Monroe County.

About four miles up Chatham river is a series of shell fields owned by Mr. Watson who resides on the place.

Conclusions.

It is our belief, judging from the results of our work along the Florida west-coast, that archæological opportunities offered there are more for the surveyor than for the excavator. And the surveyor must have a care, while introducing into his plans all visible remains of the aborigines, not to idealize, and thus on his plans show more than is present on the various sites.

We believe Mr. Cushing's discoveries at Marco were an isolated case, and in fact, Mr. Cushing has so expressed himself to us. Perhaps a hurricane crushed in, at that particular spot, a group of dwellings, including a temple or sacerdotal house. Continuous digging in the muck of keys might reveal scattered objects, accidental losses, whose specific gravity caused them to sink when falling into the water. This would not be the case with objects wholly of wood as were the majority of those found by Mr. Cushing at Marco.

We are not prepared to believe that aboriginal objects of wood, some artistically carved, were confined, as to their use in Florida, to the keys of the southwest coast. The kitchen-middens of Europe show the preservative quality of mud for wood, and we, therefore, think that wooden objects were found at Marco, because they lay in a better medium for preservation, and not because they were in use only along the southwest coast. We know the Florida Indians of other parts of the State used wood. Ribault's French Huguenots (1564) saw in use "a little vessel of wood"[1] near the mouth of the St. Johns, where we opened two great Indian mounds. In the famous mound at Mt. Royal, farther up the river, which we believe to be the place near the lake visited by some of the Frenchmen, where lived a great king, we found a long pin, or skewer, of wood, parts of which, preserved by a coating of sheet copper, were beautifully carved.[2]

We think, therefore, it not unlikely that the sand mounds of Florida contained a store of objects carved in wood, which have long since disappeared through decay.

Certain Shell Implements of the Southwest Coast of Florida.

Florida may be called the home of the shell implement in this country, for no other State has such an extent of sub-tropical sea coast where shells abound, and in no other State is such a need created through absence of stone.

[1] "Historical Collections of Louisiana and Florida," p. 229.

[2] "Certain Sand Mounds of the St. Johns river." Part II, Fig. 15, p. 142, Journ. Acad. Nat. Sci. Phila., Vol. X.

While implements of shell are fairly numerous throughout the State, they are in most profuse abundance along the southwest coast, especially the keys of the Ten Thousand Islands. The great majority of these implements are marine univalves perforated to receive a handle. Many have beaks ground down almost to a cutting edge, while other shells, in use as hammers, have blunter beaks. It is of this form of implement, that is to say, a shell used with a handle, as a hammer, a chisel, a hoe, a gouge, an adze or the like, that we propose to speak. On Key Marco, Chokoloskee Key and other places the great abundance of conchs (*Fulgur*) and "horse conchs" (*Fasciolaria*) is a positive detriment to cultivation and great heaps of these shells, as we have previously stated, are often collected by the inhabitants before agricultural work is attempted. Among these shells a fair percentage had been used as implements, broken and thrown aside in aboriginal times, while a few, presumably lost, are still fairly perfect.

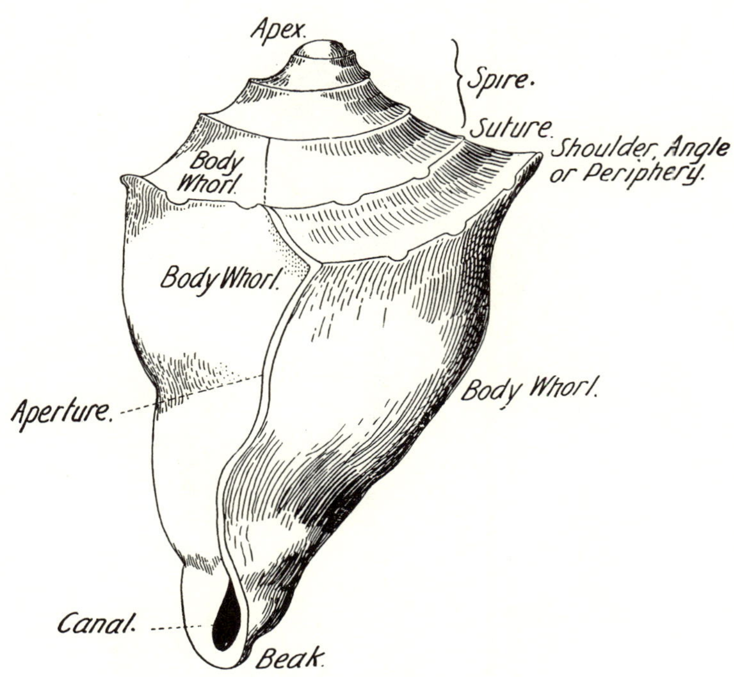

FIG. 30.—Nomenclature of parts of marine univalve.

Before going into the matter of these shell implements, it may be well to show a representation of a marine univalve with the names applied to its various parts (Fig. 30), which we have borrowed from a book by Professor Pilsbry, of the Academy of Natural Sciences of Philadelphia, to whom, with Mr. Joseph Willcox, also of the Academy, we are indebted for much information as to Florida shells.

We shall now describe a representative selection from the shell implements collected by us from the surface of the keys of the southwest coast of Florida. All are shown full size in the illustrations.

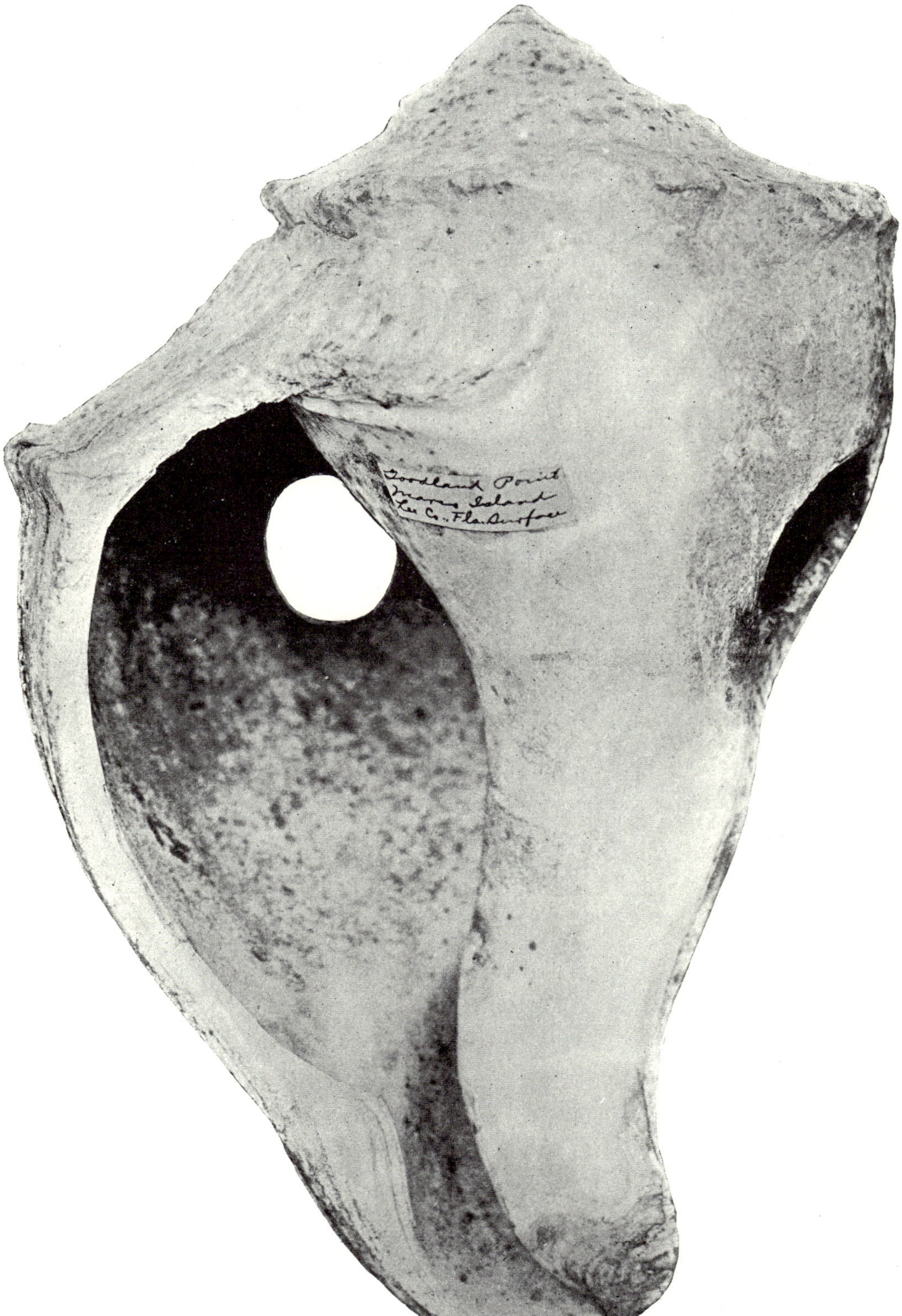

FIG. 31.—Shell implement. Goodland Point. (Full size.)

Fig. 31 is a massive conch (*Fulgur perversum*), with two round, carefully made holes to allow the handle to run diagonally to the right of the columella.[1] The beak is carefully ground almost to a straight edge which would be at an acute angle with a handle. The body whorl has been cut off several inches back. A

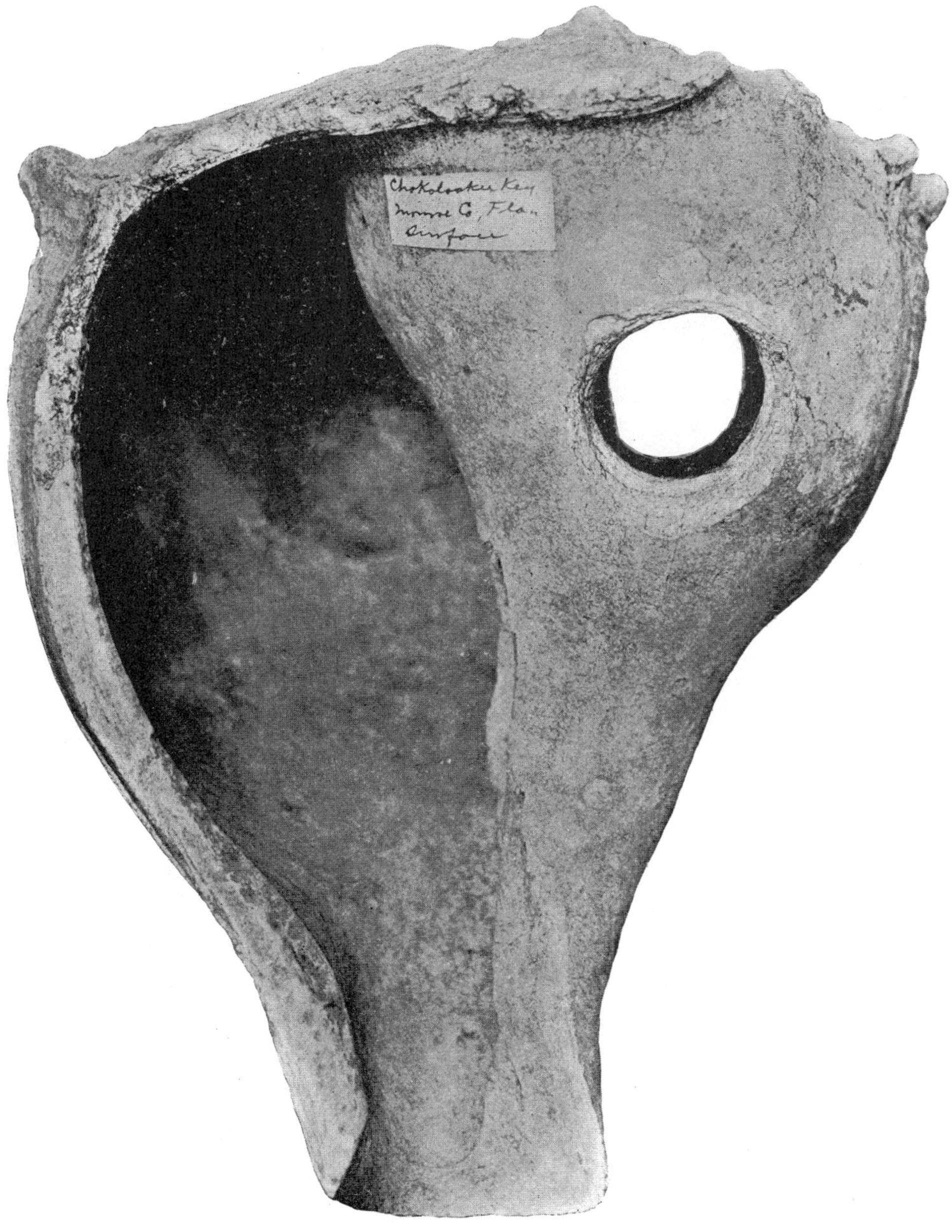

FIG. 32.—Shell implement. Chokoloskee Key. (Full size.)

small rudely made hole above the periphery, not shown in the reproduction, probably has no connection with the tool as such, as great numbers of conch shells not used as implements have similar holes presumably made to sever the muscle of the fish and facilitate its removal from the shell. This specimen came from Goodland Point.

[1] The column or axis of the shell.

Fig. 32 shows a stout *Fulgur perversum* from Chokoloskee Key. It is beautifully wrought, the two holes being round [1] and carefully cut to allow a handle to pass to the right of the columella in a way that would bring the sharp cutting edge

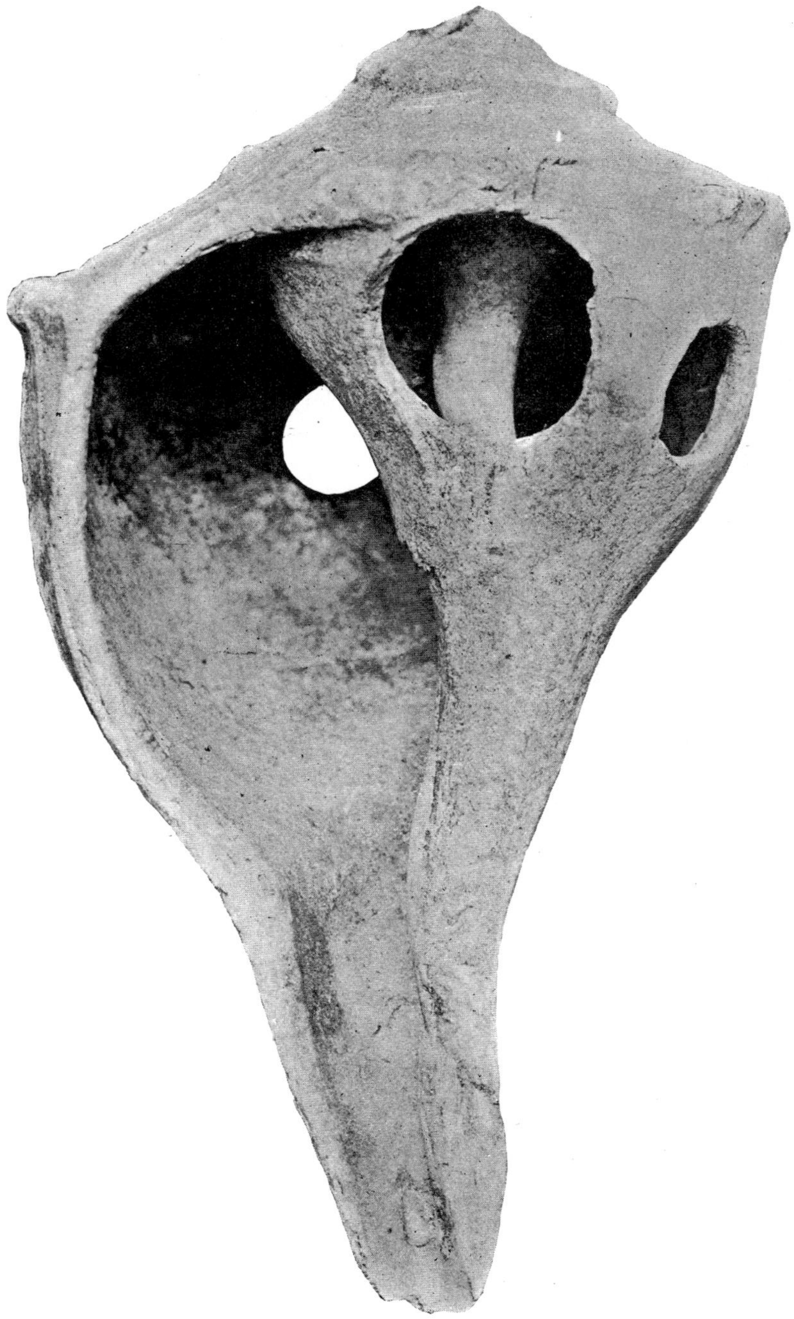

FIG. 33.—Shell implement. Chokoloskee Key. (Full size.)

at the beak at right angles to a handle. The body whorl has been cut several inches back. There is a small rude hole above the periphery of the kind we have referred to. This implement would serve admirably as a gouge.

[1] A part of the axis showing to the left of the farther hole takes away from the circular appearance in the reproduction.

Fig. 33 is of a lighter *Fulgur perversum*, also from Chokoloskee Key. Two round holes would allow a handle to pass through the shell to the right of the axis,

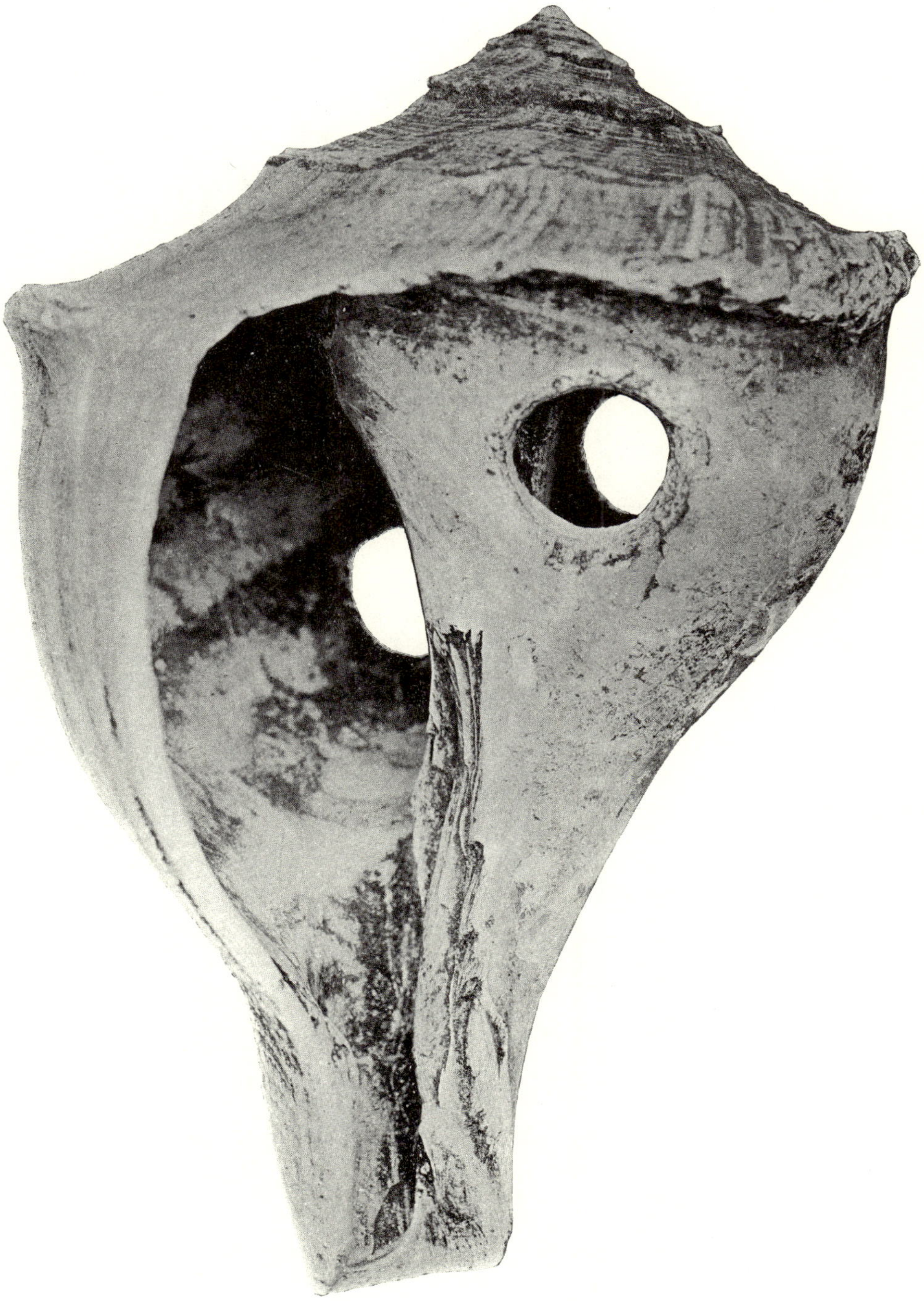

FIG. 34.—Shell implement. Goodland Point. (Full size.)

at an angle to the ground beak. A large round additional opening is present, perhaps made to allow a firmer lashing of the handle to the axis. A considerable portion of the body whorl has been removed.

Fig. 34 is a representation of a heavy *Fulgur perversum* from Goodland Point. Part of the body whorl has been removed, as in other specimens, perhaps to facilitate balance, certainly to obviate the necessity of making a second hole through the overlapping whorl. A small rude hole is above the periphery. Two round

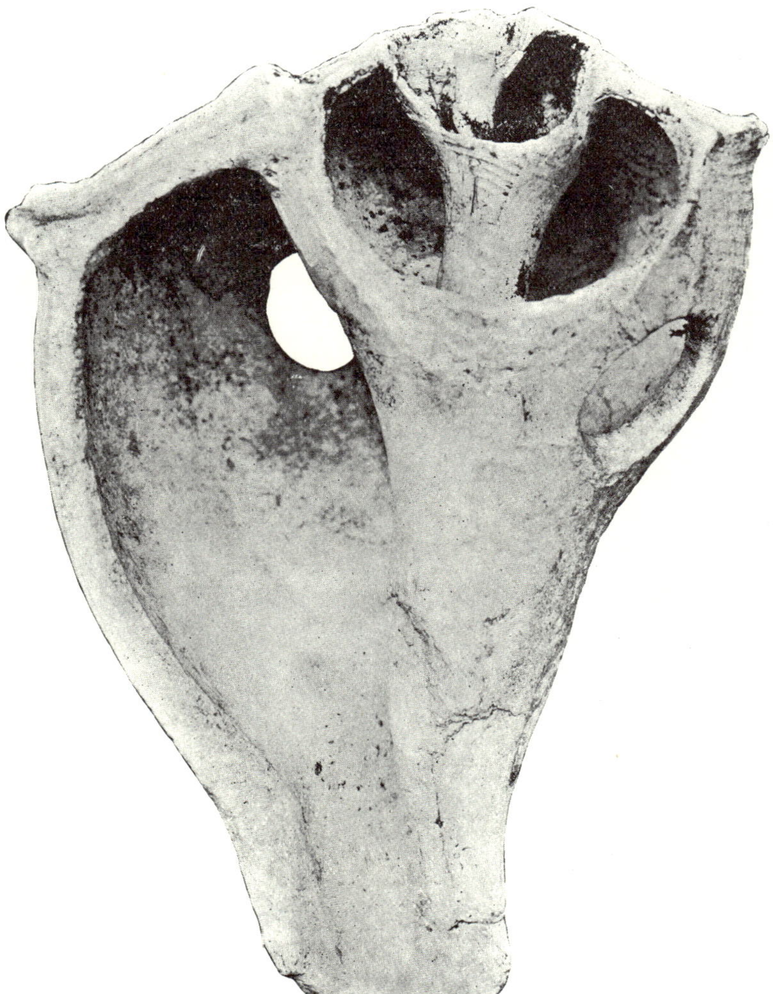

FIG. 35.—Shell implement. Goodland Point. (Full size.)

perforations have permitted a handle to pass through to the right of the axis, bringing the cutting edge, which is carefully ground from the inside, at an angle to the handle. A third hole to the left of the axis was probably for additional attachment of the handle. This implement was presumably a gouge.

In Fig. 35 we have a *Fulgur perversum* from Goodland Point, showing a modification of the two preceding types. Round and carefully made holes would bring a handle to the right of the column, at an angle to the gouge-shaped cutting edge, but, in place of an additional hole for thongs to pass through to lash the handle to the axis, the upper part of the shell, including the spire, has been removed. This is a common type along the west coast.

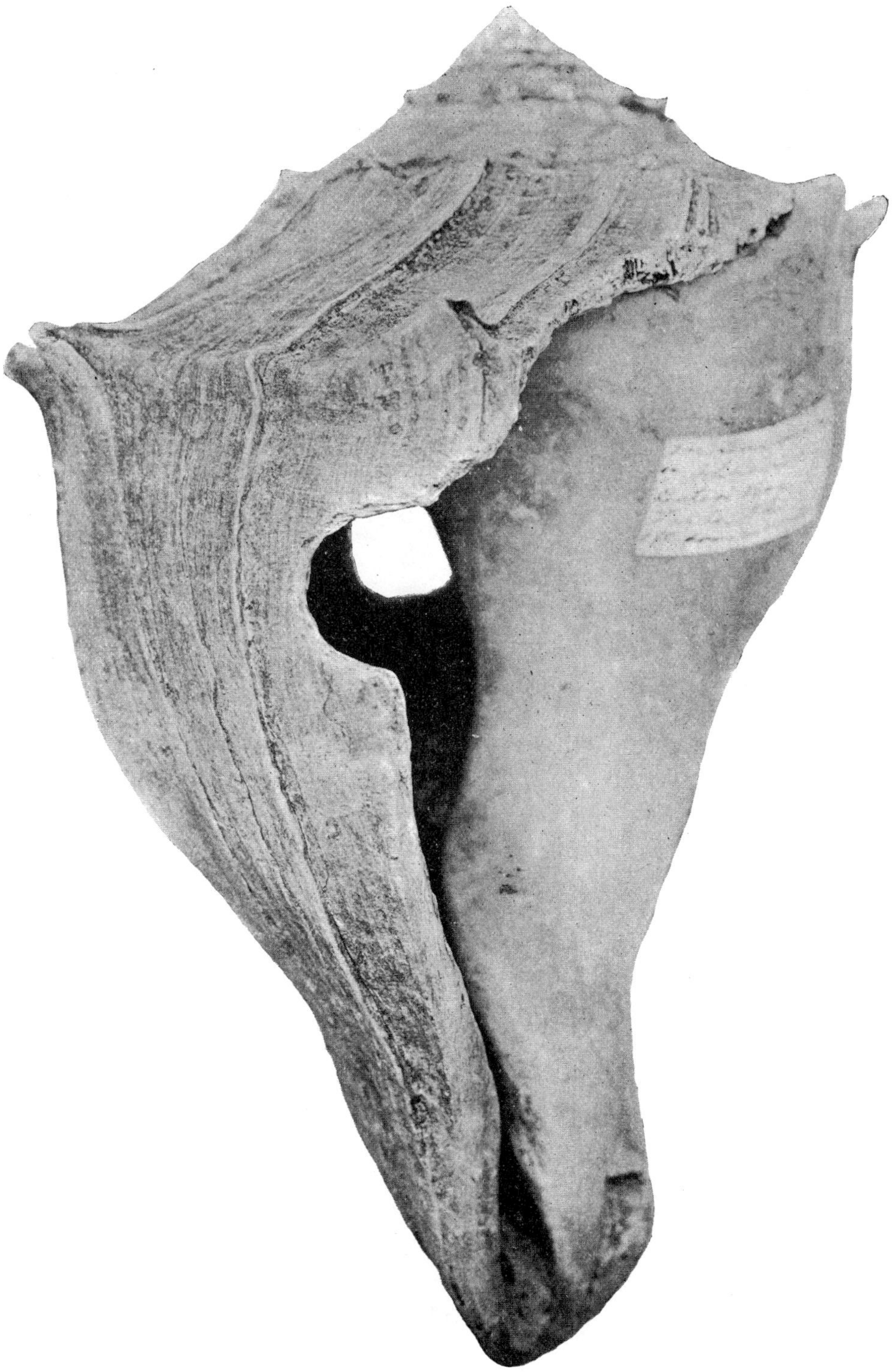

FIG. 36.—Shell implement. Mound Island. (Full Size.)

A massive *Fulgur perversum* is shown in Fig. 36, which, unlike the other shells described, did not come from the surface but lay, one foot down, in the muck in the main canal at Mound Island, Estero Bay. In this specimen are present the small hole above the shoulder and the partial removal of the body whorl from the edge back. A deep notch allowed a handle to pass to the left of the axis through a round hole in the back of the shell. The massive beak is ground to a straight cutting edge, which would be at a slight angle to a handle.

FIG. 37.—Shell implement. Mound Island. (Full size.)

Fig. 37 shows a *Fulgur perversum*, also from Mound Island, with considerable portions removed and in all respects similar to a specimen previously described save that, in place of the double perforation allowing a handle to pass to the right of the axis, the handle, resting in a notch, would pass to the left of the axis through a circular hole on the farther side.

FIG. 38.—Shell implement. Chokoloskee Key. (Full size.)

The implement shown in Fig. 38, a *Fulgur perversum* from Chokoloskee Key, is a variant in that, though deeply notched at the edge of the whorl, the hole at the other side of the shell is not in line to permit the passage of a handle. It is possible the handle abutted against the interior of the shell and was lashed to the axis through the perforation.

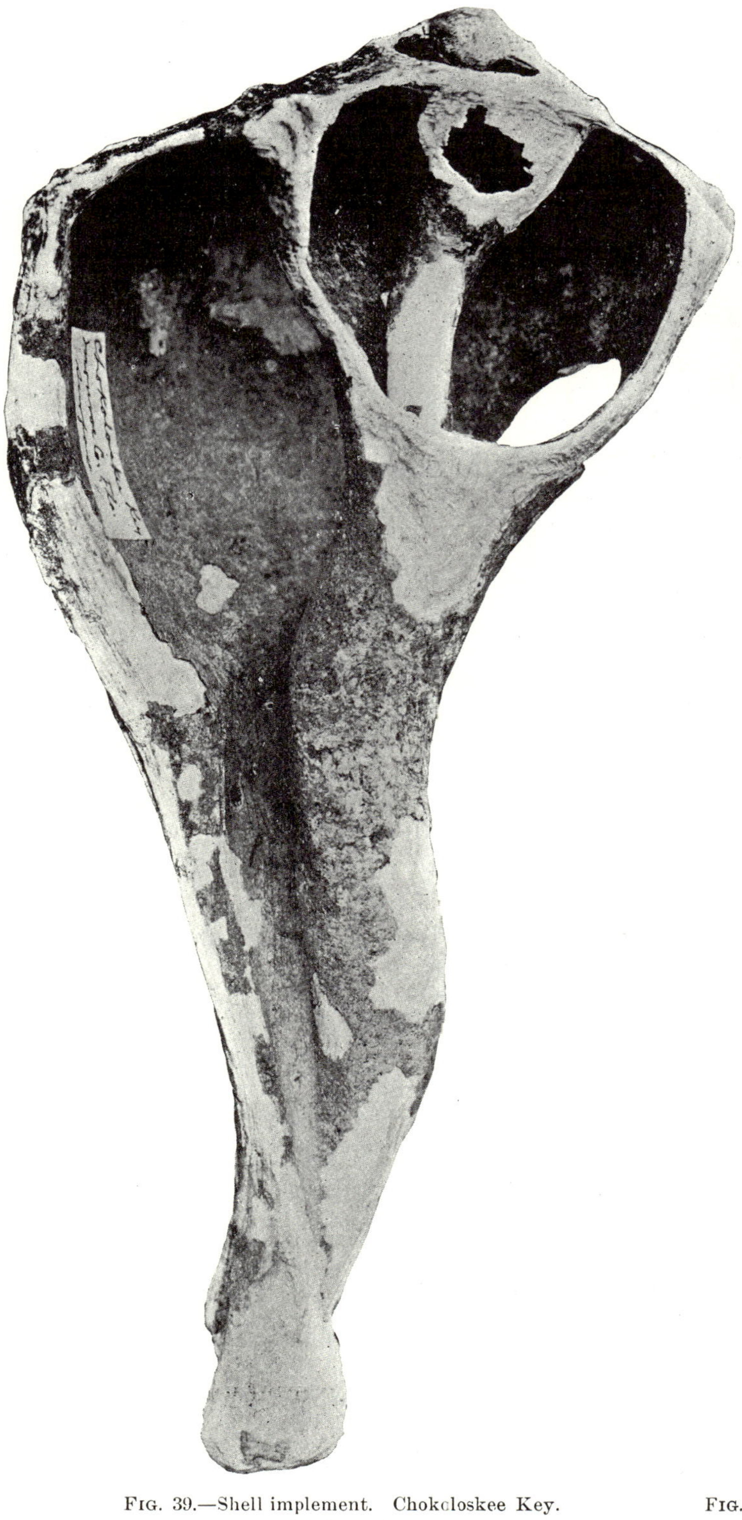

FIG. 39.—Shell implement. Chokoloskee Key. (Full size.)

FIG. 40.—Shell implement. Goodland Point. (Full size.)

Fig. 39 shows a *Fulgur perversum* with notch and single perforation. So much of the shell has been removed that the columella is exposed. The beak is rounded. This implement, which is from Chokoloskee Key, was probably used as a hammer.

Fig. 40 gives a type frequently met with on the west coast, namely, the upper portion of a *Fasciolaria gigantea* containing two holes for a handle, with the long axis extending from it, rounded at the beak by use as a hammer. This specimen comes from Goodland Point.

FIG. 41.—Shell implement. Chokoloskee Key. (Full size.)

FIG. 42.—Shell implement. Fikahatchee Key. (Full size.)

Fig. 41, from Chokoloskee Key, shows a *Fasciolaria gigantea* with somewhat more of the shell, containing two perforations for a handle and a third to allow a firmer attachment to the axis. Much of the beak has disappeared, probably through use has a hammer. This type also is frequently met with on the west coast.

Fig. 42 represents a small and light *Fulgur perversum* from Fikahatchee Key, with notch opposite the perforation. The beak is ground for use. A series of small round holes encircles the shell above the shoulder. This specimen, which is slightly foreshortened in the reproduction, is unique in our experience.

FIG. 43.—Shell implement. Fikahatchee Key. (Full size.)

FIG. 44.—Shell implement. Goodland Point. (Full size.)

FIG. 45.—Shell implement. Russell's Key. (Full size.)

Fig. 43, a *Fulgur perversum* from Fikahatchee Key, with much of the shell removed, is greatly worn and rounded at the beak. Presumably in its use a handle was dispensed with.

Fig. 44, a *Strombus gigas*, is the same type of implement as the preceding. It came from Goodland Point.

Fig. 45 is a *Strombus pugilis* from Russell's Key, with two holes to permit a handle to pass through to the left of the axis. The beak is much chipped. In all probability, this little shell was used as a hammer to open shell-fish, and is of the kind we found in such quantities at Indian Hill.

It will be noted that the type of implement of which we write, on the west coast of Florida was almost universally made from *Fulgur perversum*[1] or *Fasciolaria gigantea*.

Fulgur carica, on the average, is a much stouter shell than *Fulgur perversum*, and was very generally in use on the east coast and on the St. Johns river for the helved implements under consideration. On the west coast *Fulgur carica* is not found, so that the aborigines of these parts were compelled to look to *Fasciolaria* and heaviest forms of *Fulgur perversum*, which, however, as our illustrations show, were often amply sufficient. *Fasciolaria gigantea* is of rare occurrence on the east coast, and we have never seen these implements made from it there.

Irrespective of the shell in use, there are other points of divergence between these implements from the west coast on one hand and from the east coast and from the St. Johns river on the other.

On the east coast and on the St. Johns the shells, practically without exception, have holes for the handles rudely made,—knocked out, apparently. On the other hand, openings for the helves in the shells of the west coast are frequently round and carefully made, as may be seen by reference to the illustrations, though at times, perforations on the west coast are rude also.

A type found only on the west coast, we believe, shows the removal of a large portion of the shell on one side, as is shown in certain of the illustrations. Implements of this type were found by Mr. Cushing in the muck at Marco with wooden handles in place.[2]

Another feature peculiar to the west coast is the cutting of a notch into the margin of the aperture opposite a perforation in the body whorl, as shown in certain of our illustrations, the notch taking the place of a second perforation. We have seen this notch on the St. Johns river but once or twice, where it was present on a *Fulgur perversum* with a carefully wrought hole. The shell was associated with columellæ of *Fasciolaria*, all probably an importation from the west coast.

It is but comparatively recently that the uses of these implements wrought from entire shells have been looked into with attention.

Professor Rau figured and described[3] them as war clubs.

In the *American Naturalist* (August, 1893, p. 720, *et seq.*) we combatted this view on the grounds that many of the shells were too small to be formidable; that the size of the holes often gave evidence of handles too slender to sustain a heavy shock; that the beaks of the shells frequently showed much chipping and wear, which would not be the case if kept for use in battle. We pointed out, also, that the acute angle at which the heavy shells themselves were sometimes placed on the handles on the east coast would indicate employment as hoes rather than use as war clubs.

[1] *Fulgur perversum*, if held facing the observer, has its opening to the left, while *Fulgur carica*, held in the same position, has its opening to the right.

[2] *Op. cit.*, p. 40.

[3] Smithsonian Report, 1879, p. 222.

As we have stated, Mr. Cushing found at Marco these shell tools with handles in place. On some were remains of thongs that bound them. Mr. Cushing mentions various uses for which these tools have served.

While a few of the heaviest varieties of these implements may have seen service as war clubs, it is evident that their use was widely diverse.

Dr. Thomas Wilson of the United States National Museum, Washington, D. C., is now engaged upon an investigation of righthandedness and lefthandedness among the aborigines, and to aid him in his research is examining aboriginal implements which may furnish indications bearing upon the question. In furtherance of this we have furnished Doctor Wilson with over seventy implements of the type we have just described, about thirty of which have been retained permanently by the National Museum. The remainder have been sent to the Museum of Natural History, New York, and to the Peabody Museum, Cambridge, Mass. The shells figured in this Report with others and with the collections made by us on the west coast of Florida, are at the Academy of Natural Sciences of Philadelphia, where may be seen the result of our labors in various southern States.

Certain Aboriginal Remains of the Northwest Florida Coast. Part II [EXCERPT]

BY

CLARENCE B. MOORE

Mound on Hog Island, Levy County.

Hog Island is a small key between the eastern and western passes into the Suwanee river.

The mound, but a short distance from the marsh, is in a dense mass of trees, bushes, and palmetto scrub. Its height is 9 feet 3 inches; its basal diameter, about 50 feet.

This mound seemed to be a shell-heap covered with from 12 to 18 inches of sand. A hole put in by a former digger, showed only shell, as did a large cavity caused by the fall of a great tree. Trenches put in by us reached shell almost immediately, and, after considerable digging in this material, the investigation of the mound was abandoned.

Mound on Pine Key, Levy County.

Pine Key, a small island, lies about one-quarter of a mile from a great shell-heap on the mainland. This shell-heap, visible at a long distance from the Gulf, the northernmost of the great shell-heaps of the west coast, lies about 5 miles in a northerly direction from Cedar Keys.

Pine Key, largely marsh, has a certain amount of solid ground rising from 2 to 3 feet above the general level. About one-quarter acre of this higher ground had been used as a sort of burial place, or cemetery. There had been considerable previous digging, and fragments of human bones and bits of earthenware of the most inferior quality lay scattered over the surface.

The cemetery was trenched in all directions.

In places, bones lay in profusion, while again burials were met with singly, the flexed burial, the bunch and the lone skull being represented. No cranial flattening was noticed. The remains, as a rule, were about 1 foot below the surface, though several burials were met with at a depth of 3 feet.

A "celt" was found not far from the surface, as were a shell drinking cup with a basal perforation, and many sherds, all of poor ware, undecorated in the main, though the check stamp and the complicated stamp were represented.

Also near the surface was the lower part of a ceremonial, mortuary vessel having a basal perforation made before baking. The portion found resembled an inverted cone. Just above the base were two deep, encircling grooves made when the clay was soft. The ware and workmanship were of the coarsest description.

Mound near the Shell-heap, Levy County.

This mound is in thick scrub, about 300 yards from the homestead of Mr. W. R. Young, who lives on the great shell-heap, to which we have referred, and is the owner of the mound in the rear. This mound, 6.5 feet high, 64 feet through its circular base, had been dug into from the NE. margin previous to our coming, a trench 6 feet wide having been carried to the center where it broadened to include a space about 10 feet in diameter. A few fragments of human bones and two or three bits of rude earthenware lay on the surface.

Seven large trenches made by us, not all of which were entirely carried to the base, some having been abandoned when results of others were noted, showed the mound to be mainly of oyster shells irregularly placed.

At the center a measurement from the top showed 18 inches of sand, 22 inches of shell, 14 inches of sand, 1 foot of shell, in order, going down. Beneath, was undisturbed sand. The mound probably was built on rising ground, as its height, taken from the margin, is not accounted for by these measurements.

On the south side of the mound trenching showed 18 inches of sand on top, with a solid mass of shells below, and other trenches gave but slightly varying results.

No human remains or artifacts were met with in our digging, though one bit of human bone, just below the surface, projected from the side of the former trench.

At Cedar Keys our mound investigation for the season was brought to an end.

A continuation of our work farther south hardly would have been consistent with the title of this report. Moreover, Mr. J. S. Raybon, captain of our steamer, who had worked so successfully for us to the northward and to the westward, had been unable to locate any new mounds of importance between Cedar Keys and

Tampa bay. It is only fair to say, however, that owing to the lack of inhabitants along that part of the coast, from whom inquiry could be made, certain mounds may have escaped him. Besides, several years before, we had covered the territory from Tampa almost to Clearwater Harbor (see outline map) with but negative results, while two men in our employ, one of whom was very familiar with the coast, had searched from Tampa to Anclote Key, finding only mounds previously located and dug into by Mr. S. T. Walker,[1] whose researches were continued still farther north without discovery of importance.

Mr. Cushing,[2] it is true, opened a mound at Tarpon Springs, in which he found fragments of interesting ware, but we believe this mound to have been an exception to the general run of mounds from Cedar Keys southward. Just north of Cedar Keys the great shell-heaps of the west coast begin, and neither on the east coast, where large shell-heaps are throughout, nor in the territory of the great shell-heaps on the west coast have we found the contents of mounds to be of much interest.

As we have stated, our work of last season ended at the eastern extremity of Choctawhatchee bay and began this year at the western end of St. Andrews bay, in direct continuation (see map).

During our season's work certain points were brought to our attention.

Going eastward along the coast, we saw the waning influence of Alabama and of the middle Mississippi district as to composition of ware, the admixture of shell[3] entirely disappearing, none having been met with by us east of Choctawhatchee bay, which marks also the easternmost limit of the polished, black ware of Mississippi, as found by us.

[1] Smithsonian Report, 1879.

[2] Proceedings American Philosophical Society, Vol. XXV, No. 153.

[3] In a thoughtful article in the "American Antiquarian," May and June, 1902, entitled "Primitive Keramic Art in Wisconsin", the author of that paper is inclined to believe that a mineral substance, and not pounded shell, is used to temper earthenware through parts of the mound region, where hitherto we have been led to believe pounded shell was used.

To determine this matter, we submitted to Prof. Harry F. Keller, Ph. D., a fragment of thick, porous earthenware found by us in Alabama, which contained a considerable amount of what we have always considered broken shell used for tempering.

Dr. Keller's report is as follows:

June 24, 1902.

"The analysis of the carefully picked material (shell) from the specimen of earthenware from Alabama gave the following results:

Insoluble in dilute acid, (Silica and ferruginous clay)	3.09%
CaO (Lime)	54.07
MgO (Magnesia)	.19
MnO (Manganous oxide)	.09
Fe_2O_3 (Ferric oxide)	.11
CO_2 (Carbonic anhydride)	41.58
P_2O_5 (Phosphoric anhydride)	.62
Moisture	.11
	99.86

"The small amounts of the oxides of iron and maganese may be derived from adhering matrix. The insoluble residue contains traces of carbonaceous matter."

Here we have almost pure carbonate of lime, showing the scaly fragments in the earthenware to be shell.

The growing influence of Georgia in decoration became noticeable also, the complicated stamp, the specialty of that State and of territory to the northward, coming more and more into use. Such being the case, we should look for the clay tempered with coarse gravel, the well-known "gritty ware" of Georgia, but it is not present.

The earthenware of the northwest Florida coast is purely aboriginal in style. Probably most of the mounds there ante-dated the coming of the whites, and where they did not, their builders saw too little of the strangers to suffer modification in their art. It is true that some writers have cited the presence of feet on aboriginal vessels as an indication of European influence, and such vessels are often met with in the mounds of the northwest coast, but we have seen vessels with feet, in various localities, in too many mounds in which no European artifacts were found, to coincide with this idea.

In material and decoration the pottery of the Florida northwest coast averages far above that of such mounds of peninsular Florida, in which earthenware is met with.

For one reason or another, the occurrence of earthenware vessels is infrequent in the burial mounds of the coast of peninsular Florida. We have searched almost the entire east coast between the Georgia boundary and Lake Worth without finding a single vessel, and our good friend, the late Andrew E. Douglass, devoted many seasons to mound work along the east coast, going even as far as Miami, with a like result.

On the west coast, Mr. Cushing found fragments of important vessels in the mound opened by him at Tarpon Springs, but from near that point southward, almost to the end of the peninsula, we saw not a single vessel of earthenware, though there are a few fragments in the shell-heaps.

It is true Mr. Cushing found several vessels of earthenware in the muck at Marco, with his great discovery of objects of wood, but the vessels were few in number and unimportant as to shape and decoration.

Presumably, then, the custom to inter earthenware vessels with the dead obtained but little, if at all, along the Florida east coast, and the lower half of the west coast of peninsular Florida. If, in these districts, vessels to any extent were put into the mounds, these vessels were of wood and perishable.

Superior as is the earthenware of the northwest Florida coast to most of that of the peninsula, it does not excel a few of the finest specimens met with by us in the mounds of the St. Johns river. A duck-vessel[1] from near the mouth of the St. Johns; sherds of excellent paste and superior decoration, from near Dunn's creek[2] (see outline map); still more beautiful ones from a neighboring mound; part of a vessel and a handle representing a vulture's head, beautifully incised and showing the fine yellow of the paste, alternating with crimson pigment, from a mound near Lake Monroe, hold their own with the finest earthenware of the northwest coast of Florida.

[1] "Certain Sand Mounds of Duval County, Florida." Plate LXXXIII.

[2] "Certain Sand Mounds of the St. Johns River." Part I, Pl. II, Fig. 1. Incidentally, at this mound was the southernmost occurrence of ware bearing the complicated stamp decoration.

We have two hypotheses to offer to account for this:

1.—That the aborigines of the peninsula possessed fine ware, but did not, as a rule, inter it with the dead.

It must be borne in mind that the natives of the peninsula did not make great mortuary deposits of earthenware as did those of the Florida mainland, the vessel of earthenware being simply one of a great number of objects from which selection was made. Fewer vessels were put into the mounds, and as earthenware was not so exclusively a mortuary selection, perhaps less attention was paid to the quality of that taken for burial. Besides, the interment of "freak," or ceremonial, ware, which is always inferior to the other ware of the district where it was used, was more largely practised in the peninsula than it was on the northwest coast and, therefore, the pottery of the peninsular mounds may not be representative.

2.—That the finest vessels of the peninsula were importations.

From the island of Marco, southwest Florida, we got two large bird head handles, of excellent design, found alone, one representing the head of a turkey, the other that of a predatory bird. Around one of these heads a groove had been made to permit use as a pendant. The other head had doubtless served a similar purpose, as circular spaces, through which a cord could pass, had been left, at the time of manufacture, through the neck and through the bill. Not only was the workmanship of the heads markedly that of the middle Mississippi district or of the Gulf, but the ware was what is known as shell-tempered, which ware was in use in the districts we have named, but not in peninsular Florida. These heads were doubtless importations, and other fine specimens of ware may have been importations also.

On the whole we are inclined to believe that the best ware found in the peninsula was exceptional and perhaps got there through barter. The lower average of excellence of sherds in the peninsula argues a supply of inferior vessels, and the fact that the "freak," or ceremonial, ware is so much below the standard of that of the northwest coast might indicate a lower quality for vessels of other classes also. Had the natives of the peninsula possessed vessels of the highest grade in great numbers, we believe, in one way or another, more indication of it would have come to light.

In the first part of this report we spoke of a mortuary custom prevailing in peninsular Florida[1] to knock a hole through the base of a vessel, presumably to "kill" the pot, that its soul might accompany that of the dead man. We spoke of a refinement of this custom, and described vessels of fantastic form and flimsy material made expressly for interment with the dead, in the bases of which holes

[1] In the "American Antiquarian," Sept.–Oct., 1902, is a paper by Mr. Francis U. Duff, on the antiquities of the Mimbres valley, New Mexico, describing, among other things, the finding of "large bowls inverted over the crania of the departed. Each of these bowls, before being deposited in the grave, had a small hole broken in its bottom." It is interesting to note the occurrence of the mortuary perforation of the base of vessels in this remote region so far removed from where this mortuary custom flourished at its fullest. In the Mimbres valley, however, bowls were not inverted over lone skulls or skulls with a few scattered bones, as they were in the graves of the Florida northwest coast, but were placed over skulls interred with their skeletons.

had been made previous to the baking of the clay. Incidentally, we found this "freak," or ceremonial, ware in the peninsula, from the mouth of the St. Johns river to Lake Beresford (see outline map), going southward, and in the lake district at the head of the Ocklawaha river.

A few examples of this ready-made "freak" ware were met with by us east of Pensacola bay during our work last season. During this year's investigation, as our readers may recall, examples of this form were found in increasing numbers, and individual vessels were often of much greater size than anything of the kind we had met with to the westward on the coast, or, incidentally, in peninsular Florida, save in the mounds of Volusia, south of Lake George.

As our work progressed more to the east, a new feature in "freak" ware was encountered. In the mounds of St. Andrew's bay two vessels of a new type, and fragments of similar ones, were found, while farther to the east vessels of this kind were encountered in considerable numbers. These vessels were life-forms, usually, but differed from other life-forms of the same district, in that they were inferior to them as to ware and workmanship, and that they had various perforations made previous to baking, in the body of the vessel as well as the customary one in the base.[1]

An interesting custom noted with but few exceptions along the northwest coast was the placing in the mounds of general deposits of earthenware, nearly always in the eastern part of the mound. These deposits were found in darkened sand, often at the very edge of the mound, and continued with the blackened sand, a few vessels together, in toward the center or to it. Sometimes the deposits were met with at some little distance in from the margin, but nearly always in the eastern side of the mound.

These masses of blackened sand in which the general deposits of earthenware lay were noticed by us in the mounds during our former season's work and were referred to by us in Part I of our report. So almost universal was the juxtaposition of darkened sand and general deposits of ware in the mounds, during our work this season, that considerable thought was devoted by us to the matter. Sand of this

[1] Among numbers of small "freak" vessels found by us in the Grant mound, near the mouth of the St. Johns river, was part of a vessel filled with perforations, like a sieve. We are uncertain whether or not this vessel should be included in the same class as those having occasional perforations in the body.

The incense-cups of Mexico and of Central America, though they have perforations of the body, made before baking, do not seem to us to be of the same class as these large vessels from northwest Florida, which have basal perforations in addition to those in the body. These latter vessels with their ready-made body-perforations would seem to be intimately connected with the ceremonial vessels of peninsular Florida, since both classes possess the perforation of the base, made before the baking of the clay, though the vessels of peninsular Florida do not show the body-perforations which are probably only an amplification of the mortuary perforation of the base. Therefore, as the ceremonial vessels of peninsular Florida, being without body-perforations, could not have served as incense-burners, it is not likely that the ceremonial vessels of northwest Florida, which are so nearly related to the others, though possessed of body-perforations, were intended for the burning of incense.

The Twentieth Annual Report of the Bureau of American Ethnology will consist of Prof. W. H. Holmes', "The Pottery of the Eastern United States," a most admirable memoir, part of which it has been our good fortune to see in manuscript.

We earnestly advise those interested in the subject of aboriginal ware carefully to study this memoir, on its appearance.

kind was often carefully examined by us for charcoal, but none was found, nor was adjacent sand burnt or discolored as by fire. In our account of the mound at West Bay post-office, in the early part of this volume, we have stated that a sample of this blackened sand, examined chemically and microscopically, showed its color to be due to carbonaceous matter, very probably of animal origin, and that the material, in all probability, could not have come from anything in the vegetable line. As this report is not intended for popular reading, in all probability our readers are as able to draw conclusions as we are. It would seem to us, however, that masses of animal matter, incinerated in a way to escape mixture with charcoal, have been mingled with sand which was placed in that part of the mound devoted to deposits of earthenware, put in for the dead in common. What these masses of flesh consisted of we are unable to decide. If the flesh belonged to lower animals and the bones were not removed before burning, and it seems unlikely that they should have been, the incineration must have been complete, as particles of half-burnt bone are not present in the sand.

If we suppose, on the other hand, that the flesh which we know was sometimes stripped from human skeletons when taken from the dead-house, was cremated, the absence of particles of bone can be accounted for. We think this latter supposition the more probable since aboriginal cremation did not seem to reduce bones in a thorough way, judging from our rather extensive experience of the matter in the mounds of Georgia.

Burials of human remains, also, were in greater numbers in the eastern portions of the mounds, sometimes being there and in the central parts, exclusively. In other cases, however, human remains were met with throughout the entire mound.

No new feature as to form of burial was noted during this season's work. The lone skull, the bunch, the flexed burial, the burial at length were met with; also loose bones scattered here and there. The urn-burial, also, was found in two localities.

The question of urn-burial in Florida is an interesting one since we know the custom to have been largely in vogue in Alabama and in Georgia, and yet there is no evidence [1] of the extension of the custom into peninsular Florida.

We have seen how large bowls were put over skulls at Perdido bay, the boundary between Alabama and Florida, and how the custom, continuing eastward into Florida, was noted along Santa Rosa sound and at the eastern extremity of Choctawhatchee bay, where, also, in one instance, an inverted bowl was found covering another bowl containing human remains.

This season we have remarked the existence of a cemetery with urn-burials still farther east, at the town of St. Andrews, and have found a single urn-burial in a mound on Ocklockonee bay farther yet to the eastward, though still on the mainland.

Beyond this point, in all Florida, we have met with no example of urn-burial, nor is there one on record.

[1] With the exception of a statement made in a newspaper by an investigator of a single mound and omitted from his official report.

Cremation, which we met with so frequently in Georgia, but saw but once during our work on the Alabama and Tombigbee rivers, was not noted by us during our first year's work along the northwest Florida coast, and but twice, unmistakably, during this, our second year's work. In the peninsula of Florida we have not met with true cremation where it was evidently the purpose to burn the body as a form of burial, such cremation as is found there apparently being where single bones or parts of skeletons have lain in close proximity to ceremonial fires. These fragments of burnt bone are often found lying with bones unaffected by fire, while, at times, a skeleton is seen to have the bones of one arm burnt or calcined, or sometimes a portion of the skull, and the like.

Cremation, then, as a form of burial, cannot be said to have obtained in peninsular Florida and was practised but occasionally in the mainland, or northwestern portion.

There seems to be a possible explanation for this occasional occurrence of cremation in a district where inhumation was so generally practised. Cabeça de Vaca, who, as the reader is aware, spent some years among the aborigines of the northwest Florida coast, tells us that persons there in general were buried, but that doctors were cremated. In our work on the mounds of the Georgia coast we pointed out that this statement could not apply to that part of the country, since cremation was very widely practised there, and, moreover, often included the bodies of infants. But along the northwest Florida coast, the district of which Cabeça de Vaca's statement was made, the result of our investigations seems to bear out the assertion.

It was our intention, another season, to carry our investigation from Mobile bay westward along the coast, in the endeavor to trace connection between that district and the region we have covered to the east.

Since our return, this spring and summer (1902), Mr. J. S. Raybon, captain of our steamer, who has in previous years so successfully located mounds for us, went over part of Mobile bay and most of the Mississippi coast.

A few mounds rewarded his search on the eastern shore of Mobile bay, but along the coast of Mississippi, apart from shell-heaps, almost nothing was met with.

Certain Aboriginal Remains of the Central Florida West-Coast

BY

CLARENCE B. MOORE

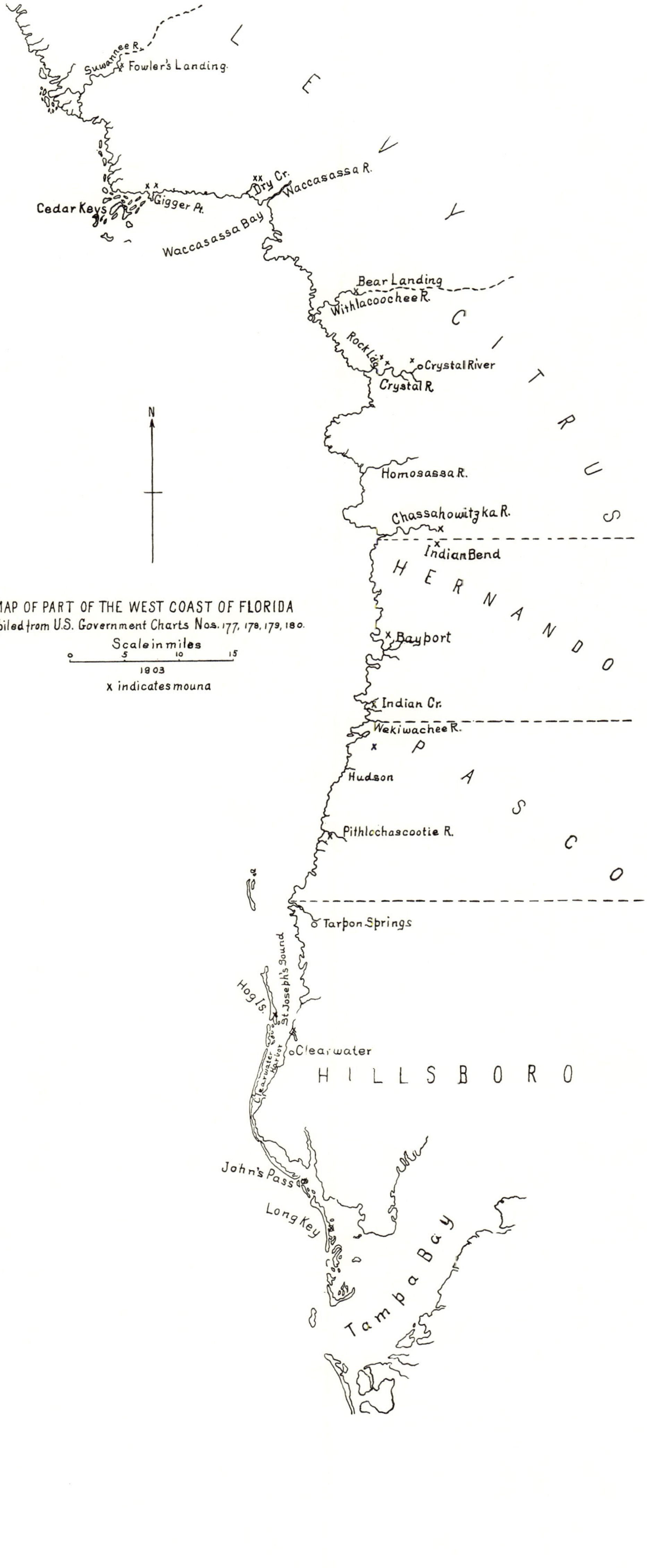

MAP OF PART OF THE WEST COAST OF FLORIDA
Compiled from U.S. Government Charts Nos. 177, 178, 179, 180.
Scale in miles
0 5 10 15
1903
x indicates mound

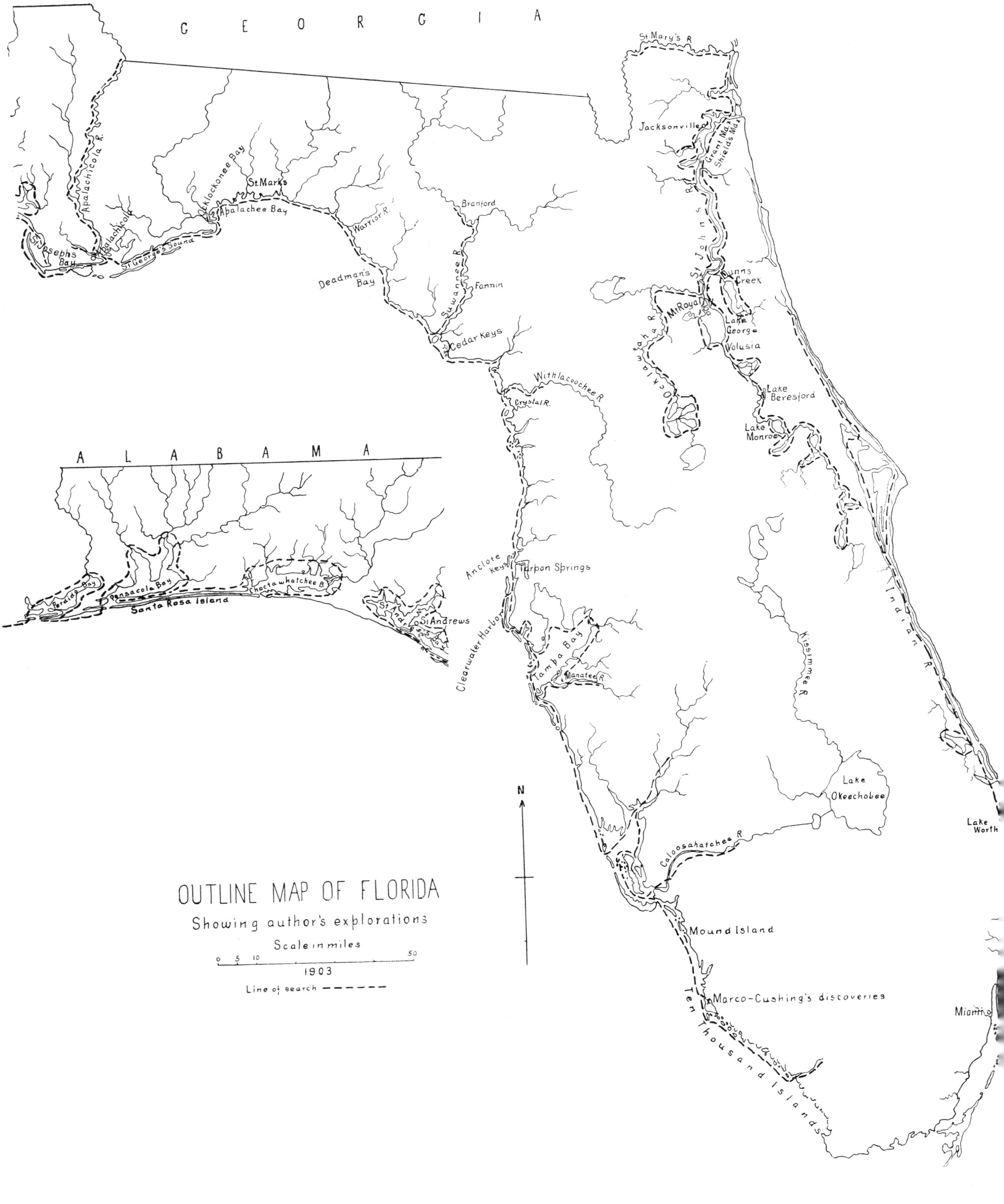

GEORGIA
ALABAMA
St. Mary's R.
Jacksonville
Grant Md.
Shields Md.
St. Johns R.
Dunns Creek
Mt. Royal
Ocklawaha R.
Lake George
Volusia
Lake Beresford
Lake Monroe
Indian R.
Kissimmee R.
Lake Okeechobee
Lake Worth
Miami
Caloosahatchee R.
Mound Island
Marco-Cushing's discoveries
Ten Thousand Islands
Apalachicola R.
Apalachicola
St. Josephs Bay
St. George's Sound
Ocklockonee Bay
St. Marks
Apalachee Bay
Warrior R.
Deadman's Bay
Branford
Suwannee R.
Fannin
Cedar Keys
Withlacoochee R.
Crystal R.
Anclote Keys
Tarpon Springs
Clearwater Harbor
Tampa Bay
Manatee R.
Perdido Bay
Pensacola Bay
Santa Rosa Island
Choctawhatchee B.
St. Andrews
N
OUTLINE MAP OF FLORIDA
Showing author's explorations
Scale in miles
0 5 10 50
1903
Line of search

CERTAIN ABORIGINAL MOUNDS OF THE CENTRAL FLORIDA WEST-COAST.

By Clarence B. Moore.

During the seasons 1901 and 1902 we investigated the aboriginal remains of the northwest Florida coast, beginning at Perdido bay, the coast-boundary between Alabama and Florida, and ending at the town of Cedar Keys[1] (see outline map).

This season (1903), our work was directly continued down the west coast of Florida, beginning at the Suwannee river, just above Cedar Keys, and continuing through Waccasassa bay, Withlacoochee bay, Crystal bay, Homosassa bay, Chassahowitzka bay, St. Joseph's sound and along the Gulf coast and islands to Tampa bay, including short journeys up the various rivers along the route.

Much of the territory covered by us is sparsely settled, so that information as to the locality of mounds is difficult to obtain and, therefore, although search had been made in advance for us by two agents, and over part of the distance by four, yet we doubt not that some mounds have escaped us, as, no doubt, have numerous cemeteries. By cemeteries, we mean where burials have been under level ground, unmarked by mounds. We do not believe these burials were enclosed in urns.

As we had anticipated, the yield of earthenware from the mounds of the central west-coast of Florida did not equal that from the mounds of the northwest Florida coast, though a few vessels found intact and many sherds, showed that the aborigines of the central west-coast had been possessed of some excellent ware bearing decorations showing no mean ability. Life-forms in earthenware were conspicuous by their absence.

In reference to the earthenware described in this report we quote from our report of last season.

"All measurements of earthenware reported in this volume are approximate.

"It must be borne in mind in respect to process work that reductions in size are made with regard to diameter and not area. If a diagram four inches by two inches is to be reduced one-half, each diameter is divided by two and the reproduction, which is called half size, is two inches by one inch. The area of the original diagram, however, is eight square inches, while that of the so-called half-size reproduction is two square inches, or one-quarter the area. To find the actual size of a design shown in diagram, multiply the length and the breadth by two, if the diagram is given 'half size;' by three, if 'one-third,' and so on.

[1] "Certain Aboriginal Remains of the Northwest Florida Coast," Parts I and II. Journ. Acad. Nat. Sci. of Phila. Vols. XI, XII.

"In a few cases partial restoration of vessels has been attempted, but always in a material differing in color from the original, so that the restoration may be readily recognized, and it has been done only when the remainder of the vessel clearly indicated the size and shape of the missing part."

All objects found by us, with the exception of certain duplicates sent to the Museum of Phillips Academy, Andover, Mass., may be seen at the Academy of Natural Sciences of Philadelphia.

Dr. M. G. Miller, who has aided us in all our previous mound work, determined as to human remains this season as before, and assisted us in a general way in the field work and in putting this report through the press.

Our warm thanks are tendered owners of the mounds investigated by us, who, to a man, when requested, accorded fullest permission to dig.

Mounds Investigated.

Mounds near Fowler's Landing, Suwannee river (2).
Mound near Cedar Keys, Gulf coast.
Mound near Gigger Point, Gulf coast.
Mounds near Dry creek, Waccasassa bay (2).
Mound near Bear Landing, Withlacoochee river.
Mound near Rock Landing, Crystal river.
Mound near the Shell-heap, Crystal river.
Mound near Crystal river settlement, Crystal river.
Mound near Chassahowitzka river.
Mound near Indian Bend, Gulf coast.
Mound near Bayport, Gulf coast.
Mound near Indian creek, Gulf coast.
Mound near Wekiwachee river, Gulf coast.
Mound near Pithlochascootie river.
Mound on Hog island, St. Joseph's sound.
Mound near Clearwater, Clearwater Harbor.
Mound near John's Pass, Gulf coast.
Mound on Long Key, Gulf coast.

Mound near Fowler's Landing, Levy County.

Fowler's Landing is about sixteen miles above the mouth of the Suwannee river, on the right-hand side, going up, though but a short distance, by land, from the waters of the Gulf, so the mound may be fairly classed as belonging to the coast. It was in thick scrub, on property of the East Coast Lumber Co., about one-quarter mile in NE. direction from the landing. Adjacent, were excavations whence material for the mound had been taken. This mound, of sand, as were all investigated by us along the coast, unless otherwise described, was circular in outline; was 7 feet high and 50 feet across the base. It had suffered considerably from previous digging. In addition to a number of smaller holes, a trench about 4 feet deep and 11 feet wide had been dug from the western margin about 20 feet in toward the center. Over the surface of the mound were fragments of human bone and bits of earthenware. This mound, which was completely dug down by us, had a clearly defined base-line, marking the original surface upon which the mound had been piled. No grave-pits were present, and of the forty-seven burials found by us, none lay upon the base and none was over 3.5 feet from the surface.

Burials were encountered near the margin and were not confined to any part or parts of the mound. They increased in number as the digging progressed, the majority of the burials being in the body of the mound. In form, the burials were of the bunched variety and consisted of certain bones without the cranium; bones with one, two or three skulls; and, in one case, a bunch with four skulls. The bones were all badly decayed. No crania were in a condition to keep, though a few calvaria, which held together temporarily, showed no cranial flattening.

Objects deposited with the dead were singularly few. Near a burial, lay fragments of a marine shell (*Fulgur*).[1] With another burial was part of an earthenware vessel having a bird-head handle but, as sherds were scattered throughout the mound, the proximity of this one may have been accidental. Hammer stones, pebbles and the like were conspicuously absent. Two "celts," not associated with burials, fell with caving sand.[2]

In the extreme edge of the mound, on the west, was an undecorated pot of very inferior ware, badly broken. With it was a vessel with globular body and upright neck around which was a complicated stamp decoration. Both these vessels had the usual mortuary mutilation made by knocking out a part of the bottom, as had all vessels met with by us in this mound.

It is interesting to note the occurrence here of the complicated stamp, the specialty of Georgia. It is frequently met with to the northward in Florida, as the readers of our two reports on the northwest coast may recall, and its occurrence much farther south along the coast will be described in this report. On the St. John's river, however, it was found by us no farther south than about ten miles above Palatka, about on a line with this Fowler's Landing mound.

Also in a marginal part of the mound, to the southeast, were many large fragments of vessels, undecorated, all of inferior ware, water-soaked and crushed. In addition, four vessels were recovered, nearly whole, with the exception of the basal perforation. Of these, Vessel No. 4, undecorated save for several encircling incised lines, somewhat resembles a dumb-bell in shape, though the base has been perfectly flat. A vessel much like this one is shown in Fig. 151 in the second part of our report on the northwest Florida coast.

[1] All determinations of shells have been made by Dr. H. A. Pilsbry and Mr. E. G. Vanatta, of the Academy of Natural Sciences of Philadelphia.

[2] Thanks are due for determination of rock material, from which objects mentioned in this report are made, to Dr. E. Goldsmith and Mr. S. H. Hamilton, of the Academy of Natural Sciences of Philadelphia. As it has not been deemed advisable to mutilate specimens, identifications are approximate only. It has not been thought necessary to give the rocks from which the "celts" found by us were manufactured. None seemed to present new features, and many were given to owners of mounds.

FIG. 1.—Vessel No. 5. Mound near Fowler's Landing. (Full size.)

FIG. 2.—Vessel No. 5. Decoration. Mound near Fowler's Landing. (Half size.)

Vessel No. 5, shown in Fig. 1, has an interesting incised decoration shown diagrammatically in Fig. 2, where restored portions are given in broken lines. There are two holes for suspension.

With these vessels was one entirely undecorated and another with a complicated stamp decoration around the neck.

Vessel No. 6, found alone in the western margin of the mound, is of most excellent yellow ware and of interesting shape and decoration. The vessel, shown in Fig. 3, is intact, save for a small basal perforation. The decoration is given in diagram in Fig. 4.

FIG. 3.—Vessel No. 6. Mound near Fowler's Landing. (Full size.)

FIG. 4.—Vessel No. 6. Decoration. Mound near Fowler's Landing. (One-third size.)

FIG. 5.—Vessel No. 7. Mound near Fowler's Landing. (Two-thirds size.)

In the margin of the eastern part of the mound were several undecorated sherds and Vessel No. 7 (Fig. 5), having two holes for suspension, on the same side and so near the base that it is plain the vessel was either ceremonial or, at all events, not intended for liquids. A part of the rim has been restored.

From near the base came an undecorated vessel in the form of a much-truncated cone.

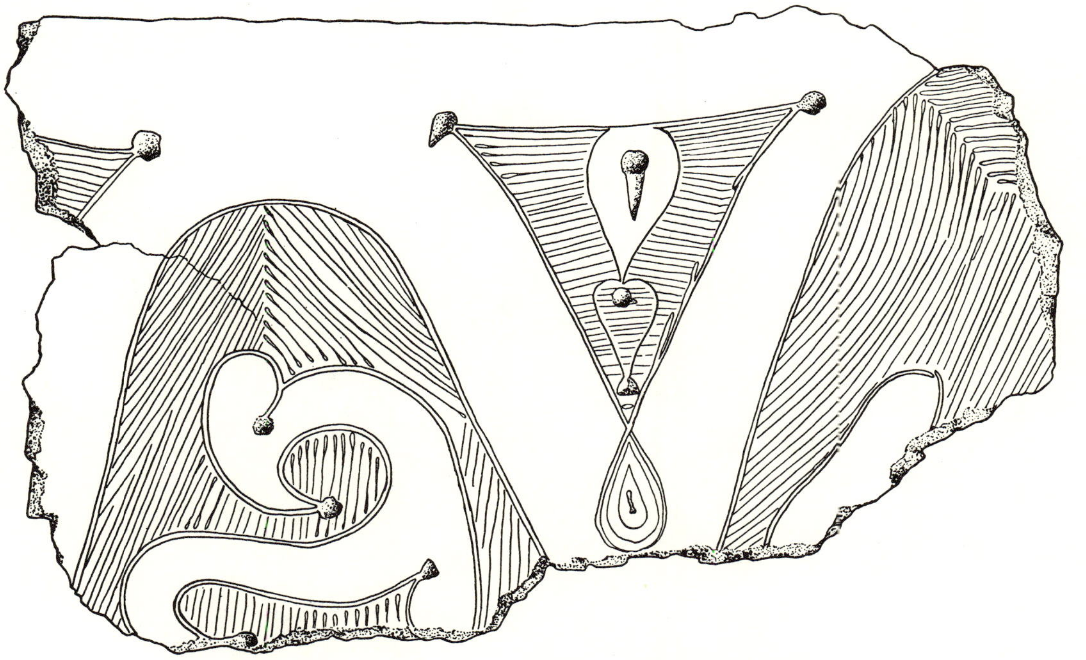

FIG. 6.—Sherd. Mound near Fowler's Landing. (Half size.)

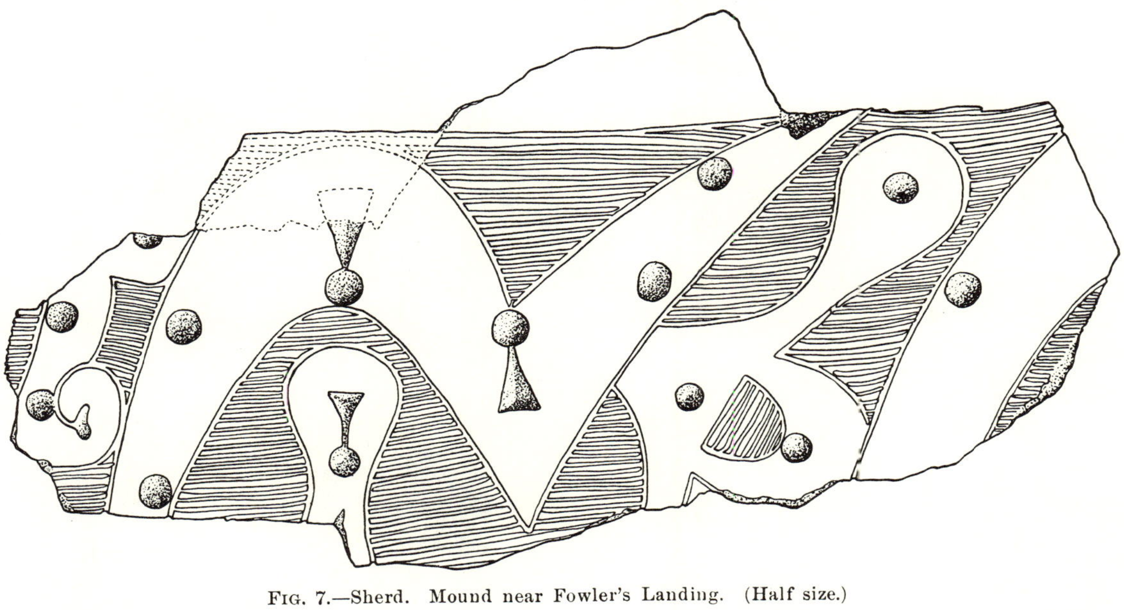

FIG. 7.—Sherd. Mound near Fowler's Landing. (Half size.)

FIG. 8.—Selection of sherds. Mound near Fowler's Landing. (Half size.)

Smaller Mound near Fowler's Landing, Levy County.

About 75 yards in a SW. direction from the other, was a low mound of irregular shape, literally dug to pieces, presumably by the ubiquitous treasure seeker, as one great central excavation extended considerably below the base. So great was the wreck that no conclusion as to the original height, diameter or shape could be arrived at. Though the surface was covered with sand from the former excavations, no fragment of bone or of earthenware was apparent and considerable digging, here and there, by us yielded but a single fragment of earthenware. Presumably, this mound was of the domiciliary class.

Near the surface were scattered parts of a human effigy-vessel. Most diligent search failed to recover the facial parts which, possibly, had not been placed in the mound.

Throughout the mound were various sherds, as a rule of inferior ware, though occasionally of excellent quality, in no case showing sand-, grit-, or shell-tempering. No small check-stamp was present, and but few sherds showed the complicated stamp.

In Figs. 6, 7, are shown, diagrammatically, two sherds from this mound, while in Fig. 8 a selection of sherds from the mound is given. It is evident that the makers of this mound favored the incised and punctate decoration.

In the mound were no masses of sand artificially colored and surrounding deposits of earthenware, such as we found in the mounds of the coast, to the northward.

The record of the discovery of a fish-spear of native copper will be given here, incidentally, as the place where the spear was found is too far up the Suwannee river rightly to be included in a description of the coast-territory.

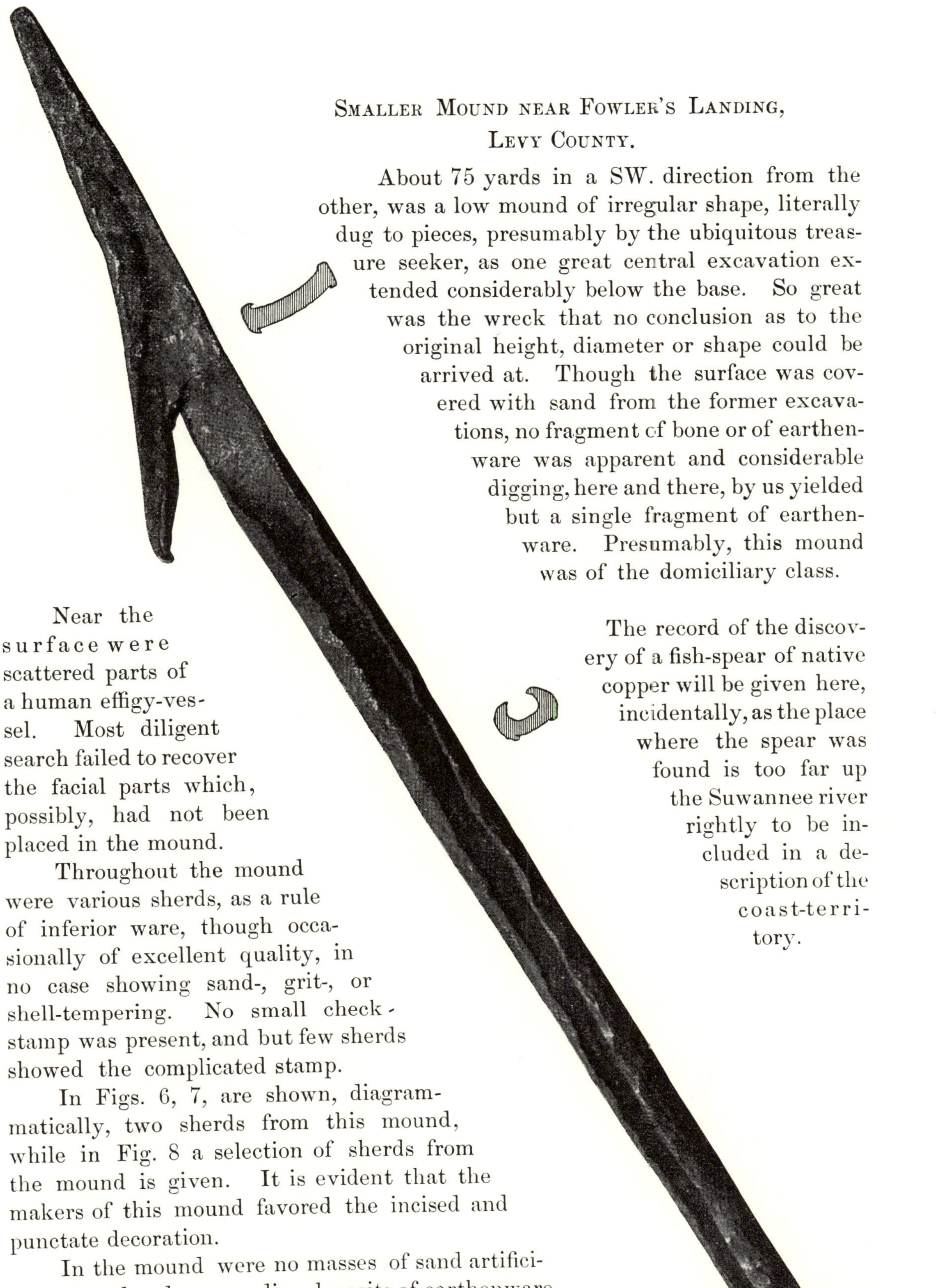

Fig. 9.—Fish-spear of native copper, from near Fannin, Suwannee river. (Full size.)

During our visit to Cedar Keys we met Decatur Pittman, Esq., of that place, Justice of the Peace, and a collector of aboriginal relics. By him we were shown a copper fish-spear 11.5 inches in length (Fig. 9), of which Mr. Pittman gives the following history :—

About seven years ago as Mr. John Clark, his father and his brother were digging in the garden of their place which is two miles below Fannin (see outline map), on the Suwannee river, they found the spear about eighteen inches below the surface.

Somewhat over two years ago Mr. Pittman heard of the finding of the spear and, at a later period, acquired it.

The value of this implement of native copper, coming from Florida, was fully appreciated by Mr. Pittman, who relinquished the spear to the Academy of Natural Sciences of Philadelphia, only because he realized, with true scientific spirit, that such a specimen was more fittingly placed in a museum in perpetuity than in a private collection.

This spear, a unique discovery as coming from Florida, would not be of unusual rarity in Wisconsin, according to Mr. H. P. Hamilton, of Two Rivers, Wisconsin, the well-known expert and collector of "coppers."

There is one point about the spear which deserves close attention. By examining the cross-sections the reader will see that a small semi-enclosed space has been left on one side of the spear, which might appear as though intended for a shaft, and yet that this space is too restricted to hold a wooden shaft of a size necessary for the work required of the spear. Neither Mr. Hamilton nor Mr. David Boyle, of the Provincial Museum, Toronto, who is very familiar with "coppers," believes that this space was intended for the insertion of a shaft. Mr. Boyle writes :

"As to the drawing you send of the fish-spear found in the Suwannee River and the question you propound respecting the small space apparently left for the insertion of a handle, I beg to give it as my opinion that it was never the intention of the maker so to use the narrow channel. The spear or harpoon has been made from a thin piece of copper and the maker had sufficient gumption, no doubt as the result of experience, to know that a piece of native copper of the size your diagram shows this to be, would bend when an attempt was made to employ it in giving an effective stroke. He has, therefore, hammered down both edges for the purpose not only of strengthening his tool, but of giving it a tolerably uniform breadth, and this shank was no doubt inserted *in* a handle rather than having been prepared for the insertion *of* a handle. Perhaps it was with only the latter object in view (*i e.* giving it a uniform breadth) that the hammering was done at all because he could reduce his material to a regular form by beating down the edges much more rapidly than by cutting away the superfluous material. I think, however, there can be little doubt that the ancient coppersmith had arrived at the knowledge that hammering the metal gave it stiffness apart from any other reason why, as in this case, such work was performed. If this tool had been inserted in a handle I suppose the handle was split, the tool being placed in the cleft, and then securely bound with either animal or vegetable fibre."

Although other mounds on the Suwannee river may not be considered coast mounds, yet, as no mound should be investigated without a public record of the fact, it has been thought best to give here, incidentally, certain work done by us on the river.

A mound near Jenning's Landing, Lafayette Co., about thirty miles by water from the mouth of the river, just bordering the swamp, about a quarter of a mile in a westerly direction from the landing, was 4.5 feet high and 62 feet across the base. Careful trenching yielded: four small bunched burials and a few scattered bones, near the surface; a few uninteresting sherds; a mass of chert; a rude arrowhead or knife, of the same material.

Fannin is at the NW. corner of Levy County (see outline map). About one-third of a mile in a northerly direction from the landing is a mound on property of Messrs. R. L. Tison & Co., of Fannin. The mound, 2 feet 8 inches high, from 46 feet to 56 feet across the base, variously measured, was carefully dug and trenched by us. One or two sherds only, were met with.

About one-half mile in an ENE. direction from Fannin is a mound showing much previous digging. Its height is 4.5 feet; its basal diameters are 46 to 64 feet. Thorough trenching yielded absolutely nothing.

At Fayetteville, Lafayette Co., about 12 miles above Fannin, is a mound on property of Mr. John E. Moriarty. The mound showed traces of previous digging in almost every part. Its height is 4 feet 8 inches; its basal diameter, 64 feet. Practically, every untouched portion of the mound was demolished by us. Remains of a disturbed skeleton were found at the beginning of the body of the mound and, farther in, were four small bunched burials, three with a single skull each, and one with two crania. Another burial consisted of a single skull with another skull immediately below it. These burials ranged from 3 feet to 4 feet 3 inches in depth. With one was a "celt" of hard rock, about 5 inches in length, and a single chip of chert. Near the base, in two places, were deposits of mussel-shells (*Unio infucatus*), unassociated with bones. There were in the mound also several flakes of chert, and two sherds, one with incised, dentate marking in a punctate field, another with rude line and punctate decoration.

Within sight of Rocky Landing, Lafayette Co., is a mound of sand, as are all we investigated on the Suwannee river, which had seen much previous digging. Its height is 4 feet; its basal diameter, 40 feet. All untouched portions, practically, were dug through by us. Near the center of the mound, 3.5 feet down, was a skull in fragments and about 1 foot distant, small fragments of bones with sand tinged with hematite, and a neatly made lance head of chert, 4 inches long. Near bits of skull and decayed fragments of other bones, with charcoal nearby, was a "celt." Another "celt" was found in sand thrown out by one of our diggers. In the SW. part of the mound, about 6 feet from the extreme margin, 3 feet 4 inches down, was a coarse bowl of somewhat over 1 pint capacity, of ordinary form and with the usual basal mutilation. The decoration consists of incised encircling lines below the rim with two additional encircling lines beneath, made up of punctate markings. With this vessel was a mass of fragments mostly of undecorated ware, among which was all or nearly all of a large bowl. There were also parts of a vessel with a decoration of rudely made incised encircling parallel lines.

The investigation was continued to Branford with negative results.

The Suwannee river, famous in song, has flat swampy banks, save in places, as far up as Branford. Beyond this point, we are informed, the river is narrow with less marshy surroundings. We have crosssed the river at Ellaville, much farther up, where the stream is picturesque and the banks rise considerably above the level of the water. This portion of the stream no doubt invited aboriginal occupation.

Mound near Cedar Keys, Levy County.

This mound, in hammock[1] land, at the edge of the salt marsh bordering the Gulf, is about 3 miles in a NNE. direction from Cedar Keys, on property of Hon. E. J. Lutterloh, mayor of that place. Great excavations near by, whence sand for the mound was taken, give to it an appearance of considerable altitude but, measured from the general level, the height is 8 feet. In shape the mound is irregular, with basal diameters of 85 feet and 133 feet.

[1] As to the meaning of the word "hammock" see pg. 140 of our second part of "Certain Aboriginal Remains of the Northwest Florida Coast."

This mound, which had every appearance of belonging to the domiciliary class, was carefully trenched by us without the discovery of even a remnant of bone or a fragment of pottery.

Mound near Gigger Point, Levy County.

Gigger Point, which extends into the Gulf, is about three miles in a NE. direction from Cedar Keys. At the rear of this point is the property of Mr. A. M. Dorsett, resident on the place. The mound, circular in outline, was in a cultivated field, and itself had been ploughed over for a considerable period. There had been much previous digging in various parts of the mound, but in a superficial way only. The diameter of base was 46 feet. The height, at the time of the total demolition of the mound by us, was 5 feet, but the original height had been lessened at least 2 feet by recent digging, as was shown by partly uncovered roots of a palmetto on the upper part of the mound. Fragments of human bones and bits of undecorated earthenware were scattered over the surface in every direction.

Burials were met with in every part of the mound, from the margin to the center, the great majority being skeletons which had been buried denuded of flesh, but held together by ligaments. This was shown in various cases where bones were inverted or otherwise out of their proper position. Two burials lay in shallow graves beneath the base. Three were associated with oyster-shells, not heavy masses of shell, but thin deposits above and on the sides. Sand, crimson from hematite, was with one burial.

Forty-six of the skeletons were flexed on the right; 34 on the left. There were also 3 skeletons full length on the back; 3 squatting; one partly flexed on the left side; and the bones of an infant. In addition, there were in the mound: many bones scattered by previous diggers; several aboriginal disturbances made by cutting through skeletons to make way for others; several skulls, each with a few small bones in association; one single skull near the base, which may have been an aboriginal disturbance. There were also several masses of bones which fell in caving sand, and three or four burials which resembled the bunched variety, but may have been aboriginal disturbances.

The bones in this mound were in excellent condition, comparatively, which may be accounted for by a deposit of shell extending through about one-half the mound, as though a smaller mound had been covered with shell and then enlarged as to height and area. It has ever been our experience that presence of shell in a mound acts as a preservative to bones, doubtless through infiltration of lime-salts.

Ten skulls were saved in good condition (Acad. Nat. Sci. Catalogue Nos. 2196 to 2205, inclusive). Neither these skulls nor any in the mound, noted by us, gave evidence of cranial compression.

Considering the number of burials present in the mound, artifacts met with were few and unimportant. Unassociated, but perhaps separated from burials by previous digging, were: one lance-head of chert; mica, in two places; a clam-shell with a neatly made circular hole near the center, probably for the insertion of a handle; a chert hammer-stone carefully worked; a shell gouge; part of a lance-head of chert, 5.6 inches long, 2.5 inches in maximum breadth, the point of which, broken by the blow of a spade, was not recovered; two masses of lime-rock, each with a circular hole, probably used as sinkers; a cigar-shaped object neatly made from the columella of a large marine univalve (Fig. 10); a columella wrought to a cutting edge at one end.

With burials were: a chert arrowhead and a shell drinking cup with perforate base; an arrowhead, of chalcedony; a conch shell and several sherds; a shell drinking cup without the basal perforation; two ornaments of shell (Figs. 11, 12).

FIG. 10.—Cigar-shaped object of shell. Mound near Gigger Point. (Full size.)

FIG. 11.—Pendant of shell. Mound near Gigger Point. (Full size.)

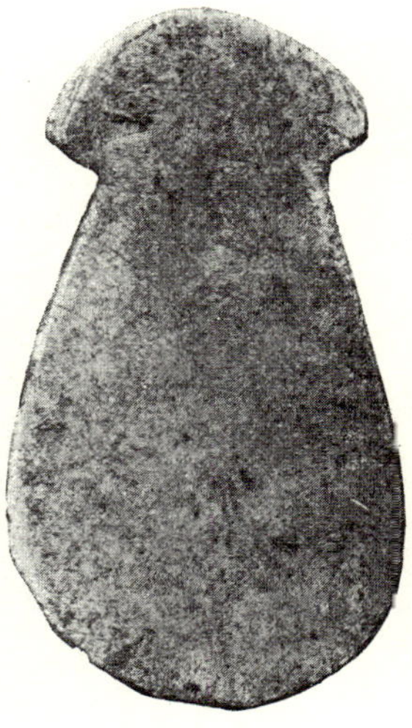

FIG. 12.—Ornament of shell. Mound near Gigger Point. (Full size.)

FIG. 13.—Object of fossil material. Mound near Gigger Point. (Full size.)

With a skeleton in a shallow grave were several mussel-shells, some on one side of the skull, some on the other; a turtle-shell with no pebbles within; parts of a conch-shell or shells; five sandstone hones; a fragment of chert; a mass of chert, about 2 inches in diameter, chipped into a circular shape; one smoothing stone; the end of an implement of bone; a small mass of serpentinous rock; two nodules of hematite; two silicious clay pseudomorphs; a bit of sandstone.

With another burial were: a bit of earthenware; mica given the outline of an arrowhead; an ellipsoidal pendant of igneous rock, with one end grooved and partly covered with bitumen, the other end broken.

An unidentified object of fossil material (Fig. 13) we are confident came from this mound, though we do not find it described in our field-notes.

At the extreme margin of the northeast part of the mound, with a burial, were two vessels of earthenware, both of which have the mortuary perforation, with this difference that, instead of the usual knocking out of part of the base, or of all of it, a carefully rounded hole is present as though, after a piece had been broken out, the edges had been worked to give a symmetrical outline.

One of these vessels had four roughly circular compartments around a larger circular one on a higher plane, almost exactly as shown in Fig. 268 of our second part of the report on the mounds of the northwest Florida coast. The vessel from the Gigger Point mound is covered with crimson pigment on the inside and on the upper half inch of the outer portion. The central compartment alone has the basal perforation.

The other vessel (Fig. 14), an oblate spheroid of about one gallon capacity, has a rather striking decoration consisting of seven encircling rows of wedge-shaped impressions between the rim and a circular band in relief.

There were in the mound, also, here and there, a moderate number of sherds, including one example of the small check-stamp, three or four of the complicated

FIG. 14.—Vessel of earthenware. Mound near Gigger Point. (About two-thirds size.)

stamp, one with ornamentation apparently made by impression of a finger-nail, and a small portion of a graceful vessel of excellent ware covered with crimson pigment, inside and out, and ornamented in places with fine, punctate markings.

One fragment of earthenware in this mound had a mingling of white material, here and there, giving it the appearance of shell-tempered ware. Expert examination, however, showed it to be pounded lime-stone, probably, since it was largely carbonate of lime, and showed no lamination under the glass. Shell-tempered ware is very unusual in Florida at any distance from Alabama where that ware was used. The material of which we speak, however, also, is exceptional in pottery of the peninsula.

Mounds near Dry Creek, Levy County.

Dry Creek enters Waccasassa bay about three miles to the westward of Waccasassa river. By following the course of the creek about 1.5 miles through the salt marsh, the Gulf Hammock is reached. The territory thus known is a strip of hammock land of varying breadth lying back of the salt marsh which borders the Gulf, between the Suwannee and Withlacoochee rivers.

Following a road entering the hammock, about .75 of a mile, we came upon a mound by the road-side, on property of Mr. Arthur T. Williams, of Jacksonville, Florida, about 2 feet high and 25 feet across the circular base. On the mound was a giant live-oak. We were unable to find either bone or artifact in this mound, in which there had been much previous digging.

About 300 yards farther along the road is an "old field," fallow for years. In this field, bordering a pond, is a mound 34 feet across the base and about 2.5 feet in height, also on property of Mr. Williams.

The mound, which was dug through by us about as extensively as a great oak growing upon it permitted, was composed of black loam from the nearby swamp. In this were masses of lime-rock similar to many in the surrounding field.

Many human bones, probably scattered by the plough, as the mound had been under cultivation, were met with by us, also three flexed skeletons and a number of bones of lower animals.

Mound near Burns' Landing, Levy County.

Burns' Landing is about seven miles up the Waccasassa river. Following a road leading into the Gulf Hammock from the landing, about 1.5 miles, we came to a small mound in sight of the road. This mound, about 25 feet in diameter and 18 inches in height, at the time of our visit, had been so thoroughly dug through that no work by us was attempted.

Mound near Bear Landing, Levy County.

This mound, about 200 yards in a northerly direction from the landing, which is about six miles up the Withlacoochee river, following the course of the stream, was in hammock land near the edge of the pine woods, on property of Mr. W. R.

Hodges, of Cedar Keys. The mound was literally honeycombed with pits and trenches, some of which, as we discovered, had been dug a second time, material from one trench filling a former one, which had again been dug by later disturbers. In fact, a strip on one side of the mound and a small portion near the base, at the center, were the only undisturbed parts. Trees growing near the top, by exposed roots, showed the mound to have been, at one time, about 2.5 feet higher than at the time of our visit when its height was about 3 feet. Its basal diameters were 58 feet by 45 feet.

The mound, new material and old, was dug through by us to the lime bed-rock found in these parts, with the exception of small portions around three trees.

Thirty-two undisturbed burials were met with by us. Twenty-eight were of the bunched variety. One skull lay with part of an ulna. One skeleton was closely flexed on the right side and two were closely flexed on the left side. One of these lay in a shallow pit, the only one met with in the mound, and had above it dark sand with scattered oyster-shells. All bones were badly decayed and no skulls were preserved. Large fragments, however, showed no cranial flattening.

FIG. 15.—Part of vessel of earthenware. Mound near Bear Landing. (Half size.)

With burials were some bits of pot, in one instance, and a "waster" of chert, in another. There were also in the mound two flakes of chert, evidently used as knives; one clam-shell; several small masses of lime-rock; a pebble with one end smoothed, as by use as a polisher; one pebble-hammer; two chert arrowheads found separately; two clam-shells with depressions at opposite sides, as for a handle.

In the SW. margin of the mound, placed in the lower part of an undecorated vessel of inferior ware, was a bowl which fell into fragments upon removal, a part having been crushed by roots. On one side of this bowl, rudely done, was part of an incised design, as though the decoration of the bowl had been started and abandoned (Fig. 15). Near this bowl were various scattered fragments of inferior ware. Two feet away was a burial.

There was also in the mound various undecorated sherds, and fragments constituting the upper part of a bowl with thickened rim, which had been decorated with red pigment.

Mound near Rock Landing, Citrus County.

Crystal river is the output of a great spring about seven miles, by water, from the Gulf.

Rock Landing is about 3.5 miles from the mouth of the river.

In scrub, about 1.5 miles in a NE. direction from the landing, on property under control of Mr. R. J. Knight, of Crystal River, was a mound 3 feet 3 inches in height, with basal diameters ef 40 and 50 feet.

Thorough investigation showed this to have been a domiciliary mound.

Mound near the Shell-heap, Crystal River, Citrus County.

In full view from the river, about 4.5 miles from the mouth, on the left-hand side going up, is a great, symmetrical shell-heap, on property under control of Mr. R. J. Knight, of Crystal River.

This shell-heap, marked A on the plan (Fig. 16) is 28 feet 8 inches in height, is oblong in horizontal section and has basal diameters of 182 feet NW. and SE. and 100 feet NE. and SW. The summit plateau is 107 feet and 50 feet in the same directions, respectively. A graded way 80 feet long and from 14 feet to 21 feet across, ascends from the level ground to the summit plateau on the NE. side of the mound.

Beginning at the NW. corner of this mound is a low, irregular shell deposit, marked B on the plan, extending to the northward then curving to the eastward and extending for a distance along the river bank.

About 115 yards in a northerly direction from the great shell-heap is a circular embankment of sand, marked C on the plan, of irregular height and width, the maximum, respectively, being 6 feet and 75 feet. Within this circle is certain territory on the general level, marked D on the plan, and an artificial elevation of sand, irregularly sloping (E). This elevation culminates in a mound of sand, marked F on the plan. While difficult to determine where the artificial elevation ended and the mound proper began, to call the diameter of the base of the mound 70 feet, would be a fairly correct estimate. The height of the mound proper from the east, where it bordered the level ground, was 10 feet 8 inches. Cross sections of the elevated ground and the mound proper are shown in Fig. 17.

In a northerly direction from the circular embankment are two ridges of shell, one (G) low and irregular, the other (H), 12 feet in maximum height, with a graded way.

Certain excavations made in the level ground outside and inside the circular embankment, yielded negative results.

Excavations in the embankment showed burials in the southerly portion where the embankment was highest and one burial in the western part. Our work, however, on the level ground and in the embankment was not exhaustive.

Eighteen men, with four men to supervise, dug seven days, demolishing the entire mound and going through much of the elevated ground surrounding it. The

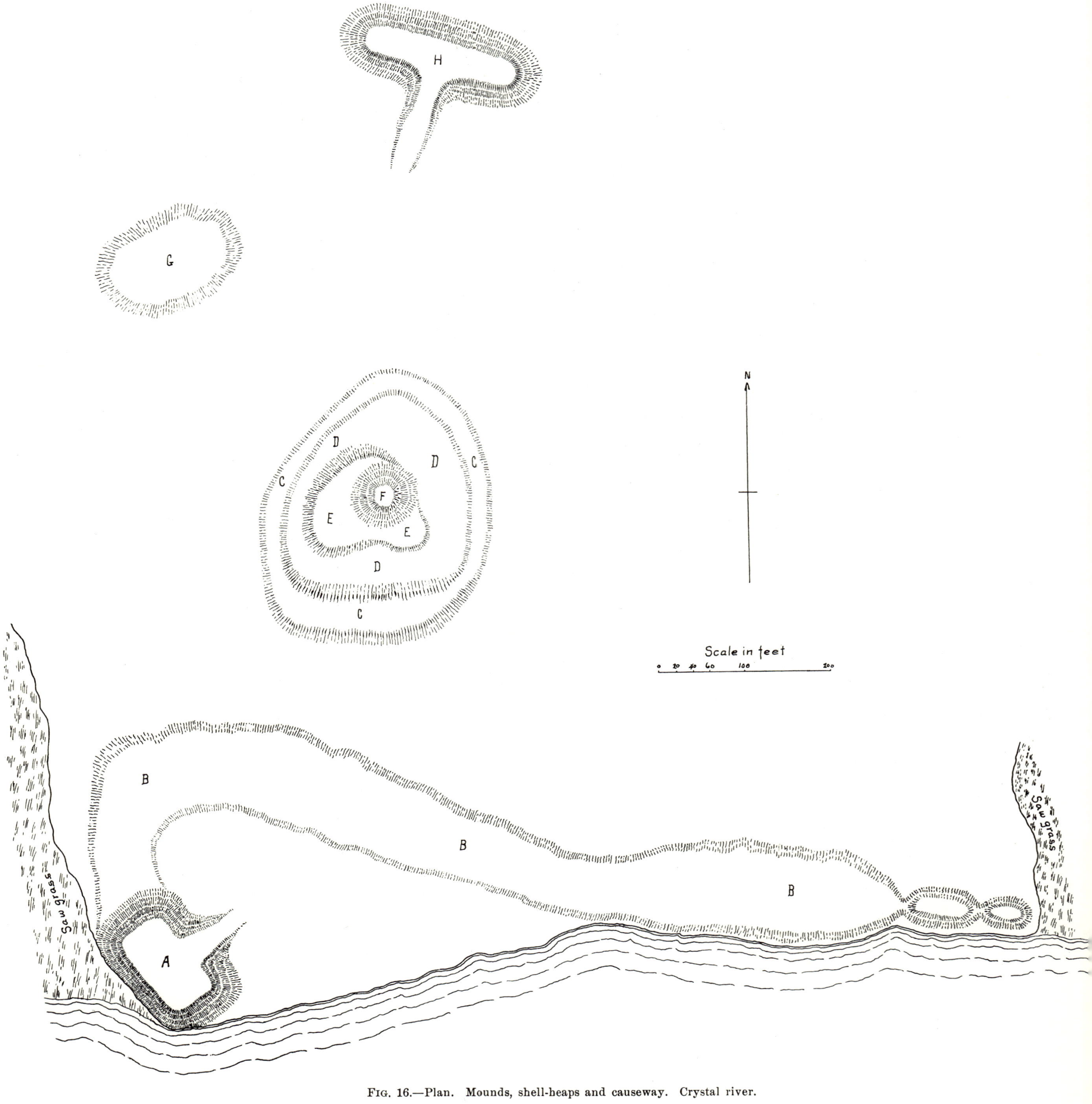

FIG. 16.—Plan. Mounds, shell-heaps and causeway. Crystal river.

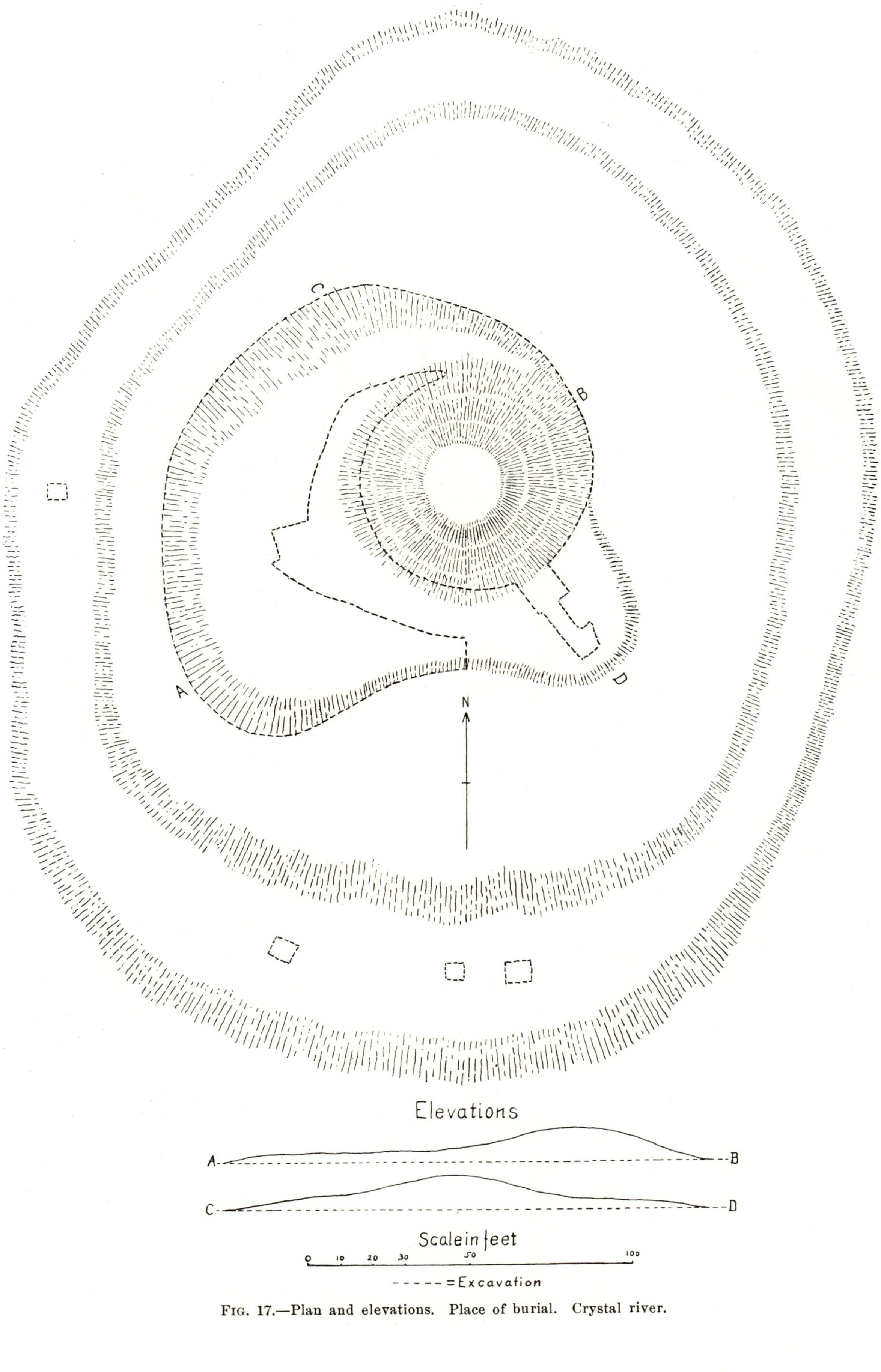

FIG. 17.—Plan and elevations. Place of burial. Crystal river.

work done by us is shown in broken lines on plan (Fig. 17), where, however, many small excavations made in the level ground and in the embankment are not given.

Though the shell-heap on Crystal river is a famous one, the sand mound was unknown to the inhabitants of the town of Crystal River, even the owner being unaware of the existence of this mound. Absolutely no digging had been done previous to our visit, which is a most important feature, and especially so when we note the interesting objects found by us and the fact that no object indicating European provenance was met with throughout the entire investigation.

In the artificial elevation, burials were very numerous, and to so great an extent had the ground been used that many graves, passing through earlier ones, had caused great disturbance. In addition, numbers of disconnected bones lay, here and there, in the sand as though they had been gathered from the dead-house and scattered while the making of the elevation was in progress. Hence, exact classification as to form of burial was impossible, nor could any estimate be arrived at as to the number of individuals originally interred, as all bones met with were so decayed that the skulls were often in small fragments. Our enumeration of burials, that is of where bones were encountered, certainly falls far short of the number of individuals interred.

The mound proper, of gray sand in the upper part and of white sand in the lower, had, running through it, along the base, from the eastern margin to the center, approximately, a ledge of shell about 2 feet high and 20 feet broad. This ledge seemed to have no particular connection with the burials.

Running for a distance of many feet into the mound were several streaks of sand dyed with hematite. One, in the southern part of the mound, from 2 to 8 inches in diameter, especially persistent, extended from the outer slope to the center. The intensity of the coloring varied considerably.

There were also pockets of scarlet sand, but these were local and in connection with burials. Once a pocket of scarlet sand was associated with sand dyed yellow by powdered limonite.

What has been said as to the difficulty of count and of classification of the burials in the elevated ground applies equally to the mound though from a different cause, in part. While burials in the mound were not unusually numerous, the height of the mound and the extreme dryness of the sand of which it was built, caused much caving and consequent disarrangement of burials.

In the elevation and in the mound, were about 225 burials, including:

Bunched burials,	42
Full length on back,	63[1]
Closely flexed on the right side,	31
Closely flexed on the left side,	26
Partly flexed on the right side,	2
Partly flexed on the left side,	7
Lone skulls,	11
Skeletons of infants, badly decayed,	7

[1] Four of these lay side by side in a single grave: seven had lower extremities cut off by later interments.

Special burials not included in the above were as follows:

Two skulls, a femur and a radius.

Four skulls with two long-bones.

Three skulls and scattered bones.

A skeleton without pelvis or lower extremities. Beneath the place where the pelvis should have been was another skull, probably an aboriginal disturbance.

Two skulls with scattered bones.

Four skulls with scattered bones and, nearby, the lower extremities of a skeleton. In place of the pelvis was a skull and beneath it another skull.

A skeleton lying on the back with the legs flexed upward.

Three skulls and one humerus.

In a grave was the skeleton of a child at full length on the back and another child's skeleton lying flexed to the left. Above these were many oyster-shells and numerous masses of lime-rock, from 3 to 8 inches in diameter.

A bunched burial with four skulls.

Various unclassified burials.

In the elevated ground surrounding the mound, masses of oyster-shells almost invariably lay above the burials and sometimes extended well to the sides. To this rule there were but three exceptions.

In the mound proper, on the other hand, forty burials unassociated with oyster-shells were noted, though there, also, many burials were covered by them.

While no crania were in a condition to save, parts of many showed no cranial flattening.

Many of the bones bore marks of pathological lesions.

Artifacts were very numerous in the elevation and in the mound, though those from the mound proper were of much higher grade, as a rule, than were the artifacts from the sloping ground around it. There was no general deposit of earthenware or of other objects. While certain artifacts were found unassociated, there was every indication that most of them had lain with burials which had suffered aboriginal disturbance.

In this place of aboriginal abode it was evident we were no longer among the mounds of the northwest Florida coast, with their great deposits of earthenware placed for the dead in common, in the eastern part of the mound. Here the vessels were widely scattered and were found singly. Outside the mound but few vessels were met with, though little piles of sherds, bits of inferior ware from various vessels, were numerous.

There were present in the elevated ground, as well as in the mound, a limited number of sherds bearing the complicated stamp, the design being chiefly one of concentric circles, a popular pattern along the central west-coast of Florida, and which we found in the great shell-heap at Cedar Keys.

From the mound proper came a number of vessels, some of inferior ware, others of excellent material.

The most striking object in earthenware met with during the investigation is part of a cylindrical vessel (Fig. 18) of excellent ware, bearing an incised design showing part of the human hand, remarkable for its boldness of execution. On the back of the hand is a curious figure which many authorities agree is not a known totemic symbol or design of any sort, hitherto met with. Some have suggested its origin from heraldry and hence early European sources, while a still greater number see nothing in the design that suggests other than an aboriginal origin. To us the figure has an aboriginal look, and as nothing of European provenance was met with during our investigation of the mound--and this counts for so much in determinations—we believe the symbol to be aboriginal in origin. Other designs, perhaps equally interesting, have been on the remainder of the vessel, which a diligent search failed to discover.

FIG. 18.—Sherd. Mound near Crytal river. (Full size.)

FIG. 19.—Part of earthenware vessel. Mound near Crystal river. (Full size.)

Throughout the mound were vessels with feet, and parts of vessels indicating the presence of feet when the vessels were whole. There was also found a part of a vessel, showing a human face (Fig. 19).

A selection of sherds found during the investigation is given in Fig. 20. The third from the left-hand upper corner shows punctate decoration between bands of crimson pigment. The sherd in the lower right-hand corner has part of another open hand.

We shall describe the vessels in detail.

FIG. 20.—Selection of sherds. Mound near Crystal river. (Half size.)

Vessel No. 1.—An oblate spheroid, of good ware (Fig. 21) lay with a burial in the northwestern border of the artificial elevation. It is entirely covered with incised and punctate decoration shown diagrammatically in Fig. 22 where the cross on the base of the vessel is spread in order to show the design in diagram. This cross is given with the remainder of the basal decoration in Fig. 23. There are two holes for suspension in the vessel, and the usual mortuary perforation.

FIG. 21.—Vessel No. 1. Mound near Crystal river. (Full size.)

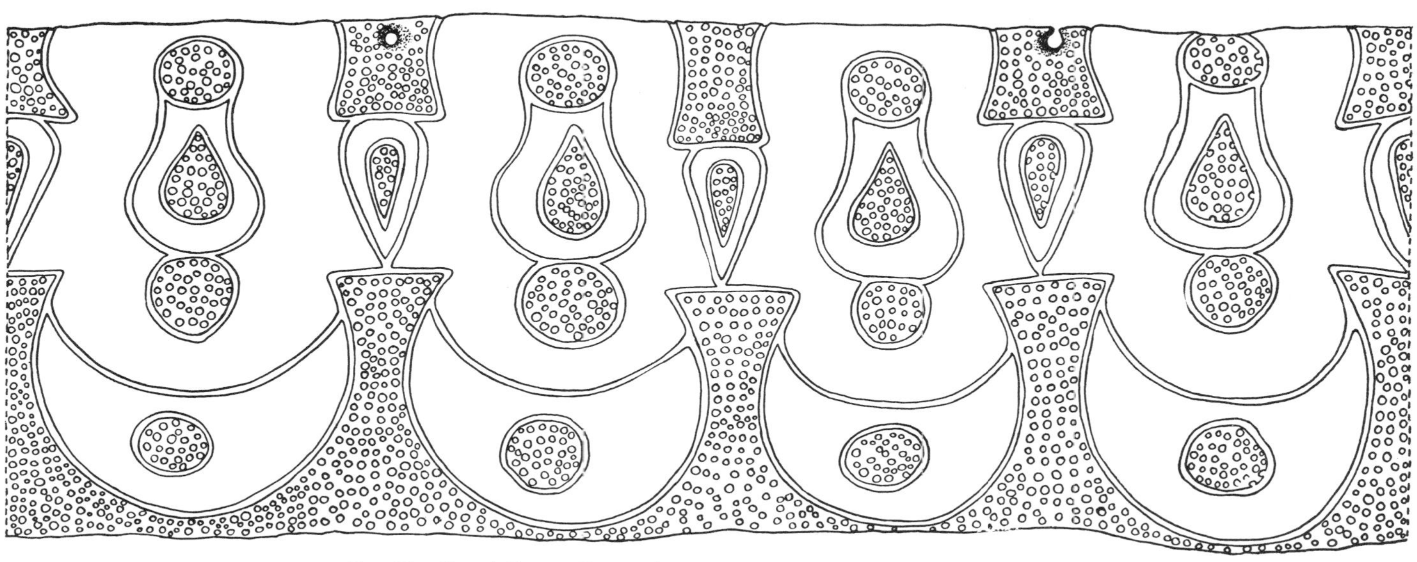

FIG. 22.—Vessel No. 1. Decoration. Mound near Crystal river. (Half size.)

Vessel No. 2.—An undecorated bowl, of most inferior ware. There is a small basal perforation, which is the case with all vessels in this mound unless otherwise described.

Vessel No. 3.—A broken bowl of inferior ware, undecorated.

Vessel No. 4.—Similar to Vessel No. 3.

Vessel No. 5.—This vessel, of dark ware, which lay about one foot from the skeleton of an infant, had with it a small, imperforate, shell drinking cup. The basal perforation had carried away two of the feet which have since been restored and a certain amount of restoration has been done to the rim. The interior of the dentate design has been colored with red pigment (Fig. 24).

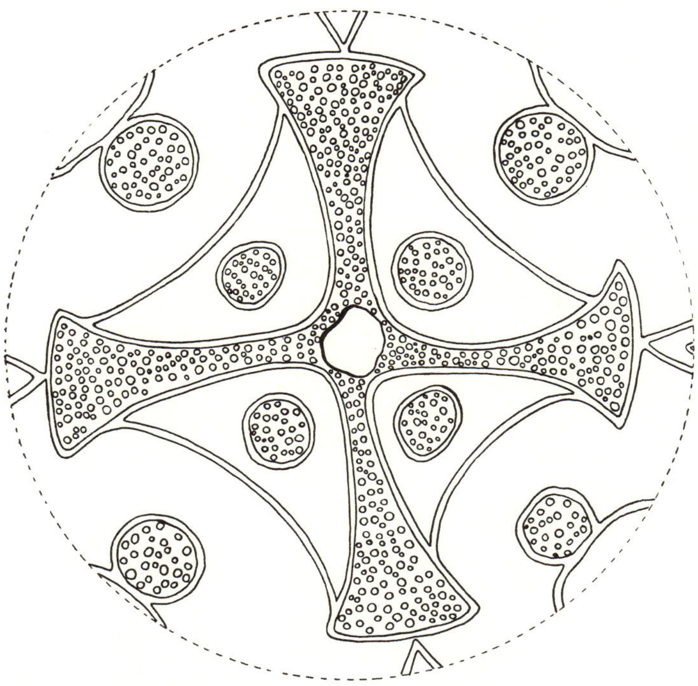

FIG. 23.—Vessel No. 1. Decoration of base. Mound near Crystal river. (Not exactly on scale.)

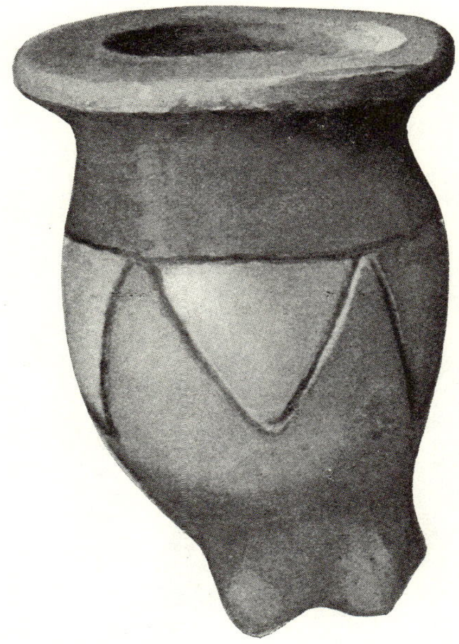

FIG. 24.—Vessel No. 5. Mound near Crystal river. (Full size.)

Vessel No. 6.—An undecorated, cylindrical jar of about one quart capacity, slightly contracted toward the base, which is flat and imperforate.

Vessel No. 7.—A toy pot of poor ware, undecorated save for notches around the margin. Two holes for suspension, on opposite sides, have been enlarged by the pulling through of the cord or sinew used. There is a carefully broken circular hole in the base. This little vessel has six feet, one somewhat within the line of the other five.

Vessel No. 8.—A bowl of excellent ware, with protruding rim (Fig. 25).

Vessel No. 9.—This vessel, undecorated, of excellent ware, lay with bones in the mound proper whence came all vesels yet to be described. In shape it is a much flattened sphere. There is a carefully rounded hole in the base and small holes for suspension on opposite sides of the opening.

FIG. 25.—Vessel No. 8. Mound near Crystal river. (Half size.)

Vessel No. 10.—A small, imperforate, undecorated bowl.

Vessel No. 11.—A pot of inferior ware, badly broken by roots, having traces of red pigment, and rough incised decoration similar on two opposite sides.

Vessel No. 12.—In fallen sand was an undecorated, imperforate vessel with ovoid body, flat base, and flaring neck, broken but since cemented together (Fig. 26).

Vessel No. 13.—A bowl of about one quart capacity, of beautiful, smooth, red ware, with thickened rim projecting slightly, horizontally (Fig. 27). The decoration, in black pigment, was not continued around the vessel, or has disappeared through wear.

FIG. 26.—Vessel No. 12. Mound near Crystal river. (Full size.)

FIG. 27.—Vessel No. 13. Mound near Crystal river. (Two-thirds size.)

Vessel No. 14.—The upper part of a vessel of beautiful red ware, with certain lower portions decorated with bands of black pigment (Fig. 28), which would give quite a classical appearance were it not for the scalloped rim.

Vessel No. 15.—Unassociated in the mound, was part of a curious vessel originally annular in shape. On the fragment is one upright neck and parts of two others. The vessel, when whole, probably resembled that shown in Fig. 164 in Part II of our "Aboriginal Remains of the Northwest Florida Coast," though in this case the body of the vessel is not flattened.

FIG. 28.—Vessel No. 14. Mound near Crystal river. (About two-thirds size.)

Vessel No. 16.—A vessel, badly broken, originally with four feet, two of which were lost at the time of the basal mutilation (Fig. 29). These feet, with certain parts of the body, have been restored.

Vessel No. 17.—A vessel of excellent ware, undecorated save for the scalloped rim. At the base, which is rounded, has been a flat, circular space in relief, 1.25 inches in diameter, which enabled the vessel to stand upright. A circular perforation has been made through this flattened part (Fig. 30).

Vessel No. 18.—A rough, undecorated vessel.

Vessel No. 19.—A wide-mouthed water-bottle, undecorated, with a portion missing.

FIG. 29.—Vessel No. 16. Mound near Crystal river. (Two-thirds size.)

FIG. 30.—Vessel No. 17. Mound near Crystal river. (Full size.)

FIG. 31.—Vessel No. 20. Mound near Crystal river. (Two-thirds size.)

Vessel No. 20.—This interesting vessel, a bowl, of superior ware, of about two quarts capacity (Fig. 31), has had for decoration a design in black pigment which, apparently, having grown faint in course of time, has had painted above it designs

FIG. 32.—Vessel No. 21. Mound near Crystal river. (Full size.)

FIG. 33.—Vessel No. 22 Mound near Crystal river. (About five-sixths size.)

FIG. 34.—Vessel No. 23. Mound near Crystal river. (About three-fourths size.)

in two shades of red. Our artist has well shown in stipple the design in black, and in lighter and darker "wash," the two shades of red. The lightest shade of all on the vessel, of course represents the natural shade of the ware. About one-third of this vessel was missing when found. There has been restoration of the missing part, but no attempt to replace the complicated design.

Vessel No. 21.—Undecorated, save for four repoussé lobes each ending at the base in a foot for the vessel's support (Fig. 32).

Vessel No. 22.—An imperforate bowl of excellent ware, undecorated. A thick rim projects laterally (Fig. 33).

Vessel No. 23.—A vessel of about three pints capacity, with a neck, first constricted, then expanded. The decoration consists of a small check-stamp. One of four feet, missing through basal perforation, has been restored (Fig. 34).

Vessel No. 24.—A vase with rude, incised and punctate decoration, shown in Fig. 35.

Vessel No. 25.—Of inferior ware, undecorated, with semi-globular body, and long neck first constricted, then flaring.

FIG. 35.—Vessel No. 24. Mound near Crystal river. (Full size.)

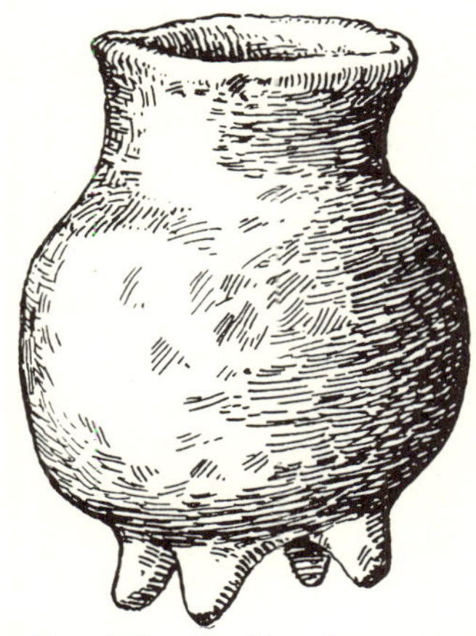

FIG. 36.—Vessel No. 26. Mound near Crystal river. (Full size.)

Vessel No. 26.—A toy vessel, undecorated, imperforate, with four feet, shown in Fig. 36.

A sherd from this mound is shown in Fig. 37.

Seven smoking pipes, all or nearly all from the mound proper, were met with during the investigation. Three are of soapstone, all of the familiar type with rectangular cross-section of the part having the bowl and of the part holding the stem. One of these pipes, showing faint incised decoration, is shown in Fig. 38. At the base of the bowl is a small circular orifice. In the second part of our "Certain Aboriginal Remains of the Northwest Florida Coast," page 256, we speak of a pipe with a basal perforation.

A rude pipe of earthenware, also of common type, has the bowl slightly flaring.

Part of a pipe of earthenware, similar in shape to those of soapstone, came from the mound. There was found also a small "Monitor" pipe of earthenware, somewhat broken. This is the first example of this type of pipe met with in penin-

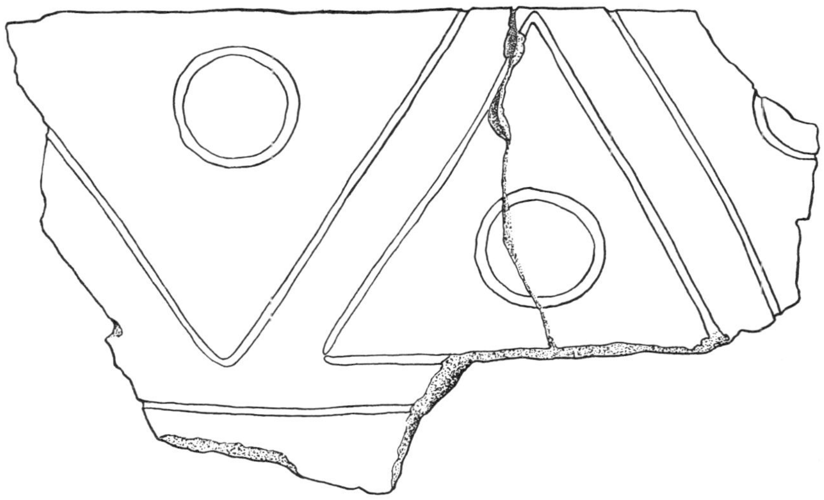

FIG. 37.—Sherd. Mound near Crystal river. (Half size.)

sular Florida. There was also in the mound a great pipe of soft lime-rock, found in pieces, but since restored. In shape it is the same as those of soapstone. Each arm is 5.5 inches in length. The measurement across each end is 2.25 inches; the openings are about 1.25 inches each, in diameter.

A flat tube of earthenware, perhaps used for a ceremony with smoke, came from the mound proper (Fig. 39).

Throughout the investigation were met with, in the elevated ground and in the mound proper, a large number of shell cups wrought from *Fulgur perversum*, some imperforate, but the great majority with the mortuary perforation. There were also eight or ten drinking cups made from what is known as the "horse-conch" (*Fasciolaria*) along the Florida coast. One of these cups is shown in Fig. 40. We do not recall before having met with a drinking cup made from this shell, although the shell was largely used in the manufacture of implements in aboriginal times.

One drinking cup wrought from *Melongena corona*, the first we have seen, was found during the investigation.

During our work, there were met with sixty columellæ of large marine univalves, sometimes a considerable number with a single burial. These columellæ had been at times ground squarely across one end to serve as chisels, and sometimes given a circular edge for use as gouges. Occasionally, a wing, or flange, was left to increase the gauge of the edge.

There were found also ten gouges made from triangular sections of the body-

FIG. 38.—Smoking-pipe of soapstone. Mound near Crystal river. (Full size.)

FIG. 39.—Tube of earthenware. Mound near Crystal river. (Full size.)

FIG. 40.—Shell drinking cup. Mound near Crystal river. (Two-thirds size.)

whorl of *Fulgur perversum* and one rectangular chisel likewise wrought from *Fulgur*, also seventeen "celts" made, as a rule, from the lip of *Strombus gigas*, 2.5 to 7 inches in length. All implements of shell from this mound were badly weathered.

Three large shells (*Cardium*) were met with, each with a hole in the centre to allow the insertion of a handle, and a number of large clam-shells, some showing wear. There were, also, triangular sections of clam-shells, doubtless tools, when hafted. Among the clam-shells was a large marine shell of the clam family (*Callista gigantea*).

There were found also three conchs (*Fulgur perversum*) variously treated for the reception of handles, and worn down at the beak by use as hammers, hoes, etc.[1]

Eleven gorgets wrought from the body-whorl of *Fulgur perversum* came from the mound, almost invariably associated with other objects near burials or near where burials had been disturbed. Only one shows decoration and none is engraved.

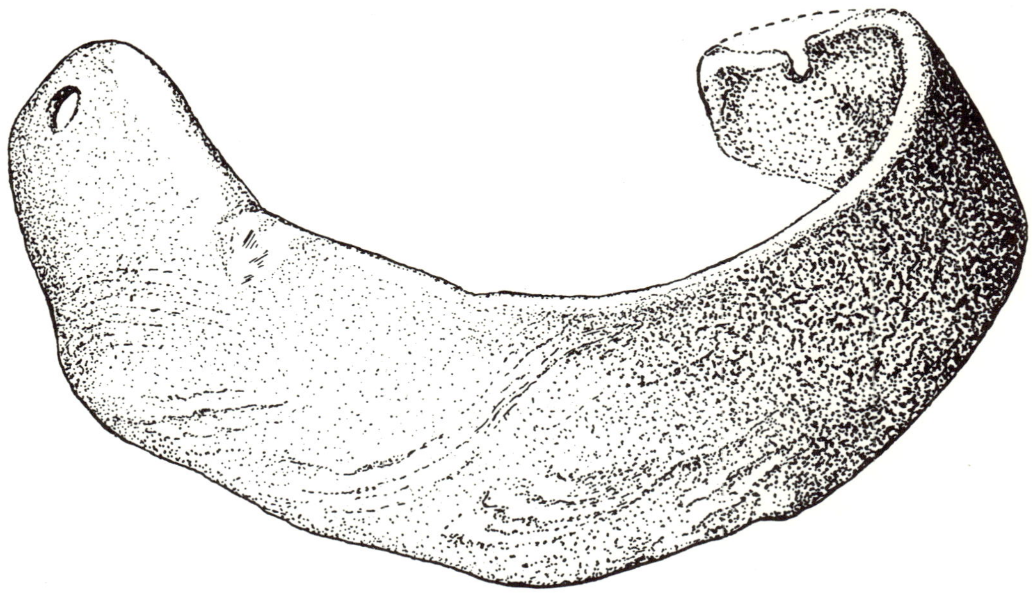

FIG. 41.—Gorget of shell. Mound near Crystal river. (Full size.)

Four are roughly circular, ranging in diameter from 2.25 to 3.5 inches. The smallest has a circular perforation in the center, about .12 of an inch in diameter. The next in size has, in the middle, three small holes in line. Two have single holes centrally, one, in addition, having two perforations side by side, at the margin. Four others are sections of the body-whorl of *Fulgur*, scoop-shaped, each with a central perforation, three about 1 inch in diameter, the fourth much smaller. One, in addition, has two small holes side by side on the broadest portion. One of these gorgets lay with the concave side upon a skull.

Two gorgets, one a curved band of shell, about 1.5 inches wide, having a hole

[1] For description and figures of many implements of this sort, see our "Certain Antiquities of the Florida West-Coast," page 380 *et seq.* Journ. Acad. Nat. Sci., Phila., Vol. XI.

for suspension and showing where another has been (Fig.41), the other, fragmentary, probably like the one just described, were found in the mound.

There was also a handsome little gorget with six rounded points, and a central perforation, shown in Fig. 42.

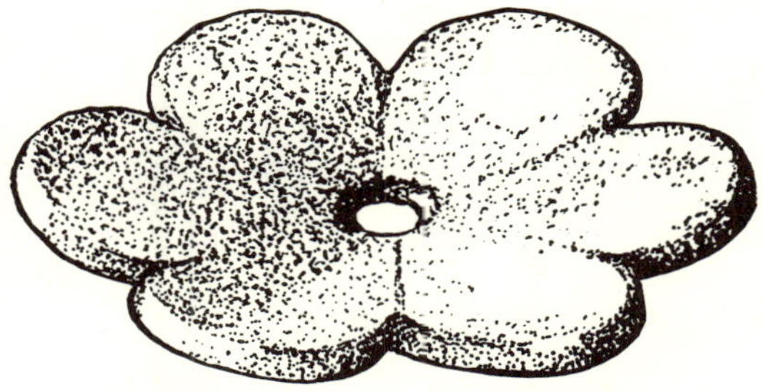

FIG. 42.—Ornament of shell. Mound near Crystal river. (Full size.)

A small number of shell beads were present with one burial, and with another were a discoidal bead of shell, about half an inch in diameter, and an imperforate shell disc of the same size. This scarcity of shell beads in a burial place teeming with objects of shell, is remarkable, and equally noticeable was the absence of shell hair-pins, which class of objects was represented by certain fragments of what may or may not have belonged to a hair-pin of shell.

Near the skull of a child, lay two shells pierced for suspension (*Oliva reticularis*, and *Cerithium*, a fossil, a large undescribed variety from oligocene beds).

Those who lay in the burial place near the great shell-heap had, in life, been given to the wearing of pendent ornaments—of shell, of stone, of copper.

Those of shell met with by us, 105 in number, were, as a rule, much affected by disintegration, and hence it is hard to say how finished their original appearance may have been. Doubtless they varied. On many is bitumen. One deposit, with a burial, consisted of ten pendants of shell, each about 5.5 inches in length. Another deposit of pendants consisted of one of lime-rock and five of shell, one being 9.25 inches in length. A selection of pendent ornaments of shell, found during the investigation, is shown in Fig. 43.

During the digging there were found: hammer-stones of chert, and several of quartz, fairly well rounded; pebble-hammers, including several of sandstone and pudding-stone; hones of sandstone and of ferruginous sandstone; flakes, and small, partly chipped, masses of chert; a "waster," of chert, 5.5 inches long; and various other fragments, and material of the class usually found in mounds. There were also fourteen entire "celts," of various rocks and a large number of "celts" badly broken. Some of these parts were afterward fitted together, which led us to believe that perhaps, also, these "celts" had been ceremonially broken before placing them in the mound. In length the "celts" varied from 2.5 to 12.5 inches. Incidentally, 13 inches is the greatest length of any "celt" met with by us in the south.

Thirty-one lance-points, arrowheads and knives, all of chert, were found during the digging, often associated with other objects. Many of these were rude, though a few were of excellent workmanship. In addition to these, from the same part of the mound whence came a number of "celts" in fragments, was a deposit of three lance-heads of brown chert, each broken in two parts; the lower half of a similar lance-head; two upper halves of lance-points of dark brown chert; three rude chert arrowheads, four chips of chert; the canine tooth of a large carnivore. Presumably the lance-heads in this deposit had been broken ceremonially.

FIG. 43.—Selection of ornaments of shell. Mound near Crystal river. (Full size.)

A neatly made blunt-pointed implement of fossil material, from the mound, with incised decoration on one side, is shown in Fig. 44. Two cigar-shaped implements, also of fossil material, are given in Fig. 45.

FIG. 44.—Object of fossil material. Mound near Crystal river. (Full size.)

A carefully smoothed ellipsoidal hammer-stone of lime-rock, about 4 inches long, shows marks of considerable use. Two bar-amulets, one of lime-rock, one of thin, banded slate, came from the mound and many sheets of mica were found during the entire investigation. None of these had any particular shape and none was perforate.

FIG. 45.—Objects of fossil material. Mound near Crystal river. (Full size.)

One hundred and eleven pendent ornaments of various rocks were met with during the investigation. As mutilation of the specimens was not deemed advisable, there has not been an exact determination as to material. Many are of the lime-rock, and some, of the ferruginous lime-rock, of the district; others are of igneous rocks; two long ones are of slate. One is of calcite and doubtless there are other rocks not included in this enumeration. Several are of quartz, including two beautifully made of rock-crystal, one of which has, presumably, a conventionalized bird-form (Fig. 46).

Ten well-made pendants, shown in Fig. 47, lay with a burial with which was sand dyed with hematite.

A selection from the various stone pendants found by us is given in Figs. 48, 49, 50, 51, among which are shown a long slate pendant similar to those found by us the preceding year along the northwest coast, one pendant with a central perforation, and several doubtless intended to represent conventionalized birds.

On the base of the mound, in the southern slope, was the skeleton of an adult, lying full length on back. Extending across the pelvis, sagging down somewhat, was a row of pendants of stone, among which were three of copper, 4.7 inches, 5.75 inches, 6 inches long, respectively, of the same type as the long ones of slate from this mound, one of which has already been figured. Seemingly, all these pendants had hung from the waist in the manner shown by Le Moyne on aborigines of the St. Johns river, Florida. Along the lower part of the left arm, which lay extended down the left side of the body, were other pendants, or charm-stones, which may have fallen over from a belt at the waist. Exclusive of the copper, 39 pendants, mostly of lime-stone and of ferruginous lime-stone, and a long one of slate, were in this interesting deposit. With them were two parts of the lower jaw of a puma, each with three molars, and each part having a hole artificially made near the foramen to aid in suspension or attachment. With these were two canines of a black bear, having the bases much ground away, and two molars, also of the bear, ground down, not on the base alone, but on certain of the sides also.[1]

About 5 feet down, in the southern side of the mound, near a skull belonging to a bunched burial, were three quartz crystals and one twin crystal of quartz, from 2.5 to 4 inches in length. The three crystals have grooves for suspension as pendants. On the twin crystal no groove is apparent, though there are traces of bitumen, at one end, where a cord has been attached.

With the crystals were sixteen ornaments of various rocks, including a small pendant of amethystine quartz,[2] a perfect gem, a triumph of aboriginal endeavor, shown fourth from the left-hand side of the upper row in Fig. 52 where all this deposit is given.

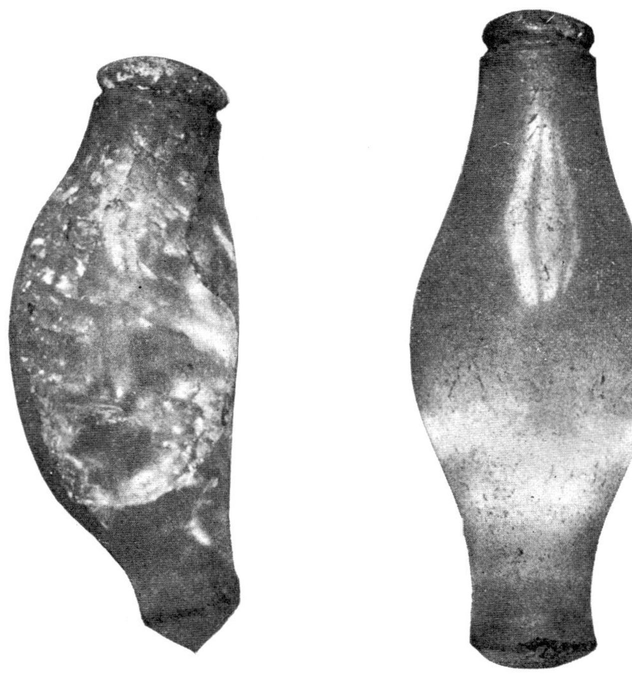

FIG. 46.—Pendants of rock-crystal. Mound near Crystal river. (Full size.)

The rocks of which these ornaments are made, which include beads, imitations of canine teeth of carnivores, and other forms, are impossible to name with any certainty, without mutilating the specimens to obtain slides for the microscope. One is surely of banded, ferruginous slate; others are of catlinite; several resemble hematite in appearance, but are not this material since they make a mark too light in color upon porcelain and do not respond to the magnet. Others are of fine-grained, igneous rock.

[1] *Vide*, "Certain Aboriginal Remains of the Northwest Florida Coast," Part II, Journ. Acad. Nat. Sci., of Phila., Vol. XII, pg. 240 *et seq.*

[2] We are indebted to Mr. Warren K. Moorehead for the following details of the discovery of a pendant of amethyst found in 1898, in a grave at the mouth of the Wabash river, west side, southern Indiana, by Mr. Clifford Anderson, acting under instructions from Mr. Moorehead. About 150 burials were found in graves at this place, having with them pottery, pipes, copper objects, etc. The graves, 2 to 4 feet below the present surface, were not stone lined. According to Mr. Moorehead, they mark the northernmost extension of the southern (Missouri–Arkansas) type of pottery. Mr. Moorehead kindly sent the pendant for our inspection. It is of a deep violet, pear-shaped, and has a perforation for suspension. It is about the same size as ours, but it is much more rudely made, showing a scratched surface without polish. The catalogue number of this specimen is 15,400, Museum, Phillips' Academy, Andover, Mass.

FIG. 47.—Pendants of stone, found with a single burial. Mound near Crystal River. (Full size)

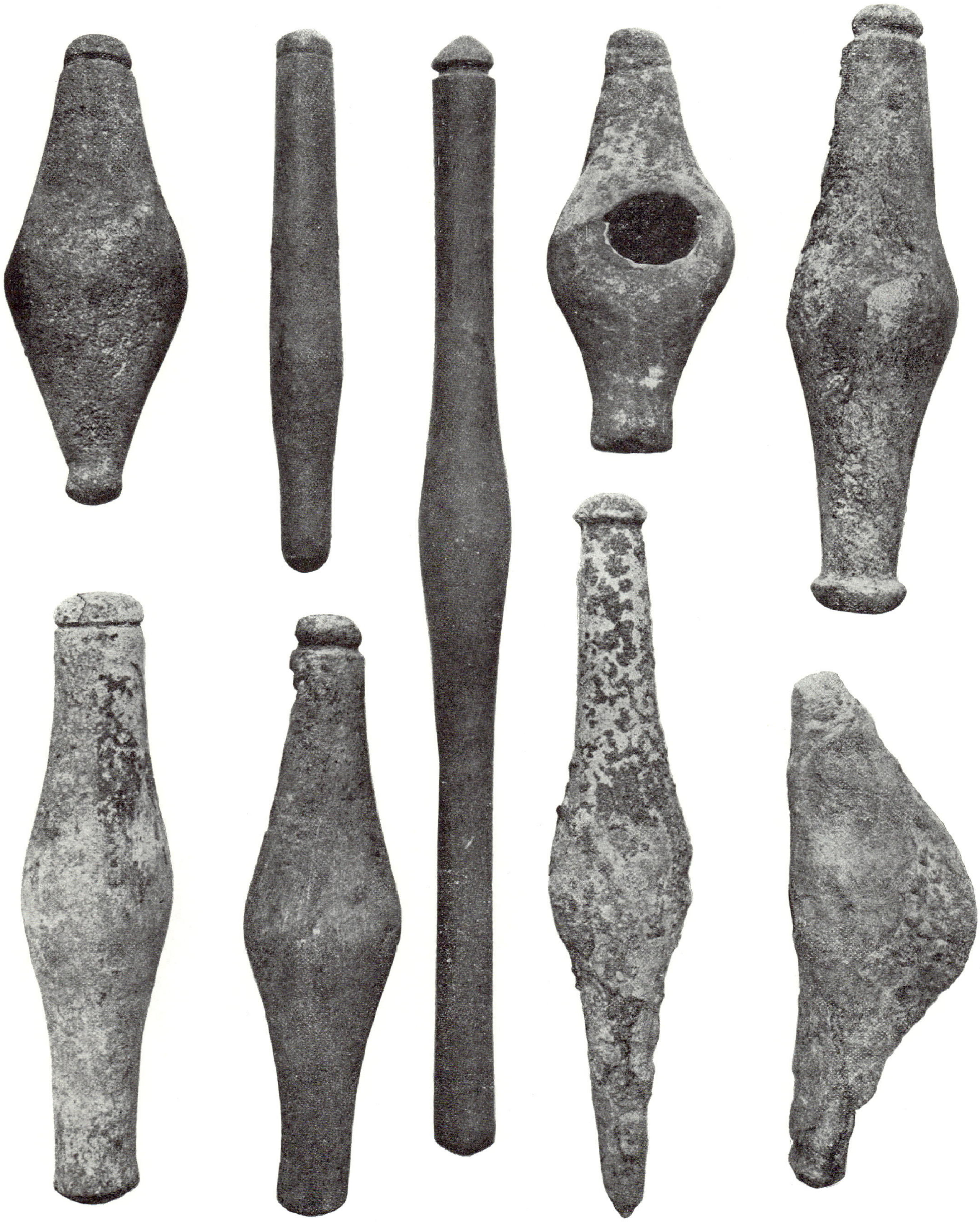

FIG. 48.—Selection of pendants of stone. Mound near Crystal river. (Full size.)

Fig. 49.—Selection of pendants of stone. Mound near Crystal river. (Full size.)

FIG. 50.—Selection of pendants of stone. Mound near Crystal river. (Full size.)

FIG. 51.—Selection of pendants of stone. Mound near Crystal river. (Full size.)

Fig. 52.—Ornaments found with a single burial. Mound near Crystal river. (Full size.)

FIG. 53.—Pendent ornaments of copper. Mound near Crystal river. (Full size.)

The perforations in these ornaments are countersunk and from large openings at the surface meet at the center in a much smaller aperture. On some are scratches which probably would be called file-marks by those disbelieving in any proficiency obtained by the natives through ages of aboriginal culture, which marks are exactly similar to those noted on certain ornaments of red jasper found by us in Florida, on which material the file leaves no mark and which was no doubt worked with the aid of hard, cutting sand.

In the southern part of the mound, whence, with the exception of two copper pendants and the deposit of ten pendants of rock, came practically all articles of especial interest met with during the investigation, were found ten copper pendants, including the three already referred to, making twelve in all from this mound, shown in Fig. 53. Three pendants were twice found together, and three times, two pendants were in association, always, of course, with burials. All came from considerable depths in the mound, from 4 to 8 feet, and nearly all were wrapped in fabrics and in bark, as is customary with "finds" of copper.

An especially noteworthy feature connected with these pendants, which are of native copper, is that all are of the same type as other pendants of stone and of shell found in this mound, even the conventional bird-form being represented.

The method of wearing these pendants was interestingly shown. Apparently, certain material, seemingly hide, was cut into a small circle. A cord was run through the center of this and knotted on the lower side. The hide was then adjusted on the end of the pendant, like a cap, and the lower portion of the hide was bound around with a cord and fastened with bitumen. The cord which ran through the hide, when fastened to a belt, would allow the pendant to hang true, which it could not do had the hide not been used and a cord been tied around the end of the pendant and knotted at one side.

But once in the elevated ground surrounding the mound proper, was copper met with, and this was so greatly corroded that it was hardly more than a paste-like substance.

Upon several occasions in the mound, copper was found in a like condition.

About 8 feet from the surface of the mound, near one of the streaks of sand dyed with hematite, to which reference has been made, was a flat mass of bitumen, about 6 inches by 8 inches and 1.25 to 2 inches in thickness. Imbedded in this was an oblong bit of sheet-copper, about 1 inch in length by .5 of an inch in breadth.

During the excavation of the mound proper there were found, always with burials, three pairs of ear-plugs of sheet-copper.

One pair has the upper and the lower discs of a similar pattern, consisting of open spaces made with considerable regularity (Fig. 54). There is a circular concavity at the center of each disc. Careful measurements show that while the four discs closely resemble each other, the openings do not exactly coincide in size or in shape, thus precluding all chance of their having been made with a die or stamp. These discs, each about 3.5 inches in diameter, were wrapped in bark. With one set of discs was a vertebra of a fish, which probably had been used to hold the pair together. The second vertebra was not found, but may have been lost in the excavation.

The interesting design of these discs was shown to Mr. Charles C. Willoughby, of the Peabody Museum, Cambridge, Mass., who writes: "Regarding the enclosed

FIG. 54.—One of four copper discs, forming a pair of ear-plugs. Mound near Crystal river. (Full size.)

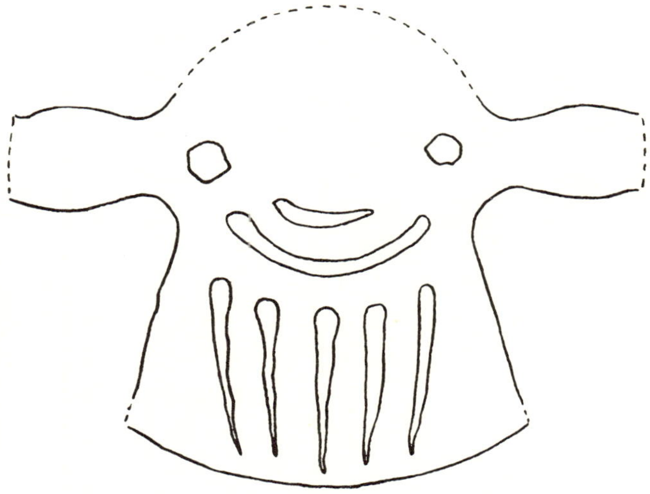

FIG. 55.—Part of copper disc showing animal head, with bear-symbol beneath. (Full size.)

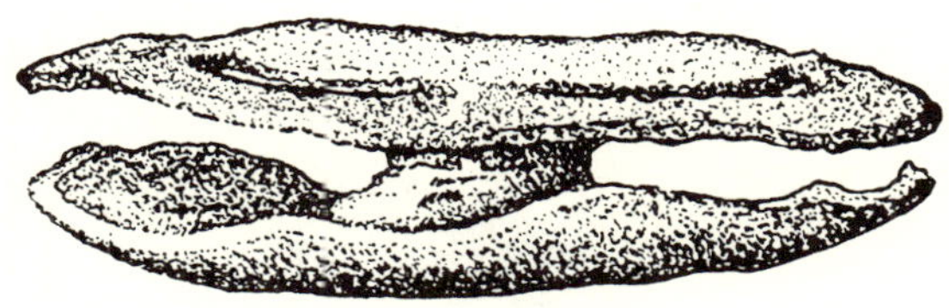

FIG. 57.—Silver-coated ear-plug of copper. Side view. Mound near Crystal river. (Full size.)

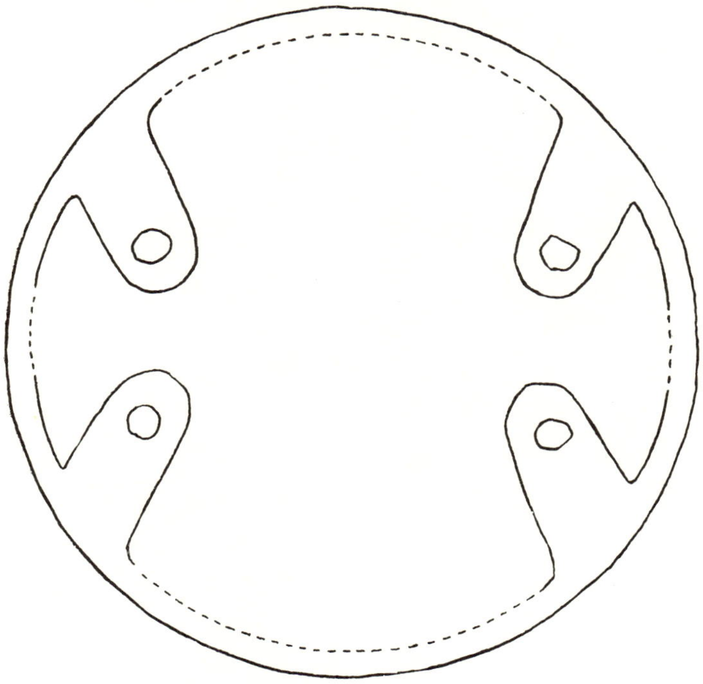

FIG. 56.—Copper disc with animal symbols removed, leaving the cosmic sign. (Full size.)

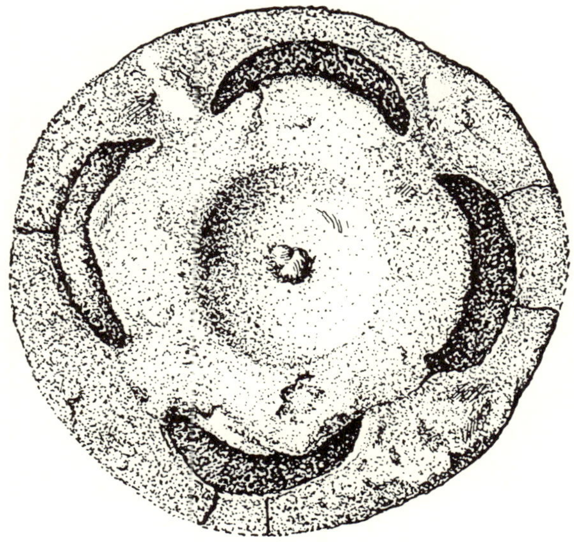

FIG. 58.—The same. Top view. (Full size.)

photograph of the copper disc from Crystal river. This seems to belong to the same type of symbolic forms as many of the sheet-copper objects from the Hopewell and Turner mounds,[1] although the mechanical execution of your ornament is inferior to similar objects from these groups.

"This may well be symbolic of an animal god, probably the bear, combined with the cosmic sign. The animal's head is drawn double, and the design appears the same when reversed. One pair of ears, two eyes and one head answer for both animals, but there are separate mouths, nostrils and necks. The five nearly parallel perforations upon the neck, also duplicated upon the opposite side, doubtless represent the claws of the bear. This symbol occurs several times in modified form in objects of bone and copper from the Hopewell group, and is still used as a bear sign by modern Indians. It seems to me that this mark may be the distinguishing mark of the animal represented.

"The outer circle and four perforated arms doubtless form a cosmic symbol representing the horizon and four directions. The central perforation may also represent the central circle usually present, especially as it seems to have no connection with the head of the animal. The arms representing the four quarters are pushed out of their normal position to make room for the central head."

In Figs. 55, 56 are given, from Mr. Willoughby's designs, part of the copper disc, showing the animal head with the bear symbol beneath, and the copper disc with the animal symbols removed, leaving the cosmic sign.

Another pair of ear-plugs, side and top views of which are shown in Figs. 57, 58, where two missing parts are represented in broken lines, had for decoration on

FIG. 59.—Silver-coated ear-plug of copper. Upper and lower parts. Mound near Crystal river. (Full size.)

top, a thin coating of sheet-silver,[2] hammered on. There is a concave circle in the center and four crescent-shaped open spaces.

The third pair of ear-plugs, wrapped in bark or vegetable fiber and in a woven

[1] For farther information on this interesting subject we would call the reader's attention to "Symbolism in Ancient American Art," by F. W. Putnam and C. C. Willoughby, "Proceedings of the American Association for the Advancement of Science." Vol. XLIV, 1896.

[2] Sheet-gold, sheet-silver, sheet iron (meteoric) have been found in various mounds in Ohio, in which no objects distinctly of European provenance have been met with.

fabric, has circular, concave spaces in the center of the upper and lower portions. The whole outer surface of the upper halves is coated with thin sheet-silver, which, loose in places, has turned up and over. The upper and lower discs were separated by a mass of vegetable fiber through which ran a cord. This cord, passing through a perforation in the middle of the central concavity, on the outside of each upper part is knotted around a pearl which is pierced. The upper and the lower part of one of these ear-plugs is shown in Fig. 59.

Fig. 60.—Ornament of sheet-copper. Mound near Crystal river. (Three-quarters size.)

Fig. 61.—Ornament of sheet-copper. Mound near Crystal river. (Full size.)

Badly broken when found, was an oblong ornament of sheet-copper (Fig. 60), rather rudely decorated with punctate markings and showing a cruder form of aboriginal effort in repoussé decoration, though in direct line with more ambitious work.

An ornament of fluted sheet-copper, badly broken, came from this mound (Fig. 61). This pattern was a popular one among the aborigines. We have met with it at least twice before, once at Apalachicola and once in the fine mound on Murphy Island, Fla.

Two tubular beads of over-lapping sheet-copper were found in caved sand.

A portion of a second ornament of fluted sheet-copper from this mound was submitted to Prof. Harry F. Keller, Ph.D., who reported on it as follows:

"As to the sheet-copper from the Crystal river mound, it is certainly made from the native metal; a very searching qualitative analysis of the cleaned specimen gave only silver and iron as metallic impurities, and demonstrated the entire absence of lead, arsenic, antimony and zinc."

Here we have native copper such as was used by the aborigines, previous to the coming of the Europeans, which copper was not obtainable in Europe in quantities sufficient for commercial purposes and which is most distinctly different from the copper brought to this country by Europeans, the European copper being the product of arsenical, sulphide ores, and teeming with impurities.

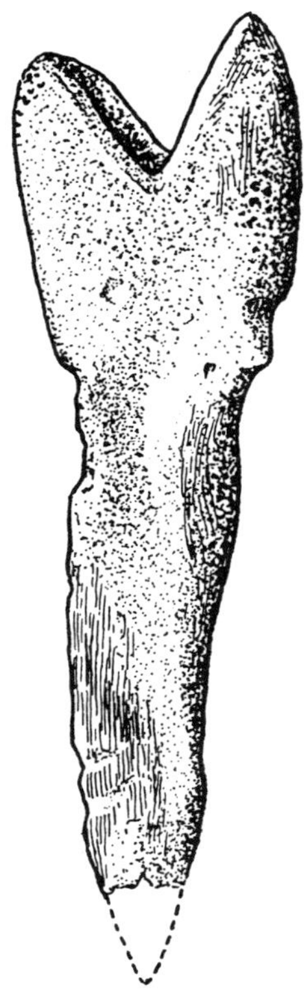

Fig. 62.—Implement of bone. Mound near Crystal river. (Full size.)

Three pointed implements made from cannon-bones of deer, and three shark's teeth of the present geological period, lay with three arrowheads or knives. Such teeth were found by Mr. Cushing at Marco, in the Ten Thousand Islands, Fla., and were shown by him to have been used for the carving of wood.

In one deposit were a number of pointed implements of bone, fragments of other bone implements of various kinds, and a fish-hook of bone, from which the pointed end, broken by the blow of a spade, was lost. With these was an object of bone, perhaps used in basketry (Fig. 62).

Half of a tooth of a fossil shark was met with in the mound.

As to note the exact association of all objects from this mound would unduly occupy our space, a few groups of artifacts, only, will be given as they were found.

With a burial were: one canine tooth of a large carnivore; two "celts" of polished rock; two sheets of mica; three lance-heads of chert; two sandstone pebble-hammers; four shell gouges; four shell "celts;" parts of other "celts" of shell; two sandstone hones; several bits of clayey material.

Together were: two pendants of shell; two pendants of igneous rock; a knuckle-bone of a deer.

Three knuckle-bones of the deer lay with two shell pendants.

With the skeleton of a child were: two pendants of rock; one pendant of shell; a knuckle-bone of a deer.

In one deposit were: half of a bar-amulet of slate; two smooth, flat fragments, one of banded slate, one seemingly of fine-grained sandstone; one pendant of sedimentary rock; one of igneous rock; one of quartz; a beautifully made one of quartz, somewhat worn.

Again we would call the attention of the reader, before ending the account of this interesting investigation, to the fact that nothing showing white provenance was met with during the work and that the entire area gone over by us was absolutely virgin.

Mound near Crystal River Settlement, Citrus County.

The settlement is at the head of Crystal river.

About 1.5 miles in a NNW. direction from the town, on property of Mr. Herman Miller, of Crystal River, in pine woods bordering a hammock, was a sand mound 4 feet 9 inches high and 70 feet across the circular base.

Thorough trenching showed this mound to belong to the domiciliary class.

Mound near the Chassahowitzka River, Citrus County.

The river has its source at a large spring, or boil, about eight miles from the Gulf.

The mound, in pine woods, about one-half mile in a E. by S. direction from the landing at the river's head, was in full view from the road. Though but comparatively little dug into before our visit, seemingly, it had been much trampled by cattle, and bits of human bone and fragments of earthenware were scattered here and there over the entire surface. It was evident that the diameter of the mound, 75 feet at the time of our visit, had been extended at the expense of the height, which was 4 feet.

Fifteen trenches were started inward from the margin and continued until human remains were encountered, when all trenches were joined and the remaining part of the mound, which had a diameter of from 50 to 54 feet, probably about the original diameter, was demolished.

Eighteen burials, all very badly decayed, including the lone skull, were met with. The bunched burial, also, was represented, sometimes without a skull, sometimes with one, and once with two.

With one burial were bits of pottery and fragments of chert. With another was an imperforate pot of inferior ware, bearing a small check-stamp. Certain decaying fragments of bone had with them bits of different vessels. The following vessels were in the mound, not as a general deposit but here and there, singly, perhaps interred with burials since decayed; a small, undecorated, imperforate vessel modelled after a gourd; an undecorated bowl with a basal perforation, having a small depression below the rim at opposite sides; a small vessel without decoration, a flattened sphere in shape, having the usual mortuary mutilation; an undecorated vessel badly broken.

A handle of a vessel, representing the head of a predatory bird (Fig. 63), was found unassociated with other ware. In the beak is a circular hole which would allow the use of the head as a pendent ornament. We got, on the Island of Marco, one of the northern-most of the Ten Thousand Islands (see outline map) a bird-head handle of a vessel, with a groove around the neck, showing the use of the head as a pendant.

Sherds in the mound were numerous but did not lie in deposits. The great majority are of ordinary ware and undecorated. Some, however, are of excellent material. Red pigment had been used in several instances and punctate markings and the check-stamp are represented. The complicated stamp was not met with.

There were also in the mound, unassociated: a small hatchet, seemingly of igneous rock; a triangular weapon or tool, of chert; a bit of fossil wood; a number of flakes and chippings, of chert; a pendant of volcanic rock (Fig. 64).

Mound near Indian Bend, Hernando County.

This name is given to a bight in the swamp bordering the Gulf, around which grow pine trees, and oaks in places. The mound at Indian Bend is about two miles in a straight line almost due south from the landing at the head of Chassahowitzka river. It had been dug into in a limited way before our visit and seemed, in addition, to have been greatly trampled by cattle. Its height was 4 feet. It was 48 feet across its circular base. Fifteen trenches were dug in toward the center until, at the union of these trenches, a portion from 32 feet to 34 feet in diameter remained. This part was entirely demolished.

Fig. 63.—Handle of vessel. Mound near the Chassahowitzka river. (Full size.)

Fig. 64.—Pendant of stone. Mound near the Chassahowitzka river. (Full size.)

Fig. 65.—Sherd. Mound near Indian Bend. (Half size.)

Burials, eight in number, in the last stage of decay, were: two lone skulls; four small bunches, each with a skull; one bunch without a skull; and, centrally, a skeleton flexed on the right side with a few shell beads at the wrist.

Exceptionally few sherds were met with in this mound. Most were undecorated; some had the check-stamp; one had encircling, parallel lines incised (Fig. 65) which gave the ware the appearance of the coil method of manufacture.

No whole vessels were found, but a portion of one, undecorated, had a basal perforation carefully rounded after the fracture.

Here and there in the mound, unassociated, were several flakes and fragments, of chert, an arrowhead or knife, and a lance-head, of the same material.

Running through the mound for a number of feet, was a deposit of sand dyed red with hematite.

Mound near Bayport, Hernando County.

Bayport is at the mouth of the Wekiwoochee river.

The mound, owner unknown, lay in scrub and pine, about one mile in a northerly direction from the town. One small hole was the only previous digging noticed by us, but, at the center, there seemed to be a certain flattening as though a building had been there, and that such had been the case was the belief in Bayport. As the mound was on a natural elevation and no base-line was at any time apparent, we found it impossible to decide as to height. Judging from appearances, the altitude was 3 feet 7 inches, but as nothing showing human origin is believed to have been found during the digging, at a depth greater than 2 feet, the mound may have been lower than it appeared. The diameters of base, as taken by us, were 84 feet N. and S., and 76 feet E. and W., but here again, our judgment may have been at fault. At all events, one burial and sherds at various points, were found soon after digging began. The area as given above was completely dug through.

Burials were found marginally in various parts of the mound and continued to be met with, occasionally, until the more central parts of the mound were reached, when they were fairly numerous. All were so badly decayed that no bones were saved. Such crania as were sufficiently preserved to allow determination showed no sign of flattening. In all but three cases, the form of burial was of the ordinary bunched variety. Of these bunches, thirty-four had one skull; four bunches had two skulls; four bunches had three skulls; one had four skulls; one had six skulls; one bunch had seven skulls. Three bunches had no crania with them.

Three other bunches had with them small deposits of fragments of calcined human bones. Twice the deposits were mingled with some unburnt bones belonging to the bunched burials. In these cases the calcined fragments were so few in number that a fractional part of the skeleton only was represented. The third deposit, near a burial, but not in contact, was somewhat larger, perhaps amounting to several quarts.

With various burials were: three conch-shells and bits of pottery; certain fragments of earthenware; two earthenware vessels in fragments; a bit of chert; six conch-shells; two implements made from marine univalves (*Fulgur perversum* and *Fasciolaria*) by removing part of the body-whorl; sand dyed with hematite; sand less deeply tinged with the red oxide; two small shells much decayed; one "celt."

Over one burial was a large fragment of what must have been a bowl of great size, of inferior ware, roughly decorated. On the fragment was one large loop-shaped handle.

FIG. 66.—Selection of sherds. Mound near Bayport. (Half size.)

There were also in the mound: marine shells, more or less broken (*Fulgur*, *Fasciolaria*) with the lower outer portions removed, and sharpened at the lower end of the columella so that, when the upper part of the shell was held in the hand, they could be used to bore or to pierce with; chips, flakes and fragments, of chert; several arrowheads or knives, also of chert, some of which were broken, some only rudely blocked out; four "celts," one showing marks of service in a handle; two very diminutive "celts;" a few fragments of what had been an crnament of sheet-copper.

At the very margin of the mound, in various directions, were small deposits of sherds made up of parts of different vessels, while single sherds and smaller deposits were met with throughout the mound. The ware, as shown by these fragments, is, in most cases, inferior, though some is of excellent quality. Much is undecorated. One sherd, seemingly, is cord-marked, though this decoration is hard to determine. A few bear traces of crimson pigment; many have the check-stamp of various sizes; several have the complicated stamp, including the design of concentric circles, so much in vogue in this district. One has a complicated pattern shown by us in Fig. 66, Part II, of our "Certain Aboriginal Remains of the Northwest Florida Coast." Some sherds from this investigation bear incised decoration alone; some, punctate decoration, in addition, but the specialty of the builders of the mound was the punctate impression in various combinations. A selection of sherds from the mound is shown in Fig. 66 and others are given in Figs. 67, 68, 69, 70.

FIG. 67.—Sherd. Mound near Bayport. (Three-fourths size.)

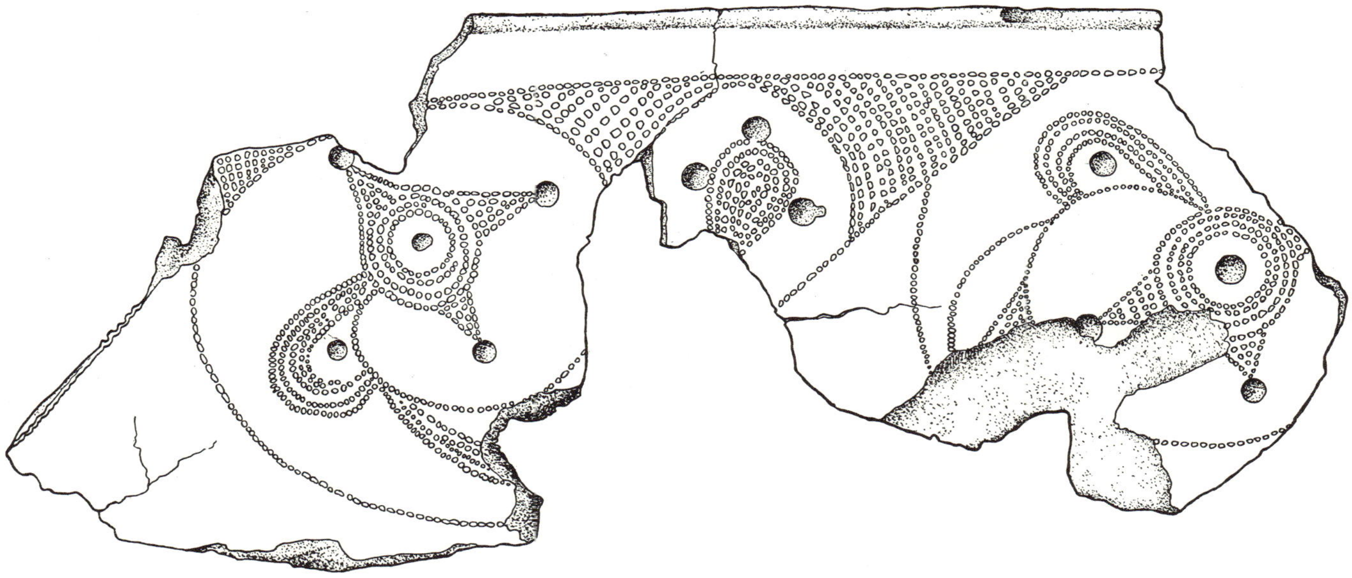

FIG. 68.—Sherd. Mound near Bayport. (Half size.)

FIG. 69.—Sherd. Mound near Bayport. (Half size.)

FIG. 70.—Sherd. Mound near Bayport. (Half size.)

FIG. 71.—Part of vessel of earthenware. Mound near Bayport. (About four-fifths size.)

Part of a vessel, found in several bits, shows an interesting decoration and indicates a graceful form though, unfortunately, the entire base and most of the neck, are wanting (Fig. 71). The sand for some distance around these fragments was carefully sifted without discovery of farther trace of the vessel and it became evident that the pieces had been interred as fragments only.

In view of the evidence furnished by some of the sherds that the makers of the mound posessed ware superior as to quality, form and decoration, the entire vessels met with by us were doubly disappointing.

Soon after the digging began, in the eastern margin of the mound, at a distance from human remains, evidently placed in the mound for the use of the dead in common, as were all deposits of vessels in this mound, with one exception, was Vessel No. 1 (Fig. 72), of most inferior ware, with six projecting knobs, undoubtedly

FIG. 72.—Vessel No. 1. Mound near Bayport. (About two-thirds size.)

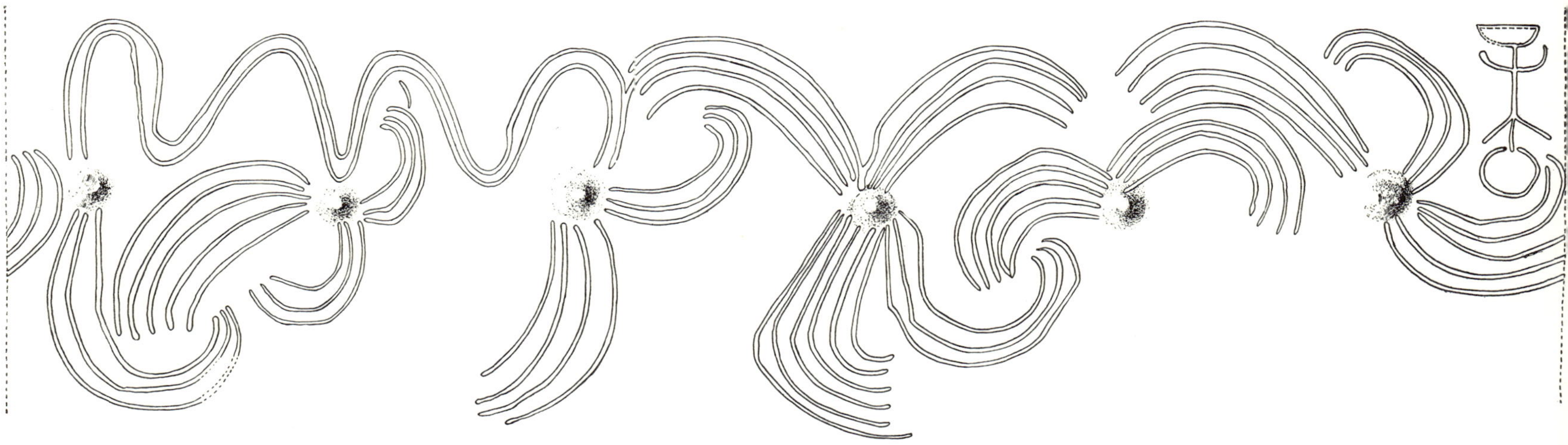

FIG. 73.—Vessel No. 1. Decoration. Mound near Bayport. (One-third size.)

FIG. 74.—Vessel No. 2. Mound near Bayport. (Full size.)

highly conventionalized head, tail and legs of a life-form. The decoration, traced on the clay before firing, is rude (diagram, Fig. 73). In the base is a carefully rounded perforation made after baking, as was the case with all vessels in this mound, except such as are described to the contrary.

With this vessel, in fragments which have since been put together, was Vessel No. 2, of excellent ware (Fig. 74), with incised and punctate decoration shown diagrammatically in Fig. 75. There are duck-head handles.

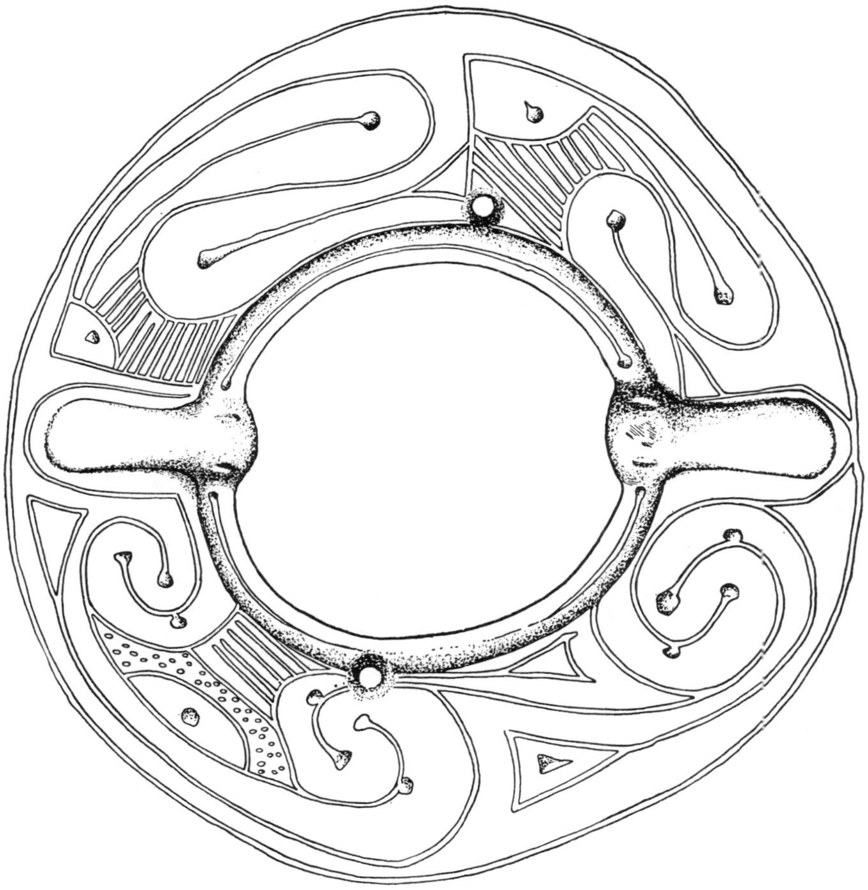

FIG. 75.—Vessel No. 2. Decoration. Mound near Bayport. (Half size.)

Somewhat farther in, still in the eastern part of the mound, unfortunately shattered by the blow of a spade, was a vessel, an inverted, truncated cone in shape, with a check-stamp decoration. This vessel was too badly broken to determine as to basal perforation.

A little later, in the same direction, an undecorated, globular vessel was met with.

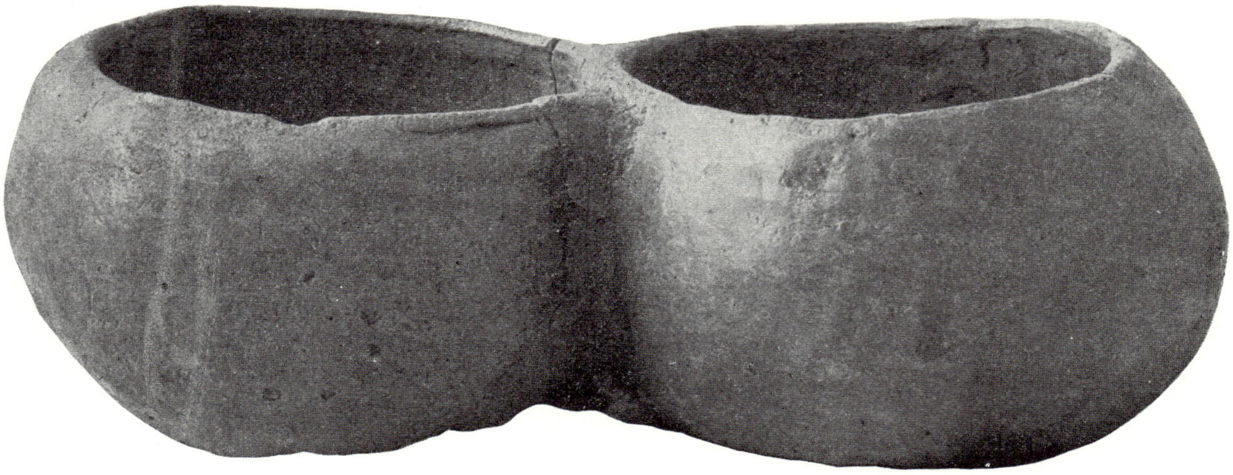

FIG. 76.—Vessel No. 5. Mound near Bayport. (About two-thirds size.)

FIG. 77.—Vessel No. 6. Mound near Bayport. (About three-fifths size.)

From the southern part of the mound came Vessel No. 5 (Fig. 76) which formerly had had double, circular compartments. The greater part of one compartment has been restored.

Still in the marginal part of the mound, the northwestern portion, but farther in than the vessels already described, together, were nine vessels, Nos. 6 to 14, inclusive, all of most inferior ware, some upright, some lying on the side, some inverted.

Vessel No. 6.—A jar of about 3 quarts' capacity (Fig. 77), undecorated, has a curious projecting base in which is a perforation made before baking. Three other vessels of this type came from this mound. Almost, there would seem to be cause to doubt whether these curious, open, projecting bases entitle the vessels to which they belong to be classed among the ready-made mortuary variety. Possibly the vessels may have been used as sieves or strainers with a fabric inserted on the bottom.

Vessel No. 7.—A globular vessel of about 6 quarts' capacity, undecorated, with a small vertical rim, a part of which was missing when the vessel was found.

Vessel No. 8.—A quadrilateral vessel with rounded base, shown in Fig. 78.

Vessel No. 9.—This vessel, similar to Vessel No. 6, was sent to the Peabody Museum, Cambridge, Mass.

Vessel No. 10.—A large bowl in many fragments, having the upper part faintly decorated with a complicated stamp composed of concentric circles.

Vessel No. 11.—A pot of about 3 gallons' capacity, having on the upper part of the body a faint check-stamp.

FIG. 78.—Vessel No. 8. Mound near Bayport. (About four-fifths size.)

FIG. 79.—Vessel No. 12. Mound near Bayport. (About three-fifths size.)

Vessel No. 12.—A jar of the same type as Vessels Nos. 6 and 9, with protruding base and ready made perforation, shown in Fig. 79, but differing slightly in outline. The reader will bear in mind that properly to show the base, the aperture of the vessel has been turned away.

Vessel No. 13.—Badly broken, similar to Vessels Nos. 6 and 9.

Vessel No. 14.—A badly broken vessel having a check-stamp decoration.

Vessel No 15.—Alone in the sand was a small vessel, oblate spheroidal, undecorated, with narrow, upright rim. The carefully-made, circular hole in the base, looking as though, after a small piece had been broken out, the margin of the break had been rounded by a cutting implement, was not present in this case, the entire bottom having been knocked out.

In the body of the mound, NE. part, with a burial, were two large, undecorated vessels in fragments (Numbers 16 and 17).

MOUND NEAR INDIAN CREEK, HERNANDO COUNTY.

Indian creek enters the Gulf about five miles south of Bayport.

Surrounded by marsh, about 400 yards ENE. from the mouth of the creek, on property of Mr. Richard A. Ellis, of Aripeka, is a small patch of solid ground on which grow a few palmettoes and pines. In the center, was an artificial elevation about 2.5 feet high and 42 feet across the base. Previous digging had been confined to a small, central hole.

The mound was entirely demolished by us except portions around several trees. The material was tough, clayey sand.

Near the center were two bunched burials, each with a skull, and a skeleton closely flexed on the right side.

No artifacts of any sort were met with.

Mound near the Wekiwachee River, Pasco County.[1]

The mound, in pine woods, in full view from the Tampa road, was about two miles in a SSE. direction from the mouth of the Wekiwachee river, also called Hammock creek.

At one side of the mound was a depression whence the sand had been taken, and about 100 yards distant was a fresh-water pond where the aborigines found a supply of water.

The mound had been dug into, centrally, to a certain extent before we came and bits of bone and fragments of pottery were scattered on the surface. The area of the base, which seemed to have been extended somewhat by the trampling of cattle, was 86 feet by 64 feet. The height of the mound was a trifle over 4 feet. What seemed to be the mound proper, was entirely dug down by us, except small parts around certain trees. Sand, apparently washed and trampled from above, presumably not belonging to the mound, though in appearance a part of it, was excluded from the investigation.

Burials were met with from the very start and continued in until a deposit of bones, spread in a layer, was encountered, which occupied all the central part of the mound, at a depth of about two feet from the surface. In this layer, with other bones, were seventy-six skulls, and, doubtless, the digging preceding our own removed certain others.

The sole, and rather incommensurate, votive offering with this great deposit of bones was a vessel of earthenware, of about one quart capacity, a flattened sphere in shape, having traces of red paint on the exterior and a small mortuary perforation in the base.

There were also in the mound:

Bunched burials each having one skull,	40
Bunched burials with two skulls each,	11
Bunched burials with three skulls each,	2
Bunched burials with four skulls each,	2
Skeletons closely flexed on the right side,	5
Skeletons closely flexed on the left side,	3
Bunched burial with no skull,	1

Four additional burials, each with a single skull, fell with caved sand.

There was also a small pocket of calcined fragments of human bone, perhaps about one quart in all, present in the mound.

The condition of the bones was such that no skull was saved. No cranial flattening was noticed on any of the fragments.

The aborigines who built this mound were not liberal in offerings to the departed, as was indicated by the comparative lack of artifacts with the great deposit. The skeleton of a child had three shell drinking-cups and two unwrought

[1] This river must not be confounded with the Wekiwoochee river, some eight miles away.

conchs (*Fulgur perversum*), while two shell-cups lay each with another burial. With one burial was sand dyed with hematite.

With a bunched burial was a gracefully made "celt;" with another, two equally as well-made.

Not immediately associated with burials were: one hammer-stone; two lance-heads, of chert, each about 3.5 inches in length; a well-made spear-head of chert, about 5 inches long and about 2 inches in maximum diameter. A grooved pendant, rather roughly made from a pebble, lay alone in the sand.

In the southern margin of the mound was a small deposit of sherds and, here and there in the mound, fragments were met with singly, bearing red pigment, the

FIG. 80.—Selection of sherds. Mound near the Wekiwachee river. (Half size.)

check-stamp, punctate markings. There were several fragments with a complicated stamp in which the concentric circle figured. A selection of sherds from this mound is shown in Fig. 80.

Part of a vessel was met with showing a basal perforation made before the firing of the clay.

MOUND NEAR THE PITHLOCHASCOOTIE RIVER, PASCO COUNTY.

This river, variously spelled on maps and charts, is commonly spoken of as the "Kootie."

About three-quarters of a mile from the mouth of the river, on the S. side, visible from the water, on property of Mr. E. B. Liles, of Ehren, Fla., is an oblong mound running almost north and south, 142 feet along the base and 70 feet across it. The summit plateau is 91 feet long and 19 feet in width. The height is 9 feet. The mound, composed of alternate layers of sand and of shell, as is shown by former excavations, is probably domiciliary.

Mr. S. T. Walker, in the *Smithsonian Report* for 1879, page 392, *et seq.*, has described, and given plans of, this domiciliary mound and of the burial mound nearby, a description of which we are about to give.

About 100 yards in an easterly direction from the domiciliary mound is a mound of sand, of irregular outline (see Plan, Fig. 81), also on property of Mr. Liles. The mound, narrowest at its western end, slopes gently upward for 58 feet,

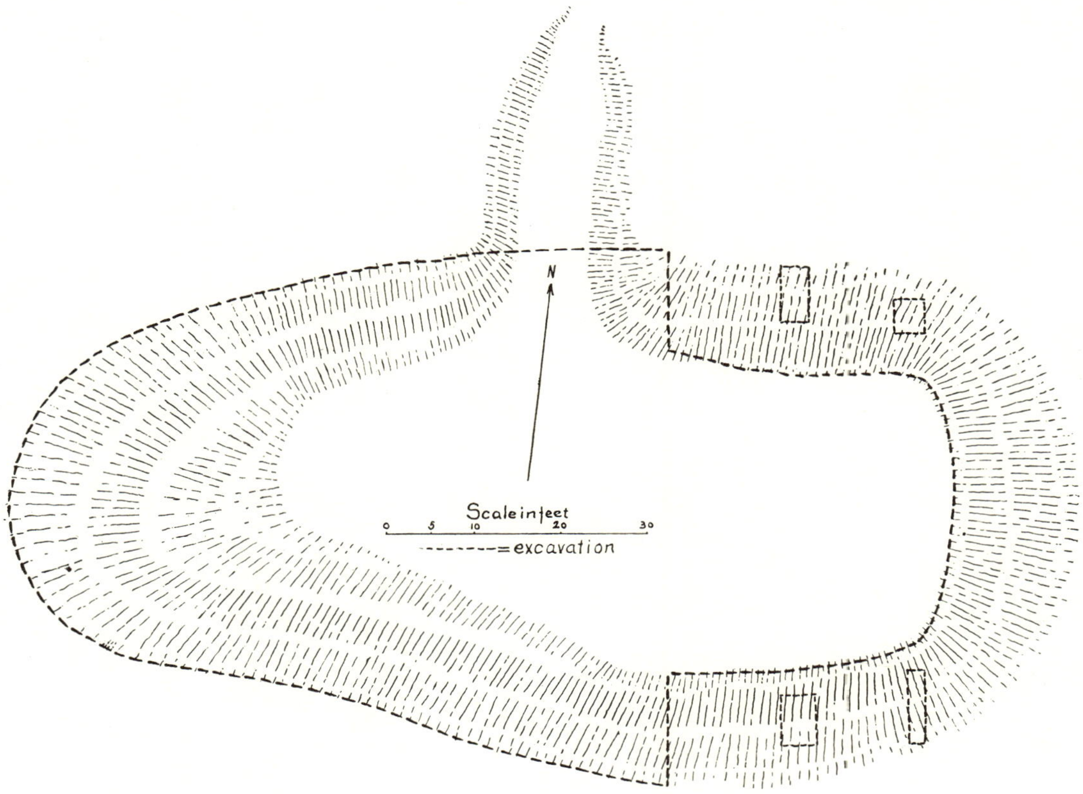

FIG. 81.—Plan. Mound near Pithlochascootie river.

when the maximum height, 4 feet, is reached. There is then a decline of 65 feet to the level ground at the eastern extremity of the mound. Mr. Walker is in error in ascribing to the sand mound a height greater than that of the domiciliary mound, and in his plan of the burial mound has reversed the position of its ends, putting the broader end at the western extremity.

There had been comparatively little previous digging, considering the size of the mound. Mr. Walker's digging, amounting to but little, was plainly traceable.

The western, or narrower part of the mound, which, however, included the highest part, was entirely dug through by us to include 76 feet of the length of the base. The remaining, or eastern portion of the mound, 47 feet in length along the base, was dug through by us with the exception of the outer parts, in which neither burials nor artifacts were found by trenching. The total area of our investigation is shown in broken lines on the plan. The arm, or causeway (see plan) having been dug by Mr. Walker, was not investigated by us.

The mound, of sand, rested upon a foundation of clay on which, here and there, were masses of lime-rock. Whether these masses were put in place by aborigines at the making of the mound, we are unable to say, though it is our opinion they were not, as an excavation made by us at some distance from the mound yielded similar masses of rock.

There were in the mound, locally, along the base, deposits of oyster-shells. These deposits had no direct connection with the burials.

Mr. Walker says, in speaking of this mound: "Excavations systematically conducted revealed human remains in vast quantities in every part of the mound."

Burials were numerous in places but were not present in others. Some of our men dug through undisturbed sand during many hours without coming upon a single bone. Mr. Walker says also, "The mode of burial was interment at full length, with the heads directed toward a common center, the body reclining on its right side; I discovered three of these circles of bodies, each containing from seven to fourteen adult skeletons."

We met with nothing in the mound to indicate this method of burial, and we may say, incidentally, we have not found it in several hundred mounds opened by us in the southern United States.

Human remains were found in the mound at sixty-two places.

The skeletons in the mound lay as follows:

Partly flexed on the right side, ...	5
Partly flexed on the left side, ...	6
Closely flexed on the right side, ...	13
Closely flexed on the left side, ...	7
Full length on back, ...	2

The heads of the skeletons pointed as follows: E., 4; E. by S., 1; ESE., 3; SE., 3; SSE., 3; S., 1; WSW., 3; W., 1; W. by N., 1; WNW., 1; NW., 1; NE., 2; ENE., 5; E. by N., 4.

The upper half of a skeleton, perhaps an aboriginal disturbance, had the cranium directed toward the south.

It was noted as an invariable rule in this mound that the skeletons lay on the base, while the lone skulls, of which there were seven, and the bunched burials, of which eighteen were met with, were considerably higher in the mound.

The bunched burials were as follows:

With no skull present,	1
With one skull,	8
With two skulls,	2
With three skulls,	4
With five skulls,	1
With eight skulls,	2

A number of scattered bones found by us at one point in the mound, was perhaps an aboriginal disturbance.

There were included in our enumeration also one recent disturbance, and one burial details as to which we do not find in our note book.

About two-thirds the length of the mound from the western extremity, well in toward the median line and continuing inward and eastward, not always in close contact but spread, was a deposit of bones with which were fifty-seven skulls. With this great mass, were three small deposits of calcined human bones. All this was scored as one burial and completes the sixty-two burials counted by us.

No skulls were saved from this mound. Judging from large fragments found, cranial compression had not been practised.

With burial No. 1, a recent disturbance, were Vessels Nos. 1, 2 and 3, all of most inferior ware, and in fragments.

FIG. 82.—Pendant of slate. Mound near the Pithlochascootie river. (Full size.)

A conch-shell lay with a lone skull, and similar shells were with burials or unassociated.

Burial No. 22, a skeleton closely flexed on the left side, had on the pelvic portion a beautiful pendant of slate (Fig. 82).

With a bunched burial was a graceful arrow- or lance-head of chalcedony, while a flake of chert, evidently used as a knife, lay with another bunched burial.

A skeleton closely flexed on the right, Burial No. 32, had with it: one hammer-stone; four small masses of cherty material; part of a lance-head or of a dagger, of chert; five fragmentary objects of shell, chisels, etc.; one tibia and one humerus, belonging to the deer; three deer tibiæ and one humerus, in fragments; one astragalus of a deer; bits of bone mainly belonging to the deer; part of a jaw of a small mammal; fragments of pointed implements of bone; five entire implements wrought from leg-bones of deer, and two, each broken into two parts; three tubes of bone, each about 1.5 inches in length.

Near Burial No. 33, a skeleton closely flexed on the right side, were three piercing implements wrought from cannon-bones of deer, and a number of fragments of bone, probably parts of implements.

In the southern part of the mound, with Burial No. 30, a skeleton flexed on the right side, was an inverted bowl, Vessel No. 4, oval in horizontal section, 13.8

inches by 15 inches in maximum diameter, 8.5 inches high, 6.5 inches by 7.5 inches in diameters of aperture, with in-turned rim and rude, incised decoration shown in Fig. 83. So stout was the ware that it resisted a number of blows of a spade, aimed at neighboring palmetto roots. There is a rounded perforation in the base, made after the completion of the vessel, and another in the side.

FIG. 83.—Vessel No. 4. Mound near Pithlochascootier iver. (About half size.)

On the base of the mound, as was the other, and about 6 feet east of it, inverted, with Burial No. 42, a skeleton closely flexed on the right side, was Vessel No. 5, a bowl of excellent yellow ware, 18 inches in diameter, 7.75 inches high and 13.8 inches across the opening. This vessel (Fig. 84) has red pigment interiorly and red coloring matter within two of each of the four triangles which make up the oblong spaces between the groups of parallel vertical lines of the decoration. With Burial No. 42 was also a small pendant of sedimentary rock, having a conventional bird-form, shown in two positions in Fig. 85, while a well-made pendant of metamorphic rock (Fig. 86) lay with another burial.

A bunched burial had near it an ungrooved quartz crystal, and a rather rude lance-head of chert was with another bunched burial.

With the large deposit were two "celts," a conch-shell, a long pendant made from a columella of a marine univalve, and three pendants of lime-rock, much the worse for age.

FIG. 84.—Vessel No. 5. Mound near the Pithlochascootie river. (About two-fifths size.)

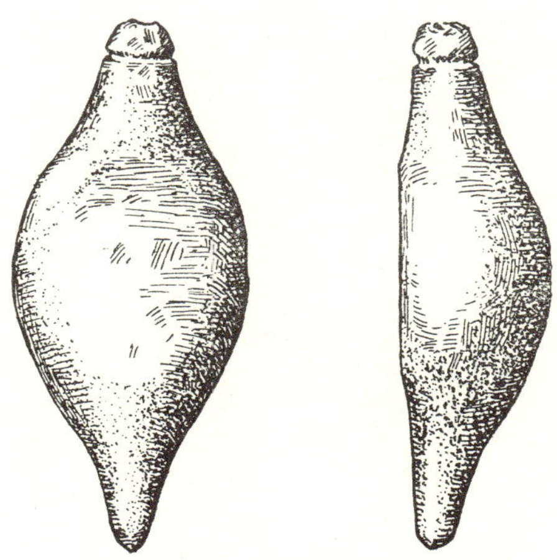

FIG. 85.—Pendant of sedimentary rock. Two positions. Mound near the Pithlochascootie river. (Full size.)

FIG. 86.—Pendant of metamorphic rock. Mound near the Pithlochascootie river. (Full size.)

At places throughout the mound, usually singly, was a considerable number of fragments of chert, also flakes of chert, evidently used as knives, and many cutting tools of chert, half wrought or very rudely worked, if complete. There were also several implements made from columellæ of marine univalves. Apparently unassociated, were: one "celt" showing much wear where the handle had been; two roughly chipped cutting implements of cherty material, each about 7 inches long and each somewhat broken at the smaller end; one graceful pendant of shell; two stone pendants found separately; seven arrow- and lance-heads, of chert, some barbed and beautifully pointed; one drill of chert; and several small cutting tools of the same material; two arrowheads which, partly broken, had been rounded for use as scrapers; the lower part of a fine lance-head of chert; an implement 5 inches long, of smoothed quartz material.

In this mound were no deposits of sherds other than, possibly, two or three fragments lying together though, here and there, sherds were met with unassociated. Some were undecorated and of inferior ware; others gave evidence that vessels of excellent ware and superior decoration had been possessed by the makers of the

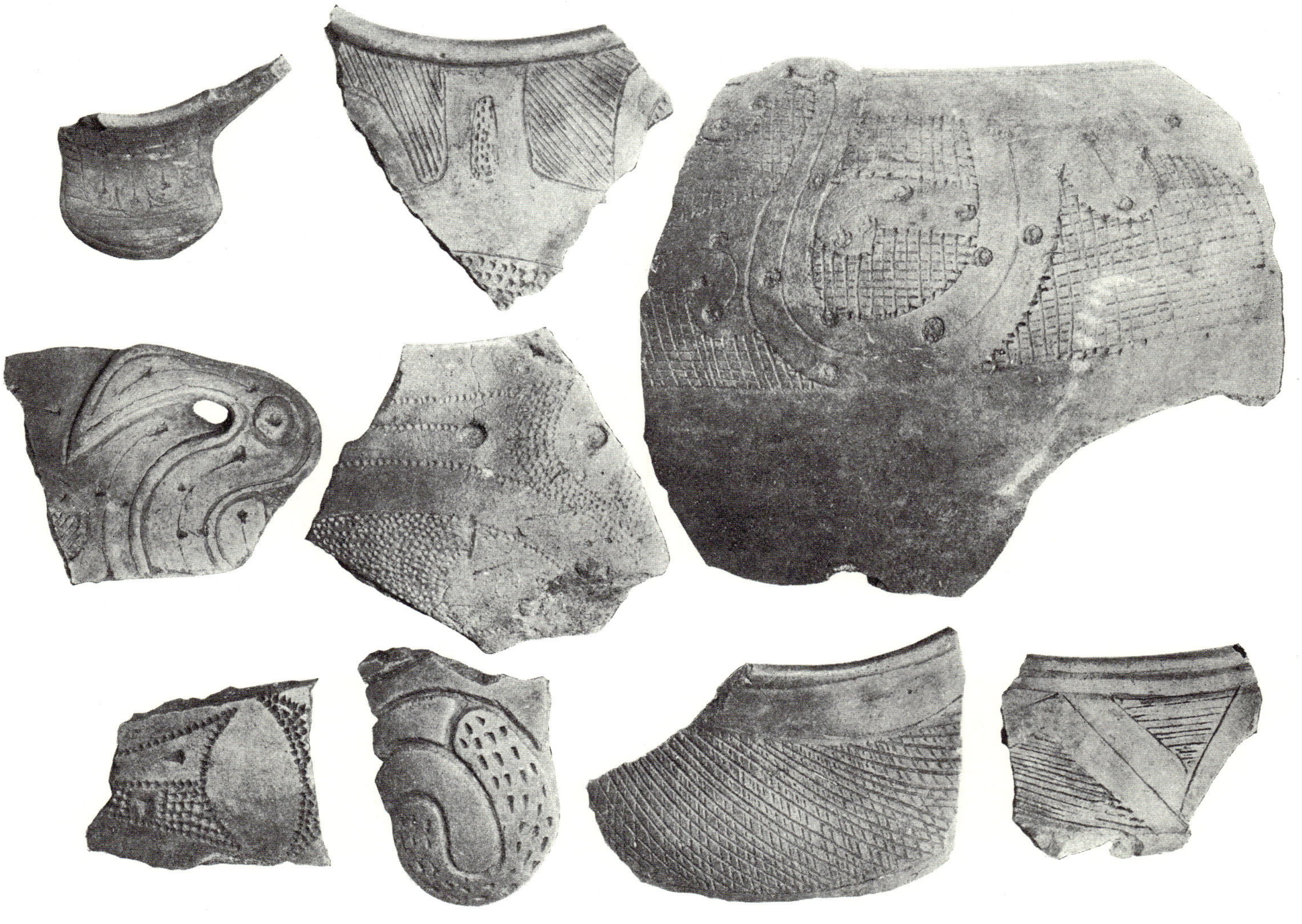

FIG. 87.—Selection of sherds. Mound near the Pithlochascootie river. (Half size.)

mound. Many sherds bore the ever-present check-stamp; the complicated stamp was on one sherd only. Some had a decoration of crimson pigment; others, incised and punctate designs. A selection is shown in Fig. 87. The reader will note in the right hand upper corner a sherd, handsomely decorated, where a portion of the design is carried above the rim. One interesting sherd, of excellent ware, shows the head of a bird with peculiarly shaped bill beneath which is a perforation which may be one of two made for the suspension of the vessel, or a single hole to allow the fragment to be worn as a pendant.

Mound near Tarpon Springs, Hillsboro County.

This mound is referred to, incidentally, as it belonged to those of the district of which we are writing.

The mound is described by Mr. S. T. Walker (*op. cit.*, page 394 *et seq.*) under the heading of the Ormond mound on the Anclote river. Such digging as was done by Mr. Walker, after members of Mr. Ormond's family had tried their hands at it, yielded nothing of importance.

In 1895, what remained of the mound was totally demolished by the late Mr. Frank Hamilton Cushing, who reported[1] the discovery of many burials and also of a pendant of crystal, a pendant of copper and many fragments of earthenware. These fragments will be figured and described in Prof. W. H. Holmes' "The Pottery of the Eastern United States," which will be published as the Twentieth Annual Report of the Bureau of American Ethnology.

Mound on Hog Island, Hillsboro County.

Hog Island lies between part of St. Joseph sound and the Gulf.

The mound, on property of Mr. Henry Scherrer, living nearby, is about one mile in a northerly direction from the southern extremity of the island. It lies on low ground which is entirely surrounded by water at high tide, and seems a curious selection for a place of burial.

The mound, composed of a mixture of sand and of small marine bivalves (*Venus cancellata*), the same genus as our round clam, had been wofully dug into, centrally, and from the sides, previous to our visit, when it was completely demolished by us, with the exception of parts surrounding two trees.

Burials in this mound lay, as a rule, near the base and in graves below the base. Many skeletons, we were told, had been removed by former diggers and many others, remaining, showed great disturbance.

Thirty-three skeletons were met with by us, buried as follows:

Closely flexed on the right side, ...	21
Closely flexed on the left side, ...	7
Partly flexed on the right, ...	1
Closely flexed, face down, ...	2
Closely flexed on the back, ...	1
Disturbance by our diggers, ...	1

[1] "Proceedings of the American Philosophical Society," Vol. XXXV, No. 153, Phila., 1897.

Two of these burials had above them a skull, and a skull with a femur, respectively, aboriginal disturbances.

There was also in the mound a burial, presumably intrusive, as it was but 2 feet below the surface and was in a better condition than the other burials, although they, owing to the infiltration of lime-salts, were in a state of preservation much superior to that usually met with.

Nineteen skulls were saved from this mound, none showing cranial flattening. Three of these, showing marked pathological changes, were sent to the United States Army Medical Museum, Washington, D. C.; four are now in our Academy of Natural Sciences (Catalogue numbers 2206 to 2209, inclusive); nine probably will be added to the collection, later. Three of the nineteen skulls subsequently fell into fragments.

In the count of burials found by us, bones scattered by former diggers are not noted. In addition, we may have passed over certain burials in graves, if any lay beneath trenches put in by former diggers.

This mound, in a negative way, is about the most remarkable one in our experience for, in the parts dug down by us, not a single fragment of pottery was met with, nor was any artifact of any sort discovered, with the exception of part of a small implement, probably of coralline lime-stone. Neither was there in the mound, according to the reports of our diggers, over whom was close supervision, in addition, any unworked pebble, conch-shell, or fragment of chert. In a word, practically nothing imperishable had been placed with the dead, if we except powdered hematite, in several instances.

Mound near Clearwater, Hillsboro County.

The mound, in sight from St. Joseph sound, and but a few feet from the N. end of the bridge across Steven's creek, about 2 miles in a N. direction from Clearwater, is 75 feet across the base and 5 feet in height. Fifteen excavations in various parts of the mound strongly suggested a domiciliary character for the mound.

Mound near John's Pass, Hillsboro County.

This mound, described by Mr. S. T. Walker (*op. cit.*, page 401 *et seq.*) lay near the SE. end of a nameless key which, extending east and west, lies just inside of John's Pass. The mound, on a low ridge, a portion of which had been dug into to make it, had sustained considerable investigation before our visit, when it was completely demolished. The diameter of the circular base was about 35 feet; the height, 2 feet 4 inches. The mound was composed of sand and of broken shells, not shell-heap material, but fragments of shells, washed up by the sea.

Although, as we have said, there had been much previous digging, a large percentage of the area of the mound was intact and afforded a good idea of what the mound and its contents had been. Burials extended more than one foot below the base, into broken shell material of the kind we have described, mixed with a little sand. In addition to disturbances by comparatively recent diggers, we noted six skeletons, three flexed on the right side, three on the left side. Also, there was on the S. side of the mound, a great number of bones, including a large number of crania, spread along the lower part of the mound. So thickly were these bones placed, at times, that eight or ten skulls were in sight within a comparatively small space. Unfortunately, though the admixture of shell in the mound tended to preserve the bones, close packing of long-bones against crania had crushed the facial bones of most of the skulls. Twelve crania, none showing flattening, were saved from this mound, six of which are now in the Academy of Natural Sciences (Catalogue Nos. 2210 to 2215, inclusive), and six, we trust, will be added later.

With certain burials, was sand dyed with hematite but no artifacts lay with the dead, though throughout the mound, were ten or a dozen shell drinking-cups (*Fulgur perversum*), some neatly made. Curiously enough, none had the usual basal perforation.

FIG. 88.—Selection of sherds. Mound near John's Pass. (Half size.)

Mr. Walker says of this mound, "The surface about the base was thickly strewn with fragments of pottery; in fact it seemed that the whole foundation of the mound was covered with broken pottery previously to the interment of any of the bodies."

There were a number of sherds in the mound, here and there, at various depths, but we saw nothing to bear out Mr. Walker's statement on the subject. These sherds, the only artifacts in the mound, except the drinking-cups, were of inferior ware and rudely decorated, when at all. The check-stamp was present in several instances, but the prevailing form of decoration was incised and punctate. A few loop-handles were found. A selection of sherds from this mound is shown in Fig. 88.

In this mound were several large fragments of shell-tempered ware, belonging to one vessel, the first we recall having met with in peninsular Florida, if we except two handsomely made bird-head handles from the Island of Marco, which had been worn as pendants, and were, doubtless, importations. Even on the Florida mainland shell-tempered ware is rarely met with until the district bordering Alabama is reached.

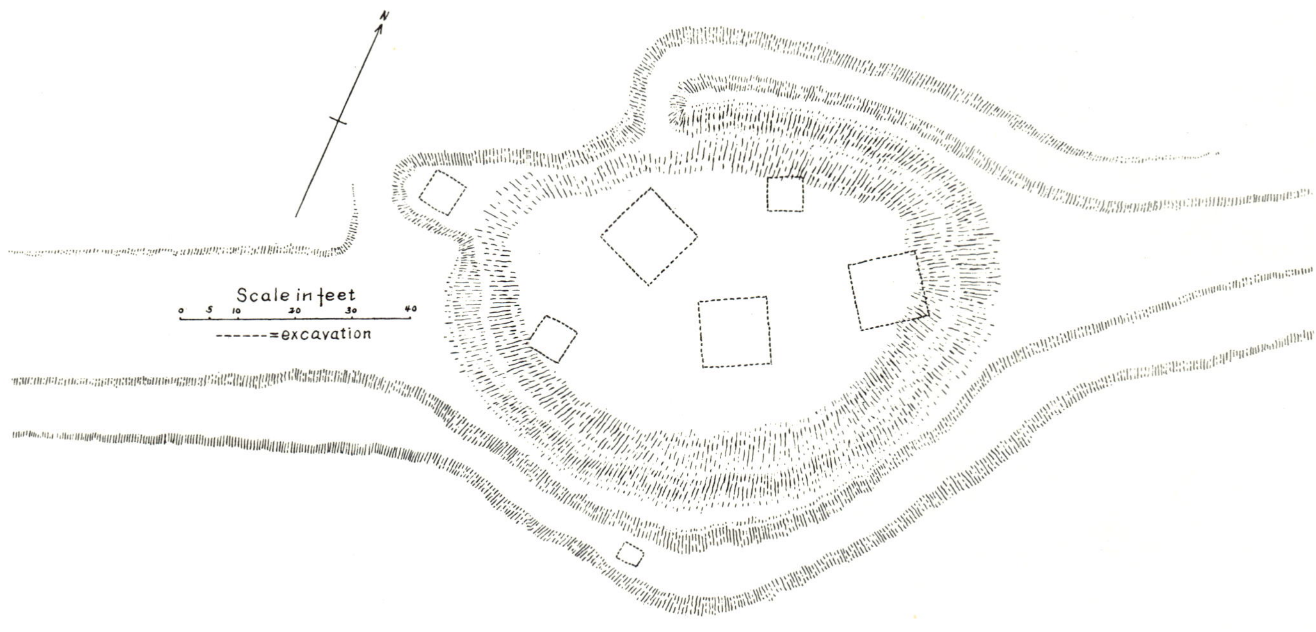

FIG. 89.—Plan. Mound on Long Key.

MOUND ON LONG KEY, HILLSBORO COUNTY.

Long Key lies between the Gulf and Boca Ceiga bay, having Blind Pass on the north and Passe a Grille on the south.

About midway from the extremities of the island, a strip of land makes into the bay in a SE. direction. About one-half mile from the end of this strip, in thick growth, is the mound, to which only good luck or a guide can lead one.

The mound is described by Mr. S. T. Walker (*op. cit.*, pg. 403, *et. seq.*) who also gives a plan of it, and ascribes to it the form of a turtle. In Fig. 89 we give the plan of the mound as it seemed to us. The material is white sand; the height somewhat under 4 feet. The length is 100 feet; the maximum breadth, about 70 feet.

Three holes, each 12 feet square, and three others, each 6 feet square, were dug by us. In several places was sand tinged with hematite and one skeleton closely flexed on the left side, about two feet from the surface, was met with. This burial had a recent appearance and impressed us as being intrusive.

No artifact of any sort was found.

For accounts of additional, but unimportant mounds in this district just north of Tampa bay, see our "Antiquities of the Florida West-Coast," Journal of the Academy of Natural Sciences of Philadelphia, Vol. XI.

In the district of which this paper treats was no new form of burial.

Calcined human bones were found upon several occasions, but these were probably connected with other burials as is usually the case when calcined remains are found in peninsular Florida.

No urn-burials were met with, nor had our previous experience in the peninsula led us to anticipate their discovery. Incidentally, the southeasternmost urn-burial we have found in Florida was on Marsh Island, Ocklockonee bay, which belongs to the mainland portion of Florida (see outline map).

Cranial flattening, which Bernard Romans says was practised by the Choctaws, was not seen by us on any skull in the mounds of the central Florida west-coast, though the reader of our reports on the northwest coast will recall that the custom was extensively practised there.

The custom to inter general deposits of earthenware in blackened sand did not obtain along the central west-coast, and the life-form in earthenware was not met with,[1] save in the case of one human effigy-vessel and a very highly conventionalized life-form consisting of six protuberances representing head, tail and four legs. Bird-head handles, however, were found. Loop-shaped handles were met with occasionally and seemingly show the influence of regions farther north.

Ceremonial vessels having, in the body, a number of large holes made before the firing of the clay, were not found along the central west-coast, though, as the reader may recall, they are present in numbers in the mounds of the northwest coast of Florida.

The small check-stamp was everywhere met with, and the complicated stamp was found once as far south as the Pithlochascootie river, which is considerably farther south than it was found by us on the St. Johns river. The complicated stamp, however, varies but slightly in pattern along the central west-coast where but little is met with that does not consist of combinations of concentric circles.

While, as we have stated, the ware, as a rule, was inferior, yet excellent ware with artistic decoration, punctate and incised, was in the possession of the aborigines

[1] Life forms in earthenware are not met with, practically, south of the Warrior river (see outline map).

of the west-coast. Gritty ware and shell-tempered ware, as might have been expected, practically were absent.

The finding of solid copper, a fish-spear along the Suwannee river, and pendants of solid copper in the Crystal river mound, came in the nature of a surprise. Though we had found several large and heavy beads of solid copper along the Ocklawaha river and near the Lakes from which the river runs, and a lance-head of thin copper near the mouth of the St. Johns, yet sheet-copper preponderated to such an extent among our discoveries of copper in Florida, that we had come to regard the territory as being so far distant from the source of aboriginal supply that the material would be used there hardly otherwise than as a veneer. It seems, however, that some solid copper was in use there, and doubtless more will be found as mound-work is continued in the State.

Miscellaneous Investigation in Florida

BY

CLARENCE B. MOORE

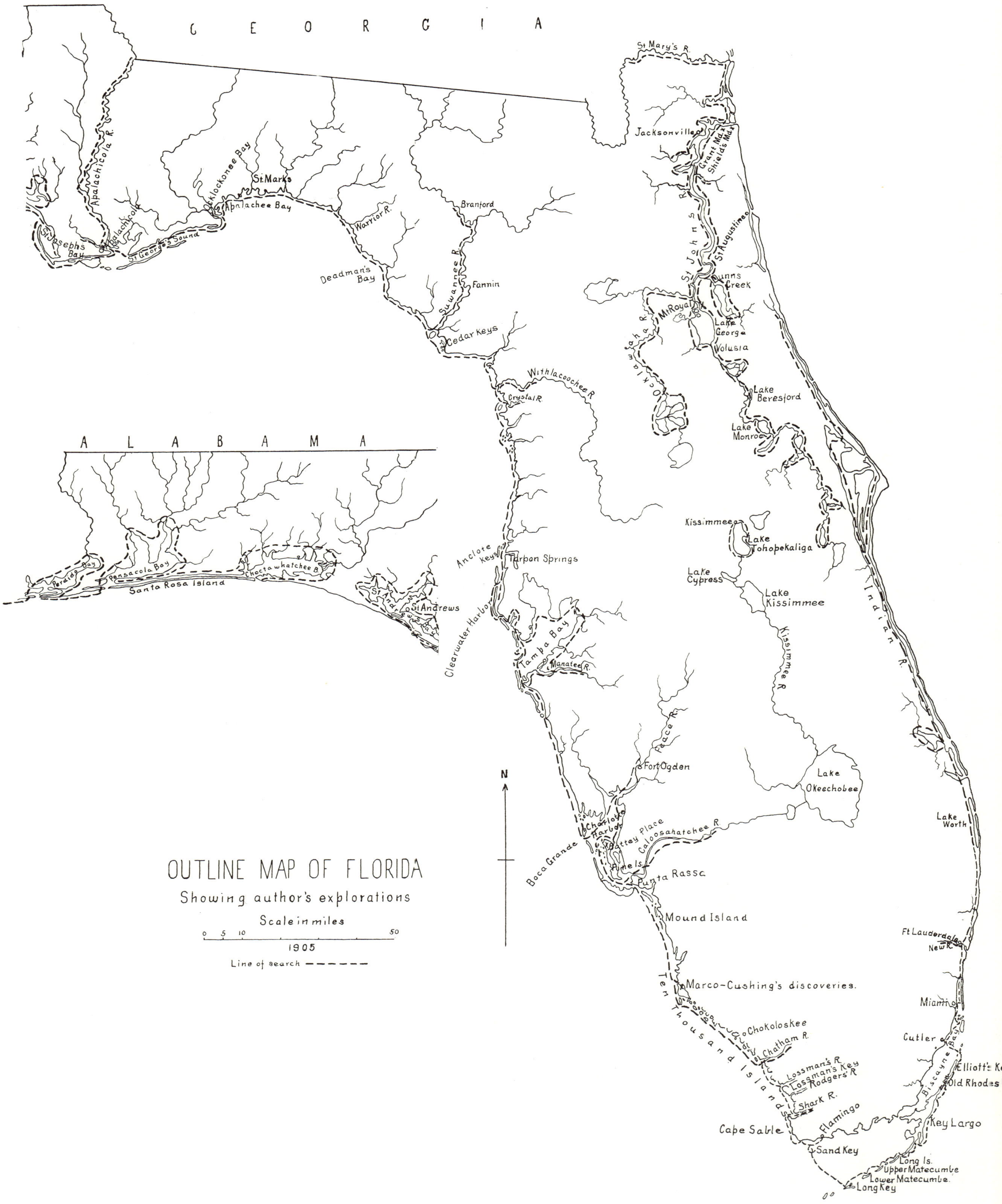
OUTLINE MAP OF FLORIDA
Showing author's explorations
Scale in miles
0 5 10 50
1905
Line of search
GEORGIA
ALABAMA
N
St Mary's R.
Jacksonville
Grant Md.
Shield's Md.
St Johns R.
St Augustine
Dunns Creek
Mt Royal
Ocklawaha R.
Lake George
Volusia
Lake Beresford
Lake Monroe
Kissimmee
Lake Tohopekaliga
Lake Cypress
Lake Kissimmee
Kissimmee R.
Indian R.
Lake Okeechobee
Lake Worth
Ft Lauderdale
New R.
Miami
Cutler
Biscayne Bay
Elliott's Key
Old Rhodes
Key Largo
Long Is.
Upper Matecumbe
Lower Matecumbe
Long Key
Sand Key
Flamingo
Cape Sable
Shark R.
Rodgers' R.
Lossman's Key
Lossman's R.
Chatham R.
Chokoloskee
Ten Thousand Islands
Marco-Cushing's discoveries.
Mound Island
Punta Rassa
Pine Is.
Caloosahatchee R.
Battey Place
Charlotte Harbor
Boca Grande
Fort Ogden
Peace R.
Manatee R.
Tampa Bay
Clearwater Harbor
Anclote Keys
Tarpon Springs
Crystal R.
Withlacoochee R.
Cedar Keys
Suwannee R.
Fannin
Branford
Deadman's Bay
Warrior R.
St Marks
Apalachee Bay
Ocklockonee Bay
Apalachicola R.
Apalachicola
St Joseph's Bay
St George's Sound
Perdido Bay
Pensacola Bay
Santa Rosa Island
Choctawhatchee B.
St Andrews

MISCELLANEOUS INVESTIGATION IN FLORIDA.

By Clarence B. Moore.

Our archæological exploration in Florida, during the season of 1904, was unsatisfactory to a certain extent; but as it has ever been our wish to let no investigation of ours pass unrecorded, we give a brief description of the season's work.

THE KISSIMMEE REGION.

The Kissimmee river, leaving the southern extremity of Lake Tohopekaliga, on which is the town of Kissimmee, flows through Cypress Lake and Lake Kissimmee, and continues in a southerly course to Lake Okeechobee. A canal connects the southwestern side of Lake Okeechobee with Caloosahatchee river, which empties into San Carlos bay, an arm of the Gulf of Mexico. These geographic features are shown on maps of Florida, and are presented on the outline map accompanying this report, which shows also the scope of all our archæological work in that State.

A few years ago it was possible, by the aid of certain canals, to make a journey by water, in a steamer of light draught, from Lake Tohopekaliga to the Gulf. Recently, however, the canals had been neglected, and an extensive growth of water-weeds, miles in extent, had formed in Kissimmee river north of Lake Okeechobee; in addition, a heavy dam[1] had been built across Caloosahatchee river, somewhat south of the lake. It was impossible, therefore, at the time of this exploration, for us to take our large, flat-bottomed steamer from the Gulf coast, where she lay, into the Kissimmee region.

Mr. J. S. Raybon, captain of our steamer, an expert in locating mounds, with a companion familiar with the territory, carefully traversed the region between Lakes Tohopekaliga and Okeechobee, inclusive. The report, however, was discouraging. Nowhere was there news of the discovery of earthenware vessels, and such few objects as were reported to have been found by the inhabitants were mainly of European make, and, perhaps, intrusive.

Lake Okeechobee was reported to be surrounded by marsh, and to be without mounds. Nevertheless, we determined to explore the region, if possible, and for this purpose chartered a small steamer which took in tow a flat-boat on which quarters had been built for the use of our colored mound-diggers.

After investigation of the mounds of Lake Tohopekaliga, which was practically without positive result, as the appended account will show, a severe accident occurred to our steam-boiler, which would have rendered the boat useless for a considerable time. No other boat being available, the investigation of the region was therefore abandoned.

[1] Since removed.

MOUNDS OF LAKE TOHOPEKALIGA, OSCEOLA COUNTY.

Mound near Kissimmee.

In a prairie, near the lake-shore, about one mile in a SSW. direction from the town of Kissimmee, on land of Mr. Walter Bass, Sr., of Kissimmee, is a mound, circular in outline, that has been much pawed and trampled by cattle. Its present height and diameter of base are 3 feet and 80 feet, respectively. It is built of sand, as are all the mounds of Lake Tohopekaliga.

Twelve excavations, each about 3 feet square, extending to the base of this mound, resulted in the finding of one arrowhead of chert, a fragment of earthenware bearing the ubiquitous small check-stamp, and several sherds of most inferior ware, each about .5 inch in thickness, with decoration of incised lines. No human remains were found. The mound was doubtless domiciliary.

Lanier Mound.

Situated in pine woods, about 6 miles in a southerly direction from the town of Kissimmee, on property of Mr. J. M. Lanier, living near by, is an artificial ridge of white sand extending almost due north and south. This ridge is 250 feet long and 90 feet in maximum basal breadth; its greatest height is 12 feet 3 inches. Previous to our visit, considerable digging had been done in this mound by persons in some cases known to the owner. No discoveries were reported by these persons.

Although the Lanier mound had every appearance of having been constructed for domiciliary purposes, and the lack of success of previous diggers tended to bear out this idea, three excavations were made by us, each 10 feet square and extending to the base of the mound. One of these was in the southern part, where the mound reached its greatest height; another, of almost equal depth, somewhat more to the north, and the third toward the northern extremity, where the height of the mound was about 8 feet.

In one excavation no relics or remains were encountered. In one was a small deposit of charcoal, and three bits of inferior, undecorated earthenware, found separately.

In the second excavation, at a depth of about 20 inches, was a "celt," with fragments of a human pelvis and parts of a femur and a humerus. About 3 feet distant, at the same level, was a human skull without the lower jaw.

Two and one-half feet down, in the same excavation, was a "celt," almost oblong in outline, with a bit of shell and two fragments of bone, too small for identification.

In our opinion this also was a domiciliary mound and the "celts" and human remains were intrusive.

Mounds near Brown's Landing.

Brown's landing is about one mile south of Edgewater, on the southwestern shore of Lake Tohopekaliga. A mound is situated in pine woods about 2 miles in a southwesterly direction from the landing, in sight from the public road, on property of Messrs. H. M. Pfann & Co., of Campbell, Fla. It is circular in outline, 5 feet 4 inches in height and 65 feet across the base. It has been dug into to so great an extent that after slight excavation it was abandoned by us. Various fragments of human bones were met with, and a number of sherds of very inferior ware, all undecorated save one upon which was a certain amount of red pigment. In addition, a single bead of blue glass, about the size of a buckshot, lay alone in the sand.

About three-quarters of a mile southwest of the mound just described, in open pine woods, in full view from the public road, is a mound of white sand, 9 feet 4 inches high and 150 feet across the circular base. This mound, which had every appearance of being domiciliary, was dug into superficially by us in many places, but no human remains or artifacts were encountered.

About three-quarters of a mile in an easterly direction from the mound just described is another, flat and irregular, evidently domiciliary.

Between these two mounds, though not directly connected with them, are two parallel artificial ridges, about 300 yards apart, extending about NW. and SE., and estimated to be from 3 to 5 feet in height. One is 200 yards, the other 300 yards, in length, approximately. These embankments do not run parallel to an imaginary line connecting the mounds, but cross it and seem to terminate in two small swamps.

The two mounds and ridges are on property belonging to Messrs. H. M. Pfann & Co.

Mound near Frier Cove.

This mound, on property of Mr. Stephen C. Partin, of St. Cloud, Fla., lies about one mile in a southeasterly direction from the cove near the SE. end of the lake. It had been long under cultivation, and, in consequence, was widely spread by the plow. Its height, at the time of our investigation, was 3 feet; its basal diameter, 83 feet. It was pitted and trenched in all directions by us, but yielded only a few, small fragments of human bone and a bit of undecorated pottery.

Mound near Lee's Landing.

Lee's landing is on the eastern shore of Lake Tohopekaliga, and the mound is situated about half a mile northwesterly therefrom, in a beautiful orange grove on the estate of Judge George F. Parker, of Kissimmee. Greatly spread by years of cultivation, its present height is only 2 feet. Its diameter, difficult to determine through irregularity of outline, may be considered about 60 feet.

This mound was carefully excavated by us in parts free from roots of orange trees. Toward the center, badly decayed, was a full-length skeleton on its back, and a second skull, without mandible, lying near the pelvic part. Near this skull was a carefully-made arrowhead or knife, of chert. Nearby were a crushed skull, and parts of two skeletons which, seemingly, had been mutilated by some modern excavation. No earthenware was found.

Mound near McCool's Landing.

McCool's landing is somewhat north of Lee's landing on the eastern lake shore. The mound, on hammock land, on property of Mr. W. A. McCool, of Beaver Falls, Pa., is about half a mile in an ESE. direction from the landing. It is 15 inches in height and 26 feet in diameter, and is thickly covered with small oaks and scrub-palmetto. Numerous carefully-made excavations yielded nothing.

Mound near St. Elmo Landing.

St. Elmo landing is near the NE. extremity of the lake. The mound, on property of the United Land Co., of Philadelphia, is about one-quarter mile in an easterly direction from the landing. Its height is 3 feet, its diameter 75 feet.

Twelve excavations, each about 3 feet square, yielded three bits of undecorated pottery. Presumably the mound was domiciliary in character.

PEACE CREEK AND CHARLOTTE HARBOR.

Leaving the Kissimmee region, we transferred our crew and the colored diggers to our steamer which lay at Fort Ogden, on Peace creek which empties into Charlotte Harbor (see outline map).

The lower part of Peace creek, previously investigated by our agents, was searched by us without discovering aboriginal mounds worthy of extended investigation.

Charlotte Harbor was examined a second time, a former visit having been made in the season of 1900, without material result. A number of reported mounds turned out to be shell-heaps only.

Mound near Hickory Bluff, De Soto County.

The remains of a mound near Hickory Bluff yielded to us only a few fragments of pottery of inferior grade, bearing crude line and punctate decoration, a selection of which is shown in Figs. 1, 2, 3.

Mound in Gasparilla Sound, De Soto County.

On a key believed to be nameless, the first large key north of Boca Grande Pass, in Gasparilla sound, were the remains of a sand burial mound almost demolished by treasure seekers, according to report. A small remaining part, dug down by us, contained the considerably decayed remains of from fifteen to twenty skeletons, some loosely, some closely, flexed; but these burials yielded only a single skull worthy of preservation (Acad. Nat. Sci. catalogue, No. 2227).

The sole artifacts found with the skeletons were three shell drinking-cups,—one imperforate, two with basal mutilation, with one burial; and two perforate ones with another burial. A number of fragments of inferior, undecorated ware lay where former diggers had left them. Two fragments of considerable size, found by us, have rude decoration, and on one is a loop-shaped handle (Figs. 4, 5). Sand tinged with hematite lay in various parts of the mound.

FIGS. 1, 2, 3.—Sherds. Mound at Hickory Bluff. (Two-thirds size.)

FIG. 4.—Sherd. Mound in Gasparilla Sound. (Half size.)

FIG. 5.—Sherd. Mound in Gasparilla Sound. (Half size.)

THE SOUTHERN FLORIDA COAST.

The remainder of the season of 1904 was devoted to exploration of the coast of southern Florida and adjacent islands. We had explored a part of this region in the season of 1900, when we investigated from a point north of Tampa bay southward to Chatham river (see outline map). A report of this work is given in "Certain Antiquities of the Florida West-Coast," Journ. Acad. Nat. Sci. of Phila., Vol. XI.

This season (1904), beginning at Charlotte Harbor, we continued southward through Pine Island sound, Estero bay and along the Gulf coast to the island of Marco, next to the northernmost key of the Ten Thousand islands. From Key Marco our course lay through the keys, including Chokoloskee Key and Lossman's Key, and along the coast to Cape Sable, the southern boundary of the Ten Thousand islands.

Rounding Cape Sable and visiting points of interest on the mainland and investigating various keys, we continued eastward, then northward, to Miami; to Fort Lauderdale on New river, where the Everglades were visited; and finally, to Lake Worth, which was the southern limit of our work during the season of 1896.

As a result of this part of our journey of the season of 1904, we formed certain conclusions, and fortified others which we had previously expressed in print, namely:

(1) That while the shell deposits of the southwestern coast of Florida are of great interest as monuments of the aborigines, their contents offer little reward to the investigator.[1]

(2) That the sand mounds of the southern Florida coast were built mainly for domiciliary purposes, and that such as contain burials yield but little pottery, whole vessels being practically absent.

(3) That these burial mounds contain but few artifacts of interest[2] and that such artifacts as are met with in the smaller ones, and superficially in the larger ones, are often of European origin, marking a strong contrast with the mounds of the northwestern Florida coast and of St. John's river.

(4) That the failure of the aborigines to place earthenware with the dead, in mounds along the southern Florida coast, did not arise through lack of its possession, but rather that the custom of doing so did not obtain there. Fragments of earthenware, though fewer in number and of far inferior quality on an average than in central and northern Florida, are met with along the southern Florida coast. Similarly, along the whole eastern coast of Florida, entire vessels seem to be absent from the mounds,[3] though inland, in the northern part of the peninsula, at least, whole vessels are fairly abundant.

(5) That while the muck, *i. e.*, mud and organic matter, which fills the canals and small artificial harbors of the Ten Thousand islands, in one instance yielded so rich a reward to Mr. Cushing's labors, it seems likely, as Mr. Cushing believed, that the objects of wood found by him at the town of Marco, Key Marco, were present there through some particular cause. Certain it is that extensive digging in the muck by Mr. Cushing and by ourselves in other localities, yielded nothing of wood, and that ditch-making and the like by the inhabitants of the Ten Thousand islands have brought to light, so far as we can learn, almost nothing of that material. An attempt to duplicate a discovery such as Mr. Cushing's would resemble a search for a needle in a hay-stack.

We shall now describe certain work in detail.

[1] Incidentally it may be said that the great shell deposit on Bullfrog creek, Tampa Bay, described and figured in the Smithsonian Report for 1879, has since been entirely demolished to furnish material for streets of the town of St. Petersburg. It was reported that in the removal of the deposit nothing of interest was found.

[2] It is said that the well-known mound at Miami, when demolished, yielded nothing except human bones.

[3] "Mound Investigation on the East Coast of Florida," by Clarence B. Moore, Phila., 1896. Privately printed.

The late Andrew E. Douglass spent years in investigating the mounds of the eastern coast, from St. Augustine in the north to Miami in the south, without finding an entire vessel.

Mound on Pine Island, Lee County.

Pine Island is a narrow island about fifteen miles long, just south of Charlotte Harbor.

About three miles below the northeastern extremity of Pine Island, just off shore, is a key[1] about three acres in extent, called "Indian Old Field," which is an aboriginal shell deposit with a shell mound upon it.

About three-quarters of a mile in a WNW. direction from the shell key, on Pine Island, was a burial mound of sand, slightly over 5 feet in height and 60 feet across the base. The mound was away from the solid ground, on what is known as a sand-spit, *i. e.*, territory not usually covered by tides, but subject to overflow during unusually high ones,—a curious spot to choose for a place of burial when solid ground was so near.

Near this burial mound is the eastern end of the aboriginal canal that extends across Pine Island, a distance of about two miles, and ends at the huge deposits of shell and mounds of sand, formerly known as the Battey Place,[2] but now called Pineland, on the western shore of the island.

The mound, then on property of the late J. H. Kreamer, Esq., of Philadelphia, was partly investigated by us in the winter of 1900.[3] During this investigation there were found burials at thirty-eight points, loosely-flexed, closely-flexed, and several masses of disconnected bones; also aboriginal disturbances.

With the burials were three "celts" of iron or of steel; glass beads, in three instances; two tubular beads of sheet-silver, with overlapping edges; one kite-shaped pendant of thin sheet-silver, decorated with a cross *repoussé*; a handsome lancehead of hornstone, 4 inches long; a lancehead of chert; two arrowheads of chalcedony; a tooth of a fossil shark, with a perforation. At the beginning of the excavation, at the northeastern side of the mound, were many fragments of pottery belonging to different vessels, placed thickly together; also several shell drinking-cups, and a number of conch-shells (*Fulgur perversum*).

In the winter of 1904 the mound was revisited by us and completely excavated, with the kind permission of Mr. and Mrs. Ferdinand Harrsen, living near-by, who had acquired the property since the former investigation.

This mound, built on lime-rock, was of gray sand except near the base where the sand was black through admixture of organic matter. In this black material, which increased in thickness from a few inches at the margin to about eighteen inches at the center, lay a number of burials, many flexed, some to the left, some to the right. In parts of the base was what seemed to be an inextricable confusion of burials; and the badly decayed condition of the bones and the presence of water, at times, made determination of the form of burial impossible. Nevertheless, it was certain that among the burials were scattered disconnected bones, sometimes singly,

[1] Key, from Spanish *cayo*, "rock," "shoal," "island."

[2] Described by Mr. Frank Hamilton Cushing, "Preliminary Report on the Exploration of Ancient Key Dweller Remains on the Gulf Coast of Florida," Proceedings of the American Philosophical Society, Philadelphia, Vol. XXXV, No. 153, p. 13 *et seq.*

[3] Described in our "Certain Antiquities of the Florida West-Coast," Journ. Acad. Nat. Sci. of Phila., Vol. XI, p. 362 *et seq.*

sometimes in masses. In other parts of the basal area of the mound were single flexed burials, as well as bunched burials with sometimes a single skull and sometimes several crania. There were, also, two closely-flexed skeletons in graves below the base, and among the skeletons at the base, which were somewhat loosely flexed as a rule, were two in a state of close flexion. In the body of the mound, but showing no sign of being intrusive, were two flexed burials and many bunched burials.

As the burials were numerous in this mound, and often encroached one upon another, it was deemed best to score singly such burials as were surely flexed and to keep a tally of the skulls found in bunched burials and where, through commingling of interments, it was impossible to say just what the form of burial had been.

There were, then : four closely-flexed burials and thirty-seven burials loosely flexed ; one skeleton with the lower part cut off by an aboriginal grave. In addition, 177 skulls were found. Thus, during our second investigation, burials representing 219 individuals were unearthed.

The bones, as a rule, showed considerable decay. But three skulls were saved in good condition ; these, preserved at the Academy of Natural Sciences of Philadelphia, are numbered 2228, 2229 and 2230, respectively.

This mound, following the rule among mounds of southern Florida, where earthenware plays but a small part among objects placed with the dead, contained but one whole vessel—a rude, undecorated bowl, about 7 inches in diameter, imperforate as to the base. This bowl, seemingly, was not associated with human remains.

There were also in the mound, scattered here and there, various sherds, as well as parts of vessels each represented by three or four fragments. In all cases, save one, the ware is inferior.

FIG. 6.—Sherd. Mound on Pine Island. (Half size.)

As might be expected in earthenware found so far south in the peninsula, but little decoration is present on the pottery from this mound. Three or four fragments of one vessel show a roughly executed, incised and punctate design (Fig. 6). The ubiquitous small check-stamp was three times encountered.

One fragment of a rim showed a series of notches, and in two cases the loop-handle decoration was met with, probably from a vessel or vessels similar to one shown in Plate CX, "Twentieth Annual Report of the Bureau of American Ethnology."[1]

With the burials along the base of the mound no implement or ornament of European origin was found, but a slab of pine wood from the basal part of the mound, showed a clean cut which could have been made only with an axe of metal.

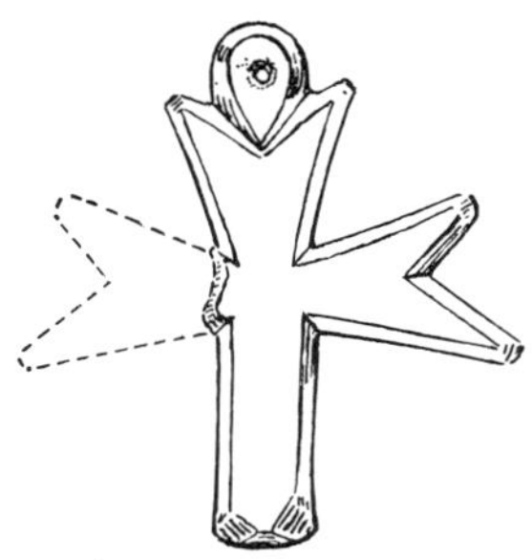

FIG. 7.—Glass cross. Mound on Pine Island. (Full size.)

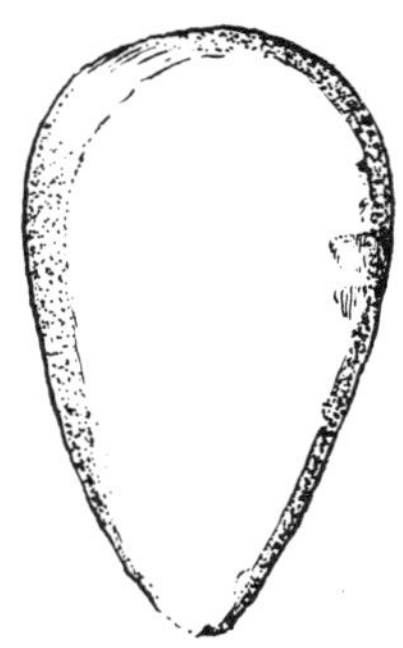

FIG. 8.—Object of earthenware. Mound on Pine Island. (Full size.)

Also on the base were found: a number of hammer-stones, some large; a bit of stone worked to a cutting edge; a thin, triangular fragment of limestone, above a burial, about 1.5 feet in length as to its sides; a small fossil shark's tooth, near a skull; a number of conch-shells (*Fulgur perversum*); drinking-cups made from the same variety of shell; one *Fulgur* with ground beak, and with body-whorl removed, probably used as a chisel. There was also an implement wrought from the heavier variety of *Fulgur perversum*, with part of the body-whorl removed and a hole below the shoulder, opposite the opening, to allow a handle to pass through at right angles, and another hole above this one and above the shoulder to facilitate the lashing of the handle. That part of the shoulder of the shell which is between these holes is greatly worn by the material used for attachment. The beak is much ground and splintered by use. A description of many shells used as implements by aborigines of southern Florida is given in our "Antiquities of the Florida West-Coast."[2]

Also at the base of the mound were found: a large clam-shell; a shell identified by Dr. H. A. Pilsbry as *Collista nimbosa*, lying beneath the shoulder of a skeleton; and a number of conchs, wrought to a certain extent but not sufficiently to show what their use had been. These conchs, all of which belong to the more delicate variety, may have been drinking-cups partly completed.

With or near burials in the body of the mound were a single glass bead, a considerable number of small glass beads, one large hammer-stone, and one sandstone hone.

There were also, variously distributed with burials, five axes of the type obtained by aborigines from early white traders; three pairs of scissors; two broad chisels; three knives; one pruning knife; one chisel or caulking-knife; one implement 28 inches long, square in cross section, about .75 of an inch in diameter, pointed at one end. This implement, of iron or of steel (as were all the foregoing), presumably intended for a drill, may have seen service as a spear, when hafted.

[1] "Aboriginal Pottery of Eastern United States," by W. H. Holmes.
[2] Journal of the Academy of Natural Sciences of Philadelphia, Vol. XI.

Three beads of sheet-silver, with overlapping edges, somewhat less than 2 inches, 1.25 inch, and 1 inch, in length, respectively, came from various parts of the mound, with or near burials, as did part of a glass cross (Fig. 7); a fragment of an earthenware vessel, about 1.5 inches in length, verging on ovoid in outline (Fig. 8), and a rude though interesting pendant of glass, showing aboriginal work on European material (Fig. 9).

With a burial was a concavo-convex pendant of thin sheet-silver, about 5 inches long, with two holes at one end for suspension (Fig. 10).

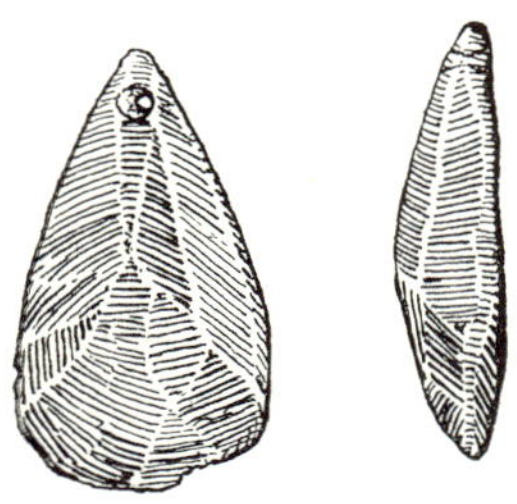

Fig. 9.—Pendant of glass. Mound on Pine Island. (Full size.)

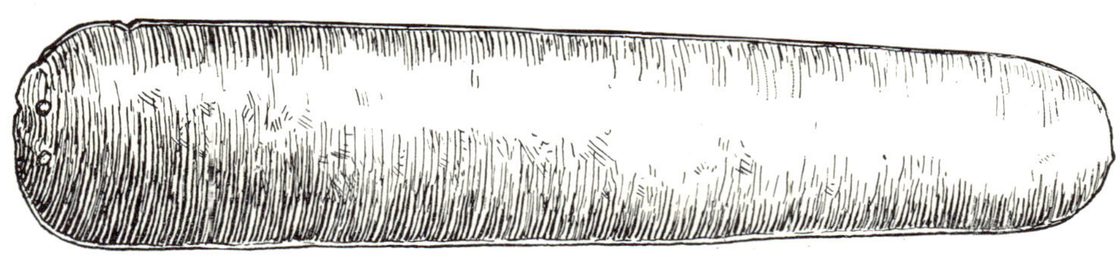

Fig. 10.—Ornament of sheet-silver. Mound on Pine Island. (Full size.)

We have here a good example of a mound distinctly post-Columbian, containing many objects as to the European provenance of which no doubt can be entertained.

Mound near Punta Rassa, Lee County.

About two miles in a northerly direction from Punta Rassa, in the heart of a mangrove swamp, a mound was reached by rowing up Shell creek a short distance, and then going into the swamp about 300 yards, from the northern side of the creek. The aid of a guide is necessary. The mound, which was kindly placed at

Figs. 11, 12, 13.—Sherds. Mound near Punta Rassa. (About full size.)

our disposal by the owner, Mr. George R. Shultz, of Punta Rassa, is of pure, white sand. The outline of the base is circular, save at one place, where a sort of flat projection extends into the swamp. The mound is 14 feet 6 inches in height. If present conditions existed when the mound was built, the sand used in its making must have been carried some distance, perhaps from the creek, as the black muck of the swamp surrounds the mound on every side.

The basal diameter of the mound is hard to determine. Either much sand has washed from the mound, forming a deposit at its base, or a sort of platform was built to serve as a base. The diameter, excluding this deposit or platform, is about 90 feet.

A great hole had been dug into the center previous to our visit.

Throughout the surrounding swamp are shell fields and numerous causeways of shell, extending in all directions. A narrow causeway, with steep sides, about 90 yards long, leaving the northwestern part of the mound, connects it with a large shell field. Another causeway extends from the same part of the mound at a different angle toward the same shell deposit, which, however, it fails to join. A third causeway leads from the mound toward Shell creek, but does not meet it.

A considerable amount of digging by us yielded 7 flexed burials, from 1 foot to 5 feet in depth. No artifacts lay with them, though previous diggers report the finding of many glass beads, and one such bead was met with by us in sand previously thrown out.

A small number of sherds were found, two or three of which are of excellent ware. Several are decorated with the small check-stamp, and others have incised and punctate decoration of inferior execution (Figs. 11, 12, 13, 14).

FIG. 14.—Sherd. Mound near Punta Rassa. (Half size.)

MOUND ISLAND, ESTERO BAY, LEE COUNTY.

This interesting key known as Mound Island, described in a former report,[1] was again visited by us. We learned from Mrs. F. M. Johnson that nothing of importance had been recovered since our previous visit, either from the shell deposits or from the famous sand mound which has yielded so many objects of European manufacture. Mrs. Johnson kindly had saved for us two bird-head decorations which had belonged to earthenware vessels, somewhat similar, though inferior, to those described in our former report as coming from Goodland Point, Key Marco, which also are referred to by Professor Holmes.[2]

MARCO, KEY MARCO, LEE COUNTY.

The Island of Marco (see outline map), otherwise known as Key Marco, is, as we have said, next to the northernmost key of the Ten Thousand islands, a group of keys bordering the southwestern Florida coast for a distance of about 70 miles in a straight line.

[1] "Certain Antiquities of the Florida West-Coast."

[2] "Aboriginal Pottery of Eastern United States," W. H. Holmes, 20th Annual Report of the Bureau of American Ethnology, p. 128.

The town of Marco, at the northern end of the island, is, as previously mentioned, where Mr. Cushing made his great collection of aboriginal objects, mainly of wood. These objects, as the reader is aware, lay in muck which forms the bottom of a small artificial basin in the shell deposit, formerly connected by a short canal with the neighboring water.

It is needless here to dwell on Mr. Cushing's archæological discoveries at Marco, the most important that have been made in Florida, as his preliminary report,[1] which his untimely end rendered final, gives a sufficiently clear description.

There is one point, however, which archæologists would gladly know: How did this great assemblage of objects come to be in this particular spot? Artificial harbors, basins and canals abound among such keys of the Ten Thousand islands as were selected by the pile-dwellers as places of residence, yet, as we have said, no collection of objects has been met with elsewhere in the muck, though considerable digging has been done by explorers and by modern inhabitants of the keys.

Objects of wood dropped or thrown ceremonially, into water, would float; and it is hardly likely that, at periods of low water, objects were buried ceremonially in the muck. It was Mr. Cushing's belief, personally expressed to us, that the objects found by him, contained in houses or in a temple on the banks of the court, or basin, had been forced down by some cataclysm of nature and subsequently held in the muck. This would seem to be a reasonable explanation, and especially so as Mr. W. D. Collier, of Marco, through whose kind permission the basin was examined, informs us that in the year 1873 a

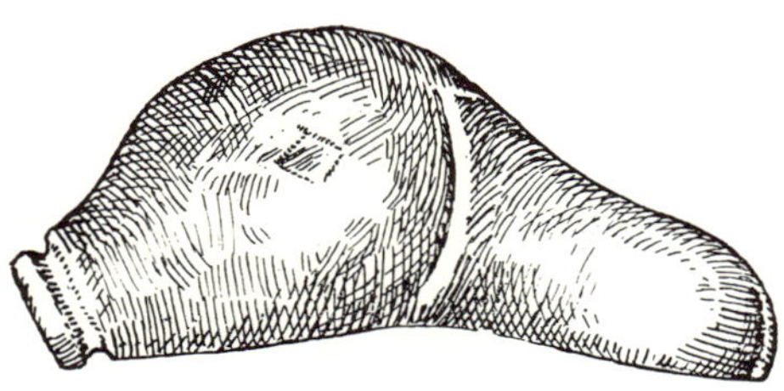

Fig. 15.—Pendant of lime-rock. Marco. (Full size.)

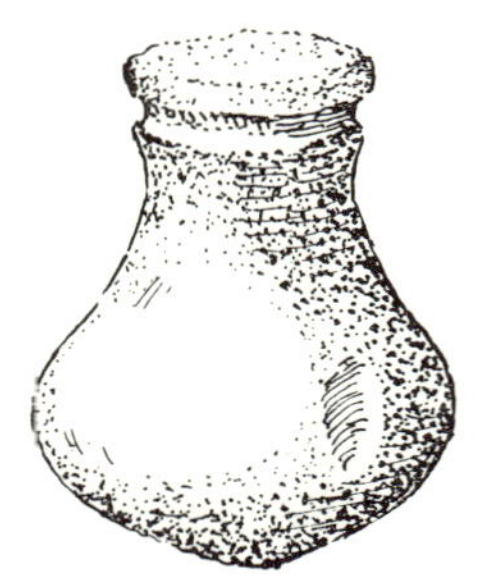

Fig. 16.—Pendant of lime-rock. Marco. (Full size.)

Fig. 17.—Pendant of lime-rock. Marco. (Full size.)

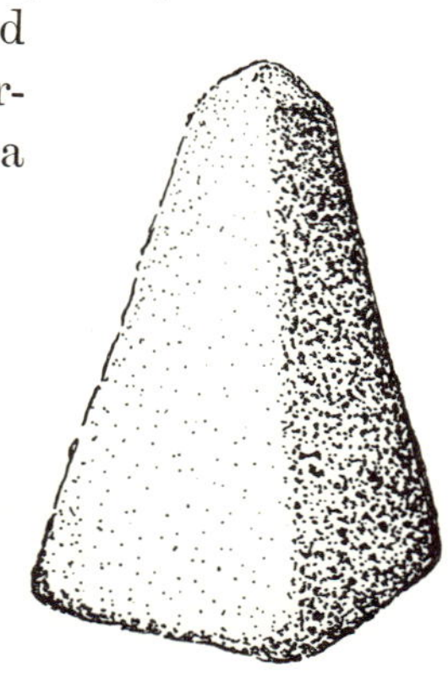

Fig. 18.—Object of clay. Marco. (Full size.)

tidal wave, brought on by a hurricane, did much damage at Marco and submerged the muck-pond in which the objects were found by Mr. Cushing.

On the other hand, it might be asked, if buildings were thus destroyed, why, in view of the preservative qualities of the muck, the debris was not preserved with the objects which were present. On the whole, the question is an interesting one.

A careful search of the surface of the shell fields of Marco resulted in the discovery of a number of tools wrought from entire shells, some of which differ somewhat from those described and figured in our former report on this region. Varieties, hitherto undescribed, from Marco; from Goodland Point, Key Marco; from Chokoloskee Key and from other localities, will be given at the close of this report.

[1] *Op. cit.*

We obtained from Mr. Collier a collection of several hundred pendants or "charm-stones," of shell, of coral, and of the coarse lime-rock found upon the keys. Most of these were of ordinary type, similar to a number figured by us in our preceding report.

Fig. 19.—Pendant of shell. Nameless Key near Key Marco. (About full size.)

Fig. 20.—Implement of bone. Nameless Key near Key Marco. (About full size.)

One pendant from this lot of surface-finds from Marco, of rather compact, yellow lime-rock, representing the head of a duck, is shown in Fig. 15. Two pendants, one of yellow, one of white, lime-rock, also from Marco, are shown in Figs. 16, 17. A pyramidal object of tenacious clay containing quartz grains and fragments of shell, molded and dried, from the same collection, is given in Fig. 18.

From a nameless shell key, near Marco, a large number of objects, similar in the main to those from Marco, were obtained from Mr. Addison, who lives on the key. One of these specimens is a pendant of shell, which in addition to the groove at one end for suspension, has another groove around the body, the use of which is uncertain (Fig. 19). An implement of bone, from the surface, with four perforations, is shown in Fig. 20.

A number of implements wrought from entire shells were found by us on the surface of this key.

GOODLAND POINT, KEY MARCO.

From Goodland point, five miles below the town of Marco, where many objects of interest were procured on our previous visit, we obtained a limited number of pendants, sinkers, etc., of stone, of shell, of coral, and one (Fig. 21) made from a fragment of an earthenware vessel. Many implements wrought from entire shells, were gathered by us from the surface at this point.

WIGGINS KEY, LEE COUNTY.

The only object of interest obtained by us on Wiggins key is a pendant of shell, having a perforation in addition to the groove at one end (Fig. 22).

Fig. 21.—Pendant of earthenware. Goodland Point. (About full size.)

Fig. 22.—Pendant of shell. Wiggins Key. (About full size.)

CHOKOLOSKEE KEY, LEE COUNTY.

The interesting Chokoloskee key, described in our previous report, has been determined, by a recent survey, to be in Lee county, and not in Monroe county, as was formerly believed to be the case.

A search, extending over a number of days, yielded many fine implements wrought from entire shells; also a number of pendants, etc., were obtained from persons inhabiting the key. Among these was a carefully wrought pendant of lime-rock (Fig. 23), presented to us by Doctor Green, postmaster of Chokoloskee, and two pendants of shell, one heart-shaped (Fig. 24), the other showing a method of suspension entirely novel in our experience of objects of shell (Fig. 25) and unusual in pendants of stone, consisting of a perforation, beginning near the end at one side, and coming out at the top. Another fine pendant of shell from this place is shown in Fig. 26.

FIG. 23.—Pendant of lime-rock. Chokoloskee Key. (About full size.)

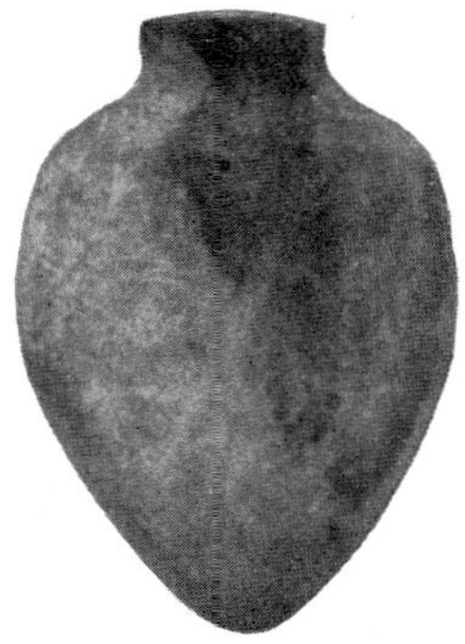

FIG. 24.—Pendant of shell. Chokoloskee Key. (About full size.)

FIG. 25.—Pendant of shell. Chokoloskee Key. (Full size.)

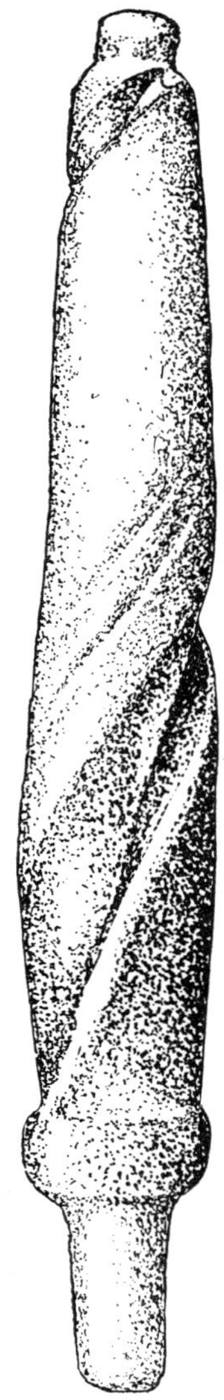

FIG. 26.—Pendant of shell. Chokoloskee Key. (Full size.)

A novel object from this key is an oyster-shell having a central perforation and, in addition, a groove at one end, as shown in Fig. 27. Presumably a handle, passing through the hole, was lashed to the shell at the groove to form a tool. A part of the shell, broken from the edge back, lends support to this supposition.

At our former visit to Chokoloskee key we made the acquaintance of Mr. C. G. McKinney, then living there. Mr. McKinney had for a long period paid close attention to aboriginal objects found upon the key. We were informed by him that, of the very many objects known as "sinkers" found on the key, none had been met with near the water, and that he was firmly convinced that these so-called "sinkers" had a use other than one pertaining to the taking of fish.

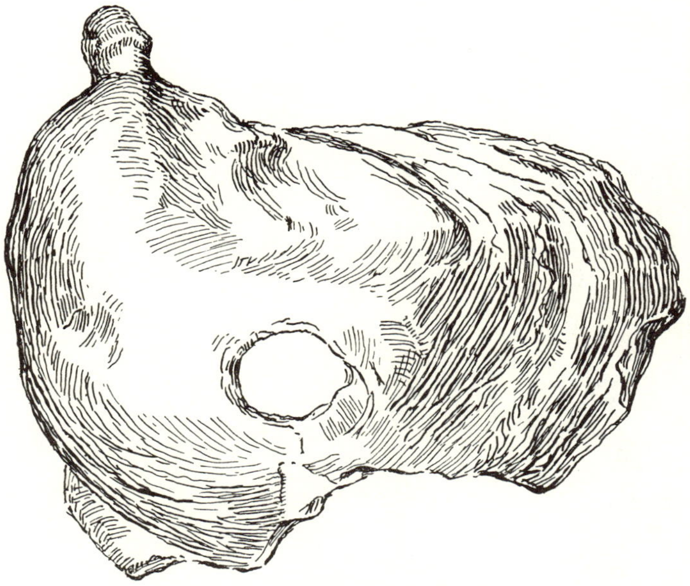

FIG. 27.—Implement of shell. Chokoloskee Key. (Full size.)

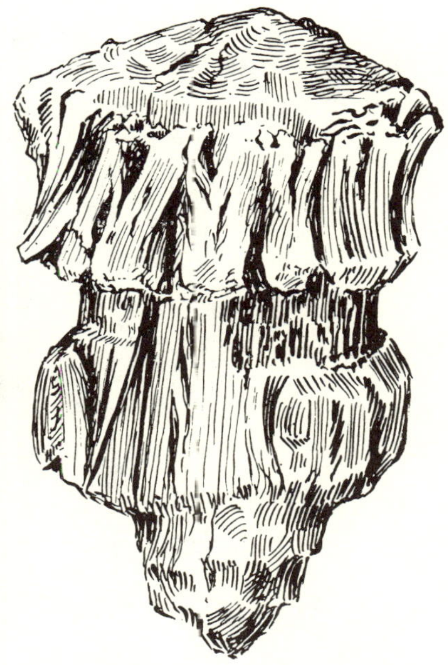

FIG. 28.—Object of black mangrove wood. Chokoloskee Key. (Half size.)

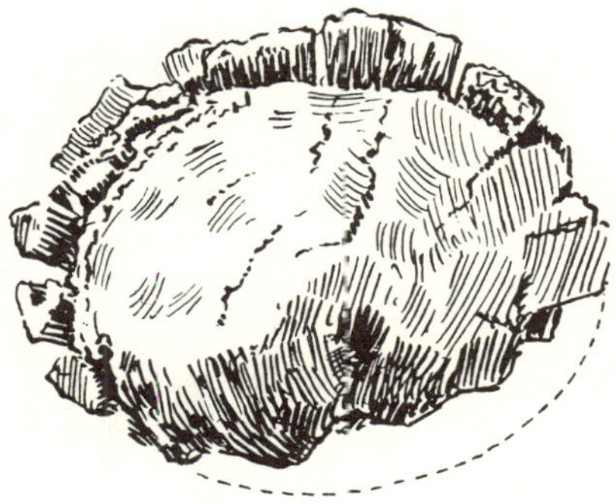

FIG. 29.—The same, end view.

FIG. 30.—Cup of wood. Chokoloskee Key. (Full size.)

In one part of the key is an interesting artificial harbor, which, no doubt, served as a shelter for canoes in aboriginal times. This harbor, protected from open water by an embankment of shell, save at a narrow entrance, was on property owned by Mr. McKinney, who, controlling the water by the insertion of a sluice, dug many trenches in the muck with the idea to pile this material above water level, and thus to gain a rich area for cultivation.

In the course of this work, Mr. McKinney, whose archæological interest was ever alert, came upon three objects of wood, which are now in possession of the Academy.

One of these, of black mangrove, shown in Figs. 28, 29, was burnt somewhat on one side by a person to whom it was entrusted by Mr. McKinney. This object, which was about 2 feet down in the muck, became cracked superficially in drying, in a way that might seem to represent carving in the figure. It has a central groove surrounding it and shows work of a blunt tool over both terminal surfaces. In shape the object resembles the head of a mace, for which the heavy mangrove wood would be especially fitted; but in the case of a mace there would be no cause to remove the handle. Possibly the object was used as a sort of hammer, with one end blunt, the other pointed, and was fastened at a right angle to a handle by means of the central groove.

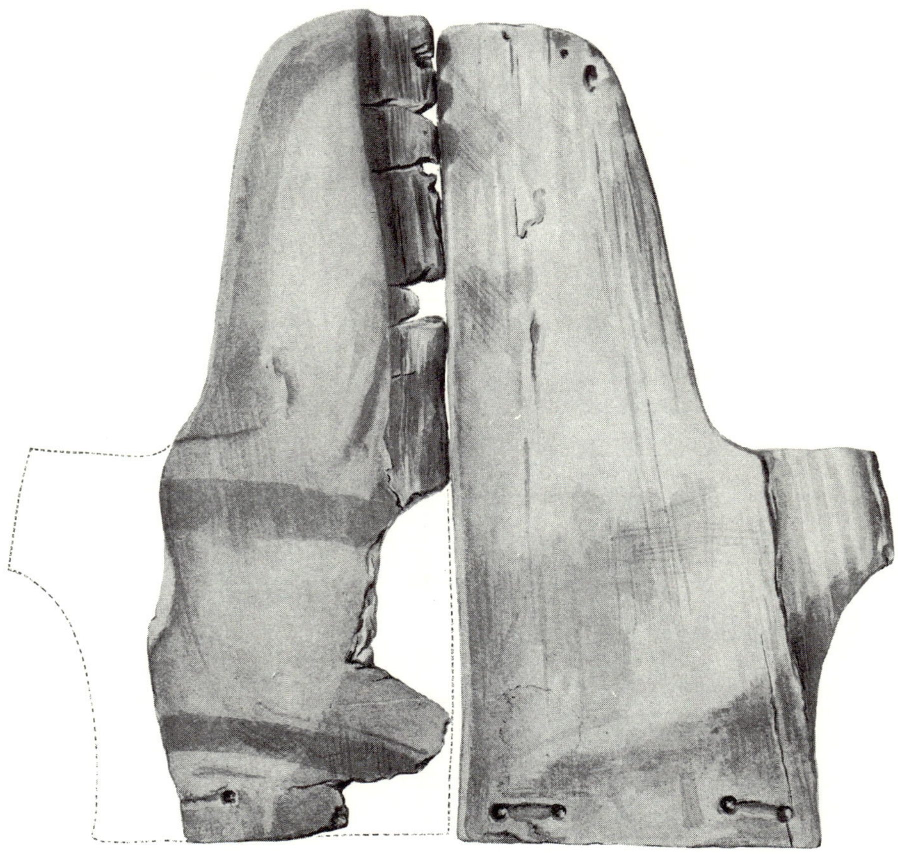

FIG. 31.—Object of wood. Chokoloskee Key. (Half size.)

A cup of a soft wood was found in the muck by Mr. McKinney (Fig. 30).

Another object, in two parts, also of a soft wood, is shown photographed from a sketch in Fig. 31. There has been a rude decoration in black pigment, still discernible in places. Holes for attachment are at the base. The purpose for which this object was made is problematical.

LOSSMAN'S KEY, MONROE COUNTY.

After investigating a number of keys which yielded nothing of interest from an archæological point of view, Lossman's key, one of the largest, if not the largest key of the Ten Thousand islands, was visited. At the northern extremity are large, level causeways and platforms, of shell, a thorough survey of which would be of interest.

South of Cape Sable and eastward among the keys and northward to Lake Worth, where our journey ended, we met with nothing of especial archæological interest. After leaving the Ten Thousand islands, no shell keys were met with by us during an extended search, all islands being of sand or of lime-rock.

IMPLEMENTS WROUGHT FROM ENTIRE SHELLS.

We shall now describe in detail certain implements of shell found by us during the expedition of 1904, which differ somewhat from implements of the same type described in our report on "Certain Antiquities of the Florida West-Coast."

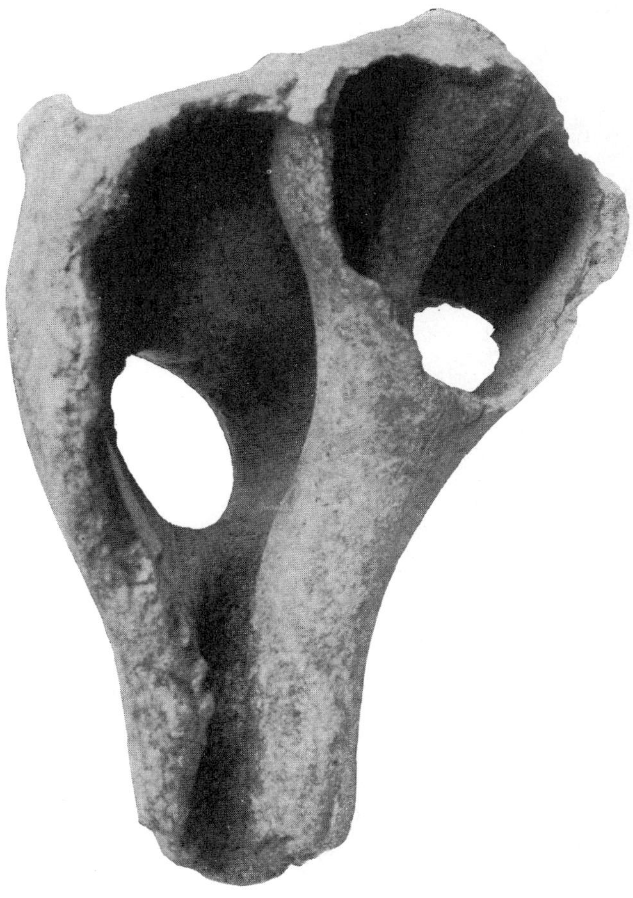

FIG. 32.—Shell implement. Russell's Key. (About full size.)

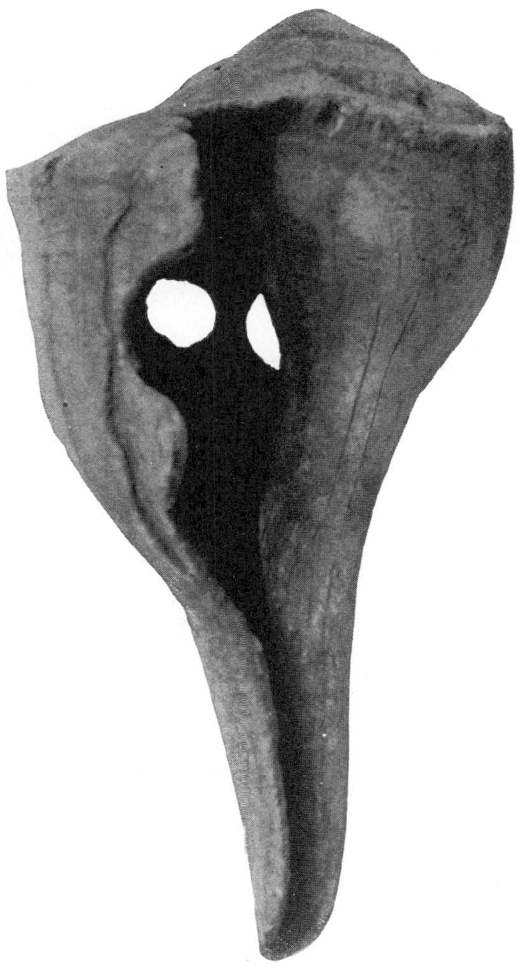

FIG. 33.—Shell implement. Marco. (About full size.)

Fig. 32 represents a fractional part of a massive *Fulgur perversum*, of a type similar to that shown in Fig. 37 of our previous report, where a hole to the right, and a notch to the left, of the axis, enabled a handle to pass behind it. In this case, however, an additional perforation, much worn, behind the axis, is present, and probably corresponded with a hole since broken away through use. When this happened, presumably, the use of the hole back of the axis was abandoned, and a new hole to the right and a notch to the left were added. This implement, which was found on Russell's key, Ten Thousand islands, probably served as a hoe.

FIG. 34.—Shell implement. Cutler. (About full size.)

In Fig. 33 is given a *Fulgur perversum* from Marco, showing the usual removal of part of the body-whorl back from the edge of the aperture. There is a small hole above the shoulder, or periphery, which seems, as a rule, to have had no connection with the tool, inasmuch as numbers of shells, not made into implements, show a similar perforation, which may have been made to sever the muscle and free the shell-fish from its shell. The feature of this particular implement is two small, circular holes, side by side, in the back of the shell, facing the notch in front. Possibly as one hole may not have given the desired angle for the handle, another hole was added.

Fig. 34 illustrates a *Fulgur perversum* from Cutler, on the mainland of the eastern coast, Dade county. It shows the usual removal of part of the body-whorl at the edge of the aperture, but no perforation above the shoulder. There are three perforations almost in line in the body-whorl, and a notch at the edge of the aperture. It would seem that the central hole which faces the notch, having become broken, was abandoned with its corresponding notch, and that two new holes were made for attaching the handle.

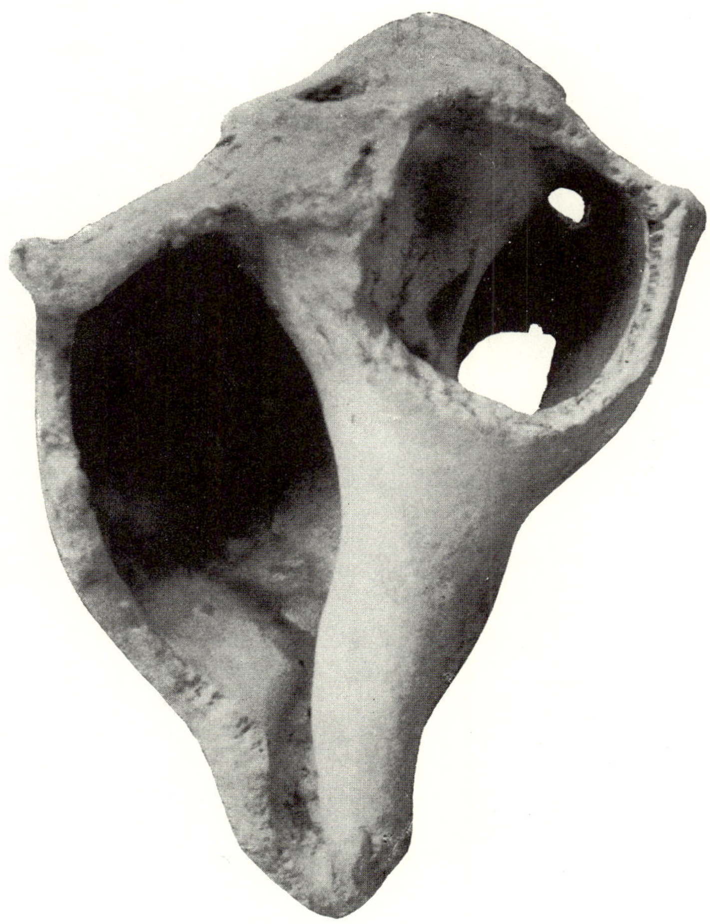

FIG. 35.—Shell implement. Battey Place. (About full size.)

The implement shown in Fig. 35, wrought from a comparatively small but heavy shell of the same species as the last, is of an ordinary type of which, in addition to the removal of part of the body-whorl, at the edge of the aperture, another part is cut away within, laying bare part of the axis. A single perforation in the body-whorl faces the notch. The peculiarity of this implement is the presence of two small perforations above the shoulder, in line, one on each side. These perforations are smaller and more regularly made than the single ones of which we have spoken as made, possibly, to free the shell-fish from the shell. Moreover, there are two holes instead of one. One, above the main hole in the body-whorl, could have aided in attaching the handle, but the other hole is shut off from the handle by the convolution of the shell. This implement is from the Battey place, Pine island, Lee county.

FIG. 36.—Shell implement. Chokoloskee Key. (About full size.)

We come next to a *Fulgur perversum* from Chokoloskee key, shown in Fig. 36, which has the usual removal of part of the body-whorl. There is but one perforation, which is to the right of the aperture. This hole, which shows no wear, cannot have been used for the insertion of a handle, as there is no corresponding hole on the opposite side, and no notch. Moreover, the hole is not in line with the required position for a notch. The cutting edge of the beak, however, shows considerable wear. Presumably, this implement was held directly in the hand.

The implement shown in Fig. 37, a heavy *Fulgur perversum*, with part of the body-whorl removed, and a small, irregular hole above the shoulder has four perforations in line in the remaining part of the body-whorl, extending from the aper-

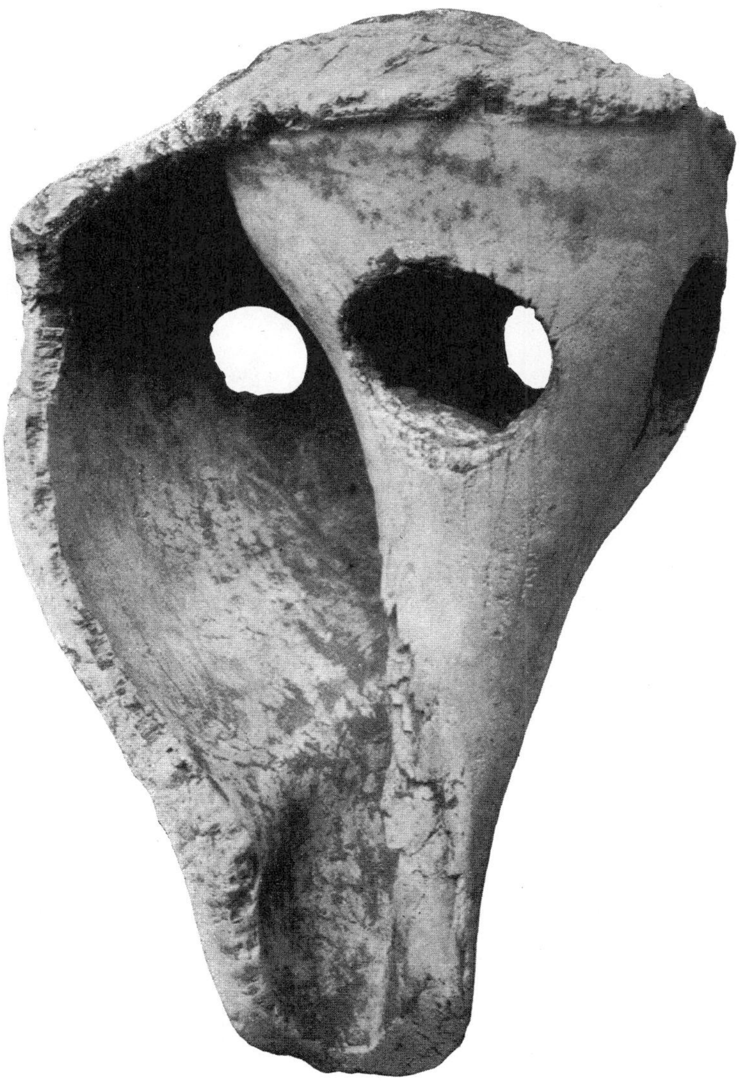

FIG. 37.—Shell implement. Chokoloskee Key. (About full size.)

ture around from left to right. The first and third holes are in line for a handle, as are the second and fourth. The third hole corresponds also with a notch in the edge of the aperture. This implement, which has a fine edge, probably served as a gouge. Like the preceding example, it came from Chokoloskee key.

In the collection is an implement from Goodland Point, Key Marco, in every way similar to the foregoing save that the notch is absent. It lay on the surface, as was the case with all the implements described in this collection.

A badly battered *Fulgur perversum*, which probably served as a hoe, came from Chokoloskee key (Fig. 38). The body-whorl has been cut away a number of inches back. The rude hole above the shoulder is present. There are three holes in line somewhat below the shoulder, and a notch. The first and third holes, counting from left to right, allowed a handle to pass to the right of, and behind, the axis, but as parts of the shell gave way at the third hole, this hole

FIG. 38.—Shell implement. Chokoloskee Key. (About full size.)

Fig. 39.—Shell implement. Chokoloskee Key. (About full size.)

FIG. 40.—Shell implement. Chokoloskee Key. (About full size.)

became useless, and, consequently, the corresponding hole became unserviceable. The tool was then utilized by making hole number two and a corresponding notch.

There is represented in Fig. 39 a *Fulgur perversum* with cleanly-ground edge at the beak, having the customary rough perforation above the shoulder, or periphery. The body-whorl is in part removed. There are two evenly-made perforations to allow a handle to pass to the right of, and behind, the columella, but there is also a notch which does not correspond with either hole. This implement came from Chokoloskee key.

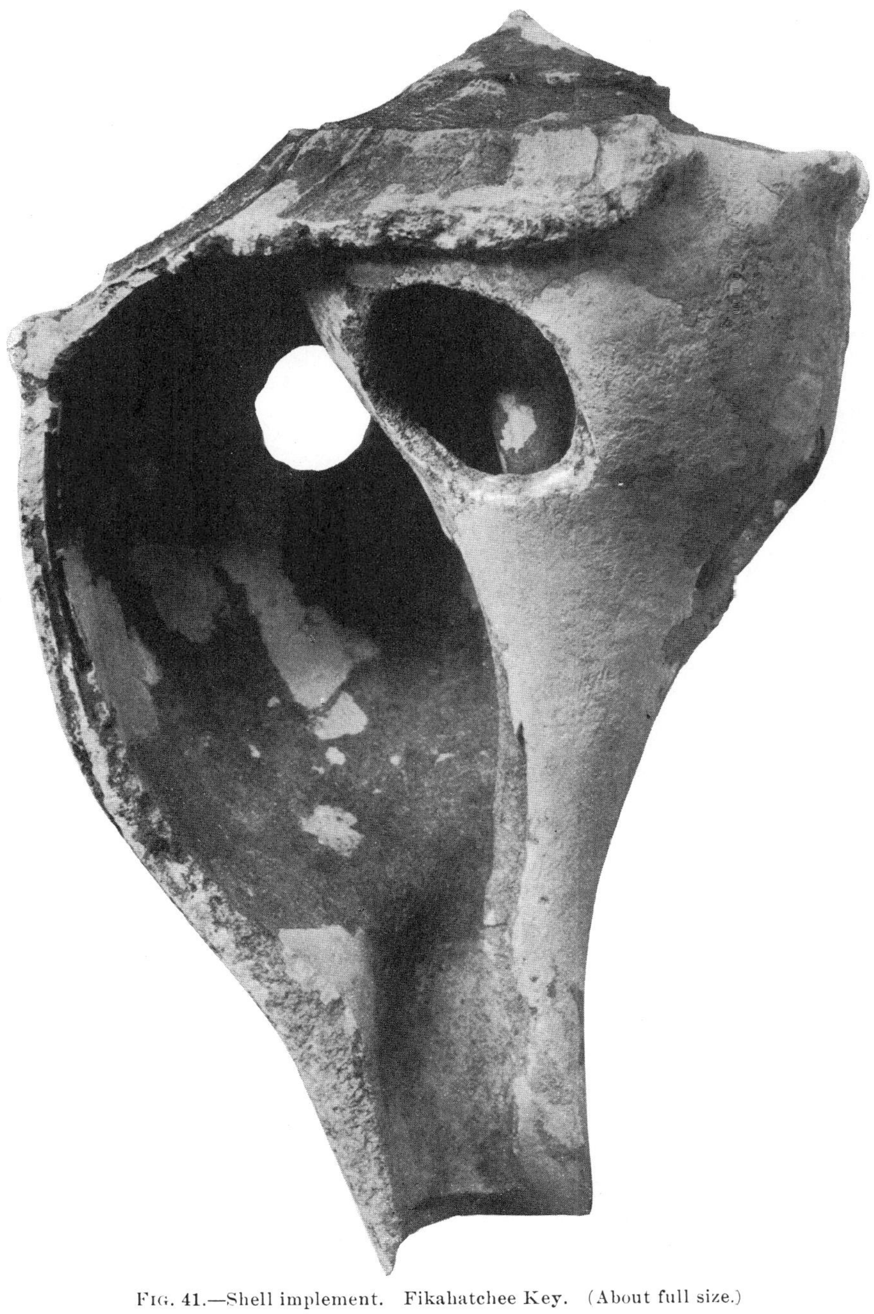

FIG. 41.—Shell implement. Fikahatchee Key. (About full size.)

Fig. 42.—Shell implement. Goodland Point.
(About full size.)

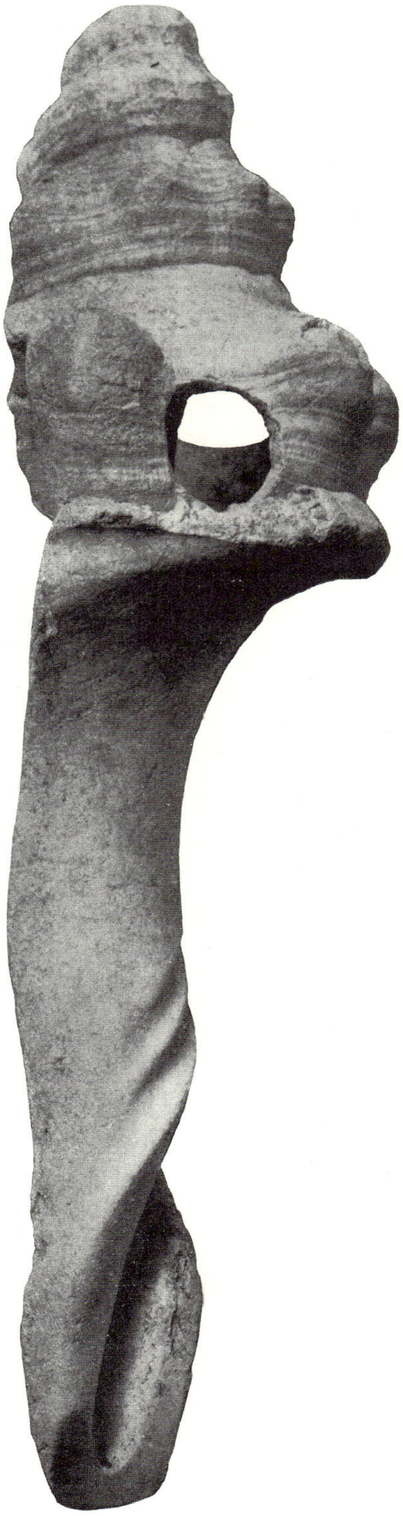

Fig. 43.—Shell implement. Goodland Point.
(About full size.)

Fig. 40 shows a *Fulgur perversum*, from the same key, with the hole above the shoulder and the body-whorl removed in part from the edge, backward. Also, as is often seen in these tools of shell, a part of the body-whorl has been cut away, exposing the upper third of the columella. There are three perforations, almost in line, somewhat below the shoulder. Numbers one and three from left to right would allow a handle to pass behind and to the right of the columella; hole number two probably corresponded with a notch on the edge which has been broken away.

Fig. 41 illustrates a *Fulgur perversum* from Fikahatchee (sometimes spelled Fakahatchee) key,[1] Ten Thousand islands. The perforation above the shoulder is present; the body-whorl has been removed several inches from the edge, backward. The beak is ground to give an excellent cutting edge for a gouge. There are two holes through which a handle could pass to the right of the axis and behind it; and there is a circular hole in the body-whorl to the right of the aperture, the use of which is not plain. This latter hole corresponds with neither of the other two holes and is entirely out of line for a notch, which, moreover, is not present. It is possible that this implement belongs to the type, where part of the body-whorl, above, has been removed, perhaps to facilitate attachment of the handle; but if so, the hole is much more evenly-made and rounder than is usually the case in openings of this kind.

Fig. 42 shows a type of implement found in abundance among the Ten Thousand islands, consisting of *Fasciolaria*, with much of the body-whorl removed and two perforations behind, to allow a handle to pass at an upward angle, behind the columella. A round hole is present in the body-whorl in front, evidently to aid in attachment. This specimen, which was used as a hammer, came from Goodland Point, Key Marco.

Fig. 43 represents an implement from Goodland Point, which, though shown in a different position, is similar to the one last described, save that it has a beautifully-ground, cutting edge for use as a chisel. This specimen is the sole example of this type that we have met during our two expeditions through the Ten Thousands islands.

Incidentally, it may be said that, as can be seen by referring to our "Certain Antiquities of the Florida West-Coast," page 393, the *Fulgur carica*, or *Fulgur* with the aperture to the right, is not found on the western coast of Florida, and hence the aborigines of that region were restricted to *Fulgur perversum* and *Fasciolaria* for use as implements.

On the eastern coast of Florida *Fasciolaria gigantea* is infrequently met with, and *Fulgur perversum* is far less massive than is that shell on the western coast of Florida. Therefore, on the eastern coast the aborigines were almost restricted to *Fulgur carica* in the manufacture of implements destined for heavy work.

All over Florida, however, *Fulgur perversum* was used for drinking cups, and "celts" made from the lip of the massive *Strombus gigas* are found.

[1] *Op. cit.*, p. 377.

Crystal River Revisited

BY

CLARENCE B. MOORE

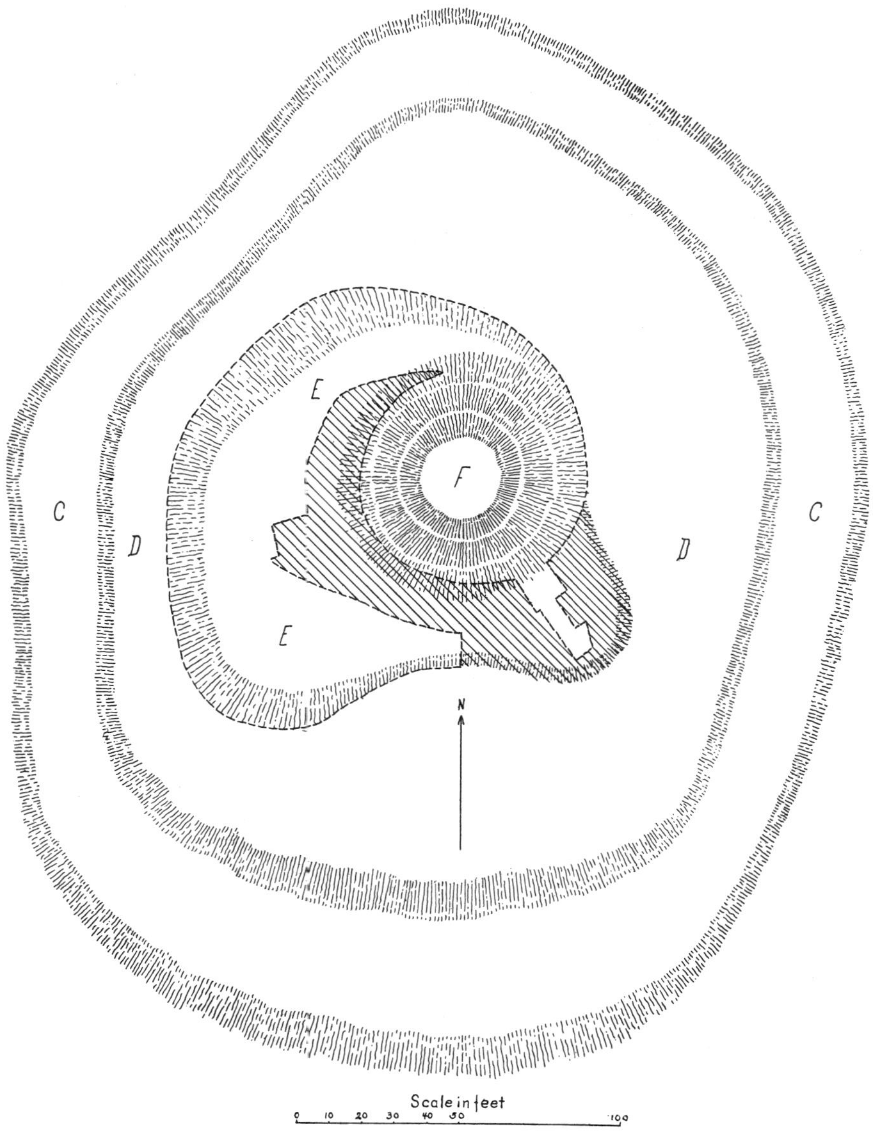

Place of burial, Crystal River. Portion dug at first visit, enclosed in broken line; at second visit, shown by diagonal lines.

CRYSTAL RIVER REVISITED.

By Clarence B. Moore.

Crystal River, on the western coast of Florida, about twenty-five miles south of Cedar Keys, was visited by us in the season of 1903. Considerable work with interesting results was done there near the well-known, rectangular shell-mound about three miles from the river's mouth. Full account of this work is given in our "Certain Aboriginal Mounds of the Central Florida West Coast."[1]

By consulting the accompanying plan it will be noted that the scene of our investigation was an enclosure surrounded by an embankment, and that the enclosure consisted of first a level space, then much ground sloping upward and, finally, a well-defined mound rising above this slope.

At our first visit, though we dug away the entire mound and a large portion of the sloping ground, we left a part of the latter uninvestigated. Therefore we revisited the place of burial near Crystal River in the winter of 1906, with the kind consent of Mr. R. J. Knight, of the town of Crystal River, the owner of the property, to whom we were indebted for permission to investigate before.

The plan given herewith shows the embankment (C C); the level ground inside the embankment (D D); the slope (E E); and the mound proper (F). The area excavated by us at our first visit, with the exception of small portions around a few trees, is shown enclosed in broken line, while the part dug through at the time of our second visit appears in diagonal lines.

This second investigation, as the plan shows, included all the sloping ground that remained, consequently the entire slope and the mound proper have been dug down by us. The maximum diameters of the area investigated are 150 feet northeast to southwest and the same distance from northwest to southeast.

The digging was begun on the margin of the slope and was carried in at a depth considerably below the surface of the surrounding level ground. The height of the mound proper above the general level was 10 feet 8 inches, and above the elevated ground which surrounded it, it was from 5 feet 8 inches to 6 feet 8 inches.

Burials, almost invariably consisting of skeletons, were found by us at our second visit to lie as a rule under deposits of shell as we found them before. These deposits of shell did not extend to the surface, but lay under the superficial sand; and the deposits were not over single burials as a rule, but were layers covering a number of burials. In the southern and southeastern part of the elevated ground a layer of shell was almost continuous, and skeletons lay here and there beneath it. A few skeletons were found in sand apart from shell, but these were met with at the border of the mound proper, and probably belonged to the mound. When digging down this mound at our first visit we found that its con-

[1] Journ. Acad. Nat. Sci. of Phila., Vol. XII.

struction differed from the sloping ground around it in that deposits of shell were much less numerous in the mound, and consequently many burials were in clear sand apart from shell.

Bunched burials, only a few of which were found at our second visit, invariably lay in sand, and were always at a less depth than the shell deposits beneath which other forms of burial lay. However, these bunched burials were found where the mound joined the sloping ground and probably were left over from the great number of bunched burials which we found in the mound proper at the time of our first visit.

There were also in the sand and in the shell layers numbers of scattered and broken human bones. It was impossible for us to classify these as to form of burial and no account of them is taken in our enumeration.

During the second visit 186 burials were met with, as follows:

Full length on back, of which 27 were children,	115
Full length, face down,	1
Closely flexed on the right side,	9
Closely flexed on the left side,	8
Partly flexed on the right side, including 4 children,	18
Partly flexed on the left side, 2 being children,	17
Partly flexed on the back, knees up,	2
In caved sand,	5
Details omitted from field-notes, a child,	1
Infant skeleton badly decayed,	1
Bunched burial with one skull,	1
Bunched burials with two skulls,	2
Bunched burials with three skulls,	2
Bunched burial with seven skulls,	1

The three remaining burials, somewhat differing from the general types, will be particularly described:

(1) Adult, trunk on back, thighs turned upward and outward at an obtuse angle, legs flexed back at an acute angle, feet crossed.

(2) Adult, full length on back, legs crossed at knees.

(3) In a pit below the base, badly decayed skeletons of two infants, together.

Throughout the second investigation but two skulls[1] in a preservable condition were found. No skulls or parts of skulls showed evidence of cranial compression.

With a number of burials was sand tinted by admixture of red hematite, and a few burials lay with sand made yellow by the addition of powdered limonite.

The artifacts found during our second investigation are practically of the same character as those found by us before, though the experience of our former visit was emphasized, namely, that objects of superior quality had been placed in the mound proper and not in the elevated area which surrounded it. On this, the second visit, when our work was of necessity confined to the sloping ground, but

[1] The Academy of Natural Sciences catalogue numbers 2231, 2232.

one earthenware vessel of superior ware and decoration was found, and this came from where the slope joined the mound proper and really belonged to the mound. Objects of crystal and of amethystine quartz, unbroken pipes, and copper (if we exclude a single object found in sand thrown out from the mound in our former visit) were not encountered on this occasion, though the yield of such objects was abundant at the time of our first investigation.

Artifacts, as before, were found with some burials and also scattered in sand and in the layers of shell. Possibly the scattered objects had belonged to burials represented by the disordered bones of which we have spoken; indeed it is likely that some of them did. We are inclined to believe that in some cases, also, artifacts

FIG. 1.—Sherds. Crystal River.

were placed in the shell layers collectively for the dead in common. At all events, on one occasion at least, a deposit of sand colored with hematite occurred in a layer of shell in connection with artifacts, and this deposit of colored sand was compact as if intentionally placed in the shells and not scattered as seemingly it must have been had it been an accidental accompaniment of disarranged bones.

Fragments of earthenware found during our second visit were inferior or were of medium excellence in the main, giving little evidence of what we know the aborigines of Crystal River could accomplish in the potter's art. The small check-stamp is represented, as is the complicated stamp to a limited extent. A selection of sherds, recovered during our second visit is shown in Figs. 1, 2.

One fragment of earthenware is of much interest. At our former visit we were fortunate enough to find in the mound proper a part of what had been a large,

FIG. 2.—Sherds. Crystal River.

cylindrical vessel of excellent ware. This fragment, which bears an incised and boldly executed design representing an open hand, and small parts of other interesting symbols, is shown in Fig. 18 of our former report, in which we set forth how we searched without avail for other parts of this vessel.

We were fortunate enough to find, this time, in sand tossed out on our former visit, another fragment which undoubtedly belonged to the same remarkable vessel. The ware is the same; the curvature is identical; and the decoration, in our opinion, is from the same bold hand that executed the design on the fragment first found by us. Unfortunately the two fragments do not join, though both belong to the upper part of the vessel and include parts of the rim. We have, altogether, less than half the circumference of the upper six inches of a vessel originally about five inches in diameter. The original height of the vessel cannot be determined, though judging from parts of the decoration which are missing, the height must have been considerably in excess of that of the fragments found by us. The fragment last found is shown in Fig. 3.

FIG. 3.—Fragment of vessel. Crystal River. (About full size.)

Professor Holmes writes that the figures on these two fragments "are probably parts of a single design, or at least a group of related designs, which covered the entire exterior surface of the vessel. They are, indeed, interesting, as you suggest, and illustrate the versatile genius of the southern potter; but they are not generically distinct in character or execution from others. * * * *

"I do not see the least reason for attributing these figures to the whites or suspecting white influence. They are aboriginal in every way."

Two sherds belonging to a vessel of coarse, porous ware seem to have borne an interesting design where what may have been intended to represent the head of a bird, front view, appears in relief on the flaring neck of the vessel. At one side is seen an incised design perhaps showing part of a wing.

FIG. 4.—Fragments of vessel. Crystal River. (About full size.)

On the second sherd is probably part of another wing which, however, by no means corresponds with the first one (Fig. 4).

A small fragment of a vessel, found in this investigation (Fig. 5 and diagram, Fig. 6) seems, judging from form and decoration, to have been the tail on a vessel representing a bird. If such is the case, the vessel was a marked exception, as the life-form, so abundant in the pottery of the northwestern coast of Florida, is conspicuously absent from the earthenware of the central western coast.

A fragment of a monitor-pipe of earthenware was found apart from human remains.

Among fragments of earthenware met with at this visit, as before, were a number of parts of vessels which had possessed four feet, and several entire vessels each having four feet also. As nothing found by us at either visit to the aboriginal place of burial at Crystal River gave distinct evidence of contact with Europeans, and as we have found vessels with feet in many other mounds, the contents of which gave no proof of the influence of white men, we believe that aboriginal vessels with feet were not of necessity inspired by contact with Europeans.

We shall now describe in detail the vessels of earthenware found by us during our second visit, continuing the enumeration from the last number in our former report.

FIG. 5.—Fragment of vessel. Crystal River. (About full size.)

Vessel No. 27.—This vessel, found in separate fragments, somewhat scattered, but since put together, is a small, undecorated bowl of excellent ware, having the rim projecting hoirzontally, as shown in Figs. 25 and 33 of our former report. The base has sustained the mortuary mutilation often practised in Florida and in parts of Georgia and of Alabama, to "kill" the pot that its soul might be free to accompany that of the departed.

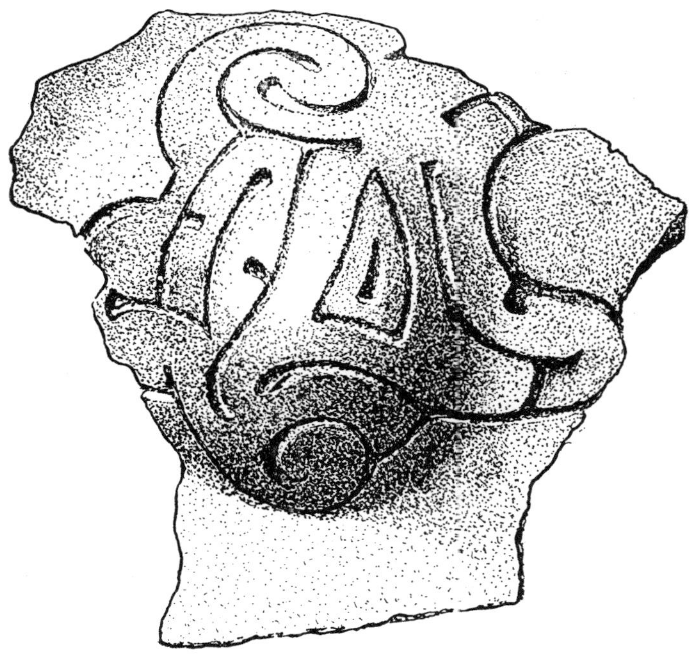

FIG. 6.—Fragment of vessel. Decoration. Crystal River. (Full size.)

Vessel No. 28.—This vase, which lay on the chest of the skeleton of a child, is a rudely-made, asymmetrical vessel of eccentric shape, having carelessly-made line decoration (Fig. 7). There are two perforations for suspension. A small, round perforation is in the base. Carefully placed on this hole was a neatly-made disc of earthenware which was distinctly not that portion of the base that had been punched out in order to make the opening.

FIG. 7.—Vessel No. 28. Crystal River. (Height 5 inches.)

Vessel No. 29.—An undecorated, imperforate bowl of inferior ware, found at the head of a skeleton.

Vessel No. 30.—A rude, undecorated bowl, from a shell layer, having a small, round perforation cut through the base.

Vessel No. 31.—A diminutive, imperforate toy pot with four feet, found apart from human remains.

Vessel No. 32.—An undecorated, imperforate toy vessel,

constricted around the middle and having a hole for suspension on two opposite sides of the aperture (Fig. 8).

Vessel No. 33.—A small, undecorated, perforate bowl of coarse ware, found at the ankle of a skeleton.

FIG. 8.—Vessel No. 32. Crystal River. (About full size.)

Vessel No. 34.—A pot of coarse ware, undecorated save for notches at the margin, found near scattered human bones. The usual mortuary mutilation is present.

Vessel No. 35.—A graceful, oblate-spheroidal vessel of excellent ware (Fig. 9), with basal perforation, having a short, upright neck and scalloped rim projecting horizontally; found in caved sand. The interesting line and punctate designs, each of which appears four times on the vessel, are shown in diagram in Fig. 10.

Vessel No. 36.—A small, undecorated, imperforate pot with four feet.

Vessel No. 37.—A small, imperforate vessel having four lobes and rude line and punctate decoration,

FIG. 9.—Vessel No. 35. Crystal River. (Diameter 6.5 inches.)

with four feet (Fig. 11). A part, missing when the rest of the vessel was found, has been restored.

Throughout this second investigation we unearthed fifty-three drinking cups wrought from conch-shells (*Fulgur perversum*),[1] of which twenty-one are imperforate and thirty-three bear the mortuary mutilation of the base. This number of cups, however, by no means represents the total of such cups in the tract dug through by us, inasmuch as many, probably as many again as we have noted, were found badly decayed and broken into fragments. Five other drinking cups were made respectively from *Fasciolaria gigantea*, *Fasciolaria tulipa*, *Cassis cameo*, *Fulgur pyrum*, and *Fulgur carica*. The last shell is of extreme rarity on the western coast of Florida so far as our experience has gone.

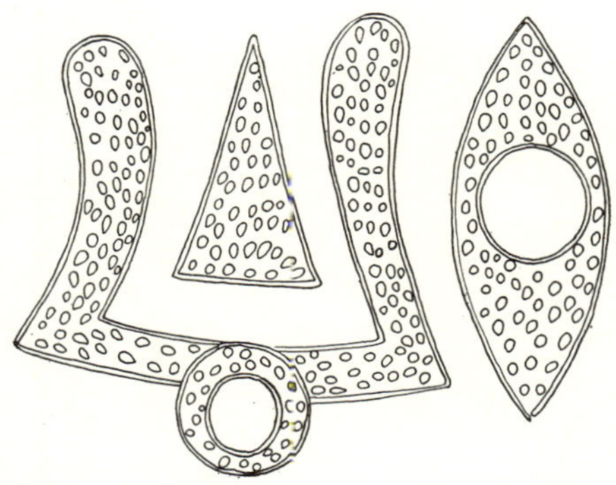

FIG. 10.—Vessel No. 35. Decoration. (Half size).

Thirty-three chisels and gouges, made from columellæ of large marine univalves, were found during our work. As we noticed before, these columellæ occasionally had a wing or flange left at the cutting edge to increase the gauge.

Seven gouges were met with, made from roughly triangular sections of the body whorl of *Fulgur perversum*. Several of these are unfinished, the grinding of the cutting edge apparently having been omitted.

FIG. 11.—Vessel No. 37. Crystal River. (About full size.)

There were found also seven "celts" fashioned from the thick lip of *Strombus gigas*. Most of these, as well as the majority of other objects of shell found during this investigation, were badly affected by lapse of time, some being covered with a thick coating of patina, which, peeling off in places, left them in a rather sorry condition.

During the digging were found: clam-shells showing wear; triangular sections of clam-shells; cockle-shells (*Cardium*) perforated for the reception of handles; a conch (*Fulgur perversum*) with two perforations for insertion of a handle at right-angles to the shell.

No fewer than forty gorgets of shell were found during our second visit to Crystal River, and had the aborigines who lived near the great shell-heap made use of engraved designs on these ornaments, as was sometimes the aboriginal custom elsewhere, the yield would have been interesting indeed. Unfortunately, most of the gorgets from Crystal River lacked decoration

[1] Dr. H. A. Pilsbry kindly has determined all shells referred to in this paper.

of any sort. The favorite form seems to have been a section of the body-whorl of a conch, sometimes including part of the shoulder, with one, two, or three perforations for suspension. Series of two and of three gorgets were found, usually with burials, and in one instance four gorgets lay together. Each series had gradation of size, the smaller lying within the larger. A few gorgets, wrought from considerable parts of body-whorls of *Fulgur*, somewhat resemble shallow drinking-cups, though the presence of small perforations for suspension places them in the gorget class. There are also circular gorgets variously perforated for suspension, some having large central holes in addition; and annular ones having a projection to which a cord could be attached. A few of the gorgets have on the convex side a series of concentric circles rudely executed—the only form of incised decoration met with on the gorgets at Crystal River. A selection of these gorgets is shown in Figs. 12, 13, 14, 15, 16.

FIG. 12.—Ornament of shell. Crystal River. (Full size.)

As in our former investigation, the yield of shell pendants on our second visit was large, seventy-two being found—in some cases a number with a single burial. All are of the same type as those found during our preceding visit, and all are grooved at one end for suspension. On many are traces of bitumen by the aid of which the cord or sinew had been attached.

Two oblong strips of body-whorls of *Fulgur perversum* were met with, each with a projection at one end for suspension, as shown in Figs. 17, 18.

In several instances small marine shells perforated for use as beads were found; and in one case a considerable number (*Marginella apicina*) lay with gorgets near scattered bones.

Where pendent ornaments were so much in vogue, one naturally would look

FIG. 13.—Ornament of shell. Crystal River. (Full size.)

FIG. 14.—Ornament of shell. Crystal River. (Full size.)

FIG. 15.—Ornament of shell. Crystal River. (Full size.)

for an ample yield of shell beads, since by strings of these such objects often were suspended. With three burials only did a few small beads of shell occur; these beads and four large shell beads, also with burials, were the sum total of our discovery in the way of ordinary beads of shell. At our first visit to Crystal River this dearth of beads was noted and commented on.

Shell hair-pins, as before, were conspicuously absent.

An object of shell of eccentric form and problematical use, found by us at the time of the second investigation, is shown in Fig. 19.

Fig. 16.—Ornament of shell. Crystal River. (Full size.)

Fig. 17.—Ornament of shell. Crystal River. (Full size.)

Fig. 18.—Ornament of shell. Crystal River. (Full size.)

On one edge are nicks or tally marks such as often are found on ceremonial objects.

Four small ornaments of shell, found lying together with a burial, are shown in Fig. 20.

A shell, a young *Fasciolaria gigantea*, ground smooth over its entire outer surface, has a round hole on one side for suspension.

During the second investigation were found in the sand and in the shell deposits the usual hammer-stones, hones, flakes of chert, parts of arrowheads or knives, and fragments of "celts." There were also two small balls of stone and half of a bar-amulet of slate.

Four "celts" were found, the largest having a length of 6.5 inches. These were presented to Mr. Knight, the owner of the property, without determination of the stone of which they are made.

Altogether, fifteen lanceheads, arrowheads, and knives were met with, some with burials and some apart from human remains. Five lanceheads, four of chert,

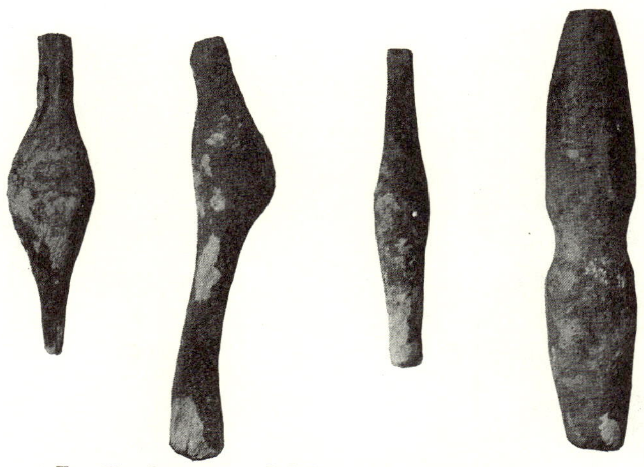

FIG. 20.—Ornaments of shell. Crystal River. (Full size.)

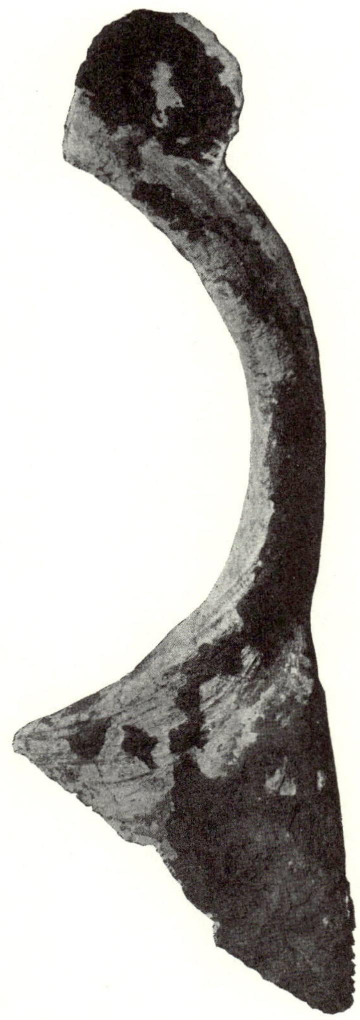

FIG. 19.—Ornament of shell. Crystal River. (Full size.)

one of quartzite, lay with a skeleton. The remaining points—nearly all lanceheads—are of chert save one, an arrowhead of chalcedony. Several of the lanceheads, none of which exceeds 6.5 inches in length, are beautifully wrought, one of medium size being finely pointed and barbed.

With many burials were sheets of mica of irregular outline, some of them dyed red from contact with hematite. Other sheets, in abundance, lay apart from human remains.

A beautiful little ornament representing a turtle (Fig. 21), perforated for suspension, doubtless came from the neighborhood of a skeleton, though the ornament apparently lay alone. The material probably is catlinite. Various ornaments of this stone from Minnesota were found during the first investigation at Crystal River.

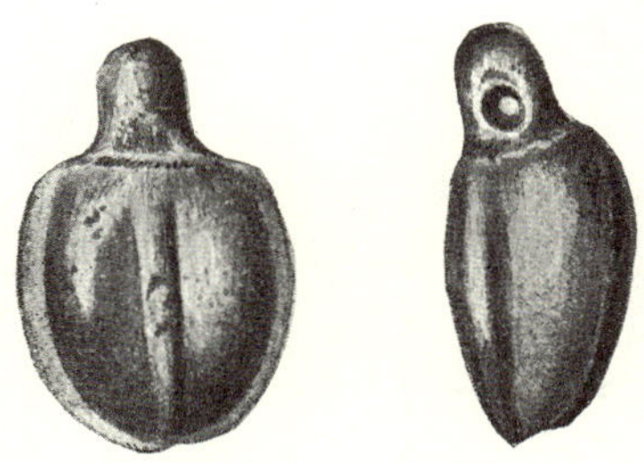

FIG. 21.—Pendant in form of turtle. Two positions. Crystal River. (Full size.)

Seventy-three stone pendants or charm-stones were found during our second visit, some with burials, others apparently not directly associated with human remains. These pendants, which do not present any particularly new form, are mostly of the limestone and of the ferruginous limestone found near the Crystal River region, and one is of chert. One pendant is of calcite; one is of quartz, and a few are of other hard stones not found in

Florida. One of these pendants (Fig. 22) is almost a facsimile of the type of the two curious pendants of copper, each having two projections, found by us on our first visit to Crystal River and shown, one above the other, in Fig. 53 of our former report. A selection of four pendants found at the time of our second visit is shown in Figs. 23, 24, 25, 26.

In a deposit, together, were three pendants, probably of slate, of the same type as the long ones shown in Fig. 48 of our former report. Their lengths are 8.3 inches, 8.5 inches, 8.9 inches, respectively.

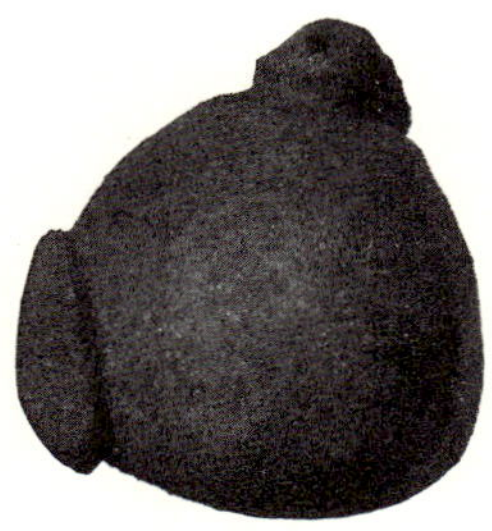

Fig. 22.—Pendant. Crystal River. (About full size.)

Fig. 23.—Pendant. Crystal River. (About full size.)

Fig. 24.—Pendant. Crystal River. (About full size.)

In Fig. 27 is shown a fossil shark's tooth which has been used as a pendant, as two encircling grooves, one at each corner of the root of the tooth, clearly prove. In a mound of the Georgia coast we found a fossil shark's tooth from which part of the root had been cut on two sides to facilitate hafting. The end ot this tooth was splintered by use.

Fig. 25.—Pendant. Crystal River. (About full size.)

Fig. 26.—Pendant. Crystal River. (About full size.)

Fig. 27.—Fossil shark's tooth used as a pendant. Crystal River. (Full size.)

Several masses of coral, hemispherical in shape, lay in the sand or in the shell layer, the flat surface of each mass showing marks of use as a smoothing-stone.

In sand thrown out at the time of the former investigation was part of an ear-ornament of sheet-copper, of the form sometimes designated "spool-shaped." The under portion of the ornament is somewhat defective by reason of former breakage; the upper part is entire.

On the upper surface of this upper part is a thin sheet of material resembling iron rust. That this material was not deposited after the ornament was placed in the mound (and we know that bog-iron sometimes is deposited in this way) is shown by two facts: The material does not lie over the entire ornament, but is symmetrically placed on the upper, outer surface, just as silver plating has been found upon similar aboriginal ornaments; and, secondly, an even covering of decayed wood is still present above the material. Evidently an even deposit of bog-iron would not form on one part of an ornament alone, and especially below a portion protected by a covering of wood. Therefore the plating was artificial.

As the ores of iron are not malleable and, therefore afford no material from which a coating of the kind found by us could have been directly made, the original plating must have been of metallic iron.

Small fragments of this coating, analyzed by Dr. H. F. Keller, proved it to be hydrated oxide of iron, containing nickel. This hydrated oxide could well be a derivative of metallic iron which had rusted through and through, and this hypothesis is strengthened by the fact that the material on the ornament is magnetic, while hydrated oxide ores of iron are non-magnetic, as a rule.

As it is practically certain that at Crystal River we have to do with a pre-Columbian site, we must reckon with the fact that this sheet-iron was of aboriginal origin solely.

It was not in the power of the aborigines to recover the metal iron from iron ore, and terrestrial native iron is not found in various localities in masses as the native, metallic copper is found; consequently, it is necessary to explain how pre-Columbian aborigines in Florida became possessed of iron in its native, metallic form.

Fortunately this can be done with the aid of Prof. F. W. Putnam[1] and Dr. L. P. Kinnicutt,[2] who have shown that iron from the Turner group of mounds in Ohio is meteoric iron, containing a large percentage of nickel, and showing other distinctive features.

In the plating of our specimen, which is rusted through and through, and from which only minute fragments could be taken, exact determination of component parts could not be made, but Doctor Keller has noted the presence of nickel[3]

[1] Sixteenth Report, Peabody Museum, Cambridge, 1882.

[2] Seventeenth Report, Peabody Museum, Cambridge, 1883.

[3] Doctor Keller found but a small quantity of nickel in our specimen, while the amount of nickel in the Ohio nuggets is relatively large. The analysis of the iron from Ohio was confined to nuggets of metallic iron. Doctor Keller thinks much nickel must have washed from the thin plating of our specimen during the transformation from metallic iron into iron rust.

in it, and to our mind there remains no doubt that the plating on the ear-ornament found by us at Crystal River was originally meteoric iron (which is metallic) similar to that found in the Ohio mounds in small masses and as plating on copper ornaments.

Professor Putnam writes:

"I have read your notice of the finding of an ear-ornament overlaid or covered on the upper surface with meteoric iron, and I am much interested in this very decided proof of the close connection of the prehistoric peoples of Florida who buried their dead in earth mounds, with those of the Ohio Valley region. You have shown, by many other objects which you have found in the Florida mounds, that this connection is exemplified by the arts of the people, and that there was much in common between some of the peoples of Florida and Ohio. This use of meteoric iron in covering the characteristic ear-ornaments, which are so common in the ancient mounds of Ohio and have not to my knowledge been found in the burial places of the recent Indian tribes, is very strong evidence of the unity of the ancient culture of the two regions. In other Florida mounds you have found such ear-ornaments made of copper. * * * The fact that the ancient Floridians made these copper ornaments in the same manner as did the builders of the ancient earthworks of Ohio, and that both used meteoric iron for covering the outer surface, is most instructive in tracing the connection of these ancient peoples.

"Similarly covered ear-ornaments have been found in considerable number in the Ohio mounds. I first found them on the altar of the Great Mound of the Turner Group and afterward with skeletons under the Great Mound of the Liberty Group (afterward known as the Harness Group). While Mr. Moorehead was working under my direction for the World's Columbian Exposition he found a number of these ornaments in a mound of the Clark, or Hopewell Group.

"Not only have we these ear-ornaments made in part of meteoric iron, but, on the altar of the Turner Group, we found other ornaments made of meteoric iron, as well as pieces of meteorites, while in the Liberty and Clark Groups celts made of meteoric iron were also found.

"This shows that the ancient people must have found masses of meteoric iron which they treated by hammering as they did native copper and native silver; and the great interest of your discovery in the Florida mound is that the people who made that mound at Crystal River had either found a mass of meteoric iron which they utilized in the same manner as did the ancient earthwork builders of Ohio, or else this ear-ornament which you found must have been obtained from the latter.

"It is probable that the meteoric iron from the Turner Group was derived from two distinct meteorites, as there is a slight difference between two of the smaller masses. The larger mass from the altar is known in the catalogues of meteorites, as the *Andersonville* Prehistoric Meteorite (Andersonville being the township in Ohio where the Turner Group is located in the Little Miami Valley)."

The latest discovery of meteoric iron in a mound is that of Wm. C. Mills, M. Sc., in the Edwin Harness mound, Ohio.[1]

[1] "Explorations of the Edwin Harness Mound." Ohio Archæol. and Hist. Quarterly. Vol. XVI, Num. 2.

Seventy-eight pointed implements of bone, made, as a rule, from the cannon-bone of the deer, split longitudinally, were unearthed during our second visit. Some doubtless were used as piercing implements, while some with flatter points probably served in basketry. Two slender implements, round in cross-section, show various small grooves at one end, worn by attachment of thread or fine cord. Among the pointed implements of bone are a number of lancets from the tails of sting-rays (*Trygon*). These objects, with their keen points, are admirably suited for use as piercing implements for which doubtless they were employed. Excluded from our enumeration of implements of bone were very many decayed fragments which in the past, no doubt, belonged to entire implements.

With finished implements often were unfinished ones, cannon-bones split longitudinally but not pointed.

Part of a lower jaw, which Prof. F. A. Lucas kindly has identified as belonging to the Virginia deer (*Odocoileus virginianus*), had been smoothed somewhat at its lower surface; the foramen had been considerably enlarged and all that side of the jaw in front of the four back molars had been cut away.

In several instances knuckle-bones of deer lay piled together.

Variously associated were: turtle-shells; five vertebræ of an unidentified fish, found together; a vertebra which Professor Lucas considers probably to have belonged to a grampus (*Grampus griseus*).

Professor Lucas has identified certain bones from the Crystal River place of burial as follows: "The front of cranium of carnivore and jaws, are from the same animal, the short-faced dog something like a bull-terrier that seems to have been a favorite with the Indians of the south and southwest."

As full details of the association of all objects found during the second investigation would occupy undue space, certain selected examples only will be given.

A skeleton lying full length on the back had, near the proximal end of the right humerus, a shell pendant. Three marine shells (*Oliva literata*), perforated for use as beads, were at the right elbow.

Another skeleton, also at full length on the back, had, under the legs, sheets of mica; sand, some tinged with hematite, some with limonite. Below the skull were: more pink sand; a pendant of limestone; a slab of compact rock as to the identity of which there is considerable doubt; one shell pendant; one pendant of a hard stone not found in Florida; four rudely triangular gorgets made from the body-whorl of *Fulgur*, each with one hole for suspension,—the two smaller ornaments lying within the larger ones; a rude section of shell with a central semiperforation. Under the head of one femur was an annular gorget of shell with a projection for suspension and having incised concentric circles on the convex side.

Still another full-length skeleton had at the left forearm, in a small pile, six astragali of the deer and two shells (*Oliva literata*) perforated for suspension.

At the head of a skeleton partly flexed on the left side was a shell drinking-cup within a turtle-shell and a neatly-made shell pendant within another drinking-cup of shell.

Near the skull of the skeleton of a child, six or seven years of age, were one shell chisel and eight stone pendants.

With a full-length burial were: twenty-one pointed implements of bone, entire, and seventeen of the same material, some broken, some partly decayed; five lancets of the sting-ray (*Trygon*); a lot of marine shells (*Macrocallista gigantea*); a fragment of a columella of *Fulgur;* bits of stone; sand colored red with hematite and yellow with limonite; a number of astragali and phalanges, with part of a jawbone, of a deer. All this deposit lay above the legs and feet of the skeleton.

Near the skull of a skeleton at full length on the back were four lanceheads of chert and one of quartzite; also a mass of fossil wood about 4.5 inches long, square in cross section.

With certain disconnected bones in the shell layer was the skull of a child near which were two pendants, one of stone, the other of shell, the grooved ends toward the skull.

Near the skull of the skeleton of a child, lying full length on the back, were a pendant of shell and one of stone. The grooved end of one of these pendants lay toward the skull, while the corresponding end of the other was directed oppositely. Incidentally, we may say here that the exact position of pendants in relation to parts of the human skeleton was a matter carefully noted by us during our work at Crystal River. As a rule, when pendants were not ceremonial deposits apart from human remains, or were not scattered as a result of aboriginal disturbance but lay immediately associated with a skeleton, the grooved end of the pendant lay nearest the bones. Sometimes, however, the grooved end was directed outward. This variety of position, we think, readily can be accounted for by calling to mind that a suspended ornament hanging taut would have the grooved end, around which the cord was placed, directed toward the point of suspension; while, should the strain be removed, as would be the case were the skeleton placed in a recumbent position, the upper ends of some of the pendants could swing outward.

A skeleton lying at full length on its back had a shell drinking-cup near the pelvis, and under the right knee nine marine shells (*Macrocallista gigantea*), the valves tightly closed, and pierced for suspension at points below the muscular attachment.

A skeleton partly flexed on the left side had on the thorax eight chisels and gouges, three made from the axis of the conch and five from its body-whorl.

A skeleton at full length had near the skull one shell pendant and one of stone. Over the shoulder and at the pelvis were fragments of mica. A stone pendant lay below the shoulder. On the thorax was part of a lancehead of chert. Above the chest were two pointed implements of bone. At the right forearm was a mass of green material kindly identified by Dr. George P. Merrill, Head Curator of Geology, United States National Museum, as arenaceous clay colored by iron. Sand dyed with hematite lay at the feet of the skeleton.

A noteworthy fact to which reference has hitherto been made is that nearly all objects of the greatest interest found in the entire investigation came from the mound proper. In fact, in comparison with the yield of the mound proper, nothing of marked interest came from the sloping area which surrounded it.

The mound itself, as we have said, differed in composition from the sloping ground in that the mound contained much less shell and to a large extent was made up of clear sand. This sand continued to the very base of the mound on the general level of the surrounding surface, so that it seems clear that the mound was built first, and later surrounded, as to its lower part, by the sloping ground.

We know that when the mound proper was built a better class of objects was placed with the dead. Either the possessions of those living at that earlier period were of a higher grade than those of the persons who later built the cemetery around the mound, or else the makers of the mound proper were endowed with a greater spirit of liberality than were those who came later.

Before leaving Crystal River, six trial-holes, some 4 feet by 4 feet, some 4 feet by 5 feet, were made in the southern part of the embankment marked C C on the plan. Two skeletons were found, and one small pendant of limestone was met with in sand thrown out from one of the excavations.

Notes on the Ten Thousand Islands, Florida

BY

CLARENCE B. MOORE

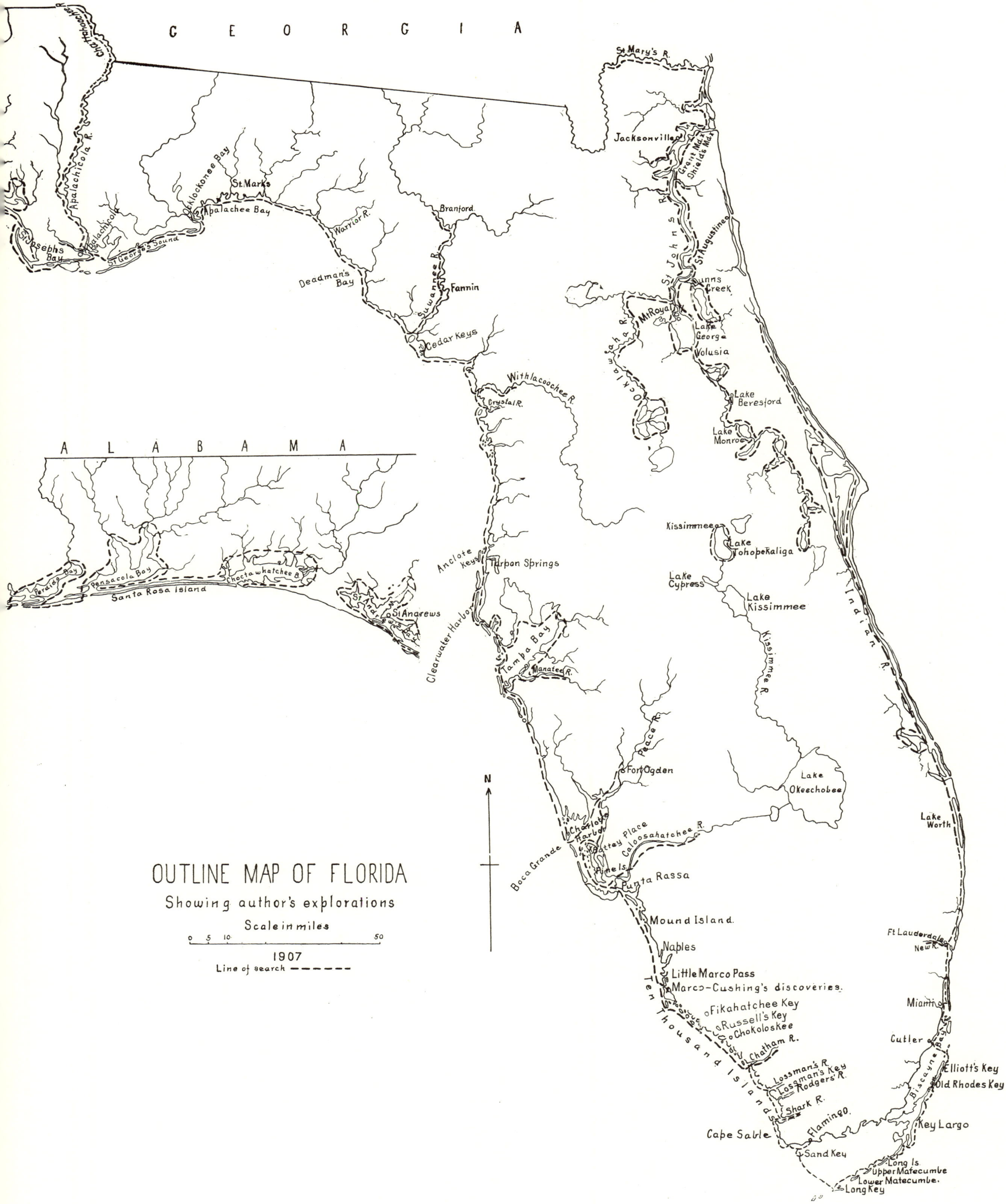

OUTLINE MAP OF FLORIDA

Showing author's explorations

NOTES ON THE TEN THOUSAND ISLANDS, FLORIDA.

By Clarence B. Moore.

The Ten Thousand Islands, which have been twice visited and twice written of by us,[1] were again the subject of our investigation during two seasons, the winter of 1906 and the winter of 1907. These islands (see accompanying map) fringe the coast of southwestern Florida for about 80 miles, along parts of the counties of Lee and Monroe, between the settlement known as Naples on the north and Cape Sable on the south.

In a former report we have spoken of Little Marco as the northern limit of the Ten Thousand Islands, but as the coast is bordered by small keys to Naples, about nine miles farther north, and as this place can be reached by an inside water-route, the most intelligent inhabitants of the Keys now speak of the Ten Thousand Islands as beginning at Naples.

Little Marco, it should be said, is not a key, but a settlement on the mainland, not far from Key Marco. The island next above Marco is not named Little Marco, but is known as "The Beach."

The settlement of Marco, at the northeastern extremity of Key Marco, the most important key of the Ten Thousand Islands, was again visited by us and a careful search made of all the shell territory adjacent. Near Marco we examined a section of a heap composed partly of shell and in part of kitchen refuse and the debris of fires, the last consisting of fine ash containing fish-bones, etc. In this midden refuse were numerous fragments of pottery of rather inferior ware, some bearing a simple incised decoration, others the imprint of cord. No doubt the key-dwellers used pottery only to a limited extent.

Among objects obtained by us at Marco were many pendants, two of which, of limestone, and two of shell, are shown in Figs. 1, 2, 3, 4.

As we have written in former reports, we gravely doubt that the grooved objects of shell and of stone, known as "plumb-bobs," among the keys, of which such great numbers have been found there, were used as sinkers for lines or fish-nets, though some are so coarsely made as to seem unfitted for ornament. Mr. Cushing,[2] among his wonderful discoveries at Marco, found fish-nets with sinkers in place, but none was in the form of the pendants found among the keys, while lines had sinkers of *Turbinella* shells with the whorls rudely battered off. The pendants are not found chiefly near the water, but distributed over such of the keys as have

[1] "Certain Antiquities of the Florida West-Coast." Journ. Acad. Nat. Sci. of Phila., Vol. XI, 1900.

"Miscellaneous Investigation in Florida." Journ. Acad. Nat. Sci. of Phila., Vol. XIII, 1905.

[2] "Preliminary Report on the Exploration of Ancient Key-Dweller Remains on the Gulf-Coast of Florida," by Frank Hamilton Cushing. Proceedings of the American Philosophical Society, Vol. XXXV, No. 153, p. 38, 1897.

aboriginal deposits of shell; some are too handsomely made to have served a utilitarian purpose; while one in our possession is of a coralline material so light that it hardly sinks in water. We found in the cemetery and mound near Crystal River,[1] Florida, in place on a skeleton, a number of stone pendants associated with others made of copper. We believe these pendants from the keys served some ornamental or ceremonial purpose—perhaps they were "charm-stones." It is true, as we have said, that many of the stone pendants of the keys are crude, but much of the stone of that locality is not of a character conducive to good workmanship.

Fig. 1.—Pendant of limestone. Marco, Key Marco. (About full size.)

Fig. 2.—Pendant of limestone. Marco, Key Marco. (About full size.)

Fig. 3.—Pendant of shell. Marco, Key Marco. (About full size.)

Fig. 4.—Pendant of shell. Marco, Key Marco. (About full size.)

Two interesting pendants from Marco probably represent ducks' heads. One (Fig. 5) is of a hard stone not found in Florida, but we have not wished to mutilate it for exact determination. The other, of limestone, is shown in Fig. 6. These pendants are another of the indications of the high esteem in which the duck was held by the ancient southern Indians.

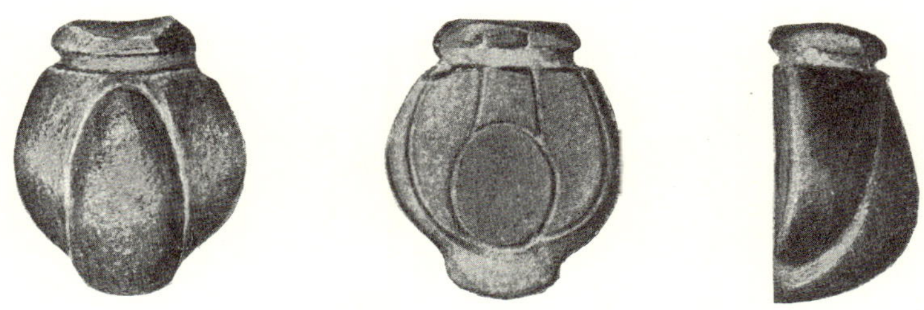

Fig. 5.—Duck-head pendant. Three positions. Marco, Key Marco. (Full size.)

A circular ornament of shell from Marco, and a curiously-shaped pendant of limestone from the same place, are shown in Figs. 7, 8, respectively.

[1] "Certain Aboriginal Mounds of the Central Florida West-Coast." Journ. Acad. Nat. Sci. of Phila., Vol. XII, p. 99, 1903.

Occasionally in the shell debris at Marco were "chipped and notched fragments of heavy clam-shells," like those found by Cushing[1] on nets in the muck at Marco; while a fossil-shark's tooth, beveled and showing signs of use, probably as a knife, was picked up by us in the shell debris of a cultivated field. Teeth of sharks, though fossil sharks are not specified, were found by Cushing,[2] set in handles for use as carving tools.

FIG. 6.—Duck-head pendant. Three positions. Marco, Key Marco. (Full size.)

FIG. 7.—Ornament of shell. Marco, Key Marco. (About full size.)

We got also at Marco—and the inhabitants say that many have been gathered from the surface near there—a fragment of clam-shell wrought on one side to a very sharp cutting edge (Fig. 9). These probably were hafted as knives or, perhaps, were the blades of small hand-adzes, as described by Cushing,[3] though "little blades made either from bits of shell, the sharp ventral valves of oysters," and not clam-shells, are mentioned by him.

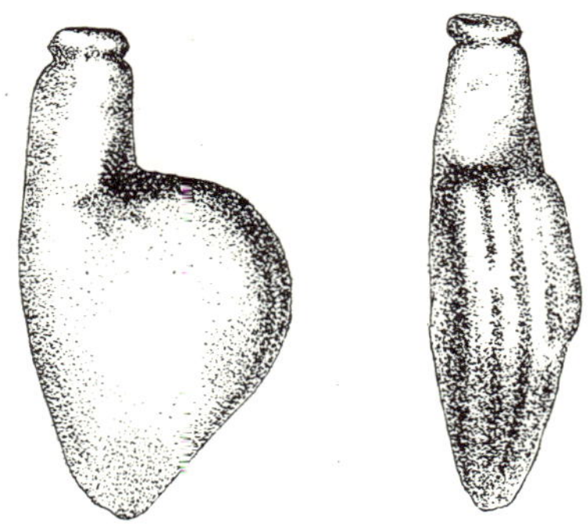

FIG. 8.—Pendant. Two positions. Marco, Key Marco. (Full size.)

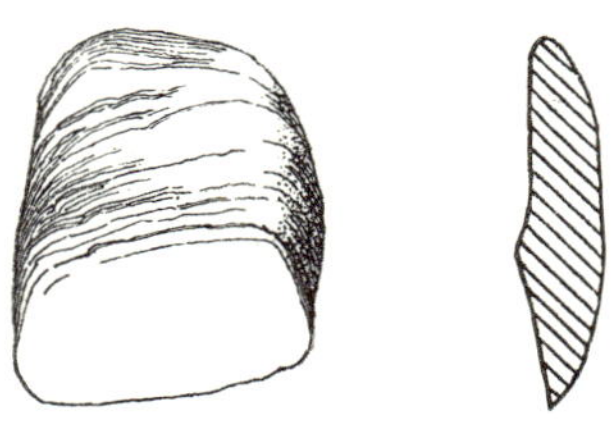

FIG. 9.—Chisel blade and section. Marco, Key Marco. (Full size.)

While at Marco we visited Little Marco; McIlvaine's Key; Addison's Key; and the Crawford place, northward toward Naples—all noteworthy, aboriginal shell deposits.

A number of interesting objects came from Goodland Point, Key Marco, among which is a gorget of shell (Fig. 10) with the aboriginal sign of the four directions.

A pendant from the same place (Fig. 11), made from fossil bone or from some coral material (we have not wished to cut into the specimen to determine it), bears an incised design on each of the four sides—two showing the eye; one, a mouth or jaws; and one being indistinguishable. Three of these designs are shown in diagram in Fig. 12.

[1] *Op. cit.*, p. 38. [2] *Op. cit.*, p. 42. [3] *Op. cit.*, p. 41.

Fikahatchee Key, and Russell's Key, large shell islands, yielded specimens of aboriginal work.

Chokoloskee Key was visited with good results. Among various objects obtained there was a gorget wrought from a considerable portion of a shell (somewhat similar to the shells we found in the great place of burial near Crystal River, Florida), which resembles a shallow

FIG. 10.—Gorget of shell. Goodland Point, Key Marco. (Full size.)

FIG. 11.—Pendant. Goodland Point, Key Marco. (About full size.)

drinking-cup and might be taken for such an object were it not for two holes for suspension bored well below the margin.

FIG. 12.—Incised decoration on pendant. Goodland Point, Key Marco. (Full size.)

An interesting object from Chokoloskee Key, a massive pick 6.7 inches in length and 1.25 inches in maximum thickness, wrought from the lip of *Strombus gigas*, is shown in Fig. 13. Much splintering at each end testifies to the amount of service to which this implement has been subjected. It is our belief, strengthened by the result of inquiry, that this shell implement is unique, though similarly shaped picks of stone are met with.

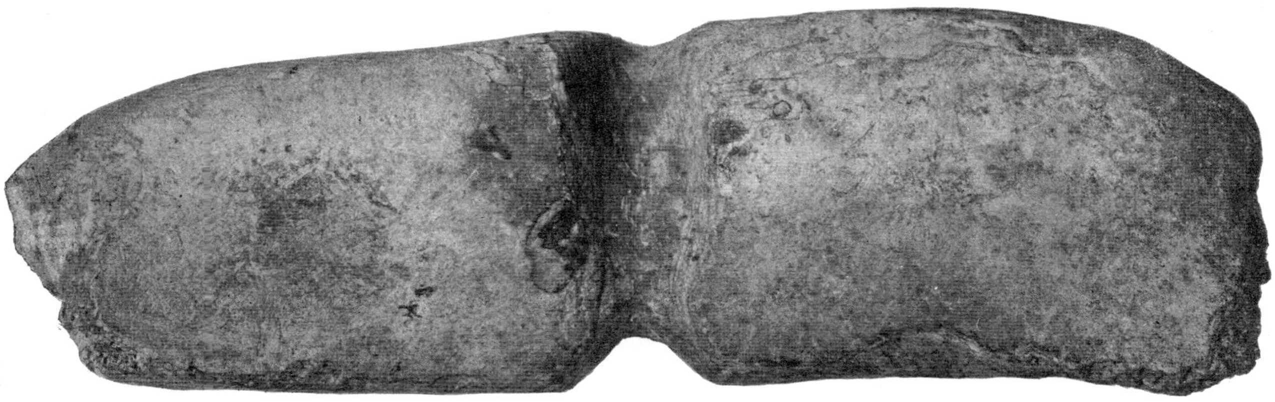

FIG. 13.—Pick-axe of shell. Chokoloskee Key. (Full size.)

A pendant from the same place is a carefully-made imitation, wrought from shell, of a canine tooth of a large carnivore. So well executed is this imitation that at first glance one might well be deceived and mistake it for a tooth in reality (Fig. 14).

Also from Chokoloskee Key came a pendant of a hard stone from a region to the north of Florida (Fig. 15); a pendant of shell (Fig. 16); a well made bead of shell (Fig. 17); an ornament of shell with the incised sign of the four directions (Fig. 18).

FIG. 14.—Pendant of shell. Chokoloskee Key. (Full size.)

FIG. 15.—Pendant of stone. Chokoloskee Key. (About full size.)

FIG. 16.—Pendant of shell. Chokoloskee Key. (About full size.)

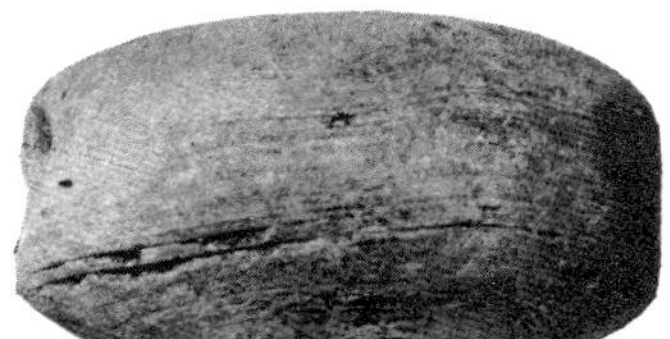

FIG. 17.—Bead of shell. Chokoloskee Key. (About full size.)

A rude effigy of a human head (Fig. 19), carved on a fragment of pumice stone, was picked up on Chokoloskee Key by a thoroughly reliable person long known to us, from whom we obtained it. This effigy has every appearance of being aboriginal work.

Lossman's Key, near Cape Sable, one of the largest keys of the Ten Thousand Islands, was again visited by us and its two shell deposits—one more than ten acres in extent—were carefully examined. The larger deposit, rich in aboriginal implements, has been recently cleared of the hammock growth formerly upon it. While there we almost walked upon the wires of a loaded spring-gun set for deer or panther—one of the chances one takes in exploring this wild and lawless region.

The reader of our former reports on the Florida Keys may recall that in the shell deposits there are many implements wrought from entire shells. These implements, sometimes whole, but much oftener broken or greatly worn, lie among great numbers of unwrought conchs and other shells, as is well shown in the picture of a cultivated field on Chokoloskee Key (Fig. 20).

FIG. 18.—Ornament of shell. Chokoloskee Key. (About full size.)

In our search for these implements we were constantly aided by the inhabitants—especially by children who, laboring in hope of substantial reward, had put aside, to await our coming, all desirable shells found on the surface or turned up by the plow. In this way, by our own efforts and by those of others we accumulated a very large collection of implements. These implements we believe to have served mainly as chisels, gouges, adzes, scrapers, hammers, and grinders, and especially as hoes and picks in the cultivation of the soil. These picks and hoes were used with fairly short handles, those employing them assuming a squatting position, after the manner of less-advanced peoples at the present time when cultivating the ground.

FIG. 19.—Head of pumice stone. Chokoloskee Key. (2.2 inches high.)

The results of our two seasons' labors were added in part to our collection in the Academy of Natural Sciences in Philadelphia and in part were sent to various museums in this country, in South America, and in Europe.

Before describing new types of shell implements found by us in our last two seasons' work, we wish to correct an error into which we have fallen. In a former report[1] we say, "There is a small hole above the shoulder, or periphery [of the shell], which seems, as a rule, to have had no connection with the tool, inasmuch as numbers of shells, not made into implements, show a similar perforation, which may have been made to sever the muscle and free the shell-fish from its shell."

[1] "Miscellaneous Investigation in Florida," page 316. Journ. Acad. Nat. Sci. of Phila., Vol. XIII, 1905.

Fig. 20.—A field on Chokoloskee Key.

While it is true that some conch shells (more from some localities than from others) which have no hole or holes in the body-whorl for the insertion of a handle, and do not seem to have served as tools, have a small hole above the shoulder, or periphery, it is equally true that a large proportion of the shells found on the keys do not have this hole, and, as the contents of these shells were brought to the keys as an article of food, it is clear that a hole above the shoulder, or periphery, was not necessary to separate the shell-fish from the shell.

Cushing,[1] who found in place in the muck at Marco shell implements pierced for handles, speaks of them as follows: "Thus the stick or handle could be driven into these perfortions, past the columella in such manner that it was sprung or clamped firmly into place. Nevertheless it was usually further secured with rawhide thongs —now mere jelly—passed through one or two additional perforations in the head, and around both the stick and the columella."

This hole above the shoulder is not always present, however, even in shells which are distinctly tools, with chisel-edge and holes, or a hole and a notch, for the insertion of a handle. This hole for the thong is absent in a small percentage of these tools among the islands generally, while at McIlvaine's, a small shell key[2] about two miles to the northeast of the settlement of Marco, a score of implements, all that were found by us of the class we have mentioned, had no hole above the shoulder of the shell.

We shall now describe in detail some of the most interesting shell implements obtained by us since the publication of our last report.

An interesting type from Marco is a pick wrought from *Fasciolaria* (Fig. 21), doubtless used in cultivating

[1] *Op. cit.*, p. 40.

[2] The reader will bear in mind that a very small proportion of the keys of the Ten Thousand Islands bear evidence of aboriginal occupancy.

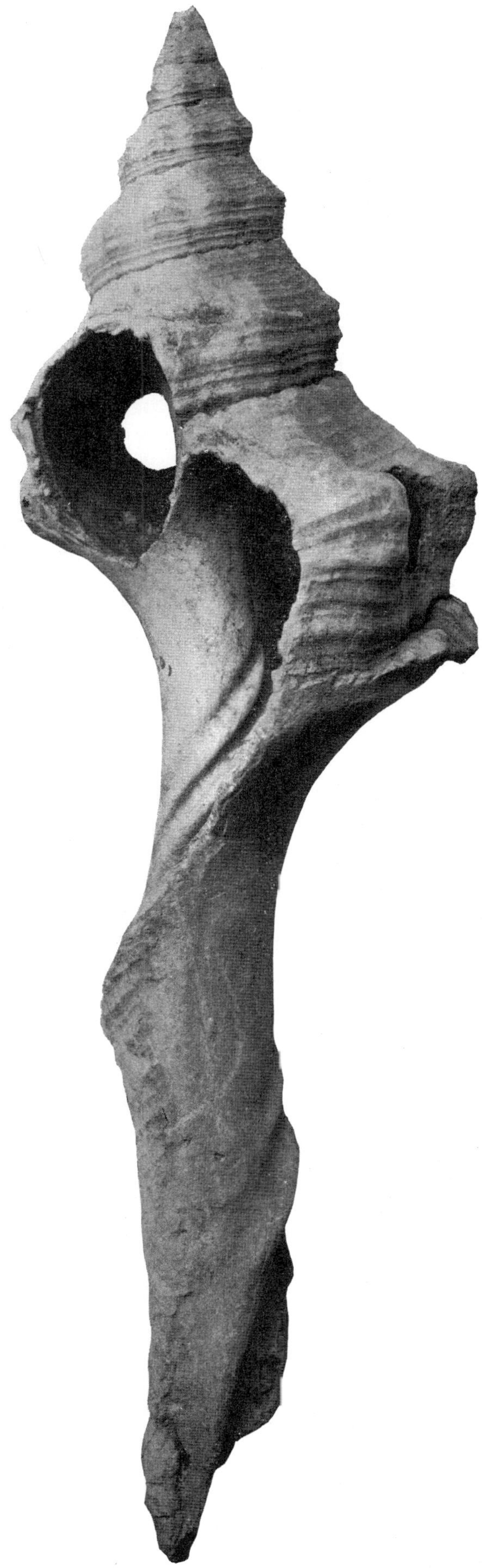

FIG. 21.—Shell pick. Marco, Key Marco. (Length 11.7 inches.)

the soil. These picks are seldom found entire, though implements of the same shell with the columella much worn away are abundant. It is likely that picks, after a certain amount of wear, were used as hammers.

The next implement to be considered, a heavy *Fulgur perversum* of moderate size, differs from types heretofore described in that there is a hole for the handle, back of the columella, and a notch on the right as shown in Fig. 22, illustrating a

FIG. 22.—Implement of shell. McIlvaine's Key. (Height 5.5 inches.)

specimen from McIlvaine's Key. Usually when a notch is present it is on the left of the shell. A number of examples similar to the one shown in the figure, however, were met with by us on McIlvaine's Key and elsewhere. There is no hole in the upper part of the shell for a thong or fiber to pass through, and none is needed in this instance as attachment can be made directly to the columella.

An interesting implement is a *Fulgur perversum* with no perforation for a handle below the shoulder, or periphery. There is, however, in addition to the usual small hole for attachment, a large one above the shoulder, a feature often found on the eastern coast of Florida, but seldom on the western coast. This tool, which came from Fikahatchee Key, perhaps was used like a spade the handle extending straight upward; or possibly the shell was placed at right angles to the handle which crossing the top of the shell entered the hole obliquely and was made fast with a thong.

An implement (Fig. 23) from Goodland Point, Key Marco, has no hole of any sort and consequently no inserted handle was used in connection with it. The upper, and heavier, part of the shell shows great wear, but as the beak is intact, bearing no trace of a cutting edge or of any use whatever, it is evident the tool was not used with the upper part held in the hand and the lower part to cut as a chisel, or to loosen the soil as a pick, as some tools closely resembling this one certainly were used. Therefore, we are inclined to believe the tool to have been employed as a kind of hammer or grinder, but as there is no evidence of chipping or battering, presumably it served in connection with some comparatively soft material, such as Indian corn.

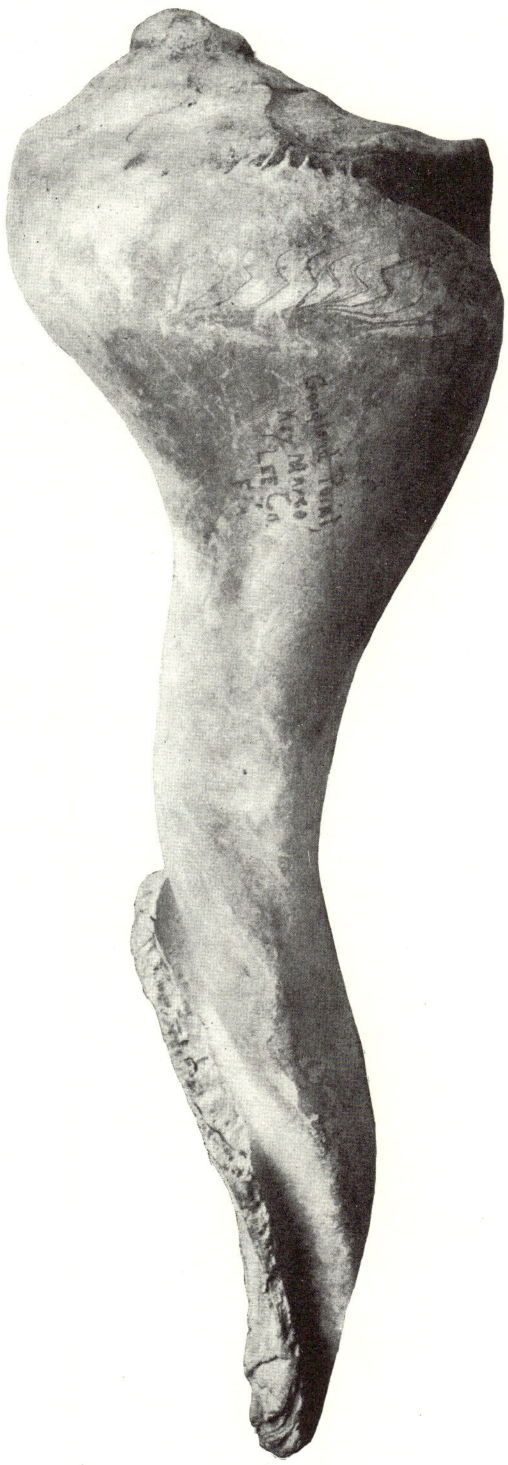

FIG. 23.—Shell implement. Goodland Point. (Length 11.35 inches.)

An implement (Fig. 24), wrought from *Fasciolaria,* is greatly cut away for convenience to the user and has a notch to the right and another to the left for the attachment of a handle. At Lossman's Key, from which this implement came, it was noted that a double notch was used more often than a hole and a notch or a double hole for the handle.

As we have said before in this report, the small hole, or sometimes two holes, in the shell above the shoulder, or periphery, through which thongs or fiber bound the handle more firmly, were not always employed. Almost invariably when these holes for attachment were not made above the shoulder, they were dispensed with, though in a few cases they are found in the body of the shell. A small number of such instances have come to our notice, and there is in our collection at the Academy of Natural Sciences a good example from Fikahatchee Key, where a shell with a fine gouge edge, and a hole and a notch to accommodate a handle, has a small, round perforation in the body-whorl—too small to have served for any purpose except for the passage of a thong.

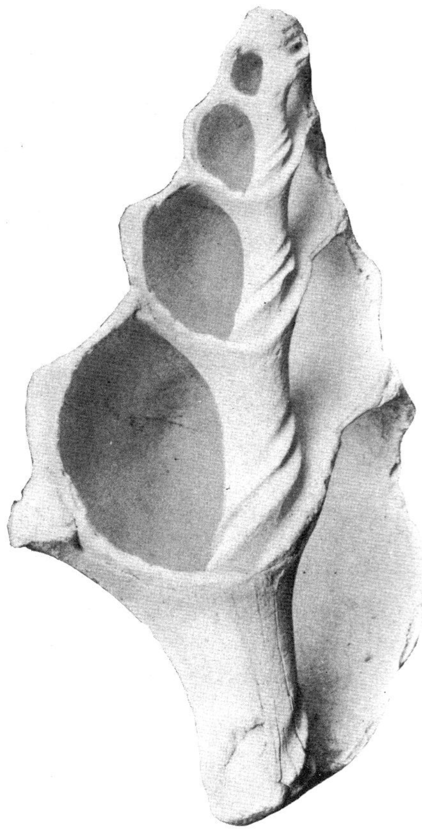

FIG. 24.—Shell implement. Lossman's Key. (Length 6.2 inches.)

Two shells (*Fulgur perversum*) added to our collection since the last report, differ from ordinary types in that while both have edges beautifully ground at the beaks, and each has a part of the body-whorl cut back from the aperture, neither shell bears hole or notch for the accommodation of a handle. One implement, however, has a hole for attachment above the shoulder of the shell, while the other is without one. These implements came respectively from Little Marco and the Crawford Place, below Naples.

As to another class of shells we are unable as yet to reach a decision. These shells, sparingly found on the Ten Thousand Islands, were fairly numerous on Wason, or Cora Key, in Pine Island Sound, north of the Ten Thousand Islands. The shells (*Fulgur perversum*) are carefully cut back from the aperture as if for use as tools and have above the shoulder usually one small hole, but sometimes two, for attachment. In certain cases some of these holes seem to bear evidence of wear. On the other hand, in no instance do these shells have any hole or notch through which a handle may be passed. The beaks are considerably chipped as if by use, but above the splintered part is no sign of the remainder of the ground surface, which is so often apparent on other tools, though they have been subjected to prolonged use. It is possible these shells were used as tools with the aid of a handle abutting against the inside of the body-whorl, the thong extending over the outside of the shell. Presumably the beaks were not ground prior to use, the implements serving as picks with unground beaks, as was the case with the large "horse-conchs" (*Fasciolaria*), one of which is shown in this report (Fig. 21).

On all the shell keys, and notably on Fikahatchee Key, we found masses of sandstone, smoothed and furrowed by use. These stones, we believe, were those used in conferring cutting edges on the shell tools of the keys.

Fig. 25 shows an ordinary southern, round clam-shell (*Venus mortoni*) from Fikahatchee Key, with a circular hole knocked from the inside through the central part of the shell or, perhaps, a little above it. Clam-shells of this kind, of which we obtained thirteen,—twelve from Chokoloskee and one from Fikahatchee,—usually show considerable wear on parts of the edge, though the shell in the illustration, probably almost an unused tool, shows but little sign of use. There seems to be, however, no evidence of wear on the sharp edges within the holes, which fact makes it still more doubtful how these shells were used, though no doubt the purpose for which they were employed was the cultivation of the soil. In "Art in Shell"[1] we see suggested various methods of hafting perforated shells.

Cushing says:[2] "Large clam-shells, deeply worn at the backs, as well as showing much use at the edges, seem to have served both as scrapers and as digging implements or hoes; for some of them had been hafted by clamping curved sticks over the hinge and over the point at the apex, or umbo—where it showed wear" . . . No reference is made by him to holes in these shells, and in point of fact repeated search made by ourselves and by the juvenile population of Marco[3] failed to discover at that place a single perforated clam-shell of the variety in question.

FIG. 25.—Shell implement. Fikahatchee. (Length about 5 inches.)

Cushing,[4] however, speaks of varieties of *Pectunculus* (which is a kind of clam) as having served as scrapers and shavers, and being "perforated at the apices, in order that a loop might be attached to them to facilitate handling," and also describes (p. 42) a variety of *Arca* shell, three and one-half or four inches long, through the aperture of which a strip of bark was passed in a way to afford an excellent grasp. Probably it was in this manner our clam-shells were used and the comparative absence of wear in the holes is owing to the soft character of the fiber.

One feature connected with the thirteen clam-shells found by us is of especial interest. Of these shells twelve are left valves, having the umbo, or beak (which in the case of the clam is above the heavy hinge-piece) turning to the right of the user, thus making it perhaps a trifle easier for a right-handed person to grasp in connection with a band. In the case of the remaining shell, a right-hand valve,

[1] W. H. Holmes. Rep. Bur. Am. Ethn., 1880–81, pp. 206–207, plate XXVI.
[2] *Op. cit.*, p. 40.
[3] Marco was the principal scene of Mr. Cushing's labors.
[4] *Op. cit.*, p. 42.

the beak turns to the left of the user, and probably was selected by a left-handed individual.

In Fig. 26 is shown a shell (*Codakia orbicularis*) which has been an implement of some sort. This shell was dug by us from one of the great ash-heaps on Chokoloskee Key, which there and on certain other keys seem to be the remains of fires long continued.

FIG. 26.—Shell implement. Chokoloskee Key. (About full size.)

Spread over the shell keys are considerable numbers of shells (*Arca ponderosa*), many with a hole below the hinge, as shown in Fig. 27.

Cushing (p. 38) speaks of nets having "sinkers made from thick, roughly perforated umboidal bivalves, tied together in bunches," no doubt referring to the *Arca ponderosa* shell.

The number of these shells having holes, when found on the shell keys, greatly preponderates over those that do not have a perforation, in which they greatly differ from the conchs and other large shells found on the keys. The reason for this is plain. The larger shell-fish were selected for food primarily, and the shells of only some of them were subsequently used as tools. The *Arca*, on the other hand, is small and moreover is found in comparatively deep water when alive. Presumably conditions were such that the *Arca* was not sought as food and the supply of shells needed for tools came from the beaches. In this event a very large proportion of the shells carried to the keys would be perforated for use.

FIG. 27.—Perforated *Arca* shell. Little Marco. (Length 2.15 inches.)

Many of the *Arca ponderosa* shells in our possession show decided wear on the edges, which leads us to believe they were used as diminutive scrapers. Probably *Arca* shells were employed for different purposes—for tools as well as for net-sinkers.

The Northwestern Florida Coast Revisited [EXCERPT]

BY

CLARENCE B. MOORE

[568]

Mounds on Hog Island, Levy County.

Hog island lies on the Gulf Coast between mouths of the Suwanee river. That part of the island on which the mounds are is owned jointly by Messrs. B. A. Thrasher, of Gainesville, Fla., and J. L. Robison, residing on the island.

The mounds are on hammock land about three-quarters of a mile northeast from the first high land up Hog Island creek, in connection with a considerable shell deposit.

One, on the shell ridge, having a diameter of 40 feet and a height of about 3 feet, had been dug into to some extent by others. Investigation by us indicated it to be of shell covered with sand to a depth of about one foot in which were burials, the bones badly broken, some by previous disturbance, other probably owing to roots of the scrub palmetto that were thickly interwoven in the mound.

Nearby was a somewhat larger mound that had been considerably dug into centrally. Seemingly it had been similar in construction to the smaller one, with the addition of some masses of limerock.

Another mound on Hog island was visited by us in 1902.[1]

Mound in Cedar Keys, Levy County.

In the town of Cedar Keys, alongside the road bordering the water and near the great shell deposits there, is a mound on the property of Mr. W. H. Hale, of Cedar Keys. This mound, about 7 feet high and having diameters of 73 and 32 feet at present, is largely of sand, though some shell is found in it in places. On the side toward the water, however, Mr. Hale informed us, much shell was hauled away for use on the streets of the town, thus accounting in part, at least, for the difference in diameters. On the water side shell must have predominated in the mound.

Much digging by others before our coming had been done in the mound, and we were shown several celts and told of others and of quantities of shell beads, celts and beads all said to have been found superficially in the mound, or, in the case of some of the beads, to have been washed from it.

Three excavations, 6 by 3.5 feet, 6 by 4 feet, 16.5 by 6 feet, were put down by us centrally in the mound to its base, a depth of 7.5 feet, all passing through sand in the main, though shell was encountered in comparatively small quantities.

About one foot down fragments of human bones having belonged to different individuals were encountered, probably a recent disturbance.

[569] Five feet down a graceful celt, apparently of sedimentary rock, was found, 7.5 inches in length.

[1] Op. cit., p. 348.

About 8 inches below and 1.5 foot away from the celt was a thigh bone and part of the base of the skull of a child, accompanied by a number of shell beads.

Five feet eight inches down, apart from bones, was a fragment of an ornament of sheet-copper.

Aboriginal Cemetery in Cedar Keys, Levy County.

In the town of Cedar Keys, in a large vacant lot, about 150 yards in a southerly direction from the principal school-house of the place, a large, brick edifice, is an aboriginal cemetery in ground on property controlled by Mr. W. R. Hodges, of Cedar Keys. This cemetery had been dug into to a considerable extent prior to our visit, though much of it remained intact. Remarkable stories of the discoveries made at the time of the earlier digging were related to us and of various interesting vessels accompanying the burials. So plentiful were the relics, it was said, that objects of interest actually had been dug out with spoons by persons living nearby. On our return to the North we addressed the Buffalo Society of Natural Sciences, of Buffalo, N. Y., for whom the work had been done, and most courteously were forwarded by Mr. W. L. Bryant, Director of the Society, who had participated in the investigation, details of the digging in the cemetery and, in addition, his illustrated catalogue, a very interesting book, and a large number of photographs of objects, mostly pottery, discovered in the cemetery.

[570] The pottery from this place presents no marked novelties though it includes specimens of the interesting incised decoration found in this region, an ex-

Fig. 39.—Vessel of earthenware. Aboriginal cemetery, Cedar Keys. (One-half size.)

ample of which, selected from the photographs sent by Mr. Bryant, is shown in Fig. 39. The projection of the decoration, also furnished by Mr. Bryant, appears in Fig. 40.

An interesting pendant[1] of diorite, in the form of a duck's head, also was found by Mr. Bryant in this cemetery.

A portion of the unexplored part of the cemetery was dug through by us. In addition to several disturbances, aboriginal or recent, we came upon eleven skeletons, closely flexed, partly flexed, at full length, none having a skull in condition to save. Eight of these burials lay in sand, each having above it a deposit of shells, indicating that interments had been made in graves which were then filled with shell almost to the surface.

At one part of the cemetery a general shell deposit was reached, which, however, was not apparent above the level. Three burials were found in that portion of this shell deposit explored by us, and these lay entirely enclosed in shell.

[571] No artifacts lay with any of the burials found by us, and but two or three bits of pottery were encountered in all our digging. One of these, however, is of excellent ware, bearing an interesting incised decoration, perhaps including the well-known step design (Fig. 41).

Fig. 40.—Projection of decoration. Vessel of earthenware. Cedar Keys.

Fig. 41.—Fragment of earthenware. Aboriginal cemetery, Cedar Keys. (About two-thirds size.)

[1] Our Academy possesses a cast of this rare piece, presented to it by the United States National Museum.

It is evident from the results of the Buffalo Society's digging and from ours that the aborigines had used one part of the cemetery in which to place burials with mortuary deposits and had selected another part to make interments without such deposits.

Aboriginal Site on Crystal River, Citrus County.

In two reports[1] we have described our investigation of the aboriginal site at the great shell mound[2] on the bank of Crystal river, about two miles from its union with the Gulf.

This site, belonging to Mr. and Mrs. Robert J. Knight, of Safety Harbor, Fla., through whose kindness all our investigations in it have been made, included as one of its component parts, as may be seen in our earlier and more complete reports on the subject, some flat ground and a rise culminating in a mound, all surrounded by an irregularly circular embankment of sand having a maximum height of about 6 feet.

The rise and the mound, entirely dug away by us during our former visits, yielded a rich harvest, consisting mainly of ornaments of copper, of shell and of stone, including several beautiful charm-stones of rock-crystal and one of amethystine quartz, a veritable gem.

In the enclosing embankment, dug into but to a very moderate extent at the time of our two previous investigations, a few burials, none accompanied by artifacts, were found.

The contrast between these burials in this respect and many of the burials in the mound and in the rise, was so marked that we determined, this season, to revisit the site in order to make a more thorough examination as to this subject.

In the southern portion of the embankment, which included its highest part, much digging was done, showing that part of the embankment to be constructed, not of white sand such as is found in the neighborhood, but of sand evidently darkened by admixture of organic matter and containing marine shells here and there, bits of pottery, other midden debris, and numerous scattered fragments of human bone, sometimes only a single one lying alone. Evidently the material for the embankment had been gathered from a dwelling-site.

Burials were numerous in the highest part of this southern portion of the embankment, nearly every trial-hole in it coming upon at least one burial (5 feet being the maximum depth), and were found here and there in other parts of it.

[572] In all twenty-four interments were unearthed, and, in addition, many skeletons parts of which had been cut away in making other graves, and bones which seemingly had been gathered up and thrown in when the embankment was made.

The form of burial was either flexed or at full length on the back, some burials being under a layer of shell.

It was impossible to determine whether the interments had been made from

[1] "Certain Aboriginal Mounds of the Central Florida West-Coast." Journ. Acad. Nat. Sci. Phila., vol. XII, pages 379-413. "Crystal River Revisited." Journ. Acad. Nat. Sci. Phila., vol. XIII.

[2] Locally known as the Spanish mound, though, of course, Spaniards had no connection with its origin.

the present surface of the embankment or in various stages of its construction, all the material being homogeneous. One burial extended about a foot into pure, white sand underlying the embankment. In this instance, at least, the interment had been made in a grave whose limits, however, we could not trace above the white sand.

With the burials were artifacts as follows:

Burial No. 5, extended on the back, had, at the outer side of the left shoulder, a small charmstone or pendant of shell.

Burial No. 6, partly flexed to the right, was accompanied by a shell tool, probably a chisel.

Burial No. 8, aboriginal disturbance, to some extent put in disorder by another burial. Under the upper part of the thorax was a drinking-cup made from a conch (*Busycon*), having a ceremonial hole knocked through the base. This cup was covered by a large fragment of pottery.

Burial No. 11, partly flexed to the left, had below it and crushed against it a skeleton of a child. Possibly at the neck of the adult, or perhaps belonging to the child, were four pendants of shell and one of limestone. With these was a gorget of shell having a large, central, circular excision and rude, incised, concentric circles on the convex side.

Under the knees of the adult was a mass of sand tinged with hematite, in which were bits of sandstone and two rude pendants, one seemingly of sedimentary rock, the other of limestone.

Burial No. 15, partly flexed to the right. Along the right forearm was an implement of bone.

Burial No. 21, partly flexed to the left, had at the thorax an arrowpoint of flint.

About 6 inches below an aboriginal disturbance were three rude limestone pendants and two of shell, all erect and grouped closely together, the grooved ends uppermost.

Apart from human remains were a number of pointed implements of bone, two shell pendants, a pendant of limestone, a shell drinking-cup having the mortuary mutilation, a gouge made from part of the body whorl of a marine shell, a number of columellae of the conch wrought into chisels.

Considerable, though not exhaustive, digging in the remainder of the embankment, most of which was decidedly lower than the southern part, failed to come upon burials, as was the case in our previous search.

In consequence of this latest investigation at the Crystal River site it [573] becomes evident that the few objects found, though showing that the burials in the embankment were not absolutely without mortuary deposits, nevertheless emphasize the discrepancy between the burials in the embankment and those found in the rise and in the mound as to abundance and quality of such deposits, and indicate that the embankment, or that part of it containing burials (the increased portion of the southern part), was made at a different time from that of the interments within the enclosure when a much greater liberality as to gifts to the dead prevailed.

About one mile in a northerly direction from the Spanish mound, on hammock land, is a mound of very irregular shape, having a large circumference and a maximum height of 6.5 feet. Extensive digging showed this mound to be of white sand without discoloration and indicated it to have belonged to the domiciliary class.

Mound on the Greenleaf Place, Citrus County.

About 3.5 miles in a southerly direction from the town of Crystal River, on hammock land on the Greenleaf Place, now belonging to Mr. J. K. Eubanks, of Crystal River, is a mound that had been greatly dug into before our investigation of it. Human bones lay in many places on its surface. Its diameters were 70 feet and 50 feet. Its original height probably had been about 4 feet, though burials were found at a greater depth than that. Whether these burials lay in graves, however, it was impossible to determine, as there was no definite baseline, and the sand underlying the mound seemed the same as that of which the mound itself was composed.

Trial-holes put down in such parts as seemed to have escaped earlier digging reached eight burials, all of the bunched variety, some representing but a small part of a single skeleton. With one burial, however, were two skulls, while three were found with another.

Burial No. 5, consisting of fragments of two femora, one tibia, and one humerus, parts of a skull lying two feet from the rest of the burial, had with it one sheet of mica and a small quantity of sand tinted a pale pink with admixture of powdered hematite.

Two arrowpoints of flint were found separately apart from burials, and two charmstones, which probably had been together, lay in sand thrown out from one of our trial-holes. These objects are now in the Museum of the American Indian, Heye Foundation, and through the courtesy of Mr. George G. Heye they were submitted to Prof. Charles P. Berkey, of Columbia University, who kindly has determined their material as follows: Museum No. 8/2054. Igneous, of basic composition, about that of basalt. Probably occurs as a dyke or sill and would be classified as a "trap" or diabase.

Museum No. 8/2055. Metamorphic sediment. Exact composition obscure, [574] but very complex. May have been associated closely with such rock as the other sample. Would be classified as a "graywacke" (which is a species of metamorphosed, very impure, grayish green sandstone).

Notes on the Archaeology of Florida

BY

CLARENCE B. MOORE

[400]

Notes on the Archaeology of Florida

By Clarence B. Moore

In "Anthropological Survey of the Southwestern Coast of Florida,"[1] p. 62, referring to recent work done for the National Museum, we find:

> The region of the coast south of Key Marco, which was supposed to be of no great account as far as aboriginal remains were concerned, was found to be full of sites, shell-heaps, platforms, and mounds with canals and other evidences of former Indian occupation, the remains covering in individual instances twenty, thirty, and even eighty acres of ground. Only the southernmost parts of the coast are poor in such remains. All of this is still intact so far as scientific exploration is concerned.

We fear that those not familiar with the literature on the subject (and it is hard to keep the run of various publications) might infer from this that the part of Florida referred to had been neglected by the numerous archaeological expeditions under the auspices of the Academy of Natural Sciences of Philadelphia, that have visited that state.

On the contrary, the hundred-foot steamer, carrying a powerboat as a tender, with an average of eleven men to dig and to supervise, has spent much of five seasons in the Ten Thousand islands, good parts of which were devoted to the region south of Key Marco, in one instance the expedition continuing around the end of the peninsula to Lake Worth, on the eastern coast.

We have published[2] the results of most of our investigations between Key Marco and Lossman's Key, the southernmost of the Ten Thousand islands, including principal sites, Dismal Key, [401] Fikahatchee Key, Russell's Key, Chokoloskee Key, Turner river and Lossman's Key.

We are not prepared to admit that

> the region of the coast south of Key Marco was supposed to be of no great account as far as aboriginal remains were concerned

[1] Explorations and Field-work of the Smithsonian Institution in 1918. *Smithsonian Miscellaneous Collections*, Vol. LXX, no. 2.

[2] "Certain Antiquities of the Florida West-coast." *Journal, Academy of Natural Sciences of Philadelphia*, vol. XI. "Miscellaneous Investigation in Florida." *Journal, Academy of Natural Sciences of Philadelphia*, vol. XIII. "Notes on the Ten Thousand Islands, Florida." *Journal, Academy of Natural Sciences of Philadelphia*, vol. XIII.

AMERICAN ANTHROPOLOGIST
N. S., VOL. 21, PL. XIV

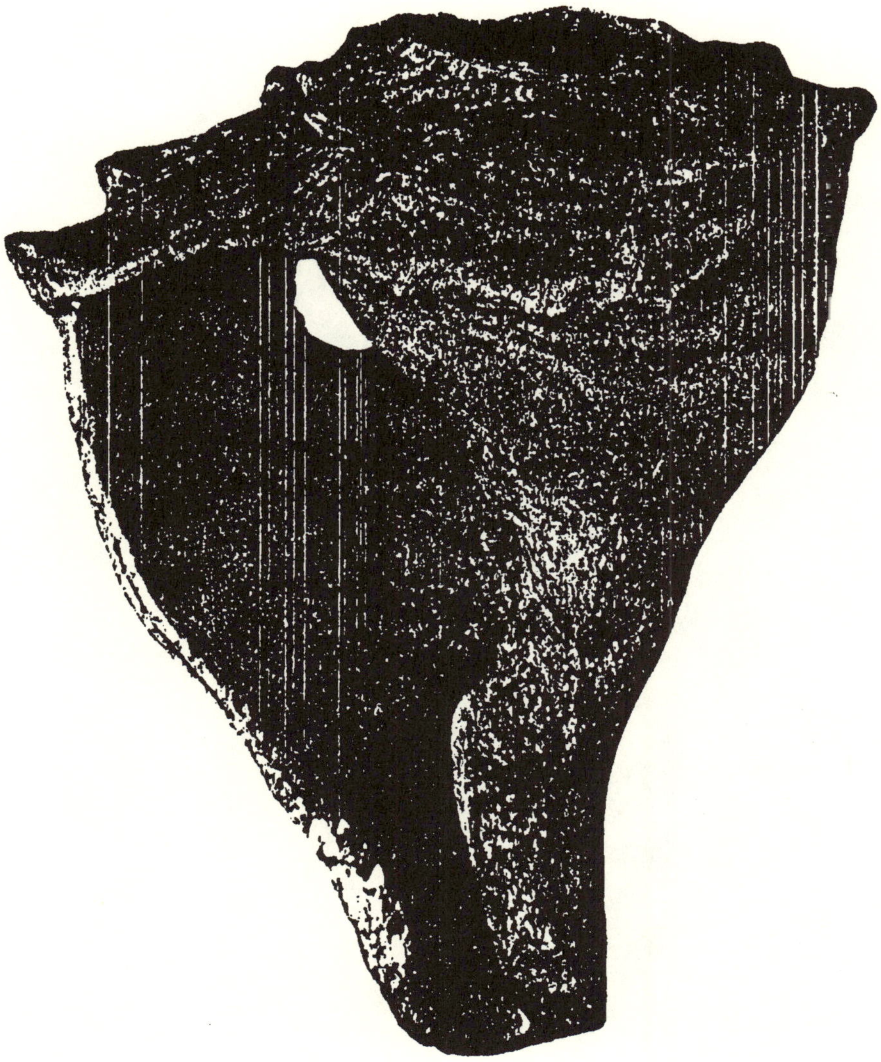

Implement of shell. Height, 7 inches.

by anyone familiar with that region through personal investigation or through comprehensive reading on the subject.

Nor, on the other hand, is it our opinion that this region is more than a continuation of the great shell deposits farther north: The huge mound above Cedar Key; those at Cedar Key; the so-called Spanish Mound, Crystal river; Indian Hill, on Tampa bay; Josselyn Key; the Battey Place, now Pineland on Pine island; Mound island; Addison's Key; Goodland Point on Key Marco; and others, all of which we have carefully examined and nearly all described in print.

The highest shell-mounds of the coast are north of Key Marco as is the best defined aboriginal canal.[1]

[1] On Mound Island, *Certain Antiquities of the Florida West Coast*, p. 366, *et seq.*

Implement of shell. Height, 6 1/2 inches.

Our own experience and that of others has convinced us that in the shell-heaps of the southwestern Florida coast, which extend southward from above Cedar Key, practically nothing of interest has been found that can begin to compensate one for the heavy outlay of time and money needed for their demolition. The great shell-mound on Bullfrog creek, ten miles southeast from Tampa, removed to furnish material for roads, was carefully watched, it is said, while the work was going on, without any discovery of importance.

An accurate survey of the shell site on Turner river might be of interest, but it is our belief that digging into the shell deposits hereafter will be more frequently suggested than done.

Incidentally we would say here, that while digging in the muck and shell in the Ten Thousand islands and somewhat north of them (Mound island) we have made also great collections of objects of shell, including many implements wrought from entire shells (*Busycon perversum*, as a rule). These implements, often made from large shells and usually found by us on the surface, have been [402] presented by us to the principal museums of North and South America and of Europe.

Though we have carefully described and figured these interesting tools, archaeologists do not seem to have devoted much attention to them, perhaps through unfamiliarity with them, owing to the limited extent of the region in which they are found.

This season (1919) we gathered at Goodland Point, Key Marco, three tools of shell, of a variety unlike any yet described. Of these shell tools, wrought from *Busycon perversum*, and with the customary removal of part of the body whorl, two are alike, while one differs from them in certain particulars. The duplicate has been sent to the Museum of the American Indian, Heye Foundation, while the other two have been placed in the Moore collection in the Academy of Natural Sciences of Philadelphia.

Each of these two has had removed the upper half of the spire, a portion of the inner part of the parietal wall, and the columella except the base. This was done, perhaps, with the exception of the partial removal of the spire, of which we shall speak later, to lessen the weight of the tool without impairing its efficiency.

The two implements, however, similar to this extent, differ decidedly in other ways. The tool shown in plate XIV, about 7 inches in length, has two round holes through which a handle readily could pass, constituting with the shell, a kind of hoe or pick for loosening the soil. The orifice left in the spire shows no mark of wear.

The other tool (plate XV) having a length of about 6.5 inches, has in the body whorl, a single, irregular hole with rough margin, seemingly unfitted for a handle and unworn by one. The periphery of the space left by the removal of the upper part of the spire, is smooth and apparently has been subjected to considerable wear. It appears likely that this tool, instead of having a handle at right angles, as had nearly all those with which we are familiar, had one inserted into the space in the spire, in line with the axis of the shell, and was used in the manner of a spade.

Notes on Shell Implements from Florida

BY

CLARENCE B. MOORE

[12]

Notes on Shell Implements from Florida

By Clarence B. Moore

Considerable has been written[1] about the interesting implements of shell, made from conchs (*Busycon*) and from "horse-conchs" (*Fasciolaria*), which are found throughout almost the entire state of Florida and sparsely in neighboring regions, but are preeminent as to numbers and quality of make in the midden sites of the aboriginal Key-dwellers along the southwestern Florida coast between Mound Key in Lee county and Lossman's Key in the county of Monroe, inclusive. (See map, fig. 7).

Farther south among the Keys, on the peninsula, and among the beautiful islands below it, these midden sites do not extend, doubtless owing to the scarcity in their waters of the oyster, the principal article of diet among the eaters of shell-fish along the coast.

This season (1920) was spent by us along the southwestern Florida coast among many aboriginal sites, most of which were familiar to us. Among these was Sandfly, formerly described by us as Wiggins Key, on Sandfly Pass, near Chokoloskee. At Sandfly we found a change of ownership[2] and name and that a considerable amount of territory had been cleared since our latest visit in 1904, all of it a midden site covered with shells left from aboriginal times.

[14] Here, on one extensive field almost exclusively covered with oyster shells, we found only two or three shell implements. These were of the ordinary type met with along the southwestern Florida coast, where almost the entire shell is used and has holes, or a hole and a notch, in the body whorl, somewhat below the shoulder, permitting the handle to enter the shell almost at right angles.

In another great field, however, abounding with implements, practically all the shell tools made from the conch (*Busycon*) proved to be variants and had either one

1. Charles Rau, *Smithsonian Contributions to Knowledge* 287, "The Archaeological Collection of the United States National Museum," p. 66, *et seq*., fig. 257.

Frank Hamilton Cushing, "A Preliminary Report on the Exploration of Ancient Key-Dweller Remains on the Gulf Coast of Florida," *Proceedings of the American Philosophical Society*, vol. XXXV, no. 153, p. 38 *et seq*.

C. B. Moore, *Journal of the Academy of Natural Sciences*, Phila.: "Antiquities of the Florida West-Coast," vol. XI, p. 380 *et seq*.; "Miscellaneous Investigation in Florida," vol. XIII, p. 315 *et seq*.; "Notes on the Ten Thousand Islands, Florida," vol. XIII, p. 463 *et seq*.

C. B. Moore, "Notes on the Archaeology of Florida," *American Anthropologist*, vol. XXI, no. 4, Oct-Dec., 1919, p. 401 *et seq*.

2. Mr. C. T. Boggess, the present owner, kindly placed the entire property at our disposal for repeated search.

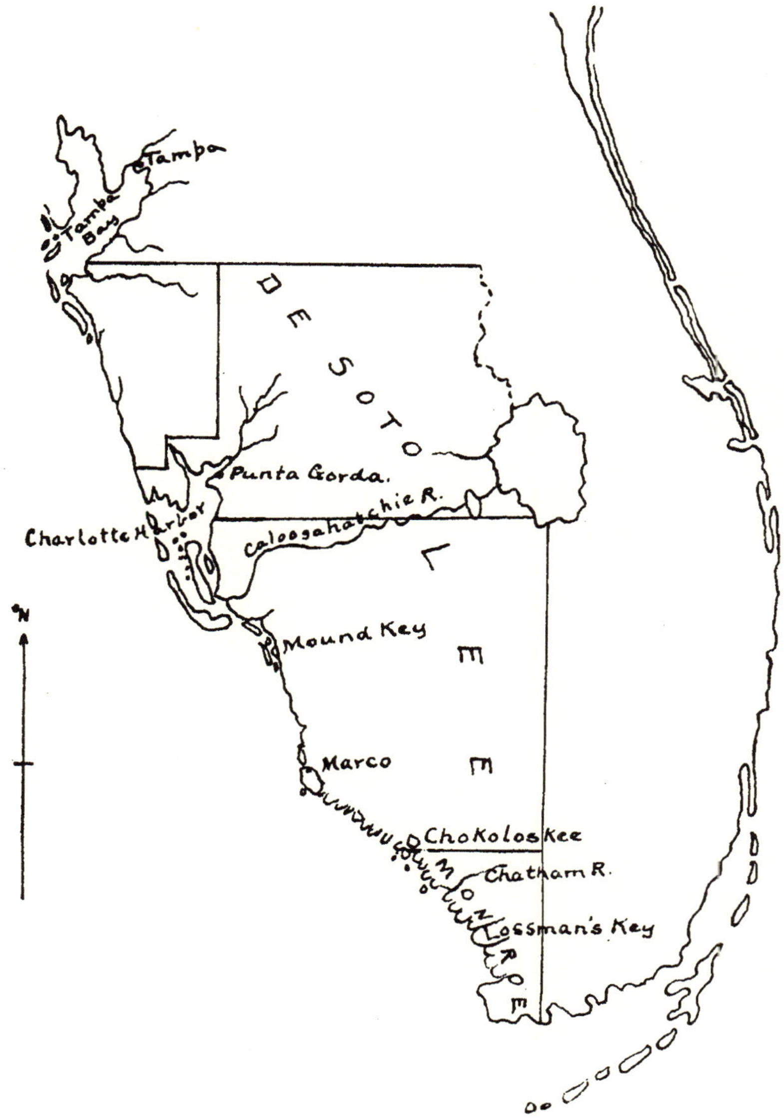

Fig. 7.—Outline map of the southwestern coast of the Florida peninsula.

or two large holes in the top of the shell above the shoulder, and none intended for handles below it.[1]

About a score of these shell tools from Sandfly, variants so far as the southwestern Florida coast is concerned, were sent to Mr. Charles C. Willoughby who very kindly has written as to the method of their hafting, and has presented to us three specimens hafted by him as shown in the illustrations, two from Sandfly and one from near the eastern coast of Florida.

1. To show how nearly universal was this rule we may say that besides many imperfect shell tools of this class, some having one hole in the top and some two holes, we got from this field, entire or almost so, twenty implements each having two holes above the shoulder, and fourteen having one hole so placed. But two exceptions were found, each having a single hole below the shoulder and none elsewhere.

The shell implements you sent for examination fall naturally into two groups—those with a single hafting perforation, and those with double perforations for hafting. All of these holes, whether single or double, are in the outer whorl of the spiral body above the shoulder. A few other minor perforations or fractures occur in the body of some of the shells, either above or below the shoulder. Judging by the weathering of their edges, some are as old as the hafting perforations, and as you suggest, may have been made to free the fish from the shell. Others are clearly of later date, for their edges show less weathering and some of the holes and fractures are relatively recent. I do not think that any of these smaller perforations had anything to do with the hafting of the implements, but that all of the twenty-two shells sent fall within one of the two above-mentioned groups.

I find practically no evidences of wear caused by the haft in any of the implements. Some of the hafting perforations are quite symmetrical with smooth edges, others are more roughly fashioned. The smoother edges, however, seem to be the result of superior workmanship rather than of wear.

It will be noticed that nearly all of the smaller implements come within the first group, and have but one perforation for the handle, while in the second group two perforations are required to insure proper rigidity for the heavier tool. The method of hafting, illustrated in fig. 8, answers well enough for the smaller tool, as the [15] upper portion of the spire prevents the looped end of the haft from working loose in the ordinary light work such as the implement would naturally be used for.

The looped end of the handle of the heavier shell, however, (fig. 9), would soon become loosened by the additional strain and turn upward over the shell's apex, were it not held securely by the binding which passes through the second perforation. Most of the implements have picklike narrow cutting edges. Some of the larger ones, however, have adze-like edges. All were ground while holding the aperture of the shell downward towards the abrading surface of the limestone, or other substance used for the purpose. The ground surface near the beak of the shell is therefore on about the same plane as the aperture. When the implement is being hafted, the handle can be adjusted so as to bring the cutting edge approximately parallel to it, or at right angles, or into almost any position desired.

With the Indian's proficiency in such work, it would not take him long to select a shell of the proper size from which the fish had been previously extracted, grind its beak to an edge, perforate the body whorl, and insert a haft. With a single blow of such a tool the body shell of a live *Busycon* could be quickly perforated to facilitate the removal of the fish, and I am inclined to think that many of the smaller tools of

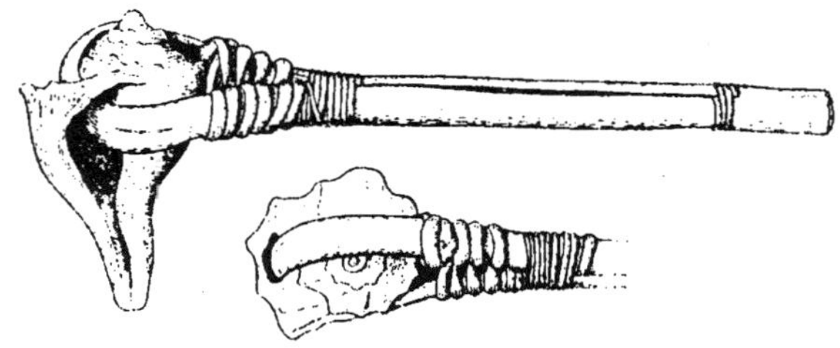

Fig. 8.—Method of hafting. About one-quarter size.

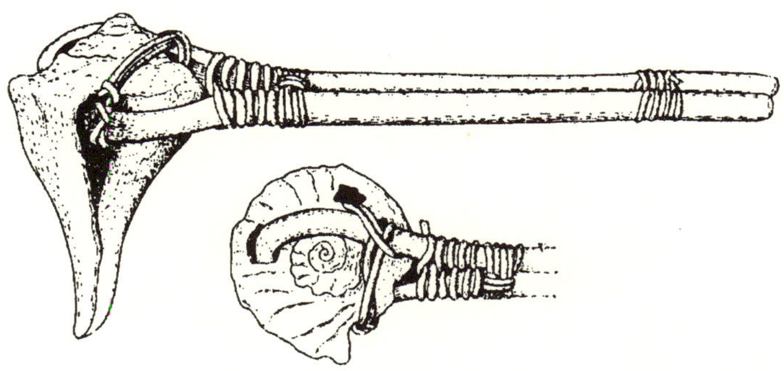

Fig. 9.—Method of hafting. About one-quarter size.

this type were often used for this purpose.

There is, of course, nothing new in the use of the looped handle such as I have [16] illustrated, except in its application to shell tools of this type for it was often employed by the Indians in hafting stone axes, mauls and clubs.

And now to take up another point in relation to tools of shell. Many of these implements have holes for the handle so carefully rounded that one is uncertain how they were made. A solution can now be offered as to some of them at least.

At Dismal Key we found a partly completed tool, evidently discarded on account of a crack accidentally developed in the making. The body whorl of the shell had been cut back about four inches from the aperture; part of the beak had been broken off to leave an end sufficiently thick to bevel into a cutting edge. The interesting point about the shell, however, is that in the place where a hole for a handle would be expected there is a round semi-perforation plainly made by pecking as shown in plate I. The margin of the hole later probably would have been ground into a regular surface.

On the top of this shell, above the shoulder, a small, irregular hole has been knocked through and this brings us to another question which, though discussed before,[1] may as well be brought to date.

We know that some of the natives around Key West, Florida, at the present time eat the conch (*Busycon*) and that, in order to aid in freeing the shell fish from its shell, they are accustomed to make a hole in it. Also we are told[2] that the aborigines of the West Indies made a small hole near the top of the shell (here the queen conch, *Strombus gigas*, is referred to) to aid in loosening the fish, and that the modern negro conch fishers there also break into the shell for this purpose but in different ways so that on finding these shells an investigator can determine by what class of persons the contents have been removed.

On such of those southwestern Florida Keys, however, where conch shells (*Busycon perversum*)[3] are found, often in great numbers, all brought there when

1. *Notes on the Ten Thousand Islands*, p. 463 *et seq*.

2. Theodoor De Booy, *Contributions from the Heye Museum*, Number 9, p. 79. Reprinted from the *American Anthropologist*, vol. XVII, no. 1, Jan.-March, 1915.

3. *Busycon carica*, having the opening to the right as one faces it, is not found on the western coast of Florida.

AMERICAN ANTHROPOLOGIST N. S., VOL. 23, PL. I

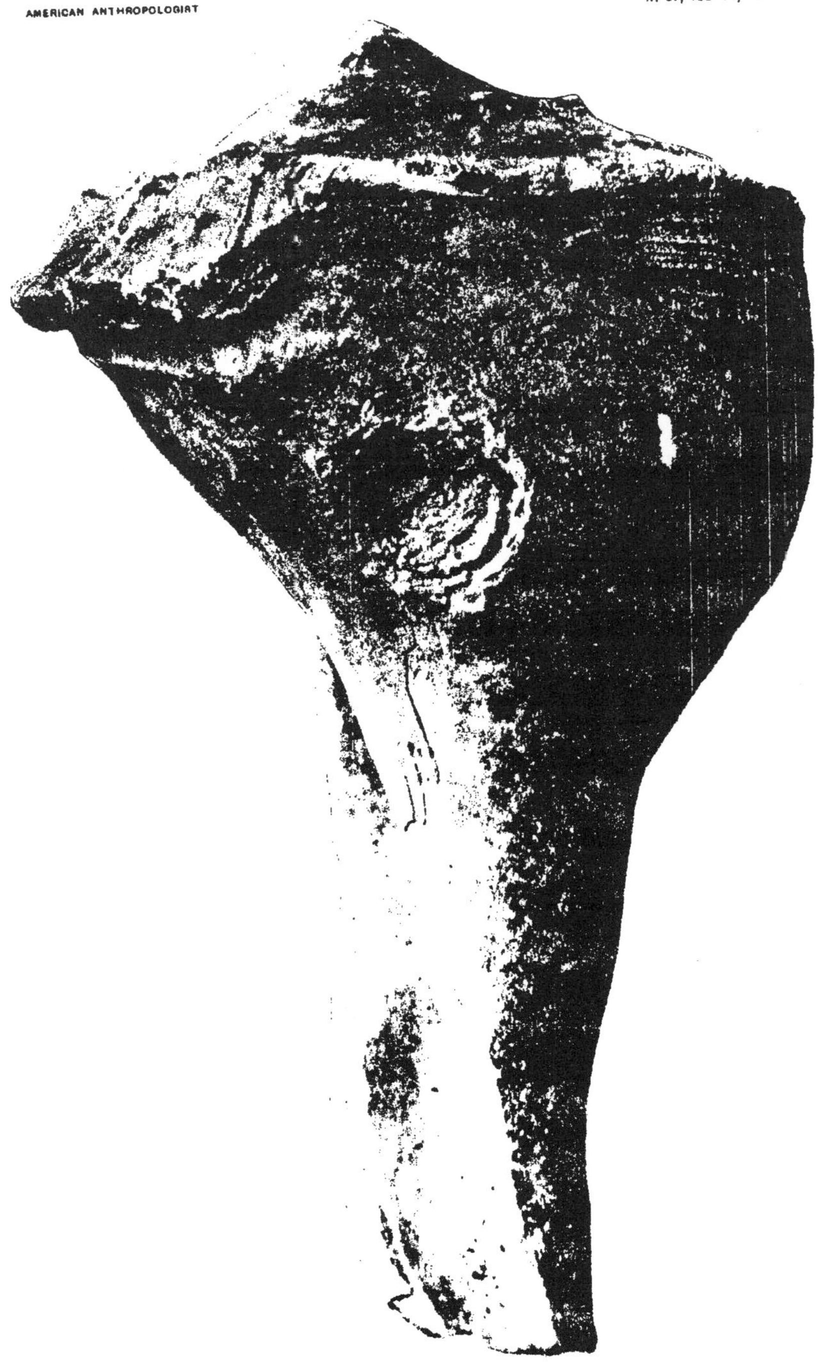

Unfinished tool of shell showing a method of making the hole for a handle by pecking. (Actual size.)

their contents were used for food by the aborigines, while many of the shells have a small hole (in the top [17] as a rule), far greater numbers are without it. Therefore in this region we see that methods other than perforation of the shell often must have been practiced to detach the fish.

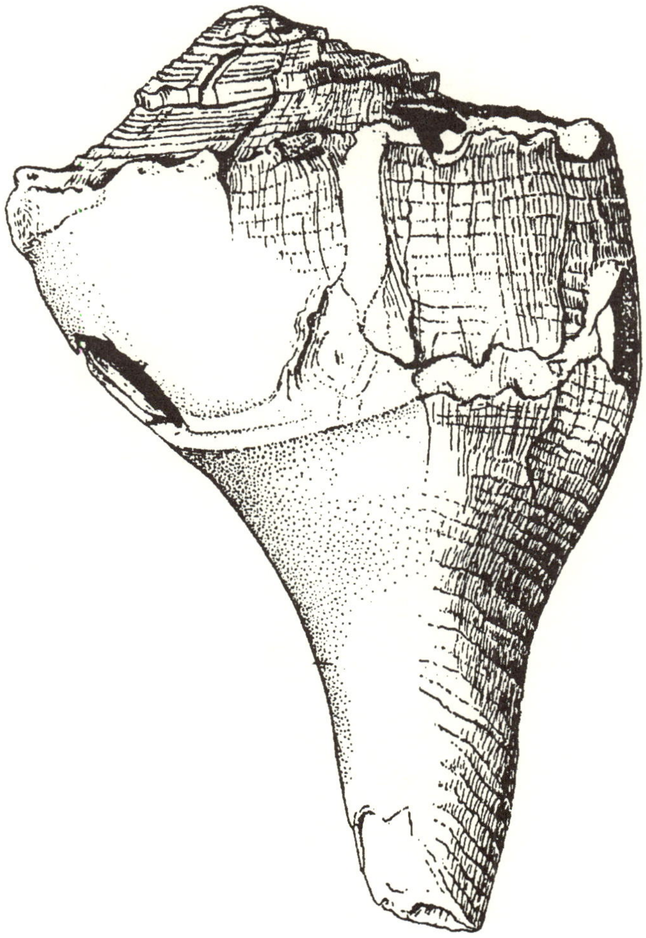

Fig. 10.—Shell tool from Marco, showing marks of thongs. Actual size.

We note also that these holes, which are small as a rule and of course are found in quantities of shells that have not been made into implements, on occasion served a secondary purpose when the shells were wrought into tools.

Cushing[1] in writing of his wonderful discoveries in the muck at Marco, a settlement at the northern end of Key Marco, tells us:

> Thus the stick or handle could be driven into these perforations [the large holes for the handle] past the columella in such manner that it was sprung or clamped firmly into place. Nevertheless it was usually further secured with rawhide thongs—now mere jelly—passed through one or two additional perforations in the head, and around both the stick and columella.

The present writer is fortunate in having received as a gift from Mr. Cushing a conch-shell implement from the Marco exploration (fig. 10) having part of the wooden handle and showing plainly deep furrows indicating the former presence of the thongs described by him. The reader will see that probably starting from what is now a deep, central depression, evidently the location of a knot, a thong was carried to the reader's left, wound around the handle, brought back (as shown by the double groove), carried to the opening at the right where it was again looped around the handle, was led upward over the shoulder, part way not in contact with the shell, to the small opening above the shoulder, through which it was drawn around the handle inside the shell and then, returning through the same opening, was directed down over the shoulder to the starting point where the marked depression is apparent, and was there knotted to the other end and to the cross thong below.

On all the hundreds, or probably thousands, of shell implements, dry surface finds, with one exception, that we have examined, no such furrows were apparent and we believe the marks on the shell in question were created by corrosive action in connection with the decomposition of the thongs, the acid affecting the lime of the [18] shell lying in the wet muck, and were not the result of wear. The large tool found by us in the muck of the canal on Mound Key[1] perhaps had been dropped there without a handle and the accompanying thongs.

1. *Op. cit.*, p. 40

1. *Certain Antiquities of the Florida West-Coast*, p. 388.

Shell Implements from Florida

BY

CLARENCE B. MOORE

[1]

Shell Implements from Florida[1]

By Clarence B. Moore

Within the confines of what is now the State of Florida (United States of America) but comparatively little stone is found and almost all such as is met with there is unsuitable for use as implements.

We know that Florida has a most extensive littoral in proportion to its area and that no part of the state is far distant from the sea and the conch (*Busycon*), *Fasciolaria* and other shells that could be utilized in making aboriginal implements were numerous in these waters.

In the northern and central parts of the state abundance of implements of hard rock, probably obtained through barter, have been found, and supplementing these, tools of shell in limited numbers, which, however, are often carelessly made and only of moderate size.

In southern Florida, however, implements of stone are rarely seen. Perhaps owing to the size and massive character of some of the shells met with there no imperative need for implements of stone was felt, those of shell being almost exclusively employed in their place.

For extensive use of implements of shell, for their size, and for care and skill displayed in their making, the sites of the former abodes of the Key-dwellers on the southwestern Florida coast bordering much of the county of Lee and the upper part of Monroe county, are preeminent.

[2] From Mound Key in Lee county to Lossman Key[1] in the county of Monroe inclusive (being the geographical limits of this marked culture in shell implements) those sent you were personally collected by the donor who has, to some extent, made implements of this class a specialty.[2]

These Key-dwellers (Key, as you know, is an island) whose homes probably were

1. El presente estudio, que juntamente con la hermosa colección de instrumentos de conchas, que se publican en las Láminas que lo acompañan, debo a la gentileza del señor Moore, que con tan precioso obsequio ha enriquecido mi museo.—J.J.yC.

1. The southern limit of aboriginal shell deposits on the Western coast of Florida, doubtless owing to the scant supply of oysters farther south.

2. "Certain Antiquities of the Florida West-Coast." *Journal Academy of Natural Sciences of Philadelphia*, Vol. XI.

"Miscellaneous Investigation in Florida." *Journ. Acad. Nat. Sci. Phila.* Vol. XIII.

"Notes on the Ten Thousand Islands, Florida." *Journ. Acad. Nat. Sci. Phila.*, Vol. XIII.

on piles until the shells, refuse from their meals, accumulating, afforded them a more solid place of abode, had a bewildering variety of implements of shell. Conchs (*Busycon perversum*), massive on occasion but of all sizes, have two holes, or a hole and a notch (some finished with great care) through which a handle was inserted, having the shell nearly at right angles; others with either one or two good sized holes in the top of the shell above the shoulder, and none elsewhere. This style is exceptional on the southwestern Florida coast and the method of hafting has not been determined. On most all these, when unimpaired by rough usage, the beak has a beautifully beveled cutting-edge.

Many implements have large portions of the shells removed for greater convenience in handling, some being used as hammers, having the hole and notch, or a notch on two opposite sides, for the handle.

The *Fasciolaria*, its lower body portions removed leaving a projecting columella, was used as a pick, and later as a hammer when the end of the axis was blunted.

Columella separate from the rest of the shell and given a cutting edge at one end probably saw service as chisels.

Also there were conchs with all outer parts carefully removed, and ground smooth as to the upper portions, which presumably were used grasped in the hand.

There were also great clam-shells perforated for use as hoes and *Arca ponderosa* shells strung as weights on fish nets, and small hammers probably for cracking shell-fish, fashioned from the diminutive *Busycon pugile*.

Shell drinking-cups, not very carefully made as a rule, are fairly numerous, and pendants of shell, ornaments of charms, until [3] lately were found on the Keys in abundance, but are much scarcer at present. With these sometimes were rude pendants of porous stone, probably charm-stones, found often away from the shore and occasionally made from material that will hardly sink in water.

In most of the shell implements which have not been so cut away as to remove it, is a hole, usually small and not carefully rounded, present as a rule in the upper part of the shell above the shoulder, or periphery. Some shell implements, however, of a kind where we would expect one, are without this hole, while others, a small proportion that come from certain localities, have it near, but below, the shoulder. These small holes, wherever placed, presumably in some instances were made to aid in freeing the fish from its shell for use as food, for they are often seen on these sites in conch-shells that have not been made into tools. Moreover, there is ample evidence that persons who eat the conch at the present time make such a hole in the shell to aid in the removal of the fish.

Cushing, however, who got such wonderful objects from the muck at Marco,[1] tells us, in speaking of tools of this kind which he found with wooden handles in place, "Thus the stick or handle could be driven into these perforations (the large holes), past the columella in such a manner that it was sprung or clamped firmly into place. Nevertheless it was usually further secured with rawhide thongs—now

1. Frank Hamilton Cushing, "A Preliminary Report on the Exploration of Ancient Key-dweller Remains on the Gulf Coast of Florida," page 40. *Proceedings of the American Philosophical Society*, Vol. XXXV, No. 153.

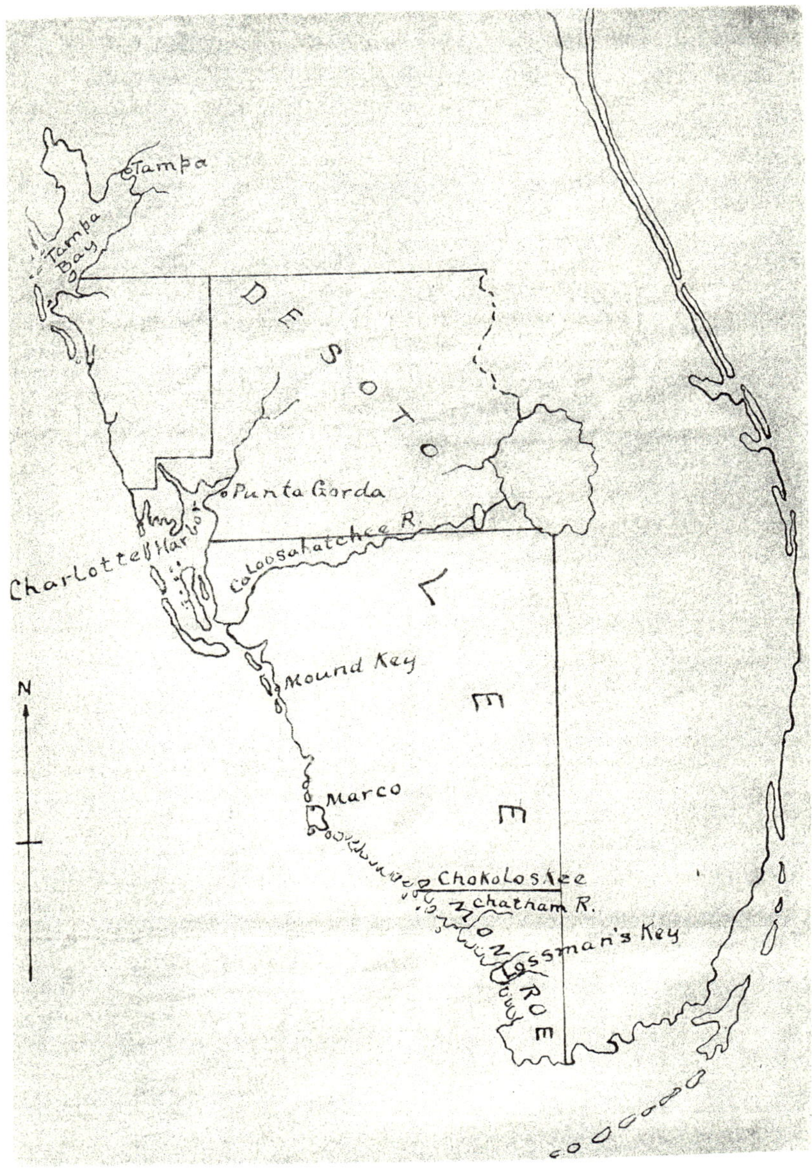

Moore.—Lam. 1. Outline map of southwestern Florida coast.

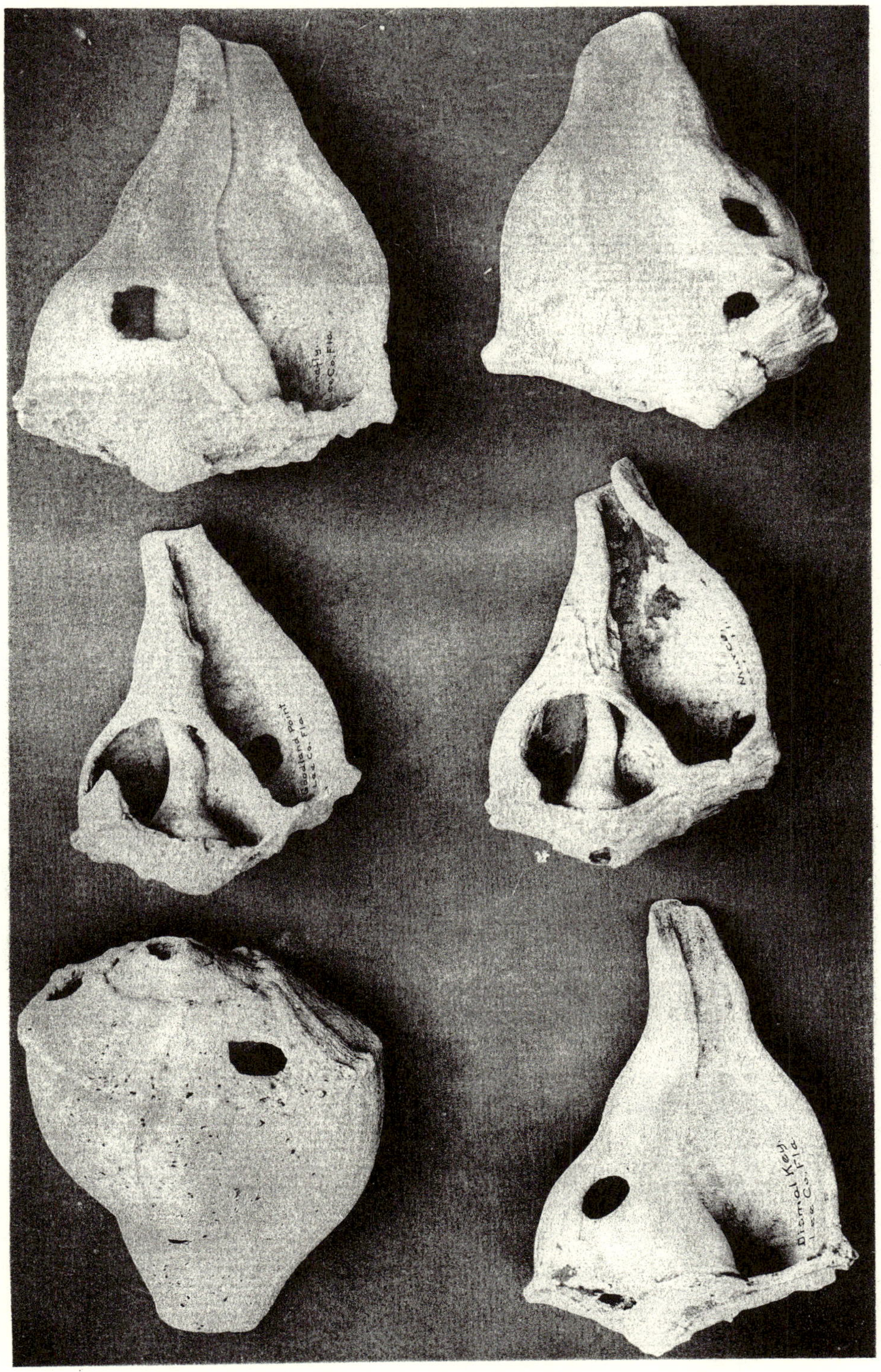

Moore.—Lam 2. Fig. 1a: Sandfly.—Fig. 2a: Mound Key.—3. Goodland Point 4: Marco.—5: Sandfly.—6: Dismal Key

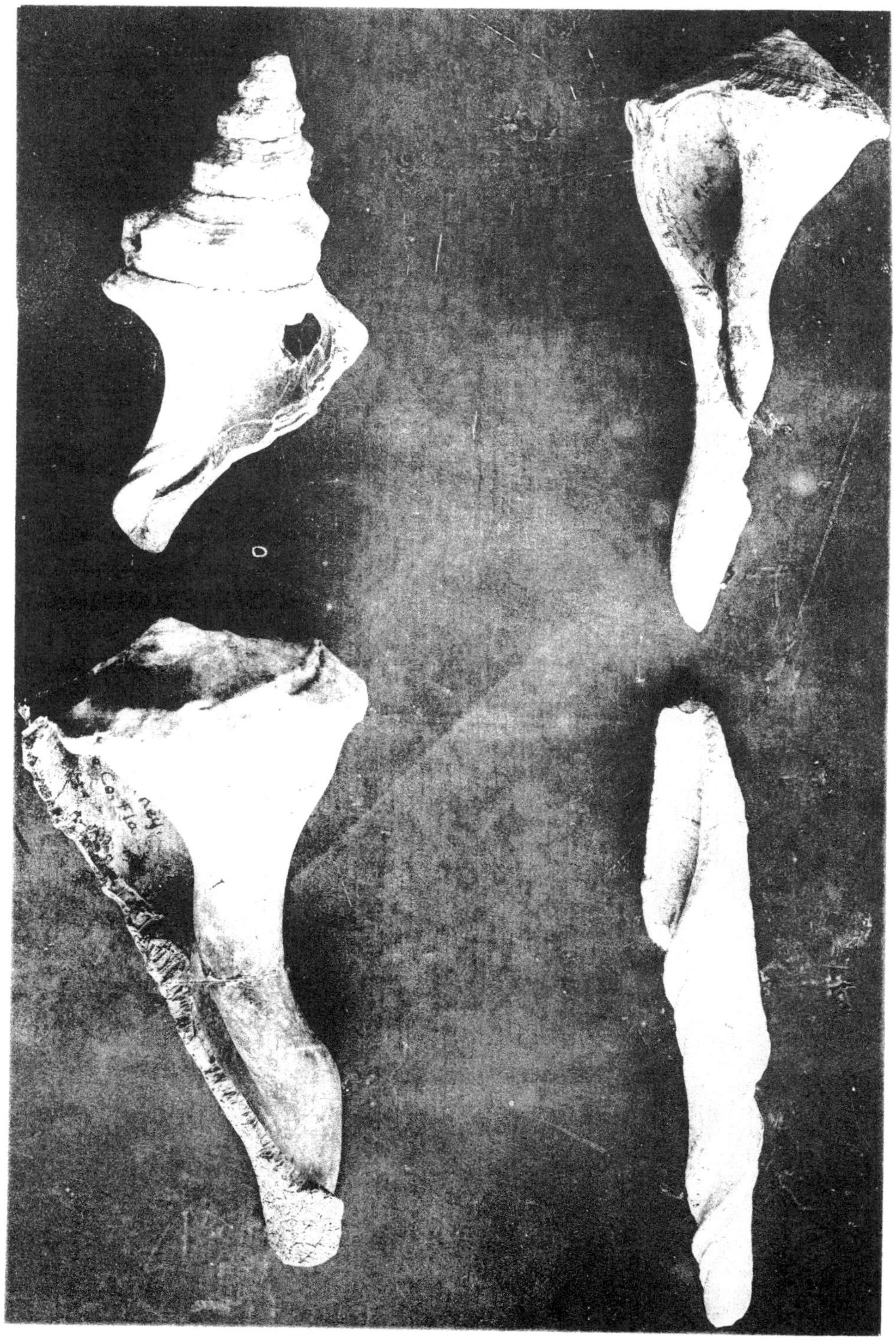

Moore.—Lam 3. Fig. 1: Sandfly.—2, 3 y 4: Pumpkin Key.

Moore.—Lam. 4. Fig. 1: Mound Key.—2: Sandfly.—3: Marco.—4: Chokoloskee.—5: Marco.—6. Goodland Point.—7: Pumpkin Key.—8 y 9: Sandfly.—10: Pumpkin Key.—11: Chokoloskee

mere jelly—passed through one or two additional perforations in the head (of the shell), and around both the stick and the columella," so it is evident that these holes often served a dual purpose.

Clarence B. Moore.

Index

INTRODUCTION: CLARENCE B. MOORE'S WORK IN WESTERN AND CENTRAL FLORIDA, 1895–1921

(by Jeffrey M. Mitchem)

Index

Works by Moore